The *Femtech* REVOLUTION

HARNESSING TECHNOLOGY TO SUPERCHARGE WOMEN'S HEALTHCARE

Bethany Corbin

WILEY

Library of Congress Cataloging-in-Publication Data is Available:

ISBN 9781394330911 (Cloth)
ISBN 9781394330928 (ePub)
ISBN 9781394330935 (ePDF)

Cover Design: Wiley
Cover Images: © venimo/Shutterstock, © Zee Shan 56/Shutterstock
Author Photo: © Carrie Allen

SKY10123512_080125

*For every woman who dares to imagine
a future where her health is a priority and
her voice is heard. This is your revolution.*

Contents

Introduction

Femtech Rising

The first time I faced the dire state of women's healthcare, I was eight years old. My mom was my world—fierce, capable, working two full-time jobs, and full of life. But then, little by little, something started to change. Her speech would slur without warning. Her eyelids drooped like they couldn't bear the weight of her exhaustion. Some days, she'd grow so weak she could barely lift her arms.

Then came the scarier moments. She'd forget how to get home from the grocery store, confused and lost in places that were once second nature. I can still see her from the window on her weekend walks, pacing up and down the street, searching for something familiar—unable to remember which house was hers. And then she started falling. The sound of her body hitting the ground, sharp and gut-wrenching, was always followed by an eerie stillness as she lay there, paralyzed. That sound lives rent-free in my mind. It haunts my nightmares and lingers in the symptoms of the illness that continues to torment her today.

For seven years, this became our life—a cycle of uncertainty, fear, and helplessness. We searched for answers in doctors' offices and hospital rooms, clinging to the hope that someone would finally piece together the puzzle. But test after test came back normal or inconclusive, and the experts we trusted failed her. Instead of solutions, she got skepticism. Instead of a diagnosis, she was dismissed. And instead of a carefree childhood, I became her caretaker.

"It's all in your head," the doctors said. "You're imagining it. Seeking attention." They discounted her pain as though it were a nuisance, a fabrication. An outright lie. I watched as the vibrant woman I adored was diminished—not just by her illness, but by a healthcare system that refused to see her. She lost her jobs, going from a driven career woman to someone they labeled an invalid. Without a diagnosis, she couldn't qualify for disability, leaving our family in financial freefall. My dad had no choice but to move to another state for a higher-paying job, desperately trying to fill the financial void, while I lay awake each night, wondering if my mom would survive until morning.

By the eighth year of trial and error—eight long years of misdiagnoses, indifferent shrugs, painful tests, and a parade of doctors who made my mom feel like a mystery no one cared about enough to solve—we finally had an answer. At the Mayo Clinic, a specialist diagnosed my mom with hypokalemic periodic paralysis. It was a moment of relief and rage all at once. Because here's the maddening truth: Her condition wasn't hidden or impossible to detect. Sure, it was rare, but the clues were there from the very first appointment. Low potassium levels? Check. Thyroid issues? Noted. Muscle weakness that came and went? Textbook. In hindsight, her charts practically screamed the diagnosis.

And yet, for nearly a decade, no one was listening. Instead of connecting the dots, doctors ignored them. Each missed opportunity felt like a betrayal—not just by one doctor, but by a system designed to overlook women like my mom. It wasn't that her condition was too complex; it was that no one thought her story was worth piecing together.

My mom's experience left a mark on me that never faded. As I grew older, I started to see the same patterns everywhere. Women were being overlooked, underserved, and dismissed—not just in healthcare, but across industries that claimed to help them. It wasn't subtle, either. The stories piled up, each one more infuriating than the last. I realized I couldn't sit by and watch it happen. Those experiences lit a fire in me, one that carried me all the way to law school. I wanted to fight for women like my mom. I wanted to fight for *all* women.

In 2018, while teaching law at Wake Forest University, I came across a term that changed everything for me: *femtech.* The word was still new, but it immediately caught my attention. It felt like a glimpse of what could be—a chance to rewrite the script for women's health and wellness. I dove in, dedicating my scholarship to studying this emerging industry. But research wasn't enough. I didn't just want to analyze femtech from a distance; I wanted to be part of it, to immerse myself in the waves these innovative founders were making.

For three years, I poured myself into femtech. When the COVID-19 pandemic hit, the world of digital health exploded almost overnight, and with it came a surge of opportunities—and challenges—in femtech. Suddenly, my workload multiplied as I raced to keep up with the rapid growth and innovation happening in the industry. By 2021, my schedule was so packed that I almost canceled my annual physical just to buy myself an extra hour. Ironically, I was so busy that I forgot to cancel in time. Not wanting to pay the no-show fee, I begrudgingly kept the appointment, expecting nothing more than a quick in-and-out visit.

"Are you pregnant?"

This question caught me off guard, coming from my doctor as her cold, gloved hands pressed firmly on my abdomen during a pelvic exam. I let out a short laugh.

"Not a chance."

"Are you sure?" she pressed, her voice firm but with an odd undertone I couldn't quite place. For a fleeting moment, it almost sounded like hope—like she *wanted* me to say yes. As if being pregnant was the only explanation she was prepared to accept for whatever she had just felt inside me.

"I'm positive," I replied. "There's no way I could be pregnant."

She paused, her hands still for a moment, then disappeared briefly. When she returned, she held a flexible tape measure. Without a word, she stretched it across my stomach, glanced at the number, then at my chart, and finally shook her head.

"You have a pelvic mass," she said, snapping the tape shut.

I was stunned. The words *pelvic mass* echoed in my mind, heavy and ominous. My thoughts immediately jumped to my aunt and a high school classmate, both of whom had recently passed away from ovarian cancer. Could this be the same thing? Panic hit me like a wave, my heart racing as

I frantically searched my memory for any warning signs—pain, discomfort, *something*—but I came up empty. That's why I'd planned to cancel the appointment in the first place. I felt fine.

But as my mind spiraled, fragments of the past few years began to surface—symptoms I had casually dismissed, convincing myself they were normal. The bloating that seemed constant. The stubborn weight gain no doctor or nutritionist could explain. Stretch marks that appeared overnight as my lower stomach grew quickly in size. Waking up multiple times at night to use the bathroom. Even my inability to lay on my stomach without feeling like *something* was pressing back at me.

And then it hit me: I had ignored and dismissed my own symptoms in the same way doctors had ignored and dismissed my mom's symptoms. In a world where women's healthcare isn't prioritized, we're even taught to devalue our own pain, to downplay our own bodies' warnings. I had absorbed that message without even realizing it, pushing aside what should have been red flags until they were impossible to overlook.

"I've scheduled you for an emergency OB/GYN appointment this afternoon," my doctor continued. "It's probably a fibroid. They're common—lots of women have them."

"Oh," I sniffled, trying to process. "So there's an easy treatment? Like a pill or something to get rid of it?"

The doctor let out a soft laugh, the kind that stings. "Oh, no," she said, shaking her head. "We don't even know what causes fibroids. You'll need major abdominal surgery. And even then, there's a good chance they'll grow back."

Dazed, I nodded and gathered my things. The weight of her words didn't fully hit me until I was in my car, tears streaming down my face. It wasn't sadness—it was fear. Fear of what this meant for my childbearing years. Fear of whether I would make it through *major* surgery. I had so many questions, and I already knew how few answers I could expect.

The pelvic mass was indeed a fibroid—a giant one, about the size of a melon and comparable to a six-month pregnancy. It was crushing my bladder, intestines, and uterus. Five smaller fibroids, ranging from the size of a golf ball to an orange, were also growing inside the uterine wall. Left untreated, they would have kept growing, further displacing my organs and eventually requiring a hysterectomy, permanently ending my ability to have children. To make matters worse, doctors couldn't definitively rule out cancer until the tumors' pathology was analyzed after surgery.

Due to the size of the fibroids, laparoscopic surgery—a minimally invasive option—wasn't available locally, leaving major open abdominal surgery as my only path forward. With my experience in healthcare, I knew I had to advocate for myself, determined to find the best procedure and surgeon to minimize risks and shorten my recovery time. While I trusted my local OB/GYN, I opted to pursue a laparoscopic approach at the institution that had helped my mother: Mayo Clinic. Thanks to advancements in digital health, I was able to consult virtually with the doctor who literally wrote the book on fibroids and collaborate with surgeons to map out the best possible care plan. What I discovered during my consultations and research shocked me.

"There hasn't been much innovation or change in fibroid care in the last 30 years," the Mayo Clinic doctor told me. "Up to 80 percent of women will experience fibroids, but treatment options are still limited to surgery or uterine artery embolization—a procedure that, unfortunately, isn't recommended in your case."[1]

She reiterated what my primary care physician had said: No one knows what causes fibroids, and mine would almost certainly grow back. The myomectomy I was scheduled for—widely considered one of the top ten most painful surgeries[2]—was only a temporary solution. If the fibroids returned before I reached menopause, I'd likely face another major surgery. And there was nothing I could do about it. The only permanent solution was a hysterectomy.

Sitting in my purple gown in the pre-op room, trying desperately not to think about the six-hour surgery ahead, a sobering truth hit me: If 80 percent of men had tumors growing on their reproductive organs, we would know the cause. There would be a pill to cure it. There would be advanced, minimally invasive treatments that didn't risk their ability to procreate. Men wouldn't be told to prepare for another surgery in five years because "these things just grow back."

But for women, this was the reality. Fibroids are met with limited innovation, minimal prevention options, and a glaring lack of urgency. And they're not the only ailment relegated to this fate. The current state of women's health has a clear message: Accept your lot in life, don't ask too many questions, and endure. After all, the medical industry invests more in erectile dysfunction—a noncritical condition that affects far fewer people—than in conditions like fibroids, endometriosis, polycystic ovary syndrome, and more, each of which measurably impacts the lives of millions of women.[3]

Yet it wasn't before or during the surgery that I felt my anger finally rise. It came during the recovery.

At 6:30 p.m., I was rushed out of the operating wing because the doctors and nurses wanted to go home. I screamed in pain, begging for a morphine pump, but the bare minimum was offered. My surgeon prescribed just three days of painkillers, despite the fact that my surgery had lasted longer than a routine heart transplant. When the pain was still unbearable after the third day, I called and pleaded for more medication.

The male resident on the phone dismissed me outright. "It shouldn't hurt that much."

"Do you have a uterus?" I snapped. "Were the multiple layers of *your* uterus cut into in six different spots?" He couldn't relate. After a moment of silence, he reluctantly prescribed one more day of painkillers.

Even so, it took 10 days before I could move well enough to board a flight home. When I finally checked in with my local OB/GYN six weeks later and recounted my story, she confirmed what I'd suspected all along: I'd been severely undermedicated—by almost two weeks.

At the end of the visit, she asked me something I wasn't prepared for: "Having gone through it, would you do it that way again?"

I couldn't answer her. I had done everything right. I'd researched my options extensively, advocated for myself, and found the least invasive, least risky surgical procedure. I'd saved up money to travel for my medical care, a privilege many people can't afford. I'd followed every step to set myself up for a successful surgery and recovery.

And yet, despite all of that, I couldn't escape the harsh truth: Because I am a woman, my pain had been ignored, dismissed, and minimized by a system that is trained not to believe women. Four years later, my fibroids are growing back, but standard treatment options remain the same. The medical world continues to view women's suffering as an afterthought, a problem to endure rather than solve.

It was no longer just frustration that bubbled inside me—it was fury. Fury at a system that let this happen to me, to my mom, and to so many other women. Fury at a system that *still* doesn't care.

That's when I got angry. Really angry.

Rebellious Women

Unfortunately, stories like mine and my mom's are far too common. One in five women report having their symptoms ignored by healthcare providers.[4] Even worse, 15 percent of women said their doctors didn't believe their symptoms were real and 29 percent said that their providers dismissed their concerns.[5] It's no surprise, then, that 80 percent of women's health issues go undiagnosed.[6]

When our pleas for help continually fall on deaf ears, we are forced to take matters into our own hands. Historically, this has always been the case. When faced with a broken system, women don't sit back—we rise up. Whether in quiet defiance or bold revolution, women have always fought for change.

In ancient Rome, for example, women organized protests against the Oppian Law, a wartime measure that restricted their financial freedoms. By blockading the Forum, they forced the law's repeal and proved the power of collective resistance.[7] Later, in 60 CE, Boudica, the Celtic warrior queen of the Iceni tribe, led a massive uprising against Roman occupation, fueled by the brutalities inflicted on herself and her daughters.[8] During the abolitionist movement, Harriet Tubman and Sojourner Truth risked their lives to fight against slavery.[9] Suffragettes in the early 20th century demanded the right to vote through protests and demonstrations. During World War II, the Soviet "Night Witches" conducted stealth bombing raids against Nazi forces, helping turn the tide of the war.[10]

But not all rebellions are fought on the battlefields or in public spaces. Women have also resisted oppression in quieter but equally powerful ways. During the colonial revolts in the Americas, enslaved women resisted their oppressors by refusing to cook or serve in their masters' homes.[11] In 1936, Iranian women protested Reza Shah's forced unveiling policy by staying indoors, refusing to run errands or appear in public.[12] In Soviet-occupied Eastern Europe, women played key roles in underground resistance movements, smuggling banned literature and using their homes as safe havens for dissidents. Similarly, in the early 20th century, British suffragettes engaged in hunger strikes while imprisoned, using their own bodies as a means of protest against a government that denied them basic rights.[13]

These acts of defiance—both grand and subtle—have shaped the course of history. And this spirit of revolution is alive and well today. Movements like #MeToo have brought abuse into the spotlight, forcing institutions to confront the truths women have long known. By sharing their stories online and in courtrooms, women are demanding to be seen, heard, and valued.

Today, femtech represents the next wave of this revolution—one that is long overdue. It is a direct response to centuries of neglect and systemic bias in medicine, offering women solutions that the traditional healthcare system has failed to prioritize. By closing gaps in knowledge, resources, and care, femtech is not just challenging the status quo—it's transforming it.

This isn't just innovation for the sake of progress; it's a seismic shift in how we approach women's health. Femtech puts power back into the hands of women, equipping us with tools, data, and resources to understand and take control of our own bodies. It represents a rebellion against a system that has ignored us for too long, proving that women's health is not an afterthought—it is essential. With femtech, we are no longer asking for solutions; we are building them ourselves. This movement is more than a technological advancement—it is a declaration that the health, dignity, and futures of women everywhere are nonnegotiable.

We Ride at Dawn

I am deeply passionate about women's health—so much so that I became a lawyer specializing in femtech and founded a company dedicated to promoting ethical, equitable innovation in this field. Every day, I work with creative individuals across the globe, helping them navigate the complex world of healthcare laws so they can build groundbreaking medical technologies for women.

A significant portion of my work focuses on advising founders who are determined to disrupt the way women's healthcare is delivered. In this role, I guide my clients through legal gray areas that have yet to catch up with the rapid pace of technological development. Together, we create structures and processes that not only comply with the law but are also designed to scale responsibly. My goal is simple: to advance healthcare solutions by supporting bold thinkers and ensuring their products are built with integrity and accountability.

At the heart of everything I do is one driving mission: keeping you, the femtech consumer, safe. Femtech has the power to revolutionize the healthcare industry, but only if we approach it the right way—the *SAFE* way. Like any emerging industry, femtech has its share of bad actors, misguided money grabs, and misleading claims. But it also holds the potential to deliver life-changing and life-saving solutions to some of women's most pressing health issues. To allow this potential to be derailed by missteps or mistrust would be a tragedy.

In the pages ahead, I'll chart a path forward for femtech, centered on the four pillars of my *SAFE* method: Security, Accuracy, Foundation, and Equity. By focusing on these principles, we can confidently create a new era in women's health—one that bridges the many gaps left by traditional healthcare and puts women's needs at the forefront.

Before diving in, it's essential to acknowledge that the impact of women's healthcare extends far beyond those who identify as female. The physical, mental, and emotional effects of this industry touch individuals across the spectrum of gender identity, including those who don't fit neatly into the male/female binary. While I'll use terms like "female" and "woman" for simplicity, this book is for anyone who relates to the stories, statistics, or inequities explored within these pages. These challenges affect people, not just categories, and the solutions must be inclusive of everyone who has been left behind by the current system. To that end, I have also changed the names of many women used within the coming stories, to protect the privacy of the fearless women who shared their stories with me. Name changes are designated with an asterisk (*) the first time the name is used.

This book is about navigating a new and rapidly evolving industry. But more than that, it's about reclaiming control over our health and our futures. It's about demanding innovation that prioritizes our well-being, challenges outdated norms, and treats women's health as the essential nonnegotiable priority it has always deserved to be. Together, we can reshape the narrative that has too often sidelined women in medicine. We can hold companies accountable, reward innovation that truly serves us, and build a foundation of trust that empowers every woman to access the care she deserves with confidence and dignity.

This is more than a guide—it's a call to action. Femtech isn't just a revolution in how women are cared for; it's a revolution in how we care for ourselves and each other. The solutions are here, the tools are within our grasp, and the future is ours to build. Let's move forward boldly, with the knowledge that the revolution in women's health starts now—and it starts with us.

The Past and Present of Women's Health and Femtech

1 | The Hidden Revolution in Women's Health

From Infertility to Innovation

Jennifer Hintzsche reluctantly handed over her laboratory keys.

"You're not smart enough to be here," her academic advisor said with a sigh, as she collected the keyring.

As Hintzsche walked off campus, her mind swirled with frustration and self-doubt. She was a cancer researcher, dismissed from her master's biology program after a single failed experiment. With less than a semester left to complete her degree, Hintzsche lost years of hard work, thousands of dollars in tuition, and the self-confidence she had spent her entire academic career building. Her advisor's cruel parting words were the knockout punch in a series of painful blows.

But Hintzsche refused to give up.

In the months that followed, she channeled her shame and disappointment into action. Determined to stay in cancer research, Hintzsche discovered a new path: bioinformatics, a field that merges biology with computer science. She knew she'd have to learn to code, so she poured herself into mastering programming languages, retaking classes, and restarting her master's degree from scratch.

Four years later, Hintzsche became the first person to earn a doctorate in bioinformatics from Northern Illinois University. As she walked across the stage at graduation, she locked eyes with her former academic advisor. Her expression said it all: I *am* smart enough to be here.

After earning her doctorate, Hintzsche quickly climbed the ranks of the healthcare industry. Her rare combination of skills made her indispensable, and she built a reputation for solving complex problems. Yet, despite her success, Hintzsche found herself facing a new, deeply personal struggle—one that left her feeling the same mixture of shame and unworthiness she'd experienced years earlier.

Why? She was infertile.

"Here I was, a PhD in biology but unable to conceive a child," Hintzsche confessed to me. "[That's] like Biology 101."

After trying to get pregnant for more than a year, Hintzsche and her partner turned to specialists for help. But instead of solutions, they were met with the same vague assurances and noncommittal answers many women hear. In one appointment, Hintzsche was greeted with a plush robe, a glass of cucumber water, and a pamphlet on women's health. The consultation itself was shockingly brief. When it was over, the specialist delivered a diagnosis with a shrug: unexplained infertility.

Hintzsche laughed in disbelief. "[At] the time, I was working on precision oncology—matching individual patient tumors with potential drug targets to treat their cancer. Meanwhile, this doctor looked me over for a couple of hours and said, 'Yeah, I don't know.'"

The diagnosis wasn't just a dead end—it also meant her insurance wouldn't cover additional testing or infertility treatments. Any further investigations would need to be paid for out-of-pocket. As Hintzsche checked out of her appointment, the receptionist handed her a loan application for $10,000, as though this were a routine next step toward becoming a mother.

Hintzsche's experience isn't unique. About 30 percent of infertile women receive the same diagnosis of "unexplained infertility."[1] What sets Hintzsche apart is what she decided to do next.

Hintzsche refused to accept her vague "diagnosis." Instead of admitting defeat, sacrificing a quarter of her income, or falling into despair, Hintzsche did what she does best: She started researching.

But what Hintzsche found—or rather, what she *didn't* find—was infuriating. Her dive into fertility research and women's health literature was more of a shallow splash; the information just wasn't there. Women weren't even required to be included in clinical trials until 1993. For centuries, the healthcare system has been built on the assumption that the male body is the default, with women viewed only as deviations from the norm. Research on women's health exists almost exclusively in the context of reproduction, as if that's all women's bodies are meant for.

As Hintzsche dug deeper, she came face-to-face with modern medicine's gender data gap—a void created by decades of neglect in clinical trials, testing, and development focused on women's health. The statistics are staggering: Excluding cancer, only 1 percent of biopharma projects and 2 percent of new medical devices address conditions specific to women.[2] Meanwhile, less than 5 percent of global healthcare research and development funding goes to women's health.[3]

The gaps aren't just theoretical; they have devastating real-world consequences. Women make up 51 percent of the global population but are grossly underrepresented in medical research. Take chronic pain, for example: Women are 70 percent of those affected, yet 80 percent of pain studies are conducted on men.[4] In cardiovascular medicine, heart disease is the leading cause of death for women in the United States, yet only 33 percent of clinical trial participants are female.[5] Similarly, in the early stages of drug development—when doses and safety are determined—far more men participate, even though women are 60 percent more likely to have adverse reactions to prescription drugs.[6] Comparable figures plague other common health conditions, including autoimmune diseases, sleep apnea, and osteoporosis.

The lack of understanding of the female body has far-reaching consequences. On average, women spend nine years of their lives in poor health, with significantly worse healthcare outcomes than men.[7] According to a groundbreaking report by the McKinsey Health Institute, the women's health gap equates to 75 million years of life lost annually due to poor health and early death.[8] Diseases like endometriosis and polycystic ovary syndrome (PCOS) take 7–10 years to diagnose, and women's health conditions are five times more prevalent than their documented diagnoses.[9]

Even when women know something is wrong, they're often ignored. Twenty-five percent of women report their healthcare providers have dismissed or ignored their symptoms, and 45 percent say they've been labeled as "chronic complainers."[10] Alarmingly, more than 70 percent of women say they've been gaslit by healthcare professionals—told their pain is "all in their head" or "just stress."[11]

Whether it's infertility, chronic migraines, chest pain, or weight management, women navigate the healthcare system with a quiet frustration that's become all too familiar. We endure appointments where our concerns are minimized, our pain is trivialized, and our experiences are reduced to hormones or stress. We leave with more questions than answers, overwhelmed by a system—including doctors (both male and female)—that seems to know so little about female biology.

But there's hope. A quiet revolution is brewing, fueled by people like Hintzsche who are tired of hitting dead ends, talking to brick walls, and watching doctors shrug. Women are fed up with being ignored, dismissed, and underserved by the medical establishment.

This revolution isn't about marches or petitions; it's about leveraging technology and data to close the gender gap in healthcare. It's about empowering women to take control of their health with tools, apps, and devices designed specifically for the female body. This revolution is called femtech, and it's changing the game for women everywhere.

Seeds of Change: Emergence of the Femtech Revolution

In 2012, Dutch entrepreneur Ida Tin created Clue, a period-tracking app born out of frustration that this technology didn't already exist.[12] By 2015, Clue had attracted two million users across 180 countries,[13] and by 2024, it boasted more than 10 million active users.[14] It's estimated that 50 million people worldwide use period-tracking apps today, making them the fourth most popular app for adults and second most popular app for adolescents.[15] Clue's explosive popularity not only proved the demand for women-centered health solutions but also ignited something far greater: the largest movement in women's health technology to date, called femtech.

Femtech, short for "female health technology," encompasses a broad spectrum of products and services designed to address health challenges unique to women. While most people associate femtech with reproductive health innovations like period trackers, fertility apps, and menstrual products, the industry goes far beyond that. As Tin herself put it, femtech refers to "products and services leveraging technology to address needs specific to people with female biology."[16]

You may have already encountered femtech without realizing it. Popular apps like Clue, Flo, Glow, Natural Cycles, Ovia Fertility, or period-proof underwear brands like Thinx and Knix, are just the beginning. Menopause tools like Embr Wave have transformed how women experience hot flashes, while breast-health devices like AI-powered gloves and smart bras offer more accurate detection and monitoring for breast cancer than traditional methods. Femtech is addressing everything from early-stage ovarian cancer detection via simple blood tests to innovative intrauterine devices for managing endometriosis, fibroids, and abnormal bleeding. This isn't just innovation—it's a reimagining of healthcare for women.

Yet, like many women, Hintzsche had never heard of femtech when she faced her infertility diagnosis. Turning to traditional medicine, Hintzsche researched her options, diving into the scientific literature on conception and intrauterine insemination. But the more she learned, the more frustrated she became. The available treatments were invasive, expensive, and often came with limited success rates. She wasn't satisfied with the one-size-fits-all approach to women's reproductive health.

Determined to find another way, Hintzsche analyzed the effectiveness of different fertility treatments and uncovered a method called intracervical insemination (ICI). Simpler, less invasive, and more affordable than IVF, ICI involves placing sperm directly into the cervix using a syringe. While the DIY version—commonly known as the "turkey baster method"—is widely recognized, its success rates are dismally low due to the lack of sterility. However, Hintzsche discovered a game-changing detail: When ICI is performed in a sterile, controlled environment, its success rate skyrockets.

The revelation sparked an idea. What if Hintzsche could create a safe, sterile at-home ICI kit? It would be a solution that could bypass the invasive nature and high cost of IVF, providing an affordable, accessible option for women like her. And she wouldn't need a $10,000 loan to do it. Fueled by frustration and hope, Hintzsche got to work.

With her husband—a mechanical engineer—by her side, Hintzsche researched materials, developed prototypes, and conducted rigorous testing. She collaborated with the US Food and Drug Administration (FDA) to ensure her product met safety and efficacy standards. Her work culminated in the launch of the only FDA-cleared and sterile at-home insemination kit.

Hintzsche herself was the first customer to use the kit. On her second attempt, she became pregnant and later gave birth to a healthy baby girl. While her joy was immeasurable, her frustration with the medical system lingered. She wasn't just angry with the specialists who dismissed her and encouraged her to go into debt to conceive—she was angry with an entire industry that routinely overlooks women's needs.

That anger became a mission. Naming her company "PherDal" as a nod to her PhD and the word "fertile," Hintzsche launched a crowdfunding campaign, raising more than $600,000, which allowed her to produce 200 proof-of-concept kits. In just 90 days, every kit sold out, resulting in 34 successful pregnancies.

A quick look at the statistics and costs associated with infertility treatments shows just how powerful and accessible Hintzsche's kit is for women. ICI boasts a 37.9 percent success rate after six attempts, according to a study of more than 1,000 women.[17] With PherDal, women can achieve six attempts for just $400, compared to $10,000 for a single round of IVF, which has a similar success rate of 46.7 percent.[18] Hintzsche's innovation wasn't just a product—it was a lifeline for women who felt overlooked, dismissed, or priced out of motherhood.

Hintzsche's story exemplifies the rise of femtech. Faced with dismissive doctors and inadequate solutions, women like Hintzsche are stepping up to create the answers themselves. Increasingly, when traditional medicine fails to meet women's needs, they turn to outside experts—or become experts themselves. But what's striking is that even women like Hintzsche, deeply embedded in healthcare, often have no idea the femtech movement exists.

Why Haven't I Heard About Femtech?

If you haven't heard of femtech before, you're not alone. Many women are unfamiliar with the term, even as the industry experiences rapid growth.[19] By 2021, femtech surpassed $1 billion in funding, and the global market is projected to skyrocket from $50 billion in 2023 to $177 billion by 2032—a more than threefold increase in less than a decade.[20]

So why haven't more people heard of femtech?

The biggest reason is censorship, particularly online. Women's health is often stigmatized and labeled as inappropriate, while ads for prostate exams, testosterone enhancers, and Viagra are widely accepted. Smart bras, menopause kits, and pelvic health products, however, are routinely flagged as explicit content. Even when femtech companies create valuable products, they're rarely visible to potential users because search engines, social media platforms, and advertising networks reject the posts and advertisements as "adult" material. A 2022 study by the Center for Intimacy Justice found that 100 percent of femtech companies surveyed had their ads rejected on Meta platforms like Facebook and Instagram.[21] Over half had their accounts suspended entirely, often for ads addressing topics like breast cancer symptoms, menstruation facts, pelvic floor health, fibroids, or endometriosis.[22]

The digital gatekeeping of women's health doesn't just stifle awareness; it perpetuates harmful stigmas, equating essential health education with taboo topics like pornography and sex advertisements. These policies make it nearly impossible for femtech companies to reach their audiences, forcing them to fight an uphill battle to simply inform women about their own bodies. To see how pervasive this issue is, take a look at some of the femtech advertisements and content that were flagged as inappropriate and banned:[23]

- "It takes 3.5 years to sail around the world. It takes 7–10 years to get an endometriosis diagnosis."
- "75% of women report experiencing pain with intimacy at some point, and it's a chronic problem for some. Learn more."
- "Many have already grabbed their spots for our breast/chest feeding workshops this week. If you are a new or expecting parent and would like to participate, make sure you register."
- "Run. Dance. Play. Love. Don't let intimate health concerns get in the way. vFit's new patented technology helps strengthen pelvic floor muscles so you can live life fully."
- "Don't wait another minute. You deserve to live your best life without embarrassing leaks. You can have stronger pelvic muscles and more bladder control in two weeks."
- "Hot flashes, headaches, crazy moods, no sleep? Consult with a specialist doctor or nurse practitioner for answers and solutions, for FREE."

In contrast, men's health advertisements that included language such as "get hard or your money back," "Say Goodbye to Nicks and Snags while Shaving Your Balls," "hard made easy," "Empower Your Balls Now," "My husband is having S** with me for 2 hours straight, and isn't getting tired," and more were approved by these platforms.[24]

This widespread censorship creates a significant barrier. Many femtech products aren't discovered unless you already know what you're looking for or hear about them through word of mouth. For countless women searching for solutions, the silence surrounding these innovations only adds to the frustration of feeling ignored by traditional healthcare. The stigma and taboo surrounding women's health means you're unlikely to encounter the full range of femtech out there today.

Hintzsche faced similar challenges. "I need all the help I can get spreading the word," she shared. "This product can help so many people, but they still don't know about it. Between the censorship and advertising barriers, we have a really hard time reaching consumers. But we want women to know that this product exists for them."

Beyond censorship, mainstream media has contributed to misconceptions about femtech, often dismissing it as unsafe, untested, or unreliable. While there are some misleading products on the market, this isn't a problem unique to femtech—every industry has bad actors. Safe, clinically effective femtech solutions do exist, but they're hard to find amid advertising bans, algorithm biases, and misinformation. The result? Women are left unaware of the groundbreaking tools available—or worse, they believe femtech can't be trusted at all.

Finding Femtech SAFEly

Women's lack of awareness and trust in femtech doesn't exist in a vacuum—it's the result of deeper frustrations with traditional healthcare and the absence of reliable guidance. This gap often leaves women to take matters into their own hands. After a frustrating or inconclusive doctor's appointment, many women find themselves diving into an all-too-familiar ritual: hours of relentless internet scrolling through forums, social media threads, and short videos desperately searching for answers, solidarity, and support. This phase, which I call the "Internet Research Storm," often provides a sense of comfort. Women find connection and validation from others who share their struggles. However, it also comes with significant risks: Misinformation spreads quickly, and poorly informed decisions can lead to wasted money, ineffective treatments, or—worse—compromised health.

In the chaos of the Internet Research Storm, women are bombarded with products and services that fail to deliver. Some don't work, others aren't safe, and many exploit desperation for profit. Targeted ads, influencer endorsements, and flashy marketing often steer women toward pseudo-femtech products that undermine trust in the entire industry. At the same time, the censorship on search engines and social media platforms makes it harder to find reputable femtech options, burying the very solutions that could genuinely help. This can make it difficult to know which femtech products to trust, but fear shouldn't hold women back from exploring solutions. Instead, we must arm ourselves with the tools to make informed decisions, demand better from the industry, and reclaim our power in healthcare. We must learn to critically evaluate femtech offerings—whether found during an Internet Research Storm, through targeted searches, or even word of mouth. By identifying credible and innovative solutions, women can ensure their choices support their well-being.

That's why I created the SAFE method—a simple, practical framework to help you navigate femtech safely and effectively. As a lawyer, my core values center on safety, compliance, and transparency. The SAFE method reflects those values, offering a roadmap for you to evaluate femtech products with confidence. SAFE stands for:

- **Security:** How well does the product protect your data and personal information?
- **Accuracy:** Is the product backed by research, clinical trials, and validated scientific data?
- **Foundation:** Do the company's mission, leadership, and values align with ethical and user-focused innovation?
- **Equity:** Is the product accessible, affordable, and inclusive, designed to meet the needs of diverse consumers?

Though designed with femtech in mind, the SAFE framework can also be applied to other health technologies. Most products can be evaluated in 15 minutes or less, and throughout the book, we'll explore each of these pillars in depth. I'll provide actionable tips and strategies to help you assess products quickly and effectively, equipping you to demand transparency, accountability, and ethical practices from healthcare and tech companies.

By embracing the SAFE method, you can engage with femtech confidently and unlock its transformative potential. Femtech is poised to revolutionize the healthcare landscape, but we must embrace it, and demand continued innovation for the industry to succeed. The possibilities are vast and empowering, promising a future where women are no longer dismissed by doctors, where their pain is acknowledged and treated, and where open discussions about their bodies are met with support, not stigma. Together, we'll navigate this exciting new era of women's health, empowering you to become both an informed consumer and an active participant in the femtech revolution.

Conclusion

This transformative combination of medicine, autonomy, and technology empowers women to shift from being passive recipients of care to active participants in their health journeys. Femtech has the potential to fill the gaps left by traditional healthcare, not by replacing compassion and expertise but by enhancing and personalizing the care women receive. It offers tools to bridge the divide between outdated systems and the unique, evolving needs of women, opening the door to better outcomes and greater empowerment.

To fully grasp the significance of femtech and its promise, we must first examine the history that shaped today's healthcare system. Centuries of neglect, bias, and inequality have left a profound mark on women's health. In the next chapter, we'll trace this journey from ancient remedies to groundbreaking modern innovations, exploring the societal forces that deepened the disparities between men's and women's health. This story of resilience and progress will set the stage for understanding how femtech is uniquely positioned to drive lasting, meaningful change—and why it's more crucial now than ever.

2

Legacy of Neglect

Why Women's Health Needs a Revolution

A Timeless Struggle

In 1845, 18-year-old Lucy knelt on the rough wooden table, her bare knees digging into its unforgiving surface.[1] Her arms trembled as she leaned forward, resting her head on folded hands, her body completely exposed. The position was degrading, stripping her of dignity as well as comfort. The air was thick with the metallic tang of iron and sweat. Soon, the stench of blood—her blood—would overwhelm them both.

J. Marion Sims stood behind her, holding a strange metallic instrument—a prototype of what would one day become the modern speculum. He did not offer Lucy comfort or reassurance. Sims rarely spoke to the women he experimented on, except to bark orders or dismiss their cries of pain.

Lucy flinched as the cold metal entered her body, followed by an explosion of pain. Sims had no use for anesthesia during his experiments. He believed Black women like Lucy didn't feel pain the way white women did—a lie rooted in the racist pseudoscience of the time.[2] Her screams tore through the room. For an hour, Sims worked to perfect a surgical technique to repair vesicovaginal fistulas—a common complication of childbirth that left women incontinent. Nearly a dozen white male doctors stood in the room, observing.

"Lucy's agony was extreme," Sims would later admit in his writing, though not with regret.[3] His controversial use of a sponge to drain urine from Lucy's bladder led her to contract blood poisoning. For three months, she hovered between life and death, her body racked with infection.[4] Sims himself doubted she would survive.

Lucy's experience was far from unique. Sims performed dozens of experimental surgeries on enslaved women, including more than 30 on 17-year-old Anarcha, until he finally perfected his technique.[5] These women were his unwilling subjects, enduring unimaginable pain for medical advancements they would never benefit from.

Sims would later be celebrated as the "father of modern gynecology." His innovations, including the speculum and the surgical repair of fistulas, became cornerstones of women's healthcare. But the true cost of his achievements—the suffering, exploitation, and dehumanization of Lucy, Anarcha, and countless others—was deliberately erased from the narrative. Their names, their voices, and their pain were buried in the margins of history, dismissed as necessary sacrifices for progress.

Lucy's voice, like so many others, was silenced. But her story echoes through history, a haunting reminder of how women—especially women of color—have been marginalized and dehumanized in the pursuit of medical progress.

And yet, as we reflect on Lucy's experience, it's impossible not to wonder how much has truly changed. Danielle's* story, unfolding centuries later, suggests the answer might be unsettlingly familiar.

In 2020, Danielle stared at the ceiling tiles, her breath shallow as she lay on the exam table. The paper sheet beneath her crinkled with every small adjustment. She clutched the flimsy hospital gown tighter across her chest, painfully aware of how exposed she was.

Her gynecologist entered with a curt smile. "Let's get started," she said, pulling on a pair of latex gloves. Danielle scooted down on the table, her feet awkwardly finding their place in the cold metal stirrups.

"This might feel a little uncomfortable," the doctor remarked as she reached for the speculum. Danielle flinched as the cold, rigid device was inserted. The pressure was sharp, unnatural, and invasive. She gritted her teeth as the doctor adjusted it, performing a routine pelvic exam and pap smear. Danielle clenched her fists, digging her nails into her palms. *Uncomfortable* wasn't the word for it. It was painful.

"Everything looks normal." The doctor smiled at the conclusion of the exam.

Danielle pushed herself up on her elbows. "But I've been in so much pain," she said, her voice shaking. "It's not just my periods. I have pain all the time—sharp cramps that come out of nowhere. I'm exhausted, my lower back is killing me, and I can barely eat without getting bloated or nauseous. This isn't normal."

The doctor sighed and looked through her chart. "It could be stress. Or maybe irritable bowel syndrome or a food sensitivity. Have you tried eliminating gluten?"

Danielle felt her throat tighten. "This has nothing to do with gluten."

"Well," the doctor replied, "we can do some testing, but nothing's jumping out at me right now."

Over the next three years, Danielle endured an endless barrage of tests and procedures. Each one felt more invasive than the last. There were transvaginal ultrasounds, where the long, wand-like device was inserted to capture grainy images of her reproductive organs. There was the colonoscopy, ordered after a gastroenterologist suggested her pain might stem from a gastrointestinal issue. There were countless blood draws. Yet, each time, the results came back negative or inconclusive.

When the pain became too much to bear, Danielle was rushed to the emergency room, where doctors ran more tests. Still, they found nothing. "It's likely hormonal," one emergency room physician told her. Another handed her a prescription for birth control. Danielle began to dread every medical appointment. She felt like a specimen rather than a person, her pain brushed aside as an inconvenience.

Finally, Danielle's OB/GYN suggested laparoscopic surgery to look for signs of endometriosis. Her symptoms had worsened by then: stabbing pelvic pain radiated into her legs, her abdomen was tender to the touch, and she couldn't lie on her stomach without discomfort. Desperate for answers, Danielle agreed. The last thing she remembered before surgery was the anesthesiologist's voice, calm and steady as she counted down.

What Danielle didn't know—and what her surgeon didn't tell her—was that while she was unconscious, her body was used to train medical residents. Multiple pelvic exams were performed without her knowledge or consent, a routine practice in some teaching hospitals.[6] The residents practiced inserting speculums, examining her cervix, and palpating her uterus, all while she lay unaware.

When Danielle woke in recovery, the doctor reassured her that the surgery had gone well. They had confirmed she had endometriosis, with scar tissue fusing parts of her ovaries and uterus. Danielle left the hospital feeling a mixture of vindication and devastation. She finally had a diagnosis after years of being dismissed—but the journey had cost her years of pain, invasive procedures, and an irreversible toll on her fertility. And even worse, her body had also been used without her permission, another violation in a long line of indignities.

Like Lucy, Danielle's story is not an isolated one. It's part of a broader failure to respect women's autonomy and address their healthcare needs. The same speculum Sims designed in 1845 remains the standard tool for gynecological exams, unchanged in nearly two centuries. The same dismissive attitudes toward women's pain persist, with symptoms too often minimized or blamed on stress. And just as Lucy was used without consent in the name of medical progress, Danielle's body was treated as a teaching tool without her knowledge. This disappointing state of women's health persists not because it's the best we can do, but because the system has never been forced to do better.

Historical Patterns: The Roots of Modern Myths

The story of Lucy and the modern-day experience of Danielle reveal an uncomfortable truth: Systemic biases in women's healthcare have persisted for centuries. Despite strides in technology and understanding, the journey toward equitable healthcare has been marked by neglect, bias, and inequality. To grasp the significance of femtech—and why it represents such a transformative shift in women's healthcare—we must first understand how we arrived here. The story begins thousands of years ago and winds through triumphs and tragedies that have shaped, and often undermined, women's well-being.

Ancient Wisdom and Early Marginalization

In ancient civilizations, women were at the heart of healthcare, often serving as primary caregivers and healers. Egyptian healers like Peseshet trained midwives, and in Greece, midwives and herbalists provided reproductive care.[7] Similarly, Mesopotamian priestesses of the goddess Gula, revered as the deity of healing, combined spiritual rituals with practical treatments, bridging the gap between medicine and religion. Ancient Indian Ayurvedic texts and traditional Chinese Medicine also recognized the distinct health needs of women, addressing conditions such as menstruation and fertility with herbal remedies and holistic approaches.[8] Even the famed *Hippocratic Corpus*—a cornerstone of Western medicine— included a section on gynecology.

Yet even in these early records, women's roles in healthcare were often tied to their reproductive functions. The Kahun Gynecological Papyrus from ancient Egypt (c. 1800 BCE), one of the earliest medical texts dedicated to women's health, primarily focused on fertility, menstrual disorders, and pelvic pain, underscoring how women were largely seen through the lens of reproduction.[9] This reductive view of women as vessels for childbirth rather than individuals with complex and diverse health needs set the stage for centuries of bias.

Over time, this limited perspective deepened. By the Middle Ages, as medicine became increasingly dominated by men, the contributions of female healers were systematically erased. Midwives and herbalists, who had been pillars of community healthcare, were branded as witches and persecuted. The Church and other institutions denounced women healers, while universities excluded them from medical training, consolidating male authority in the field.

This exclusion not only silenced women's voices but also left them dependent on male physicians, who often ascribed illnesses to "inherent female weakness" or a faulty womb. These ideas were influenced by thinkers like Aristotle, who described women as biologically inferior to men, reinforcing harmful stereotypes about the female body that persist today.[10] Across much of the world, women were increasingly relegated to passive roles in their own healthcare, with their bodies viewed as pathological and in need of control.

Progress Built on Exploitation

The professionalization of medicine in the 19th century marked a turning point in healthcare, bringing both groundbreaking progress and devastating exploitation. Innovations such as anesthesia and antiseptics revolutionized surgery, reducing pain and infection rates. However, many of these medical advancements came at the expense of vulnerable populations, particularly women, whose bodies were treated as experimental sites rather than as individuals deserving of care and dignity.

Across the medical field, women's bodies were subjected to invasive and often unnecessary procedures, reflecting a troubling disregard for their autonomy. As we saw with Lucy, experimentation on enslaved Black women without their consent was used to lay the groundwork for modern gynecology, exposing the dehumanizing practices of the time.[11] But Sims was not alone. Ovariotomies—surgical removal of the ovaries—became disturbingly common, performed for vague or pseudoscientific diagnoses like "hysteria" or "nervous disorders."[12] Surgeons like Robert Battey and Ephraim McDowell undertook these operations with limited understanding of their long-term effects. Many women suffered chronic pain, infertility, and even death as a result. Similarly, clitoridectomies were promoted as cures for perceived sexual deviance or excessive libido, reinforcing harmful stereotypes that women's bodies were unruly and in need of control.[13]

This exploitation extended beyond surgeries to medical training and experimentation. Poor immigrant women and incarcerated women were frequently coerced into becoming subjects for medical students' practice, unnecessary procedures, or clinical trials.[14] For example, immigrant women in urban centers were lured into hospitals under the guise of receiving charity care, only to find themselves used for untested procedures. These practices reflected not only the gender biases of the time but also deeply entrenched class and racial inequities, as marginalized women were deemed expendable in the pursuit of medical advancement.

Childbirth practices also underwent significant changes during this period. The shift from home births, typically managed by midwives, to hospital deliveries led by male obstetricians was framed as progress. However, it often disregarded the expertise of midwives, whose holistic approaches to care were replaced with interventions that sometimes introduced more harm than good. Forceps, for instance, were widely adopted without a full understanding of their risks, leading to complications like infections, perineal tears, and maternal injuries. Moreover, the lack of hand hygiene among physicians moving between autopsies and deliveries caused rampant infections and maternal deaths.[15]

Amid these failures, the seeds of change began to take root. Elizabeth Blackwell, the first woman to earn a medical degree in the United States, founded the New York Infirmary for Women and Children, creating a space where women physicians could practice and serve underserved populations.[16] Mary Edwards Walker, a Civil War surgeon and recipient of the Medal of Honor, defied gender norms to provide critical battlefield care while advocating for women's rights.[17] Harriet Tubman, celebrated for her work on the Underground Railroad, also served as a nurse and healer during the Civil War, using her knowledge of herbal remedies to care for soldiers and formerly enslaved individuals.[18] Meanwhile, Florence Nightingale revolutionized nursing, transforming it into a respected profession and emphasizing sanitation practices that saved countless lives.[19]

The 19th century was thus a paradoxical era for women's health. While it brought monumental medical advancements, it also exposed and deepened the inequities that marginalized women—particularly those of color and lower socioeconomic status. The efforts of pioneering women laid the groundwork for progress, but the abuses and biases of the time underscore how often those advancements came at an unacceptable cost.

Advances Without Equity

The 20th and 21st centuries brought remarkable medical breakthroughs, yet women's health consistently lagged behind, sidelined by outdated assumptions and biases. Women were often excluded from critical medical conversations, their unique needs dismissed as secondary or unimportant. This neglect wasn't just a missed opportunity—it entrenched inequalities that continue to shape healthcare today.

A stark example is the development of the birth control pill, approved in 1960 and hailed as a groundbreaking step toward reproductive autonomy for women. Beneath this scientific triumph, however, lies a darker history. The pill's development relied on unethical clinical trials conducted on impoverished Puerto Rican women who were not fully informed of the risks.[20] Participants suffered severe side effects, including nausea, blood clots, and strokes. Tragically, three women died during the trials, but their deaths were never thoroughly investigated.[21] While the pill revolutionized reproductive choices, its development exposed the disturbing reality that medical progress often came at the expense of vulnerable populations.

Forced sterilizations further exemplified the violations of women's reproductive autonomy during this period. From the 1930s to the 1970s, eugenics programs in the United States targeted tens of thousands of Black, Latina, Indigenous, and low-income women, coercing or forcing them into sterilization under the guise of public health.[22] For example, in North Carolina alone, more than 7,600 sterilizations were performed as part of state-sanctioned eugenics programs.[23] Similar abuses occurred in California, which led the country in sterilizations, often targeting Latina women.[24] These practices robbed women of their ability to make reproductive choices, perpetuating cycles of systemic oppression.

Even widely adopted treatments often came with hidden dangers. Diethylstilbestrol (DES), prescribed to millions of pregnant women from the 1940s to the 1970s to prevent miscarriages, was later linked to vaginal cancer, infertility, and other reproductive complications in both mothers and their children.[25] The thalidomide disaster of the 1960s, in which a drug used to treat morning sickness caused severe birth defects, further exposed the risks of insufficient safety testing.[26] Following this disaster, the FDA issued a policy excluding women of childbearing age from clinical trials.

While the FDA's policy aimed to protect women and their future children, it had long-term consequences. From the 1970s to the early 1990s, clinical trials focused almost exclusively on men, leaving critical gaps in understanding how diseases, medications, and treatments affected women. However, biological uniqueness means drugs affect males and females differently. Women, for example, generally have larger stores of fat than men,[27] meaning drugs that dissolve in fat storage before reaching the brain (e.g., antidepressants, anti-anxiety, and antipsychotic medications) are distributed differently in women.[28] Similarly, women tend to produce less gastric acid than men, resulting in slower digestion.[29] This means medications that require gastric acid for absorption are often less effective in women. Comparably, women's fluctuating hormones can impact how well drugs are metabolized in the liver, which can cause drugs to be more concentrated—and thus more dangerous—for women even if the dosage is the same as men.

As a result, women experience disproportionately higher rates of adverse drug reactions and are frequently prescribed treatments that are inappropriate or ineffective for their bodies. Between 1997 and 2000, 10 drugs were withdrawn from the market, with 8 of them causing more severe adverse effects in women than men.[30] Despite this, at least four of those drugs were prescribed more frequently to women and were more likely to cause potentially fatal cardiac arrhythmias in women than in men.[31] Since 1980, medications have been 3.5 times more likely to be removed from the market due to safety risks that disproportionately affect women.[32] This glaring disparity highlights the long-standing neglect of women's health in medical research and emphasizes the critical importance of addressing gender differences in clinical trials.

Amid these failures, the feminist health movement of the 1970s emerged as a powerful force for change. Women's health collectives provided contraception, abortion services, and education, and books like *Our Bodies, Ourselves* empowered women to advocate for themselves in medical settings.[33] These efforts led to significant policy changes, including the passage of Title X in 1970, which funded family planning services, and the 1993 NIH Revitalization Act, which mandated the inclusion of women in federally funded research.[34] The FDA also rescinded its 1977 policy that excluded women from participating in clinical trials.

Despite these victories, progress was uneven. A 2001 Government Accountability Office audit revealed that many clinical trials—despite allowing women to participate since 1993—still failed to account for sex-based differences, leading to dangerous outcomes.[35] Four years later, another report revealed that only 3 percent of research funded by the National Institutes of Health (NIH) analyzed sex differences, widening the knowledge gaps for women with conditions such as heart disease, autoimmune disorders, and chronic pain.[36] By 2015, Congress was still calling on federal agencies to improve oversight of sex inclusion in research. It wasn't until

2016—the same year that the term "femtech" was coined—that the NIH required grant applicants to account for sex as a biological variable in their research designs.[37]

Even today, the gender data gap continues to harm women's health in profound ways. The neglect of conditions like menopause, which every woman experiences, remains a glaring oversight. A 2023 study revealed that only 31 percent of OB/GYN residency programs in the US include a formal menopause curriculum, leaving many doctors ill-equipped to diagnose and treat menopausal symptoms.[38] As a result, 8 in 10 women experiencing menopause remain undiagnosed or improperly treated.[39] Similarly, the Centers for Disease Control and Prevention estimates that four out of five pregnancy-related deaths in the US are preventable,[40] yet at least 50,000 women suffer life-threatening complications from childbirth each year.[41]

Consent issues in women's health also remain a significant concern today, reflecting the troubling legacy of paternalism in medicine. One stark example, as we saw in Danielle's story, is the practice of performing pelvic or vaginal exams on women under anesthesia without explicit consent. Studies have revealed that medical students in some hospitals are even allowed to conduct these exams during surgeries or procedures unrelated to gynecology.[42] While some states have passed laws requiring explicit consent for these exams, gaps in regulation persist, leaving many women vulnerable to these unethical practices. Beyond this, broader consent issues include insufficient disclosure of risks associated with women's health treatments, such as contraceptive devices like intrauterine devices (IUDs) or long-acting implants. As of 2022, forced sterilization was still legal in 31 states and Washington, DC, with some laws being passed as recently as 2019.[43]

These examples highlight how women's health has been treated as an afterthought throughout much of the 20th century and beyond. From the lack of representation in clinical trials to the ongoing neglect of critical health issues, countless women have been left to navigate a medical system that fails to meet their needs. This legacy of neglect not only has caused direct harm but has also fueled pervasive medical myths about women's bodies—misconceptions that continue to shape healthcare practices and reinforce inequities today.

Conclusion

The historical neglect of women in healthcare has had far-reaching consequences, impacting not only individual outcomes but also the way society and the medical community perceive women's bodies and health. This has given rise to persistent myths about women's pain tolerance, reproductive health, and even basic anatomy. These misconceptions have become deeply entrenched in modern medicine, influencing everything from medical education to research priorities and clinical care. The result is a system that too often dismisses women's concerns, delays critical diagnoses, and offers inadequate treatments.

This failure isn't just about the past—it's about the ongoing inequities that continue to affect women today. Conditions like endometriosis, menopause, and autoimmune diseases remain underdiagnosed, underfunded, and misunderstood. This perpetuates a cycle of exclusion that leaves millions of women without the care they need.

Understanding this history is critical because it illuminates how deeply rooted these issues are—and why they're so difficult to overcome. Yet it also provides an opportunity for change. In the next chapter, we'll explore the modern myths that stem from this history and reveal how they continue to harm women's health. More importantly, we'll set the foundation for discussing how femtech offers a powerful solution: a way to dismantle these misconceptions, challenge systemic biases, and finally place women's health at the forefront of medical innovation. The future of healthcare depends on recognizing and addressing these long-standing injustices, and femtech is poised to lead the way.

3

Myths, Misconceptions, and Misogyny in Women's Health

Modern Medical Mythology

For women, navigating the healthcare system often feels like walking into battle—armed with little more than persistence and hope. Even today, with all the advancements in modern medicine, we face a system that devalues our health and forces us to fight for the care we deserve. It's a battle fought on many fronts: first, convincing doctors to take our concerns seriously; then navigating the maze of bureaucracy and insurance policies seemingly designed to deny rather than deliver care; and finally, grappling with the reality that many solutions for women's health are underdeveloped or not designed with our unique needs in mind.

The story of my friend Amber* is a stark illustration of how deeply biases against women are woven into the fabric of healthcare. When

Amber became pregnant with her first child, she was overjoyed. Like many first-time mothers, she prepared for the journey ahead with excitement and a healthy dose of caution. But as her pregnancy progressed, she began experiencing sharp, tearing pains that left her breathless. Something felt wrong. At every appointment, she tried to describe the pain to her doctors, only to be met with condescension and dismissal. "Pregnancy can be uncomfortable," the doctors told her with a smile. "Try to rest more."

By the time Amber reached the emergency room, doubled over in agony, the situation was impossible to ignore. Tests revealed a mass growing on the outside of her uterus. It was impossible to know if the mass was cancerous without a biopsy, but because she was pregnant, no one wanted to risk intervention. Doctors sent her home with instructions to rest and wait. While she waited, her baby grew, the mass expanded, and her fear of what might be happening inside her body deepened with each passing day.

The months that followed were excruciating. By her final trimester, Amber's pain was unbearable. She couldn't sleep, couldn't move, and couldn't shake the fear that she was carrying something malignant alongside her child. When it was finally time for delivery, the doctors prepared her for an emergency C-section. Amber seized the moment to ask what she thought was a no-brainer question.

"You're going to remove the mass at the same time, right? Or at least biopsy it so we know if I have cancer?"

Her doctor's answer stunned her. "I'm sorry," he said, avoiding her eyes. "You're here for a C-section. Insurance won't cover tumor removal or biopsy at the same time."

"What do you mean you can't do both?" Amber asked, stunned. "You're cutting into my uterus anyway!"

"We can't," her doctor repeated. "The system isn't set up for it."

The system. That faceless entity dictating her care, controlling her options, and, in that moment, forcing her to undergo two separate invasive surgeries instead of one. Amber delivered her baby girl that day. During the delivery, the top of her uterus—and the mass that grew on it—was pulled outside Amber's abdominal cavity to allow the surgeons better access and space to deliver her baby. Following the delivery, the mass was then placed back inside Amber's body. It would be two more months before the doctors reopened her body—along her same C-section incision line—removed the tumor, and finally confirmed that it was benign.

Amber's story is an absurd, infuriating example of how biases against women are embedded not just in attitudes, but in the very structure of the healthcare system. These biases are driven by powerful myths about women's health—myths that devalue women's pain, trivialize their concerns, and prioritize bureaucracy over their well-being.

This chapter examines three of the most pervasive myths about women's health, exposing how they create and perpetuate the inequities women face every day. These myths don't just shape the way women are treated; they shape the way women view their own health, often leading to shame, dismissal, or a sense of helplessness. Once we understand these myths, we can begin to dismantle them—and explore how femtech offers a transformative solution to rewrite the story of women's healthcare.

The Myth: Medical Equality Exists

One of the most pervasive myths in modern medicine is the belief that the healthcare system treats men and women equally. This assumption—that medicine is neutral and objective—obscures a glaring reality: Healthcare has long centered on male physiology as the default, leaving women's unique health needs undervalued, misunderstood, or outright ignored. The result? Inequities that delay diagnoses, deprioritize care, and lead to preventable harm for millions of women worldwide.

These disparities are perhaps most visible in the prioritization of treatments and surgeries. Conditions like pelvic floor disorders and endometriosis—issues that can devastate a woman's quality of life—are routinely labeled as "elective" and pushed to the bottom of priority lists. But this isn't just a scheduling issue; it's economic. For centuries women's health has been so undervalued that it has created a system where surgeries addressing female-specific conditions are reimbursed at significantly lower rates than procedures seen as more universal or "essential."

The problem is rooted in the Relative Value Unit (RVU) system, the framework that determines how much physicians are reimbursed for specific procedures. When the RVU system was formalized in the 1990s, gynecological surgeries were largely overlooked in the original calculations, leaving them undervalued from the start. Although initially designed for Medicare and Medicaid, the RVU system now shapes reimbursement across virtually all insurance providers, embedding systemic inequities into the healthcare economy. Procedures that primarily benefit women—like endometriosis excisions—receive fewer RVUs than procedures benefiting men or procedures that are gender-neutral. The math is simple: Fewer RVUs means lower reimbursement rates, which means hospitals, often operating under tight margins, are incentivized to prioritize higher-paying procedures.

Consider a complex endometriosis excision surgery, which can take anywhere from one to eight hours and is life-changing for the patient. This procedure earned 12.15 RVUs in 2023.[1] Compare that to a shoulder arthroscopy, a procedure lasting only 30–60 minutes, which earned 15 RVUs.[2] This discrepancy is even more apparent when we consider the difference in pay for a scrotal biopsy versus a vulvar biopsy. The scrotal biopsy pays 123 percent more than the vulvar biopsy.[3] The higher reimbursement attached to male surgeries, which are often quicker and less complex, means hospitals naturally favor them, leaving women with conditions like endometriosis to wait years for care, enduring debilitating pain in the meantime.

But inequity in healthcare isn't just a matter of dollars and cents; it's deeply personal, affecting lives in profound ways. Take the story of Rebecca,[*] a 29-year-old elementary school teacher who had been living with debilitating pelvic pain for years. After countless appointments and tests, she was diagnosed with severe endometriosis. Her gynecologist recommended excision surgery to remove the adhesions and prevent further complications, but scheduling the procedure was a nightmare. The wait time for the procedure was two years.

In the meantime, Rebecca's condition worsened. The pain became so severe that she couldn't work, sleep, or eat without agony. Doctors put her on hormone replacement therapy to treat the pain, but it caused premature menopause, jeopardizing her ability to have children. By the time her surgery was finally performed, the endometriosis had spread further, requiring additional operating time and a partial bowel resection—complications that could have been avoided if her surgery had been performed earlier.

Rebecca's experience exemplifies how historic biases in healthcare continue to result in devastating consequences for women today.

These inequities extend beyond surgeries and insurance to diagnostic processes. For example, sleep apnea—a condition affecting millions—is diagnosed based on symptoms like loud snoring and breathing pauses, which align with how the condition presents in men. Women, who often experience subtler symptoms like fatigue or insomnia, are misdiagnosed or overlooked entirely. An estimated 90 percent of women with sleep apnea remain undiagnosed, leaving them at risk for complications like heart disease and cognitive decline.[4]

Autoimmune diseases further highlight the failures of gendered healthcare. Conditions like lupus, rheumatoid arthritis, and multiple sclerosis disproportionately affect women, yet they are among the most misdiagnosed and misunderstood illnesses. Women with these diseases often endure years of unnecessary treatments or dismissal before receiving an accurate diagnosis. Similarly, ovarian cancer, often referred to as the "silent killer," is frequently caught too late because symptoms like bloating and pelvic pain are dismissed as digestive issues. Seventy percent of ovarian cancer cases are diagnosed at advanced stages, drastically reducing survival rates.[5]

Jordan,* my high school classmate, is a heartbreaking testament to the devastating consequences of dismissing or delaying women's healthcare. The day before Jordan's 29th birthday, she was diagnosed with stage four ovarian cancer. For months, she had experienced symptoms like fatigue, bloating, severe abdominal pain, and limited appetite. But by the time doctors pieced her symptoms together, it was too late for early intervention. What makes this story even more surreal is that both her parents are doctors—yet even with that level of medical awareness and advocacy in her family, the biases and misconceptions surrounding women's health still delayed her diagnosis. Jordan passed away at the age of 32.

This inequity isn't just a moral failure—it's an economic one. Despite the fact that women are responsible for 80 percent of healthcare decisions, women's health receives just 4 percent of all healthcare research and development funding.[6] Take Alzheimer's disease as an example: Two-thirds of the 5.8 million Americans with Alzheimer's are women, and women have a 30 percent higher risk of dying from the disease than men.[7] Yet only 12 percent of the NIH's external research portfolio for Alzheimer's disease focuses on women.[8] Similar figures are seen in the field of cardiology. Cardiovascular disease is the number-one killer for women in the United States, yet only 4.5 percent of coronary artery disease funding is targeted at women.[9]

The economic impact of this neglect is staggering. Women spend $500 billion annually on healthcare, yet their unmet health needs cost the United States billions more in lost productivity.[10] Maternal mortality alone results in $6.6 billion in productivity losses annually.[11] Menopause-related health issues cost employers $27 billion annually, with $1.8 billion in lost working time.[12] Endometriosis patients report healthcare costs three times higher than average and significant income loss due to debilitating symptoms.[13] More than $80 billion is spent annually on autoimmune condition management for women.[14] Overall, healthcare spending for women ages 18–44 is 84 percent higher than their male counterparts, and healthcare spending for women ages 44–64 is 24 percent higher than their male counterparts.[15]

The financial toll isn't limited to women themselves; it impacts the broader economy. A study found that a single day without working women in the United States would result in $21 billion in lost gross domestic product.[16] Conversely, investing in women's health yields extraordinary returns. For instance, a $300 million investment in women's health research could generate $13 billion in economic benefits.[17] Small improvements in managing diseases like rheumatoid arthritis or coronary artery disease could similarly save billions in healthcare costs and add years of productivity to women's lives.[18]

The message is clear: The myth that healthcare treats men and women equally is not only false but dangerous. Women's health inequities cost lives, livelihoods, and billions of dollars annually. Change is long overdue, and it requires systemic reform to ensure that women's health is prioritized—not just for the sake of equity, but for the well-being of everyone.

The Myth: Women's Pain Is Normal or Overstated

Building on the myth of medical equality, the second myth is equally damaging: the belief that women's pain is either normal or exaggerated. This assumption has shaped the way society and medicine have viewed women's health for centuries. From childbirth to chronic illness, women's pain is too often dismissed, minimized, or outright ignored, leaving countless women to suffer in silence.

The roots of this myth trace back to ancient Greece. As we saw in Chapter 2, early physicians like Hippocrates attributed women's ailments to a "wandering womb." This pseudoscientific theory gave rise to the term "hysteria," a label used for centuries to dismiss women's health concerns as emotional instability. Women were painted as unreliable narrators of their own bodies, their pain dismissed as an overreaction or a symptom of their so-called fragile emotional state. Tragically, these archaic beliefs continue to cast a long shadow over modern medicine.

Take Lisa,* who endured debilitating migraines for over a decade. Each episode left her confined to a dark room, unable to work or care for her children. When she finally sought help, her doctor told her she was likely stressed and prescribed meditation and hydration. It wasn't until years later, after switching physicians, that Lisa was diagnosed with migraines triggered by hormonal changes. In that time, she had missed countless workdays, birthdays, and family events—all because her pain wasn't taken seriously.

This pattern of dismissal extends to life-threatening conditions and surgical recovery. In emergency rooms, women presenting with acute abdominal pain wait an average of 65 minutes for pain relief, compared to 49 minutes for men.[19] Similarly, women experiencing heart attacks are seven times more likely than men to be misdiagnosed and discharged from emergency departments because their pain presents differently.[20] A study from King's College London further found that women are less likely to receive pain relief prescriptions than men, with 26 percent of women receiving prescriptions compared to 31 percent of men.[21] The researchers suggested that pre-existing biases, such as the perception that women are more emotional and likely to overreport pain, may contribute to this disparity. This bias often leaves women to manage their illnesses and surgical recoveries with insufficient medication,[22] prolonging their suffering and delaying their return to normal activities. These disparities are not only harmful but deeply demoralizing, reinforcing the notion that women's pain is less deserving of care and attention.

The story of Katrina* exemplifies how devastating this can be. After starting a new form of birth control, Katrina experienced intense menstrual cramps and pain during sex. Her OB/GYN waved off her concerns, telling her she would "get used to it." Months later, she collapsed at home from a ruptured ovarian cyst—a known side effect of her medication. Instead of receiving early intervention, Katrina endured months of unnecessary pain until her condition became an emergency.

This disbelief of women's pain disproportionately affects women of color and those from lower socioeconomic backgrounds, compounding already stark health disparities. Studies show that Black women are systematically undertreated for pain compared to white women, often due to deeply ingrained racist stereotypes. A 2016 study revealed that nearly 40 percent of first- and second-year medical trainees still believed harmful myths, such as Black patients having a higher pain tolerance, thicker skin, or less sensitive nerve endings than white patients.[23] These falsehoods not only reflect historical biases, but they also directly affect clinical decision-making today, leading to disparities in pain management.

For example, Black patients are 22 percent less likely than white patients to receive pain medication in emergency rooms, and when they do, they are often prescribed lower doses.[24] A study by the *Journal of the American Medical Association* exemplifies this point, finding that Black children presenting with appendicitis in emergency departments were far less likely to receive opioid pain relief compared to white children with the same condition.[25] Such patterns persist across medical contexts, with Black women facing even greater barriers to care due to the intersection of racial and gender bias.

The consequences are profound. Consider Serena Williams, who nearly died after childbirth due to a pulmonary embolism. Despite her clear understanding of her body and her history of blood clots, her concerns were dismissed by healthcare providers. Her life-threatening condition was only addressed after she repeatedly insisted on further testing and refused to accept the dismissal of her pain. While Williams is alive today because of her advocacy, the delay she faced in receiving appropriate care led to complications that kept her bedridden for the first six weeks of her daughter's life. If one of the most famous and influential women in the world can struggle to have her health concerns addressed, it speaks volumes about the systemic inequities faced by millions of Black women in healthcare. Against this backdrop, it's not difficult to understand why Black women are three to four times more likely than white women to die during childbirth, even though many of these deaths are preventable with proper care.[26]

The myth that women exaggerate their pain isn't just harmful—it's a foundational barrier that undermines the entire healthcare experience. When women's pain is dismissed, it creates a ripple effect that devalues all their symptoms, making it harder for them to receive accurate diagnoses and effective treatments. Instead of addressing what hurts, women are told things *shouldn't* hurt, leaving their suffering unacknowledged and untreated. This reinforces the damaging belief that women can't be trusted to understand or articulate their own bodies. It's a cycle that not only delays care but erodes the trust women have in a system designed to protect their health.

The Myth: Women's Health Means Reproductive Health

Beyond the myths of equality and pain tolerance lies another harmful misconception that disadvantages women today: that women's health means reproductive health. While menstruation, pregnancy, and childbirth are undeniably critical aspects of women's health, this narrow definition ignores the vast and complex medical needs of women throughout their lives. It perpetuates the idea that women's value is tied solely to their reproductive capabilities and sidelines essential areas of research, treatment, and innovation. This myth reduces women's health to a biological function, erasing their worth before puberty and after menopause, and falsely assumes that all nonreproductive health conditions affect men and women in the same way. Nothing could be further from the truth.

This reductive view has deep historical roots. For centuries, societal norms and medical practices framed women's health through the lens of reproduction. Medical literature from the 18th and 19th centuries treated women's bodies as vessels for childbirth, devoting pages to the uterus and ovaries while largely ignoring other systems. Symptoms unrelated to reproduction were dismissed as "nervousness" or "hysteria." By the Victorian era, women were warned that intellectual pursuits or employment would drain energy from their reproductive organs, leading to infertility or illness. These ideas shaped the foundation of modern medicine, embedding the belief that women's bodies are valuable only when performing reproductive functions.

Even in the 20th century, this outdated perspective persisted. Clinical research, which became more standardized in the 1950s and 1960s, systematically excluded women—even before the FDA's 1977 policy. Researchers justified this exclusion by claiming that fluctuating hormones made women unreliable test subjects. One NIH-supported study in the 1960s on how obesity affected breast and uterine cancer enrolled 8,341 men and 0 women, despite its explicit focus on female cancers.[27] This exclusion wasn't just a missed opportunity; it solidified the misconception that women's health beyond reproduction wasn't worth studying and that women's unique physiology could be overlooked even in research on conditions specific to their bodies. By neglecting to include women in widespread research, medicine effectively equated women's health with their reproductive systems, leaving gaps in knowledge that continue today.

Ironically, even reproductive health—supposedly the focus of women's healthcare—is riddled with neglect and misunderstanding. Conditions like endometriosis, polycystic ovary syndrome (PCOS), and uterine fibroids are prime examples. Endometriosis, affecting 1 in 10 women, often takes 7–10 years to diagnosis.[28] During this time, women endure chronic pain, infertility, and organ damage while their symptoms are dismissed as "normal period cramps." Despite its prevalence and severity, endometriosis research receives only $1–$2 per affected individual annually in the United States, compared to $31 per diabetes patient and $130 per Crohn's disease patient—all diseases that have a similar prevalence in women.[29]

Similarly, PCOS affects approximately 1 in 10 women of reproductive age and has long-term complications such as type 2 diabetes and cardiovascular disease.[30] Yet studies show that up to 70 percent of women with PCOS go undiagnosed.[31] Symptoms like irregular periods, acne, and weight gain are often dismissed as cosmetic issues or lifestyle problems rather than indicators of a serious hormonal disorder. The lack of standard diagnostic criteria only exacerbates this problem, leaving millions of women without answers or proper treatment.

Even conditions like uterine fibroids, which affect up to 80 percent of women by age 50, are often overlooked or trivialized.[32] Despite causing heavy menstrual bleeding, pelvic pain, and even infertility, fibroids are frequently met with a "wait and see" approach that delays care. Recent studies show that, on average, women wait about 3.6 years before seeking treatment for fibroids, with Black women waiting 4.45 years.[33] Even when women do seek treatment, 41 percent had to see two or more doctors before receiving a diagnosis, with 5 percent seeing five or more providers.[34] By the time some women are finally treated, their fibroids have grown so large that invasive surgery becomes the only option—a preventable outcome if the condition had been prioritized earlier.

This systemic under-diagnosis exposes a glaring contradiction: While women's health is improperly reduced to reproduction, even reproductive health conditions are routinely ignored, misunderstood, or minimized. Far from being a priority, these conditions are treated as inconveniences rather than urgent medical concerns. This sends a devastating message: Women's health matters only insofar as it relates to reproduction, and even then, not enough to warrant adequate care.

The broader harm of this myth is that it erases the full scope of women's health. Autoimmune diseases, for example, disproportionately affect women and are among the most misdiagnosed and poorly understood conditions in medicine. Lupus, rheumatoid arthritis, and multiple sclerosis are up to nine times more common in women than men, yet women with these diseases often endure years of unnecessary treatments before receiving a diagnosis.[35] These delays allow conditions to progress, causing irreversible damage and worsening quality of life. This myth also affects how we perceive women's aging. Osteoporosis, a condition that predominantly affects postmenopausal women, is frequently overlooked until fractures occur—despite being partially preventable through early intervention. These examples highlight how the conflation of women's health with reproduction diminishes women's access to comprehensive care, regardless of age.

Conclusion

The myths surrounding women's health have shaped medical practices, research priorities, and societal attitudes for centuries, often to the detriment of countless women. The belief that women's health and men's health are fundamentally the same has masked crucial gender-specific differences in symptoms, diagnoses, and treatments, leading to gaps in care and poorer outcomes for women. The idea that women's pain is either normal or exaggerated has invalidated their experiences, leading to dismissals, delays, and inadequate care for millions experiencing chronic pain, illness, or life-altering conditions. Finally, the notion that women's health is limited to reproduction has ignored the broader medical needs of women, sidelining research into conditions that affect them throughout their lives.

These myths are harmful because they dismiss the complexity of women's health, perpetuate inequity in medical treatment, and reinforce a culture that undervalues women's experiences beyond reproduction. They fail to account for the nuanced ways that women experience health, illness, and care, often treating women's bodies as afterthoughts or anomalies in a male-default medical system. By perpetuating these flawed ideas, we have normalized a status quo that underserves women, undermining the fundamental principle of equitable healthcare.

Dispelling these myths requires a shift in mindset—one that recognizes the scale, significance, and profitability of addressing women's health. It means challenging outdated assumptions and pushing for meaningful change in healthcare, research, and funding. It also requires embracing the promise of innovation and looking to new solutions that directly target the unmet needs of women. The myths of women's health have persisted for too long, and it is time to replace them with a narrative of opportunity, equity, and growth.

The rise of femtech represents a pivotal opportunity to overcome these challenges. By driving innovation and investment in solutions tailored to women's unique needs, femtech is poised to shatter these myths and usher in a new era of growth, equity, and progress in women's healthcare.

4 | The Femtech Frontier

A New Era in Healthcare

When Technology Saves Lives

Ruby* was 47 when she noticed the changes to her body. At first, it was a few extra days of spotting between cycles. Then, when her period arrived, the bleeding was heavier, more intense, and longer than ever before. She knew her body. This wasn't normal.

When she mentioned it to friends, they shrugged. "That's just part of getting older," one said. "It could be perimenopause," another suggested. Still, the unpredictability made Ruby uneasy. So she booked an appointment with her OB/GYN.

Her doctor was kind but dismissive. "This is all perfectly normal," she reassured Ruby after a pelvic exam. "It's just hormones shifting at your age. Nothing to worry about."

But Ruby *was* worried. What if this wasn't just the early signs of menopause? What if something was really wrong?

She started tracking everything—her cycles, her symptoms, her moods—using a period-tracking app she found online. A few months later, she noticed a pattern. Her data wasn't just confirming her suspicions; the app itself flagged her symptoms as abnormal for someone her age and recommended she see a doctor. This time, Ruby wasn't going to be brushed off.

At her second appointment, Ruby arrived prepared. When her doctor once again tried to dismiss her concerns, she pulled out her phone. She showed her doctor her tracked symptoms, pointed to the flagged irregularities, and even read aloud the app's recommendation to seek medical attention.

"Now, are you going to take this as seriously as I am, or do I need to find another doctor?" Ruby asked.

Her OB/GYN hesitated, then ordered a round of tests—bloodwork, an ultrasound, and a pap smear. Two weeks later, after several follow-up tests, the results came back.

Ruby didn't have perimenopause. She had cervical cancer.

The diagnosis was terrifying, but the news could have been much worse. Thanks to her diligence and refusal to ignore her symptoms, the cancer was caught early, before it had spread. A hysterectomy removed the cancer and Ruby recovered fully. Today, she is cancer free.

Ruby still uses the app, tracking her menopause symptoms with the same vigilance. If something ever seems off again, she won't wait for a doctor's approval to act. Without femtech, however, Ruby's cancer might have gone undetected for years. She might have faced grueling treatments or a dire prognosis. But because she had access to technology that helped her understand her body, she saved her own life.

Ruby's story is just one example of how femtech is revolutionizing healthcare. Instead of relying solely on a medical system that wasn't built for women, Ruby empowered herself with technology designed specifically for her needs. Instead of waiting for research to catch up, she created her own dataset—proving that personalized, real-time health tracking is more than just a convenience. It can be lifesaving.

This is the true power of femtech. It's not just about new gadgets or wellness trends—it's about giving women the tools to advocate for themselves, to track and understand their bodies, and to push back against a healthcare system that has historically underserved them. As we dive into the femtech landscape, we'll explore what this industry is, where it's grow-ing, why it's the solution to dismantling outdated myths about women's health, and how it's reshaping healthcare across the world.

The femtech revolution isn't on the horizon. It's already here.

Giving Women's Health a Name—and a Future

Breaking away from the limitations of traditional healthcare was no small feat. As we saw in Chapter 2, women's health concerns have been sidelined, dis-missed, and folded into male-centered medical research for centuries, leaving critical gaps in care. Pushing back against these historic failures required persis-tence, advocacy, and innovation, eventually leading to the rise of femtech. But even after this industry emerged, defining its scope became a challenge. What exactly qualifies as femtech? Does it only include digital health tools, or does it extend to physical products? How is femtech different from healthcare as a whole? And why isn't there a corresponding "mentech" industry?

The truth is, there is no need for a "mentech" industry—we already have one. It's called healthcare. As we explored earlier, medical research and treatment guidelines have long been centered on men's bodies. While healthcare is often framed as gender-neutral, we saw in Chapter 3 that healthcare is a male-dominated industry that has systematically deprior-itized, underfunded, and overlooked women's health. This is why having a term like *femtech* matters. It doesn't just define an industry—it creates visi-bility for women's unique health needs, ensuring they are no longer lost within a system that was never designed for them.

Without a distinct category for innovation in women's health, many advancements would continue to go unrecognized and underfunded. Femtech challenges the long-standing assumption that women's bodies are simply variations of men's or that women's health is a niche concern. It gives us the language to name the bias, identify the gaps, and rally behind a cause that has been neglected for too long. By carving out space in an industry that has failed to prioritize women's health, femtech helps ensure that these innovations are recognized, invested in, and delivered to those who need them most.

Yet, despite its increasing prominence, femtech still lacks a universally agreed-upon definition. Some define it narrowly, restricting it to digital health tools—software, apps, and data-driven platforms—primarily focused on reproductive health. Others take a broader view, arguing that femtech includes any technology-driven innovation addressing health issues that affect women, even if the product is not directly intended for women. For example, one femtech accelerator program included a startup focused on pre-ejaculation solutions, claiming that the product supported "climax control" for women by minimizing sperm pre-ejaculation in men.[1] Most experts in the industry disagree with this categorization, viewing it as a stretch that dilutes femtech's core mission. However, without a standardized definition, such broad interpretations remain part of the ongoing debate over what truly qualifies as femtech.

The best working definition of femtech is one that captures its true purpose: It refers to products and services that leverage technology to address the unique health needs of people with female biology. This definition is significant for three reasons. First, it recognizes that femtech is not limited to digital platforms but encompasses *all* forms of technological innovation. Second, it keeps the focus on women's unique anatomy and health rather than diluting the term to include unrelated health solutions. Finally, it acknowledges that femtech is not just about fertility or menstruation; it spans the entire spectrum of women's health, including cardiovascular care, autoimmune disorders, and mental health—areas that have long been under-researched and underserved.

Beyond defining an industry, femtech serves another critical function: It breaks down deeply ingrained taboos. For centuries, women's health topics—including menstruation, menopause, and sexual wellness—were considered embarrassing, unmentionable, or even shameful. This stigma has had real-world consequences, discouraging women from discussing their health concerns and delaying the development of solutions. Many women hesitate to talk to their doctors about issues like chronic vaginal dryness, painful sex, or urinary incontinence, fearing judgment or embarrassment. But the impact of this silence extends beyond the doctor's office—it has also shaped the way women's health solutions are perceived and prioritized in the broader healthcare and investment landscape.

Before femtech existed, women's health entrepreneurs struggled to gain traction in a system that largely overlooked their innovations. With most investors being men, securing funding for women-focused products was often an uphill battle—not because there wasn't a need, but because the problems these products addressed were misunderstood, trivialized, or considered too "uncomfortable" to discuss. Take the experience of Janica Alvarez, a women's health founder who developed a smart breast pump. When she pitched her product, investors Googled the device, landed on a porn site, and cracked jokes instead of discussing the business opportunity. One investor even scoffed at the pump, saying, "I'm not touching that. It's disgusting."[2] Without a recognized industry or the language to legitimize these innovations, women's health solutions are often dismissed as unprofitable, unnecessary, and too awkward to talk about—further delaying progress in an already neglected space.

The introduction of femtech has started to change this landscape. It has given legitimacy to an entire field of innovation that was once invisible. With this new framework, investors and founders can discuss breast pumps, period-tracking apps, and sexual health devices without as much discomfort or embarrassment. The impact of this shift has been obvious—within a few years, smart breast pumps like Elvie raised tens of millions of dollars in funding and landed on *Time* magazine's Best Inventions list. By 2024, *Time's* list was filled with femtech breakthroughs, including PherDal, the sterile at-home insemination kit discussed in Chapter 1. While naming and defining femtech didn't solve every problem in women's health, it broke down enough barriers to allow critical innovations to finally reach the market.

Some critics, however, argue that the term *femtech* is exclusionary, particularly because "fem" suggests it applies only to cisgender women. The concern is that this term alienates the health experiences of LGBTQ+ and trans individuals. While this concern is understandable, it overlooks a crucial reality: Femtech is not about exclusion—it's about correcting a long-standing imbalance in healthcare. No term can fully capture the complexities of gender and healthcare, but for the reasons discussed, it is important to have a term that we can rally behind. Femtech is not about limiting care—it's about expanding it. Many femtech companies are actively working to close healthcare gaps for ethnic minorities, LGBTQ+ individuals, and other underserved populations. Rather than excluding non-cisgender women, femtech is often more inclusive than traditional healthcare, designing solutions that prioritize the needs of *all* individuals who have historically been overlooked.

While femtech was created to address critical gaps in women's health, its impact extends far beyond any single group. More than 70 percent of femtech startups have at least one female founder[3]—compared to just 20 percent of startups in other sectors[4]—yet the solutions they develop often benefit a much broader population. Research shows that women-founded innovations are more likely to address overlooked health concerns in ways that improve outcomes for *everyone*, not just women. For example, pelvic floor therapy devices, initially designed to help women with postpartum recovery and incontinence, have also proven effective for men dealing with pelvic pain or recovering from prostate surgery. Similarly, advancements in hormonal tracking technology, originally developed for fertility and menstrual health, are now being explored for applications in men's health, including testosterone regulation and metabolic monitoring. These examples illustrate how femtech's innovations often extend beyond their intended audience, filling gaps in healthcare that benefit a wider population.

Put simply, *femtech* is a new name for an old problem. Women's health has been ignored for centuries, and as a result, critical innovations have been delayed or dismissed. Some critics argue that the term is unnecessary or even sexist, but its impact speaks for itself. By creating a distinct category for women's health innovation, femtech has forced the medical and investment communities to finally take women's health seriously. Defining this industry bridged a gap too wide for consumers, investors, and policymakers to cross on their own.

For these reasons, *femtech* is more than a name—it's a declaration that women's health is real, valuable, and worthy of investment. Language shapes perception and naming this industry has helped shift the conversation from neglect and stigma to innovation and action. By defining and legitimizing this space, femtech has opened doors that were once shut, forcing the medical and investment communities to finally listen. And now that the world is at last paying attention, there is no turning back.

Welcome to the femtech revolution.

Mapping the Femtech Revolution

Femtech has evolved into a global force, driving innovation and expanding access to healthcare solutions designed specifically for women. Across continents, the industry is growing at an unprecedented rate, fueled by technological advancements, shifting consumer expectations, and long-overdue recognition of the disparities in women's healthcare. While the need for better women's health solutions is not new, the increasing investment in and adoption of femtech are transforming how these solutions are developed, delivered, and integrated into everyday life. As awareness rises and barriers to innovation continue to break down, femtech is reshaping the future of healthcare on a global scale.

The Femtech Map: A Global Look at Innovation Hubs

Femtech is thriving worldwide, but its growth and adoption vary significantly by region. Some countries have emerged as global leaders in femtech investment and innovation, while others are rapidly catching up, tailoring solutions to fit cultural, economic, and regulatory landscapes.

Policy, Power, and Progress: The United States Leads the Global Femtech Charge   The United States is at the center of the global femtech revolution, home to more than half of all femtech startups.[5] As of February 2025, 798 of the 1,550 femtech startups worldwide are based in the United States, a testament to the country's role as an innovation powerhouse.[6] Cities like New York and San Francisco have become hotspots for groundbreaking women's health technologies, with startups tackling everything from mental health and menopause to cardiovascular and autoimmune disorders. Silicon Valley, already known for its deep expertise in digital health and biotech, has become a hub for AI-driven femtech, powering advanced fertility tracking, precision medicine tailored to female biology, and noninvasive diagnostic tools for endometriosis and PCOS.

One of the biggest shifts in recent years has been the flood of investment into femtech. In 2024 alone, femtech startups raised a collective $1.19 billion—a dramatic change from the past.[7] The federal government has also supported funding initiatives for women's health, with former President Joe Biden issuing a 2024 Executive Order directing federal agencies to expand funding for women's health research.[8] This led to major investments from the NIH and the Department of Defense. To further encourage innovation, the Advanced Research Projects Agency for Health (ARPA-H) announced a $110 million "Sprint for Women's Health," a funding initiative aimed at advancing research in conditions that uniquely or disproportionately affect women, including autoimmune diseases, heart disease, and menopause-related health challenges.[9] These efforts marked a turning point in the national approach to women's healthcare, emphasizing that femtech extends far beyond reproductive health to include chronic conditions.

Cultural shifts are also accelerating femtech's momentum in the United States. Once-taboo topics like menopause, period pain, and pelvic floor dysfunction are now being discussed openly, thanks in part to social media advocacy, femtech startups, and celebrity-led awareness campaigns. More women are using digital health platforms to access expert guidance, connect with others facing similar health challenges, and normalize discussions around issues that were once brushed aside. Community-driven wellness brands are also helping to reshape how women access information, demand better care, and take charge of their well-being.

Additionally, femtech is making waves in mainstream retail and corporate benefits. More companies are integrating femtech products into their employee healthcare plans, giving women access to menopause support programs, fertility preservation benefits, and reproductive health telemedicine services—all covered by employers. Some companies are even partnering with femtech startups to provide personalized hormone testing, pelvic floor therapy, and lactation support as part of their wellness initiatives. At the same time, major retailers are expanding access to femtech products in pharmacies and grocery stores, making everything from period underwear to urinary tract infection tests available on everyday shopping trips.

With strong policy support, a booming startup ecosystem, and rising consumer demand, the United States is leading the femtech revolution. The next decade will determine just how far this movement can go, but one thing is clear: Women's health is no longer an afterthought—it's front and center in the future of US medicine.

From London to Estonia: The European Femtech Boom   While the United States may be the powerhouse of femtech, Europe is proving that innovation can thrive when technology and healthcare systems work together. With one in four femtech startups based in Europe, the region has emerged as the second-largest femtech market and has become a major force in reshaping women's health.[10] Unlike the United States, where private investors and corporate partnerships fuel much of the industry, Europe's femtech boom is driven by a combination of strong public healthcare systems, government-backed initiatives, and progressive policies designed to prioritize women's health.

At the forefront of this transformation is the United Kingdom (UK), which has established itself as Europe's femtech capital. London is home to the highest number of femtech startups of any city worldwide, fueled by a robust digital health ecosystem, strong policy support, and access to funding from both private and public sources. The National Health Service (NHS) has played a pivotal role in integrating femtech into mainstream care, making fertility treatments, menopause support, and telehealth services more accessible without excessive out-of-pocket costs. With the UK government prioritizing women's health through initiatives like the Women's Health Strategy, femtech companies are increasingly collaborating with the NHS to bring innovative products and services directly to patients.

Beyond the UK, France and Germany have also become major players in the femtech space. France is making waves in fertility technology, menstrual health, and AI-powered diagnostics. The French government has also introduced financial incentives to encourage investment in femtech and feminist solutions, signaling a long-term commitment to female-centered innovation. Germany, on the other hand, is pioneering digital health solutions. Thanks to its DiGA program, femtech apps can be prescribed by doctors and reimbursed by public health insurance. This means women in Germany can access AI-powered fertility trackers, digital menopause coaching, and hormonal health apps—all covered by the healthcare system. It's a game-changing approach that makes femtech more accessible and mainstream than ever before.

Even countries that were once slow to embrace femtech are now becoming key players. Spain, for example, made headlines when it became the first country in Europe to pass paid menstrual leave legislation.[11] This policy ignited a continent-wide conversation about how workplaces should support women's health, especially when it comes to periods, menopause, and fertility treatments. Femtech startups in Spain are riding this wave of change, developing innovative solutions for digital menopause care, hormone health, and cycle tracking. Meanwhile, Poland and Estonia are emerging as unexpected femtech hubs, with Estonia's digital-first healthcare system allowing femtech startups to integrate their platforms directly into electronic medical records and telehealth services.

Looking ahead, Europe is set to continue leading the way in femtech growth. The European Medicines Agency is making it easier for digital health products to be approved across multiple countries, and the European Commission is investing in female-led startups to close the gap in health-care innovation. With government backing, a tech-driven startup culture, and increasing public demand for better women's health solutions, Europe is proving that femtech isn't just about gadgets and apps—it's about trans-forming healthcare at every level.

Emerging Markets and the Future of Femtech: Asia, Africa, the Middle East, and Latin America   While the United States and Europe have led the global femtech movement, some of the most exciting and impactful growth is now happening in emerging markets across Asia, Africa, the Middle East, and Latin America. These regions are home to bil-lions of women who have historically had limited access to healthcare. Unlike wealthier countries, where femtech may focus on convenience and personalized wellness, in emerging markets, it is a lifeline—helping women access critical health services in places where doctors and clinics may be too far away or too expensive.

Asia, for example, is quickly becoming a hotspot for femtech innova-tion, thanks to large populations, rising smartphone use, and growing aware-ness of women's health needs. With many regions facing gaps in reproductive and maternal healthcare, femtech solutions are stepping in to provide acces-sible, tech-driven alternatives. Some of the biggest opportunities exist in countries like India, China, and across Southeast Asia, where millions of women struggle to access gynecologists, fertility specialists, and preventive care due to cost, distance, or cultural barriers. As governments invest in digi-tal health infrastructure and private investors pour funding into women's health startups, Asia is poised to become one of the largest and fastest-growing femtech markets in the world.

The Middle East is also experiencing a major shift in the femtech land-scape. Femtech has historically faced challenges in this region due to cultural sensitivities around reproductive health and limited access to women's health-care services. However, the UAE has become a regional leader in digital health, with cities like Dubai and Abu Dhabi actively encouraging healthcare startups to develop AI-driven diagnostic tools, telemedicine platforms, and personalized wellness services. While some topics like contraception and sex-ual health remain taboo in parts of the Middle East, femtech startups are now finding ways to work within cultural norms to improve access to care. Governments are also investing heavily in digital transformation, which means femtech will likely play a bigger role in healthcare in the coming years.

Similarly, Africa presents one of the biggest opportunities for femtech to transform healthcare delivery, especially in regions where traditional medical infrastructure is limited. With over 230 million women of reproductive age across sub-Saharan Africa,[12] the demand for maternal care, contraception, and gynecological health solutions is immense. However, financial barriers, rural healthcare shortages, and cultural stigmas have long prevented women from accessing critical health services. Instead of relying on traditional healthcare systems, femtech startups like Grace Health, Kasha, and Musana Carts are using mobile technology to reach women directly.

Finally, Latin America and Mexico are quickly becoming exciting regions for femtech, thanks to rising digital health adoption and policy shifts that are improving access to reproductive care. Brazil, Mexico, and Argentina are leaders in this region, with femtech startups focused on fertility, period health, and telemedicine. Throughout Latin America, telehealth adoption is increasing, and governments are updating digital healthcare regulations to make it easier for femtech companies to work within the public health system.

Femtech is proving that technology can overcome many of the challenges that have historically limited women's access to healthcare. While each region faces unique hurdles—whether cultural stigma, lack of investment, or regulatory barriers—the momentum is clear: Women around the world are demanding better healthcare, and femtech is stepping up to provide it. As these innovations continue to grow, they won't just shape the future of femtech—they'll redefine what healthcare looks like for women everywhere.

Health Without Limits: The Reach of Femtech

Femtech's rapid expansion isn't just about geography—it's about reshaping how women experience healthcare at every stage of life. While reproductive health remains a cornerstone of the industry, femtech's reach extends far beyond it. Innovations are now tackling menopause, mental well-being, chronic disease management, and early cancer detection, transforming the way women access and experience healthcare. As the industry continues to evolve, femtech is bridging critical gaps in care and redefining what personalized, accessible, and effective healthcare looks like for half the world's population. The innovations emerging today are not just filling long-standing voids in women's healthcare—they're setting a new standard for the future.

Reproductive and Maternal Care

Pregnancy and maternal health are a major focus of femtech, accounting for almost 20 percent of the total market and driving innovations that support women throughout every stage of motherhood.[13] Companies like Kindbody, which provides comprehensive fertility care, and Elvie, known for its smart breast pumps and pelvic floor trainers, have gained widespread recognition for enhancing maternal and postpartum health. But femtech's impact extends far beyond fertility counseling and nursing support—new technologies are making pregnancy safer, improving early risk detection, and giving women more control over their prenatal and postnatal care.

As femtech continues to evolve, one of the most groundbreaking advancements in maternal health is the rise of AI-powered pregnancy monitoring. These technologies are progressing prenatal care, giving expectant mothers real-time insights into their health and their baby's development. Apps like Bobi Health leverage AI to analyze fetal growth patterns and maternal health data, helping identify potential complications early. At the same time, wearable devices are making it easier than ever to track vital signs and detect risks like preeclampsia, gestational diabetes, and irregular fetal heart rates before they escalate into serious concerns.

Several startups are leading the charge in making at-home pregnancy monitoring more accessible. Owlet and HeraMED offer remote maternal health tracking, allowing women—especially those with high-risk pregnancies—to monitor key health metrics without constant hospital visits. Bloomlife's prenatal wearable enables continuous, at-home tracking of fetal heart rate and contractions, helping expectant mothers and their doctors detect early signs of preterm labor. Similarly, Nuvo's Invu system features a wearable monitoring band equipped with 12 sensors that use electrocardiogram (ECG) and acoustic technology to measure both fetal and maternal heart rates in real time. Sera Prognostics is developing predictive tests to assess preterm birth risk, providing an earlier window for intervention. These innovations not only improve pregnancy outcomes but also empower women to take a more active role in their prenatal care, bridging gaps in access and ensuring high-risk pregnancies receive appropriate attention.

But femtech's impact doesn't stop at childbirth—it is also redefining postpartum care, a stage of motherhood that has historically been overlooked. Digital platforms are emerging to support women during the critical recovery period after birth, providing tools for tracking postpartum healing, monitoring mental health, and connecting new mothers with professional care. Companies like Mahmee offer personalized postpartum support, helping women access lactation consultants, OB/GYNs, and mental health specialists through a single platform. Maven Clinic's postpartum programs similarly provide on-demand virtual care, including guidance on physical recovery, sleep coaching for newborns, and nutrition plans for postpartum healing.

Mental health is also a growing focus within maternal femtech, because perinatal depression and anxiety affect up to one in seven women.[14] Startups like Canopie and Woebot Health use AI-driven chatbots and cognitive behavioral therapy programs to offer on-demand mental health support to pregnant and postpartum women. Wearable devices like HeraBEAT integrate stress tracking into pregnancy monitoring, allowing doctors to quickly identify women at risk for perinatal anxiety and depression.

By leveraging AI, remote monitoring, and digital healthcare tools, femtech is reshaping the entire journey of motherhood—from conception to postpartum recovery. These advancements are not only improving health outcomes for mothers and babies, but are also making maternal healthcare more accessible, proactive, and personalized than ever before.

Menstrual Health and Contraceptive Innovation

As femtech transforms maternal health, it is also driving major advancements in menstrual health and contraception. Menstrual health alone accounts for approximately 14 percent of the femtech market,[15] with brands like Clue and Flo Health leading the way in period tracking and reproductive health management. These apps have helped millions of women better understand their cycles, predict ovulation, and track symptoms related to hormonal fluctuations, providing a level of insight into menstrual health that was previously unavailable outside of a doctor's office.

Beyond cycle tracking, startups are reshaping menstrual care itself by making products that are more sustainable, accessible, and stigma-free. Companies like Sunny Period, Here We Flo, and Awkward Essentials are developing eco-friendly period products, reusable menstrual solutions, and discreet, subscription-based care models. Thinx and Knix have led the charge in pioneering period underwear, offering leak-proof, reusable options that provide a more sustainable and comfortable alternative to traditional pads and tampons. Meanwhile, Aunt Flow is tackling period equity by providing freevend menstrual product dispensers for schools, workplaces, and public restrooms, ensuring that access to period products is treated as a necessity, not a luxury. These brands are not only expanding choices for consumers; they are challenging outdated narratives around menstruation and advocating for better accessibility and inclusivity in menstrual care.

At the same time, contraceptive innovation is seeing a surge in development, making up 17 percent of the femtech market.[16] Traditional birth control options have remained largely unchanged for decades, relying on hormonal methods that don't work for all women or come with unwanted side effects. Femtech startups are challenging the status quo, introducing hormone-free contraceptive options, AI-powered fertility tracking, and digital birth control solutions. One of the earliest breakthroughs in this space came from Natural Cycles. Using temperature tracking and AI-driven predictive analytics, the app determines a woman's fertile window, giving her a noninvasive, data-backed way to prevent or plan pregnancy. Other companies, like Dama Health, are taking a personalized approach to contraception, using genetic testing and hormonal profiling to help women find the birth control method best suited to their unique biology.

Femtech is also making contraception more accessible. Companies like OUI and Emme are developing smart pill-tracking systems, digital prescription services, and streamlined access to birth control pills without the need for a doctor's visit. Meanwhile, nonhormonal innovations, like Phexxi, an FDA-approved vaginal gel that alters pH to prevent sperm mobility, offer women alternatives beyond the pill, IUDs, or implants.

These advances in menstrual and contraceptive care are giving women more control over their reproductive health with smarter, more personalized solutions. As innovation continues, these advancements are not just improving convenience—they're making menstrual care and birth control more accessible, sustainable, and tailored to individual needs.

Menopause and Longevity

Femtech is also tackling how women navigate the next stage of their health journey: menopause and aging. For decades, menopause was a silent struggle, dismissed as an inevitable phase women simply had to endure. But femtech is changing the conversation, bringing long-overdue innovation and support to a stage of life that affects over a billion women worldwide. Since 2019, menopause-focused startups have surged, with 74 percent of them founded in just the last few years.[17] As more companies recognize the glaring gaps in care, femtech is stepping in with solutions that help women track symptoms, access expert care, and manage hormonal changes with confidence.

Companies like Elektra Health and Midi Health are at the forefront of this sector, offering digital menopause clinics that provide personalized hormone therapy plans, AI-driven symptom tracking, and access to specialists. These platforms help women navigate everything from hot flashes and brain fog to bone health and cardiovascular risks. Meanwhile, FemGevity is taking a longevity-focused approach to menopause care, using biomarker testing, hormone optimization, and personalized longevity plans to help women manage symptoms and improve long-term health.

Wearable technology is also advancing menopause care, offering noninvasive solutions to manage symptoms in real time. Embr Wave is a temperature-regulating wearable that provides cooling or warming sensations on the wrist to help alleviate hot flashes and night sweats without medication. Similarly, Thermaband Zone functions as a personal thermostat using AI to detect body temperature changes and deliver instant relief. Meanwhile, Midday pairs with commercial wearables like Fitbit to use AI-driven algorithms that personalize menopause management strategies.

The conversation around women's health in midlife and after is expanding beyond menopause. Aging brings a unique set of health challenges, including osteoporosis, heart disease, metabolic changes, and cognitive decline. Bone Health Technologies has developed Osteoboost, the first FDA-cleared, nondrug medical device designed to treat osteopenia and prevent osteoporosis using targeted vibration therapy to stimulate growth and reduce density loss. IBEX Innovations is similarly transforming osteoporosis detection with its IBEX Bone Health software, which integrates with standard x-ray equipment to assess bone density during routine screenings, enabling earlier diagnosis and intervention. Cognitive health is gaining comparable traction, with companies like BrainCheck, which uses digital cognitive assessments to detect early signs of decline, helping women be proactive about their brain health. As longevity-focused femtech continues to grow, these innovations are ensuring that women move through midlife and beyond with strong bodies, healthier hearts, and sharper minds.

Uterine and Breast Health

Femtech is also advancing the standard of care for uterine and breast health, offering much-needed innovation in the diagnosis, treatment, and management of conditions like fibroids, endometriosis, PCOS, and breast cancer. For uterine health, OCON Healthcare is redesigning intrauterine devices with its IUB Ballerine, a spherical intrauterine device designed to adapt to the shape of the uterine cavity. This reduces the discomfort and side effects commonly associated with traditional IUDs. Additionally, the company's technology may soon allow for the delivery of drugs and other medical treatments directly into the uterus.

For fibroid care, Ablatus Therapeutics is developing Luna, a radiofrequency ablation technology aimed at providing minimally invasive, fertility-preserving procedures for treating uterine fibroids. Similarly, Gynesonics has developed the Sonata System—the first FDA-cleared medical device for diagnostic intrauterine imaging and transcervical treatment of symptomatic uterine fibroids. This incisionless procedure combines ultrasound imaging with radiofrequency energy to reduce fibroid size in a 45-minute outpatient setting, allowing most patients to resume regular activities the next day.

Femtech is also making significant progress in other uterine disorders. Hera Biotech is developing the world's first nonsurgical test for diagnosing and staging endometriosis. Butterfly Therapeutics developed Endocare, a medical device that uses sounds and images to alleviate chronic pain in patients suffering from endometriosis. Elanza Wellness and Lasa Health have built virtual chronic care platforms for people with endometriosis, providing access to AI-powered screening tools, multimodal support, medical specialists, clinical decision support, evidence-based treatment plans, and more.

For PCOS, companies like PERLA Health offer evidence-based, integrative approaches to PCOS education and care delivery, while companies like Allara develop nutrition plans for patients, connect them with gynecologists, and offer mental health support.

For breast health, early detection remains the most critical factor in improving survival rates, yet many women still lack access to affordable and radiation-free screening options. iBreastExam is a handheld device that uses tactile sensing technology to detect breast lesions quickly and painlessly. Unlike traditional mammograms, iBreastExam is radiation-free and can be used in low-resource settings, making breast cancer screening more accessible worldwide. Similarly, DeepLook Medical has created the first FDA-cleared AI technology designed to detect cancer in dense breast tissue. The company's technology integrates seamlessly into existing breast imaging workflows, assisting radiologists with detecting cancers that might otherwise go unnoticed—especially in women with dense breasts where visualization is more challenging.

UK scientists are also in the process of developing a smart textile that could fit inside a bra and monitor breast tumor growth. The technology works using an electric current that can scan and detect changes in fluids inside and outside the cells, measuring tumor changes. This technology could reduce the need for constant MRIs, ultrasounds, and mammograms for individuals being treated for breast cancer. Additionally, companies like Cairn Surgical are working to enhance the precision of breast-conserving surgery for women who need lumpectomies. With these advancements, femtech is not only improving access to better screening and diagnosis but also redefining what proactive care looks like for women's uterine and breast health.

Chronic Illnesses, Cardiovascular Disease, and Cancer

Finally, femtech is stepping into the realm of chronic illnesses, cardiovascular disease, and cancer care. Autoimmune diseases affect women at significantly higher rates than men, yet diagnosis and treatment remain fragmented. Hashiona has developed the first Hashimoto's thyroiditis management app that helps women track their symptoms, diet, and lifestyle to better manage their condition, beat brain fog, regain their energy, and lose weight. Meanwhile, Grace & Able is developing wearable joint support solutions to help women with autoimmune arthritis manage pain, mobility, and daily function. WellTheory has developed a collaborative care model that helps women identify the root causes of their chronic illnesses, learn simple lifestyle habits to help manage their diseases, and heal between doctor's appointments with continuous video and messaging support. Similarly, Ampersand Health helps women self-manage chronic conditions like arthritis and irritable bowel disease by tracking symptoms, medications, and activities to build healthier habits.

Cardiovascular disease is also attracting more attention in femtech through innovative tools that help women monitor their heart health and detect early warning signs before they become life-threatening. Adesso by Heart-Tech Health is a digital health platform that offers personalized prevention programs, risk assessments, and lifestyle recommendations tailored specifically to female cardiovascular physiology. Similarly, Systole Health is leveraging AI to provide women with continuous cardiovascular monitoring, risk evaluations, and targeted interventions to prevent heart disease. By focusing on early detection and proactive care, these solutions are closing critical gaps in women's heart health.

Cancer detection is another area benefiting from femtech. AOA Dx is developing a noninvasive blood test to detect ovarian cancer in its earliest stages, potentially revolutionizing early detection and survival rates. Meanwhile, Teal Health has introduced an at-home cervical cancer screening device that allows women to self-collect samples, making screenings less invasive. Companies like MobileODT are using AI-powered imaging technology to make cervical cancer screenings more accurate, efficient, and available.

In this manner, femtech is transforming how chronic illnesses, cardiovascular diseases, and cancer are diagnosed, managed, and treated. These innovations are not only improving health outcomes but are also empowering women with the tools to take control of their long-term health in ways that were never possible before. The coming years will shape the future of this movement, but one thing is certain: Femtech is here to stay.

What Femtech Means for You

Femtech is more than just gadgets, apps, and biotech breakthroughs—it's redefining women's health. For too long, pain, discomfort, and medical dismissal have been treated as inevitable. Femtech is shifting this reality, offering solutions that go beyond traditional healthcare. While some integrate with existing medical systems, many are designed for direct access, giving women more control over their well-being. These innovations help us understand our bodies, address long-ignored health concerns, and take charge of our physical, mental, and emotional well-being. Here's what that means for you.

Finally Understanding Our Bodies

Femtech is giving women the tools to finally understand their bodies with clarity, turning guesswork into actionable insights. For generations, women have been left in the dark about their own health, dismissed with vague reassurances instead of real answers. Menstrual cycles were a mystery, hormone fluctuations felt random, and symptoms that signaled deeper health issues were often brushed aside. Without data to back up their concerns, women were left wondering if their instincts were wrong, if their symptoms were normal, or if they were simply imagining things.

Ruby was one of those women. When she first noticed spotting between cycles and heavier, more unpredictable bleeding, she knew something felt off. But when she brought it up with her doctor, she was told it was normal. A generation ago, that might have been the end of the story. But instead of being left without answers, Ruby turned to femtech. She tracked her cycles, recorded her symptoms, and watched as patterns emerged. When she returned to her doctor, she wasn't just explaining a feeling—she was presenting evidence.

Femtech is helping women reconnect with their bodies in ways that were never possible before. Period-tracking apps don't just help predict when your next cycle will start—they reveal irregular patterns, hormonal imbalances, and potential signs of reproductive conditions. At-home hormone tests allow women to measure their estrogen, progesterone, and cortisol levels, giving them insights into how their hormones fluctuate throughout the month. Wearable devices are tracking temperature, heart rate, and metabolic changes, showing how the menstrual cycle influences everything from energy levels to sleep quality. Instead of relying on generic medical advice, women now have the power to understand their unique biology, track what's normal for them, and recognize when something feels wrong.

What happened to Ruby can happen for women everywhere. A vague sense that something is off is no longer the only proof we have to offer. Femtech is bridging the gap between intuition and evidence, giving women the tools to advocate for themselves in a healthcare system that has failed them. We're no longer left to navigate our health in the dark—femtech is finally turning on the lights.

Taking Action Against Health Concerns

Having more information is only useful if we can do something with it. One of the biggest flaws in traditional healthcare is its reactive nature— waiting until symptoms become unbearable before offering treatment. Too many women have been forced to push through pain, brush off concerns, and accept long delays before getting the care they need. Femtech is shifting the model toward prevention and early intervention, ensuring that women can address health concerns before they escalate.

Tracking cycles, monitoring symptoms, and getting at-home test results is only the first step. Once we have that data and knowledge, we need to know what to do with it. This is what sets femtech apart. It doesn't just provide information—it guides women toward solutions. A period-tracking app, for instance, doesn't just confirm irregular bleeding; it flags potential issues and advises users to seek medical attention when necessary. An at-home hormone test doesn't just show estrogen fluctuations; it offers insights on whether those levels are within a healthy range. Smart wearables don't just track vitals; they alert users when readings are abnormal, giving them the confidence to act before a small concern turns into a crisis.

Femtech is also making it easier to take the next step when action is needed. Many women hesitate to seek care because they don't have easy access to specialists, can't afford repeated doctor visits, or feel dismissed during these visits. In the United States, nearly half of all women reported skipping or delaying necessary healthcare because of cost, time, or lack of access.[18] Even more troubling, a staggering 72 percent of Millennial women say they have felt dismissed by a medical provider at some point in their lives.[19] These barriers don't just lead to frustration—they delay diagnoses, prolong suffering, and increase the risk of serious health complications.

Now, instead of being stuck in a cycle of uncertainty, women can use telehealth platforms to consult with medical professionals who specialize in women's health. Instead of waiting months for a doctor to order lab work, they can order at-home tests that give them a clearer picture of their health. Even in clinical settings, femtech is making procedures less invasive, more accurate, and more comfortable, removing another barrier that keeps women from obtaining care.

For many conditions that disproportionately affect women, early intervention is critical, yet most diagnostic pathways are outdated, designed with men in mind, or require years of persistent advocacy. Femtech is shortening that timeline by identifying risk factors earlier and providing tools for continuous monitoring. Femtech is also empowering women to act in everyday ways—whether that means adjusting lifestyle habits based on cycle tracking, using digital coaching for mental health, or proactively screening for conditions they might be genetically predisposed to. Instead of relying solely on a healthcare system that wasn't built with their needs in mind, women now have the power to take charge of their health on their own terms.

Empowering Holistic Wellness

Women's health isn't just about managing illness—it's about feeling strong, energized, and in tune with the body's natural rhythms. Yet for decades, wellness has been treated as something separate from traditional medicine, with little attention paid to how hormones, metabolism, mental health, and recovery are interconnected. Femtech is changing that, offering a more complete, personalized approach that allows women to proactively manage their well-being rather than just reacting to problems.

One of femtech's biggest contributions is shifting the focus from treatment to prevention. Many chronic health conditions, such as osteoporosis, cardiovascular disease, and autoimmune disorders, develop gradually, beginning with subtle shifts in metabolism, bone density, inflammation, or sleep patterns. Historically, these early warning signs were overlooked, leaving women without the ability to act until the damage was done. Now, with continuous tracking, AI-driven diagnostics, and personalized health insights, women can recognize changes in their bodies early and make informed decisions before small issues become serious health crises.

Even for those already managing chronic conditions, femtech is providing new ways to take control. Instead of waiting for symptoms to worsen, real-time monitoring allows women to track inflammation levels, heart rate, blood sugar, and hormonal fluctuations, helping them adjust their diet, exercise, and stress management strategies in real time. These tools empower women to recognize triggers, prevent flare-ups, and maintain stability, turning unpredictable conditions into something more manageable.

Jordan—my high school classmate diagnosed with ovarian cancer—was a testament to how technology can help women maintain control of their wellness, even in the face of serious illness. Jordan used every tool available to manage her treatment, track symptoms, optimize her health, and maintain her quality of life. She relied on health-tracking apps to monitor her energy levels, nutrition, and medication side effects, adjusting her routines to stay strong during chemotherapy. She also used a cold-cap—an innovative device that helps reduce chemotherapy-induced hair loss—which allowed her to maintain a sense of normalcy throughout treatment. Her ability to integrate technology into her care—and its impact on maintaining her wellness—was so effective that most people didn't even realize she was sick until just six weeks before her passing. Jordan's journey wasn't just about endurance—it was about using technology to preserve dignity, independence, and a sense of control in a situation that so often takes those things away. Her story highlights the life-changing impact of femtech, not just in early detection and prevention, but in helping women maintain agency over their bodies and their lives, even in the face of a devastating illness.

Femtech is redefining the way we think about women's health as a whole. Mental and emotional well-being are no longer afterthoughts but integral parts of overall health. Hormonal fluctuations, reproductive transitions, and lifestyle stressors all shape how women experience anxiety, depression, and burnout. Femtech is bridging this gap, normalizing the idea that emotional health is just as important as physical health and providing smarter, more accessible solutions that adapt to women's real lives. By shifting from reactive to proactive care, women can move beyond survival mode and toward a life where they feel informed, empowered, and in control of their long-term health.

Collective Wins for Healthcare

At first glance, femtech might seem like it only benefits women. But the reality is, investing in women's health has ripple effects that improve healthcare and the economy for *everyone.* When we close the gaps in women's health, we don't just improve outcomes for women—we strengthen health-care systems, lower medical costs, fuel economic growth, and make scientific discoveries that help all patients, regardless of gender.

One of the biggest reasons to use and invest in femtech is its direct impact on the economy. Closing the women's health gap could boost the global economy by at least $1 trillion annually by 2040.[20] When women have access to better healthcare, they can stay in the workforce longer, take fewer sick days, and contribute more to economic growth. Businesses also benefit—when companies offer health benefits that support women, like fertility treatments, menopause care, and better maternal health coverage, they see higher employee retention and productivity. Healthy workers mean a stronger economy, and that benefits everyone.

Beyond economic growth, adoption of femtech and investment in women's health leads to groundbreaking medical discoveries that improve care for everyone. For example, the Women's Health Initiative (WHI), a long-term national health study, provided critical insights into disease pre-vention that have influenced public health guidelines and clinical practices worldwide.[21] WHI research led to groundbreaking changes in the way doctors approach hormone therapy, heart disease prevention, and osteopo-rosis treatment. These findings did not just benefit women—many of the insights gained from studying female patients have improved cardiovascular care, cancer prevention, and metabolic health strategies for all patients.

Another major area where women's health research has led to broader medical advancements is cardiovascular disease. As more research has focused on how heart disease presents differently in women, it has resulted in better diagnostic tools and treatment protocols that now benefit all heart patients, regardless of gender. For example, studies on women's microvascular dysfunction have improved the understanding of coronary artery disease in both men and women. Additionally, research into pregnancy-related conditions like preeclampsia and gestational hyperten-sion has provided valuable insights into long-term cardiovascular risks, leading to better prevention and early intervention strategies for all patients at risk of heart disease.

Cancer research has also seen major advancements due to women's health studies and investment. The push to understand breast and ovarian cancer led to the discovery of BRCA gene mutations, enabling early genetic testing to assess cancer risk. While initially focused on women, this research also identified genetic markers linked to prostate, pancreatic, and other hereditary cancers in men. Similarly, advancements in hormone receptor research for breast cancer paved the way for targeted therapies, such as tamoxifen, which later influenced treatments for hormone-driven cancers like prostate cancer. In other words, funding research into female-specific diseases doesn't just help women—it drives medical discoveries that improve healthcare for all.

Beyond medical discoveries, investing in women's health saves money. The World Economic Forum found that a $300 million investment in women's health research could generate a $13 billion economic return.[22] How? By reducing hospital visits, preventing chronic diseases, and improving early detection so that conditions are treated before they become expensive, long-term problems. A more efficient healthcare system means lower costs for insurance companies, government programs, and taxpayers.

At its core, femtech isn't just about advancing women's health—it's about improving healthcare overall. By addressing long-standing gaps in research, developing technology that serves all bodies, and pushing for more inclusive medical innovation, femtech is transforming outcomes for all patients, regardless of gender. A healthcare system that prioritizes women's health is one that is more advanced, more equitable, and more effective for everyone.

What's the Catch? Navigating Femtech Safely

At this point, you might be thinking: *This all sounds amazing—but what's the catch?* After all, we've spent decades watching women's health get overlooked. Now, suddenly, there's an entire industry dedicated to solving the very problems that have plagued us for generations. As women, we've learned to approach medical advancements with a healthy dose of skepticism. We've seen too many so-called "revolutionary" health solutions turn out to be unproven fads, exploitative scams, or products designed without real scientific backing. So, while femtech is making real, meaningful strides in healthcare and is an exciting and transformative movement, it's important to acknowledge that not all femtech is created equal.

Like any rapidly growing industry, femtech has its fair share of opportunists—companies that slap the "femtech" label on products that aren't scientifically tested, ethically developed, or truly designed to help women. Some prioritize profits over patient well-being. Others fail to protect sensitive health data, leaving consumers vulnerable to privacy breaches. And in some cases, companies roll out flashy new products without the rigorous clinical testing needed to ensure safety and efficacy. As femtech continues to grow, so will the number of bad actors trying to exploit its success. That's why, as consumers, we need to be proactive in distinguishing legitimate, well-researched femtech innovations from those that are untrustworthy or even harmful.

So, how do we navigate femtech? By staying SAFE.

Before engaging with any femtech product or service, it's essential to assess whether it meets four key standards:

- **Security:** A trustworthy femtech company prioritizes data privacy and uses strong security measures to protect sensitive health information. Femtech should be transparent about how data is collected, stored, and shared, with clear policies that empower users to control their own information.
- **Accuracy:** The best femtech products are grounded in science, backed by peer-reviewed research, clinical trials, or input from medical professionals. Legitimate companies provide evidence for their claims and avoid misleading marketing that prioritizes profit over patient well-being.
- **Foundation:** Ethical femtech companies have leadership teams that include healthcare experts, scientists, and medical professionals guiding their decisions. Their products are developed with input from specialists to ensure safety, efficacy, and adherence to medical standards.
- **Equity:** True femtech innovation is designed to serve all women, not just a select few. The best companies prioritize inclusivity, ensuring their products address the needs of women across different racial, socioeconomic, and gender backgrounds, rather than reinforcing existing healthcare disparities.

By keeping the SAFE method in mind, you can confidently navigate the femtech space, embracing the innovations that truly prioritize health, safety, and inclusivity—while avoiding those that fall short. In the coming chapters, we'll take a closer look at each aspect of SAFE, equipping you to make informed choices about the products and services you trust with your health.

Conclusion

Femtech is not just an industry—it is a revolution. For too long, women's health has been sidelined, misunderstood, and underfunded. But through technology, innovation, and advocacy, femtech is dismantling these barriers and forcing a long-overdue reckoning in healthcare. It is shifting power back into the hands of women, giving them the tools to track their bodies, demand better care, and make informed decisions about their health.

This revolution is not limited to reproductive health, nor is it confined to developed nations—it spans the entire spectrum of care across all continents. What's more, the breakthroughs in women's health research are not just benefiting women; they are unlocking critical medical advancements that improve healthcare for *everyone*. Investing in femtech is investing in a stronger, more inclusive healthcare system, one that finally acknowledges and addresses the unique needs of half the population. The momentum is undeniable, and the demand for change is louder than ever. The question is no longer whether femtech will reshape the future of women's health—the question is how far we are willing to take it.

5 | Femtech's Invisible Currency

The True Value of Your Health Data

The Data We Give Away—And What It Costs Us

"This is absurd. We can't afford this."

Rachel* stared at the document in her hands, her stomach twisting. Her new Summary of Benefits—the breakdown of her work-sponsored health insurance—showed an increase in premiums. Specifically, for women aged 21–35, the cost had jumped by $58 per month.

"Why would they do this?" she asked aloud. Her partner shrugged, but Rachel wasn't ready to let it go.

She skimmed the document, searching for an explanation. What she found instead was a vague reference to "complex calculations" and "risk-predicting algorithms." No specifics, no transparency—just numbers that had real consequences for her bank account.

Rachel wasn't alone in her frustration. Other women at her workplace were equally outraged about the spike in premiums. But here's the part that no one realized: They had all played a role in this decision. Even Rachel, despite her anger, had unknowingly contributed to the data that determined her new, higher premium. By simply tracking their symptoms, they had helped write the algorithm that worked against them.

Months before this moment, Rachel visited her OB/GYN. Sex with her partner had become painful and she needed answers. Was it something serious or simply the result of changing up their sexual routine?

When her doctor asked about symptoms, Rachel pulled up her tracking app—the one she used religiously. For weeks, she had documented every detail she could think of—frequency and duration of sex, positions used, number of orgasms per partner, cramps, spotting, and other side effects. Rachel had also tracked a particularly bad episode the week before when her cramps were so severe she had to miss two days of work.

Her doctor nodded, impressed by her diligence. "Keep tracking everything and bring me updates at your next appointment," she said.

But just as Rachel was about to leave, her doctor hesitated. "By the way, which app are you using?"

Rachel told her. Her doctor frowned. "Ah. That one's ... not the most secure. I'd recommend switching to something with better privacy protections."

Rachel meant to look into it. She even skimmed a few other apps while sitting in her car. But starting over felt exhausting. She had already learned this app's interface and knew how to enter her data quickly. A new app would have another learning curve. It would cost her more time. And honestly? She wasn't worried.

So what if this one app knows about my sex life? Rachel thought as she drove home. She was in a committed relationship and didn't mind speaking openly about sex. *It's not a secret. I'm 30 years old. I'm allowed to have sex.* Rachel wasn't ashamed of her body. She had nothing to hide.

Rachel's mindset seemed harmless—her data, her choice.

But Rachel's data wasn't just *hers.*

She wasn't the only person using that app. Hundreds of thousands of women were feeding similar information into the same system. And when data at that scale is collected, it creates a pattern—one that companies can use to make decisions that affect real lives.

Here's what Rachel didn't know: The tracking app sold user data to third-party brokers. Those brokers, in turn, packaged the data and sold it to interested companies—advertisers, research firms, and yes, insurance companies.

Rachel's insurance provider bought that data. Their risk-predicting algorithm scanned through thousands of reports from women just like Rachel. It flagged a trend: Women in Rachel's age group, especially those who were sexually active, reported more cramping than previous years and some even documented missing work due to the pain. For the insurance provider, that meant one thing: higher future costs. More pain meant more doctor visits. More missed work meant increased financial risks. Cramps had become an expensive symptom.

So the insurance company adjusted their calculations. And just like that, Rachel's premium went up.[1]

Rachel, like most of us, wasn't careless. She wasn't trying to overshare or make herself vulnerable. She was simply doing what she'd been encouraged to do—track her symptoms, take control of her health, and be proactive about her well-being.

But this is where the system can fail us.

Some femtech apps promise empowerment but turn around and sell that empowerment to the highest bidder. Rachel didn't consciously agree to let her health data be used to raise her insurance premiums. But by agreeing to the app's privacy policy and terms of use, she gave permission for her data to be sold.

And she's not alone. Millions of women are making the same trade-off every day. We tell ourselves it doesn't matter. So what if a company knows when you have your period? So what if they know you experience cramps?

But it *does* matter.

Because it's not just about you. When hundreds of thousands of users log similar symptoms, their collective data becomes a weapon—one that companies can use to make real decisions that impact our lives.

As consumers, we have a choice in how our data is used and disclosed. Our choices help set the standards for the systems that affect our everyday lives. Yet we live in a society that has taught us to devalue our data, even though it's one of our most powerful assets. We give our data away for free and then we're surprised when it is used against us.

Sharing information isn't inherently bad—in fact, it's a part of life. But we need to do it with intention. Giving our data to the right organizations can help close the gender data gap and improve women's health. But giving our data to the wrong companies feeds a system that makes healthcare more restrictive, more expensive, and more discriminatory. Our data isn't just information. It's power. And we should decide—consciously—who gets to hold it.

This is why security is the first pillar of the SAFE method. Security isn't just about avoiding risk—it's about controlling how your data is collected, stored, and used so that it isn't weaponized against you. A secure system should be transparent about its data practices, give users control over what they share, and have strong safeguards in place to prevent misuse.

Because privacy and security are such key components of femtech, the next three chapters will focus on how to protect your data and evaluate femtech companies based on their security practices. In this chapter, we'll explore the bigger picture of data privacy—who actually controls your health information, what laws exist to protect it, and where those laws fall short. The truth is, the regulations designed to safeguard your data are full of loopholes, and many companies take full advantage of them. Understanding this landscape will help you see just how easily your most personal information can be collected, shared, and even sold—sometimes without you realizing it.

Once you understand what's really happening behind the scenes, you'll be able to make smarter choices about which femtech apps and devices prioritize your privacy—and which ones might be putting it at risk. Then, in Chapter 6, we'll explore data privacy concerns in a post–*Roe v. Wade* environment, separating fact from fear to determine whether femtech is safe to use in this changing reproductive health climate. Finally, in Chapter 7, we'll go deeper, breaking down how to assess femtech companies' security standards so you can take control of your data and choose products that align with your values.

Data Is a Currency—And We're Spending It Blindly

Most of us don't think twice about handing over our health data to an app—especially a free one. After all, it's just information—right? A few details about your period, fertility tracking, pregnancy symptoms, or even sexual health might not seem like a big deal. Like Rachel, we may even think about our data in terms of secrets—as if privacy only matters if we have something to hide. But what if I told you that your health data is one of the most valuable commodities you own?

Health data isn't just numbers and charts—it's a highly lucrative asset that companies, insurers, advertisers, researchers, and even political organizations are willing to pay top dollar for. It can predict your future health risks, shape your access to care, influence the ads you see, affect insurance rates, and impact financial opportunities. Yet many people tend to think of data as valueless—just numbers, information, and facts about our bodies. We trade it freely for the convenience of new technologies that promise deeper health insights or greater control over our well-being. But unlike a credit card number, which can be canceled or changed, health data is permanent. Once it's out there, you can't take it back. And that's what makes it so powerful.

The true value of health data lies in what it reveals. A single medical record is far more than an ID number or transaction history—it's an intimate blueprint of your body, behaviors, long-term health patterns, and financial history. It contains everything from diagnoses and prescriptions to insurance details, billing histories, and even genetic data. This makes it one of the most sought-after commodities. A 2021 report estimated that a single healthcare record is worth up to $250 on the black market, compared to just $5.40 for a credit card number.[2] In other words, your health data is nearly *50 times* more valuable than your financial data.

Why? Because, unlike financial data, which becomes worthless once a compromised credit card is canceled or a password is changed, health data is permanent. You can reset a PIN, close a bank account, or get a new credit card in minutes. But you can't erase your medical history. Once your personal health details are collected, they become part of a lasting digital record—one that can follow you indefinitely, influencing decisions about your insurance coverage, healthcare costs, and employment opportunities.

And that's where the problem begins. You may think your data is only being used for your benefit—to improve health outcomes or provide personalized insights—but once it's shared, it enters a marketplace that extends far beyond your control, where companies you've never heard of are buying, selling, and profiting from the most intimate details of your life. Your menstrual cycle, fertility history, pregnancy status, medical usage, and even symptom patterns can be bundled into anonymous datasets and sold to data brokers, who then repackage and distribute that information to advertisers, pharmaceutical companies, and other third parties.

These transactions happen behind the scenes, often without your awareness. The data may be stripped of direct identifiers like your name or email, but that doesn't mean it's truly anonymous. Studies have shown that with just a handful of data points, individuals can often be re-identified with alarming accuracy.[3] A 2019 study revealed that 99.98 percent of Americans could be accurately re-identified in any dataset using only 15 demographic attributes.[4] Once your health information is out there, it's nearly impossible to track where it goes or who ultimately has access to it.

At first, some of these uses may seem harmless—or even beneficial. Researchers might analyze data to better understand women's health conditions, making strides to bridge the gender data gap. Pharmaceutical companies may use aggregated data to develop more effective treatments. But not all uses of health data are so noble. Too often, this information is leveraged in ways that shape real-life decisions about you.

For example, health insurers, employers, and mortgage lenders all use data to make decisions. These companies don't just evaluate you as an individual. They analyze patterns—trends revealed through millions of data points collected from people just like you. The result? They decide how much of your medical bills are covered, whether you get hired for a job, what kind of interest rate you qualify for on a loan, and much more.

In Rachel's case, her insurer inferred health conditions based on consumer-generated health data (CGHD). For years, health insurers have increasingly leveraged vast amounts of data to set premiums, adjust rates, and manage risk.[5] However, the rise of CGHD from wearable devices and femtech applications has significantly expanded the range of information insurers can access, enabling more dynamic pricing models. When combined with data from traditional sources, such as brokers' client information and electronic health records, femtech platforms provide unprecedented visibility into a policyholder's health.

For instance, irregular menstrual cycles or a diagnosis of PCOS could indicate potential fertility treatments or metabolic disorders, leading to higher premium costs. Similarly, pregnancy-tracking apps that monitor blood pressure and glucose levels can flag individuals as high risk for gestational diabetes or preeclampsia—conditions that may result in increased healthcare costs and premium hikes. Although insurers are prohibited from directly discriminating based on genetic or health conditions under the Genetic Information Nondiscrimination Act and the Affordable Care Act, they can still indirectly use CGHD to assess long-term costs and modify pricing.

Insurers aren't the only companies leveraging femtech data. Employers also have access to data-driven decision-making tools that use health-related information in ways that employees never intended. While federal laws such as the Americans with Disabilities Act prevent employers from discriminating based on medical history, there are growing concerns that companies could use alternative data sources—such as consumer health apps, fitness trackers, or wellness program participation—to make hiring, promotion, and benefits decisions without employees even realizing it.

Some employers have already integrated fertility tracking apps and femtech products into their workplace wellness programs. In 2019, Ovia Health allowed employers to access aggregated and de-identified data about employees' reproductive health trends.[6] While companies claim that such insights help tailor benefits and improve workplace policies, the practice raises concerns about privacy and potential discrimination. Even when data is anonymized, patterns in reproductive health trends could influence employer decisions about healthcare coverage, parental leave policies, or even workplace advancement opportunities. Employees may also feel pressured to participate in these programs, fearing that opting out could signal a lack of engagement in workplace wellness initiatives. Without strong privacy protections in place, the line between corporate wellness and corporate surveillance blurs.

Advertisers also use health data to target consumers with precision, influencing everything from the products you see online to the political ads that appear in your social media feed. A person tracking their pregnancy might suddenly be bombarded with baby product ads, while someone logging symptoms of menopause may see endless promotions for hormone therapy. Sometimes, this level of targeting can be so advanced that it reveals personal information before individuals have even shared it themselves.

The impact of data collection and selling isn't just intrusive. It can lead to potentially dangerous outcomes or legal liability, depending on the data involved. For example, in 2022, journalists discovered that data brokers were actively selling location data from people who had visited abortion clinics.[7] For as little as $160, anyone could purchase detailed information on where individuals traveled before and after their visit.[8] It wasn't just a violation of privacy—it was a weapon that could be used against people seeking reproductive care. And what's worse? This data was being sold *legally*.

In a world where data is currency, health data is among the most valuable assets a person has. Yet most consumers assume that agreeing to a privacy policy means their data is protected. In reality, consent is often buried in lengthy, complex agreements designed to discourage scrutiny. Weak data privacy laws offer little protection, leaving most users vulnerable to a system where companies dictate the rules. But this isn't just about privacy; it's about control. The moment you share your health data with an untrustworthy app, you lose the ability to decide where it goes, who profits from it, and how it might be used in the future. And once it's out there, there's no getting it back.

The answer, however, isn't to abandon femtech. Instead, the solution is to become informed consumers—to understand how our data is collected, who has access to it, and what protections are in place. The more we educate ourselves about our rights and risks, the more power we have to make choices that align with our values. This allows us to fully embrace femtech without placing our privacy and safety at risk.

It's time to stop treating our personal health information as disposable and start demanding transparency, accountability, and control. But to do that, we first need to understand the legal landscape that governs health data—where protections exist, where they fall short, and what rights we have as consumers. While many people assume that privacy laws safeguard all health-related information, the reality is far more complicated. By understanding the privacy frameworks that govern femtech, you'll be better equipped to make informed decisions about your data.

The Privacy Myth: What Femtech Users Get Wrong About Their Data

When Mia* downloaded a new period-tracking app, she barely glanced at the privacy policy before hitting "Agree." She assumed her data—her cycle dates, ovulation symptoms, even notes about her sex life—was protected.

After all, it was health information. And wasn't health information protected by the Health Insurance Portability and Accountability Act (HIPAA)?

It wasn't until later, when she read a news article about apps selling user data to third-party brokers, that she started to worry. She asked her neighbor, a healthcare attorney, whether her data was secure. What she discovered was alarming: Her data wasn't covered by HIPAA at all. The company could legally share her personal health details with advertisers, insurers, and even law enforcement in certain situations.

Mia's mistake is a common one—many people assume that because femtech apps collect intimate health data, they must follow the same privacy rules as doctors and hospitals. But that's not how the law works. In reality, most femtech data falls into a legal gray area. Unlike medical records stored in hospitals, which are protected under HIPAA, health data collected by apps, wearable devices, and direct-to-consumer services often has little legal protection.

While HIPAA doesn't cover most femtech data, it's not the only law at play. The Federal Trade Commission (FTC) and state consumer protection agencies have begun cracking down on health apps for misleading users about how their data is collected and shared. However, enforcement is limited, and most femtech companies still operate with few restrictions, giving them enormous freedom to collect, use, and sell deeply personal data. Without strong, proactive oversight, the burden falls on consumers to understand where their health data is protected—and where it's not.

How Privacy Laws (and Loopholes) Shape Femtech

In the United States, data privacy is not governed by one comprehensive law. Instead, it's regulated through a patchwork of federal, state, and industry-specific rules, creating gaps and inconsistencies—especially when it comes to femtech. At the federal level, two key agencies regulate health data privacy—the Department of Health and Human Services (HHS), which enforces HIPAA, and the FTC, which oversees consumer protection. State laws may also come into play, offering additional protections—or in some cases, introducing even more complexity. To understand the risks femtech users face, let's break down how each of these regulators protects health data and where the biggest gaps remain.

HIPAA and Femtech: A Law with Limits

Like Mia, most people assume that HIPAA protects all health-related data. Indeed, a survey of 2,000 adults found that 81 percent mistakenly believed the health data collected by digital health apps is covered by HIPAA.[9] But HIPAA's scope is far more limited than most consumers realize.

It often comes as a surprise to learn that HIPAA wasn't even created with data privacy in mind. When Congress passed HIPAA in 1996, its main goal was to address health insurance portability—making it easier for people to keep their health insurance when switching jobs—and increase the administrative efficiency of healthcare transactions. Privacy and security rules were only added later—in the early 2000s—as healthcare providers shifted to electronic medical records. However, the HIPAA Privacy Rule (2002) and HIPAA Security Rule (2003) only apply in specific circumstances—they don't apply to all health data in all settings. This is where many people misunderstand HIPAA's reach.

HIPAA's Applicability   First, the HIPAA Privacy and Security Rules only apply to specific organizations, known as "covered entities" and their "business associates."[10] A covered entity includes only the following three types of organizations:[11]

- **Healthcare providers:** Any individual or organization that bills insurance for medical or health services (e.g., hospitals, doctors, and clinics). If a healthcare provider does not process insurance claims or is cash pay only, then HIPAA does not apply.
- **Health plans:** Any organization that pays for or manages healthcare costs. This includes private insurance companies, employer-sponsored health plans, and government-funded programs such as Medicare and Medicaid.
- **Healthcare clearinghouses:** Entities that process medical transactions between providers and insurers. Clearinghouses are often perceived as a go-between for healthcare providers and health plans. As such, they rarely deal with patients directly. For example, these could be billing service providers, community health management information systems, repricing companies, or data intermediaries.

A business associate is a third-party company that handles protected health information (PHI) on behalf of a covered entity.[12] In simpler terms, a business associate often works with a covered entity as a contractor or subcontractor and has access to health data to perform specific tasks for the covered entity. For example, a business associate might be an electronic prescription platform that transmits medication orders for a hospital, a law firm or consulting company that reviews patient records for legal or compliance purposes, a billing or medical coding company that processes insurance claims for a doctor's office, and more. The key distinction is that business associates are not collecting health data for their own use—they are processing, storing, or transmitting it as part of a service for a covered entity. Because business associates handle PHI, they must follow HIPAA's rules for the work they perform for the covered entity.

If a company or individual does not meet the definition of a covered entity or a business associate, they are not required to comply with HIPAA's Privacy and Security Rules. It's that simple.

Second, the HIPAA Privacy and Security Rules only apply to a specific subset of data known as protected health information. PHI refers to health information that can be linked to an individual and is created or received by a healthcare provider, health plan, employer, or healthcare clearinghouse.[13] The information must relate to a person's past, present, or future physical or mental health, the medical care they receive, or the payment for healthcare services.[14] Additionally, it must identify or be capable of identifying the individual.[15] If health data does not satisfy these requirements, then it does not constitute PHI, and HIPAA's protections do not apply.

Why Most Femtech Companies Are Not Covered by HIPAA
Although femtech companies handle personal health information, most do not fall under HIPAA's jurisdiction. The first and most fundamental reason is that most femtech companies are not considered covered entities. HIPAA was designed to regulate traditional healthcare institutions—meaning medical providers, insurance plans, and intermediaries that process health-related transactions. This is why the definition of covered entity is purposefully narrow. By contrast, femtech companies typically fall into the category of consumer technology businesses. Most do not provide direct medical

treatment to patients. Most do not bill insurance. And most do not interact with health plans in a way that would bring them under HIPAA's oversight. Even in cases where a licensed doctor or medical professional founds or operates a femtech company, the business itself may remain outside HIPAA's jurisdiction unless it directly participates in billing insurance or delivering care through the regulated healthcare system.

Another key reason HIPAA does not apply to most femtech data is that the information collected by these apps and devices does not necessarily qualify as PHI. HIPAA only covers individually identifiable health information when it is created or received by a covered entity or its business associates.[16] Because most femtech companies do not fall into either of these categories, the data they collect is classified as consumer-generated health data rather than protected health information. This distinction means that femtech users often do not have the same privacy protections as patients receiving care from a healthcare provider.

Let's revisit Rachel's story. She used a free app to track some of her most personal health and sexual experiences, assuming her data was protected. However, because the femtech company operating the app was neither a covered entity nor a business associate, none of the information she entered was safeguarded by HIPAA. If, instead, Rachel had recorded the same details on paper and given it to her doctor during her visit, and her doctor added it to her medical records, that exact same data would now be protected under HIPAA.

If you're thinking this outcome is absurd, you're not alone. The data is the same—word for word—but whether it's protected depends entirely on where the data is created and stored. When input into a medical record at a doctor's office, it becomes federally protected. When entered into a femtech app, it can be collected, shared, or sold with no HIPAA oversight. That's the legal loophole femtech companies operate within, and it's why users often have far less privacy protections than they assume.

The third reason HIPAA typically does not apply to most femtech companies is that, unlike traditional healthcare services, which operate within the regulated healthcare system, most femtech products are currently designed as direct-to-consumer (DTC) platforms. DTC femtech companies sell their products directly to users, bypassing the need for involvement from healthcare providers, insurers, or other covered entities. As a result, they remain outside HIPAA's jurisdiction.

DTC femtech products typically operate under a terms of service and privacy policy model, meaning that users must agree to the company's data practices when enrolling. This model places the responsibility for data privacy entirely in the hands of the company, rather than within a standardized federal framework. Because these DTC companies do not operate within the traditional healthcare system, they are not subject to the same privacy obligations as doctors, hospitals, or insurers. Instead, their data practices are dictated by corporate policies, which can vary significantly. As such, the burden of determining whether your data is protected falls almost entirely on you.

The FTC's Role in Femtech Privacy: A Safety Net with Holes In the absence of a comprehensive federal privacy law, the FTC has stepped in as the primary enforcer of consumer privacy protections in the United States. Unlike HIPAA, the FTC's reach is much broader, covering most businesses engaged in commerce—including femtech companies. However, while the FTC has the power to hold companies accountable, it does not proactively regulate how businesses handle consumer health data. Instead, its authority stems from the Federal Trade Commission Act, which prohibits unfair or deceptive acts or practices in commerce.[17] This means the FTC's role in femtech is focused on enforcement rather than regulation, stepping in only when companies mislead consumers or fail to properly protect sensitive information.

Because femtech companies fall under the FTC's jurisdiction, they can be subject to enforcement actions for unfair or deceptive practices related to user data. Unfair practices occur when a company's actions cause substantial harm to consumers without enough benefits to justify the risks. For instance, if a femtech company fails to implement any adequate security measures, leading to a data breach that exposes sensitive health information, the FTC could act. Deceptive practices, on the other hand, involve misleading consumers about data use. If a femtech app claims it won't share user data but secretly sells it to data brokers, the FTC can hold the company accountable.

One area where the FTC does set more specific requirements is the Health Breach Notification Rule, which applies to companies handling personal health information outside of HIPAA regulations. If a femtech app experiences a breach, exposing sensitive user data, the company may be legally required to notify affected consumers, the FTC, and, in some cases, the media.[18] However, this rule applies only after a breach has already occurred, reinforcing the FTC's reactive rather than proactive role in consumer protection. For many femtech users, this means that recourse comes only after harm is already done.

The FTC also does not prohibit the sale of consumer health data. If a femtech company chooses to sell user data, it is perfectly legal—as long as the company discloses this practice in its privacy policy. The FTC does not regulate what femtech companies can or cannot do with consumer data—it only intervenes when companies break their own promises. If a company falsely guarantees user privacy but secretly monetizes health data, it becomes a deceptive practice, triggering FTC enforcement. However, there are no baseline privacy requirements preventing femtech companies from profiting off user data, as long as they are transparent about it.

Further complicating matters, the FTC is responsible for overseeing the entire US commercial marketplace—not just femtech. With limited resources, it can only investigate the most egregious violations or high-profile cases, meaning smaller femtech companies or lesser-known breaches may go unnoticed unless consumers file significant complaints. This enforcement gap leaves many violations unchecked, making it possible for companies to continue questionable data practices as long as they avoid major scrutiny.

Ultimately, while the FTC plays a critical role in consumer protection, its ability to safeguard femtech users is limited. It can hold companies accountable for misleading practices, but it does not create proactive privacy regulations or dictate how consumer health data should be handled. This means the burden still falls on consumers to understand the limitations of femtech privacy policies, recognize potential risks, and make informed decisions before sharing their sensitive health data.

State Privacy Laws: A False Sense of Security? While federal privacy laws leave significant gaps in health data protection, some states have stepped in with their own regulations aimed at giving consumers more control over their personal information. As of February 2025, at least 19 states have passed their own privacy legislation.[19] Laws like the California Consumer Privacy Act (CCPA) and the Virginia Consumer Data Protection Act are designed to increase transparency, allowing people to see what data companies collect, request its deletion, and opt out of certain data-sharing practices. On the surface, this sounds like progress. But for most femtech users, these laws offer little to no real protection.

The problem isn't that these laws fail to recognize health data as sensitive—rather, like HIPAA, the problem is that these state laws only apply to certain businesses, and most femtech companies don't meet the legal thresholds to be covered. The CCPA, for example, only applies to businesses that make over $25 million in annual revenue; buy, sell, or share the personal data of at least 100,000 consumers per year; or earn at least 50 percent of their revenue from selling personal data.[20] Most femtech companies, especially the smaller startups that dominate the industry, don't satisfy these thresholds. As a result, even if an app collects highly sensitive health data, it may still be exempt from these laws simply because it doesn't make enough money or process enough user data to qualify. This means that even in states with so-called "strong privacy laws," most femtech apps are not legally required to follow them. Some companies may choose to comply voluntarily, but others operate with few meaningful restrictions, deciding for themselves how much privacy users get.

This patchwork approach to data privacy leaves femtech users in a vulnerable position. Without clear, industry-wide regulations, privacy protections remain inconsistent, reactive, and largely dictated by the companies themselves. Consumers are forced to decipher complex privacy policies, rely on company promises, and hope that their sensitive health data isn't being exploited behind the scenes. But history has shown that hope is not a strategy. Time and time again, companies have prioritized profit over privacy, quietly sharing, selling, or mishandling user data while claiming to uphold high standards of security. When privacy violations do come to light, it's usually only after millions of users' data has already been compromised.

One of the most recognizable privacy scandals in femtech revealed just how fragile consumer trust can be—and how easily companies can exploit sensitive health data without users realizing it. What happened next served as a wake-up call, exposing the glaring gaps in data privacy protections and forcing many consumers to reconsider how much personal information they were willing to share. The fallout from this case sent shockwaves through the femtech industry, but the real lesson isn't just about what went wrong—it's about what every user can learn from it to protect themselves moving forward.

The Flo Fallout: What It Taught Us About Data Privacy

When Flo Health launched its period-tracking app in 2015, it positioned itself as a revolutionary tool for reproductive health. Using AI, Flo promised users a highly accurate predictor for their menstrual cycles, fertility windows, and pregnancy tracking. As the app expanded its features, it skyrocketed in popularity. By 2022, it had been downloaded over 220 million times and held a top spot in the App Store.[21] As of June 2024, Flo had more than 70 million monthly users actively logging some of their most personal health details—secure in the belief that their data was private.[22]

Flo's privacy policy reassured users that their health data would remain confidential, stating that under no circumstances would the app share intimate health information without user consent. There was a small caveat— Flo mentioned it might share certain information with third parties for technical reasons like web hosting—but it explicitly promised not to share details about users' cycles, pregnancies, symptoms, or notes.

For users like Jaime Lam, this promise was enough.

Jaime downloaded Flo in 2016 when she and her husband began trying to conceive. Like many users, she quickly skimmed the privacy policy, reassured by Flo's emphasis on confidentiality. The app prompted her to enter her name, birthdate, height, weight, and email address—and even encouraged her to link her husband's email so he could receive notifications about her cycle.

For two years, Jaime used the app daily. She logged her period dates, tracked her ovulation, and recorded every time she and her husband had sex. When she started taking ovulation tests, she entered the results into Flo. Every aspect of her reproductive health was carefully documented in the app she had grown to trust.

In July 2018, Jaime conceived her first child. She switched the app to "Pregnancy Mode," logging details about her pregnancy week by week. Even after giving birth, Jaime continued using Flo, documenting postpartum symptoms and tracking her cycle again. She had every reason to believe that the data she shared was hers alone—until 2019, when she learned the truth.

That year, a *Wall Street Journal* investigation revealed that Flo had been secretly sharing sensitive user data with Facebook, Google, and other third parties.[23] These companies weren't just receiving general app data—they had access to users' menstrual cycle logs, fertility tracking, and pregnancy statuses. *The Wall Street Journal* tested multiple period-tracking apps, including Flo, to see whether they were leaking user data to Facebook. Their findings were shocking: Flo notified Facebook whenever a user was on her period or had logged an intent to get pregnant.[24]

Flo immediately denied wrongdoing, insisting that any data shared with third parties was "depersonalized" and stripped of identifying details. But the *Journal's* investigation found that the app was linking shared health data to unique advertising identifiers, which could be matched back to individual users or their devices.[25]

Jaime was horrified. The personal details she had entrusted to Flo had been quietly sent to third parties, potentially used to target ads or build consumer profiles without her knowledge.

Flo's data sharing practices caught the attention of the FTC, which launched an investigation. In 2021, the FTC formally charged Flo with deceptive business practices, alleging that Flo had misled users into believing their health data was private when, in reality, it was being shared with advertisers.[26] Flo never admitted fault but entered into a settlement agreement with the FTC.[27] The settlement agreement required Flo to notify all affected users that their health data had been improperly shared, obtain explicit consent before sharing any health information with third parties in the future, and undergo independent privacy audits for 20 years to ensure compliance.[28] While the FTC's intervention forced Flo to change its practices, it couldn't undo the damage. Users like Jaime had no way to retrieve or erase their data from the third parties that had already received it.

The FTC wasn't the only entity investigating Flo. A class-action lawsuit was filed in California against Flo, consolidating seven separate lawsuits from users who felt their privacy had been violated.[29] By 2023, another class-action lawsuit was filed in Canada, with Jaime as the lead plaintiff.[30] While lawsuits like these may result in financial settlements, they can't restore the trust that was lost. Even if Jaime's personal health data wasn't sold to an insurance company or linked to her name, the risk of exposure was enough to change how she viewed femtech forever.

The fallout from the Flo case revealed a deeper truth about health data privacy: Most violations happen long before consumers realize. What seemed like a reliable and discreet tracking app was, in reality, funneling sensitive information to third parties. This case, however, wasn't just about one company's misstep—it exposed larger data privacy issues in femtech and digital health, serving as a wake-up call for both consumers and other femtech companies. In particular, the Flo case taught us three key lessons about how companies handle health data and what consumers need to do to stay safe.

The first lesson from the Flo fallout is that privacy violations often happen quietly, and by the time they come to light, the damage is already done. Flo users had no idea their data was being shared until a journalistic investigation exposed it. Even then, many people only learned about the breach when the FTC stepped in. Companies may not be upfront about how they handle user data, and without strong federal protections, it's often left to investigative reporters, lawsuits, or regulatory agencies to uncover the truth after the fact.

The second key takeaway is that even the most popular, well-reviewed apps aren't necessarily the safest. Flo was one of the most widely used period-tracking apps in the world. It wasn't an obscure company or a shady knockoff app—it was a go-to choice for period and pregnancy tracking. This shows that size, reputation, and popularity don't always equal security. Consumers can't assume that just because an app is widely used it follows the best privacy practices.

Most importantly, the final lesson is that no one is looking out for your privacy more than you. While the FTC eventually acted against Flo, millions of users already had their sensitive health data shared. Class-action lawsuits were filed, but they won't erase the fact that this information is out in the world. Regulators and courts can step in after privacy violations occur, but they can't prevent companies from making decisions that put user data at risk in the first place.

As a result, the burden of protecting our data ultimately falls on us as consumers. If we don't take a proactive role in evaluating femtech apps, companies will continue to exploit legal loopholes, vague policies, and weak regulations to justify invasive data practices. We have the power to reshape standards for health data privacy—to expect more, push for stronger protections, and reject a system that treats our most personal information as just another commodity. But if we don't use this power, nothing will change. Without stronger expectations of privacy and security, the industry will continue to put profit over protection. It's time we demanded better for our data.

Conclusion

Our health data is far more valuable—and vulnerable—than most of us realize. We've seen how companies can exploit, monetize, and even share deeply personal health information under the guise of providing a helpful service. We've also seen that privacy protections in femtech are inconsistent at best and nonexistent at worst. The reality is that most of these companies operate in a legal gray zone, where they set their own rules and face few consequences for mishandling user data.

But that doesn't mean we're powerless. Privacy laws may be lagging, but we, as consumers, still have choices. The power to protect our health data starts with awareness and action—understanding which companies take privacy seriously, recognizing red flags, and refusing to support platforms that don't respect our information. The more informed we are, the more we can push the industry toward stronger protections and demand accountability where regulations fall short.

6 | Data, Danger, and the Post-*Roe* World

What's Real, What's Hype, and What You Can Do

When Data Becomes a Threat

In the days following the 2022 *Dobbs v. Jackson Women's Health Organization* decision,[1] Sara* sat at her kitchen table, her fingers wrapped tightly around a mug of coffee that had long since gone cold. Her phone screen glowed in the dim light, filled with an endless scroll of breaking news updates, opinion pieces, and frantic social media posts. The headlines were everywhere: CNN, *The Washington Post*, Vox, *Newsweek*, and more. "White House Says Americans Should Be 'Really Careful' About Using Period Tracker Apps."[2] "The Danger of Period-Tracking Apps in a Post-*Roe* World."[3] "Why Delete Period Tracking App? *Roe v. Wade* Ruling Sparks Panic Over Data."[4] "Why US Women Are Deleting Their Period Tracking Apps."[5]

Sara's stomach twisted as she read each article. She had never thought about her period-tracking app as a threat before. It was just part of her routine, a quiet background habit she barely considered. She had used the app for three years, carefully logging every detail of her cycle. A few months earlier, after a late period sent her into a spiral of anxiety, she had even searched "Plan B effectiveness" in the app's forums. She had nearly forgotten about it. But now it was all she could think about.

Her best friend, Megan,* had already deleted her app.

"It's not safe," Megan had texted her the night before. "If you ever need an abortion, you don't want that data out there."

Sara had scoffed at first. *Is this really where we are now?* It felt dramatic. But as she sat there, scrolling through the warnings from privacy experts and lawyers, the pit in her stomach deepened. Maybe it wasn't paranoia. Maybe it was just reality now.

She thought about the stories. Latice Fisher, the Mississippi woman who had been arrested after law enforcement pulled her internet search history to charge her with killing her infant child.[6] Purvi Patel, an Indiana woman who was charged, convicted, and sentenced for feticide in ending her own pregnancy based on texts discussing her plans to take abortion-inducing pills.[7] Sara's stomach continued to churn.

Her hands felt clammy as she set her coffee down and tapped open the app. The interface was familiar, comforting even, with its soft colors and neat little charts mapping out her cycle. But suddenly, it didn't feel so harmless. She clicked into her history and scrolled back.

There it was. Three months ago. "Missed period."

It hadn't meant anything at the time. Sara had been a few days late, probably stressed, and had logged it absentmindedly. When her period arrived, she had marked it like normal and moved on. But now, staring at those two words, she felt something close to panic.

She clicked into the privacy settings, something she had never bothered to check before. The legal jargon blurred together, but certain phrases jumped out at her. "May share anonymized data with third-party users." "Law enforcement requests will be processed in compliance with applicable laws."

Her pulse thudded in her ears.

Could this be used against her? Her name wasn't attached to the data, but what if it didn't have to be? What if a prosecutor somewhere could match her location, her app usage, and her browser history and make a case?

Her thumb hovered over the "Delete Account" button.

Then another thought hit her. Even if she deleted the app now, would it even matter? Her data was already stored. Her searches, her logged symptoms, her cycle history—it wasn't just on her phone. It was sitting on a server somewhere, waiting to be accessed, analyzed, and interpreted. She swallowed hard. The walls of her apartment felt smaller.

And for the first time in her life, Sara wasn't sure if she was the only one watching her body.

Sara wasn't alone. In the days following the Supreme Court's decision, thousands of women across the country deleted their period-tracking apps, overwhelmed by the fear that their most intimate health data could one day be used against them. Privacy experts warned that data collected by femtech companies was often unprotected by health privacy laws, while headlines cautioned that law enforcement could subpoena app data in states where abortion was now illegal.

But how much of this was *actual* risk, and how much of it was speculation? In this chapter, I'll unpack the exact ways data can—and can't—be used against you in a post-*Roe* world. I'll explore what risks are real, which ones are theoretical, and what you can do to protect yourself while still maximizing your use of femtech. Femtech has never been under more scrutiny, but that doesn't mean we should abandon it altogether. Instead, we need to understand how to navigate this new landscape, separating fear from fact while making informed choices about our own digital safety.

The Legal Shift That Put Reproductive Data at Risk

For nearly 50 years, *Roe v. Wade* was the legal foundation for abortion rights in the United States.[8] Decided in 1973, the Supreme Court ruled that the right to an abortion was protected under the US Constitution through the Due Process Clause of the Fourteenth Amendment, which guarantees a right to privacy.[9] *Roe* established that a woman had the right to terminate a pregnancy before fetal viability—typically considered around 24 weeks—without excessive government interference.[10] While states could regulate abortion to some degree, they could not ban it outright before viability.

In 1992, *Planned Parenthood v. Casey* reaffirmed *Roe* but changed how abortion restrictions were evaluated.[11] Instead of requiring the government to prove a law was necessary, *Casey* allowed states to regulate abortion as long as they did not impose an "undue burden" on someone seeking the procedure.[12] This ruling gave states more power to pass laws that made abortion harder to access, such as waiting periods, mandatory counseling, parental consent requirements for minors, and limits on when and how the procedure could be performed. Even so, abortion remained a federally protected right. No matter how many restrictions a state imposed, *Roe* and *Casey* ensured that a person could not be completely denied the ability to terminate a pregnancy before viability.

That all changed on June 24, 2022, with *Dobbs v. Jackson Women's Health Organization.*

In *Dobbs*, the Supreme Court held that abortion was not a constitutionally protected right and that individual states could regulate it however they chose. The majority opinion declared that *Roe* had been "egregiously wrong from the start" and that abortion rights should never have been recognized under the Constitution.[13] By overturning *Roe*, the Court gave full power to state governments to determine whether abortion should be legal, restricted, or entirely banned.

The ruling had immediate and far-reaching consequences. Thirteen states had "trigger laws" on the books, meaning their abortion bans would automatically take effect as soon as *Roe* was overturned.[14] In some states, clinics stopped performing abortions within hours of the decision, and many patients who had already scheduled appointments were turned away. Other states rushed to pass new restrictions, with at least 19 states eventually enacting bans or severe limitations on abortion.[15] The result was a country where reproductive rights were no longer consistent—where a person's ability to access an abortion depended entirely on their zip code.

For those living in states with bans, the decision meant that abortion was no longer a legally protected medical procedure but, in many cases, a potential crime. Some states enacted laws that not only banned abortion but also imposed criminal penalties on those who performed or facilitated one. In Texas,[16] Oklahoma,[17] and Idaho,[18] laws allowed private citizens to sue anyone who helped a person obtain an abortion, creating a bounty system that encouraged neighbors, coworkers, and even family members to report one another. Other states pushed laws that could allow prosecutors to charge women with murder or child endangerment if they ended a pregnancy outside legal channels.

Beyond the bans themselves, the *Dobbs* decision created widespread confusion about what was still legal. The ruling didn't just eliminate abortion rights—it reshaped the entire landscape of reproductive healthcare, leaving doctors, hospitals, and patients unsure of what care could be provided without risking criminal charges. Doctors who once provided essential reproductive care now found themselves navigating a legal minefield, where a single medical decision could land them in court or cost them their medical licenses.

For patients, this uncertainty has devastating consequences on necessary care. The same medications and procedures used in abortions are also used to treat miscarriages, uterine fibroids, Crohn's disease, lupus, eczema, and endometriosis.[19] Restricting access to these medications can harm people who are not seeking abortions by preventing them from receiving essential treatment or subjecting them to unnecessary scrutiny and legal investigations for using prescribed medication.

In states where doctors fear prosecution, the outcomes can be even worse. Numerous doctors in abortion-restrictive states have hesitated to provide necessary reproductive healthcare services—even when a woman's life is at risk. One Texas woman, Amanda Zurawski, experienced a miscarriage at 18 weeks.[20] She went to the emergency room in excruciating pain, only to be told she had to wait until she was actively crashing—meaning experiencing life-threatening complications—before doctors could legally treat her. Three days after her water broke, she spiked a 103-degree fever and was too weak to walk on her own.[21] By the time doctors agreed she was sick enough to legally terminate the pregnancy, Amanda was so ill that antibiotics and blood transfusions couldn't stop the bacterial infection raging through her body. She became septic and doctors had to insert an intravenous line near her heart to deliver medication to stabilize her blood pressure.[22] Amanda lived, but the delay caused significant scarring on her uterus. Another woman was denied miscarriage medication at her pharmacy and bled at home for days, developing an infection before she was finally given care.

Some doctors have reported that they now wait longer than ever before treating patients with pregnancy complications, because they fear legal consequences if they intervene too soon.[23] Some hospitals require ethics committees or legal teams to sign off before doctors can perform procedures that would have been routine before *Dobbs*. These delays have led to unnecessary suffering, increased risks of infection, and in some cases preventable deaths.

The *Dobbs* decision didn't just criminalize abortion—it created a chilling effect that has bled into every aspect of reproductive healthcare. Women seeking treatment for pregnancy loss, life-threatening conditions, or even standard OB/GYN care are now facing longer wait times, unnecessary legal roadblocks, and the fear that the care they need may no longer be available. In a post-*Roe* world, the issue is no longer just about abortion rights—it's about whether women can still rely on a medical system to protect their health and their lives.

When Doctors Disappear, Femtech Steps In

The *Dobbs* decision has forced millions of women to seek alternative ways to manage their reproductive health, making femtech more essential than ever. With abortion bans and restrictions limiting access to in-person care, digital health solutions are filling critical gaps by providing discreet, accessible, and often more affordable options for contraception, pregnancy monitoring, and abortion services. For many, these platforms offer a crucial alternative to overwhelmed or unavailable medical providers, particularly in states where clinics have shut down or doctors fear legal repercussions. By leveraging technology, women can now obtain the reproductive healthcare they need on their own terms, without the barriers of cost, location, or political interference.

Telehealth platforms in particular have become a lifeline for those living in restrictive states. Through services like Aid Access, Hey Jane, and Choix, women can consult with licensed medical professionals and receive prescriptions for birth control, emergency contraception, and abortion pills—without stepping into a clinic. For those in states with bans, some organizations help patients navigate legal pathways to obtain care, such as prescriptions from out-of-state providers who can ship abortion pills to forwarding addresses. These workarounds are becoming one of the safest and most effective ways for women to access reproductive care in states where abortion is criminalized.

Femtech platforms are also helping women secure contraception without relying on in-person visits to a doctor or pharmacy. Digital health services like Nurx and the Pill Club allow women to order birth control pills, patches, and even prescriptions for IUD insertions without the need for a clinic appointment—a critical solution in states where Planned Parenthood and other providers have been forced to shut down. Many services now encourage preordering Plan B so women have emergency contraception readily available,[24] avoiding the risk of being denied at a pharmacy or facing restrictions on over-the-counter purchases.

Cycle-tracking apps have also taken on a new level of importance in the post-*Roe* era. With limited access to OB/GYNs and emergency reproductive care, women can utilize these apps to closely monitor their periods, helping them identify a pregnancy as early as possible—a necessity in states with six-week abortion bans, where options disappear before many even realize they are pregnant. Early detection gives women precious time to make decisions about their healthcare, whether that means traveling out of state, seeking telehealth services for abortion medication, or preparing for a pregnancy in an environment where maternity care is also under strain.

Beyond pregnancy tracking, these apps help women spot signs of reproductive health issues that may go untreated due to restrictive medical policies. Beyond knowing the date of one's last period, tracking ovulation, pregnancy, symptoms, and bleeding patterns helps women demonstrate the progression—or lack thereof—of a pregnancy when seeking emergency care. This can be especially important in cases where doctors refuse to intervene and delay care until a patient develops an infection or other life-threatening complication. By logging symptoms, such as severe cramping, prolonged bleeding, temperature, or abnormal discharge, women can provide a clear, time-stamped medical history that may compel hesitant providers to act sooner. Some cycle-tracking apps are also integrating with telehealth services and miscarriage support networks, offering medical guidance and connections to providers who can help women navigate restrictive hospital policies and access care before their condition worsens.

Another critical way femtech is stepping up in the post-*Roe* era is by providing medication safety guidance for those self-managing their reproductive healthcare. While many women now rely on telehealth to obtain abortion pills, some do not have access to follow-up care if they experience complications. Platforms like Plan C and Reprocare provide detailed, evidence-based guidance on safely using abortion pills, explaining how to manage symptoms, recognize warning signs, and understand when medical intervention is necessary. Some services even connect users with aftercare support via encrypted messaging or telehealth consultations, ensuring women are not left without medical help during the process.

Femtech is also providing education and support for women navigating an increasingly complex legal landscape. Many platforms now include legal hotlines, encrypted chat groups, and connections to advocacy organizations that help women understand their rights, locate safe providers, and avoid legal risks. Some digital tools even offer step-by-step guidance on traveling for care, connecting women with out-of-state abortion funds, transportation networks, and lodging assistance programs.

As access to traditional reproductive healthcare continues to erode, femtech is no longer just a convenience—it's a necessity. But as more women turn to femtech, a pressing question remains: How safe is it to use these digital tools in a post-*Roe* world, particularly where data could be weaponized? In states where abortion is restricted or criminalized, many women fear that their health data could be requested by law enforcement, used in legal cases, or accessed by third parties without their knowledge. With so many conflicting reports about digital surveillance, subpoenas, and law enforcement tactics, it's essential to separate real risks from overblown fears. Understanding the true risks—and how to navigate them—can help you make informed choices without sacrificing necessary care.

Subpoenas, Warrants, and Loopholes: How Law Enforcement Can Access Your Data

In a post-*Roe* world, digital footprints matter more than ever. While many assume their health data is private, the reality is that law enforcement has multiple ways to access and use reproductive health information. Whether through phone records, app data, location tracking, or purchased consumer data, reproductive health information can become evidence in an investigation. Understanding how this data is obtained is the first step in knowing how to protect it. There are four main ways law enforcement can access your data, but not all of them pose the same level of risk. In the following sections, I'll break down these methods, how likely each one is to happen, and what's a real concern versus what might be overblown or theoretical at this time.

Method 1: Law Enforcement's Access to Your Phone and Stored Data

The first way law enforcement can access reproductive health data is straight from your device. Phones, tablets, and computers store vast amounts of information—search histories, text messages, app activity, and location data—all of which can be used to track or reconstruct someone's reproductive choices. Law enforcement does not always need sophisticated hacking tools to get this information; sometimes they obtain it simply by asking. For example, if you voluntarily hand over your phone during an encounter with police, officers may search through messages, call logs, notes, apps, and browsing history for evidence. In states where abortion is criminalized, text conversations about obtaining abortion pills, Google searches for clinic locations, or period-tracking data showing a missed cycle could all become pieces of a larger investigation. In some cases, law enforcement officers may pressure individuals into unlocking their phones, sometimes implying that they are required to comply when, in reality, they have the right to refuse. This tactic is particularly effective in high-stress situations, where a person may feel intimidated or too overwhelmed to assert their rights.

Even without voluntary access, law enforcement can seize a phone if they obtain a warrant, which allows them to search the device for evidence. Once a phone is in their possession, investigators use forensic tools to extract data, including deleted text messages, private browsing histories, and even location records stored in hidden system files. These tools allow authorities to recreate a person's digital activity over weeks, months, or even years, uncovering information that the user may have believed was erased.

These forensic tools can also expose a person's digital footprint in ways they might not expect. Even messages sent through supposedly "private" platforms may not be fully secure. While some encrypted messaging apps delete conversations automatically, many default phone messaging systems store backups that can be retrieved. Investigators can recover timestamps of when messages were sent, metadata showing who a person was communicating with, and, in some cases, the actual contents of messages themselves. Location tracking adds another layer of risk. Many smartphones passively log a user's movements, and unless these features are disabled, a phone may store detailed records of visits to reproductive health clinics, pharmacies, or out-of-state abortion providers. This information can allow law enforcement to establish a timeline of someone's actions, which prosecutors may attempt to use as evidence of intent in states where abortion is criminalized.

So how big a risk is this really? While law enforcement does have the ability to seize and search a phone under the right circumstances, the reality is that this isn't happening to most people. A device typically only becomes a target after other evidence already points to potential criminal activity and a warrant has been obtained—meaning that it's rarely the first step in an investigation. For most people, the chances of having their phone searched remain low, but that doesn't mean it's impossible.

For law enforcement to seize and search a phone, they first need a warrant, which requires probable cause.[25] This means they can't just take a phone at random or demand access without justification unless you consent. Investigators will almost always have some other source of evidence first—whether that's messages obtained from a tech company, location data purchased from a third-party broker, or a tip from an informant—before they can prove probable cause to a judge and obtain a warrant that allows them to search a physical device. In most cases, a phone is only targeted if there is already a strong reason to believe it contains relevant information that could further an investigation.

Even when law enforcement does suspect someone of a crime, seizing and searching a phone is generally not a simple process unless the person hands over their device. There is no requirement that you voluntarily surrender your device unless you're presented with a legally binding court order. If law enforcement requests your device without a court order, you can—and should—decline to turn over your device. If you refuse to voluntarily surrender your device, then law enforcement officers will need a warrant, which requires them to justify to a judge why they believe the phone contains pertinent evidence of illegal activity. Courts do not approve these requests automatically—there must be specific and credible evidence supporting the claim that the device is relevant to a crime. This legal hurdle makes it far less likely that someone who has merely searched for abortion-related information or used a period-tracking app would have their phone targeted without other supporting evidence. As such, for the average person, the risk of law enforcement taking their phone remains extremely low.

Although the risk is low, you may still wish to take precautions to ensure that your health data is protected. Make sure that you lock your device so that even if it is seized, the data remains inaccessible without your password. Enabling full-disk encryption, if available, further ensures that even if data is extracted from your device, it remains unreadable without the proper credentials.

Beyond securing the device itself, limiting the amount of reproductive health data stored on your device is another smart precaution. Turning off location tracking can prevent the device from logging visits to clinics or out-of-state providers. Checking and restricting app permissions can stop femtech apps from collecting unnecessary data. Deleting sensitive messages and using encrypted messaging apps with disappearing messages can further reduce the risk of personal health data being used as evidence. Thus, while the likelihood of law enforcement seizing a device without probable cause is extremely low, taking these steps helps ensure that even in the worst-case scenario, your personal reproductive health information remains private and secure.

Method 2: The Data Broker Loophole—How Police Buy Personal Information

The second way in which reproductive health data can end up in the hands of law enforcement is through third-party data brokers—companies that collect and sell personal data. Some femtech apps share user data for marketing and analytics purposes, often claiming it is anonymized. But once that data is sold, consumers have no control over who buys it or how it is used. Law enforcement agencies, private actors, and anti-abortion organizations can all legally purchase this information, potentially using it to track or report individuals seeking reproductive care.

Data brokers gather information from a variety of sources, including location-tracking services that log movement patterns, search engines that store queries related to reproductive healthcare, and credit card transactions that reflect purchases such as pregnancy tests or emergency contraception. What makes this particularly concerning is that law enforcement does not need a warrant to obtain this data.[26] Because data brokers operate in the private sector, authorities can bypass legal oversight entirely by simply purchasing access. In states where abortion is restricted, law enforcement could theoretically use this method to track individuals without their knowledge or consent. Unlike traditional investigative techniques, this approach does not require reasonable suspicion of a crime, judicial approval, or notification to the person being investigated. The data is treated like any commercial product—available to anyone who can pay.

While this is a real risk, the likelihood of an individual being targeted in this way depends on several factors. Law enforcement agencies often have limited budgets and prioritize investigative techniques that provide clear leads. Buying raw, anonymized, or de-identified data from brokers is not always the most efficient way to identify individuals and their crimes, particularly when such data may need to be combined and cross-referenced with other data sources and re-identified. There are more efficient and less costly methods that law enforcement can use to obtain identifiable user data—such as subpoenaing data from tech companies. However, this does not fully eliminate the risk, especially as data tracking technologies become more advanced. As such, this is a moderate-level risk, and it's recommended that you take precautions to guard your data.

You can take several steps to protect yourself from this form of data collection and minimize the risk of your data being sold to law enforcement. The most effective measure is to avoid using apps that sell data to brokers. Apps that prioritize user privacy will explicitly state that they do not sell data to third parties, making these apps safer and more privacy-friendly than products that sell your data or are silent on this topic. We'll talk more about how to identify whether an app sells data in Chapter 7.

Another way to reduce exposure is to limit location tracking on mobile devices. Many apps request location access unnecessarily, and disabling this feature can prevent them from collecting detailed movement data that isn't necessary to the app's core functionality. Turning off ad personalization and opting out of data-sharing programs through your phone's settings or browser extensions can also reduce the amount of information available to brokers. For those who need to access reproductive health services discreetly, using privacy-focused browsers and encrypted messaging apps can minimize digital footprints.

While avoiding data brokers entirely is difficult in the modern digital landscape, being intentional about privacy choices can significantly reduce this risk. In a post-*Roe* world, choosing platforms that prioritize user security and minimize unnecessary data sharing is one of the best ways you can protect your reproductive health information while still using and embracing all femtech has to offer.

Method 3: When Femtech Apps Hand Over Your Data

The third way law enforcement can access reproductive health data is directly from femtech companies. Typically, this occurs through subpoenas and court orders, though some companies may comply with less formal law enforcement requests. Femtech apps store sensitive health data, including cycle-tracking information, pregnancy logs, and medication usage, making them a potential source of evidence in investigations. Whether a femtech company complies with a subpoena depends on its internal policies, because there are no universal legal protections preventing disclosure.

That said, there have been no widely publicized cases of law enforcement subpoenaing reproductive health data directly from a femtech company. Law enforcement would first need to know exactly which apps a person uses before attempting to obtain those records. Unlike mainstream search engines and social media platforms, which store vast amounts of easily accessible user data, femtech usage is highly individualized, making it less likely to be an immediate target. As such, while this is technically an avenue through which law enforcement could obtain data, it is not one that is being widely used at this time.

However, this does not mean there is no risk. Femtech apps that store user data on company servers rather than on a user's device could theoretically be subpoenaed. This is why it's important to choose apps that prioritize strong encryption, local data storage, and minimal data collection. By selecting privacy-focused platforms and being mindful of digital security, you can better protect sensitive reproductive health information in an evolving legal landscape.

Method 4: Hacked Health Data—A Tool for Blackmail and Extortion

Finally, reproductive health data may be stolen through a breach or cyberattack and disclosed to law enforcement by a cybercriminal. As states continue to criminalize abortion, the value of reproductive health data on the dark web has increased, making it a potential target for cybercriminals. Hackers who gain access to femtech apps may be able to steal reproductive health information. If the stolen files contain any data points related to abortion, cybercriminals may attempt to blackmail or extort both femtech companies and the individuals whose data they possess. This could put women in a vulnerable position, facing threats of exposure or even legal consequences based on stolen and potentially misinterpreted health data.

This concern is not entirely unfounded, as many femtech companies have weaker security protocols compared to larger, more established tech and healthcare companies. Some femtech startups operate with limited resources, prioritizing product development and user experience over cybersecurity. There is no universal standard for how femtech companies should store or protect user data, leading to inconsistencies in encryption practices, data retention policies, and breach notification procedures. Without strong security frameworks in place, these apps can become attractive targets for hackers looking to exploit vulnerabilities and access reproductive health information.

However, in most cases, hackers targeting femtech companies are not interested in blackmailing individual users or handing over data to law enforcement. In fact, unless they could do so anonymously, disclosing stolen data to authorities would risk exposing their own criminal activities, making it an unlikely motive for most cybercriminals. Instead, cybercriminals often breach femtech apps as a steppingstone to access larger healthcare networks and datasets. Some femtech platforms are connected to broader digital health ecosystems, including electronic health records and insurance databases, which contain far more lucrative data for financial fraud and identity theft. Cyberattacks on healthcare providers have surged in recent years, with hackers often using smaller, less secure companies as an entry point into larger systems.[27] Despite concerns, there have been no publicly reported cases of women being blackmailed by hackers based on their reproductive health data.

It's also important to recognize that health data is never 100 percent secure—even within hospitals and major healthcare organizations. Large-scale data breaches have occurred at some of the most well-protected institutions, exposing millions of patient records. For example, in 2023, HCA Healthcare, one of the largest hospital networks in the United States, suffered a breach that exposed the personal data of 11 million patients.[28] Similarly, in 2022, a cyberattack on Shields Health Care Group, a medical imaging company in New York, compromised the sensitive health information of over two million patients.[29] Even Change Healthcare, a subsidiary of UnitedHealth Group, was recently hit by a ransomware attack that disrupted medical claims processing nationwide.[30] These breaches demonstrate that no healthcare organization is immune to cyber threats, and femtech is not necessarily more vulnerable or more targeted than the broader medical industry. While security should always be a consideration, it is not a risk unique to femtech, nor is it the most likely way reproductive health data would be accessed by law enforcement.

Debunking the Common Myths About Femtech Risks in a Post-*Roe* World

With growing concerns about digital privacy and reproductive rights, many women are questioning whether femtech apps are still safe to use in a post-*Roe* world. Misinformation has fueled anxiety, leading to widespread misconceptions about how law enforcement accesses data, what can realistically be used against someone, and whether deleting an app truly protects you. While it's crucial to be aware of risks, not all fears are grounded in reality. Instead of abandoning these tools entirely, let's break down the four most common misconceptions and explore what you can do to protect your privacy while still benefiting from femtech.

Myth 1: Law Enforcement Is Actively Targeting Femtech Apps to Track Abortion Seekers

One of the biggest fears circulating online is that law enforcement is using femtech apps to proactively track and prosecute individuals who seek abortions. While it is true that femtech data could be subpoenaed, there have been no publicized cases of law enforcement targeting users specifically through femtech apps. For police officers to subpoena a femtech app, they would first need to know that a person is using it, which is highly unlikely unless other evidence has already led them to that conclusion. Femtech apps are therefore not the primary tool law enforcement uses in abortion-related cases. Rather, the real risk comes from mainstream tech companies, which routinely provide user data to authorities upon request.

Search history is one of the most frequently subpoenaed data points, and Google has a long history of compliance with law enforcement demands. In the first half of 2023 alone, Google received over 216,000 data requests from government agencies, covering 441,296 accounts, and complied with 80 percent of them.[31] While these requests covered a wide range of crimes, some involved reproductive health. In multiple instances, law enforcement has used Google search history to build cases against people suspected of self-managing abortions, flagging searches for terms like "abortion pill," "misoprostol," "mifepristone," and "how to end a pregnancy."

Similarly, Apple and other major tech companies provide user data when served with legal demands. Between January and June 2023, Apple received more than 18,000 account requests globally, covering 56,692 accounts, and complied with 78 percent of those requests.[32] Despite its reputation as a privacy-focused company, Apple still provides data in response to legal requests, particularly for iCloud backups, which store messages, photos, and other sensitive information. This means that even if you delete a message or remove an app from your phone, a copy may still exist in cloud storage—where it can be accessed by authorities.

Facebook (Meta) has also played a significant role in law enforcement investigations. In the second half of 2023, Meta received over 301,553 government data requests for information on 528,232 users and accounts and complied with nearly 77 percent of those requests.[33] Because most Facebook messages are not end-to-end encrypted by default, law enforcement can easily obtain them with a subpoena.

Accordingly, law enforcement is not proactively monitoring femtech apps to build abortion-related cases. Instead, law enforcement relies on widely used digital platforms that collect and store vast amounts of personal data, often without users realizing how accessible that information is to authorities.

Myth 2: Deleting Your Femtech App Protects You from Digital Surveillance

After the *Dobbs* decision, many women rushed to delete their period-tracking and fertility apps, believing this would prevent law enforcement from accessing their reproductive health data. While this reaction is understandable, deleting an app does not necessarily erase previously collected data. If an app has already stored information on a company's servers, that data may still exist and could be accessible if the company complies with a subpoena. Some femtech companies retain user data for extended periods, even after an account is deleted, meaning personal health information could still be retrieved long after you stop using the app. Additionally, if you've backed up your phone to the cloud, records of your app activity, including notifications or logged information, could still be available through services like iCloud or Google Drive.

The real privacy concern isn't the app itself but how it stores and shares data. Many femtech apps collect more information than users realize, which can be shared with third parties or advertisers. Some apps explicitly state in their privacy policies that they will comply with law enforcement requests. This is why choosing the right femtech app is crucial. Instead of focusing on deleting apps out of fear, you should prioritize apps that emphasize local storage, encryption, and reasonable data retention timeframes. While no digital tool is entirely risk-free, making informed choices about which apps to trust can significantly reduce the chances of sensitive reproductive health information falling into the wrong hands.

Myth 3: Femtech Apps Are More Dangerous Than Other Digital Tools You Use Daily

Many people assume that femtech apps pose a unique risk, but the real privacy threats come from the everyday digital tools we rarely think twice about. Platforms like Google, Facebook, and Apple collect vast amounts of personal data, making them far more likely to be used in law enforcement investigations. While concerns about femtech privacy are valid, there are no widely known cases of law enforcement subpoenaing period-tracking or fertility apps for abortion-related prosecutions. Meanwhile, Google search history, iCloud backups, and Facebook messages have already been used in criminal cases—including those related to reproductive health.

The real danger isn't downloading a femtech app—it's the digital footprint we leave everywhere else. Searching for abortion services on Google, discussing reproductive care over Messenger, or automatically backing up sensitive data to the cloud pose far greater risks than any single femtech app. These platforms are already embedded in law enforcement investigative strategies, yet they often escape scrutiny in privacy discussions. It's easy to fixate on deleting a period tracker, but true digital security requires a broader awareness of how our everyday tech choices expose us.

For example, in 2017, Mississippi prosecutors charged Latice Fisher with second-degree murder after reviewing her phone's search history, which contained queries about how to buy abortion pills online. Investigators also retrieved text messages discussing her pregnancy. This type of digital evidence—taken directly from a person's phone and search history—has been used in multiple cases involving pregnancy outcomes, proving that anything that leaves a digital trail could be obtained and used against someone, particularly if it is backed up to the cloud or not encrypted.

Another widely publicized case involved Meta, which provided Nebraska police with private messages between a teenager and her mother discussing plans to obtain abortion pills.[34] In 2022, law enforcement requested Messenger logs, which revealed that the teen had discussed her pregnancy termination plans with her mother. These messages were used to charge the teenager with multiple felonies related to an illegal abortion and improper disposal of the baby's remains.[35] Because these messages were stored on Meta's servers rather than being encrypted or deleted after a set period, law enforcement was able to obtain them.

While femtech apps may feel like a heightened risk due to the sensitivity of the data they collect, the reality is that mainstream tech platforms pose a far greater threat. Law enforcement already knows how to access data from Google, Apple, and Meta, and these companies have repeatedly provided user data when subpoenaed. The biggest risk isn't femtech—it's the everyday platforms we rely on without a second thought, often assuming our data is private when in reality it is stored, accessible, and vulnerable to legal requests.

Myth 4: If a Femtech App Is Subpoenaed, It Will Automatically Hand Over Your Data

Just because a company receives a subpoena does not mean it will automatically comply. Some companies fight back against law enforcement requests, while others have privacy policies that limit the amount of data they store in the first place. Apps that store data locally on the user's device rather than in the cloud cannot provide data they don't have—meaning that even if subpoenaed, they have no information to share. Similarly, some companies locate their data servers in privacy-protective states, which may—by law—be inaccessible to law enforcement seeking to prosecute reproductive health crimes.

This means that femtech companies vary widely in their responses to legal demands, with some choosing to comply fully while others resist. Some startups, particularly those that are smaller and have fewer legal resources, may comply with subpoenas and other requests without challenging them, simply because fighting a request can be costly and time-consuming. On the other hand, larger or more privacy-focused companies may push back, requiring law enforcement to meet a higher legal threshold before handing over data.

Another factor that influences a company's response is where it is headquartered and the laws governing data access in that jurisdiction. Some femtech companies are based in states with strong digital privacy protections or reproductive health shield laws, which can make it more difficult for law enforcement from restrictive states to successfully obtain that data. These companies may use state-level legal protections as justification for rejecting subpoenas or requiring law enforcement to go through a more burdensome legal process. In contrast, companies operating in states with strict abortion bans may face more pressure to comply with legal demands, particularly if local authorities are aggressively prosecuting abortion-related cases. In general, be wary if a femtech company is headquartered in Alabama, Arkansas, Idaho, Indiana, Kentucky, Louisiana, Mississippi, Oklahoma, or Texas unless the company states that its data is housed in a more privacy-friendly state.

Ultimately, a femtech company's response to subpoenas is shaped by a combination of legal, financial, and strategic factors, making it difficult to predict how any one company will act. While some fight back against law enforcement requests, others may comply quickly, whether due to limited resources, legal pressure, or internal policies that allow for data disclosure. The lack of universal legal protections for reproductive health data means that responses will vary widely across the industry. This uncertainty underscores why it is essential to be aware of how different femtech companies handle legal demands and to choose platforms that align with your privacy expectations using the SAFE framework.

Safe Harbors and State Protections: Defending Digital Privacy

Despite the fears surrounding reproductive health data privacy in a post-*Roe* world, it's important to recognize that legal protections do exist. While law enforcement has multiple tools to access digital information, state governments, advocacy groups, and federal agencies have taken steps to create safeguards that limit how reproductive health data can be obtained and used against individuals. These protections, while not uniform across the country, provide critical legal barriers that can prevent sensitive health information from being easily accessed or weaponized in abortion-related prosecutions. Understanding these laws helps paint a more complete picture—one that includes not only risks but also the growing number of defenses available to protect reproductive privacy.

One of the most powerful legal protections to emerge in the wake of *Dobbs* is the wave of shield laws passed by several states. These laws act as a firewall, preventing law enforcement in abortion-restrictive states from reaching across state lines to investigate or prosecute people seeking or providing abortion care. As of mid-2024, 18 states and the District of Columbia have enacted these protections, including California, Colorado, Connecticut, Delaware, Hawaii, Illinois, Maine, Maryland, Massachusetts, Minnesota, Nevada, New Jersey, New Mexico, New York, Oregon, Rhode Island, Vermont, and Washington.[36] Their goal is simple: to stop out-of-state authorities from using legal loopholes to go after doctors, clinics, and individuals who legally obtain reproductive healthcare in a shield law state. California, for example, has passed a robust package of legal protections that not only safeguard in-state providers but also extend to those offering telehealth services to patients in states with abortion bans. Similarly, Massachusetts' shield law ensures that reproductive health consultations with patients in restrictive states are treated as local medical encounters, effectively preventing authorities in abortion-hostile states from prosecuting providers who follow their home state's laws.

These shield laws don't just protect clinics and doctors—they also have important implications for femtech companies and the data they store. Many of these laws explicitly restrict the sharing of medical records with law enforcement or prosecutors from anti-abortion states, which means that if a femtech company is based in a shield law state, it may be less likely to comply with subpoenas seeking reproductive health data. If a company's data servers are housed in one of these protected states, that could also offer an extra layer of security, since law enforcement from abortion-restrictive states may not have legal authority to access them. However, these protections are still being tested, and legal battles continue to play out. The case of Dr. Margaret Carpenter, a New York physician who was fined by a Texas court for prescribing abortion pills via telemedicine to Texas residents,[37] underscores just how complex and unpredictable interstate enforcement can be.

Beyond shield laws, some states have taken proactive measures by enshrining reproductive rights in their state constitutions.[38] These amendments ensure that the right to make decisions about one's reproductive health is protected from fluctuating political climates. For example, states like Vermont have passed amendments explicitly guaranteeing personal reproductive autonomy, offering an added layer of protection against potential infringements. Some constitutional safeguards not only fortify the legal standing of reproductive rights but also serve as a clear statement of a state's commitment to upholding these freedoms.

While these legal frameworks represent significant strides in protecting reproductive health data, their practical application is still evolving. The interplay between state and federal laws, coupled with ongoing legal challenges, means that the landscape remains complex. It's still up to us to take charge of our data privacy and ensure we are using apps and solutions that give us the most protection.

Conclusion

Understanding the risks of reproductive health data exposure is important, but it's just as critical to know how to take control of your digital footprint rather than operating from a place of fear. In a post-*Roe* world, abortion access is deeply divided across state lines, and data privacy must be a key part of reproductive healthcare and our use of femtech. We must be proactive about how and where we share our reproductive health information, which means thinking beyond how we use femtech and focusing on where those companies operate and store our data.

One of the best ways to protect yourself is by choosing femtech companies that are headquartered in states with strong reproductive health protections. Companies based in states that have enacted shield laws may be legally restricted from cooperating with out-of-state law enforcement seeking to prosecute abortion-related cases. On the other hand, if a femtech company is headquartered in a state with strict abortion bans, it may be more likely to comply with legal demands from prosecutors in that jurisdiction. Before using a femtech app, find out where the company is based by checking the terms of service or privacy policy. Typically, companies will include their primary address at the end of these documents or in a "contact us" section. This simple step can give you insight into how much legal protection your data has from outside interference.

Where a femtech company stores its data is just as important as where it is headquartered. Many femtech platforms use cloud-based storage, meaning that your data could be housed on servers located in states with strict abortion laws or in jurisdictions where law enforcement can more easily obtain access. Femtech companies that store data in states with privacy or shield laws will be better equipped to safeguard your data from law enforcement investigations. This will make it harder for out-of-state authorities to retrieve your reproductive health records. Some femtech companies may even store their data internationally, such as in Europe, which can create additional legal barriers to access. If you want to maximize your privacy protections, choose femtech companies that store data in states with shield laws or that store data in the European Union. To check where a company's data is stored, search the privacy policy or the company's website for terms like "data storage" or "servers." If a company does not disclose this information, that lack of transparency could be a red flag.

Taking these steps can help you navigate the post-*Roe* digital landscape without panic or misinformation dictating your choices. The goal is not to abandon femtech altogether but to be strategic about the platforms you trust with your health data. By considering where a company is headquartered and where its data is stored, you can take charge of your reproductive health privacy, ensuring that your information remains in your control, not in the hands of those who may seek to use it against you.

PART

II

Supercharge Your Health with the SAFE Method

7

The SAFE Method

Security

Your Health App Knows You—So Does Everyone Else

Emma* had always been careful about what she shared online. She didn't post about her personal life on social media, kept her location settings turned off, and used strong passwords. But when she started struggling with anxiety, she let her guard down.

The therapy waitlist was months long, and she needed help now. So when she came across an ad for an app that offered AI-powered mental health coaching for women and a space to privately journal her feelings, it felt like the perfect solution. It wasn't therapy, exactly, but it was something.

When she signed up, the app asked for a few details—her age, Zip Code, and general health history. There was even a field to enter her primary health-care provider's information. She hesitated for a moment but typed in the name of the clinic she visited for annual checkups. It seemed harmless enough.

For months, Emma poured her heart into the app. She logged her panic attacks, wrote about the nights she couldn't sleep, and tracked the days when she felt too exhausted to function. The app responded with soothing encouragement, mindfulness exercises, and affirmations that made her feel seen. It felt safe. Private.

Until the day it wasn't.

Emma had been experiencing migraines lately, something she had never dealt with before, so she scheduled an appointment with a neurologist. She filled out the usual forms, sent her medical records over to the practice, and completed the onboarding process. When it was finally time for her visit, she sat nervously in the exam room while the doctor scrolled through her file on the tablet. When he glanced up, he said something that made her heart stop.

"I see you've been experiencing increased panic attacks and insomnia. Are your anxiety symptoms worsening?"

Emma stiffened. She hadn't mentioned her anxiety. It wasn't even the reason she was there. And more than that, she had never told *any* doctor about the frequency of her panic attacks. She had only ever written about them in the app.

"How do you know that?" she asked.

The doctor barely looked up. "It's in your medical records."

Emma felt a rush of nausea. What records? She had never been formally treated for anxiety, had never gone on medication. How had this information made its way into her file?

Her mind raced as she drove home. The moment she walked through her door, she opened the app and scrolled through its privacy policy for the first time. That's when she saw the truth hiding in plain sight.

Because she had entered her healthcare provider's information during the sign-up process, she had authorized the app to share her health insights directly with her provider and the provider's digital records system under the guise of "integrated wellness data." Unlike de-identified research sharing, this was explicitly linked to her name and medical profile. The privacy policy stated that users who voluntarily entered their provider's information consented to the transmission of select behavioral health insights for the purpose of "enhanced care coordination." Her clinic, in turn, had an electronic health record (EHR) system designed to aggregate data from trusted health apps. It was meant to be a seamless way for doctors to obtain a full picture of a patient's health, but Emma had never intended for her journal entries to become part of her official medical record.

And now they were.

At first, Emma tried to convince herself it wasn't a big deal. But the more she thought about it, the more the consequences began to unfold in her mind. This wasn't just about her doctor knowing more than she wanted. It was about the fact that, from now on, every provider she saw would have access to that information. Her anxiety was no longer a private struggle; it was a documented part of her medical history.

That meant if she ever applied for life insurance, she could be flagged as a higher-risk applicant, leading to higher premiums or even denial of coverage. If she needed to switch health insurance plans, her history of anxiety and panic attacks might be used to justify increased costs or limited coverage for mental health treatment. If she ever applied for a job that required a health screening, an employer could take her documented anxiety into account when making hiring decisions.

Emma had always assumed that her health record belonged to her—that it was something she controlled. But now she realized just how permanent it was. She had thought she was writing to a private journal. Instead, she had unknowingly created a medical record that could follow her for the rest of her life.

Emma never would have handed over her private thoughts to her doctor, let alone a neurologist she had never met. But by clicking "I Agree" on the app, she had done exactly that.

Most of us don't think twice before downloading a health or wellness app and agreeing to the privacy policy and terms of use. The process is almost automatic—one tap to install, another to create an account, and a final, thoughtless click on "I Agree." The permissions requests blend into the background, drowned out by sleek designs, reassuring language, and promises of "personalized insights" and "AI-powered wellness." If an app looks polished and professional, if it has been recommended by influencers or ranks high in the app store, it's easy to assume it's safe.

And why wouldn't it be? These apps are marketed as tools to help, to empower, and to put users in control of their own health. They offer something modern medicine often lacks—immediacy. No waiting weeks for an appointment, no awkward conversations, and no barriers between the person and the information they need. Just an easy-to-use interface and the promise of better health at your fingertips.

But convenience comes at a cost. And too often, that cost is invisible, hidden in the fine print, buried in complex legal language that few people take the time to read. The risks don't feel immediate. There's no flashing warning sign when an app quietly shares your data with third parties. There's no instant notification when it feeds your health patterns into an algorithm that determines your insurance rates. The harm is slow and creeping, often unnoticed until it's too late.

The good news is that you don't need a law degree or hours of research to protect yourself. With the right approach, you can evaluate an app's privacy and security in minutes—before you ever hit download. In this chapter, I'll show you exactly how to spot the red flags, decode the jargon, and take control of your data before someone else does.

Data Privacy, Protection, and Transparency

To fully embrace the femtech revolution and shape the future of women's health, we need to trust that the technologies designed to empower us won't put us at risk. If women don't feel safe using these tools, progress stalls, and the promise of innovation falls flat. No amount of advanced features, AI-driven insights, or sleek user interfaces can outweigh the fundamental need for security. Without trust, even the most groundbreaking femtech solutions will fail to reach the women who need them most.

Trust, however, doesn't come from flashy branding or vague reassurances about "commitment to privacy"—it comes from real transparency and clear, enforceable protections. Women deserve to know who has access to their health data, how it's being used, and what safeguards are in place to keep it from falling into the wrong hands. Companies that truly prioritize privacy should make this information easy to find, not buried in endless pages of legal jargon. If we can't confidently say that an app respects and protects our data, then we shouldn't be using it.

That's why the first step in the SAFE framework is security—because before we can benefit from tech tools, we need to know they're protecting us, not exposing us. Security is about more than just encryption or complex passwords; it's about the entire ecosystem of how a company collects, protects, stores, and shares its users' data. If a femtech company is truly prioritizing the people it serves, these details should be straightforward, accessible, and easy to understand. When companies make it difficult to find this information or bury it in confusing legalese, it's often a sign that their priorities don't align with ours.

This means that transparency is key, and without it trust is impossible. When a femtech company is upfront about what data it collects, how it's used, and when it's deleted, it creates an environment where users can make informed decisions. This transparency makes it easier to use the app confidently. When companies take shortcuts with privacy or keep users in the dark about their data practices, they erode the very trust that makes femtech adoption possible. Women shouldn't have to wonder if their health data is being exploited. Companies should be proving, every step of the way, that it isn't.

Still, trust isn't built by companies alone—we have a role in shaping this industry, too. With more femtech products entering the market, we get to choose which companies we support with our data. Our choices shape the future of femtech, and when we opt for the companies that prioritize privacy over profits, we take a stand. That decision sends a message: We will not sacrifice security for convenience, and we expect tech companies to do better.

To make informed choices, we need a way to quickly and effectively evaluate a femtech product's security and privacy—without wasting hours combing through dense legal documents. That's why the security step of the SAFE framework exists. It breaks down privacy and security vetting into a simple, four-step process that makes it easy to determine whether an app is likely to be trustworthy before you share your data. These four steps are:

1. Decide your data preferences and risk tolerance.
2. Analyze the privacy policy for red flags.
3. Explore the FAQs for additional clarity.
4. Investigate the company's privacy track record.

By following this method, you can confidently decide which femtech tools are worth your time and trust, and which ones aren't.

Step 1: Decide Your Data Preferences and Risk Tolerance

Before you can evaluate whether a femtech app's privacy and security meet your needs, you must first determine what those needs are. Not every person has the same risk tolerance when it comes to sharing health data, and that's okay. Some people are comfortable with their data being used for research or personalized recommendations, while others want the strictest level of privacy. The key is understanding *your* personal boundaries so that you can make informed decisions before an app makes them for you.

Determine What Types of Data You're Comfortable Sharing   Every time you use a femtech app, you're sharing data. Some of this information might feel routine, like tracking your water intake or sleep habits. But other details, like your sexual activity, pregnancy status, or mental health history, may feel more personal. Most people never stop to think about what they're truly comfortable sharing until after they've already handed over their data. Apps make it easy to input information without much thought, often encouraging users to provide more details for "better insights" or "personalized recommendations." But by taking the time now to decide where your boundaries are, you can save yourself time later when evaluating privacy policies and security practices. Instead of getting lost in the fine print, you'll already know exactly what you're okay with—and what's a dealbreaker.

Femtech companies collect many different types of data, and each category varies in sensitivity. The following are the most common types of data these apps and products may request from you. Review each category and consider whether you'd feel comfortable sharing this information and in what circumstances, keeping in mind how it might be stored, used, or shared with third parties.

- **General health and wellness data:** This includes lifestyle-related metrics that track your overall well-being and daily habits. It's typically considered low-risk data but can still reveal patterns about your health. For example, this may include your exercise routine, step counts, hydration levels, sleep duration, energy levels, nutrition habits, weight fluctuations, heart rate, and more.
- **Reproductive health data:** Many femtech products focus on reproductive health, collecting data related to menstrual cycles, fertility, and pregnancy. While this data is often necessary for the app's function, it can also be sensitive, especially in states with restrictive reproductive health laws. Carefully consider whether you're comfortable providing data on miscarriages and abortions, if those apply to you, along with other personal metrics like cervical mucus

thickness, which is often used to help track ovulation. Examples of other types of data within this category include cycle dates, PMS symptoms, basal body temperature, postpartum recovery, hormone fluctuations, contraceptive use, breastfeeding, and more.

- **Sexual health data:** Depending on the type of femtech product and its purpose, you may be asked to input details about your sexual activity and libido. While this data can provide insights into reproductive health, hormonal changes, and fertility, it is highly personal and could be misused if shared improperly. Examples of sexual health data include type and frequency of sexual activity, number of partners, sexual positions, condom use, contraceptive use, libido fluctuations, sexually transmitted diseases, sexual discomfort or pain, and more.

- **Mental health data:** Mood and mental health tracking features are increasingly common in femtech apps, but this data can be sensitive, especially if shared with insurers or employers. Some apps also include journaling or therapy-related features, which could store personal reflections. For example, these apps may collect mood data, self-reported stress and anxiety levels, depression symptoms, therapy session notes, journal entries, mental health triggers, mindfulness or meditation habits, and self-harm risk assessments.

- **Medical data:** Some femtech apps integrate with medical devices or allow users to track symptoms related to chronic conditions. While this can be useful for managing health conditions, it also creates a digital record of medical history that could be accessed by third parties. Examples of medical data that might be collected include diagnoses, chronic pain symptoms, migraine tracking, prescription medications, over-the-counter medications and supplements, vaccination records, test results, and family medical history.

- **Biometric data:** Biometric data is increasingly being used to provide health insights. This data often involves direct physiological measurements from wearable devices or manual tracking. Examples include resting heart rate, body temperature, blood glucose levels, blood pressure, oxygen saturation, and more.

- **Payment and financial data:** If an app offers premium features or subscription services, it will need to collect payment-related information. Please be mindful that this data may also be shared with third-party payment processors. Types of data that may be collected include credit card details, billing address, saved payment methods, PayPal or Apple Pay usage, insurance billing information, and transaction history within the app.

- **Location data:** Some femtech apps track your real-time location or store records of past locations. This data can be used for helpful features, like finding nearby healthcare providers, but it can also reveal patterns about your movements. Examples of location data include GPS-based location tracking, home and work addresses, frequent travel routes, clinic visit history, pharmacy visits, travel history, proximity to reproductive health centers, location-based health alerts, geofencing activity, and more.

- **Device and usage data:** Most apps automatically collect information about your device and how you interact with the app. While this may seem harmless, it can be used to track behaviors or for advertising purposes. For example, an app may collect your IP address, device model, operating system, app crash reports, frequency and time of app usage, interactions with app features, advertising identifiers, browsing and search history within the app, and more.

Now that you understand the types of data femtech companies collect, it's time to define your boundaries. What types of data feel acceptable to share, and which ones cross the line? Take a moment to list the information you're comfortable providing—but don't stop there. Context matters. Ask yourself under what circumstances you'd be willing to share it.

For example, you might feel comfortable logging your reproductive health data in a period-tracking app, but would you want a mental health app to have access to that same information? You may not think twice about sharing your pregnancy and miscarriage status with a fertility app, but would you hesitate to provide it to a general wellness tracker? The purpose of the app, who has access to your data, and how it might be used all shape what feels acceptable.

For each category of data that you're willing to share, consider the specific situations where you're comfortable disclosing it—and where you're not. If you have a particular health issue you're looking to solve now, evaluate your data preferences in light of the solutions you're hoping to find.

Your data preferences can change—and likely will—depending on the app. By thinking through these boundaries now, you'll be able to make informed decisions about which apps align with your comfort level, rather than realizing too late that you've shared more than you intended.

Determine How Your Data Can Be Used

Once you've determined the types of data you're comfortable sharing and the circumstances under which you'd share that data, the next step is to consider how your data may be used, who may access it, and what level of risk you're willing to accept. Every femtech company operates differently, and while some prioritize privacy, others may use your data in ways you might not expect or be comfortable with. The best way to define your comfort level is by understanding the most common ways femtech companies use and share data. Some of these practices are essential for the app to function as intended, while others may feel excessive or intrusive.

The following list contains the most common ways femtech products use and disclose data. Just as you did with the data collection categories, take a moment to read through this list and determine which disclosures you find acceptable and which ones cross the line. Keep in mind that some of these uses and disclosures are standard across most products and apps, meaning there may not always be a meaningful choice. But understanding them will help you make more informed decisions.

- **Using your data to provide the product or service:** This is the most fundamental and expected use of your data—it's what enables the app to function as intended. When you sign up for a femtech app, you're voluntarily providing information in exchange for its features, whether that's cycle predictions, fertility tracking, pregnancy insights, or symptom monitoring. If you use a period-tracking app, for example, it needs access to your cycle data to predict your next period or ovulation window. A pregnancy-tracking app similarly analyzes your health inputs to offer guidance for different stages of pregnancy. Because this type of data use is directly tied to the app's core function, it is generally required and accepted. Without consenting to this type of data disclosure, you likely won't be able to fully use the app's features (or use the app at all).

- **Sharing data with the company's business advisors:** Femtech companies typically need to disclose certain data to their advisors and business partners to ensure the overall functioning of their company. These disclosures often happen when a company needs to comply with business regulations, manage its finances, or handle legal matters. For example, if a femtech company undergoes a financial audit, an external auditor may review records that include subscription transactions or user purchase history. If the company is involved in a lawsuit, its legal team may need access to user records as part of its defense or compliance with court proceedings. In general, this type of data sharing is usually low risk because it occurs under controlled, necessary circumstances.

- **Disclosing data when required by law:** Almost every privacy policy includes some language stating that the company will disclose user data if required by law, such as in response to court orders, subpoenas, legal investigations, or national security requests. While companies are legally obligated to comply with legitimate legal demands, the level of discretion and resistance they apply can vary significantly. Some companies will only release data when presented with a formal court order, while others may voluntarily provide information in response to informal requests. For users in states where abortion or reproductive healthcare is criminalized, you may flag this as a potential unacceptable risk and look for apps that implement strong privacy protections to guard against the risk of disclosure without a valid court order. If you don't live in a state with restrictive reproductive healthcare laws or don't plan to use femtech for reproductive health tracking, this risk may be less concerning. In that case, you can assess the level of risk based on your own comfort and privacy preferences.

- **Using data to improve the product or service:** Many femtech companies analyze user data to refine their algorithms, improve product accuracy, or develop new features. This allows apps to become more personalized and effective over time. For example, a period-tracking app may review anonymous user data to improve its cycle predictions. This type of data use is generally considered low risk and favorable to consumers because it can result in better products and features for the company's consumers. The data also generally stays within the company's walls. If you're not comfortable with your data being used for ongoing product development, you'll want to check whether the app allows you to opt out of this type of data analysis.

- **Sharing data with third-party vendors and service providers:** Most femtech companies rely on external vendors to operate their apps efficiently. These third-party service providers may handle functions like payment processing, cloud storage, customer support, analytics, and advertising. For example, if you pay for a premium version of a femtech app, your payment information may be processed by Stripe, PayPal, or another third-party provider. The risk with this type of data sharing depends on how broadly the company defines third-party partnerships. Some companies limit data sharing to essential business functions—which is generally accepted—while others include marketing firms, advertising networks, or data aggregators in their vendor list—which substantially increases exposure and risk. If a privacy policy mentions sharing data with "affiliates" or "third-party vendors" without clear limitations, that can be a red flag and may mean your data is being shared more widely than you realize.

- **Transferring data in the event of a merger, acquisition, or sale:** Femtech is a rapidly growing industry, and many companies are startups seeking acquisition or investment opportunities. If a femtech company merges with another business, is acquired, or undergoes a change in ownership, your data may automatically transfer to the new company. This means that the privacy protections you originally agreed to could suddenly change, depending on the policies of the acquiring company. For example, if a small, privacy-conscious maternal health app is acquired by a large tech corporation, the new parent company will now have access to your data, and your information will be subject to its privacy policies—which may not be as strict as those of the original company. If you're concerned about who might ultimately control your data, this is an area of risk to flag. Some companies promise to notify users before a data transfer occurs, giving them time to delete their accounts. Others may automatically transfer all data to the new owner without giving users a chance to opt out.

- **Selling or sharing data with data brokers and unrelated third parties:** One of the most controversial data practices in femtech is selling user data as part of a company's business model. Some femtech companies generate revenue by selling de-identified or aggregated health data to advertisers, research firms, or data brokers. While companies often claim this data is anonymized or de-identified, research has shown that data can frequently be re-identified when combined with other datasets.[1] Once your data is provided to brokers or unrelated third parties, it is nearly impossible to track how it is used or prevent further distribution or reidentification. For many women, this category of data sharing raises significant privacy concerns, because it creates the possibility of their health information being used in ways they never intended or approved.

- **Using data for scientific research:** Some femtech companies share data with research institutions, universities, or public health organizations to contribute to studies on women's health. This data is often used to advance medical research on menstrual cycles, fertility, pregnancy, menopause, and chronic conditions such as PCOS. Companies that participate in these research partnerships may share de-identified user data to help scientists identify trends, improve diagnostic tools, or develop new treatment options. While contributing to medical research can benefit public health, the level of anonymization and user control varies between companies. Some femtech apps allow users to opt into research participation, while others automatically include all users unless they actively disable data sharing in their settings. Since research data often has long-term value, you'll want to think about how comfortable you are having your data used for this purpose and whether this information could be used in future studies beyond what you originally intended.

Understanding how femtech companies use and share your data is essential to making informed choices about which apps to trust. While some data disclosures are necessary for an app to function, others—such as sharing information with data brokers, advertisers, and law enforcement—may raise concerns depending on privacy preferences and personal circumstances.

By reviewing these common data usage and disclosure categories, you can start identifying which practices align with your comfort level.

Now that you've flagged the data collection and usage categories that you may not be willing to accept, the next step is learning how to evaluate a femtech company's privacy to determine whether it meets your standards. In the next section, I'll walk you through how to analyze an app's privacy policy quickly and efficiently based on the categories of risk you identified earlier. This will help you decide whether a company's data practices are acceptable or whether it's better to look elsewhere.

Step 2: Analyze the Privacy Policy for Red Flags

Reading a full privacy policy is unrealistic for most consumers, yet these documents are often the only way to understand how a company collects, uses, and shares your data. Fortunately, you don't need to read every word to determine whether an app aligns with your privacy preferences. Most privacy policies follow a predictable structure, covering what data is collected, how it is shared, what rights users have, security measures, disclaimers and warnings regarding data misuse, and updates to privacy terms. By focusing on specific sections, searching for key terms, and watching for red flags, you can efficiently assess an app's privacy practices. The following sections are a step-by-step approach to evaluating an app's privacy policy without getting lost in legal jargon.

Identify the Data the App Collects

Before diving into the privacy policy, refer back to your checklist from the previous section. Which types of data did you flag as high-risk? Those categories should be your priority.

Rather than reading the entire privacy policy, use the Find function (Ctrl + F or Command + F) to search for key terms related to the data categories you're concerned about. If the Find function isn't available, scroll to the data collection section—often labeled as "What Data We Collect," "Information We Collect," or "Collection of Personal Data." If the privacy policy has a table of contents, you may be able to click directly into this section.

Each company phrases its data collection policies differently, so terminology can vary. The following are the key search terms to locate whether the app collects specific types of data:

- **General health and wellness data:** Search for "wellness," "fitness," "exercise," "activity tracking," "weight," "sleep," or "heart rate." These are the terms most likely to be used in privacy policies that describe the general health and wellness category. However, some apps may also refer to this as "lifestyle data" or "health metrics," so if you don't receive results, try using these alternative terms.
- **Reproductive health data:** Search "reproductive health," "menstrual tracking," "fertility," or "pregnancy." The term you use will depend on the purpose of the app.
- **Sexual health data:** Search for "sexual health," "sexual wellness," "sexual activity," "intimacy," or "relationship insights."
- **Mental health data:** Search for "mental health," "mood tracking," "therapy," "behavioral health," or "stress management."
- **Medical data:** Search for "health data," "medical information," "medical history," "diagnoses," "symptoms," "medications," "treatment," or "test results."
- **Biometric data:** Search for "biometric," "body metrics," "body temperature," or "wearable device integration."
- **Payment and financial data:** Search for "credit card," "billing," "subscription," "insurance," or "financial transactions." The term "insurance" will be more limiting because many apps are cash-pay only.
- **Location data:** Search for "location tracking," "GPS," "geofencing," or "real-time location."

The goal is not to search for every term, but instead to focus on key words and phrases that will lead you to the relevant section of the privacy policy. If your first search doesn't return results, try a related term before assuming the app doesn't collect that type of data.

Determine the Scope of Data Collection

Once you locate the data collection section, don't stop at just confirming whether a category is collected—read further to determine exactly what data is being gathered.

Privacy policies sometimes list broad data categories without specifying details. If you only see vague wording like "We collect reproductive health data," that could be a red flag. Companies that value transparency often list the specific types of data they collect within that category (for example, "We collect reproductive health data, including cycle dates, contraception use, and PMS symptoms"), while less privacy-conscious companies may use general terms that make it difficult to understand what is actually being tracked (e.g., "We collect a wide range of menstrual health information"). Broad, vaguely worded categories give companies significant flexibility to decide what information falls within them and to expand the types of data they collect—often without providing additional notice to consumers. For example, a period-tracking app collects "reproductive health data." When you first used the app, you were asked to provide your cycle dates, PMS symptoms, and birth control information. A year later, the app now requires you to input miscarriages and abortions. The app can require this additional information under the broad "reproductive health data" category without providing additional notice to you.

Analyzing the specific types of data within each category can also help you determine if that category poses as big a risk as you initially thought. For instance, let's say you're evaluating an app's payment and financial data practices. You're worried about the app having access to your insurance information. When you search for "payment," you see that the app collects credit card data because it operates on a subscription model. However, the privacy policy does not mention collecting insurance information or processing insurance claims. As a result, this data category may not pose the risk you were worried about since it is not collecting insurance information.

The more specific a company is about the data they collect, the greater the likelihood that the company prioritizes transparency. This makes it easier to determine whether the company's data collection practices align with our comfort level. Be wary of apps that only use broad data categories without examples or specifics, because this does not benefit consumers and instead provides significant protection for the companies.

Identify Whether Data Collection Is Optional or Automatic

If you're still concerned about any of the data categories after performing the previous searches, the next step is to analyze whether the app's data collection is optional or automatic. Some apps require certain data to function, while others allow users to opt out of sharing sensitive information. This distinction determines how much control you have over what the app knows about you.

When reviewing the data collection section of the privacy policy, look for language that indicates whether data collection is mandatory, optional, or automatic, such as:

- **"You may choose to provide this information" or "With your consent, we may share your data with your healthcare provider."** These suggest that data collection and sharing are optional and can be skipped, providing you with significant control over how your data is used and disclosed.
- **"This data is required for core app functionality."** This indicates that opting out may limit key features. You will likely not be able to withhold this data, because providing the data is mandatory for you to use the app. This suggests you have limited or no choices with respect to providing this data.
- **"We automatically collect this data when you use our services."** This suggests the data is collected in the background and may not be controllable. If the app automatically collects data that you consider sensitive, perform an additional search for the phrase "opt out" to determine whether the app allows users to disable tracking. If you can opt out of automatic tracking, then it typically poses little risk, and you retain control over your data and choices (assuming you remember to opt out).

Knowing whether data collection is optional or automatic gives you greater control over what information you share and how it's used. If an app requires data that you're uncomfortable providing or lacks clear opt-out provisions for that data category, it may be worth reconsidering whether it aligns with your privacy expectations.

Check Data Retention and Deletion Practices

Even if you're comfortable with an app collecting certain data, you should know how long it keeps your information and whether you have control over deleting it. Some companies store user data indefinitely, even after you stop using the app, while others allow you to delete your data or automatically erase it after a set period of inactivity. To determine how an app handles data retention and deletion, search for key terms such as:

- **"Data retention"** This will explain how long your data is stored and under what circumstances it is deleted. Skim this section until you either find a number (typically in years) for how long data is retained or find language like "indefinitely" or "as long as necessary." Companies that retain data "indefinitely" are not complying with best practices regarding privacy and data maintenance and you should be wary of trusting your data to those apps. If a company retains your data indefinitely, not only can it access and use your data forever, but your data also continues to live on their servers. If the company experiences a breach—even years after you've stopped using the app—your data could be compromised. Companies that state reasonable and specific time periods for data retention are more likely to comply with best data practices.

- **"Data deletion" or "Right to be forgotten"** These phrases indicate whether you can request the permanent removal of your data from the company's systems. A strong privacy policy will explicitly state that users can delete their data at any time and that the company will erase the data from its servers, including backups. This is the gold standard if you're looking for control over your data. Some policies may allow for immediate deletion upon request, while others require a waiting period or specify conditions under which deletion requests will be honored. Some companies may also implement automatic deletion processes, where data is erased after a set period of inactivity or after you cancel your account. Be wary of policies that don't offer you a right to delete your data from their systems—this is a red flag.

A company dedicated to preserving the privacy of its users will allow you to delete your data from its servers upon request and will specify how long data is stored before erasure. Depending on the systems involved, it's possible that full erasure may be technologically impossible for some companies; however, those companies should make this clear in their privacy policies and explain why full erasure cannot be accomplished. If a company does not provide clear answers on data retention and deletion, or proposes to keep your data indefinitely, that is a privacy risk.

Determine How Your Data Is Used or Shared

Once you know what data an app collects and how long that data is stored, the next step is to determine how that data is used and whether it is shared with third parties. Privacy policies outline this information under sections like "How We Use Your Information," "Data Sharing & Disclosure," or "Third-Party Sharing." This section is crucial because it tells you whether your personal health data stays within the app or if it's being sold, shared with advertisers, or provided to law enforcement.

Since privacy policies can be intentionally vague, you'll need to search for specific terms to pinpoint whether your data is at risk of being shared in ways that go beyond the core function of the app. The following sections highlight the highest-risk categories of data sharing that we discussed earlier, along with tips for finding and evaluating them quickly in a privacy policy.

Data Disclosures Required by Law

Some privacy policies state that they will only release user data if legally required, such as in response to a valid subpoena or court order. Others leave the door open to voluntary cooperation with law enforcement, government agencies, or legal investigations—even when not required by law. If you're concerned about the possibility of your data being used in legal proceedings or shared with government agencies, search for these terms: "subpoena," "law enforcement," "government authorities," "judicial proceedings," and "court order."

When reviewing this section, look specifically for how a company will respond if your data is requested by law enforcement or as part of a judicial proceeding. Companies that state they will only comply with formal, legally binding court orders or subpoenas are going to be more protective of consumer rights than companies that allow for voluntary compliance with a broader range of nonbinding requests. Be wary if a privacy policy includes phrases like "We may disclose information if we believe it is necessary," or "We may share data at our discretion to assist law enforcement," because this suggests the company can hand over your data even if they are not legally required to do so.

If you're worried about reproductive health data, skim this section for any mention of how the company will respond if law enforcement requests that data. Companies that are particularly privacy conscious will directly address this given the post-*Roe v. Wade* landscape. Companies that are most protective of your privacy will likely reference some type of security measures or data scrambling technology that would make it difficult or impossible to provide data to law enforcement. Alternatively, the company may explain that such data cannot be provided to law enforcement because it is stored locally on the user's device rather than a cloud-based server. These are green flags and show that a company is attuned to the risks associated with sharing reproductive health data.

Additionally, some companies may attempt to notify users before sharing their data with authorities, unless prohibited by law. This is another green flag and offers you more privacy protections. If this is not mentioned, then you should assume that your data could be handed over without your knowledge. Further, if a privacy policy does not mention government or legal disclosures at all, that does not mean the company won't comply—it just means they aren't being transparent about their policies. Lack of transparency is always a risk because you don't know how the company will respond in this type of situation, and you can't make an informed choice about whether you're okay with that response.

Data Transfers in the Event of a Merger, Acquisition, or Sale

The femtech landscape is rapidly changing, with many startups seeking funding, acquisitions, or partnerships. If an app is sold, merges with another company, or undergoes a change in ownership, your data could be transferred to the new entity. If this concerns you, search for these terms: "merger," "reorganization," "change of control," "joint venture," "acquisition," "assignment," "transfer," or "bankruptcy."

When reviewing this section of the privacy policy, the gold standard is for companies to give you a choice in whether your data is transferred to the new company. This allows you to delete your data and account if you don't agree with the new owner's privacy practices. It's a red flag if a policy states, "We reserve the right to transfer user data in the event of a business transaction" without giving users any notification or opt-out. This means your data could be handed over to a completely different company without your knowledge or consent. Similarly, if a policy doesn't specify whether privacy protections will remain the same after an acquisition, this could indicate that the new company will have full control over your data and could change privacy practices without restriction. Think of it this way: If Facebook acquired your period-tracking app, would you want it having access to your reproductive health data? What about Google? You can't predict which company might acquire the femtech app you're using, so it's important to consider all possible outcomes.

If you're uncomfortable with your sensitive health data being transferred to an unknown company in the future, look for an app that promises to notify users before a data transfer occurs and allows them to delete their data in advance.

Selling or Sharing Data with Data Brokers and Unrelated Third Parties

Some femtech apps—especially free ones—make money by selling user data to advertisers, data brokers, or other third parties. As a lawyer, I consider any femtech company that sells user data to brokers or leaves even the slightest loophole for third-party sales to be an instant dealbreaker for me.

To determine if a company is selling your data, search for these terms: "data broker," "sale," "sell," "selling," "monetization," "aggregate data," "de-identify," or "anonymize." A clear statement that the company does not sell user data is a good sign. It's a red flag if a company includes language such as:

- **"We may share de-identified or aggregated data with trusted partners for research and business development."**
  This is often a legal loophole that allows companies to sell user data

while claiming it is anonymized. It also permits the selling of information to data brokers without explicitly calling them out in the policy (making it more difficult for you to identify and flag this type of data transfer).

- **"We do not sell personal information, but we may share certain user insights with third-party partners."** The phrase "user insights" is intentionally vague and could mean selling certain health trends, behavioral data, app activity logs, or anonymized data.
- **"We may transfer anonymized user data to affiliates, business partners, and other organizations for legitimate business purposes."** This language is relatively common, but the broad wording allows the company to sell your data under the guise of "business purposes" without specifying what those purposes are and who the recipients are. For instance, is selling information to data brokers a "legitimate business purpose"? It may be if that's part of the company's revenue model. It's the breadth of this statement that makes it concerning.

If a company doesn't explicitly state that it doesn't sell user data, or if it uses vague phrases that seem overly broad and undefined—such as "trusted partners," "business purposes," or "enhancing services"—it's safest to assume that your data could be monetized.

Evaluate Security Protections

Before you exit the privacy policy, there's one final aspect to examine: security. Even if an app collects sensitive data, the risk to your privacy depends on how well that data is protected. A strong security infrastructure can make the difference between your health data remaining private or falling into the wrong hands due to weak safeguards or a data breach.

Security provisions are often buried in the middle or near the end of a privacy policy. In most cases, this section outlines baseline security measures the company implements. However, this is an area where vague language is a major red flag. If a company provides only generic statements—such as "We take reasonable measures to protect user data"—that tells you almost nothing about what protections are actually in place. For instance, what counts as "reasonable"? There is no universal definition. The company has full discretion to decide what level of security is acceptable. This could be anything from world-class encryption to basic password protection—or virtually nothing at all.

By contrast, a privacy policy that explicitly identifies security measures—such as encryption, authentication safeguards, and access controls—offers stronger protections and a higher level of transparency. Companies that take security seriously will want to reassure users by specifying the steps they take to safeguard their most sensitive data. To assess whether a company prioritizes security, search for the following key terms:

- **Encryption:** This is one of the most basic and critical protections. If a company doesn't mention that it encrypts your data, this is a red flag. Look for end-to-end encryption or zero-access encryption, which prevents even the company from accessing your data. If encryption is not mentioned, assume your data is not encrypted and consider finding a different app.
- **Authentication:** Search for "multi-factor authentication" or "two-factor authentication," which adds an extra layer of security when logging in. This is relatively easy for companies to implement and should be considered an essential security feature for any app you use. If the policy does not mention authentication safeguards, the app may only require a simple password, which is much easier to breach.
- **Access controls:** This term refers to who within the company can view or handle user data. Strong privacy policies limit access to authorized personnel only and may specify that data access is restricted to employees with a legitimate business need. However, some companies may opt not to include this language in their consumer-facing privacy policies and instead may include it in their internal privacy documents. The absence of this language doesn't necessarily mean that a company allows all employees to access data, but you should proceed with a bit more caution.
- **Industry standard:** At a minimum, look for statements that the company adheres to industry-standard security measures. While this is still somewhat vague, it at least shows a commitment to following reasonable safeguards. If this term is absent, the company may not follow any recognized security protocols.

- **Server(s):** While optional, checking for server location can be important, particularly when it comes to reproductive health data. Some users may prefer apps with servers located in Europe or in US states that are more protective of reproductive health data following the overturn of *Roe v. Wade*.
- **Scramble:** This refers to data obfuscation techniques that make information unreadable to outsiders. This is not required, but if the term appears, check whether the company explains how it scrambles or secures data.
- **Unreadable:** A privacy policy that states data is "rendered unreadable" through encryption or other security measures is stronger than one that simply says data is "secured."

When performing this review, here are a couple of additional red flags to watch out for:

- **"We strive to use industry best practices where possible."** This language suggests that best practices are not applied consistently. There's ambiguity around the phrase "where possible," which makes it unclear when industry best practices would be implemented.
- **"We cannot guarantee the security of your data."** This is a common phrase in privacy policies because it allows the company to avoid liability in many instances in which a data breach or other security incident occurs. While no system is 100 percent secure, strong privacy policies emphasize clear, proactive security measures rather than simply shifting liability onto users. If a company includes a broad disclaimer stating it cannot guarantee security, look for whether it also outlines specific protections. A company that truly prioritizes security will go beyond disclaimers and detail the steps it takes to safeguard your data.
- **"Your data is secured using methods we deem appropriate."** This statement is vague and not protective of your security. For instance, who decides what's appropriate and under what circumstances? If this is the only security language in the policy, assume weak protections.

By searching for key security terms, recognizing vague or misleading language, and ensuring an app implements protections like encryption, you can make a more informed decision about whether an app is truly safe to use. If a privacy policy doesn't provide clear security assurances, the safest choice may be to look for an alternative.

Step 3: Explore the FAQs for Additional Clarity

Some companies provide a separate section for frequently asked questions (FAQ) on their website that explains their data practices in more consumer-friendly terms than the privacy policy. FAQs are typically designed to offer straightforward answers to common concerns about data use, retention, sharing, and security. Companies that value transparency are more likely to have FAQs related to privacy on their websites. If you have any lingering questions about how the company uses your data, jump on the company's website to see if they have an FAQ section and, if so, whether it addresses your questions. While the lack of an FAQ section isn't a dealbreaker, its presence can be a dealmaker because it demonstrates the company's commitment to transparency for its users.

Step 4: Investigate the Company's Privacy Track Record

The final step in evaluating a company's security is to run a quick search to see if the company has been involved in any past privacy or security incidents. A company's history can provide valuable insights into how seriously it takes user privacy and whether it has a track record of mishandling sensitive data.

To start, run the following quick searches in your preferred search engine:

- [Company Name] Data Privacy
- [Company Name] Data Security
- [Company Name] Data Breach
- [Company Name] Privacy Scandal
- [Company Name] Lawsuit
- [Company Name] FTC Investigation

These searches can help uncover any reports of privacy violations, legal actions, or security failures. In most instances, your search won't yield any significant results. In some cases, you may even find positive stories about the company's commitment to data privacy and security, which can be a sign that the company is reliable.

If a company has been involved in a security incident, take time to understand what happened, how the company responded, and whether any changes were made to improve future security. For example, has the company admitted fault and committed to change, or has it dismissed concerns and continued with business as usual? How a company responds to an incident says a lot about its integrity and how it will handle future incidents, if they ever occur.

However, it's important to remember that a past privacy or security issue doesn't necessarily mean an app is unsafe today. In some cases, companies that have been caught violating user privacy are under greater scrutiny and stronger regulatory oversight than those that have never been investigated. We discussed Flo's privacy scandal earlier, and as part of that incident, the company entered into a settlement agreement requiring it to undergo regular privacy audits and implement stronger protections for user data. Flo is subject to stringent data-sharing restrictions that do not extend to other companies in this space. Because of this oversight, Flo may actually have stronger privacy protections today compared with many other femtech apps that have never faced legal action.

By contrast, companies that haven't been investigated may be engaging in questionable data practices—they just haven't been caught yet. A company that has never been fined or sued could be selling user data to third parties in violation of its privacy policy or failing to properly secure sensitive information. Just because a company hasn't been in the news for privacy violations doesn't mean it isn't engaging in shady data practices behind the scenes.

As such, the goal of this search isn't to automatically rule out companies based on past security incidents or rule in companies that don't appear in the news. Rather, the goal is to provide you with a fuller picture of the company's history and how they have responded to any incidents that occurred. If a company has a history of misleading users, failing to protect data, or ignoring privacy concerns, it's more likely to put your information at risk in the future. However, a company that has taken meaningful steps to improve its privacy practices after an investigation may be a safer choice than one with an unclear or untested track record. If your search returns results, it will come down to balancing your personal risk tolerance and preferences against the other information you've found in the privacy policy and FAQs.

By following this four-step framework, you can quickly and confidently evaluate the privacy and security standards of a femtech company—often in less than 10 minutes. This framework is designed to help you make informed decisions on whether an app meets your personal privacy and security goals without conducting a time-intensive review of all the company's documents. While this method isn't foolproof—and perfection isn't possible in today's digital world—it creates an efficient and workable foundation that all consumers can implement to begin regaining control over their data.

Staying Vigilant: Monitoring Updates

Even when an app starts out secure, there's no guarantee it will stay that way. Companies evolve, leadership changes, and business models shift—sometimes in ways that make user privacy an afterthought. When it comes to femtech, the solutions we trust today may not be as secure tomorrow. That's why staying informed about privacy policy updates, app changes, and company news is essential to protecting our data for the long term.

Privacy Policies Aren't Set in Stone

Most of us ignore the "We've updated our privacy policy" emails that land in our inboxes. But these updates can introduce major shifts in how our data is collected, used, or shared. A company that once promised not to sell user data could quietly remove that clause or a new feature could require expanded tracking permissions. Simply skimming update notifications or privacy policy change logs can help flag potential risks before they become a problem.

Similarly, when an app releases an update, don't just install it blindly. Take a moment to review what's changed. Companies that prioritize transparency will clearly state what's different and how it affects users. If an update introduces new permissions, sharing policies, or vague wording around data retention, it's worth taking a closer look and re-running your searches from the prior sections to ensure the app still aligns with your privacy expectations.

Security Updates versus Privacy Risks

Not all updates are bad. Many software updates include critical security patches that fix vulnerabilities and protect against cyber threats. Ignoring updates can leave your data exposed to breaches, so it's important to keep your apps current. However, some updates may quietly introduce new privacy risks, such as expanded third-party data sharing, additional tracking permissions, or integrations with other platforms that increase surveillance.

A good rule of thumb is to check the app's privacy settings after each major update. Some companies reset user preferences when they roll out new features, automatically opting users into more data collection or tracking without explicit consent. Taking a minute to review and adjust your settings ensures you're not unknowingly sharing more than you intended.

Keeping an Eye on Company News

Beyond privacy policies and app updates, it's also important to monitor the company itself. Businesses change ownership, merge with larger corporations, or shift their revenue models—all of which can impact how data is handled. A femtech startup that once championed user privacy may change direction after an acquisition, prioritizing profit over protection.

One of the easiest ways to stay informed is to set up a Google Alert for the company name along with key terms like "privacy policy," "data breach," "lawsuit," "investigation," "merger," and "acquisition." This way, if a news story breaks about a femtech app you're using failing to protect user data, changing its privacy terms, merging with another company, or facing a regulatory investigation, you'll know right away.

Conclusion

As consumers, we have more influence than we realize over how femtech companies handle privacy. Every time we speak up about concerning changes, switch to a more transparent app, or warn others about questionable data practices, we send a message that privacy matters.

Femtech companies that want to earn and keep users' trust will take privacy concerns seriously. The ones that thrive will be those that engage with their users, explain updates clearly, and provide meaningful choices.

The companies that ignore privacy concerns may survive for a while, but eventually, they'll lose users to better alternatives.

We don't have to be privacy experts or read every line of every legal document, but staying aware, staying vocal, and staying informed helps ensure femtech evolves in a way that protects our data. Femtech's future will continue to bring exciting innovations but also new challenges. By staying vigilant and advocating for strong privacy protections, we ensure that these changes serve women's real needs. Our health data is far too valuable to be left unprotected, and together, we have the power to demand better.

8 | The SAFE Method

Accuracy

Clickbait or Breakthrough? The Battle for Trust in Femtech

Twenty-four-year-old Melanie* stared at her open laptop, fingers hovering over the keyboard. Sweat clung to her forehead, dried from her post-gym commute. After months of strict dieting, grueling workouts, and endless restrictions, she was exhausted. No matter how disciplined she had been, nothing changed. The scale refused to move, her energy levels swung unpredictably, and despite everything, she had *gained* weight. The program she followed—one she later learned was designed by men—was failing her.

She leaned back in her chair, frustration curling in her chest. There had to be a better way. She clicked into the search bar and typed "weight loss for women." The results loaded instantly, a flood of promises and solutions crowding her screen. Products claimed to have cracked the code to "hacking female fat loss." Influencers boasted meal plans "scientifically designed to work with your cycle." Subscription boxes filled with supplements guaranteed to "balance your hormones naturally" lined the margins of her screen. Every company claimed scientific backing, but the details were always vague. Melanie scrolled, searching for something that felt *real*, something that offered more than just another marketing gimmick.

Determined to dig deeper, she refined her search. This time, she typed "femtech weight management." The results shifted, replacing influencers and meal plans with tech solutions that promised precision and personalization. One company claimed its smart ring could track metabolism in real time, adjusting recommendations based on daily fluctuations. Another boasted an AI-powered app that could predict exactly when a woman would gain or lose weight based on her hormonal cycle. A third insisted its groundbreaking blood tests could unlock the secret to permanent weight loss. Melanie's stomach twisted as she skimmed the claims. Some of it sounded revolutionary. Some of it sounded ridiculous. But how was she supposed to know the difference?

Melanie was trapped in what so many women experience every day—the Internet Research Storm. As discussed earlier, when traditional healthcare fails to provide answers, women turn to the internet, searching for solutions in a sea of options. Some are legitimate, backed by rigorous science and capable of making a real difference. Others are nothing more than overpriced gimmicks, snake oil wrapped in sophisticated branding. Separating fact from fiction isn't just frustrating; it can feel nearly impossible.

Femtech is a rapidly growing industry, and with that growth comes opportunity—but also exploitation. Every emerging market attracts bad actors looking to capitalize on consumer desperation. The lack of regulatory oversight in femtech has made it easy for companies to rush untested, inaccurate, or misleading products to market.[1] Many of these solutions aren't designed to deceive outright, but they are built on shaky foundations, using limited studies or incomplete data to justify their claims. Consumers are left to navigate this landscape alone, forced to distinguish between revolutionary tools and expensive placebos.

This issue isn't exclusive to femtech. The broader health technology industry has long struggled with accuracy and reliability. For example, a study from Stanford University found that while wrist-worn fitness trackers measured heart rate with reasonable accuracy, they were far less reliable in estimating calorie expenditure. The most accurate tracker still had an error rate of 27 percent, while the least accurate was off by a staggering 93 percent.[2] Similarly, the Mayo Clinic found that many wrist blood pressure monitors provide falsely high readings due to improper positioning.[3] If inaccuracies are this prevalent in general health technology, it's no surprise that femtech—an industry still fighting to be taken seriously—faces similar challenges, if not greater.

For women, the stakes are even higher. We rely on these tools not just for fitness tracking, but for essential healthcare decisions. When these technologies fail us, the consequences go beyond frustration. A faulty fertility tracker can result in an unplanned pregnancy. An inaccurate hormonal diagnostic tool can lead to misdiagnosis, delayed treatment, and prolonged suffering. A misleading weight loss program can push women further into cycles of guilt, self-blame, unhealthy supplements, and bad habits.

Femtech has the potential to revolutionize women's health, but only if it is built on accuracy, transparency, and trust. Women don't just need more health solutions. We need the right ones. And in a world where misinformation is everywhere, finding the right solutions is more essential than ever.

Femtech's Accuracy Problem

The femtech solutions women seek out are only as useful as the insights they provide. A period-tracking app is pointless if it can't accurately predict a woman's next cycle. Ovulation-tracking apps fail if they don't incorporate the latest medically backed insights. Unproven supplements do little for women's health—except leave them frustrated, skeptical, and discouraged from trying new solutions.

Women don't want to trade their valuable data for products that don't deliver on their promises. And yet the growing potential to capitalize on the women's health market has led some companies to enter the femtech space solely for profit, with little regard for whether their products work. This isn't just a question of wasted money—it's a matter of trust. The result is a cycle of skepticism, frustration, and ultimately, disengagement from a sector that was supposed to empower them.

The demand for femtech is undeniable. From April through December 2021, three menstrual-tracking apps were downloaded 250 million times.[4] That's 250 million attempts by women to better understand their bodies—250 million moments of trust placed in technology to fill the knowledge gap left by traditional healthcare. Yet studies have revealed that many of the available period-tracking apps were wildly inaccurate at predicting when women were most fertile.[5] The reason? Women's cycles and ovulation days are not as predictable as app developers often assume. Medical research has confirmed this since the 1930s, yet may apps still use outdated and disproven assumptions to make their predictions.[6]

Despite the fact that only about 30 percent of women have a fertile window that falls between days 10 and 17 of their cycle, most fertility apps still rely on calendar-based ovulation predictions.[7] When researchers examined these apps in 2018, none accounted for the full variation of cycle characteristics.[8] Instead, they layered basic algorithms over outdated assumptions. Unsurprisingly, most were off by more than a few days—an alarming margin of error for women trying to conceive or avoid pregnancy. That same year, a study published in *Current Research and Opinion* evaluated 73 menstrual cycle apps and found that none correctly predicted ovulation.[9] The most accurate app achieved only a 21 percent success rate.[10] Another study by Columbia University Medical Center examined 108 femtech apps and found that 95 percent of free smartphone period-tracking apps were inaccurate.[11] Most of these apps had little to no oversight from healthcare professionals or evidence-based medical research, meaning they weren't just flawed—they were actively misleading the women—like Melanie—who relied on them.

The problem persists, even as the femtech industry continues to grow. In 2019, the Organization for Review of Care and Health Applications (ORCHA) evaluated the clinical accuracy of 200 femtech apps. The results were disappointing. More than 85 percent of the apps tested failed to meet ORCHA's quality thresholds, which assess safety, effectiveness, and data protection.[12] Only three of the 200 apps—Natural Cycles, Baby Buddy, and Mum & Baby— exceeded these rigorous standards.[13] This means that despite the explosion of interest and investment in femtech, some apps still lack the clinical validation necessary to ensure reliability. Women seeking trustworthy digital health solutions are often left navigating a market flooded with ineffective or misleading products, with little guidance on which ones they can trust.

When the solutions we trust fail us, they don't just disappoint us— they push us away from seeking help at all. Each device that doesn't deliver accurate results erodes consumer confidence.[14] Repeated inaccuracies can ultimately result in product abandonment and stifle femtech adoption rates across the market. Many women are willing to experiment with a few different solutions in search of answers, but our patience runs out when those solutions repeatedly fail. Disillusionment builds. Trust erodes. Eventually, we disengage from femtech altogether, resigning our-selves to the limited solutions available within the traditional healthcare industry that has neglected us.

Accuracy isn't just a technical benchmark for femtech—it's the foun-dation of trust. If femtech is to fulfill its promise of revolutionizing wom-en's health, companies must prioritize rigorous clinical validation, transparency about product limitations, and a commitment to scientific integrity. Without these efforts, femtech risks undermining its own credi-bility and losing the very people it set out to help. Worse, it risks reinforc-ing the same cycle of misinformation and neglect that has plagued women's health for generations.

Ensuring Accuracy: How to Separate Science from Hype

When evaluating a femtech product for accuracy, distinguishing reliable companies from less trustworthy ones can be easier than it seems. The most reputable brands take pride in their scientific backing, clinical partnerships, and research initiatives—so they make this information easy to find. A com-pany that genuinely values accuracy won't bury its studies in obscure foot-notes or rely solely on flashy testimonials. Instead, clear evidence of medical validation should be readily available, typically on their website's home page, within the navigation menu, or linked in the footer. Just as individuals showcase what they're most proud of, companies do the same. When trans-parency is lacking, it's often a red flag.

During her research, Melanie came across two hormone-focused nutri-tion apps that appeared promising. But she knew better than to stop at a surface-level comparison. Effective research requires digging deeper, espe-cially in an industry where marketing can blur the line between fact and fiction. She started by verifying their claims.

The first app prominently advertised that its recommendations were "based on clinically validated diagnostics." The app encouraged users to complete and upload at-home hormone test results for AI-driven insights, suggesting a level of medical credibility. That sounded impressive—until she looked closer. When Melanie checked the company's website, she found no mention of the company working with a certified lab, nor any clear infor-mation about whether its recommendations were reviewed by healthcare professionals. The company was silent on which aspects of its diagnostics were "clinically validated."

The second app took a different approach. Instead of referencing diagnostic tools, it cited "clinical studies proving 97 percent effectiveness." But when Melanie clicked the link, expecting peer-reviewed research, she found only a blog post summarizing internal company testing. No published studies. No independent verification. Just carefully worded marketing copy designed to *look* like scientific evidence. When she Googled the company's technology, she finally learned that one very minor component of the product was 97 percent effective, but this did not extend to the majority of the app's features and recommendations. Melanie felt as though she had been cruelly misled.

This kind of in-depth research might seem tedious, but in an industry where anyone can claim expertise, it's necessary. A company that prioritizes accuracy doesn't make consumers hunt for proof—it makes proof impossible to miss. Kindbody, for example, provides a strong model of transparency. The company offers fertility services and runs its own Preimplantation Genetic Testing laboratories.[15] Kindbody employs an in-house team of scientists and doctors overseeing lab operations, and its website features direct links to detailed information about the company's experts, research, and publications. When a company makes it easy to verify its credibility, it's a sign that it takes accuracy seriously.

Ultimately, accuracy in femtech isn't just about technical precision—it's about trust. Women deserve solutions that are rooted in real science, not vague promises or misleading marketing. In an industry that holds so much potential, accountability is everything. If a product or service claims to be backed by research, it shouldn't take more than a few clicks to find proof. If that proof isn't there, it's safest to assume the science isn't, either. When looking for proof that a company's product is accurate, here are four steps you can perform quickly. This part of the SAFE framework will help ensure you're using products that are grounded in science and legitimacy.

Step 1: Check for Regulatory Approval

Regulatory approval from agencies like the FDA can be a reliable indicator of a femtech product's accuracy and safety. Products that receive FDA approval or clearance are subject to testing and regulatory oversight to ensure they meet specific standards for performance, consistency, safety, efficacy, and risk management. These evaluations determine whether the device functions as advertised and whether it provides accurate, reliable results under typical usage conditions. Beyond the initial approval process, the FDA also conducts post-market surveillance, monitoring existing devices for potential safety concerns. This level of oversight minimizes the chances of misleading claims, false readings, or harmful inaccuracies, offering consumers greater confidence in a product's reliability.

The FDA's Role in Overseeing Femtech Devices

The foundation of medical device regulation in the United States is the Food, Drug, and Cosmetic Act (FDCA).[16] The FDCA gives the FDA authority to oversee the safety of food, drugs, medical devices, and cosmetics. Medical devices, including some femtech innovations, are categorized into three risk-based classes.[17] Class I devices pose the least risk to safety and well-being and include simple, noninvasive tools like stethoscopes, thermometers, and bandages. Since these devices are considered low risk, they typically don't require clinical trials or extensive safety studies, though they must still comply with FDA labeling and manufacturing standards. Class II devices—such as menstrual cups, tampons, heart rate monitors, and glucose monitors—pose a moderate risk. These devices typically undergo a streamlined premarket approval process known as 510(k) clearance. This means the company must prove its device is as safe and effective as a similar, already-approved product. Class III devices are the highest risk and include life-sustaining or implantable devices, such as pacemakers. These devices require a rigorous premarket approval process, often involving clinical trials to ensure safety and efficacy.

A device's classification depends on two key factors: risk and intended use.[18] Risk refers to the potential harm a device could cause if it malfunctions or provides inaccurate readings. The higher the risk, the stricter the FDA's oversight. For example, a pacemaker, which is implanted inside the human body, has a higher risk of harm or malfunction compared to a general wellness app on your phone. As a result, the pacemaker will be classified at a higher risk level compared to the wellness app. Intended use, on the other hand, describes what the device is designed to do—whether it's for general wellness tracking or diagnosing and treating medical conditions. The FDA determines intended use by analyzing not just the device but also how the company markets it. Product labeling, promotional materials, and even company websites play a role in this classification. This means two seemingly similar devices can actually fall under different regulatory categories depending on how they're positioned and advertised.

Consider two hypothetical femtech startups: Alva and Zephyr. Both companies develop wearable devices for pregnant women, monitoring key maternal health indicators. Alva's device is marketed and intended to be used as a general wellness tool that helps expectant mothers track their vitals for general awareness. Zephyr's device, however, goes a step further—it not only collects vital signs but also analyzes the data and provides medical recommendations to patients using its AI algorithms and clinician teams, such as flagging potential pregnancy complications and diagnosing symptoms. Because Zephyr's device is intended to support medical decision-making, it will require more oversight from the FDA than Alva's device, which is just intended to collect consumer-generated data and provide general educational resources.

Many real-life femtech companies have successfully navigated this process to receive FDA approval or clearance. Sequel's spiral tampon, a Class II device designed with diagonal grooves for enhanced absorption, earned FDA approval after demonstrating its safety and efficacy. Sunny Period's combined menstrual cup and applicator became the first product of its kind to receive 510(k) clearance. Mosie Baby, which offers an at-home insemination kit, and PherDal's FDA-cleared sterile at-home insemination kit are additional examples of femtech products that have met stringent regulatory requirements.

However, not all femtech products require FDA approval—especially software-based tools like mobile apps. The FDA primarily regulates medical devices, including a category called Software as a Medical Device (SaMD). Apps that make medical claims—such as diagnosing conditions or recommending treatment—may fall under this classification and require regulatory review. But general wellness apps, which simply track behaviors like menstrual cycles or daily habits, or provide educational resources, are usually exempt from FDA oversight.[19] This lack of regulation means accuracy can vary widely among these apps, making independent verification even more critical.

Given the fact that certain femtech apps and products can come to the market without FDA clearance or approval, it's not surprising to see some femtech companies intentionally design their productions to avoid regulatory oversight—at least at the beginning. One reason many femtech companies delay or avoid FDA approval is cost. Obtaining 510(k) clearance or full FDA approval can be expensive, with application fees alone ranging from $6,000 to over $24,000.[20] But these fees only scratch the surface—clinical trials (if necessary), product testing, and legal compliance costs can push total expenses into the hundreds of thousands, even millions, of dollars. For femtech startups, this financial burden can be unsustainable, at least until initial funding is secured. As a result, many companies launch with general wellness products that don't require FDA approval, allowing them to enter the market quickly, gather user feedback, and refine their offerings. Once the company secures additional funding, it may expand into FDA-regulated products, increasing its credibility and market potential.

Checking for Regulatory Oversight

Because FDA approval is a strong marker of a product's reliability and safety, verifying a company's claims is a crucial step in evaluating accuracy. Some companies falsely or confusingly advertise their FDA status, relying on misleading labels or ambiguous wording to appear more legitimate. For this reason, it's important that you independently verify whether a company is FDA "approved" or "cleared." The best way to verify this is through the FDA's Medical Device Database (Devices@FDA), available at https://www.accessdata.fda.gov/scripts/cdrh/devicesatfda/index.cfm. By visiting Devices@FDA and searching for the product or company name, you can confirm whether the device has been cleared or approved. If it appears in the database, the entry will include the device's approval date, classification, and intended use.

You should also be wary of misleading terms like "FDA-registered." This phrase does not mean a product has been tested or approved—it simply means the company has notified the FDA of its existence and listed its products for tracking purposes. Registration is a purely administrative process and does not involve any safety or accuracy testing. A company that touts "FDA registered" status without further explanation may be attempting to create a false sense of security about its product's legitimacy.

If a device does not appear in the FDA's database, that doesn't necessarily mean it's inaccurate or ineffective. It simply means the company hasn't pursued FDA approval, often due to cost or classification exemptions. In these cases, further steps—such as reviewing clinical studies and independent research—are essential for determining a product's reliability before using it.

Step 2: Search for Clinical Validation Studies

Clinical validation studies are another critical tool for determining whether a femtech product delivers accurate, reliable, and meaningful results in real-world conditions. These studies assess how well a device performs compared to gold-standard medical tests or protocols. A fertility-tracking app, for example, might be tested against hormone blood tests, while a wearable heart monitor could be evaluated against an electrocardiogram. When studies are published in peer-reviewed scientific journals, they provide independent confirmation of a product's effectiveness, reinforcing its credibility and ensuring that its claims are backed by real evidence.

Finding clinical validation studies might sound daunting, but it's easier than you think. The first place to look is the company's website. Companies with FDA approval or scientifically validated products often display this information prominently, either on the home page, within the navigation menu, or in a dedicated section labeled "Research," "Science," or "Clinical Studies." If a company has invested in research, it wants customers to see it. The transparency in sharing research is a strong indicator of a company's commitment to accuracy and scientific integrity.

However, some companies rely on vague language to create an illusion of credibility. Be wary of phrases like "evidence-backed" or "scientifically proven" when there are no direct links to studies or supporting data. If a company makes bold claims but offers no references, it's worth questioning why. A truly research-backed product should make its studies easy to find. If you locate links to peer-reviewed publications, make a quick note of the journal name and any relevant study details—you may need these later for conversations with your healthcare provider (more on this in Chapter 11).

If you can't locate scientific studies on a company's website, try searching PubMed at www.PubMed.gov or Google Scholar at www.scholar.google.com, both of which are accessible to the public. PubMed, run by the NIH, focuses on peer-reviewed medical research, while Google Scholar provides a broader range of sources, including scientific journals, conference papers, and institutional reports. In the search fields, perform one or more of the following searches:

- [Company Name or Product Name] Clinical Validation
- [Company Name or Product Name] Peer-Reviewed Study
- [Company Name or Product Name] Peer-Reviewed Research

If nothing appears in reputable journals, that may be a sign the product has not undergone rigorous scientific evaluation. This means that unless the company has transparently described its processes and methodologies elsewhere on its website, you have very little insight into whether the product is accurate.

It's also important to remember that not all studies are created equal. Knowing what to look for is just as important as finding the research itself. A strong study should be published in a peer-reviewed journal, meaning it has been evaluated by independent experts before publication. Articles that are written by independent researchers, not just employees of the company producing the product, are more objective and reliable. Studies that are recent and build on established science carry more weight than outdated or overly promotional research. If you find a study but don't have time to read the entire paper, focus on three key sections: Abstract, Discussion, and Conclusion. These parts summarize the study's findings and are usually written in clearer language, making it easier to understand the key takeaways.

If a study still feels overwhelming, trusted sources like Healthline or Mayo Clinic often summarize research findings in simpler terms. A quick search on these sites can provide additional context and highlight products that have been validated by medical professionals. Taking a few extra minutes to verify clinical research can help ensure that the femtech products you use are based on real science—because when it comes to health, accuracy isn't optional.

Step 3: Evaluate Partnerships with Medical Institutions

If a femtech product does not have FDA approval or clearance, another strong indicator of credibility is its partnerships with medical institutions. These collaborations demonstrate a company's commitment to accuracy and clinical validation, even if they haven't yet undergone formal regulatory review or published clinical studies.

Many femtech companies work with universities, teaching hospitals, and research organizations to conduct studies, validate their technology, and improve their products. These institutions maintain strict standards for partnerships, because their reputation depends on associating only with scientifically sound initiatives. Before agreeing to collaborate, medical institutions typically conduct thorough evaluations to ensure a company's technology aligns with evidence-based medicine and meets compliance requirements. This level of scrutiny means that a femtech product with strong institutional partnerships is more likely to be built on scientific rigor rather than marketing hype.

Some of the most well-known femtech brands have established partnerships with top-tier research institutions. Clue collaborates with Stanford University, Oxford University, and Oregon Health & Science University to study reproductive health. Their research initiatives include studies on how COVID-19 affects menstrual cycles, demonstrating their commitment to advancing scientific understanding in this space.[21] Ava, a fertility-tracking bracelet, partners with the University of Zurich to refine its ovulation prediction algorithms through clinical research. Partnerships like these enhance credibility by showing that a company values accuracy and continuous improvement. They also allow femtech companies to access large-scale clinical trials, experienced researchers, and high-quality data that strengthen their products.

Identifying these partnerships is similar to finding clinical validation studies. Start by checking a company's official website—many highlight their research collaborations on the home page or in sections labeled "Research," "Science," "Partners," or "About Us." If this information isn't easily available, look at the "News," "Press," or "Blog" sections for partnership announcements. If nothing appears, a quick Google search with the following terms can help confirm a company's affiliations:

- [Company Name] Partnership
- [Company Name] Collaboration
- [Company Name] Medical Partnership
- [Company Name] Research Partnership
- [Company Name] Affiliations
- [Company Name or Product Name] Endorsements
- [Company Name] and Medical Organizations
- [Company Name] Science Team Affiliations

Be wary of companies that make bold claims about scientific accuracy and cutting-edge technology if there are no verifiable partnerships or research affiliations. This can be a red flag that the product may not be as reliable as advertised.

Step 4: Check Product Review Websites

Beyond scientific validation and institutional partnerships, independent product reviews offer another way to assess a femtech product's accuracy. Third-party reviews provide valuable insights into a product's real-world performance, usability, and reliability. Unlike company-controlled testimonials, which can be biased or manipulated, independent reviews consolidate expert analysis and user feedback to offer a more objective perspective.

It's important to distinguish between genuine third-party reviews and promotional content. Many femtech companies display user testimonials on their website, but these reviews can be curated, incentivized, or even artificially generated. Instead, focus on reviews from well-known health and technology publications. Websites like CNET Health, PCMag, Verywell Health, and Healthline evaluate how well products function, often comparing them to other validated medical tools. Health-focused platforms frequently consult medical experts to assess accuracy claims, making them a reliable resource for understanding whether a product lives up to its promises.

Finding these reviews is simple. A quick Google search using the following terms can surface independent assessments:

- [Company Name or Product Name] Accuracy Review
- [Company Name or Product Name] Validation
- [Company Name or Product Name] Product Comparison

If you already know of a well-established competitor, you can also search for direct comparisons to see how a newer product stacks up against proven alternatives. Searches like "[Product Name] vs [Competitor Name]" can help determine whether the product is on par with industry leaders.

For those who prefer trusted review platforms over general searches, some of the reputable websites for health technology reviews include WebMD, Healthline, Mayo Clinic, Medical News Today, Harvard Health, and MedlinePlus (NIH). While tech-oriented sites like The Verge and TechRadar may focus on design and features, health-focused platforms take a deeper look at clinical reliability, user outcomes, and expert opinions.

It's worth noting that newer femtech products may not yet have extensive independent reviews. This doesn't necessarily mean they are inaccurate—it may simply reflect the industry's rapid growth. You should weigh your personal preferences for using tech that may be newer and more sophisticated against the possibility that the tech may not be tested for accuracy yet. As femtech expands, so will the number of comprehensive product evaluations. Until then, using a combination of scientific research, medical partnerships, and third-party reviews remains the best way to assess a product's legitimacy before trusting it with your health.

Conclusion

Taking just a few minutes to evaluate the accuracy of a femtech product can make all the difference in determining whether it's a valuable tool for your health. A device or app that provides reliable, science-backed data empowers you to make informed decisions about your body. Without accuracy, even the most innovative technologies lose their value, turning into sources of confusion rather than clarity.

Checking for accuracy is also essential when it comes to getting your healthcare provider to take your data seriously. Many women turn to femtech because they feel unheard or dismissed in medical settings, but bringing data from an app or device won't guarantee that a doctor will accept it as valid. When you know a product is backed by clinical research, regulatory approval, or reputable medical partnerships, you're in a much stronger position to advocate for yourself and integrate that data into your healthcare conversations. We'll dive deeper into how to effectively present your femtech data to your provider in Chapter 11, but taking these steps now will ensure you have accurate, credible information when the time comes to discuss your health with a professional.

9 | The SAFE Method

Foundation

Why a Company's Foundation Determines Its Future

On a bright California day in June 2014, the air inside Apple's Cupertino headquarters buzzed with anticipation. Engineers and designers were putting the final touches on what they believed would be a revolutionary step forward in health tracking. The new Apple Health app (part of a suite of tools known as HealthKit) was set to be a game changer—a sleek, all-in-one dashboard that could monitor key metrics about the human body.

Craig Federighi, Apple's senior vice president of software engineering, took the stage.[1] With a few taps, he demonstrated the app's capabilities—tracking everything from calorie intake and heart rate to blood alcohol content and respiratory rate. The crowd applauded as he scrolled through dozens of metrics the app could monitor—metrics he claimed that users were most interested in.[2]

But within hours, a glaring omission became apparent. Apple's state-of-the-art health tracker could measure sodium intake, remind asthma patients to use their inhalers, and even determine body fat percentage. Yet, it completely ignored one of the most fundamental aspects of women's health: menstruation.[3]

151

Consumers took to Twitter (now X) to express their frustration. One commenter remarked, "Further evidence that tech doesn't care about women: no period tracking in HealthKit in iOS8."[4] Another tweeted, "Steve Jobs didn't have periods so Health[K]it doesn't need a period tracker."[5] It was an oversight so egregious, so absurd, that it could only mean one thing: No one in the room—at least no one with decision-making power—had thought to ask a woman what *she* needed in a health app.[6]

It wasn't just a fluke. At the time, women made up only 23 percent of technical roles at Apple and held just 29 percent of the company's leadership positions.[7] The absence of women in decision-making roles wasn't merely a corporate diversity issue—it was shaping the very products Apple put into the world.

Women noticed the gap immediately. But Apple? It took them a *full year* to add a reproductive health tracking feature.[8] By then, apps like Clue had already gained millions of users—because they actually understood what women needed from health technology.[9]

Apple wasn't the only company to make this mistake. Fitbit also failed to include menstrual health tracking for years. Despite offering detailed insights on steps taken, calories burned, and heart rate monitoring, Fitbit didn't introduce menstrual cycle tracking until 2018—more than a decade after its founding.[10] For years, users had to rely on third-party apps to track their reproductive health, even though it was just as crucial to overall wellness as the metrics Fitbit *did* track. The omission was another glaring example of what happens when women's health isn't prioritized in tech development. It wasn't until persistent feedback from users that Fitbit finally integrated the feature, proving once again that when diverse voices aren't in leadership or product design, women's health needs are often an afterthought.

The blunders by Apple and Fitbit weren't just a wake-up call—they were a warning. A company's foundation—its leadership, values, and decision-making processes—shapes the products it creates. A strong foundation doesn't just support innovative solutions; it ensures those solutions are inclusive, representative, and impactful. When that foundation lacks diverse voices, the results are often exclusionary, ineffective, or even harmful. This makes consumers feel as though their needs are secondary to profit. In femtech, where the goal is to improve women's health, a weak foundation isn't just a business misstep. It's a betrayal of the very people the industry is meant to serve.

Any company can claim to care about women's well-being. But their actions—whom they hire, whom they listen to, and how they design their products—are what reveal their true priorities. If you want to understand whether a femtech company is serious about improving women's health, start with their leadership. Who founded the company? Do they have medical or scientific expertise? If not, have they built a team of experts to guide them? Does their approach account for diverse needs across race, gender identity, and socioeconomic background? If the answers to these questions are vague, weak, or nonexistent, chances are the company is more interested in chasing a trend than solving real problems.

Representation and foundational stability in femtech aren't just bonuses—they're the difference between success and failure. Consider a femtech company developing a fertility tracking app. If the team lacks awareness of the unique needs of trans and nonbinary individuals, women with PCOS, or those from marginalized communities, the product may inadvertently exclude large segments of its intended audience. This often happens when a company's leadership and advisory teams lack representative voices who can advocate for these populations during product development. Without internal champions to push for broader inclusivity, key features—such as cycle tracking for people on testosterone, considerations for irregular ovulation patterns, or cultural sensitivities around reproductive health—never make it onto the roadmap. Worse, without ethical guidelines embedded in the company's foundation, inclusivity becomes an afterthought, addressed only when users complain rather than being proactively built into the product's evolution. This means that even if an exclusion is recognized later, ongoing updates and developments may still fail to fully correct it, reinforcing the cycle of neglect.

Additionally, a weak foundation can perpetuate device inaccuracies. Imagine a scenario where a menopause app is developed by a team without a scientific or medical background. Without the necessary expertise, the team might overlook critical differences in how menopause manifests across populations. For example, research shows that Indian women tend to experience menopause earlier than their Western counterparts, with an average onset age of 46.2 years compared to 51 years in Western populations.[11] If the app's algorithms and recommendations are based solely on Western data, they could miscalculate key milestones, provide inaccurate guidance, or fail to recognize symptoms at the right stages for certain users. This kind of oversight wouldn't just be a minor inconvenience—it would lead to frustration, mistrust, and even real health risks for users who rely on the app for accurate tracking and insights.

On the other hand, companies that prioritize representative leadership, equitable product design, and scientific accuracy are far more likely to create solutions that work for all women. They build trust with their users, foster strong communities, and iterate on feedback. These aren't just good business practices; they're the foundation of safer, more effective, and more accessible healthcare solutions.

Whom We Trust with Women's Health

Do femtech founders have to be women? No.

Do they have to be doctors, mothers, or have firsthand experience with the issues they're trying to solve? Not necessarily.

But here's the thing: Most femtech founders do fall into one of those categories. Why? Because they *get it*. They understand, on a personal level, what it means to navigate a healthcare system that has historically overlooked and misdiagnosed women. As consumers, we tend to trust them when they say they're invested in their company's success—not just for profit, but because the problem they're solving matters to them in a way that's personal, not just professional.

When we see women leading femtech companies, we're more inclined to instinctively trust that they have a stake in the outcome. Maybe the founder has struggled with endometriosis, faced fertility challenges, or spent years feeling dismissed by doctors. That lived experience makes femtech founders more likely to approach product development with empathy, urgency, and a deeper understanding of what's at stake.

When we see men leading femtech companies, we don't necessarily question their intentions—but we do ask what drives their commitment to women's health. Impactful innovations in femtech have come from male founders who have seen the challenges women face—through their partners, daughters, mothers, or colleagues—and have committed themselves to making a difference. The key is whether a founder, regardless of gender, is building with intention, collaborating with experts, and ensuring women's voices are at the center of the innovation process.

That's why well-rounded and competent leadership in femtech is so essential. It's not about excluding men—it's about ensuring that the people shaping women's healthcare solutions understand, respect, and prioritize women's lived experiences and the need for accurate and reliable products. It's about making sure femtech products aren't just marketed to women but rather built *for* them, with real consideration for their diverse needs.

When women are in leadership roles, the conversation shifts. And when companies foster diverse, inclusive teams—whether led by women, men, or a mix of both—their products are more likely to be innovative, effective, and truly representative of the people they serve. At the end of the day, trust isn't just given—it's earned. And the companies that truly deserve women's trust are the ones proving, through leadership, innovation, and action, that women's health is more than just a business opportunity. It's a mission.

Weak Founders: Mistrust, Misuse, and Misunderstanding

Trust is the cornerstone of every successful femtech company. Women don't just use health-tech products—they rely on them to track their bodies, manage their health, and make informed decisions about their well-being. That kind of relationship requires more than a sleek interface or clever branding. It demands transparency, respect, and a deep commitment to ethical responsibility. Without that, trust breaks down. And when trust breaks down, women walk away.

Unfortunately, where there's a booming industry, there are always those looking to capitalize. The femtech market is projected to reach \$103 billion by 2030,[12] and with that level of financial potential, companies that lack a genuine commitment to women's health will inevitably enter the space. These businesses may see opportunity, but they don't always see responsibility. When that happens, it has the potential to alienate and insult core user groups.

Glow, a menstrual tracking app founded in 2013 by PayPal's Max Levchin and four other men, serves as a striking example.[13] Instead of centering women's health, the company initially approached fertility tracking from a less than fully inclusive perspective. In its early years, Glow sent notifications reminding women to wear nice underwear when their ovulation window began.[14] It also notified their partners to bring home flowers.[15] A fertility tracker reducing ovulation to lingerie and date nights wasn't just outdated—it was an oversimplification of reproductive health. The assumption that every user wanted to conceive (and do so within a stereotypically romantic dynamic) alienated many, sending a clear message: This product was designed with a narrow, traditional view of women's experiences in mind.

Glow wasn't alone. Flo Health made similar missteps. When the company introduced its "Flo for Partners" feature, its marketing framed the update as a tool for men to "plan surprise date nights" and "see when your period has started" (complete with a chili pepper emoji implying "spicy" sex).[16] The tone of these notifications reinforced the idea that menstrual tracking existed to help men navigate relationships, rather than serving as an educational resource for helping women manage their health.[17] While there is certainly a place for male education about menstrual cycles and fertility, the initial branding undermined the larger importance of this new feature and, in doing so, alienated a portion of its user base.

Problematic design isn't limited to messaging—it's often baked into the product itself. Some femtech apps still rely on outdated, infantilizing aesthetics, using hearts, flowers, and pastel palettes that make women's health feel lighthearted, even trivial.[18] Others use demeaning and reductive language—such as calling users "girls," describing sex as "hookups," or designing sexual activity logs around a banana icon to indicate condom use.[19] When apps do this, they aren't just being quirky. They're excluding users. Not every sexual relationship involves a heterosexual male partner. Not every woman navigating femtech identifies with traditionally feminine aesthetics. These design choices tell users exactly who the app was built for—and who it wasn't.

And here's the most telling part: These issues don't show up nearly as often in health-tech products designed for men. A University of Washington study found that healthcare apps marketed to women were far more likely to suffer from flawed design elements, including a lack of scientific citations, condescending and cliched branding, and reductive assumptions about their users.[20] A separate study in 2016 found that only 5 percent of femtech apps provided users with referenced medical literature to support their health insights[21]—reinforcing the stereotype that women's health issues are somehow less medically significant than men's.

These problems occur when femtech companies lack a leadership team that understands, firsthand, the nuanced realities of women's health. They happen when companies prioritize marketability over medical accuracy, or when decision-makers don't think beyond their own assumptions about what "women's health" should look like. They result when companies build products *for* women, without taking the time to build them *with* women.

The best femtech companies—the ones earning real trust—don't just aim to capture a market. They aim to serve it. And that means ensuring that inclusivity and scientific integrity aren't just marketing slogans, but core values embedded in every stage of development. Women's health is vast, varied, and deeply personal. The founders who truly understand that are the ones who will shape the future of femtech the right way.

"Othering" Women

The consequences of failing to build an appropriate foundation for a femtech product are more than just poor design choices—they actively alienate the very users femtech claims to serve. When companies build products based on narrow assumptions about what a "typical" woman's health journey looks like, they don't just overlook those with different experiences; they tell them, intentionally or not, that they don't belong. This kind of exclusion isn't always obvious at first. It's often disguised as cheerful messaging, soft aesthetics, and seemingly harmless notifications—until a user like Zara* opens her femtech app one morning and finds herself staring at a happy little stork, delivering a message that couldn't be further from her reality.

Like most mornings, 26-year-old Zara woke up to the sound of her alarm, rubbed her eyes, and reached for her phone. She scrolled through her notifications—a few emails, a text, and her daily reminders. But one message made her stomach drop: "Congratulations, you're late!"

Zara's health tracker was alerting her that she was now 10 days late. When she tapped the notification, her app opened with a smattering of flowers, hearts, and a tiny stork, soaring happily across her screen with a bundle in its beak. Yes, Zara's period was late. But she wasn't pregnant. She never would be.

Weeks earlier, Zara had undergone a hysterectomy to stop her uterine cancer from spreading. She had barely begun to process her infertility, and until that moment, she hadn't even thought about missing a period. At first, she almost laughed—at least she'd never have to deal with the pain of menstruation again. But then the weight of it settled in. The bright, cheery stork suddenly felt like a cruel joke.

She closed the app, forcing herself to move on with her day. But the next morning, the notification was waiting for her again. And the next morning. She ignored it at first, swiping it away, and continued to log her other health metrics. But by the fourth day, she couldn't take the daily reminders anymore. She tapped into the app, stared at the stork one last time, and deleted her account.

Zara didn't quit because she disliked the app. She left because the app made it clear that someone like her—someone who could no longer conceive—wasn't part of its intended audience. The developers hadn't designed that smiling stork out of malice. But by assuming that every late period was cause for celebration—that a "normal" woman would desire a pregnancy—they had unintentionally alienated an entire population of women: those who couldn't or didn't want to get pregnant.

This is what happens when femtech companies don't consider the full spectrum of women's experiences. They don't just exclude certain users. They "other" them.

The term "othering" refers to the process of marginalizing people by defining them not by what they are, but by what they are not.[22] We've already discussed how the male-as-default approach in medicine has excluded women, but even within femtech—an industry created *for* women—the same exclusion happens in more subtle ways.

When a product is designed with a single type of user in mind, it creates an invisible divide: those who fit within the "standard" experience and those who do not. A one-size-fits-all jumpsuit makes anyone who can't fit feel like their body is defective and abnormal. For example, a pair of headphones that only works for one ear shape implies that any other anatomy is incorrect. Similarly, when a femtech app claims to serve all women but only includes women who are fertile, menstruating, or in heterosexual relationships, it sends a clear message: If you don't fit into our model of womanhood, this isn't for you.

What makes othering so damaging is how it normalizes exclusion over time. When certain characteristics become the assumed standard, anything outside of them becomes invisible. In femtech, this kind of unconscious bias can play out in both language and design. Sometimes it appears in the form of pastel-colored apps decorated with hearts and flowers, where health is treated as something lighthearted and feminine. Other times it's built into the very functionality of the product itself. Fitbit's first attempt at a menstrual tracker, for example, didn't allow users to input a period longer than 10 days.[23] Women with conditions like PCOS, endometriosis, or perimenopause—who often experience prolonged or irregular bleeding— found themselves unable to accurately track their cycles. Their experiences weren't accounted for, effectively rendering them invisible.

These oversights are not inevitable. They are the result of weak foundations—of leadership teams that fail to include diverse voices, of rushed development cycles that prioritize aesthetics over inclusivity, and of companies that don't take the time to test their products on a broad enough range of users. Femtech companies with strong foundations do it differently. They welcome diverse perspectives during the design and testing phases, ensuring that real users—not just assumed ones—shape the final product. They listen to feedback, adjust their messaging, and create tools that serve the full range of women's health experiences.

Identifying these strong, ethical companies requires looking beyond marketing hype. In the next section, I'll walk you through how to identify companies with strong foundations that have your best interests in mind.

Evaluating a Company's Foundation

A femtech company's foundation is rooted in its leadership, values, and approach to product development. A strong foundation is built on ethical leadership, scientific integrity, and a commitment to inclusivity. Evaluating a company's foundation helps determine whether it prioritizes medical accuracy, data security, and ethical business practices, or whether it's simply capitalizing on a growing market. By understanding how a femtech company is structured, and what it truly stands for, you can make informed decisions about which products deserve your trust. Here are five simple and effective steps you can take to evaluate a company's foundation.

Step 1: Investigate the Company's Leadership and Governance

The first step is to find out who is leading the company. The foundation of a femtech company starts at the top with its leadership. The individuals at the helm shape decision-making at every level, from research priorities and product design to marketing strategies and corporate policies. Their values and expertise influence not only how the company operates but also how it prioritizes user needs, medical accuracy, and ethical business practices. A company led by individuals with backgrounds in women's health, medical research, or ethical tech design is far more likely to create safe, effective, and inclusive products. On the other hand, a leadership team with little to no relevant experience in these areas may be more focused on capturing market share than making meaningful improvements in women's healthcare.

However, leadership isn't just about experience and credentials—it's also about representation. A homogeneous leadership team, whether in gender, race, or professional background, can create blind spots in product development and reinforce existing biases. A femtech company that claims to serve all women should have decision-makers who reflect the diversity of its user base. If the leadership team consists of a small, unrepresentative group, the products they develop are more likely to exclude, misunderstand, or oversimplify the wide range of women's health experiences.

To assess a company's leadership and governance, start by visiting the company's website and navigating to the "About Us," "Team," or "Leadership" page. Review the profiles of at least the top three executives and the founders. In early-stage startups, founders are often central to daily decision-making, but as companies grow, they may transition into advisory or board roles, shifting direct leadership to other executives. For each of the founders and the three most senior leadership officers (which, depending on the company's structure, may include the chief executive officer, chief financial officer, chief technology officer, chief legal officer, chief product officer), assess the following three questions.

First, what is their experience? A capable leadership team should include individuals with expertise in women's health, medical research, healthcare technology, ethical product design, or consumer advocacy. While not every executive needs direct experience in these fields, at least one senior decision-maker should have a deep understanding of the healthcare challenges the company is aiming to solve. A leadership team with no apparent connection to women's health, medicine, or technology raises red flags, because it may indicate an opportunistic rather than a mission-driven approach to the industry.

Another red flag is serial entrepreneurs. While business acumen is important, a founder who has built multiple companies in completely unrelated industries may be more focused on market trends than solving real healthcare problems. If the leadership team is composed primarily of individuals whose expertise lies in rapid startup growth, it raises concerns about their ability to develop a scientifically sound and ethically responsible product. For example, if a company's CEO previously founded a ride-sharing app, a cryptocurrency platform, and a meal kit service before launching a menstrual health startup, it's worth questioning whether the company is truly invested in advancing women's healthcare or simply capitalizing on femtech's rapid growth.

An effective femtech leader doesn't have to be a doctor or researcher, but they should demonstrate a clear and sustained commitment to improving healthcare outcomes, whether through prior work, partnerships with medical experts, or deep understanding of the challenges facing their users. It's a good sign when founders acknowledge their gaps in expertise and actively fill them by hiring professionals with backgrounds in women's health or bringing on an advisory board of experts.

Second, how diverse is the leadership team? A variety of perspectives ensures a company is more likely to consider a broad range of user experiences and avoid narrow, one-size-fits-all solutions. A lack of diversity, whether in terms of gender, race, socioeconomic background, or lived experience increases the risk of products that fail to address the real needs of varied populations. If a company's leadership is overwhelmingly white, male, or comes from similar backgrounds, it may indicate that women's health is being treated as a market opportunity rather than a priority.

Another warning sign is the lack of transparency. If a company does not publicly share information about its leadership team or avoids addressing diversity altogether, it may suggest that inclusivity is not a real priority. Leadership teams that feature women, people of color, LGBTQ+ individuals, and those with lived experience in the healthcare challenges they are trying to solve are most likely to develop products that are inclusive, medically relevant, and responsive to the unique needs of their user base. Another positive indicator is when a company actively collaborates with advocacy groups, medical professionals, and community organizations to ensure their solutions are accessible, effective, and relevant for all women.

Third, what is their track record? Past leadership decisions can indicate how the company will navigate challenges in the future. Research key executives and founders to see if they have a history of ethical decision-making, advocacy, or involvement in organizations that align with their mission. A quick Google search of the leaders' names alongside terms like "controversy," "scandal," or "unethical" can surface past misconduct or questionable business practices.

Additionally, look for patterns in leadership behavior. Has the leadership team demonstrated a long-term commitment to improving women's health, or have they moved between unrelated industries, hopping onto the femtech trend with no clear expertise or passion for the space? Do they have a track record of building ethical, user-centered products, or have they previously been involved in companies that prioritized profit over people? If a leader has launched a company that faced backlash for misleading claims, exploitative practices, or mishandling of user data, this is a strong indicator that the current venture may follow a similar path.

Further, examine whether the company's founders and executives have been recognized for their contributions to healthcare innovation or patient advocacy. Do they engage with research institutions, policymakers, or medical professionals to improve access to care? Do they perform community service in healthcare? A Google search of the leaders' names and terms like "advocacy," "community service," "pro bono," and "giving back" can provide a better sense of their philanthropic initiatives. A leader who actively participates in shaping the industry and giving back beyond their own company is more likely to be invested in long-term, meaningful change.

Finally, pay attention to how a company responds to criticism. Did the leaders acknowledge past mistakes and take measurable steps to improve, or did they deflect responsibility? Companies that listen to user feedback, admit missteps, and make genuine changes to better serve their audience are far more trustworthy than those that ignore complaints, delete negative reviews, or rely on superficial public relations statements to manage public perception. A solid foundation is built on accountability, and a company's track record—both of its leadership and its actions—reveals whether it is truly dedicated to advancing women's health.

Step 2: Read the Company's Mission and Vision Statements

Once you've investigated the company's leadership, the next step is to examine what the company stands for. A company's mission and vision statements reveal its core purpose, values, and long-term goals. These statements should express a clear, actionable commitment to advancing women's health.

Most companies include their mission and values on their website, typically under an "About Us" or "Mission" section. When reading these statements, look beyond vague promises or trendy buzzwords. A powerful mission statement will acknowledge specific challenges in women's health, advocate for underserved populations, or emphasize fairness, transparency, and inclusivity. Companies that build with intention make it clear what they're fighting for, whether it's better access to gynecological care, data privacy protections, or solutions for overlooked health conditions. Be cautious of mission statements that focus on "disrupting" the industry or making things "better" without explaining how. Innovation without a clear purpose often signals that a company is more focused on market dominance than on real healthcare impact.

If a femtech company doesn't have a mission or vision statement readily available, that's also a red flag. In that case, look at their press releases, marketing, and product descriptions to see if they align with ethical, research-backed business practices. A company that is committed to improving women's health will make its mission obvious—not just in a tagline, but in everything it does.

Step 3: Review Public Speaking and Thought Leadership

In today's world, CEOs and executives do more than just run companies— they act as public voices shaping industry narratives. Their speeches, interviews, and published insights provide valuable clues about their priorities, ethical stance, and level of expertise. This means that effective leaders don't just talk about their products—they talk about the larger systemic challenges women face in healthcare and advocate for meaningful change. They may participate in panel discussions, publish opinion pieces in medical or tech journals, collaborate with health professionals, or push for policy improvements that benefit users beyond their own company's bottom line.

Conversely, some leaders use public platforms to focus solely on business metrics, growth strategies, and investor appeal while avoiding discussions about the ethical and social implications of their work. If a CEO is constantly promoting "industry disruption" without mentioning health equity, women's health pain points, or underserved populations, it's a sign that the company may be more focused on market expansion than genuinely improving women's lives.

This is why the next step in assessing a company's leadership is to learn what the executives are speaking about. Most people won't have time to analyze all the materials a leader puts online. Instead, I recommend a simple search and skim approach. Your goal is to find proof these leaders have spoken publicly on the topics of women's health and that there are no major red flags in the results. Search for the company's founders and leaders using one or more of the following terms:

- [Name] women's health speaking
- [Name] diversity in healthcare
- [Name] speaking engagements
- [Name] keynote speech
- [Name] podcast interview
- [Name] thought leadership
- [Name] women's health interview

When reviewing the results, consider whether the leader's statements reflect a deep understanding of the issues they claim to be solving. Does the leader discuss women's health with nuance and insight or are they sticking to surface-level talking points? Do they acknowledge gaps in research and advocate for inclusivity, or do they focus only on their company's achievements? Thought leaders who meaningfully engage in these conversations are more likely to be invested in long-term progress rather than short-term gains. If your search doesn't return any results, that's a red flag.

Step 4: Investigate Advisory Boards and Consultants

Femtech companies don't operate in isolation—their strength comes from the expertise they bring in through their advisory boards and consultants. While full-time executives handle the company's day-to-day operations, advisory boards play a crucial role in shaping product development, guiding ethical considerations, and ensuring medical accuracy. This is especially important in the early stages of a company, when leadership may lack direct experience in women's health. A company's choice of advisors reflects not only its commitment to scientific and medical integrity but also its willingness to be held accountable by those with deep expertise in the field.

A well-structured femtech company should have advisors with backgrounds in women's health, medical research, bioethics, health technology, and/or regulatory affairs. You can often find these individuals listed on the company's website, usually under the "About Us," "Team," or "Advisory Board" section. Depending on the company's focus, a strong advisory board may include professionals such as OB/GYNs, endocrinologists, reproductive health researchers, data privacy specialists, and regulatory consultants who understand the complexities of health technology. It's a red flag if a company's advisory board lacks these voices or is composed mainly of business executives without medical or scientific backgrounds.

However, just because a company lists advisors on its website doesn't necessarily mean those individuals are actively shaping the company's direction. Some companies add high-profile names to their advisory boards purely for marketing appeal without actually engaging them in product development or decision-making. It's possible for a celebrity or high-profile individual to be listed as an advisory board member and never to have attended a board meeting. To assess whether an advisory board is truly contributing, look beyond the company's website. Search for the advisors' names alongside the company's name to see if they have participated in interviews, posted about their affiliation on social media, authored research papers related to the company's products, or spoken publicly about their involvement. If they appear to be figureheads with little visible engagement, that's a cause for concern.

If a company has no visible advisory board or medical consultants, that's another red flag. It suggests that leadership is either overconfident in their own expertise or unwilling to bring in external voices that might challenge their assumptions. In femtech, where health outcomes and personal data are on the line, strong advisory boards are not just a bonus—they are a necessity. A company that actively collaborates with respected experts and integrates their insights into product developments is far more likely to build a foundation of trust and credibility.

Step 5: Evaluate Marketing Materials for Insights into Company Leadership

The final step is to analyze the company's marketing materials. Marketing materials are more than just advertisements—they are a window into how a company perceives and engages with its audience. The language, imagery, and themes in social media campaigns, product descriptions, and promotional content reveal whether a company genuinely understands and respects the diversity of its users or whether it relies on outdated stereotypes and superficial branding.

Start by searching for the company on social media platforms and reviewing its website and digital content. Pay close attention to the imagery used. Does it showcase a diverse range of women—different ages, ethnicities, body types, and abilities? A company that values inclusivity will ensure that its marketing represents the broad spectrum of people who use its products. If the visuals primarily feature thin, young, conventionally attractive white women, it suggests a narrow and exclusionary perspective on women's health. A company that fails to acknowledge diversity in its marketing is likely to do the same in its product development.

Beyond imagery, the language a company uses speaks volumes about how it views its customers. Some companies overcomplicate their messaging, using highly technical jargon that makes their products inaccessible. Others take the opposite approach, using infantilizing or overly simplified language that underestimates the intelligence of their users. A potential red flag is marketing that relies on euphemisms or emojis instead of using correct medical terminology—such as referring to menstruation as "that time of the month" or using a banana emoji in place of anatomical terms. Companies that prioritize open, honest, and scientifically accurate communication show respect for their users and demonstrate a commitment to education and empowerment rather than just sales. The one caveat to this is that companies may be forced to use euphemisms or emojis on social media given the wide censorship of women's health and barriers to using medically correct language. However, if this occurs beyond the context of social media, consider it a red flag.

Additionally, look for patterns in the tone of a company's messaging. Does it encourage empowerment, education, and autonomy over personal health? Or does it lean heavily into patronizing phrases that reduce complex health concerns to casual, surface-level branding? Thoughtful, well-founded companies take the opportunity to educate their users, offering clear and reliable health information rather than relying solely on aesthetics and trendy marketing tactics.

Finally, examine whether the company's messaging excludes certain groups. Does the language assume all users are heterosexual and cisgender? Are LGBTQ+ individuals, nonbinary users, and women with disabilities acknowledged in any meaningful way? A femtech company that overlooks entire populations in its marketing materials is unlikely to have built products that truly serve their needs. True inclusivity isn't just about who appears in promotional images—it's reflected in the language, accessibility, and intentionality of the entire brand.

Founders who care about their company's mission strike a balance between aesthetics and accuracy, ensuring that their messaging reflects real-world health concerns. Look for companies that provide educational content—such as blog posts, infographics, or expert interviews—rather than relying solely on lifestyle-driven branding. A femtech company that invests in users' education demonstrates a deeper commitment to women's health beyond just selling a product.

Conclusion

The strongest femtech companies are those that prioritize women's health through their leadership choices, business practices, and user engagement. The foundation of a company determines whether it is genuinely working to improve healthcare or simply capitalizing on a growing industry. By critically evaluating a company's leadership, mission statement, public engagement, advisory boards, and marketing materials, you can identify the companies that are truly committed to inclusivity, medical integrity, and ethical innovation. As the industry grows, supporting companies with strong foundations will help shape a future where all women's health needs are respected.

10 | The SAFE Method

Equity

When Health Tech Fails the Women Who Need It Most

When Ama* first saw the ad for a new wearable health band, she felt like she had finally found something designed for her. The sleek, AI-powered wearable promised to track menstrual cycles, monitor stress levels, and predict potential hormone imbalances—all features that felt transformative for women's health at the time.

The marketing campaign was everywhere: Influencers were raving about it, glossy magazine ads declared it a game changer for women's wellness, and even doctors were cautiously optimistic about its potential. Finally, a piece of health-tech that wasn't just repurposed from a men's fitness tracker. Ama, like thousands of other women, eagerly preordered.

But within a few weeks of using it, something seemed off. The band frequently failed to detect her heart rate during workouts. Some mornings it would tell her she hadn't slept, despite the fact that she felt well-rested. The temperature tracker was wildly inconsistent, giving her erratic readings. At first she thought her device was defective. But when she researched online, she realized she wasn't alone.

Women with darker skin tones were reporting the same issues. The health band had been tested primarily on lighter-skinned women, and its optical sensors struggled with melanin-rich skin. The product's breakthrough health insights, it turned out, only worked accurately for some women—and for some not at all.

The company scrambled for damage control, issuing statements about "future updates" and promising improvements. But the damage was done. Trust was lost. The very people who could have benefited most from personalized health insights had been excluded from the start.

The "equity" portion of the SAFE method comes last, but not because it's the least important. It can be tempting to think of equity as a minor consideration, but in reality it's typically underestimated by those in the most represented groups. Straight, white, middle-class women of childbearing age might not be as concerned with equity as women who don't fit into those categories. But as consumers, it's on all of us to drive change toward more equitable products, services, and solutions.

Even as new medical innovations emerge today, some of them are still showing early signs of bias. For example, thermometers, pulse oximeters, and even x-ray machines are less accurate when used for patients with darker skin.[1] One study found that forehead thermometers were about 26 percent less accurate than oral thermometers in detecting fevers in Black women.[2] Similarly, pulse oximeters have been found to overestimate oxygen saturation in Black and Hispanic patients, leading to delays in care for conditions like COVID-19 and respiratory failure.[3] When new products like these are released without diverse population testing, they end up slowing down healthcare; they delay diagnoses, treatments, and improvement for illnesses and diseases.

The femtech revolution is not immune to the biases and inequities that plague so many growing industries. If we want to help femtech thrive, we must support not just the products that work for us, but the products that work for *everyone*, regardless of their size, shape, color, or location. On the other hand, if we allow inequities to persist in products designed to transform the women's health industry, we not only limit the impact and accuracy of solutions—we also risk leaving the most vulnerable populations behind.

It doesn't matter how well a product solves a problem if the people who need the solution can't reliably use or access it. Not only do these populations miss out on opportunities for early intervention, preventive care, and self-management of illnesses, but we also risk deepening existing health disparities and perpetuating cycles of poor outcomes. Without equitable access, the data collected and analyzed by digital health tools reflects only a privileged subset of the population, skewing research findings and enhancing biases in healthcare delivery. This means that if a product's not equitable, it's not a real solution. It's a diamond-studded Band-Aid.

Equity versus Equality: Why the Difference Matters

Femtech has been heralded as the great equalizer in women's health. But *equal* access to a product doesn't always mean *equitable* healthcare outcomes. The difference between equality and equity is the difference between making a health tool available and ensuring that it actually works for the women who need it most.

Take, for example, a newly launched AI-powered fertility tracker. If it is sold for $899, marketed primarily in the United States, and optimized for Apple devices, it is technically available to any woman who can afford it. That is equality. Every customer is given the same opportunity to purchase the product. But not every woman starts from the same place. A low-income woman without health insurance may be unable to justify the cost. A woman living in a rural area may not have a nearby retailer or reliable internet access to use the device's full features. A Black or South Asian woman may discover that the product's biometric sensors fail to measure her basal body temperature accurately because the technology was only tested on lighter skin tones. The product may be *available*, but it is not *accessible* to everyone in a meaningful way.

This is where equity comes in. While equality focuses on giving everyone the same thing, equity ensures that each person gets the support they need to achieve the same outcome. A truly equitable approach to femtech means designing devices to work across all populations and skin tones, pricing them in ways that allow for broader affordability, translating content into multiple languages, and ensuring they are compatible with various technological products and internet access levels. It means conducting clinical trials that include women of different ethnic backgrounds, income levels, and geographic locations, rather than relying on a narrow subset of users. The femtech industry cannot afford to make the same mistakes as traditional healthcare, where bias has long dictated who receives quality care and who is left behind. If femtech simply creates more tools that only serve the most privileged users, it isn't fixing the problem—it's repeating it with better branding.

Equity and Intersectionality in Women's Health

Equity in women's health is complex and multifaceted, shaped by economic, geographic, cultural, racial, and identity-based barriers. These categories don't fully capture all challenges women face in accessing healthcare, but they provide a broad framework for assessing whether new femtech solutions are truly equitable. Understanding these key aspects of equity can help ensure you find solutions that provide benefits for the widest possible audience. Let's look at each component of equity in more depth.

Economic equity addresses the financial barriers that prevent women from accessing healthcare or using health technologies. Affordability is one of the biggest roadblocks, as many digital health tools require subscriptions, out-of-pocket purchases, or access to private healthcare. Women with lower incomes, those without insurance, and those in marginalized communities often cannot afford cutting-edge fertility monitors, hormone tracking devices, or telehealth services. Economic equity means creating financial models that allow more women to benefit from these innovations, whether through subsidized options, tiered pricing, or partnerships with community health programs. When femtech products include free or low-cost options for underserved communities, they embody economic equity in action.

Geographic equity ensures that women living in rural or remote areas have the same access to healthcare innovations as those in urban centers. Where a woman lives directly impacts her ability to see a doctor, visit a specialist, or even access a pharmacy. Geographic disparities arise when digital health tools assume users have high-speed internet access or live near healthcare providers. Women in rural areas often travel long distances for reproductive care, face physician shortages, or lack broadband connectivity. Femtech solutions that prioritize geographic equity take these barriers into account by designing for low-bandwidth connections, offering offline modes for apps, deploying mobile health services, and integrating with community clinics.

Cultural equity focuses on ensuring that healthcare solutions are respectful, inclusive, and responsive to the diverse beliefs, practices, and backgrounds. Cultural expectations can shape how women approach healthcare, whether due to religious beliefs, family traditions, or community norms. A woman from a culture where menstrual health is taboo may feel uncomfortable using a period-tracking app with overtly sexualized branding, while another may require a pregnancy care app that accommodates dietary restrictions based on religious guidelines.

Language is another crucial factor in cultural equity. Some femtech platforms are available only in English, automatically excluding non-English speakers. Recent estimates suggest that almost 66 million people in the United States—around 22 percent of the population—speaks a language other than English at home.[4] A culturally equitable approach means offering health tools in multiple languages, providing education tailored to different communities, and ensuring that health advice is not one-size-fits-all.

Racial equity acknowledges that healthcare access, treatment, and outcomes differ dramatically across racial groups. Women of color are disproportionately affected by systemic biases in medicine, leading to higher maternal mortality rates, greater misdiagnosis risks, and lower-quality care. Racial inequities become apparent when products fail to consider the needs of diverse populations. Health monitoring wearables that cannot accurately detect heart rates or oxygen levels in women with darker skin tones are not just technological flaws—they are failures of racial equity. Similarly, when AI-driven health tools rely on datasets primarily trained on white populations, their predictive models become less effective for women of color, resulting in racial inequity. True racial equity means ensuring that research trials include diverse participants, that algorithms are trained on a wide range of data, and that technology works effectively across all racial and ethnic groups.

Finally, sexual orientation and gender identity equity addresses the unique health barriers faced by LGBTQ+ individuals. Traditional definitions of women's health often exclude people who do not fit within a narrow, cisgender framework. Many health apps, wearable devices, and digital services default to binary gender categories, leaving transgender and nonbinary people with little guidance on how a product applies to them. LGBTQ+ individuals frequently experience discrimination in healthcare settings, making them less likely to seek medical care and more hesitant to share personal health data with femtech companies. A truly equitable approach to femtech means designing tools that are inclusive, affirming, and adaptable to different identities. This could mean allowing users to customize app settings to reflect their gender identity, providing hormone tracking options that include transgender health needs, or ensuring that interfaces are welcoming to all users. Small design choices can make the difference between an inclusive product and one that alienates entire groups of users.

These facets of equity do not exist in isolation. A woman might simultaneously face economic, racial, and gender identity inequities, and the barriers she encounters are compounded by these overlapping challenges. A low-income Latina woman living in a rural area may struggle with affordability, language barriers, internet access, and medical bias all at once. If a femtech product is not designed with multiple layers of equity in mind, it will fail her. This is why intersectionality is critical in health technology design—focusing on just one aspect of equity is not enough.

The most effective way to achieve true equity in femtech is to design and use solutions that serve the most marginalized groups first. When a product is built for the most vulnerable users, it naturally becomes more accessible for everyone. An app with an offline mode benefits women in rural areas, but it also helps travelers, those with unreliable Wi-Fi, and anyone who prefers to save mobile data. A telehealth service that offers multilingual support helps non-English speakers, but it also benefits bilingual families and global users. An interface that avoids hyperfeminized imagery or rigid gender markers makes healthcare more inclusive for transgender and nonbinary users but it also serves cisgender women who don't want their reproductive health reduced to pink flowers and baby emojis.

Equity in femtech is not about making products available to everyone in the same way—it's about making them usable, effective, and accessible for all women, regardless of their background, identity, or circumstances. The goal is not just to close gaps in healthcare but to ensure that technology works for the people who need it most. If we don't demand equity from the femtech products we use, we risk stalling the progress of women's health by turning a blind eye to those populations the medical system has historically ignored. It's up to individuals with the most privilege to use their influence and ensure no woman is left behind in the future of healthcare.

Digital Health Equity

When the five facets of equity—economic, geographic, cultural, racial, and identity-based—come together in the medical industry, they form what's known as digital health equity. Digital health equity is the idea that all people, regardless of income, location, language, or digital literacy, should have access to and benefit from digital health technologies. It's not a bonus feature of innovation; it's a fundamental requirement for transforming healthcare.

Nowhere is this more critical than in femtech. A substantial number of women's health innovations rely on digital platforms, wearable devices, mobile apps, and AI-driven data analysis. If women can't access these technologies, they're shut out from the very advancements designed to improve their health.

There are three ways to test for digital health equity: access, usability, and meaningful engagement. For a femtech product to truly serve its users, women must be able to find it (access), understand how to use it (usability), and feel confident and empowered enough to keep using it (meaningful engagement). If a product fails at any of these levels, it isn't a solution—it's just another barrier disguised as innovation.

Access: Finding Femtech

Access is the foundation of equity in femtech. It doesn't matter how advanced or groundbreaking a product is—if women can't find it, afford it, or confidently use it, then it's not truly serving them. Equity in access means more than just making a product available; it means ensuring that all women can obtain it. In theory, this should be a simple problem to solve—most industries rely on digital advertising, influencers, and retail partnerships to reach their target audiences. But femtech currently faces significant barriers that disproportionately exclude women who are already underserved in healthcare.

One of the biggest barriers to access is visibility. Women's health products, particularly those related to menstruation, sexual health, and menopause, face persistent censorship in digital spaces. When companies can't advertise their products, women—especially those outside of major cities or without disposable income for trial and error—lose the opportunity to discover and benefit from new solutions. The result is a widening health gap, where only the most well-connected or privileged consumers have access to cutting-edge femtech.

The issue isn't just limited to digital spaces. Retail gatekeeping plays a major role in restricting who can access femtech solutions. Pharmacies, big-box retailers, and supermarkets often hesitate to stock women's health products, particularly those related to sexual wellness or reproductive care. Emergency contraception, for example, remains locked behind pharmacy counters in some locations, requiring women to ask for it—an added step that can create discomfort, delays, or even prevent access altogether. The same limitations affect newer femtech products. If menstrual health innovations, menopause solutions, or pelvic floor trainers aren't available in mainstream stores, then only the women who are already aware of these products and comfortable shopping online will have access to them. Women without reliable internet access, credit cards, or trust in online shopping are left behind. Similarly, women who need solutions quickly are unable to obtain them in a timely manner. True equity means making sure these products are available where women are already shopping, not just in exclusive digital storefronts.

But availability means nothing without affordability. This is one of the most significant ways femtech can fail at equity. Some femtech products are priced as luxury items, making them accessible only to high-income consumers. A woman with a high-paying corporate job might be able to afford a $500 fertility tracker or a $250 pelvic floor device without hesitation, but a single mother working two jobs may not have the same flexibility, even if she has the exact same health needs. Low-income women, uninsured women, and those who rely on public healthcare systems are often the ones who would benefit most from femtech innovations, but if those products are financially out of reach, they are not truly solutions—they are privileges.

The lack of insurance coverage for some femtech products further deepens these inequities. If a wearable that tracks heart health isn't eligible for insurance reimbursement, only the wealthiest consumers will be able to incorporate it into their healthcare routine. The same goes for telehealth services that charge out-of-pocket fees. If a woman must choose between paying for a virtual gynecology consultation or covering groceries for the week, the decision is clear, and her health takes the hit. True equity in access means ensuring that cost is not a barrier to care by making more femtech products affordable, covered by insurance, or available through community health or discount programs.

Femtech has the potential to close healthcare gaps, but without equitable access, it risks widening them instead. To achieve true equity, femtech companies must do more than just make their products available; they must actively break down the barriers that prevent underserved women from finding and using them. This means fighting for visibility in retail spaces, designing branding that is clear and inclusive, and ensuring affordability so that all women can benefit from the future of digital health.

Usability: Understanding Femtech Features

Usability is just as critical to equitable access as affordability and visibility. A femtech product may be available to all women, but if they can't understand how to use it or if the design makes it inaccessible to certain groups, it still fails at equity. A well-intentioned innovation can become functionally useless if it doesn't meet the needs of the people it was meant to serve.

For technology to be accessible, it must be intuitive. It should not require a medical degree or hours of troubleshooting for women to understand how to use it (assuming the product is not an advanced medical device that requires clinician handling). If a femtech company develops an app to help women track menopause symptoms, but the interface is cluttered with confusing charts, clinical terminology, and cryptic data points, it will push women away rather than empower them. Many health apps fail not because they lack useful features, but because they assume that their users are already health-tech experts.

Equity in usability also means designing for the *actual* users, not just the assumed ones. Many femtech companies market their products toward younger, tech-savvy consumers, yet fail to account for the fact that older women, disabled women, and non-native English speakers also need access to these solutions. For example, a longevity app that assumes all users are comfortable navigating complex digital interfaces will alienate older consumers who are unfamiliar with digital technology. Similarly, a wearable fertility tracker that requires frequent manual input or difficult adjustments may work for a young woman familiar with fitness gadgets, but it may not be practical for someone with arthritis or dexterity challenges.

True equity in femtech means designing solutions that are functionally diverse and widely usable. A product that is difficult to navigate, not adaptable to different users' needs, or too complex is just as inaccessible as one with a price tag that's too high. The best femtech products meet women where they are—with interfaces that are clear, features that are adaptable, and designs that empower rather than frustrate. When femtech prioritizes usability for all women, it moves from being an exclusive tool for a select few to a true force for equity in healthcare.

Meaningful Engagement: Confidently Using Femtech

Finally, equity in femtech isn't just about making products available or easy to use—it's about ensuring that women actually *want* to use them. The best femtech solutions don't just function well; they create an experience that makes women feel empowered, understood, and valued in their healthcare journeys. Meaningful engagement happens when a woman doesn't just use a product because she has to or because it's the only app on the market, but because it actively improves her well-being, deepens her understanding of her body, and makes her feel seen.

For femtech to be equitable, it must create a space where every woman, regardless of her background, feels like she belongs. If a woman sees a product that doesn't reflect her experiences or needs, she is far less likely to engage with it—no matter how innovative it may be. A menstrual tracking app that assumes all users have 28-day cycles alienates the millions of women with irregular periods, PCOS, or perimenopause. A fertility app that only presents heterosexual conception paths erases the experiences of LGBTQ+ couples and single parents by choice. A tele-health platform that offers an incredible range of services but lacks cultur-ally competent doctors may leave BIPOC women feeling unheard and hesitant to trust the care they receive.

When a woman finds a femtech solution that acknowledges and respects her identity and lived experiences, she is far more likely to engage with it long-term. Not only that, but she is more likely to explore other digital health tools, expanding her engagement with technology-driven healthcare solutions. Women who feel seen and heard by femtech companies are also more likely to advocate for those products, driving word-of-mouth adop-tion and normalizing conversations around women's health. When women are comfortable sharing their data with femtech platforms, they contribute to better research, improved AI models, and more inclusive innovations—all of which help future generations of users.

Evaluating Equity in Femtech Products

Throughout this chapter, we've seen how equitable practices in femtech aren't just a moral imperative—they are a prerequisite for building trust. This trust is more than a marketing advantage; it's the foundation for repair-ing centuries of medical neglect, bias, and systemic exclusion that have fos-tered deep distrust among marginalized communities. Femtech, however, has a rare opportunity to change this narrative. By prioritizing equity, trans-parency, and accessibility in its solutions, femtech can begin to bridge the gap between these communities and the broader healthcare system, creating renewed confidence in women's health innovation.

But equity doesn't happen by accident. It requires conscious effort—from both companies and consumers. If we want femtech innovators to keep equity at the forefront of their growth strategies, we must be inten-tional with our dollars, our data, and our support. The products and ser-vices we choose to invest in should demonstrate a true commitment to inclusion, addressing health disparities head-on rather than reinforcing existing barriers. We should champion companies that design with the needs of *all* women in mind, not just those who already have the easiest access to healthcare.

When evaluating femtech companies, we should ask ourselves whether they are committed to real, measurable change or whether they are simply applying a uniform approach across women's health. Even if a product works for you, it's important to consider whether the company behind it is pushing the industry forward or simply maintaining the status quo. As you work to evaluate the final step of the SAFE method, here are three quick and easy steps you can take to determine whether a company prioritizes equity.

Step 1: Check the Product's Features for Inclusivity

The first and most direct way to assess a femtech company's commitment to equity is by looking at the product itself. An inclusive femtech solution should reflect an understanding of the diverse experiences, identities, and needs of its users. An equitable product will provide flexible, customizable features that adapt to different health conditions, lifestyles, and accessibility needs.

If you've already purchased or downloaded a femtech app, start by exploring the product's interface and functionality. An inclusive product will allow users to tailor or customize their experience. If a device forces users into rigid categories or arbitrarily limits certain data inputs, it is failing to serve the full spectrum of experiences in women's health. Tracking features should allow for irregular data input, giving users the ability to log outlier symptoms, changes due to chronic illness, or hormonal fluctuations caused by medications. Having an open notes section, the ability to toggle data points on or off, and options for personalized reminders helps ensure that the product is adaptable rather than restrictive.

Femtech products should also account for the diverse ways women engage with technology based on their language, culture, and physical abilities. Language accessibility is a critical factor. Check whether the app offers multilingual support, culturally relevant health recommendations, or customer assistance in multiple languages. If so, this is a green flag. At the same time, accessibility for users with disabilities is just as essential. Examine whether the app includes voice commands, screen reader compatibility, high-contrast visuals, and alternative text for images—all of which help make digital health tools usable for individuals with visual, auditory, or motor impairments. If so, the app is demonstrating a commitment to equity.

Step 2: Check the Website for Diversified Representation and Affordability

A company's commitment to equity goes beyond the features built into its products. It's reflected in whom they design for and how they ensure accessibility. A company that prioritizes inclusivity will integrate both representation and affordability into its core business strategy. If a product is designed in a way that only serves a narrow, privileged demographic—whether through exclusive branding, selective testimonials, or high-cost barriers—it's not breaking down healthcare disparities; it's reinforcing them.

Start by looking at whom the company showcases in its imagery, language, and testimonials. An inclusive femtech company will reflect the full spectrum of real-world users—women of different races, body types, abilities, and gender identities. If a product claims it is designed for all women but is only visually marketed to young, white, able-bodied, cisgender women, that's a disconnect. Representation matters because it signals whom the company is designing for. If diverse voices and experiences aren't reflected in marketing materials, it raises a question: Are those same groups being ignored in product development as well?

Beyond seeing who is represented, skim through the company's website to see how it talks about its users. An equitable company will use inclusive, non-stigmatizing language—avoiding assumptions about gender, sexuality, or reproductive goals. Consider whether the company acknowledges non-binary users, provides language options beyond English, and describes medical conditions in a way that is respectful and empowering across cultures. Language that excludes or stereotypes is a sign that a company may not be genuinely invested in serving all women equitably.

Representation alone, however, is not enough. A femtech product may look inclusive on the surface while still being financially inaccessible. If a company claims to serve all women but only offers high-priced, out-of-pocket solutions, it is excluding low-income users. To assess whether a company is prioritizing economic accessibility, look at the pricing models on its website. If a company offers a free version of the app, sliding-scale pricing, payment plans, or subscription tiers for different income levels, that's a green flag. Similarly, it's a green flag if the company is working to get its product covered by insurance, Medicaid, and public health programs.

Another marker of financial accessibility is whether the company engages with community health programs. Some companies partner with nonprofits, public health initiatives, or women's clinics to distribute products at reduced costs—or even for free—to underserved populations. Others provide discounts to students, low-income individuals, or those using government assistance programs. These initiatives demonstrate that a company isn't just selling a product but is invested in making healthcare solutions available to those who need them most.

Finally, testimonials and reviews can provide insight into who is actually using the product. A diverse range of user feedback—from people of different races, ages, income levels, and geographic locations—suggests that a product is reaching a broad audience. If reviews overwhelmingly come from one specific type of user, it may indicate that the company's reach is limited to a privileged demographic. Additionally, be wary of testimonials or reviews that sound overly polished and inauthentic. If a testimonial sounds generic, is from an influencer, or fails to showcase real-world usage of the device, that is a red flag.

Step 3: Assess the Company's Advocacy and Industry Influence

A femtech company's commitment to digital health equity must extend beyond its own products. Femtech companies should be actively working to advance equity across the entire women's health industry. An equitable company will advocate for policy changes, industry-wide improvement, and systemic reforms that make healthcare more accessible and inclusive for all women, not just its customers.

One way to evaluate this is by looking at whether the company supports or advocates for broader healthcare equity initiatives. Does it support legislative efforts that improve reproductive rights, maternal health, or access to affordable care? Does it participate in industry discussions on equity, inclusion, and accessibility in women's health? Does it sponsor events that promote these same objectives? Companies that value equity often collaborate with public health organizations, have a presence at industry conferences, or contribute to research on gender health disparities.

Additionally, look at whether the company supports regulatory changes that benefit marginalized groups. Some femtech companies actively push for better insurance coverage of digital health tools, increased funding for women's health research, or expanded access to telehealth services in rural and low-income communities. A company that is silent on major health equity issues may not be as committed as it claims.

Another indicator is whether the company partners with global health initiatives or offers its products in developing nations. Equity isn't just about serving customers in high-income countries—it's about ensuring women in lower-income regions also benefit from innovation. Some companies donate technology to underserved areas, collaborate with international health organizations, or develop versions of their products that are accessible in regions with limited medical infrastructure. If a femtech company only operates in wealthier countries and makes no effort to expand access globally, its commitment to equity may be limited.

To assess a company's industry influence and advocacy, check its press releases, blog posts, or interviews with its leadership team. Companies that are actively working toward systemic equity will talk about these efforts publicly. They will participate in panels, write about healthcare disparities, and engage in conversations that push the industry forward.

In addition to reviewing the materials on the company's website, consider running the following Google searches:

- [Company Name] women's health equity
- [Company Name] healthcare policy
- [Company Name] equity pledge
- [Company Name] women's health sponsorship
- [Company Name] low-income program
- [Company Name] cultural competency

Finally, consider following the company on social media. Companies will regularly post about their new partnerships, expansions, programs, benefits, speaking opportunities, and sponsorships. Follow the company's social media channels to see what conversations it engages in with its broader community.

Conclusion

As consumers, we play a powerful role in shaping the future of femtech. The companies we support—through our purchases, our engagement, and our recommendations—determine which businesses succeed, which innovations gain traction, and which standards become the industry norm. By making informed decisions about where we invest our dollars and data, we can help ensure that femtech companies prioritize equity, accessibility, and inclusion. Supporting businesses that uphold the SAFE tenets pushes the entire industry forward for all women.

To see real, lasting change in women's healthcare, we must choose to support companies that are actively working to eliminate barriers to access. The future of femtech isn't just about innovation—it's about who that innovation serves. By holding companies accountable and choosing solutions that prioritize equity, we can help build a healthcare system that empowers every woman, everywhere.

The Future of Women's Health and Femtech

11 | Overcoming Medical Dismissal

How Femtech
Strengthens Your Case

The Woman Who Refused to Be Ignored

Sophia* sat at her kitchen table, her laptop open, phone beside her, and a pile of printed reports spread out in front of her. She took a deep breath and ran her fingers over the neatly stapled pages—the symptom logs, the cycle-tracking charts, the screenshots from her smartwatch app showing spikes in her heart rate, and the at-home lab results that suggested something was off with her hormone levels.

Tomorrow morning, she had a doctor's appointment.

She had been there before—too many times. The last three doctors she had seen all told her the same thing. Her symptoms—months of crushing fatigue, dizzy spells so intense she had nearly passed out in public, and a menstrual cycle that had become wildly unpredictable—were nothing to worry about. One doctor said it was stress. Another suggested she try eliminating caffeine. The last one had barely looked up from his clipboard before telling her it was just part of being a woman.

But Sophia *knew* this wasn't normal.

The first few times she had gone to the doctor, she had simply described her symptoms. She sat there, hands folded in her lap, trying to be the kind of patient who was easy to deal with—concise, agreeable, understanding. And each time, she had left the office feeling smaller, unheard, and no closer to answers. But now, things were different.

She had spent the past four months collecting hard data, and she wasn't going to walk into that office tomorrow with vague complaints and a desperate hope that this doctor might finally take her seriously. She was walking in with *proof*.

Sophia reached for her symptom-tracking app, scrolling through the notes she had taken. She had recorded everything—when her fatigue was the worst, how often she felt dizzy, the exact days her period started and ended, and the unusual shifts in her body temperature throughout her cycle. She tracked her heart rate fluctuations using her smartwatch, noticing that it spiked every time she went from sitting to standing, something she now suspected could indicate POTS (postural orthostatic tachycardia syndrome), a condition she had never even heard of until she started digging into her own health.

She had also taken an at-home hormone test, skeptical at first, but when her results had come back showing low progesterone and signs of estrogen dominance, she knew she had something real to bring to the table. It wasn't just *I feel off*. It was *Here is measurable evidence that something is not right with my body.*

Sophia picked up her pen and underlined three sentences in her notes.

- My cycle has increased from 32 days to 50 days over the last four months, with no clear explanation.
- I experience a 30+ BPM heart rate increase when I stand, accompanied by dizziness.
- My hormone panel shows low progesterone and high estrogen, which could indicate a hormonal imbalance that needs further investigation.

She exhaled. This time, she wouldn't be brushed off. She had seen how easily doctors dismissed women who came in with "I don't feel right" and no concrete evidence to back up their concerns. She had been one of those women before. Tomorrow she was going in with facts, patterns, and data that couldn't be ignored. And if this doctor tried to tell her once again that this was "just stress"?

Then she was ready to fight for the care she deserved.

Taking Control of the Conversation

Women's symptoms are dismissed at alarming rates. Studies show that women in pain are less likely than men to receive adequate treatment, their symptoms often minimized as normal, exaggerated, or purely psychological. As a result, many women spend years misdiagnosed—or not diagnosed at all—left searching for answers in a medical system that repeatedly overlooks them.

Thankfully, the pattern of dismissal is beginning to change. Femtech is giving women the tools to track their health in ways that were once impossible. By identifying patterns, spotting red flags, and collecting objective evidence, women can now walk into a doctor's office with measurable data rather than vague complaints. Yet despite this progress, a significant challenge remains: Most doctors are not trained to interpret data from femtech devices, and many reject it outright.

More than 7 out of 10 clinicians have admitted they are inundated with more data than they can effectively analyze, leading to what they describe as data overload.[1] Many acknowledge uncertainty about how to integrate data from wearables and consumer health technology into patient care plans, with some even expressing intimidation at the sheer volume of information these devices produce. In fact, 94 percent of surveyed clinicians reported feeling overwhelmed by the influx of data from apps and wearables, often questioning its reliability and clinical usefulness.[2] This disconnect between technological advancement and medical practice has left many patients struggling to bridge the gap between the insights they gain from femtech and the recognition they seek from their doctors.

This is why simply bringing femtech data to a medical appointment isn't enough. It's not just about *having* information—it's about knowing how to present it effectively, how to push back when dismissed, and how to demand action. To do this, you need to approach your appointment with the same level of preparation and strategy that a lawyer would use when presenting a case—structured, evidence-based, and impossible to ignore. You can't just hope that a doctor will listen; you must be prepared to *make* them listen.

Prepare Like a Lawyer, Not a Patient

Walking into a doctor's office as a woman with unexplained symptoms can feel like stepping into a courtroom where you're expected to defend your own health concerns. Too often, doctors—especially those unfamiliar with femtech—default to skepticism, downplaying symptoms, or dismissing consumer-collected data as unreliable. To counter this, you need to prepare like a lawyer building a case. That means structuring your health data in a way that mirrors clinical reasoning, so that your doctor has no choice but to take it seriously.

Step 1: Define Your Chief Complaint

Doctors are trained to diagnose conditions by identifying a chief complaint—the primary health issue that requires medical attention. This is the foundation of your visit, and how you frame it can significantly impact how your doctor approaches your case. Many patients make the mistake of presenting a scattered list of symptoms without a clear central issue, which can lead to confusion, dismissal, or a lack of focused investigation.

Sophia had tried the laundry list approach with her doctors before. She had listed every symptom she experienced over the past six months—exhaustion, dizziness, irregular cycles, brain fog, and unpredictable heart rate spikes—and each time, her doctors had looked overwhelmed and disinterested. The doctors often nodded absentmindedly, jotting down a few notes before attributing her symptoms to stress. This time, to get the answers she needed, Sophia was going to be more precise.

Instead of listing every discomfort she had experienced in the past few months, Sophia sat down with her symptom logs and anchored her visit around her central problem that tied everything together. She thought about how her dizziness and fatigue were her most debilitating symptoms—the ones that affected her daily life the most. While her cycle changes and heart rate spikes were important, they were supporting symptoms rather than the core issue. Centering her visit around her two most pressing symptoms would allow doctors to assess her case methodically rather than as a collection of unrelated complaints.

As a result, Sophia revised how she would explain her concerns. She moved away from a laundry list of symptoms and toward a structured statement centered on her primary issues while still acknowledging the broader impact her secondary symptoms had on her health. Instead of saying, "I feel exhausted all the time, my heart sometimes races, my cycles are weird, I can't sleep, I get dizzy, and my skin is breaking out," Sophia refined her statement to: "For the past four months, I have been experiencing increasing fatigue and frequent dizziness, along with a lesser concern of irregular menstrual cycles and a fluctuating heart rate. These symptoms have progressively worsened and are now affecting my ability to function in daily life."

This revised statement did three important things:

- It clearly defined a timeline (four months), which helped Sophia's doctor assess whether this was a chronic issue.
- It prioritized the most concerning symptoms (fatigue and dizziness), making it easier for the doctor to focus on potential underlying causes.
- It established the impact on Sophia's quality of life, reinforcing that this was a significant medical issue, not a minor inconvenience.

Once Sophia established her chief complaint, she made sure to organize her supporting symptoms and femtech data in a way that strengthened her case. She planned to back her statement up with:

- Cycle-tracking data showing increased cycle length and irregular ovulation patterns
- Sleep-tracking data indicating a decline in sleep quality and increased nighttime awakenings
- Heart rate variability showing an increase in resting heart rate, which could correlate with stress or hormonal imbalance
- At-home hormone test results that indicated low progesterone or high cortisol levels

After compiling and structuring her data, Sophia felt more confident. The key was keeping her chief complaint focused and succinct and using her femtech data to reinforce her concerns. This approach made it harder for the doctors to dismiss Sophia's concerns, as they were presented in a way that aligned with medical reasoning.

You should approach your medical care in the same manner as Sophia. Identify your most pressing symptoms or concerns—your chief complaint—and use your femtech data as objective supporting evidence. Define the timeline during which your symptoms have occurred and be prepared to show or state the impact your symptoms have had on your life. Develop a clear one-sentence statement with this information that you can quickly memorize and recite to your healthcare provider. This will keep you focused and on target when you enter your appointment and prevent you from falling back into the laundry list method if you get distracted or nervous during the appointment.

Step 2: Translate Your Symptoms into Measurable Patterns

Doctors are trained to analyze objective data—measurable changes in health markers—rather than rely solely on a patient's description of how they feel. While your personal experience is valid and important, some doctors are hesitant to act based on subjective symptoms alone. This is where femtech gives you a powerful advantage. It allows you to track and document measurable patterns over time, transforming subjective experiences into data-backed trends that are harder to dismiss. The key to making this information effective is organization and presentation.

In previous appointments, Sophia had tried to explain her symptoms verbally, using phrases like "I just don't feel like myself," or "something is off, but I don't know what." She had seen the way doctors' faces changed when she said that—the way their expressions shifted from concern to polite dismissal. She had learned the hard way that doctors prefer objective data, not just subjective descriptions of how patients feel. While her personal experience was valid, she knew that many doctors hesitated to treat her based on how she *felt* unless there was measurable evidence to support it. This time, Sophia was determined to show her doctor objective patterns and trends over time to ensure she was taken seriously.

The first step in translating symptoms into patterns is maintaining consistent records. Whether you're using a cycle-tracking app, a wearable device, or a symptom journal, logging your health concerns systematically will allow you to identify trends that might otherwise go unnoticed. Instead of trying to recall from memory when your symptoms began or how frequently they occur, you will have clear, timestamped data to reference. Before your appointment, take time to review your records and identify the most significant changes or trends that align with your concerns. If your energy levels have declined over the past six months, note whether this decline is steady or occurs in specific phases of your cycle. If your heart rate has increased, determine whether the spike occurs at certain times of the day or in response to specific activities. These details will make your case stronger and more structured when speaking with your doctor—especially since most patients get less than 20 minutes total with their doctor during a visit.

Before her appointment, Sophia did just this. She sat down with her phone and journal and reviewed the trends she had logged over the past four months, hoping to translate her symptoms into concrete, trackable evidence. She identified three key questions that would help frame her case:

- When did my symptoms start?
- How frequently do they occur?
- How have they changed over time?

With these questions in mind, she went back through her cycle-tracking app, sleep data, and wearable metrics to pull out the most relevant trends. Her cycle-tracking app showed that over the last four months, her periods had gone from being 32 days to being wildly unpredictable—one cycle lasting 50 days, another just 21. Ovulation was inconsistent, and her premenstrual symptoms had worsened. Her wearable sleep tracker showed that her deep sleep had declined from an average of 1.5 hours per night to just 30 minutes. She also logged frequent nighttime awakenings, which correlated with her rising fatigue. Her heart rate data revealed an unexpected pattern—her resting heart rate had increased by 10 beats per minute over the last three months, and she consistently experienced a 30+ BPM spike when moving from sitting to standing. Her at-home hormone test results also confirmed that her progesterone was low, and her estrogen was unusually high.

She exhaled. Seeing it all laid out like this, she felt a sense of confidence. This was objective proof that her body was experiencing real changes. She hoped this level of preparation would make all the difference. Instead of relying on memory or vague descriptions, she now had a clear, structured picture of her health—one that showed undeniable shifts over time. Armed with this information, she felt more in control of the upcoming conversation, hopeful that this data would force her doctor to take her concerns seriously.

Like Sophia, you can turn your symptoms into measurable patterns by tracking them consistently and focusing on key data points. Choose your tracking methods—for example, apps, wearables, journals, spreadsheets, at-home testing—and use them consistently. This will make it easier to identify trends and discrepancies. Focus on logging measurable factors that align with your concerns rather than trying to track everything. This will give you a clearer, more digestible picture that you can present to your doctor. Once you have a few months of data, review it and ask yourself when your symptoms started, how frequently they occur, and whether they have changed over time. These connections will help your doctor see the bigger picture and allow you to confidently and concisely explain your concerns during an appointment. By translating your symptoms into measurable patterns, you'll be able to transform your personal experience into medical evidence that your doctor will take seriously.

Step 3: Create and Print a One-Page Summary of Your Findings

While identifying and translating your symptoms and supporting data into a cohesive argument is an important step, it's not enough. You must present the information to your doctor in a way that is persuasive and easily digestible. An effective way to do this is to summarize your findings in a succinct one-pager that you can hand your clinician during the appointment.

Raw data alone can be overwhelming, and most clinicians won't have the time or interest to sift through app screens filled with numbers. This is particularly true if the doctor is not familiar with the app's interface or if the doctor doesn't know how to locate and move between different data sources on the app. There's also a general level of discomfort associated with reviewing data on a patient's phone, where personal notifications, texts, and emails may pop up during the review. However, most doctors *are* accustomed to reviewing printed lab reports or patient charts, so presenting your tracked data in a similar format increases the likelihood that they will engage with it.

Given this, it's important to create a one-page summary that you can hand your doctor. Before your visit, compile your findings into a clear, easy-to-read document that outlines your chief complaint (a one- or two-sentence statement of your main concern), a timeline of symptom progression (when symptoms began, how they have progressed, and any patterns you've observed), a summary of your femtech or health data (this can include short tables or bullet points with your key data and metrics), at-home test results (if applicable), and requests for next steps (including any specific tests or referrals you believe are warranted based on your data). If possible, print out graphs or charts from your apps, as visual representations of trends can be even more compelling. The goal is to present your information in a way that supports your chief complaint and makes it easy for your doctor to recognize potential red flags.

When you enter your appointment, hand this summary to your doctor and frame it as a tool to help streamline the appointment. For example, you could say, "I know we have limited time, so I put together a summary of my symptoms and tracked data to make it easier to review. I'd like to go over these findings and discuss next steps." This not only demonstrates that you have done your research but also shifts the conversation toward objective review rather than subjective dismissal.

Sophia took these exact steps. Once she had the data before her, she compiled her information into an easy-to-digest structured summary:

- Chief Complaint: Fatigue and dizziness
- Symptom Onset: Six months ago
- Fatigue & Sleep Issues: Deep sleep dropped from 1.5 hours to 30 minutes per night, with frequent awakenings
- Heart Rate Data: Resting heart rate increased by 10 BPM over time; noticeable spikes of +30 BPM when standing
- Hormone Test Results: Low progesterone, high estrogen
- Desired Outcome: Follow-up testing to determine underlying cause

The way Sophia structured her summary made it easy for her doctor to review her chief complaint and identify red flags from her supporting data. Sophia also printed her most recent cycle charts and heart rate graphs to have on hand if her doctor needed additional information or had follow-up questions about her metrics. This summary also prepared Sophia to better articulate her concerns and symptoms. Instead of saying, "I haven't been sleeping well," Sophia was able to say, "Over the past four months, my sleep tracker has recorded a decline in deep sleep from 1.5 hours per night to just 30 minutes. I've also logged frequent awakenings, which align with worsening fatigue." Rather than saying, "I've been getting dizzy a lot," she said, "My wearable device has recorded a consistent pattern where my heart rate increases by 30+ beats per minute when I move from sitting to standing, which correlates with my dizziness."

By structuring her case this way, Sophia wasn't just telling her doctors how she felt—she was showing them documented patterns that demanded further investigation.

Step 4: Anticipate and Address Doctor Skepticism

Even with well-organized data, some doctors will remain skeptical of femtech tools. This is especially true if they are unfamiliar with consumer health technology or if they have concerns about the reliability of nonclinical data. Many physicians were trained in an era when medical decisions were based solely on in-office exams and lab results, and they may not know how to interpret information from apps, wearables, or at-home tests.

Sophia reminded herself of this as she sat in the waiting room, clutching her printed summary. Her goal wasn't just to present her case—it was to ensure it couldn't be ignored. But Sophia *had* been ignored before. She had walked into past appointments with her symptoms carefully explained, only to be dismissed. And she couldn't help but fear that even with her data organized, her summary printed, and her argument ready, that this doctor might push back or dismiss her again.

To prevent your concerns and data from being dismissed, anticipate potential pushback and prepare to counter it with evidence. Think of it as responding to a cross-examination. You have presented your case, and your doctor may challenge your data and assumptions. Being ready with a calm, confident rebuttal makes it far more likely that your doctor will engage with your findings.

The first way to counter clinician skepticism regarding femtech is to have your research regarding device accuracy and validation on hand. You've already performed this step as part of the SAFE framework to ensure that your device is medically and scientifically accurate. Now you just need to compile that data. Before your appointment, take time to gather the research you initially performed regarding whether your femtech device has been clinically validated and identify any additional supporting evidence to bring with you. Prepare a list of published studies conducted on your femtech app or device and note whether any of the research has been referenced in peer-reviewed studies. If the company provides documentation on how its device aligns with clinical testing, bring that as well.

Here's how to prepare for different types of femtech skepticism:

- **If you use a wearable health tracker** (such as the Apple Watch, Fitbit, Oura Ring, or WHOOP), look up studies that validate the device's accuracy in monitoring heart rate, sleep cycles, or body temperature (depending on the metric you're measuring). Some wearables have been studied for their ability to detect early illness or menstrual cycle changes, which can be useful if you're using them to track hormonal fluctuations.
- **If you use a cycle-tracking or femtech app**, print out any available scientific literature that supports the reliability of the device. For example, some fertility apps have been tested against clinical ovulation detection methods, and bringing this research can help establish their credibility, especially since some apps use outdated methodologies that have been scientifically disproven.
- **If you have taken an at-home test** (such as a hormone or vitamin test), verify whether the lab processing your test is CLIA-certified (Clinical Laboratory Improvement Amendments) or CAP-accredited (College of American Pathologists). This certification ensures that the lab meets clinical testing standards. Print documentation showing that your test meets regulatory guidelines to demonstrate its reliability.

After being pulled back into the exam room, Sophia opened her femtech app's website and clicked on the "research" tab. She scrolled down to the section on clinical studies and scientific support, which detailed the app's proven methodologies and accuracy. She also opened the website for the at-home hormone test she took and verified that the tests were sent to a CLIA-certified lab. She felt a quick wave of relief, ready to defend her data if challenged. This time, if her doctor questioned the validity of her data, she would confidently respond, "I understand that not all consumer health data is clinically validated, but this device has been tested in multiple studies for accuracy. Here's some research that supports its use in tracking health metrics. I'd like to use this information as a starting point for further investigation with standard testing." By showing that she had done her homework and that her femtech tools were backed by science, Sophia reinforced the credibility of her data, making it much harder for her doctor to disregard her concerns.

Sophia's experience is not unique, but her preparation made her confident to handle the pushback. Many doctors unfamiliar with femtech may have a range of objections. Rather than feeling frustrated, defensive, or dejected, anticipate these objections ahead of time and be ready with clear, confident responses. Here are some common statements you may hear and how to push back effectively:

- **"These apps and devices aren't accurate."** Some doctors believe that consumer health devices are not as precise as clinical tests. While it's true that femtech tools are not meant to replace professional diagnostics, they are valuable for tracking trends over time and providing insights that may lead to faster diagnoses and more accurate clinical testing. If your physician pushes back against your use of femtech for this reason, you can respond, "I understand that this isn't a clinical-grade device, but it provides consistent data that shows patterns over time. I'm not using this data as a diagnosis—I'm using it to highlight a trend that I believe warrants further investigation. Can we use it as a starting point for clinical testing?"

- **"At-home test results aren't as reliable as lab tests."** Physicians may be hesitant to rely on at-home hormone or vitamin tests, particularly if they are unfamiliar with how they are processed. This is where it can be beneficial to show that the test is processed by a CLIA-certified or CAP-accredited laboratory. If you still receive resistance from your clinician, try responding, "I understand that at-home testing can have limitations, which is why I'd like to confirm these results with in-office lab work." If applicable, you can also add, "This test was processed by a CLIA-certified lab, which meets the same standards as many traditional medical labs. Since my results showed abnormal levels, I believe it's worth following up with further testing."

- **"Your symptoms or results are within the normal range."** Some doctors may compare your test results or symptoms to population averages rather than your personal baseline. If you have tracked your health over months or years, you have a unique advantage—you can show that your individual baseline has changed. Just because a value is considered "normal" for the average population doesn't mean your symptoms aren't valid, and you should push back to receive the care you deserve. Try responding, "I understand that my numbers may fall within the general reference range, but I am experiencing symptoms that are abnormal for my body. I'd like to discuss further testing and, if results are still normal, treating my symptoms rather than relying on the reference value."

- **"Your symptoms are probably due to stress."** This is one of the most common ways women's health concerns are dismissed. Doctors may default to stress or lifestyle factors instead of considering underlying medical issues. You know your body and the levels of stress you can and can't handle. If your stress level hasn't changed or if you don't feel your symptoms are a result of your stress tolerance, then push back. Consider responding, "I completely agree that stress can impact health, but I don't believe stress is the cause of my symptoms. My symptom tracking shows a pattern that doesn't align with general stress responses. I'd like to investigate possible underlying causes before assuming this is purely lifestyle related."

By preparing for these objections in advance, you can keep the conversation focused on the need for further testing and solutions rather than letting your concerns go unresolved. Too often, we adopt a passive stance with doctors, assuming they know best. We may hesitate to speak up out of fear that we will be perceived as difficult or confrontational. Preparing in advance can help the encounter feel less stressful and give you the confidence to ensure your needs are addressed. A lawyer would never go into a courtroom without data, questions, and rebuttal points. If you think of your healthcare encounter like building and defending a case, you're much more likely to be successful.

Step 5: Prepare Your Ask—and Make It Specific

Doctors are more likely to act when patients request clear and specific next steps rather than making vague statements like "I just want to know what's wrong," or "I just want some tests done." However, many patients don't know exactly what is wrong with them or what tests to request. That's completely understandable—after all, the whole point of seeking medical care is to get professional guidance. You don't need to have all the answers, but you do need to ensure that your concerns are fully explored.

If you have done your own research, received abnormal results from at-home testing, or strongly suspect a particular issue, being specific in your requests can be helpful. Instead of saying, "I think something's off with my hormones," you might say, "Given the irregularities in my cycle and my worsening fatigue, I'd like to explore whether a hormonal imbalance is contributing to my symptoms. I'd like to request a full hormone panel, including progesterone, estrogen, LH, FSH, testosterone, and DHEA." If you have noticed symptoms that suggest thyroid dysfunction, you could say, "I've tracked my symptoms over the past six months, and they align with potential thyroid issues. I'd like to rule this out with a full thyroid panel." By directly tying your request to your tracked symptoms, you increase the likelihood that your doctor will take your concerns seriously and order the appropriate tests.

Most patients, however, don't know what specific tests to ask for, but that shouldn't stop you from advocating for yourself. If you aren't sure which tests are appropriate, you can still ensure that your doctor takes your concerns seriously by framing your request in a way that encourages investigation rather than leaving the decision entirely in their hands.

This is the approach Sophia took. Based on her cycle-tracking data, sleep disruptions, and at-home hormone test results, she suspected an underlying hormonal imbalance—but she wasn't entirely sure which tests were needed to confirm it. Instead of freezing up or leaving the decision solely in the doctor's hands, she framed her ask strategically: "I've been experiencing severe fatigue, irregular cycles, and dizziness for four months, and my symptoms are worsening. I'd like to understand what might be causing this. Can we do a comprehensive workup to check for possible underlying issues, including hormonal imbalances?" By phrasing it this way, she put the responsibility back on the doctor to offer diagnostic options, rather than passively waiting for the doctor to suggest testing on their own.

If you don't have a clear ask and your doctor does not immediately suggest next steps, you can still salvage and redirect the conversation by asking, "What tests do you recommend to rule out potential underlying conditions?" If your symptoms are impacting your daily life, make sure to state that directly. Saying, "These symptoms are affecting my ability to function, and I'd like to explore diagnostic testing to understand what could be contributing," makes it clear that this is not a minor issue that can be ignored. Even if you don't know exactly what you need, this type of direct and structured approach makes it harder for your doctor to ignore your concerns.

If your doctor refuses a test you've requested, ask them to explain their reasoning. A simple "Can you help me understand why these tests wouldn't be necessary, given my tracked symptoms?" shifts the burden back onto the doctor to provide a valid medical justification. If the doctor insists that your results or symptoms fall within the normal range, push back by reminding them that medical averages don't always reflect individual baselines. You want to keep the conversation focused on what is different for *you* specifically. If your doctor attempts to attribute your symptoms to stress, redirect the conversation back to your tracked data and reiterate your request for further testing to rule out underlying issues.

If your doctor still refuses to order appropriate testing, you should create a medical record of your request by asking the doctor to document their decision. Saying, "Can you note in my chart that I have requested further testing based on my tracked symptoms and that this request has been declined?" can be effective. Many doctors will reconsider their position when they realize their refusal is being documented, particularly given the legal liability this can raise if there is an underlying issue, and the doctor dismissed you.

You don't need to walk into your doctor's office knowing exactly what's wrong, but you do need to be proactive in ensuring that your concerns are fully investigated. If you are confident in your requests, present your data clearly, and push for further evaluation, you can significantly increase the chances of getting the answers you deserve.

Refusing to Be Dismissed

Even after presenting your data, advocating for yourself, and pushing for further testing, there is always a chance that your doctor may still dismiss your concerns. This can be frustrating, disheartening, and even infuriating. But this doesn't mean you are out of options. If your doctor refuses to take your symptoms seriously, it's time to take additional steps to ensure you receive the care you deserve.

The first thing to do is document everything. Keep a record of your appointment, noting what was discussed, any tests or treatments that were denied, and the reasoning given for those denials. If your doctor refused testing or dismissed your symptoms, make sure to request that this be documented in your medical record. If the doctor refuses to document it or tries to downplay your request, you can take your own notes and ask for a copy of your medical records after the appointment. Having this document can be valuable if you decide to seek a second opinion or need to escalate your concerns.

Next, consider requesting a referral. If your doctor is not interested in following up on your concerns, they may be open to referring you to a specialist. You can ask, "If you don't believe further testing is needed, can you refer me to a specialist who has more experience with these symptoms?" This shifts the burden onto your doctor to either acknowledge that a specialist may have more expertise or further justify why they are refusing to escalate your care. If your doctor refuses to refer you to a specialist, this can be a red flag that they are not taking your case seriously, and it may be time to move on.

If you are unable to get a referral through your doctor, take matters into your own hands. Many specialists, particularly those in fields like endocrinology, gynecology, and functional medicine, accept self-referrals. Research providers in your area, particularly those who specialize in the symptoms you are experiencing. If you can, look for doctors who specifically state that they take a patient-centric or data-driven approach. Online patient reviews can also be a helpful way to gauge whether a doctor is likely to be dismissive.

Telemedicine can be another excellent option. Many online health platforms, such as those specializing in women's health, hormone balancing, and functional medicine, offer virtual consultations with doctors who are well-versed in femtech and patient-tracked health data. If you've hit a wall with traditional in-person care, exploring a virtual option could provide new insights and a fresh approach.

If you suspect that racial or gender bias is playing a role in your dismissal, consider seeking out a different doctor, preferably one with a history of working with patients on complex or chronic health issues. Some patients find that switching to a female provider, a provider with a background in integrative medicine, or one who explicitly specializes in the condition they suspect can make a significant difference. Unfortunately, not all doctors are trained to recognize patterns in women's health (including female doctors), and finding a provider who is knowledgeable and willing to investigate further is crucial. It is *never* wrong to request a second opinion or switch providers if your health concerns aren't being appropriately addressed.

If you feel that your doctor's dismissal was unethical or negligent, you also have the option of filing a complaint. In some cases, advocating for yourself is not just about getting the care you need but also about holding medical providers accountable for dismissing patients without proper investigation. You can report your experience to your healthcare provider's office, hospital administration, or even state medical boards if you feel that you were not given appropriate care.

Above all, do not let one doctor's opinion be the final say on your health. You know your body better than anyone, and if you feel something is wrong, you have every right to keep searching for answers. Advocate for yourself, seek second opinions, explore alternative providers, and do not stop until you get the care and attention you deserve. Persistence is often the key to finally getting the right diagnosis and treatment. If one door closes, find another. Your health is too important to accept being ignored.

Conclusion

Femtech is more than just a tool for tracking health—it's a way to transform personal experiences into objective evidence that demands attention. By collecting and presenting data in a structured, measurable way, you can shift the conversation from vague complaints to medically relevant patterns, making it harder for doctors to dismiss your concerns. A well-documented record of symptoms, cycle changes, or biometric trends turns a subjective experience into something tangible, increasing the likelihood of receiving appropriate testing and treatment.

However, data alone isn't enough. Knowing how to present it effectively, anticipate skepticism, and persist when met with resistance is just as important. Doctors are trained to follow clinical reasoning, and the more closely your data aligns with that structure, the more seriously it will be taken. If a doctor refuses to listen or dismisses your concerns despite clear evidence, you now have the tools to push back—whether that means requesting documentation of their refusal, seeking a second opinion, or continuing to build your case. Your symptoms matter, your data matters, and most importantly, *you* matter. Never let anyone tell you otherwise. If you do, the price you pay may be your life.

12

The Future of Femtech

A Revolution in Motion

The Personal Journey and the Collective Impact

Throughout this book, we've traced the long history of women fighting to be heard in healthcare. We've seen how traditional medicine has dismissed or misunderstood women's experiences. We've witnessed the rise of new technologies promising to bridge these long-standing gaps. But perhaps most importantly, we've explored how femtech is shifting the power dynamic, giving women the tools to move from feeling unheard and powerless to becoming informed, activate participants in their own healthcare.

This transformation isn't just about adopting new technology—it's about changing how we approach our health entirely. Where once we might have accepted a dismissive doctor's assessment, we now have tools to document, validate, and understand our experiences. Where we once struggled alone with confusing symptoms, we can now connect with communities of women sharing similar experiences. And where we once relied solely on medical institutions that often overlooked our needs, we now have options for taking control of our own health data and decisions.

Yet with these new opportunities come real concerns. We may be hesitant about sharing our health data online. We may question the accuracy of symptom tracking apps. We may wonder whether digital health platforms truly understand our needs. These concerns aren't just reasonable—they're necessary. They reflect an awareness that health data is valuable and should be protected.

This is precisely why the SAFE method is so powerful. It provides a clear, structured way for women to evaluate healthcare technologies and make informed choices. Instead of relying on marketing claims or word-of-mouth recommendations, SAFE helps women assess security, accuracy, foundation, and equity—the four pillars that determine whether a product is truly trustworthy. By empowering women with this knowledge, the SAFE method enables them to take control of their personal healthcare journeys with confidence. It shifts the balance of power, ensuring that patients become active participants in their care rather than passive recipients of information.

Beyond individual decision-making, the SAFE method has broader implications for the femtech industry as a whole. When women feel empowered to research, assess, and make informed decisions about femtech solutions, their choices create a ripple effect. Every time a woman selects a secure, accurate, well-founded, and equitable solution, she strengthens its impact. Every dollar spent on a SAFE femtech solution is a vote for better women's healthcare. Every subscription to a research-backed platform is an investment in future innovations. Every decision to walk away from a lackluster or underperforming product raises the bar for the entire industry. Women aren't just improving their own healthcare experiences—they're shaping the future of women's health technology for everyone.

We're already seeing the results of this collective power. As femtech prepares to enter its second decade as a recognized industry, businesses in the space have increased by 1,000 percent.[1] The femtech market has expanded into a multi-billion-dollar industry and is expected to keep growing. Major players—from health insurers to universities—are recognizing the value of femtech and integrating it into their policies, offerings, research, and education.

For example, health insurers are increasingly partnering with femtech companies to expand affordable access to digital health solutions. In 2022, Minnesota's Blue Cross and Blue Shield teamed up with Health in Her HUE to provide women of color with free access to its digital health platform.[2] In 2024, Aetna became the first major insurer to cover intrauterine insemination as a medical benefit, helping more patients access fertility testing and treatment.[3] And this is only the beginning.

Medical schools are also integrating femtech into their curricula to ensure that the next generation of doctors understands the latest innovations in women's health. Johns Hopkins University's Innovator Program encourages students to develop new femtech solutions.[4] In February 2024, the school also launched the Center for Global Women's Health and Gender Equity, leveraging research and training resources from the larger Johns Hopkins ecosystem to further gender equity.[5] The University of Pittsburgh established the Repro-Techquity Collaborative, developing and using technology to improve and advance reproductive health equity.[6] Other universities are also adding new courses focused on women's health to help close the gender data gap.

These advancements didn't happen in a vacuum. They happened because millions of women demanded better healthcare solutions. By supporting reputable femtech companies, participating in research initiatives, and advocating for change, women are driving the momentum that fuels these breakthroughs. And as femtech continues to grow, it gains traction within major institutions that once overlooked women's health.

This is the collective impact of femtech. By making informed choices about our healthcare, we fuel a larger transformation. When we demand higher standards in critical areas, we push companies to create more secure, accurate, and equitable solutions. This ripple effect has the potential to elevate the entire field, fostering trust, transparency, and innovation across the industry. And the SAFE method equips us with the essential tools to responsibly bring this vision for femtech to life.

Shaping a SAFE Future

Women's healthcare is evolving, and it will continue to do so for years to come. As the landscape shifts, barriers that once seemed insurmountable—censorship, the lack of women-centric health data, and minimal research funding—are gradually coming down. Femtech founders and companies are not just working around these challenges; they're finding creative ways to push past them entirely. Playground (a sexual wellness brand co-founded by Christina Aguilera), for example, turned censorship restrictions into an opportunity with its 1-888-PLY-GRND hotline.[7] NextGen Jane transformed a traditionally overlooked resource—menstrual products—into a powerful tool for scientific research.[8] Rather than avoiding obstacles, these companies are facing them head on and creating new avenues for growth.

These innovations aren't just clever marketing strategies—they mark the maturation of the femtech industry. We've moved beyond basic period trackers and fertility monitors to address the full spectrum of women's health—from cardiovascular care and autoimmune diseases to mental health and aging. Each breakthrough redefines what femtech can accomplish and expands its role in modern medicine.

Barriers to progress in women's health still exist, but they are becoming more navigable. When social media platforms block advertisements for women's health products, companies find alternative ways to connect with consumers. When traditional funding sources dry up, femtech founders pioneer new investment models. When healthcare access remains uneven, developers create solutions with built-in accessibility—offline functionality for areas with limited internet, multilingual interfaces for diverse communities, and sliding scale payment options to accommodate different financial situations.

This evolution reflects a deeper understanding of what women need from health technology. It's not enough to create solutions that work—they must also be accessible, trustworthy, and inclusive. The future of femtech isn't just about innovation—it's about responsibility. It's about ensuring that new technologies are developed with security, accuracy, foundation, and equity at their core.

Throughout this book, we've used the SAFE method to evaluate today's femtech solutions. But SAFE is more than just a framework for assessment—it's a blueprint for building better health technology. Each of its four pillars serves as a guide for shaping the future of women's health:

- **Security** in femtech's future means putting women in control of their health data. Digital privacy must be a built-in standard, not an afterthought. Companies are now developing privacy-first platforms that allow users to selectively share information—contributing valuable health insights without compromising their personal data.

- **Accuracy** is evolving as femtech moves beyond basic tracking tools and preliminary studies. The industry is shifting toward clinically validated, research-backed solutions. Stronger partnerships between femtech companies and medical institutions are leading to more rigorous studies, helping close the gender data gap and improving the precision of healthcare tools.
- **Foundation** is becoming a priority for femtech companies, with leadership teams that reflect the diversity of the communities they serve. More startups are building advisory boards that include medical professionals, patient advocates, researchers, and accessibility experts to ensure their products are developed through an inclusive lens.
- **Equity** remains at the heart of femtech's evolution. Companies are taking deliberate steps to ensure their solutions are widely accessible—offering multilingual support, flexible payment models, and designing for economic, geographic, racial, and cultural inclusivity. This ensures that the experiences and circumstances of all applicable users are understood, acknowledged, and integrated.

The future we're building through SAFE isn't just about better technology. It's about designing solutions that recognize and respect the full range of women's needs. It's about creating systems that support women at every stage of life, from adolescence to post-menopause. And most importantly, it's about making sure that as femtech continues to grow, it does so responsibly.

Our Role in the Revolution

Women's health is undergoing an undeniable transformation, and we are all part of it. Every time we make an informed decision about our health technology, we contribute to the future of women's health. Each time we evaluate a femtech solution using the SAFE method, provide feedback on a product's effectiveness, or share our experiences with other women, we help shape the industry.

For these reasons, each of us has a role to play in the femtech revolution, even if those roles look different from person to person. Some contributions are small but meaningful: choosing femtech solutions that align with our values, prioritizing products that meet our needs while protecting our data, and supporting companies that demonstrate a real commitment to the SAFE principles. Others might take a step further and become femtech advocates, sharing their experiences online, through word-of-mouth, or at industry events. Advocates join communities dedicated to educating and supporting women making their own healthcare choices. They push for better research funding, more inclusive technology, and stronger patient protections. And some of us? We might even be the next femtech founders. If that's you, then you now have a blueprint for building one of the SAFEst femtech businesses out there—one that prioritizes security, accuracy, foundation, and equity in everything it creates.

And yet none of this progress happens in isolation. Each of us has the ability to channel our personal experiences into advocacy and action. By taking the time to educate ourselves about the femtech solutions available and how they measure up against SAFE principles, we not only make better decisions for our own health but also encourage collective progress. These efforts make the industry more transparent and drive developers and companies to do better and think bigger.

There's also power in connecting with others. When we open up about our journeys and share lessons we've learned, we empower more women to embrace their health experiences. This knowledge-sharing strengthens the communal foundation of the femtech movement. From small acts like recommending a trusted product to a friend, to larger contributions like collaborating with advocacy groups, each of us plays a crucial part in advancing this revolution. Together, these actions remind us that while the tools and technology are important, it is the people who use them and demand better that ultimately redefine the future of women's health.

We are all part of the femtech revolution, and every action we take shapes its future. This isn't just a movement; it's a call to action for all of us to actively participate in building a future where healthcare works better for every woman. Our decisions today are the foundation of a healthier, more inclusive tomorrow.

Conclusion

The journey we've explored throughout this book—from uncovering historical neglect to examining modern solutions—is just the beginning. New technologies will continue to emerge. Some will bring long-overdue advancements, while others will fail to live up to their promises. The challenges we fight today—bias in medical research, privacy concerns, and lack of accessibility—won't disappear overnight. Instead, they will evolve, presenting new obstacles that demand new solutions. But with SAFE as our guide, we are equipped to navigate this shifting landscape. We know how to separate meaningful innovation from empty marketing. We know how to protect our data, demand accountability, and advocate for equity in the technologies that are shaping our future.

The femtech revolution isn't something happening to us—it's something we are actively creating. Every time we choose a secure platform, we raise the standard for privacy. Every time we support accurate, research-backed technology, we push the industry forward. Every time we demand ethical leadership and inclusivity, we ensure that innovation serves all women, not just a privileged few. Every time we share knowledge with others, we strengthen our collective power. And every time we refuse to settle for less than we deserve, we take one more step toward a future where women's healthcare is not just an afterthought but a priority.

The future of women's healthcare isn't something we have to wait for—it's something we are building, right now. The revolution is here. Let's embrace it, wisely, together.

Notes

Introduction: Femtech Rising

1. Research shows that 70 to 80 percent of women will develop fibroids before age 50. Most women will experience fibroids before age 40. See "Fibroids: More Common Than You Think," OHSU Center for Women's Health, accessed February 2, 2025, https://www.ohsu.edu/womens-health/fibroids-more-common-you-think#:~:text=%22Fibroids%20are%20extremely%20common%2C%22,have%20fibroids%20before%20age%2050.

2. On a list of the top five most painful surgeries published by *Medical News Today*, myomectomies ranked as number 3 on the list, ahead of complex spinal reconstruction. "What Are the Most Painful Surgeries?" *Medical News Today*, accessed February 2, 2025, https://www.medicalnewstoday.com/articles/321779#most-painful-surgeries.

3. A study by McKinsey & Company found that from 2019 to 2023, funding for companies focused on erectile disfunction (ED) was six times higher than that for endometriosis ($1.24 billion invested in ED compared to $44 million invested in endometriosis). In 2022, the ED drug market was valued at $2.46 billion compared to $1.22 million for endometriosis treatments. Kweilin Ellingrud et al., "Closing the Women's Health Gap: A $1 Trillion Opportunity to Improve Lives and Economies," McKinsey Health Institute, January 17, 2024, https://www.mckinsey.com/mhi/our-insights/closing-the-womens-health-gap-a-1-trillion-dollar-opportunity-to-improve-lives-and-economies.

4. Emily Paulsen, "Recognizing, Addressing Unintended Gender Bias in Patient Care," Duke Health, January 14, 2020, https://physicians.dukehealth .org/articles/recognizing-addressing-unintended-gender-bias-patient-care#:~:text=One%20in%20five%20women%20say,of%20gender%20 bias%20are%20correct.

5. The study also found that nearly 50 percent of women ages 18 to 35 reported having a negative healthcare encounter or negative experience with a healthcare professional. Almost 20 percent reported that their doctor assumed something about them without asking, and 13 percent said that their healthcare provider suggested they were personally to blame for a health problem they were experiencing. Kaiser Family Foundation, "Women's Experiences with Provider Communication and Interactions in Health Care Settings: Findings from the 2022 KFF Women's Health Survey," KFF, March 22, 2023, https://www.kff.org/womens-health-policy/issue-brief/womens-experiences-with-provider-communication-interactions-health-care-settings-findings-from-2022-kff-womens-health-survey.

6. According to U.S. claims data from January 2019 through August 2022, women's health conditions are roughly five times more prevalent than their documented diagnoses. This means that for every one woman diagnosed with a women's health condition, approximately four more go undiagnosed. "Unseen and Untreated," McKinsey & Company, accessed February 2, 2025, https://www.mckinsey.com/featured-insights/sustainable-inclusive-growth/charts/unseen-and-untreated.

7. Lucy R. Nicholas, "The Women's March on Rome," *History Today*, accessed January 10, 2025, https://www.historytoday.com/history-matters/womens-march-rome.

8. Erin Blakemore, "How Boudica Led Britain's Revolt Against Rome," *National Geographic*, accessed January 10, 2025, https://www.national geographic.com/history/history-magazine/article/boudica-britain-revolt-against-rome.

9. Deborah Gray White, "Old Age, Justice, and Black Feminist History: Sojourner Truth's and Harriet Tubman's Final Years," University of Virginia, Department of Women, Gender & Sexuality, accessed January 10, 2025, https://wgs.as.virginia.edu/news/story/old-age-justice-and-black-feminist-history-sojourner-truth%E2%80%99s-and-harriet-tubman% E2%80%99s.

10. Rosie Lesso, "The Women of the Red Army in WWII," *The Collector*, accessed January 10, 2025, https://www.thecollector.com/women-red-army-wwii.

11. Angela Y. Davis, "Reflections on the Role of Black Women in the Community of Slaves," Freedom Archives, accessed January 10, 2025, https://www.freedomarchives.org/Documents/Finder/DOC46_scans/46.RoleBlackWomenSlavery.pdf.

12. Parnian Moudi, "Uses and Abuses of Fashion: Veiling and State Power in Iran," *Harvard Political Review*, accessed January 10, 2025, https://harvardpolitics.com/uses-and-abuses-of-fashion-veiling-and-state-power-in-iran.

13. "Why Did Suffragettes Go on Hunger Strike?" London Museum, accessed February 2, 2025, https://www.londonmuseum.org.uk/collections/london-stories/why-did-suffragettes-go-on-hunger-strike/.

Chapter 1: The Hidden Revolution in Women's Health

1. Alan Penzias et al., "Evidence-Based Treatments for Couples with Unexplained Infertility: A Guideline," Fertility and Sterility vol. 113, no. 2 (February 2020): 305–22, https://doi.org/10.1016/j.fertnstert.2019.10.014.

2. When oncology is included, the rates increase from 1 percent to 5 percent of biopharma pipeline assets and from 2 percent to 4 percent of medtech approvals. Burns, Delaney, et al., "Closing the Data Gaps in Women's Health," McKinsey & Company, April 3, 2023, https://www.mckinsey.com/industries/life-sciences/our-insights/closing-the-data-gaps-in-womens-health.

3. "Funding Research on Women's Health," *Nature Reviews Bioengineering* 2, no. 10 (October 2024): 797–798, https://doi.org/10.1038/s44222-024-00253-7.

4. "Women and Pain: Disparities in Experience and Treatment," Harvard Health Blog, Oct. 9, 2017, https://www.health.harvard.edu/blog/women-and-pain-disparities-in-experience-and-treatment-2017100912562.

5. "The Case to Fund Women's Health Research," WHAM, last accessed February 2, 2025, https://thewhamreport.org/report.

6. Katherine Dainty, "Women's Health, AI and the Data Gap," Venner Shipley, August 10, 2023, https://www.vennershipley.com/insights-events/womens-health-ai-and-the-data-gap.

7. Kweilin Ellingrud et al., "Closing the Women's Health Gap: A $1 Trillion Opportunity to Improve Lives and Economies," McKinsey & Company, January 17, 2024, https://www.mckinsey.com/mhi/our-insights/closing-the-womens-health-gap-a-1-trillion-dollar-opportunity-to-improve-lives-and-economies.

8. *Ibid.*

9. Halle Tecco and Julia Cheek, "Women's Health Is More than Female Anatomy and Our Reproductive System—It's about Unraveling Centuries of Inequities Due to Living in a Patriarchal Healthcare System," Harvard Business School: Health Care, January 18, 2022, https://www.hbs.edu/healthcare/blog/post/defining-womens-health-womens-health-is-more-than-female-anatomy-and-our-reproductive-systemits-about-unraveling-centuries-of-inequities-due-to-living-in-a-patriarchal-healthcare-system.

10. Marya Shegog, "Medical Gaslighting of Women Is Real and So Is Its Toll," *DC Journal*, March 27, 2023, https://dcjournal.com/medical-gaslighting-of-women-is-real-and-so-is-its-toll/.

11. Chloe Castleberry, "Know the Facts: A Deeper Look Into Medical Gaslighting," SheKnows, December 28, 2022, https://www.sheknows.com/health-and-wellness/videos/2687700/medical-gaslighting-statistics/.

12. Charmaine Li, "A Close-up of Clue, the Startup That Aims to Help Women Make Sense of Their Fertility Cycle," Tech.eu, February 6, 2022, https://tech.eu/2014/09/05/clue-app-profile-ida-tin.

13. Natasha Lomas, "Period Tracker App Clue Gets $7M to Build a Platform for Female Health," TechCrunch, October 9, 2015, https://techcrunch.com/2015/10/09/clue-series-a/?guccounter=1.

14. "About Clue," Hello Clue, accessed February 2, 2025, https://helloclue.com/about-clue.

15. Bridget G. Kelly and Maniza Habib, "Missed Period? The Significance of Period-Tracking Applications in a Post-*Roe* America," *Sexual and Reproductive Health Matters* 31, no. 4 (Dec. 2023), https://pmc.ncbi.nlm.nih.gov/articles/PMC10494721/.

16. Ida Tin, "Maybe helpful to add to this conversation what my definition of Femtech is," LinkedIn Posts, May 23, 2024, https://www.linkedin.com/posts/idatin_maybe-helpful-to-add-to-this-conversation-activity-7200920413994917888-R1Y4/.

17. P. Kop et al., "Intrauterine Insemination or Intracervical Insemination with Cryopreserved Donor Sperm in the Natural Cycle: A Cohort Study," *Human Reproduction* 30, no. 3 (January 29, 2015): 603–7, https://doi.org/10.1093/humrep/dev004.

18. "What Are My Chances of Success with IVF?" UT Health, accessed September 18, 2024, https://uthscsa.edu/physicians/services/assisted-reproduction/what-are-my-chances-success-ivf.

19. Conor Stewart, "Use and Awareness of Femtech in the U.S. 2021, by Age," Statista, November 9, 2024, https://www.statista.com/statistics/1323194/use-and-awareness-of-femtech-in-the-us-by-age. In a separate online questionnaire distributed to over 10,000 women between the ages of 20 and 60, only 7 percent recognized the term *femtech*. "Consumer Questionnaire on Feminine Care & FemTech (Consumer Goods & Services) Market: Key Research Findings 2023," Yano Research Institute, December 8, 2023, https://www.yanoresearch.com/en/press-release/show/press_id/3384.

20. "FemTech Market—Industry Dynamics, Market Size, and Opportunity Forecast to 2032," Astute Analytica, January 2024, https://www.astuteanalytica.com/industry-report/femtech-market#:~:text=Global%20FemTech%20Market%20was%20valued,the%20forecast%20period%202024–2032.

21. Center for Intimacy Justice, "Meta's Censorship of Health Ads for Women and People of Diverse Genders," January 2022, available at https://docsend.com/view/phfstt65wzta5nw7 and https://www.intimacyjustice.org.

22. Ibid.

23. Ibid.

24. Ibid.

Chapter 2: Legacy of Neglect: Why Women's Health Needs a Revolution

1. This story of Lucy is compiled and dramatized from historical texts. See, e.g., Nikki Rojas, "How Lucy, Betsey, and Anarcha Became Foremothers of Gynecology," *Harvard Gazette*, March 30, 2023, https://news.harvard.edu/gazette/story/2023/03/how-lucy-betsey-and-anarcha-became-foremothers-of-gynecology/; "Life Story: Anarcha,

Betsy, and Lucy," Women & The American Story, accessed February 2, 2025, https://wams.nyhistory.org/a-nation-divided/antebellum/anarcha-betsy-lucy/; Brynn Holland, "The 'Father of Modern Gynecology' Performed Shocking Experiments on Enslaved Women," *History*, December 4, 2018, https://www.history.com/news/the-father-of-modern-gynecology-performed-shocking-experiments-on-slaves.

2. Holland, *supra* note 1.
3. Ibid.
4. See sources cited in note 1.
5. Holland, note 1.
6. One study estimates that more than 3.5 million patients have been given pelvic exams without consent. "More Than 3.5 Million Patients Given Pelvic Exams Without Consent, Study Estimates," NBC News, September 19, 2023, https://www.nbcnews.com/nightly-news/video/more-than-3-5-million-patients-given-pelvic-exams-without-consent-study-estimates-193321541876; Meghan Rosen, "Pelvic Exams at Hospitals Require Written Consent, New U.S. Guidelines Say," *Science News*, April 24, 2024, https://www.sciencenews.org/article/pelvic-exam-informed-consent-guidelines. *Elle* conducted a separate survey of 101 medical students from seven major American medical schools. Ninety-two percent of respondents reported performing a pelvic exam on an anesthetized female patient. Of those who performed the pelvic exam, 61 percent said they did so without explicit patient consent. Jennifer Tsai, "Medical Students Regularly Practice Pelvic Exams on Unconscious Patients. Should They?" *Elle*, June 24, 2019, https://www.elle.com/life-love/a28125604/nonconsensual-pelvic-exams-teaching-hospitals/.
7. Peseshet is credited with being one of the earliest known female physicians in ancient Egypt. Joshua, Mark, "Female Physicians in Ancient Egypt," *World History Encyclopedia*, February 22, 2017, https://www.worldhistory.org/article/49/female-physicians-in-ancient-egypt/; Matthew Turner, "Healer of Pharaohs: History's First Woman Doctor," *Hektoen International*, accessed February 2, 2025, https://hekint.org/2022/12/13/healer-of-the-pharaohs-historys-first-woman-doctor/.
8. Chukwuka Elendu, "The Evolution of Ancient Healing Practices: From Ahamanism to Hippocratic Medicine: A Review," *Medicine* (Baltimore) 103, no. 28, July 12, 2024, https://pmc.ncbi.nlm.nih.gov/articles/PMC11245246/.

9. Lesley Smith, "The Kahun Gynaecological Papyrus: Ancient Egyptian Medicine," *Journal of Family Planning and Reproductive Health Care* 37, no. 1 (January 2011): 54–55. https://doi.org/10.1136/jfprhc.2010.0019; "A Brief History of Women's Health," Aspivix, March 21, 2021, https://www.aspivix.com/a-brief-history-of-womens-health.

10. "Sexist Science: From Aristotle to the Modern Day," The Week, July 25, 2017, https://theweek.com/87121/sexist-science-from-aristotle-to-the-modern-day. For a more in-depth look at the historic biases and sexist assumptions that have led to modern day claims of female inferiority, consider reading Angela Saini's book *Inferior: How Science Got Women Wrong—and the New Research That's Rewriting the Story* (May 30, 2017).

11. See citations in note 1.

12. Chloe Nobuhara, "Battey's Operation Was an Experiment in Human Endocrinology," American College of Surgeons, October 9, 2024, https://www.facs.org/for-medical-professionals/news-publications/news-and-articles/bulletin/2024/october-2024-volume-109-issue-9/battey-s-operation-was-an-experiment-in-human-endocrinology/; Tomoko Komagamine, Norito Kokubun, and Koichi Hirata, "Battey's Operation as a Treatment for Hysteria: A Review of a Series of Cases in the Nineteenth Century," *History of Psychiatry* 31, no. 1 (March 2020): 55–66, https://pubmed.ncbi.nlm.nih.gov/31538814/; Thomas Schlich, "Cutting the Body to Cure the Mind," *The Lancet Psychiatry* 2, no. 5 (May 2015): 390–392, https://www.thelancet.com/journals/lanpsy/article/PIIS2215-0366(15)00188-1/fulltext.

13. Agnes Arnold-Forster, "Clitoridectomies: Female Genital Mutilation c.1860–2014," NOTCHES, November 18, 2014, https://notchesblog.com/2014/11/18/clitoridectomies-female-genital-mutilation-c-1860-2014/.

14. For example, a congressional investigation into medical abuse allegations at a Georgia detention center found that immigrant women underwent "unnecessary" invasive gynecological procedures, including, in some cases, questionable procedures without patient consent. Montoya-Galvez, "Investigation Finds Women Detained by ICE Underwent 'Unnecessary Gynecological Procedures' at Georgia Facility," CBS News, November 15, 2022, https://www.cbsnews.com/news/women-detained-ice-unnecessary-gynecological-procedures-

georgia-facility-investigation/; Joel Rose, "Dozens of Women Allege Unwanted Surgeries and Medical Abuse in ICE Custody," NPR, December 22, 2020, https://www.npr.org/2020/12/22/949257207/dozens-of-women-allege-unwanted-surgeries-and-medical-abuse-in-ice-custody.

15. Peter Poczai, "The Little-Known History of Cleanliness and the Forgotten Pioneers of Handwashing," Front Public Health, October 20, 2022, https://pmc.ncbi.nlm.nih.gov/articles/PMC9632745/; Didier Pittet and Benedetta Allegranzi, "Preventing Sepsis in Healthcare—200 Years After the Birth of Ignaz Semmelweis," *Euro Surveillance* 23, no. 18, May 3, 2018, https://pmc.ncbi.nlm.nih.gov/articles/PMC6053623/.

16. Alice Duer Miller, "Dr. Elizabeth Blackwell NY Infirmary," Hobart and William Smith Colleges, accessed February 2, 2025, https://www.hws.edu/about/history/elizabeth-blackwell/ny-infirmary.aspx.

17. Dr. Mary Walker was the only female to receive the Medal of Honor among 3,500 recipients. In 1855, she was the only female doctor to graduate from her class at Syracuse Medical College and volunteered as an unpaid field surgeon near the frontlines. In 1863, she became the first female surgeon in the US Army before being taken as a prisoner of war by Confederate troops. She received the Congressional Medal of Honor a year later, in 1865. Though her Medal of Honor was rescinded in 1917, it was reinstated by President Jimmy Carter in 1977. "Dr. Mary E. Walker: The Sole Female Medal of Honor Recipient," Wounded Warrior Project, accessed February 2, 2025, https://newsroom.wounded warriorproject.org/Dr-Mary-E-Walker-The-Sole-Female-Medal-of-Honor-Recipient.

18. Harriet Tubman served in Freedmen's Hospital in Washington, DC, using home remedies to help treat infectious diseases. She traveled to Beaufort, South Carolina, to be a nurse and teacher to the Gullah people, who were abandoned on South Carolina's Sea Islands. In 1865, she was appointed matron of a hospital in Virginia, where she cared for Black soldiers. Singleton, Maura, "Flashback Friday—Harriet Tubman's Overlooked Story as a Nurse," UVA School of Nursing, November 8, 2019, https://nursing.virginia.edu/news/flashback-harriet-tubman-nurse/#:~:text=African%20Americans%20tended%20to%20the,Hospital%20in%20Washington%20and%20elsewhere.&text=But%20she%20never%20received%20pay,wartime%20service%20as%20a%20nurse.

19. Jennifer Matthews, "Florence Nightingale: Visionary for the Role of Clinical Nurse Specialist," *Online Journal of Issues in Nursing*, May 2020, https://ojin.nursingworld.org/table-of-contents/volume-25-2020/number-2-may-2020/nightingale-visionary-for-clinical-nurse-specialist/.

20. "Past as Present: America's Sordid History of Medical Reproductive Abuse and Experimentation," National Partnership for Women & Families Fact Sheet, October 2020, https://nationalpartnership.org/wp-content/uploads/2023/02/past-as-present-americas-sordid-history-of-medical-reproductive-abuse-and-experimentation.pdf; Theresa Vargas, "Guinea Pigs or Pioneers? How Puerto Rican Women Were Used to Test the Birth Control Pill," *Washington Post*, May 9, 2017, https://www.washingtonpost.com/news/retropolis/wp/2017/05/09/guinea-pigs-or-pioneers-how-puerto-rican-women-were-used-to-test-the-birth-control-pill/.

21. Vargas, note 20.

22. Lisa Ko, "Unwanted Sterilization and Eugenics Programs in the United States," PBS, January 29, 2016, https://www.pbs.org/independentlens/blog/unwanted-sterilization-and-eugenics-programs-in-the-united-states/. In the case of *Relf v. Weinberger*, the US District Court for the District of Columbia found that doctors threatened to withhold welfare benefits or medical care unless poor women in the South agreed to forced sterilization. Maya Manian, "Immigration Detention and Coerced Sterilization: History Tragically Repeats Itself," ACLU, September 29, 2020, https://www.aclu.org/news/immigrants-rights/immigration-detention-and-coerced-sterilization-history-tragically-repeats-itself. An estimated 100,000 to 150,000 people were sterilized annually under these federally funded eugenics programs. "Relf v. Weinberger," SPLC, last accessed February 2, 2025, https://www.splcenter.org/resources/civil-rights-case-docket/relf-v-weinberger/.

23. Hayley Fowler, "Act of Genocide: Eugenics Program Tried to 'Breed Out' Black People in NC, Report Says," *The News & Observer*, August 18, 2020, https://www.newsobserver.com/news/state/north-carolina/article244411987.html.

24. Nicole Novak and Natalie Lira, "California Once Targeted Latinas for Forced Sterilization," *Smithsonian*, March 22, 2018, https://www.smithsonianmag.com/history/california-targeted-latinas-forced-sterilization-180968567/.

25. "Diethylstilbestrol (DES) Exposure and Cancer," National Cancer
    Institute, accessed February 2, 2025, https://www.cancer.gov/about-
    cancer/causes-prevention/risk/hormones/des-fact-sheet.

26. James Kingsland, "How the Thalidomide Scandal Led to Safer Drugs,"
    Medical News Today, December 15, 2020, https://www.medicalnew
    stoday.com/articles/how-the-thalidomide-scandal-led-to-safer-drugs.

27. Ellen Blaak, "Gender Differences in Fat Metabolism," *Current Opinion
    in Clinical Nutrition and Metabolic Care*, 4, no. 6 November 2001:
    499–502, https://pubmed.ncbi.nlm.nih.gov/11706283/#:~:text=
    Women%20generally%20have%20a%20higher,the%20visceral%20
    (abdominal)%20depot.

28. "Are Medications and Medical Devices More Dangerous for Women?"
    Canadian Institutes of Health Research, accessed February 2, 2025,
    https://cihr-irsc.gc.ca/e/51569.html#; Carol Gillette, "Do Drugs Act
    Differently in Men and Women?" *Alternative to Meds Center*, June 2,
    2022, https://www.alternativetomeds.com/blog/do-drugs-act-differently-
    in-men-and-women/.

29. Robyn Karlstadt, Daniel Hogan, and Amy Foxx-Orenstein, "Normal
    Physiology of the Gastrointestinal Tract and Gender Differences," Mayo
    Clinic, accessed February 2, 2025, https://mayoclinic.elsevierpure
    .com/en/publications/normal-physiology-of-the-gastrointestinal-
    tract-and-gender-differ.

30. Marjorie Jenkins et al., "Food and Drug Administration Beyond the
    2001 Government Accountability Office Report: Promoting Drug
    Safety for Women," *Journal of Women's Health* (Larchmont), 30, no. 7
    (July 2021): 927–934, https://pubmed.ncbi.nlm.nih.gov/33635140/;
    Robinton, Daisy, "POV: The Global Economic Impact of Ignoring
    This Aspect of Women's Health Is $150 Billion. We Can Do Better,"
    Fast Company, March 21, 2023, https://www.fastcompany.com/
    90868245/global-economic-impact-of-ignoring-this-aspect-
    of-womens-health-is-150-billion-we-can-do-better.

31. US General Accounting Office, "Women Sufficiently Represented in
    New Drug Testing, but FDA Oversight Needs Improvement," July
    2001, https://www.gao.gov/assets/gao-01-754.pdf.

32. Kweilin Ellingrud et al., "Closing the Women's Health Gap: A $1 Tril-
    lion Opportunity to Improve Lives and Economies," McKinsey Health
    Institute, January 17, 2024, https://www.mckinsey.com/mhi/our-insights/

closing-the-womens-health-gap-a-1-trillion-dollar-opportunity-
to-improve-lives-and-economies#.

33. "History & Legacy," Our Bodies Ourselves, last accessed February 2,
2025, https://ourbodiesourselves.org/history-legacy.

34. "NIH Policy and Guidelines on the Inclusion of Women and Minorities
as Subjects in Clinical Research," NIH, accessed February 2, 2025,
https://grants.nih.gov/policy-and-compliance/policy-topics/inclusion/
women-and-minorities/guideline#:~:text=The%20NIH%20
Revitalization%20Act%20of,and%20minorities%20in%20clinical%
20research.&text=The%20statute%20includes%20a%20specific,and%2C
%20in%20particular%20clinical%20trials.

35. US General Accounting Office, note 31.

36. Viviana Simon, "Scientific Report Series: Understanding the Biology
of Sex Differences," Society for Women's Health Research, May 2005,
https://swhr.org/wp-content/uploads/2024/12/CRISPreport.pdf.

37. "Consideration of Sex as a Biological Variable in NIH-Funded
Research," NIH, accessed February 2, 2025, https://orwh.od.nih.gov/
sites/orwh/files/docs/NOT-OD-15-102_Guidance.pdf; "NIH Policy
on Sex as a Biological Variable," NIH, accessed February 2, 2025,
https://orwh.od.nih.gov/sites/orwh/files/docs/SABVPoster508C.pdf.

38. Celeste Krewson, "Survey Shows Menopause Curriculums Lacking in
Residency Programs," *Contemporary OB/GYN*, August 11, 2023,
https://www.contemporaryobgyn.net/view/survey-shows-menopause-
curriculums-lacking-in-residency-programs.

39. Delaney Burns et al., "Closing the Data Gaps in Women's Health,"
April 3, 2023, https://www.mckinsey.com/industries/life-sciences/
our-insights/closing-the-data-gaps-in-womens-health.

40. Deeptha Khanna, "Women's Health: Why Is the Health of at Least Half
the Global Population So Often Overlooked?" World Economic Forum,
January 2, 2023, https://www.weforum.org/stories/2023/01/women-
health-gap-davos-2023/.

41. Katherine Ellison, "Nearly Dying in Childbirth: Why Preventable
Complications Are Growing in the U.S.," NPR, December 22, 2017,
https://www.npr.org/2017/12/22/572298802/nearly-dying-in-
childbirth-why-preventable-complications-are-growing-in-u-
s#:~:text=But%20more%20than%20135%20expectant,more%20
children%2C%20or%20searching%20in.

42. See discussion and citations in note 6.

43. "Forced Sterilization of Disabled People in the United States," National Women's Law Center, January 24, 2022, https://nwlc.org/resource/forced-sterilization-of-disabled-people-in-the-united-states/; Sara Luterman, "31 States Have Laws that Allow Forced Sterilizations, New Report Shows," 19th News, February 4, 2022, https://19thnews.org/2022/02/forced-sterilization-guardianship-reproductive-justice/.

Chapter 3: Myths, Misconceptions, and Misogyny in Women's Health

1. CPT code 58662 corresponds with laparoscopic excision of lesions of the ovary, pelvic viscera, or peritoneal surface and has an RVU of approximately 12.15. Lisa Rome, "Coding for Laparoscopy for Endometriosis," NASPAG, accessed February 3, 2025, https://www.naspag.org/index.php?option=com_dailyplanetblog&view=entry&category=uncategorized&id=34:coding-for-laparoscopy-for-endometriosis; "Physician Fee Schedule—January 2023 Release," Centers for Medicare & Medicaid Services, accessed February 3, 2025, https://www.cms.gov/medicare/medicare-fee-service-payment/physicianfeesched/pfs-relative-value-files/rvu23a.

2. CPT code 29827 corresponds with shoulder arthroscopy with rotator cuff repair and has an RVU of approximately 15.59. "Physician Fee Schedule—January 2023 Release," note 1.

3. Erin Fennern and Sharon Stein, "Gender Inequity in the Clinical Setting," *Clinics in Colon and Rectal Surgery* 36, no. 5: 309–314, March 8, 2023, https://pmc.ncbi.nlm.nih.gov/articles/PMC10411211/.

4. "Sleep Health," Society for Women's Health Research, accessed February 3, 2025, https://swhr.org/health_focus_area/sleep-health/.

5. Jeremy Chien and Elizabeth Poole, "Ovarian Cancer Prevention, Screening, and Early Detection: Report from the 11th Biennial Ovarian Cancer Research Symposium," *International Journal of Gynecological Cancer.* 27, no. 9: S20–22, November 2017, https://pmc.ncbi.nlm.nih.gov/articles/PMC6154781/#:~:text=This%20is%20mostly%20due%20to,(stages%20III%20and%20IV).&text=There%20is%20currently%20no%20approved,are%20there%20early%20detection%20modalities.

6. Fritz Heese, et al., "Closing the Gender Health Gap," Oliver Wyman, accessed February 3, 2025, https://www.oliverwyman.com/our-expertise/perspectives/health/2023/jan/closing-the-gender-health-gap.html.

7. "Women's Health Equity Initiative: Alzheimer's Disease," Society for Women's Health Research, accessed February 3, 2025, https://swhr .org/programs/womens-health-equity-initiative/alzheimers-disease/.

8. Matthew Baird et al., "The Case to Fund Women's Health Research: An Economic and Societal Impact Analysis," WHAM, accessed February 3, 2025, https://thewhamreport.org/wp-content/uploads/2022/02/ TheWHAMReport_crosscutting-compressed.pdf.

9. Ibid.

10. Ossie Ravid and Danny Tobey, "Contributed: The Rise of Femtech," *Mobi Health News*, December 11, 2020, https://www.mobihealthnews .com/news/contributed-rise-femtech; Eva, Epker, and Linda, Greub, "Why Investing in Women's Health Is Impact Investing," *Fast Company*, February 24, 2023, https://www.fastcompany.com/90855196/why-investing-in-womens-health-is-impact-investing.

11. So O'Neil et al., "The High Costs of Maternal Morbidity Show Why We Need Greater Investment in Maternal Health," The Common-wealth Fund, November 12, 2021, https://www.commonwealthfund .org/publications/issue-briefs/2021/nov/high-costs-maternal-morbidity-need-investment-maternal-health.

12. Stephanie Faubion et al., "Impact of Menopause Symptoms on Women in the Workplace," *Mayo Clinic Proceedings*, February 25, 2023, https://www.mayoclinicproceedings.org/pb-assets/Health%20 Advance/journals/jmcp/JMCP4097_proof.pdf.

13. Delaney Burns et al., "Closing the Data Gaps in Women's Health," McKinsey & Company, April 3, 2023, https://www.mckinsey.com/ industries/life-sciences/our-insights/closing-the-data-gaps-in-womens-health.

14. Heather Landi, "Parsley Health Rolls Out Comprehensive Women's Health Program as Company Rapidly Builds Out Employer-Focused Business," Fierce Healthcare, May 18, 2023, https://www.fiercehealth care.com/providers/parsley-health-rolls-out-comprehensive-womens-health-program-company-rapidly-moves.

15. Fritz Heese et al., note 10.

16. Kate Bahn and Annie McGrew, "A Day in the U.S. Economy Without Women," *American Progress*, March 7, 2017, https://www.american progress.org/article/a-day-in-the-u-s-economy-without-women/.

17. "The Case to Fund Women's Health Research: Did You Know?" WHAM, accessed February 3, 2025, https://thewhamreport.org/report/.

18. Matthew Baird et al., note 12.

19. Nicole Rideout, "OHSU Aims to Reduce Differences in How Men, Women Experience, Are Treated for Pain," OHSU, March 21, 2024, https://news.ohsu.edu/2024/03/21/ohsu-aims-to-reduce-differences-in-how-men-women-experience-are-treated-for-pain#:~:text=A%20number%20of%20studies%20show,wait%20an%20average%20of%2065; Esther Chen et al., "Gender Disparity in Analgesic Treatment of Emergency Department Patients with Acute Abdominal Pain," *Academic Emergency Medicine* 15, no. 5 (March 29, 2008): 399–482, https://onlinelibrary.wiley.com/doi/10.1111/j.1553-2712.2008.00100.x.

20. Beth Casteel, "Women Don't Get to Hospital Fast Enough During Heart Attack," American College of Cardiology, March 5, 2015, https://www.acc.org/About-ACC/Press-Releases/2015/03/05/16/33/Women-Dont-Get-to-Hospital-Fast-Enough-During-Heart-Attack.

21. "Study Finds Women Less Likely to Be Prescribed Pain Relief Than Men," King's College London, September 4, 2024, https://www.kcl.ac.uk/news/study-finds-women-less-likely-to-be-prescribed-pain-relief-than-men#:~:text=The%20finding%20was%20supported%20by,disparity%20seen%20in%20their%20results.

22. Carol Weisse et al., "Do Gender and Race Affect Decisions About Pain Management?" *Journal of General Internal Medicine* 16, no. 4 (April 2021): 211–217, https://pmc.ncbi.nlm.nih.gov/articles/PMC1495199/#:~:text=In%20general%2C%20women1–3,patients%20are%20treated%20less%20aggressively.

23. Kelly Hoffman et al., "Racial Bias in Pain Assessment and Treatment Recommendations, and False Beliefs About Biological Differences Between Blacks and Whites," *PNAS* 113, no. 16 (April 4, 2016): 4296–4301, https://www.pnas.org/doi/10.1073/pnas.1516047113.

24. Salimah Meghani, Eeeseung Byun, and Rollin Gallagher, "Time to Take Stock: A Meta-Analysis and Systematic Review of Analgesic Treatment Disparities for Pain in the United States," *Pain Medicine* 13, no. 2 (February 2012): 150–74, https://pubmed.ncbi.nlm.nih.gov/22239747/; Janice, Sabin, "How We Fail Black Patients in Pain," AAMC,January6,2020,https://www.aamc.org/news/how-we-fail-black-patients-pain.

25. Monika Goyal, et al.,"Racial Disparities in Pain Management of Children with Appendicitis in Emergency Departments," *JAMA Pediatrics* 169, no. 11 (November 2015): 996–1002, https://pmc.ncbi.nlm.nih.gov/articles/PMC4829078/#:~:text=Black%20children%20with%20appendicitis%20were,significance%20in%20the%20multivariable%20model.

26. "Working Together to Reduce Black Maternal Mortality," CDC, April 8, 2024, https://www.cdc.gov/womens-health/features/maternal-mortality.html#:~:text=Black%20women%20are%20three%20times,healthcare%20and%20underlying%20chronic%20conditions.

27. Gabrielle Jackson, "The Female Problem: How Male Bias in Medical Trials Ruined Women's Health," *The Guardian*, November 13, 2019, https://www.theguardian.com/lifeandstyle/2019/nov/13/the-female-problem-male-bias-in-medical-trials; Dusenbery, *Doing Harm: The Truth About How Bad Medicine and Lazy Science Leave Women Dismissed, Misdiagnosed, and Sick,* March 6, 2018.

28. "More Than 1 in 10," Endometriosis Foundation of America, February 23, 2023, https://www.endofound.org/morethan1in10.

29. Monica Lefton, "Rewriting Endometriosis Education for Providers and Policymakers," Society for Women's Health Research, October 30, 2023, https://swhr.org/rewriting-endometriosis-education-for-providers-and-policymakers/?utm_source=chatgpt.com; "Endometriosis Foundation of America: Our Commitment to Research," Endometriosis Foundation of America, accessed February 3, 2025, https://www.endofound.org/research.

30. "Polycystic Ovary Syndrome," Office on Women's Health, accessed February 3, 2025, https://womenshealth.gov/a-z-topics/polycystic-ovary-syndrome.

31. Amanda Johnson, "Up to 70% of Women with PCOS Remain Undiagnosed | Polycystic Ovary Syndrome Affects 1 in 10 Women," U.S. Department of Veterans Affairs, September 23, 2024, https://www.va.gov/sheridan-health-care/stories/up-to-70-of-women-with-pcos-remain-undiagnosed-polycystic-ovary-syndrome-affects-1-in-10-women/#:~:text=Surprisingly%2C%20up%20to%2070%25%20of,"female"%20sex%20hormones).

32. Bijan Borah et al., "The Impact of Uterine Leiomyomas: A National Survey of Affected Women," *American Journal of Obstetrics and Gynecology*, vol. 209, no. 4, October 2013, https://pmc.ncbi.nlm.nih.gov/articles/PMC4167669/#:~:text=Uterine%20leiomyomas%20(fibroids)%20are%20benign,affect%20approximately%2080%25%20of%20women.&text=Most%20leiomyomas%20are%20asymptomatic%2C%20and,severe%20enough%20to%20require%20treatment.

33. Ibid.

34. Ibid.

35. Between 24 and 50 million Americans have an autoimmune condition, and as many as four of five of those individuals are women. While the female-to-male ratio for a disease like lupus is 9:1, the ratio is much higher for other autoimmune diseases like Sjogren's syndrome, which has a 19:1 ratio. Bruce Goldman, "Stanford Medicine-Led Study Shows Why Women Are at Greater Risk of Autoimmune Disease," *Stanford Medicine*, February 1, 2024, https://med.stanford.edu/news/all-news/2024/02/women-autoimmune.html#:~:text=As%20many%20as%204%20out,syndrome%2C%20it's%2019%20to%201.

Chapter 4: The Femtech Frontier: A New Era in Healthcare

1. "Open Accelerator: Zcube Announces 5 Startups Selected for the New Edition Focused on Women's Health and Femtech," Zambon, September 23, 2024, https://www.zambon.com/en/media/press/2024-09-23-open-accelerator-zcube-announces-5-startups-selected-new-edition-focused; Kadence Bio, "Home Page," last accessed February 17, 2025, https://www.kadencebio.com.

2. Emily Chang and Ellen Huet, "A Smart Breast Pump: Mothers Love It. VCs Don't." Bloomberg.com, September 21, 2017. https://www.bloomberg.com/news/articles/2017-09-21/a-smart-breast-pump-mothers-love-it-vcs-don-t.

3. Selin Bucak, "Even in Femtech, It Still Pays to Be a Male Founder," Sifted, October 18, 2023, https://sifted.eu/articles/even-in-femtech-it-still-pays-to-be-a-male-founder. Dr. Brittany Barreto's *2023 Femtech Landscape Report* estimates that up to 85 percent of femtech startups have at least one female founder. Brittany Barreto et al., "2023 FemTech Landscape Report," *FemHealth Insights*, March 2024, https://www.femhealthinsights.com/reports/p/2023-femtech-landscape-report.

4. "Female-Founded Startups: 3 Things Female Founders Must Know Before Raising Money," Founders Network, last accessed February 17, 2025, https://foundersnetwork.com/blog/female-founded-startups/#:~:text=Globally%2C%2020%20percent%20of%20startups,States%20have%20a%20female%20CEO.

5. Barreto et al., note 3.

6. Ibid.

7. Eva Epker, "How Venture Capital Investment in Women's Health Changed in 2024," *Forbes*, January 11, 2025, https://www.forbes.com/sites/evaepker/2025/01/11/was-2024-truly-womens-healths-much-needed-and-awaited-standout-year/.

8. "Executive Order on Advancing Women's Health Research and Innovation," The White House, March 18, 2024, https://bidenwhitehouse.archives.gov/briefing-room/presidential-actions/2024/03/18/executive-order-on-advancing-womens-health-research-and-innovation/.

9. "Sprint for Women's Health Awards Aim to Close Gaps in Women's Health Research," ARPA-H, October 23, 2024, https://arpa-h.gov/news-and-events/sprint-womens-health-awards-aim-close-gaps-womens-health-research.

10. Barreto, note 3.

11. Camille Bello and Laura Llach, "Painful Periods? Spain Just Passed Europe's First Paid 'Menstrual Leave' Law," *Euro News*, February 16, 2023, https://www.euronews.com/next/2023/02/16/spain-set-to-become-the-first-european-country-to-introduce-a-3-day-menstrual-leave-for-wo.

12. Marrium Habib et al., "The Challenges for Women's Health in Sub-Saharan Africa: Lessons Learned from an Integrative Multistakeholder Workshop in Gabon," *Journal of Global Health* 11, September 4, 2021, https://pmc.ncbi.nlm.nih.gov/articles/PMC8442509/#:~:text=

Joint%20senior%20authors.&text=Collection%20date%202021
.&text=This%20work%20is%20licensed%20under%20a%20Creative
%20Commons%20Attribution%204.0%20International%20License
.&text=The%20sub%2DSaharan%20African%20(SSA,and%20
economic%20challenges%20%5B1%5D.

13. Ariella Tal and Brittany Barreto, "Maternal Health," September 2024,
available at https://www.femhealthinsights.com/reports/p/maternal
health; "US FemTech Trends and Competitive Analysis," Grand View
Research, July 2024, https://www.grandviewresearch.com/market-
trends/us-femtech-market-trend-analysis.

14. "What Is Perinatal Depression?" American Psychiatric Association, last
accessed February 17, 2025, https://www.psychiatry.org/patients-families/
peripartum-depression/what-is-peripartum-depression?utm_source=
chatgpt.com; Brenda Bauman et al., "Vital Signs: Postpartum Depressive
Symptoms and Provider Discussions About Perinatal Depression—
United States 2018," CDC, May 15, 2020, https://www.cdc.gov/
mmwr/volumes/69/wr/mm6919a2.htm?utm_source=chatgpt.com.

15. "US FemTech Trends and Competitive Analysis," Grand View Research,
July 2024, https://www.grandviewresearch.com/market-trends/us-
femtech-market-trend-analysis.

16. Ibid.

17. Barreto, note 3.

18. Lunna Lopes et al., "Americans' Challenges with Health Care Costs,"
KFF, March 1, 2024, https://www.kff.org/health-costs/issue-brief/
americans-challenges-with-health-care-costs/#:~:text=The%20cost%
20of%20health%20care,year%20because%20of%20the%20cost.

19. Shelby Hale, "Medical Gaslighting: Study Reveals 72% of Millennial
Females Feel Dismissed by Doctors, Mira, February 11, 2025, https://
shop.miracare.com/blogs/resources/medical-gaslighting?srsltid=AfmB
Ooqpmx1HCYMmdpqLcV7F-Nj4vh2A8g0UeybuXIXGZNebbv3T
iF9E&country=US.

20. Kweilin Ellingrud et al., "Closing the Women's Health Gap: A $1 Tril-
lion Opportunity to Improve Lives and Economies," McKinsey &
Company, January 17, 2024, https://www.mckinsey.com/mhi/our-
insights/closing-the-womens-health-gap-a-1-trillion-dollar-
opportunity-to-improve-lives-and-economies.

21. "Women's Health Initiative (WHI)," NIH, last accessed February 17, 2025, https://www.nhlbi.nih.gov/science/womens-health-initiative-whi.
22. "The Case to Fund Women's Health Research: Did You Know?" WHAM, accessed February 3, 2025, https://thewhamreport.org/report/.

Chapter 5: Femtech's Invisible Currency: The True Value of Your Health Data

1. For more information on how insurers can use femtech and other data sources in their risk stratification process, along with ethical concerns about such data use, see Danielle Keats Citron, "A New Compact for Sexual Privacy," *William & Mary Law Review*, no. 62: 1770 (2021); Marshall, Allen, "Health Insurers Are Vacuuming Up Details About You—And It Could Raise Your Rates," ProPublica, July 17, 2018, https://www.propublica.org/article/health-insurers-are-vacuuming-up-details-about-you-and-it-could-raise-your-rates; Rebecca Robbins, "Insurers Want to Nudge You to Better Health. So They're Data Mining Your Shopping Lists," *Stat News*, December 15, 2015, https://www.statnews.com/2015/12/15/insurance-big-data/#:~:text=Insurance%20companies%20have%20always%20had,shop%20and%20what%20you%20buy.
2. "Hackers, Breaches, and the Value of Healthcare Data," Imprivata, June 30, 2021, https://www.imprivata.com/blog/healthcare-data-new-prize-hackers.
3. "Guidance Regarding Methods for De-Identification of Protected Health Information in Accordance with the Health Insurance Portability and Accountability Act (HIPAA) Privacy Rule," Department of Health and Human Services, last updated February 3, 2025, https://www.hhs.gov/hipaa/for-professionals/special-topics/de-identification/index.html#:~:text=Although%20the%20risk%20is%20very,patient%20to%20which%20it%20corresponds; Katharine Miller, "De-Identifying Medical Patient Data Doesn't Protect Our Privacy," Stanford University, July 19, 2021, https://hai.stanford.edu/news/de-identifying-medical-patient-data-doesnt-protect-our-privacy; Amitai Richman, "Re-Identification of Anonymized Data: What You Need to Know," K2view, September 11, 2023, https://www.k2view.com/blog/re-identification-of-anonymized-data#:~:text=One%20of%20the%20main%20ways,the%20identity%20of%20the%20subjects.

4. Rocher, Luc, et al., "Estimating the Success of Re-Identifications in Incomplete Datasets Using Generative Models," *Nature*, vol. 10, no. 3069, 2019, https://www.nature.com/articles/s41467-019-10933-3.

5. According to a 2023 report by the Organisation for Economic Co-operation and Development, insurance companies are leveraging external data sources and applying analytical tools based on artificial intelligence to enhance risk assessment and policyholder risk reduction. OECD, "Leveraging Technology in Insurance to Enhance Risk Assessment and Policyholder Risk Reduction," 2023, https://www.oecd.org/content/dam/oecd/en/publications/reports/2023/12/leveraging-technology-in-insurance-to-enhance-risk-assessment-and-policyholder-risk-reduction_4844de05/2f5c18ac-en.pdf?utm_source= chatgpt.com. Additionally, a 2018 ProPublica article highlighted that insurers and data brokers are predicting health costs based on data about factors such as race, marital status, and even consumer behaviors like television viewing habits. Marshall Allen, "Health Insurers Are Vacuuming Up Details About You—And It Could Raise Your Rates," ProPublica, July 17, 2018, https://www.propublica.org/article/health-insurers-are-vacuuming-up-details-about-you-and-it-could-raise-your-rates?utm_source=chatgpt.com. Life Insurers could also access results of at-home genetic tests—like those provided by 23andMe or Ancestry.com—by asking you for those test results or buying the information from data brokers. Zack Sigel, "Can Your DNA Change How Much You Pay for Life Insurance?", Investopedia, January 6, 2025, https://www.investopedia.com/can-your-dna-change-how-much-you-pay-for-life-insurance-8768536?utm_source=chatgpt.com; Kristen Brown, "Genetic Discrimination Is Coming for Us All," *The Atlantic*, November 12, 2025, https://www.theatlantic.com/health/archive/2024/11/dna-genetic-discrimination-insurance-privacy/680626/?utm_source=chatgpt.com.

6. Drew Harwell, "Is Your Pregnancy App Sharing Your Data with Your Boss?" *Washington Post*, April 10, 2019, https://www.washingtonpost.com/technology/2019/04/10/tracking-your-pregnancy-an-app-may-be-more-public-than-you-think/.

7. Joseph Cox, "Data Broker Is Selling Location Data of People Who Visit Abortion Clinics," VICE (May 3, 2022), https://www.vice.com/en/article/location-data-abortion-clinics-safegraph-planned-parenthood/.

8. Ibid.

9. Steve Alder, "Majority of Americans Mistakenly Believe Health App Data Is Covered by HIPAA," *HIPAA Journal*, July 26, 2023, https://www.hipaajournal.com/americans-mistakenly-believe-health-app-hipaa/.

10. To learn more about the HIPAA Privacy and Security Rules and their applicability, see 45 C.F.R Part 164 (2024), available at https://www.law.cornell.edu/cfr/text/45/part-164.

11. 45 C.F.R. § 160.103 (2024).

12. Ibid.

13. Ibid.

14. Ibid.

15. Ibid.

16. Ibid.

17. 15 U.S.C. § 57b (2024); "A Brief Overview of the Federal Trade Commission's Investigative, Law Enforcement, and Rulemaking Authority," FTC, accessed February 7, 2025, https://www.ftc.gov/about-ftc/mission/enforcement-authority.

18. "Health Breach Notification Rule," FTC, last accessed February 19, 2025, https://www.ftc.gov/legal-library/browse/rules/health-breach-notification-rule.

19. C. Kirby, "US State Privacy Legislation Tracker," IAPP, last accessed February 7, 2025, https://iapp.org/resources/article/us-state-privacy-legislation-tracker/.

20. "California Consumer Privacy Act (CCPA)," California Office of the Attorney General, March 13, 2024, https://oag.ca.gov/privacy/ccpa.

21. "Flo Health Inc. Company Update, March 2022," Flo Health, March 16, 2022, https://flo.health/newsroom/flo-company-update.

22. Heather Landi, "Flo Health Banks $200M to Reach Unicorn Status," Fierce Healthcare, July 30, 2024, https://www.fiercehealthcare.com/digital-health/fertility-and-period-tracking-app-flo-health-bank-200m-reach-unicorn-status.

23. Sam Schechner, "You Give Apps Sensitive Personal Information. Then They Tell Facebook," *The Wall Street Journal*, February 22, 2019, https://www.wsj.com/articles/you-give-apps-sensitive-personal-information-then-they-tell-facebook-11550851636.

24. Ibid.

25. Ibid.

26. "In the Matter of Flo Health, Inc.," FTC, Docket No. C-4747, Complaint, June 17, 2021, https://www.ftc.gov/system/files/documents/cases/192_3133_flo_health_complaint.pdf.

27. "FTC Finalizes Order with Flo Health, a Fertility-Tracking App that Shared Sensitive Health Data with Facebook, Google, and Others," FTC, June 22, 2021, https://www.ftc.gov/news-events/news/press-releases/2021/06/ftc-finalizes-order-flo-health-fertility-tracking-app-shared-sensitive-health-data-facebook-google.

28. Ibid.

29. *Frasco v. Flo Health Inc.*, No. 3:21-cv-00757-JD (N.D. Cal.); "Frasco v. Flo Health Inc.," Labaton Keller Sucharow, September 23, 2024, https://www.labaton.com/cases/frasco-v-flo-health-inc.

30. *Lam v. Flo Health Inc.* (Supreme Court of British Columbia 2024); Rhianna Schmunk, "Lawsuit Claiming Flo Health App Shared Intimate Data with Facebook Greenlit as Canadian Class Action," CBC, March 18, 2024, https://www.cbc.ca/news/canada/british-columbia/flo-health-privacy-class-action-1.7137600.

Chapter 6: Data, Danger, and the Post-*Roe* World: What's Real, What's Hype, and What You Can Do

1. *Dobbs, State Health Officer of the Mississippi Department of Health et al. v. Jackson Women's Health Organization et al.*, 597 U.S. 215 (2022), https://www.supremecourt.gov/opinions/21pdf/19-1392_6j37.pdf.

2. Jasmine Wright and Maegan Vazquez, "White House Says Americans Should Be 'Really Careful' About Using Period Tracker Apps," CNN, July 8, 2022, https://www.cnn.com/2022/07/08/politics/white-house-period-tracker-apps/index.html.

3. Katherine Yao, and Megan Ranney, "Opinion: The Danger of Period-Tracking Apps in a Post-*Roe* World," CNN, June 16, 2022, https://www.cnn.com/2022/06/16/opinions/period-trackers-app-roe-abortion-ranney-yao/index.html.

4. Darragh Roche, "Why Delete Period Tracking App? *Roe v. Wade* Ruling Sparks Panic Over Data," *Newsweek*, June 25, 2022, https://www.newsweek.com/why-delete-period-tracking-app-roe-v-wade-ruling-sparks-panic-data-1719167.

5. Flora Garamvolgyi, "Why US Women Are Deleting Their Period Tracking Apps," *Guardian*, June 28, 2022, https://www.theguardian.com/world/2022/jun/28/why-us-woman-are-deleting-their-period-tracking-apps.

6. Cat Zakrzewski et al., "Texts, Web Searches About Abortion Have Been Used to Prosecute Women," *The Washington Post*, July 3, 2022, https://www.washingtonpost.com/technology/2022/07/03/abortion-data-privacy-prosecution/.

7. Emily Bazelon, "Purvi Patel Could Be Just the Beginning," *New York Times Magazine*, April 1, 2015, https://www.nytimes.com/2015/04/01/magazine/purvi-patel-could-be-just-the-beginning.html. Purvi Patel's conviction was later overturned by the Indiana Court of Appeals, which ruled that the state legislature did not intend for the feticide law to be used to prosecute women for their own abortions. "Indiana Court Tosses Purvi Patel Feticide Conviction," NBC News, July 22, 2016, https://www.nbcnews.com/news/asian-america/indiana-court-tosses-purvi-patel-s-2015-feticide-conviction-n615026.

8. *Roe v. Wade*, 410 U.S. 113 (1973).

9. Ibid.

10. Ibid.

11. *Planned Parenthood of Southeastern Pa. v. Casey*, 505 U.S. 833 (1992).

12. Ibid.

13. *Dobbs, State Health Officer of the Mississippi Department of Health et al. v. Jackson Women's Health Organization et al.*, 597 U.S. 215 (2022).

14. Elizabeth Nash, "13 States Have Abortion Trigger Bans—Here's What Happens When *Roe* Is Overturned," Guttmacher Institute, June 2022, https://www.guttmacher.org/article/2022/06/13-states-have-abortion-trigger-bans-heres-what-happens-when-roe-overturned.

15. Annette Choi and Devan Cole, "See Where Abortions Are Banned and Legal—and Where It's Still in Limbo," CNN, last updated February 11, 2025, https://www.cnn.com/us/abortion-access-restrictions-bans-us-dg/index.html#:~:text=See%20where%20abortions%20are%20banned,where%20it%27s%20still%20in%20limbo&text=Following%20the%20US%20Supreme%20Court%27s,limited%20access%20to%20the%20procedure.

16. Texas, S.B. 8, https://capitol.texas.gov/tlodocs/87R/billtext/pdf/SB00008F.pdf; Emma Bowman, "As States Ban Abortion, the Texas Bounty Law Offers a Way to Survive Legal Challenges," NPR, July 11, 2022, https://www.npr.org/2022/07/11/1107741175/texas-abortion-bounty-law#:~:text=SB%208%20bans%20abortions%20following, be%20sued%20under%20the%20law.

17. Oklahoma passed two "bounty hunter" laws after the *Dobbs* decision; however, they were both struck down in May 2023. Becca Damante and Kierra Jones, "A Year After the Supreme Court Overturned *Roe v. Wade*, Trends in State Abortion Laws Have Emerged," *American Progress*, June 15, 2023, https://www.americanprogress.org/article/a-year-after-the-supreme-court-overturned-roe-v-wade-trends-in-state-abortion-laws-have-emerged/#:~:text=Most%20bans%20are%20enforced%20through,struck%20down%20in%20May%202023.

18. "Idaho Governor Signs Bounty-Hunting Abortion Ban," ACLU, March 23, 2022, https://www.aclu.org/press-releases/idaho-governor-signs-bounty-hunting-abortion-ban.

19. Brittni Frederiksen et al., "Abortion Bans May Limit Essential Medications for Women with Chronic Conditions," KFF, November 17, 2022, https://www.kff.org/womens-health-policy/issue-brief/abortion-bans-may-limit-essential-medications-for-women-with-chronic-conditions/; "Mifepristone: Questions and Answers with Rollins Researchers," Emory University Rollins School of Public Health, December 13, 2023, https://sph.emory.edu/news/news-release/2023/04/mifepristone-questions-answers.html#:~:text=Additionally%2C%20mifepristone%20has%20important%20uses,the%20medication%20for%20any%20reason.

20. Elizabeth Cohen and John Bonifield, "Texas Woman Almost Dies Because She Couldn't Get an Abortion," CNN, June 20, 2023, https://www.cnn.com/2022/11/16/health/abortion-texas-sepsis/index.html.

21. Ibid.

22. Ibid.

23. Selena Simmons-Duffin, "Doctors Who Want to Defy Abortion Laws Say It's Too Risky," NPR, November 23, 2022, https://www.npr.org/sections/health-shots/2022/11/23/1137756183/doctors-who-want-to-defy-abortion-laws-say-its-too-risky#:~:text=Why%20doctors%20

don%27t%20openly%20defy%20abortion%20laws%2C,provide%
20abortion%20care%20in%20a%20medical%20emergency
.&text=Jack%20Resneck%20recently%20recounted%20how%20
doctors%20around,practicing%20medicine%20in%20states%
20that%20ban%20abortion.

24. Hannah Smothers, "Should We All Be Stockpiling Plan B Right Now?" *Self*, July 8, 2022, https://www.self.com/story/buying-plan-b-emergency-contraception-in-advance; Claire Bugos, "What You Should Know About Stockpiling Plan B," Verywell Health, June 24, 2022, https://www.verywellhealth.com/stockpiling-plan-b-5271334.

25. *Carpenter v. United States*, 585 U.S. 296 (2018); *Riley v. California*, 573 U.S. 373 (2014).

26. Emile Ayoub and Elizabeth Goitein, "Closing the Data Broker Loophole," Brennan Center for Justice, February 13, 2024, https://www.brennancenter.org/our-work/research-reports/closing-data-broker-loophole.

27. "Healthcare Sees 300% Surge in Ransomware Attacks," Dark Reading, October 24, 2024, https://www.darkreading.com/cyberattacks-data-breaches/microsoft-healthcare-300-percent-surge-ransomware-attacks; John Riggi et al., "A Look at 2024's Health Care Cybersecurity Challenges," American Hospital Association, October 7, 2024, https://www.aha.org/news/aha-cyber-intel/2024-10-07-look-2024s-health-care-cybersecurity-challenges.

28. Steve Alder, "11.27 Million HCA Healthcare Patients Affected by Recent Cyberattack," *HIPAA Journal*, July 11, 2023, https://www.hipaajournal.com/hca-healthcare-cyberattack-data-breach-2023/#:~:text=Largest%20Healthcare%20Data%20Breaches&text=On%20July%2010%2C%202023%2C%20HCA,HCA%20Healthcare%20programs%20and%20services.

29. Rebecca Pifer, "2 Million Patients' Data Exposed in Cyberattack on New England Health Services Provider," Healthcare Dive, June 9, 2022, https://www.healthcaredive.com/news/cyberattack-shields-2-million-patient-data-breach/625132/.

30. "Change Healthcare Cyberattack Support," Change Healthcare, last accessed February 20, 2025, https://www.unitedhealthgroup.com/ns/health-data-breach.html.

31. Yohan, Yun, "How Big Tech Handles Privacy and Governments' Data Demands," *Coin Telegraph*, August 29, 2024, https://cointelegraph.com/news/big-tech-privacy-government-data-regulation.

32. Ibid.

33. Ibid.

34. Kevin Collier and Minyvonne Burke, "Facebook Turned Over Chat Messages Between Mother and Daughter Now Charged Over Abortion, NBC News, August 9, 2022, https://www.nbcnews.com/tech/tech-news/facebook-turned-chat-messages-mother-daughter-now-charged-abortion-rcna42185.

35. Sara O'Brien and Clare Duffy, "Nebraska Teen and Mother Facing Charges in Abortion-Related Case that Involved Obtaining Their Facebook Messages," CNN, August 10, 2022, https://www.cnn.com/2022/08/10/tech/teen-charged-abortion-facebook-messages/index.html.

36. "Interstate Shield Laws," Center for Reproductive Rights, June 26, 2024, https://reproductiverights.org/interstate-shield-laws/.

37. Jack Queen, "Texas Judge Fines NY Doctor at Least $100,000 for Prescribing Abortion Pills," Reuters, February 13, 2025, https://www.reuters.com/legal/texas-judge-fines-ny-doctor-least-100000-prescribing-abortion-pills-2025-02-14/.

38. "State Constitutions and Abortion Rights," Center for Reproductive Rights, last accessed February 20, 2025, https://reproductiverights.org/maps/state-constitutions-and-abortion-rights/.

Chapter 7: The SAFE Method: Security

1. Katharine Miller, "De-Identifying Medical Patient Data Doesn't Protect Our Privacy," Stanford University, July 19, 2021, https://hai.stanford.edu/news/de-identifying-medical-patient-data-doesnt-protect-our-privacy.

Chapter 8: The SAFE Method: Accuracy

1. Bethany Corbin, "Why Is Femtech Software Unreliable? + 3 Strategies for Improvement," May 4, 2023, https://www.meddeviceonline.com/doc/why-is-femtech-software-unreliable-strategies-for-improvement-0001.

2. Jennie Dusheck, "Fitness Trackers Accurately Measure Heart Rate But Not Calories Burned," *Stanford Medicine*, May 24, 2017, https://med .stanford.edu/news/all-news/2017/05/fitness-trackers-accurately-measure-heart-rate-but-not-calories-burned.html.

3. Francisco Lopez-Jimenez, "Wrist Blood Pressure Monitors: Are They Accurate?," Mayo Clinic, July 6, 2024, https://www.mayoclinic.org/ diseases-conditions/high-blood-pressure/expert-answers/wrist-blood-pressure-monitors/faq-20057802; see also Edoardo, Casiglia, et al., "Poor Reliability of Wrist Blood Pressure Self-Measurement at Home," *Hypertension*, vol. 68, no. 4 (October 2016): 896–903, https://doi .org/10.1161/hypertensionaha.116.07961.

4. "New Study Reveals Global Trends for Menstrual Tracking App Use," University of Oxford, November 21, 2024, https://www.ox.ac.uk/ news/2024-11-21-new-study-reveals-global-trends-menstrual-tracking-app-use.

5. Jennifer Langston, "Period Tracking Apps Failing Users in Basic Ways, Study Finds," University of Washington, May 2, 2017, https://www .washington.edu/news/2017/05/02/period-tracking-apps-failing-users-in-basic-ways-study-finds/; Marguerite Duane et al., "The Performance of Fertility Awareness-Based Method Apps Marketed to Avoid Pregnancy," *Journal of the American Board of Family Medicine* 29, no. 4 (July 1, 2016): 508–11, https://doi.org/10.3122/jabfm.2016.04.160022.

6. A. J. Wilcox, "The Timing of the 'Fertile Window' in the Menstrual Cycle: Day Specific Estimates from a Prospective Study," *BMJ*, vol. 321, no. 7271 (November 18, 2000): 1259–1262, https://doi.org/10.1136/ bmj.321.7271.1259; Sarah Johnson, Lorrae Marriott, and Michael Zinaman, "Can Apps and Calendar Methods Predict Ovulation with Accuracy?" *Current Medical Research and Opinion* 34, no. 9 (May 25, 2018): 1587–94, https://doi.org/10.1080/03007995.2018.1475348.

7. A. J. Wilcox, note 6.

8. Ibid.

9. Johnson, Marriott, and Zinaman, note 6.

10. Ibid.

11. Michelle Moglia et al., "Evaluation of Smartphone Menstrual Cycle Tracking Applications Using an Adapted Applications Scoring System," *Obstetrics & Gynecology* 127, no. 6 (June 2016): 1153–1160, https://doi .org/10.1097/aog.0000000000001444.

12. "Femtech Apps Rating Map," ORCHA, July 24, 2019, https://orchahealth
    .com/femtech-apps-rating-map/.
13. Ibid.
14. Melissa Hartley, "The Hidden Costs of Inaccurate Sensors in Wearable
    Health Tech," Novo Sound, December 16, 2024, https://novosound
    .net/the-hidden-costs-of-inaccurate-sensors-in-wearable-health-tech/.
15. "Welcome to Kindlabs," Kindbody, last accessed February 20, 2025,
    https://kindbody.com/kindlabs/.
16. "Federal Food, Drug, and Cosmetic Act (FD&C Act)," FDA, last updated
    March 29, 2018, https://www.fda.gov/regulatory-information/laws-
    enforced-fda/federal-food-drug-and-cosmetic-act-fdc-act.
17. Center for Devices and Radiological Health, "How to Determine If
    Your Product Is a Medical Device," US Food and Drug Administration,
    last accessed January 8, 2025, https://www.fda.gov/medical-devices/
    classify-your-medical-device/how-determine-if-your-product-
    medical-device.
18. Center for Devices and Radiological Health, "Classify Your Medical
    Device," US Food and Drug Administration, last accessed January 8, 2025,
    https://www.fda.gov/medical-devices/overview-device-regulation/
    classify-your-medical-device.
19. "Examples of Software Functions for Which the FDA Will Exercise
    Enforcement Discretion," US Food and Drug Administration, last
    updated September 29, 2022, https://www.fda.gov/medical-devices/
    device-software-functions-including-mobile-medical-applications/
    examples-software-functions-which-fda-will-exercise-enforcement-
    discretion.
20. "Medical Device User Fee Amendments (MDUFA)," FDA, last accessed
    March 20, 2025, https://www.fda.gov/industry/fda-user-fee-programs/
    medical-device-user-fee-amendments-mdufa#:~:text=Annual%
    20Establishment%20Registration%20Fee:%20$9%2C280,
    %2Daccredited%20third%2Dparty%20reviewer.
21. Amanda Shea, "Scientific Research at Clue," Clue, May 31, 2024,
    https://helloclue.com/articles/about-clue/scientific-research-at-clue.

Chapter 9: The SAFE Method: Foundation

1. Jemima Kiss, "WWDC 20214: Apple Reveals 'Health,' Its New App for Tracking Fitness and Wellbeing," *The Guardian*, June 2, 2014, https://www.theguardian.com/technology/2014/jun/02/apple-reveals-health-its-entry-into-fitness-tracking.

2. Rose Eveleth, "How Self-Tracking Apps Exclude Women," *The Atlantic*, April 5, 2018, https://www.theatlantic.com/technology/archive/2014/12/how-self-tracking-apps-exclude-women/383673.

3. Ibid.

4. Tanya Lewis, "Apple's Health App Tracks Almost Everything, Except Periods," NBC News, September 26, 2014, https://www.nbcnews.com/id/wbna56126216.

5. Ibid.

6. Andrew Griffin, "Your iPhone Will Now Track Periods," *The Independent*, June 9, 2015, https://www.independent.co.uk/tech/apple-s-health-data-app-gets-period-tracking-10307363.html.

7. Leif Johnson, "The Women of Apple," *Macworld*, March 8, 2017, https://www.macworld.com/article/673893/the-women-of-apple.html.

8. Griffin, note 6.

9. Clue launched its app in 2013 and by 2015, it had more than two million active users in over 180 countries. Natasha Lomas, "Period Tracker App Clue Gets $7M to Build a Platform for Female Health," *Tech Crunch*, October 9, 2015, https://techcrunch.com/2015/10/09/clue-series-a/.

10. Maria Mellor, "Fitness Trackers and Wearables Are Ignoring a $50bn Market: Women," *Wired*, November 27, 2019, https://www.wired.com/story/health-tech-fitness-trackers-women/#:~:text=It%20wasn%27t%20until%202018,women%20and%20gather%20their%20data.

11. Maninder Ahuja, "Age of Menopause and Determinants of Menopause Age: A PAN India Survey by IMS," *Journal of Midlife Health* 7, no. 3 (July 2016): 126–131, https://pmc.ncbi.nlm.nih.gov/articles/PMC5051232/.

12. Angela VanScoy, "Growing Femtech Investment Brings Solutions to Underserved Women's Health Challenges," Deloitte, March 18, 2024, https://www2.deloitte.com/us/en/blog/accounting-finance-blog/2024/femtech-growth-investment.html; "The Femtech Industry: Statistics and Facts," Statista, January 10, 2024, https://www.statista.com/topics/10267/femtech/#editorsPicks.

13. Mick Champayne, "How Femtech Is Capitalizing on Women," Papaya .Rocks, March 17, 2019, https://papaya.rocks/en/trendbook/w-jaki-sposob-femtech-zarabia-na-kobietach.

14. Kaitlyn Tiffany, "Period-Tracking Apps Are Not for Women," Vox, November 16, 2018), https://www.vox.com/the-goods/2018/11/13/18079458/menstrual-tracking-surveillance-glow-clue-apple-health.

15. Ibid.

16. Christine Olivas, LinkedIn post, accessed November 19, 2024, https://www.linkedin.com/feed/update/urn:li:activity:7231750331854954496/.

17. Bella Wigley, "The World's Most Popular Female Health App Was Made by Men, for Men," Polyester, last accessed February 20, 2025, https://www.polyesterzine.com/features/the-worlds-most-popular-female-health-app-was-made-by-men-for-men.

18. Rebecca Jennings, "Your Period Tracker App Could Be Selling Your Data," Vox, November 13, 2018, https://www.vox.com/the-goods/2018/11/13/18079458/menstrual-tracking-surveillance-glow-clue-apple-health.

19. Ibid.

20. Jennifer Langston, "Period Tracking Apps Failing Users in Basic Ways, Study Finds," University of Washington, May 2, 2017, https://www.washington.edu/news/2017/05/02/period-tracking-apps-failing-users-in-basic-ways-study-finds/.

21. Jenny McGrath, "With Period-Tracking Apps, the Fate of Your Fertility Is Far from Clear," Digital Trends, September 2, 2019, https://www.digitaltrends.com/mobile/the-problems-and-promises-of-period-tracking-apps/#dt-heading-hundreds-of-uncertified-apps.

22. The term "othering" refers to "a set of dynamics, processes, and structures that engender marginality and persistent inequality across any of the full range of human differences based on group identities." John Powell and Stephen Menendian, "The Problem of Othering: Towards Inclusiveness and Belonging," *Othering & Belonging*, Summer 2016: 17. As a result, othering results in the construction of an identity in reference to others, thus propagating group-based inequality and marginality. Natalie Grove, and Anthony Zwi, "Our Health and Theirs: Forced

Migration, Othering, and Public Health," *Social Science & Medicine* 62, 2006: 1931–34; Joy Johnson et al., "Othering and Being Othered in the Context of Health Care Services," *Health Comm* 16, 2004: 253–54. Through this process, a virtuous "self" and a lesser "other" are created. Susan Stabile, "Othering and the Law," *University St. Thomas Law Journal*, no. 12, 2016: 381–83. In this manner, othering operates by defining and securing a person's identity by stigmatizing and distancing those who are different, resulting in exclusion, devaluation, and dehumanization of others.

23. "Does Digital Health Technology Know Women?" Medical Futurist, February 21, 2019, https://medicalfuturist.com/femtech-womens-health/; Jane Wakefield, "Period-Tracking Apps 'Not for Women,'" BBC News, August 2, 2018, https://www.bbc.com/news/technology-45043399.

Chapter 10: The SAFE Method: Equity

1. "How FemTech Is Transforming Healthcare for BIPOC Communities," World Economic Forum, May 2023, https://www.weforum.org/stories/2023/05/femtech-healthcare-bipoc.

2. "Racial Bias Is Deeply Rooted in Healthcare Technology and Medical Devices," Chartis, last accessed November 19, 2024, https://www.chartis.com/insights/racial-bias-deeply-rooted-healthcare-technology-and-medical-devices.

3. Annalies Winny, "The Problem with Pulse Oximeters: A Long History of Racial Bias," Johns Hopkins, July 8, 2024, https://publichealth.jhu.edu/2024/pulse-oximeters-racial-bias; Sylvia, Sudat, et al., "Racial Disparities in Pulse Oximeter Device Inaccuracy and Estimated Clinical Impact on COVID-19 Treatment Course," *American Journal of Epidemiology* 192, no. 5 (May 5, 2023): 703–713, https://pubmed.ncbi.nlm.nih.gov/36173743/.

4. Laura Jones, "How Many People Don't Speak English in the US?," Lingoda, January 3, 2024, https://www.lingoda.com/blog/en/how-many-people-not-speak-english/#:~:text=It%27s%20very%20difficult%20to%20know,other%20than%20English%20at%20home.

Chapter 11: Overcoming Medical Dismissal:
How Femtech Strengthens Your Case

1. Maria Whitman et al., "ZS Future of Health Report," ZS, last accessed February 20, 2025, https://www.zs.com/consumer-survey-on-the-future-of-connected-health; Ben Leonard et al., "Buried in Data: A Doctor's Lament," *Politico*, February 8, 2023, https://www.politico.com/newsletters/future-pulse/2023/02/08/buried-in-data-a-doctors-lament-00081673.

2. Evan Sweeney, "Data Overload, Access and Affordability Limit Patient Monitoring Technology," Fierce Healthcare, June 1, 2017, https://www.fiercehealthcare.com/mobile/data-overload-access-and-affordability-limit-home-health-monitoring.

Chapter 12: The Future of Femtech: A Revolution in Motion

1. "How Femtech Startups Transform Women's Healthcare," Vention Teams, November 16, 2023, https://ventionteams.com/blog/femtech-startups.

2. Sorina Mihaila, "US Health Insurance Company Partners with Health in Her Hue to Connect Black Women with 'culturally Sensitive' Providers," *FemTech World*, October 4, 2022, https://www.femtechworld.co.uk/news/us-health-insurance-company-partners-with-health-in-her-hue-to-connect-black-women-with-culturally-sensitive-providers.

3. "Fertility Care More Within Reach for Everyone," Aetna, last accessed February 20, 2025, https://www.aetna.com/individuals-families/womens-health/iui-intrauterine-insemination-coverage.html#:~:text=Fertility%20care%20more%20within%20reach,medical%20benefit%20on%20eligible%20plans.

4. "For Women, by Women: Femtech Innovation Grows at Johns Hopkins University," Johns Hopkins Technology Ventures, March 26, 2024, https://ventures.jhu.edu/news/for-women-by-women-femtech-innovation-grows-at-johns-hopkins-university.

5. "Johns Hopkins Launches Center for Global Women's Health and Gender Equity," Johns Hopkins Bloomberg School of Public Health, February 2, 2024, https://publichealth.jhu.edu/2024/johns-hopkins-launches-center-for-global-womens-health-and-gender-equity.

6. "The ReproTechquity Collaborative," University of Pittsburgh, last accessed February 20, 2025, https://www.converge.pitt.edu/reprotechquity-collaborative.

7. "Playground Teams Up with Center for Intimacy Justice to Destigmatize Conversations About Sexual Wellness," *Femtech Insider*, June 12, 2024, https://femtechinsider.com/playground-center-for-intimacy-justice/.

8. To see what studies NextGen Jane is sponsoring and apply to participate, visit https://www.nextgenjane.com/clinical-studies.

Acknowledgments

This book is the product of countless voices, stories, struggles, and triumphs in the fight for better women's health. It stands as both a testament to the injustices so many have endured and a celebration of the resilience and brilliance that continues to fuel the femtech revolution. I am deeply grateful to every individual working in women's health and femtech, to those tirelessly innovating, advocating, challenging systems, and creating solutions. You are the architects of a future that empowers women, honors their needs, and restores their dignity. Thank you for your courage, your vision, and your unwavering dedication to transforming a system that has failed for far too long.

To my parents, whose love and encouragement are the bedrock of everything I do, thank you for being my constant source of strength. Your belief in me has propelled me forward even when the road was unclear, and your unwavering support of my work has meant more to me than words can express. You have given me the courage to pursue this mission with everything I have. Thank you, a thousand times.

To my friends Lauren, Corrine, Virginia, and Bea, thank you for walking this path with me. Your patience, honesty, and willingness to listen transformed my thoughts into focused ideas. You were my sounding board when I needed clarity and offered thoughtful feedback that helped shape this book. Your support and input along the way have been invaluable, and this book is better because of you.

To my editors and publisher, thank you for believing in me and this project, and for your support in bringing this book to life. Your trust and dedication have made all the difference, and I'm especially thankful for your efforts in championing the femtech revolution and helping this work find its place in the world.

Women's health deserves a revolution, and I am forever grateful to everyone striving to deliver it. You are the reason this book exists, and you are the reason I believe in a brighter, stronger, and healthier future for women everywhere. With deepest gratitude, I extend my heartfelt thanks to everyone who made this journey possible and believed in this vision. Thank you, from the bottom of my heart.

About the Author

Bethany Corbin, JD, LLM, is a healthcare innovation, femtech, and privacy attorney on a mission to help thought-leading companies revolutionize the global women's health sector. Through her company, FemInnovation, Bethany helps unite the women's health ecosystem to drive meaningful and sustainable change in women's digital health and femtech. She is a recognized thought leader at the intersection of women's health, law, and technology, and was a 2023 recipient of the American Bar Association's On the Rise Top 40 Young Lawyers Award. Her strategic insights have been featured in top news outlets, including *Forbes, Fortune,* BBC, NPR, *Cosmopolitan, Bustle, Teen Vogue, The Atlantic,* and more. Bethany has testified about the importance of data privacy for reproductive health before the Maryland Cybersecurity Council's Ad Hoc Committee on Consumer Privacy and her guest episode on the *HIT Like a Girl* podcast discussing the impact of the overturn of *Roe v. Wade* won a 2022 Power Press Award.

Index

Making Ireland Irish

Irish Studies
James MacKillop, *Series Editor*

Selected titles from Irish Studies

Making Ireland
IRISH

Tourism and National Identity since the Irish Civil War

Eric G. E. Zuelow

Syracuse University Press

First Edition 2009

09   10   11   12   13   14   6   5   4   3   2   1

The following previously published material by the author was modified for this work, and its use herein is gratefully acknowledged: (1) "Enshrining Ireland's Nationalist History Inside Prison Walls: The Restoration of Kilmainham Jail," *Éire-Ireland* 39 (Fall–Winter 2004): 180–201. Copyright © 2004: Rish American Cultural Institute, 1 Lackawanna Place, Morristown, N.J. 07960; (2) "'Ingredients for Cooperation': The Role of Irish Tourism in North-South Relations, 1924–1998," *New Hibernia Review* 10, no. 1 (Spring 2006), 17–39.

∞ The paper used in this publication meets the minimum requirements of the American National Standard for Information Sciences—Permanence of Paper for Printed Library Materials, ANSI Z39.48–1992.

For a listing of books published and distributed by Syracuse University Press,
visit https://press.syr.edu.

ISBN-13: 978-0-8156-3225-2   ISBN-10: 0-8156-3225-8

Library of Congress Cataloging-in-Publication Data

Zuelow, Eric.
Making Ireland Irish : tourism and national identity since the Irish Civil War / Eric G. E. Zuelow. — 1st ed.
p. cm. — (Irish studies)
Includes bibliographical references and index.
ISBN-13: 978-0-8156-3225-2 (hardcover : alk. paper)
ISBN-10: 0-8156-3225-8 (hardcover : alk. paper)
1. Tourism—Social aspects—Ireland—History—20th century. 2. Tourism—Social aspects—Ireland—History—21st century. 3. National characteristics, Irish. 4. Nationalism—Ireland—History—20th century. 5. Nationalism—Ireland—History—21st century. 6. Ireland—History—Civil War, 1922–1923—Influence. 7. Ireland—Cultural policy. 8. Ireland—Intellectual life. 9. Ireland—Politics and government—1922– I. Title.
G155.I7Z84 2008
338.4'79417—dc22
2008043217

For my parents,
Helen and Richard

Eric G. E. Zuelow is assistant professor of European history at the University of New England. He has presented his research internationally and has published a number of articles and book chapters on both Scottish and Irish history. Zuelow is coeditor of *Nationalism in a Global Era: The Persistence of Nations* (2007). He is the editor/creator of The Nationalism Project (<http://nationalismproject .org>), a leading Web site devoted to the study of ethnicity and nationalism in global perspective.

Contents

Illustrations

Acknowledgments

Just as Irish tourism and national identity grew from ongoing dialogue and discussion, so too did this book. The project started as a Ph.D. dissertation at the University of Wisconsin-Madison, and I benefited greatly from conversations with University of Wisconsin-Madison faculty and fellow graduate students. A number of faculty members were especially helpful in focusing my ideas. George L. Mosse, Rudy Koshar, Frank Solomon, Johann Sommerville, David McDonald, Stan Schultz, and Thongchai Winichakul were each influential in the framing of this project. I benefited greatly from countless discussions with Robert J. Kaiser both during and after an immensely valuable semester spent doing independent reading under his guidance; he has done much to help define my ideas about place, space, and national identity. My graduate advisor, James S. Donnelly Jr., deserves special recognition. His patience, advice, encouragement, and exceptional editing skill dramatically improved the quality of my work. His influence on my approach to history has been profound.

While I conducted my research for this project, Irene Furlong, Mike Cronin, Eunan O'Halpin, Michael Kennedy, Ruth McManus, Robert McNamara, Spurgeon Thompson, and Anne Dolan all offered advice at various points about documents to consult, possible interview subjects, and questions to consider. I am deeply indebted to Irene Furlong and her husband, Frank, for their hospitality during my initial week in Dublin; without them I might never have found a place to live, let alone commenced research. I also owe thanks to Franz and Peggy Geiselbrechtinger for their friendship and hospitality during my time in Ireland.

Rudy Koshar, Roy Foster, Shelley Baranowski, and Jim Rogers all read an early draft of this book and provided me with invaluable feedback. The anonymous peer reviewers for Syracuse University Press also provided me with useful suggestions that helped further improve the manuscript. While I am responsible for any and all errors, their suggestions made this a much better volume than it otherwise would have been.

The staffs of the National Library of Ireland, Irish National Archives, Public Records Office of Northern Ireland, National Photographic Archives of Ireland, and the University of Wisconsin Libraries were all exceptionally accommodating during my research. All documents from the National Archives of Ireland are published with the permission of the Director of the National Archives of Ireland and I would like to extend my deepest thanks for this assistance. Clive Brooks and Derek Cullen of the Bord Fáilte Photographic Archives were more helpful than they can imagine. Clare Hackett of the Guinness Ireland Archives was especially helpful in locating and scanning photographic images. Eugene Finn and Sunniva O'Flynn made my research at the National Film Center of Ireland a real pleasure. Brian McGee of the Cork Archives Institute was most helpful despite the extraordinary workload that he shouldered as the only archivist managing a massive and invaluable collection. Niamh O'Sullivan of the Kilmainham Jail Archives saved me significant time by providing me with copies of all the relevant documents available in her collection. I also received considerable assistance from the staff of Dúchas—The Heritage Service and especially from Joan Murphy, who both answered my questions and provided me access to closed files regarding the state purchase of Poulnabrone. Kevin O'Doherty, Michael Gorman, and Jan de Fouw were generous with their time and extraordinary recollections of their lives at Bord Fáilte. I would also like to thank both *Éire-Ireland* and *New Hibernia Review* for allowing me to republish material covering the restoration of Kilmainham Jail and North/South tourism relations respectively.

I have had useful conversations with many people over the course of my research, but the friendship and comments offered by Michael Chamberlain, Stephen E. Hanson, David Burrow, Brian Covey, Joel Green, Tara Keenan, Scott Moranda, Robert Kruse, and David Tenenbaum stand out. I am especially grateful for the hospitality, friendship, and extraordinary discussions that I was fortunate to have with Dr. Aoife Bhreatnach, whose thinking about Irish Travellers often sparked my own ideas about tourists and tourism. Brian

Covey's comments on the earliest draft of this book led to a judicious period of editing that dramatically helped the finished product.

I could not have successfully weathered the long passage from dissertation to book without the love and support of Katie Burns. Her good humor, kind words, editing skill, and constant encouragement not only contributed to this project but brighten all aspects of my life.

I owe an extraordinary debt of gratitude to my grandfather, the late Gerald E. Zuelow, without whose financial support the research and initial writing of this book would have been impossible.

Finally, although the ideas contained in the following pages developed from my experiences in graduate school at the University of Wisconsin-Madison and while conducting research in Ireland, this book has much deeper roots. I owe more to my parents, Helen and Richard Zuelow, than I can possibly acknowledge or express. My interest in history is the result of the trips to Great Britain they took me on during my early adolescence. I will not soon forget the thrill of exploring British castles and cathedrals, and wandering along Roman roadbeds, nor my feeling of pride when I was able to share my newfound knowledge with others. My parents added to the gift of travel by encouraging me to express my nascent knowledge and excitement through writing. I dedicate this book to them.

Introduction

On 11 November 1996, "Tourism Brand Ireland," a new marketing campaign, was launched in Dublin; its first and most visible project was a seven-minute promotional video. It is easy to get lost in the footage. As viewers, we are immediately struck by a blast of vibrant color and feel the thumping drumbeat of "Dreams" by the popular Irish rock band The Cranberries. We see blue skies, smiling faces, and pints of Guinness. A woman in romantic nineteenth-century dress rides down an apparently deserted beach on the back of a beautiful horse, only to be followed by a herd of wild horses frolicking in the surf. A girl, atop a vintage bicycle, rides in circles on the firm sand as the camera gazes through the spokes of her front wheel at the playing horses. Then we are in a small town in County Cork where a pack of dogs is racing down a pastel-painted street as onlookers cheer. One dog, evidently thinking better of the madness, breaks from the pack and disappears into a pub for a pint. We then soar over the ocean waves toward the Skellig rocks off County Kerry. Seabirds glide on the air around us as we pass over Great Skellig, the site of one of Ireland's most breathtaking and sublime collections of monastic remains; the camera pivots backward and we see the striking rocks disappearing behind us. The same camera technique later finds us zooming over a young couple lying at the edge of the four hundred-foot-high Cliffs of Moher. The woman, wearing a flat cap, turns to her partner and the pair shares a romantic look. Many more striking images pass quickly before our eyes: a brilliantly lit Glendalough round tower seen rising above picturesque gravestones, currachs (traditional Irish boats) racing, a young student sprinting into his exam hall at Trinity College, Dublin doorways and Georgian architecture in an environment apparently free of traffic, fresh seafood, dancing, red-haired colleens. As the song ends, we see two animated figures embrace, swinging around and then exchanging a shamrock with the word "Ireland" below. In the European version we read, "Ireland: Lead a Different Life," while in the American edition, where "lead a different life" might imply "find a gay lover," the viewer is told to "Awaken to a Different World."[1]

The images presented in those seven minutes are not entirely new. Guinness, blue skies, secluded beaches, romantic ruins, red-haired girls, friendly people, and the rest have long been a part of Irish tourism marketing. But if one were to look only at tourist guidebooks or advertisements, the complexity and sociocultural implications of Irish tourism would be lost and the historical context omitted.

The Tourism Brand Ireland campaign was announced eighteen months before the video was released; it was the brainchild of a group of tourism interests and the minister for tourism and sport, who felt that Ireland needed a new "brand strategy." Although Bord Fáilte's international marketing director, Noel Toolan, acted as project coordinator, Tourism Brand Ireland was a joint effort among Bord Fáilte (the Republic's official tourist body), the Northern Ireland Tourist Board (NITB), industry representatives in both countries, and overseas marketing partners: a collaborative effort from beginning to end.

The images presented, while similar to those imagined by late-Victorian visitors, showed a greatly expanded range of destinations and sites/sights that often bore little resemblance to those enjoyed by the first large influx of nineteenth-century tourists. Before the early 1950s most visitors went to Killarney, Galway, Dublin, Cork, and a handful of historic sites such as Glendalough, Newgrange, and Clonmacnois, or perhaps a seaside resort such as Bray, Tramore, or Kilkee. Following the Irish Civil War a series of programs and schemes emerged that ultimately sparked the expansion of tourist resources, the transformation of landscapes and townscapes, and the creation of new "traditions." The small street with its racing dogs, for example, would have looked drab and grey in the years before 1958, given that the pastel colors in the film were the product of a campaign started in the late 1950s to brighten Ireland's townscapes.

If only statutory tourist bodies were involved, few of the changes in Irish tourism since the early 1920s would have been possible. The government showed little concern with tourism until the end of the 1930s, and even thereafter it was often half-hearted as the role of tourism as a national interest was debated. Free State tourism development started life as a private campaign waged by a collection of patriotic businessmen. Following the formation of the first statutory tourist board, tourism officials still had to depend on the public to carry out much of the work required to make Ireland a successful destination. Buildings had to be painted, streets cleaned, behavior modified, landscapes preserved, and historic sites maintained and made accessible. Despite the fact that many of these projects originated in Dublin, people with parochial interests never failed to pursue their own agendas, and the dependence of tourism promoters on local cooperation ensured that these concerns were taken seriously. Tourism symbolized different things to different people; it was shorthand for a variety of ideas about the national interest that were routinely debated from the Civil War onwards. Tourism Brand Ireland is but one stage in a very complicated and still ongoing process of negotiation that helped shape and reshape Irish identity and that is explored at length in these pages. This book is about these negotiations and about how Irish men and women, together with outside interests, came together to make Ireland Irish.

The Development of Tourism

Although historians have yet to write a comprehensive history of preindependence Irish tourism, it is clear that Ireland has long been a tourist destination. For the most part, English groups, including railway companies and hoteliers, promoted pre-1921 Irish tourism for a largely English audience. Most Irish people lacked the financial resources to travel around Ireland, let alone to develop attractive tourist products crafted to charm outsiders.[2] While these realities did not eliminate tourism-inspired discourse, the pre- and postindependence periods exhibit significant differences. Following the Irish Civil War, the *Irish,* not the English, were, for the first time, completely responsible for developing their own tourist product and for determining how they wanted to present themselves to the world. Suddenly the opportunity to define Irishness was on the shoulders of Irish men and women.

Modern tourism, in Ireland as elsewhere, is a recent development with roots firmly planted in the "Grand Tour."[3] This eighteenth-century coming-of-age ritual involved sending England's young aristocrats and wealthy landed gentlemen to the European continent in order to learn languages, meet important political figures, and develop the skills that would allow them to become England's future statesmen. As it happened, the Grand Tour often devolved into a hedonistic excuse for Britannia's sons to frequent Mediterranean brothels and to consume vast quantities of alcohol—a sort of eighteenth-century "spring break."[4]

While the Grand Tour was at its height, a series of aesthetic changes gradually altered the popular attitude toward remote landscapes, beaches, and mountains. The eighteenth-century philosopher Edmund Burke's notion of the "sublime" helped to redefine what cultured Europeans found aesthetically pleasing.[5] Beaches were transformed from a transitory zone between the untamed sea and the tranquility of the land into a healthful space where people could visit to restore their strength and to take the waters.[6] Remote and mountainous areas were romanticized and recast as beautiful.[7] Ruins were reimaged as scenic rather than as eyesores or as a source of stone for local building projects.[8] Early Irish tourism developed as a direct result of these changes; the rugged beauty of the western seaboard attracted the first tourists to Ireland and the countless romantic ruins that dot the countryside also lured them.

It did not take long before Killarney emerged as the country's major tourist destination. By 1775 Killarney already provided visitors an established tourist routine. It was customary to spend two days exploring the area's beautiful lakes, a task accomplished by hiring local boatmen to row the tourist from island to island.[9] Most early tourists to Ireland seem to have been pleased by what they found. For example, Arthur Young, a famous English agriculturalist, visited Killarney in 1776 and declared it to be "the wildest and most romantic country I had any where seen; a region of steep rocks and mountains, which continued for nine or ten miles."[10] Jacques Louis de Bougrenet, a Breton Royalist who escaped to exile in England during the French Revolution, declared that "the soul most indifferent to beauty cannot but be charmed by this delightful spot (near Kenmare)."[11]

Many early English travelers found another striking attraction in Ireland: extreme poverty. The legacy of absentee landlordism, poor soil and unsophisticated agricultural techniques, a failure to industrialize, and regular famines assured that most Irish families were appallingly poor. Many tourists came to see Irish misery for themselves. British newspapers were filled with accounts of unrest and destitution, and the journalists who reported on Irish matters portrayed the country as if it were a disaster zone. According to literary scholar Melissa Fegan, English travelers "insisted that as the Irish were congenital liars, they had to come discover the truth" about Irish reality.[12]

The "romantic tourism" and outright curiosity that fueled early Irish tourism soon replaced the older Grand Tour and quickly led to the development of mass tourism. Where once the idea was to prepare for an aristocratic life, the new intent was to collect views.[13] Romantic tourism made tourists into "consumers of places, experiences, and souvenirs,"[14] and before long more and more people wanted to take part as the emerging middle class learned how to properly consume views.[15] Following the development of an efficient rail network, Thomas Cook capitalized on the growing desire for touring by launching a travel agency dedicated to providing affordable excursions and trips to exotic and not-so-exotic destinations. Initially Cook wanted only to transport teetotalers to a temperance meeting, but he quickly realized the extraordinary demand for inexpensive travel and soon was promoting tours to Scotland, continental Europe, Africa, the Middle East, America, and even Ireland.[16]

Mass tourism arrived in Ireland a few years later than it did in England, largely because railways developed at a slower pace. During the early nineteenth century, travelers in Ireland first depended on mail coaches and later on a network of inexpensive passenger carriages established by an Italian immigrant named Charles Bianconi. Bianconi's coach network crisscrossed most of Munster, Leinster, and Connacht, covering nearly four thousand miles daily. Travel in one of the Italian's carriages was inexpensive and relatively comfortable given the poor roadways, and the average speed was a blistering eight miles per hour. Even at this speedy clip, travel was time consuming and travelers needed to possess the resources necessary to take significant time away from work in order to enjoy leisure pursuits.[17]

Ireland's first railway was constructed between Dublin and Kingstown (Dun Laoghaire) in 1834, but further construction did not proceed rapidly. Between 1,829 and 2,050 miles of track were operational in England in 1843, compared with only 400 in Ireland seven years later. By 1870 the Irish rail lines were expanded to an impressive 2,000 miles, yet this distance still paled when compared with the nearly 10,000 miles of track that covered England in 1856.[18] Why did Irish railways develop so slowly? There are at least two answers. First, Ireland had precious little heavy industry and this lack reduced the demand for railways. Second, and closely related, Irish rail lines were built and managed by English companies, and these firms devoted the majority of their wealth to expanding and improving their lucrative English routes. Ireland had to wait until English lines were firmly established.

Thomas Cook was one of the first to capitalize on the expanding Irish rail network when he recommended short excursions to Ireland in 1852. He praised the construction of more and more track and expanded his Irish business accordingly. In 1856, for example, Cook conducted about 1,500 tourists in sixty packed railway cars to some of Ireland's beauty spots. Unfortunately, as in Scotland, the railway companies were impressed by Cook's success and soon became convinced that they could increase their profit by organizing their own excursion trains while refusing to sell inexpensive tickets to Cook. For seventeen painful years Cook was unable to conduct tours in Ireland while the railway companies monopolized the package tour business. Two years after the railways recognized that Cook's success actually contributed to their own, John Mason Cook, Cook's son and business partner, opened the company's first office in Ireland. By the 1880s Thomas Cook and Son enjoyed a lucrative business there.[19]

The most significant chapter of nineteenth-century Irish tourism started when Frederick W. Crossley arrived in the 1880s to manage the Thomas Cook and Son Dublin office. Crossley was convinced that Ireland had tremendous potential as a tourist destination and he encouraged his employer to dedicate resources to further development. When this support was not forthcoming, Crossley resigned in 1891. Three years later he started publishing a travel magazine called *Irish Tourist* and in 1895 he joined forces with a collection of hotel and railway companies to found the first Irish Tourist Association (ITA). Until the First World War, Crossley and the ITA worked tirelessly to lobby the government; to improve Irish roadways, hotels, and rail lines; and to assure continued public access to important sites such as the Giant's Causeway in County Antrim. At various times Crossley teamed up with British officials as well as key Irish leaders such as John Redmond. His lobbying efforts ultimately led to the 1909 Health Resorts and Watering-Places (Ireland) Act, which allowed local authorities to put aside money in support of tourist development—a special provision that was unique to Ireland and Blackpool (in England).

While the Anglo-Irish elite exhibited substantial support for Crossley's efforts, there were dissenting voices as well. University College Dublin archaeologist R. A. S. MacAlister, for example, worried that a steady stream of tourists would ultimately destroy Ireland's most cherished historic sites. He also rejected claims that increased tourism would lead to enhanced understanding between the English and Irish races. As historian Irene Furlong notes, "he [MacAlister] dreaded the arrival of what he viewed as an army of trippers who would encourage the emergence of pauperism in the Irish peasant by tipping the mobs of young children who would follow them."[20] Similarly, the Gaelic League, which was founded in the 1880s in order to promote the revival of the Irish language, expressed concern that tourists would "degrade the noble soul of the Irish peasant." This attitude greatly irritated Crossley and he shot back,

> Much has been said and written of an Irish Ireland. The Hooligans [*sic*] of the Irish gutter press having raised their inane heads from their native slush, babble re [*sic*] an Irish Ireland . . . (they) won't have foreigners coming to the island which had the honour of being selected for their place of birth . . . a great league is to be formed for keeping out foreign Englishmen and foreign Scotsmen from Irish Ireland . . . in the presence of such slavish twaddle, the average intelligent Irishman must feel ashamed unless he is saved by a sense of humour.[21]

The two sides of this debate did not vanish with Irish independence in 1921 and their respective voices became louder following independence. While English entrepreneurs led the Irish tourist industry before independence, and while most Irish people lacked the resources to take part in tourism development either as tourists or as tour operators, the tourism-related dialogue was muted. Then, when Irish men and women assumed the role of tourism developer, the lid was removed and tourism-related discourse became more widespread. Irish people from every part of Ireland could actually make a difference. Their opinions mattered.

When the First World War erupted in 1914, Crossley's tourism development efforts were subsumed by larger concerns; the 1916 Easter Rising and Irish War of Independence (1919–21) scarcely allowed for a resumption of the ITA's work. Following the ratification of the Anglo-Irish Treaty ("the Treaty") in 1921, the largely English-led ITA breathed its last. For his part, Crossley, a firm unionist, was disgusted by the turn of events and never again devoted any effort to tourism development.[22]

In 1922 Ireland plunged headlong into a traumatic period of civil war, the reason for which was inseparably connected to the terms of the Treaty. The Irish Free State had its own government, but Dáil (lower house of the Irish parliament) deputies had to swear an oath of allegiance to the Crown and the British continued to have a governor-general in Ireland who could summon, prorogue, and dissolve the Dáil. The governor-general had the power to approve money bills on the advice of the executive council, and he served as the direct line of communication between the British government and the Free State. Several British naval ports also remained in operation on Irish soil. From the moment that the Treaty came before Dáil Éireann for consideration it was clear that the country was fiercely divided by its terms. On 17 December 1921, Deputy Liam Mellows rejected the right of anybody to accept the Treaty, saying that "[w]e who stand by the Republic still will, I presume rebel against the new government that would be set up if this Treaty is passed."[23] This assumption proved prophetic: violence erupted in June 1922 after anti-treaty forces occupied the Four Courts in Dublin and after Michael Collins, the military leader who led Irish forces during the War of Independence and who negotiated the Treaty, attacked the building to remove them. Guerrilla conflict raged until 24 May 1923 when the IRA dumped arms to wait for another day. At times, especially following the assassination of Collins, the war was frighteningly violent. The Free State government responded to anti-treatyite activities by executing seventy-seven Irregular prisoners. Families split apart. Brothers fought against brothers. Although the conflict was not nearly as bloody as civil wars in other countries—roughly 927 people died during the Irish Civil War as compared with 25,000 in the Finnish Civil War and 300,000 in the Spanish Civil War[24]— the legacy of the conflict cast a long shadow over Irish history and, as will become clear in the following pages, had an impact on many aspects of Irish life including tourist development.

The Impact of Tourism

Modern travel has brought massive growth to many regions, inspired encounters between vastly differing cultural groups, and prompted a scholarly interest where previously there was little more than disdain for an aspect of the human experience deemed trivial. [25] Picking up on a long-standing tendency among the respectable to turn up their noses at participants in mass travel, scholars have painted tourists as little more than a "golden horde" invading less dynamic societies and turning them into a "pleasure periphery."[26] Like unthinking robots, they say, tourists travel a "beaten track"[27] and resemble the client in a massage parlor "more than it would be polite to emphasize."[28] Tourists do little more than mindlessly traipse to whatever sites are popular, they snap photographs, and then they go home. According to these scholars, tourism is an almost wholly inactive pursuit of pleasure tantamount to hedonistic excess.

Recently a growing number of academics have been more gracious to the lowly tourist. Dean MacCannell, for example, claims that tourists actually set out to find real artifacts, not just mechanical reproductions.[29] They are fully cognizant of what Walter Benjamin called the "aura" of authenticity;[30] they are not satisfied to rest at home with mere photographs but want to experience the real thing. Similarly, Rudy Koshar describes an "optics of tourism" through which tourists search for "meaning beyond the marketplace."[31] This meaning derives largely from the pursuit of difference. Tourists travel in order to enter into "contact with other ways of life. The most prestigious experiences are the ones that take people the furthest away from their everyday world. And the distance from home is not only measured in miles, but in cultural terms."[32] Tourists seek out the "other"—authentic representations of distinctive cultures.[33] It follows that host cultures must market themselves in such a way as to attract guests to the "other": Irish tourism officials must emphasize a distinctive Gaelicism, French villages must promote a distinctive folk heritage, and Scottish tourism must present misty bens, glens, and tartan-clad Highlanders.

The very fact that tourism promotes a process of "othering" raises worthwhile questions about the impact of tourism on native culture. In keeping with their disapproving treatment of tourists, scholars have until recently believed that tourism leads to the "bastardization" and "'commoditization' of previously authentic ethnic cultures for the purpose of touristic display."[34] Catherine A. Palmer, studying the Bahamas, goes even further, suggesting that tourism robs local people of the ability to define a national identity of their own and locks them into the perpetual use of images created during the colonial past.[35]

More recently, anthropological studies have suggested that the story is more complicated. According to Simon Abram, for example, "It is clearly not enough to question the effect of tourism on local people. This implies a one-way process by which tourists disempower the local 'hosts.'"[36] The older exploitation argument robs host cultures of agency by suggesting that once hosts begin mugging for the camera, they promptly forget that they are *acting*. Abram shows that while locals in small rural French towns are not above performing for tourists, they are fully capable of distinguishing touristic performance from local tradition, and they assign different meanings to each. These villagers have not mindlessly forgotten who they really are.

Likewise, after studying Foxwood, Ireland, a small town of 944 people in north Mayo, Moya Kneafsey concluded that while tourism has an influence on identity, this impact is very complicated. Relationships between tourism and place identities can be conceptualized in terms of social relations. On the one hand, changes to place identities occur as groups, institutions, and individuals act to commodify resources such as the local environment or heritage for tourism. The process of commodification is mediated through new social relations between individuals and groups within the town and farther afield.[37]

In other words, change is not brought about strictly by the tourist invasion; it is produced by decisions within the host community about self-presentation. At least when a local population is itself responsible for development, members of that population can choose how and if they will be altered by tourism. Producers have every bit as much control as do tourists. If scholars want to understand how tourism changes host cultures, they must adopt an approach that first pays attention to the social relations that exist in and between places, and second takes account of the other social processes that affect place identities. Taking this approach illustrates the ways in which different individuals and groups of people combine to resist or promote the commodification of cultural identity.[38]

Very little scholarship has yet followed Kneafsey's lead. Instead, the tendency has been to focus on one or two social groups, usually at the top of the social hierarchy, while ignoring the rest of society. Little attention is paid to the full range of individuals and organizations involved in creating tourist products. Yet if Kneafsey is correct and community relationships ultimately define how tourism will exert its impact on a society, it is fair to assume that such relationships must also determine the effectiveness of national tourism programs. To really understand tourism, it is necessary to examine the links between hosts and guests, between local and national groups, and among the government and local authorities, tourism bodies, and regional interest groups. The shape of the tourist product, to say nothing of the impact that tourism has on identity, is the result of these complex interactions. Ultimately tourism is a nexus at which different groups converge. Tourist guidebooks, for example, are a product of collaborative decisions about "what ought to be seen" that take place at the tourism nexus. Indeed, Irish guidebooks reflect a desire to spread wealth widely around the country, promote development in rural areas, and present a positive narrative about Irishness and Irish history. To appreciate the content chosen for these guides demands an understanding of the structure of Ireland's various tourist bodies, perceptions within Ireland about what it means to be Irish, government policies, and local concerns and political pressures, as well as global tourism trends. To comprehend the implications of tourism demands recognizing the role of the nexus between groups.

Working the Projectors?

Because of the history of colonialism in Ireland, scholarly willingness to disempower host communities by robbing them of agency is all too common. According to one postcolonial theorist,

> tourist representations hang like a weight around the neck of the cultural present in Ireland. They can be relied upon to remain resolutely cliché[d],

simplistic, and dogmatic in the worst possible ways. . . . Tourist representations were largely projected onto an Irish screen by English visitors. They served to rationalize colonialism for the home audience and, like a hotel training film, taught Irish people habits of silence and subservience. After 1921 the postcolonial bourgeoisie learned to work the projectors and bothered little with changing the reels.[39]

While this characterization might have been true during the colonial period, this book makes clear that it was not at all true after independence. Although it is right to stress the importance of the tourist product, the current tourist images of Ireland were chosen for presentation through an ongoing process by which images that were useful to the state and its people were adopted, while more harmful images were rejected and downplayed.

What is remarkable is how actively involved many people from across Irish society were in determining how their unique national identity would be shaped and presented. Consider what happened when an American travel magazine published an extensive article that depicted Ireland in an unfavorable light. The offending article was published by *Holiday* magazine and was written by Frank O'Connor, a major twentieth-century Irish short story writer; it dominated the December 1949 issue of the publication.[40] The feature sparked immediate anger on both sides of the Atlantic among Irish citizens and Irish-Americans alike. Among other complainers, the New Ross IRA Memorial Association protested;[41] Wexford Corporation passed a resolution calling for the immediate termination of any employment enjoyed by Frank O'Connor and requested that the minister for external affairs instruct the Irish ambassador to the United States to "deny the truth of the article in question";[42] and the Society of Friendly Sons of St. Patrick in Philadelphia asked *Holiday* magazine to apologize.[43] The Killarney Urban District Council declared the article to be a "lying tirade from beginning to end," and demanded that Frank O'Connor be investigated and his position at Radio Éireann terminated.[44] Even the Catholic press, which seldom commented on tourism-related issues, lambasted the piece as "a grave mistake."[45]

What was so awful? The article included a collection of gorgeous photographs in both color and black and white—the Cross of Muiredach at Monasterboice, the Book of Kells, a lovely thatched cottage, castle ruins and round towers, the Killarney lakes, and the Blarney Stone, to say nothing of women in Kinsale cloaks, manor houses, turf cutting, and smiling Dubliners going about their daily routines. It was a wonderful-*looking* article, but the text was problematic. O'Connor provided a catalogue of unpleasantness. Readers learned that "Ireland contains slums like you have not seen the like of elsewhere in Europe, with sickly looking children playing barefoot in the streets." Towns were devoid of industry and churches were in ruins. The author stressed Ireland's "sometimes dreadful poverty," while drawing attention to the "all-powerful" middle classes. O'Connor stressed the supremacy of the Catholic Church and alleged that

> infanticide in Ireland is appallingly common, though almost from the moment a girl starts walking out with a boy, she is kept under observation by the police; if she leaves the neighborhood, she is shadowed, and if she has a baby in another area, the police return and spread the news throughout her own town. Yet it never seems to have occurred to anybody that there is any other way of stopping the crime.

O'Connor even suggested that there was widespread anti-English feeling in Ireland. However true his allegations were,[46] he cast attention on aspects of life in Ireland that fell well outside of the scope of constructive "cultural propaganda." Little goodwill was to be gained from depictions of tyrannical clerics and sick and starving children.

Pressured by the tide of public outrage, the Department of External Affairs launched an investigation of the article so that the minister could determine whether it was "defamatory." The department's weekly newsletter criticized O'Connor's characterization of Ireland as "a rather moist baby," and challenged the overwhelmingly negative characterization of the country. More important, the department contrasted the piece with other articles addressing potential tourist destinations. It was easy enough to dismiss the bizarre allegations about spying on courting couples, but

> Irish readers will wonder not so much at the assertions . . . as at their context, and the general balance of the article. A tourist article on, say, France, is not likely to dwell on slum conditions in Menilmontant or lovingly recall epidemics which occurred seven years ago in Vieux Port or Marseilles, or recite statistics of abortions and alcoholism. Rather will it speak of France's attractions for the foreigner: it may say something about France's effort

of reconstruction and recovery. So why a different approach for Ireland? Carelessly, one may be inclined to answer that it is Ireland's own fault for breeding such cantankerous writers.

As it happened, the fault lay not with Ireland's "cantankerous writers," but instead with the "the creative process of an industrial age"—or so it was claimed.[47] In the wake of the outrage *Holiday* magazine supplied External Affairs with a summary description of the process used to produce the sordid article. The editors had instructed O'Connor to "steer well clear of [the] sentimental and corny approach" and demanded that he "dig into the almost hopeless economy of the country," while also exploring the "peculiar quirk of the Irish nature that has continually had them embroiled with their neighbours." To assist O'Connor, they provided him with "research" and set him loose. O'Connor duly provided a draft, but it "failed to take the expected crack at the clergy" and so required rewriting. The new draft still did not meet with the magazine's requirements, and the publisher asked for a discussion of an Irish family living in a cottage with a dirt floor and living space shared between pigs and people. O'Connor was put off by the notion of domestic pigs and refused to include them, but the editors still demanded that Irish poverty be emphasized and that priests be raised to much greater prominence in the narrative. When the great work was finished, the editors stressed, "The production of a thing like *Holiday* requires 'a lot of hard work, plus brains, plus talent.'"[48]

External Affairs was thoroughly displeased with the article, but the damage had been done. When the minister considered the situation, he decided that it was not a defamatory article, and no instructions were sent to the Irish ambassador in Washington to refute the charges.[49] One imagines that the minister recognized that to do so would only magnify the damage. Instead, the department urged *Holiday* to publish a new article about Ireland in a subsequent issue. This time the piece, written by John Horne Burns and published in 1950, was provided to the Irish ambassador for vetting. The ambassador in turn declared it to be "reasonably inoffensive," and, aside from the correction of a few factual errors, the article was returned to the magazine with the department's approval.[50] While a few cutting remarks, including the suggestion that Limerick city was not a pleasant introduction to the charms of southern Ireland, were present, there was little to condemn.

The response to the *Holiday* article does not support the view that the Irish people simply sat back and accepted older colonial views. The poverty that attracted many nineteenth-century tourists to Ireland was no longer an acceptable representation of Ireland. Indeed, what follows here is the story of a broad segment of Irish society actively working to erase either the image or the reality of Irish poverty. People from a diversity of groups and organizations wanted to present the best possible Ireland to the outside world. This book is an account of how the Irish people worked out exactly what the "best possible Ireland" actually was and the story of how Irish national identity was imagined and reimagined in the years following independence.

National Identity and Tourism

As with most studies of the impact of tourism on host cultures, the academic literature on nationalism tends to oversimplify the nationalization process. Most scholars describe nations as the result of an effort by a mysterious and undefined elite.[51] The problem with this view is that it fails to reflect the degree of horizontal dialogue hinted at by the heated response to the *Holiday* article or by the other cases described in this book. The "great man" view of nationalization does nothing to explain why the masses are willing to unquestioningly accept what they are told and in fact it robs them of any agency whatsoever. A smaller group of scholars suggests that nations are actually created from the bottom up. National communities, they say, are the product of preexisting cultural identities that are used to juxtapose indigenous identity with that of a colonial power.[52] While there is, no doubt, an element of truth in this view (as there is in the previous explanation), it is nevertheless unreasonable to assume that elites play no role at all. In the end, the bottom-up or top-down debate is little more than a straw man. Elites could not have imposed a new culture on the masses if there had not been a receptive audience. Likewise, subalterns undoubtedly adapted earlier identities to match new state-defined demands. It is simply not possible to understand the creation of nations if either group is written out of history.

If nations are a "deep, horizontal comradeship," then the history of the nation must reflect this fact by addressing society horizontally rather than vertically. Instead of being static, as suggested by Benedict Anderson's formulation of the nation as "an imagined community,"[53] nations are *perpetually reimagined communities that are maintained through a horizontal dialogue about community membership;* they are the sum total of cross-community dialogues about national membership and national interests, composed and recomposed by the very act of collectively discussing them. This dialogue can become louder or softer, more or less obvious, as conditions warrant. More often than not, nationalism is "banal" and it is hardly noticeable to observers. But other times, when a crisis occurs or other demands arise (like the need to create images for tourist consumption), the discussion can become much more noticeable.[54] Over time, competing practices and memories are woven into the fabric of national identities. Newer, more useful memories or images replace older ones, while conflicting visions of the national mythology are debated and discussed.[55] Nations are always in process, always changing.[56] To a large extent, this process is why nations persist, despite the many challenges that arise, and this is why Irish national identity was able to transform itself from a revolutionary identity to a state-building one.

Tourism is not the only nexus for national dialogue, but it is a particularly useful one for several reasons. First, tourism is often identified as a national interest because it is able to offer benefits to many different groups within the national community, while at the same time these groups often have disparate concerns in mind; the result is an immediate dialogue about exactly what the nation's priorities should be. Second, tourism, at least national tourism, requires consideration of precisely what it means to be part of the nation in question, of its defining characteristics, history, and geographic space. Consensus about the best image to present for tourist consumption is often difficult to attain, and thus tourism quite naturally prompts discussion about the nature of national identity. Finally, tourism involves the movement of people both within their own nation and between nations, and it places a premium on the interaction of people from different geographic spaces. The result of this contact is a continual exchange of ideas about mutual identities and "a dynamic between previous understanding and expectations and new observations and experiences."[57]

Between the end of the Irish Civil War and the present, tourism acted as both a subject of and a catalyst for debate about the Irish nation. Tourism inspired two closely related and coterminous debates. The first concerned whether tourism should be considered a national interest. On the one hand tourism advocates argued that tourism would help Ireland emerge from its history of colonial oppression and poverty to become a forward-looking and modern nation. On the other hand tourism opponents viewed dreams of modernization with suspicion while gazing backward toward a halcyon day when the Irish people spoke Gaelic and enjoyed a simple, straightforward existence doing as they had always done. Also part of the larger debate concerning tourism's place as a national interest was the question of who should manage tourism. Should local communities control tourism development in their areas or should the industry be administered from Dublin? To some extent this was another way of rephrasing the modernization debate. Traditionally the localities jealously guarded their distance and difference from Dublin. Regional rivalries, such as between Cork and Kerry, were long part of Irish life and they helped give many people a vital sense of place. Meanwhile, the modernizing forces behind tourism development viewed these local identities as a hindrance. Centralization allowed for a unified message, for more efficient and less fractious distribution of funds. The first three chapters of this book are organized chronologically and trace the "battle for tourism" as it evolved from the initial calls for tourism development through the start of the Celtic Tiger–related tourism boom of the mid-1990s, giving the reader an understanding of the historical evolution of Irish tourism and the actors involved in the process. Above all, these chapters describe how tourism was both a subject of and an inspiration for debate concerning the collective interests of newly independent Ireland.

The second major tourism-related debate involved determining the "best" Ireland to show visitors. As more people became convinced about the importance of tourism and more tourists visited Ireland, this question grew in importance. Not surprisingly, the "best" Ireland was composed of multiple components, the three most important of which were language/culture, heritage/history, and landscape. While the resultant debates often overlapped, different individuals and groups had their own pet issues; therefore, the next three chapters explore each issue separately.

Chapter 4 is divided into two sections. The first explores the dialogue between two groups: one that believed that being truly Irish involved a close link to the nation's Gaelic heritage and the Gaelic language, and another that felt Ireland should be progressive and seek to attain economic prosperity in preference to language preservation. Language enthusiasts, drawn primarily from the intelligentsia, argued vehemently that tourism would destroy the last refuges of Gaelic, and that the only way to prevent the end of the Irish language was to shield it from Anglophones. Meanwhile, the Gaelic speakers themselves saw little threat and demanded the wealth symbolized to them by tourists. The result was a protracted discussion about whether Ireland should be forward-looking or nostalgic, whether the language was better served by fencing it in and risking the emigration of its speakers or by encouraging tourism and risking death by drowning in an Anglophone sea. The second section of chapter 4 begins by noting that after independence many Irish adopted older stereotypes about Irish friendliness as a way to differentiate themselves from others. To encounter friendly and welcoming natives in Ireland represented a positive "other" to the harried people of industrial Europe and America. Once Irish character was defined, it was important to develop cultural events that would be widely acceptable. Traditional Irish fairs, for example, were often bawdy gatherings marked by drinking, fighting, and even some open sexuality. Some Irish people were left with deeply ambivalent feelings about presenting such scenes to outsiders, and therefore new festivals were invented and carefully made "authentic" by rooting them in the distant past.

As with Irish culture, the Irish past presented troubling challenges to tourism developers and to the Irish public more broadly. Irish history was defined by a long struggle with the English as well as by a more recent civil war, yet the priority of the new state was to create a unified citizenry and prosperous relations with England. The result was a strong desire to develop a historical narrative stressing Irish unity and deemphasizing past conflicts. Thus the primary concern when presenting Irish history was to show a united Irish people with a proud legacy of saints and scholars rather than a long standing penchant for violent confrontation. Chapter 5 examines the reformation of Irish history from early efforts at the development of preservationist legislation through the creation of a new historical narrative that stressed unity rather than conflict. The chapter concludes by exploring the role of global trends in defining how Irish history was presented to host and guest alike.

The presentation of a positive image of Irishness involved more than language and festivals or an historical narrative that stressed saints and scholars more than conflict; it was also closely connected with landownership and aesthetics. Chapter 6 explores debates about who should have access to Irish landscapes and what these landscapes ought to look like. Opinions varied between those who felt that the Irish constitution guaranteed landowners total control over their holdings and those who considered Irish spaces to be the property of the Irish people, to be exploited for the benefit of all. Closely tied to this debate was another concerning aesthetics. Should the land be translated for tourists by using signs, or left as a confusing network of seemingly aimless tracks? Should Irish towns be left unpainted and grey or made bright and cheerful with pastel paints and flowerpots? Ought builders be encouraged to consider aesthetic concerns when erecting structures, or should they be left to their own devices and allowed the freedom to cater to market forces? Finally, should Irish ecosystems be altered to match tourist tastes or conserved as true examples of the Irish environment?

The final chapter examines developments between the mid-1990s and early 2007, demonstrating that the debates described throughout this book continued unabated into the first years of the twenty-first century. Tourism-related horizontal dialogue remains the norm. The chapter begins with a brief explanation of the dramatic expansion of Ireland's tourism sector during the 1990s. It moves on to discuss how the industry was restructured yet again starting in 2001. Finally, it concludes with a detailed discussion of the "Dingle Wrangle," a debate over what to call the small tourist town of Dingle, County Kerry: an incident that made clear the continuing vitality of the tourism nexus as a vital element in the perpetual remaking of Irishness.

In the end this book shows how a very large cross-section of Irish society, irrespective of rank or social class, took part in the process of making Ireland Irish. It paints a picture of a people who were very much involved not only in defining their tourist product but in defining themselves. The Irish people were not merely projectionists, nor hapless dupes condemned to live in the shadow of a colonial legacy. Instead, men and women, Dubliners and rural dwellers, tourist boards and local committees took part in an ongoing process in which they created both a public image and a sense of self. *Making Ireland Irish* is a story of success, of indigenous agency, and ultimately of the close relationship between tourism and national identity in postindependence Ireland.

Making Ireland Irish

1

Introducing a National Interest, 1922–1939

If there had been no widespread debate about tourism in the years following the Irish Civil War, it would not have been surprising. The country was deeply wounded both physically and psychologically. Roads, especially in rural areas, were badly damaged, and there were too few workers employed in fixing them.[1] Between paying for the war itself, repairing material damage, and housing captured prisoners, the Cumann na nGaedheal government strained under serious financial handicaps.[2] In addition, much of the population suffered from deep poverty. Roughly 800,000, many of them in North Dublin City, lived in overcrowded conditions, and infant mortality was still appalling.[3] As if these adversities were not bad enough, the government lacked legitimacy in the eyes of a substantial portion of the citizenry,[4] and certain state institutions, such as the criminal-justice system, were notoriously weak[5]—hardly an acceptable state of affairs when Republican forces continued to carry out military operations, including a machine-gun attack on British soldiers at Cobh in 1924,[6] and, more famously, the assassination of Kevin O'Higgins on 10 July 1927. It helped little that much of the population was ambivalent about the future and was deeply divided as well.[7] Republicans "swarmed together" and "formed little coteries based on nothing more than good fellowship, a welcoming household, shared experiences, and a commonly held republican faith,"[8] effectively ensuring that a large section of the population was unwilling to help in reconstruction efforts. To survive, the Free State government had to do nothing less than "remake the administration of the nation and, in so doing, to assert its preeminent authority throughout the land"[9]—hardly easy when novel problems merged with old suspicions of Dublin rule in rural areas.[10]

Despite the Cosgrave government's general disinterest, others, stirred by tourist development efforts in countries such as Spain, France, Austria, and Italy, overflowed with pro-tourism enthusiasm. From 1905, Spain had its own state tourist commission while France and Austria followed within the next five years. Tourism advocates in these places viewed the industry as a harbinger of modernity and an essential national interest. In Spain, for example, advocates insisted that "those anxious for progress and for our country to figure among the most prosperous, patriots in general" should take the initiative by furthering tourism development.[11] With the Continental countries as inspiration, an important section of Ireland's bourgeoisie fully believed tourism represented a primary national interest. These middle-class people argued not only that tourism should be developed, but that it should be viewed as a patriotic crusade, a harbinger of modernity and improvement. Between late 1923 and 1939 these tourism advocates, led by the Irish Tourist Association (ITA), worked tirelessly to promote their cause as much to the Irish people as to foreign tourists. To meet their goals, the association first had to establish itself as the leading tourism voice in Ireland, winning as many adherents as possible in the process; then it had to persuade the government that the industry was worth investing in.

The ITA's work was made more challenging by the fact that tourism meant different things to different groups within Ireland. For members of local authorities and many citizens, tourism symbolized improvement and development, but for others it represented a threat to cherished ways of life or simply a waste of money. On the one hand, this set of attitudes meant that the ITA could promise something to everyone, but on the other, it sometimes led to conflict with those who found the modernist thrust of tourism threatening or who simply believed that the government had no business pursuing tourist development. This chapter traces the pro-tourism campaign from the first appearance of tourism advocacy after the Civil War to the eventual passage of substantial tourism legislation in 1939; particular attention is paid to the symbolic meanings that various groups within Irish society assigned to the nascent tourist industry, and to how these meanings were addressed by pro-tourism voices.

Unity through Tourism

If Ireland's bourgeoisie lacked self-confidence at the time of independence,[12] the lack was not visible in the zeal with which many advocated tourism development. Even during the Civil War a Dublin-based group of business and tourism interests combined to create the Tourist Organisation Society of Ireland, a body composed primarily of representatives of railway and steam-packet companies as well as hoteliers and tourist agencies. The group was chaired by Senator James Moran, the grandfatherly vice chairman of the Dublin Dockyard Company, who saw tourism as one path toward addressing Ireland's myriad problems such as the housing crisis.[13] From the outset this organization justified its existence in national terms, claiming that its efforts "saved many . . . Irish resorts from ruin," and the society sought to continue this work by promoting the flow of tourists between Northern Ireland and the Free State. The only real problem was a shortage of money. Existing legislation—the Health Resorts and Watering Places (Ireland) Act of 1909—did not provide adequate resources, and local groups were unable to raise enough capital to develop an acceptable promotional scheme. Killarney, for example, managed to garner only £30 for tourism publicity, while Bundoran in Donegal scratched up a meager £17. Such fund-raising failures supported the group's contention that tourism was a national concern that should be addressed at the national level. "If success is to be obtained," its leaders cried, "the Irish cities, with their great tourist attractions, must be grouped with lesser communities, and the attractions of the country as a whole pressed upon potential visitors for the benefit of the entire community of Ireland."[14] The Tourist Organisation Society of Ireland promised to create a national tourism coalition by drawing representatives from corporations and counties across Ireland and by lobbying the government for money, the use of which would be audited by a government-appointed civil servant.

The Tourist Organisation Society of Ireland was not the only organization with national plans and a firm belief in the need for a nationwide solution to tourism development. During 1923 and 1924 similar bodies were formed, including the Ulster Tourist Development Association (UTDA), the West of Ireland Tourist Development Association, and the Irish Tourist Association. All of these organizations largely followed the Tourist Organisation

Society of Ireland model as voluntary bodies comprised of bourgeois tourism interests, and all were born in the belief that Ireland, North and South, could develop a significant and lucrative tourism industry if the Irish people would pull together and get to work. The problem was that these groups were each fighting for the same money, the same political support, and even the same membership. While the Ulster Tourist Development Association had no competition in the North (the UTDA continued to operate into the 1980s), the Irish Free State was simply too small to support three organizations with national aspirations.

By January 1925 the Irish Tourist Association emerged as the most likely prospect to lead Irish tourism into the post–Civil War period. Cork-based tourism advocates founded the ITA at the Victoria Hotel, Cork, in 1923, although the group did not incorporate until June 1924. Like the Tourist Organisation Society of Ireland, the Tourist Association hoped to promote tourist traffic in Saorstát Éireann (the Irish Free State) and to safeguard "the interests of tourists therein." Toward this end the group planned to establish advertising agents, to set up an agency for hotel, motorcar, railway, and shipping companies, and to develop tourist information bureaus in key tourist centers. In addition, the ITA intended to purchase property that might be used to enhance the organization's liquidity while also working to acquire money from the state to better promote tourism. While in hindsight these were overly aggressive goals, they suggest a genuine feeling of optimism among an important segment of the population in spite of the problems faced by the new state.

At the time of its incorporation the ITA had only twenty members, but this number quickly expanded by the end of June 1924 to ninety-five.[15] As with the Tourist Organisation Society of Ireland, most members were drawn from the business classes, and a sizeable cross-section of Munster's financial elite was represented. Signatories on the incorporation papers include hotel owners, shipping men, and company directors. For example, the ITA's first director was Dr. J. C. Foley of Cork city. During his varied career Foley worked as managing director of the firm John Daly & Co., was a member of the governing body of University College, Cork, and acted as a director of the Electricity Supply Board, the Cork Opera House, and the Victoria Hotel. In addition, he served on the Cork Harbour Commission and the Central

Savings Committee, not to mention the Cork Corporation.[16] The ITA's second president, Howard S. Harrington, was an American-born lawyer, educated at Columbia and Georgetown, who directed the prosecution against the White Star Line in the legal hearing following the Titanic disaster.[17] In 1921 Harrington retired to his ancestral homeland and purchased Dunloe Castle in Killarney, where he quickly developed an interest in Irish tourism development as a way of building up the financial resources of his adopted country.[18] Other early members of the executive included Robert W. Sinnott, the manager of a steamship company; John J. Barry, a railway manager; and Arthur C. Freeman, the manager of Cork's Imperial Hotel.[19]

Beyond those with a direct financial interest in the development of Irish tourism, almost from its formation the ITA employed a young man named J. P. (Jack) O'Brien, a curious-looking character of average height, with a substantial pointed nose, large ears, and dark hair. His bright, lively eyes were framed by thick eyebrows, and his intense nervous energy and endless ideas tended to impress those who met him.[20] O'Brien grew up in Ballyporeen, not far from the Cork-Tipperary border, where his parents owned a small business that was not substantial enough to support all of the O'Brien children. After he fought on the anti-treaty side during the Civil War, the Irish Tourist Association hired O'Brien as its secretary. Encouraged by President J. C. Foley, O'Brien developed an overwhelming interest in the holiday business. He studied tourist literature from such important destinations as France, Switzerland, and England, and then traveled to these places to observe their promotional activities firsthand. His enthusiasm knew no bounds; he took what he learned and began to reshape it into programs for Ireland. He saw the Emerald Isle as a potential mecca for sportsmen where tourists could hunt, fish, or simply relax. He dreamed about improving hotel facilities, training hotel staffs, and establishing schools that would reinvent the country as a culinary center.[21] For O'Brien tourism represented a means to raise money to support his countrymen and a way to show outsiders the wonders of Ireland. Tourism, in fact, represented a profound example of the national interest, even if O'Brien himself was no fan of the present state or of the terms of the Treaty that had created it. Tourism was a powerful vehicle for helping his countrymen to raise their status, and thus it bolstered his already strong sense of nationalism.

Even if tourism meant a great deal to many in the bourgeoisie and encouraged the nationalism of others, and despite the fact that Continental governments such as Spain and France were increasingly convinced of the economic and political importance of the industry, tourism was not a government priority in Ireland.[22] No tourist-traffic legislation was proposed during this period and there were no debates in the Dáil solely about tourism development. Yet neither could the government ignore tourism—too many important people were already involved in the various tourist-development groups, and it was also obvious that countries like Belgium were enjoying substantial benefit from tourism income.[23] While this recognition did not lead government officials to propose sweeping tourism legislation in the 1920s, they nevertheless mentioned tourism frequently when discussing road improvements, unemployment, and the infrastructure at such important Irish ports as Dun Laoghaire. Already in March 1924 some government ministers and Dáil deputies adopted the national terms used by the ITA and the Tourist Organisation Society to discuss tourism. As one minister put it, the government had saved

> Ireland from . . . the worst consequences of that challenge [civil war and revolution], we have saved her from anarchy, we have saved her from the intervention of a hostile army, and we have saved her from famine. But we have not saved her, and we could not save her, no power on earth could save her, from a great deal of want and suffering, the inevitable consequences of the reckless defiance of political and economic laws of which during the last eighteen months we were the witnesses and the victims.

To rescue the country from poverty, the Dáil must earnestly look for ways to reduce unemployment and distress, the minister insisted. Tourism was a very logical solution because it would "certainly be a great source of wealth to Ireland, with its world-scattered race, naturally interested in Irish history, topography, and social institutions."[24]

Others, however, were far less enthralled with the prospect of shaping Ireland into a tourist utopia. During debate surrounding a new local-government bill, Daniel Morrissey, the minister for industry and commerce during the late 1940s, reasoned that the government should not be "so very keen on making this country an attractive place for tourists" but should focus its efforts on "making the country a suitable place for the people to live."[25] Ultimately, he argued, it was in the nation's best interest to solve the country's social and economic problems, not to use government resources and energy to create a tourist mecca while interfering in affairs that should be left to the operation of the free market.[26]

Though tourism lacked universal government support, pressure from newspapers and the various tourist bodies soon forced action. In late 1924 Patrick McGilligan, the minister for industry and commerce, called a conference of tourism groups to develop a unified national approach to tourist development.[27] The meeting occurred on 15–16 December 1924 at government buildings in Dublin and was presided over by E. J. Riordan of the Ministry for Industry and Commerce. After some discussion the delegations from each of the main tourist organizations agreed that the groups should combine to form a single tourism-development body, with the Irish Tourist Association formally becoming Ireland's national tourism organization. After a further five hours of negotiation a temporary standing committee was appointed so that the group could "start work immediately."[28] Senator Moran, previously the chairman of the Tourist Organisation Society of Ireland and a well-known and widely respected advocate of "the gospel of progress" after nearly thirteen years as a significant public figure,[29] was quickly elected president. The vice presidents included J. C. Foley, the driving force behind the formation of the ITA in Cork; Martin MacDonagh of the West of Ireland Tourist Development Association; and Howard Harrington, who represented not only the ITA but, more important, the Killarney area. These men went on to appoint an executive committee "representing various parts of the Free State." J. P. O'Brien was given the task of establishing an ITA office in College Street, Dublin.

Finding a compromise that would absolve the Oireachtas (Irish legislature) of unpleasant financial decision making while still securing the necessary money for tourism development was probably the single greatest reason behind the amalgamation of the various tourism bodies. On the one hand, without substantial income it would be impossible for any tourist organization "to undertake any comprehensive scheme likely to induce visitors to come to our various resorts and places of scenic attraction." On the other hand, there was no money and little political support for sweeping legislation despite a very vocal collection of important pro-tourism groups and individuals—many of them high in Ireland's social, economic, and political circles—who were demanding money for tourism development. By paving the way for the creation of a single tourism body, the government was able to placate the pro-tourism groups. At the same time the addition of Amendment 89 to the 1925 Local Government Act made it possible to shift responsibility for funding the unified association to county councils. The amendment allowed local authorities to levy rates for advertising "the attractions and scenery in their localities"[30] and to provide revenue to any association approved by the minister for industry and commerce. The minister for local government and public health would audit the approved organization. Technically, any approved tourism body could receive money, but only the Irish Tourist Association met the qualifications stipulated in the legislation. Crucially, the amendment did not require councils to levy a rate; instead, the decision rested with the councils themselves, and the Irish Tourist Association was thus forced to lobby councils in order to secure its income.[31]

The other major reason for creating a single tourism body was the need to present a unified front to English railway and transatlantic shipping companies that had already voiced a willingness to cooperate with a new Irish tourism organization.[32] A single national voice would facilitate easy communication and the efficient production and distribution of tourism materials. Likewise, centralization eliminated potential competition for distribution outlets; there would be no tendency for tourist bureaus in Galway, for example, to shun publicity materials from Killarney.

The Local Dimension

While the amalgamation of the Irish Tourist Association created a national tourism-development body (though not a statutory one), the need for local assistance was inescapable. Above all, development activities required the support of local groups. There were too many places to visit in Ireland for a single national organization with a minimal budget to promote successfully, and once tourists began to arrive in numbers, it was vital that the areas where these visitors were directed be ready to receive them. In addition, each locality had its own political concerns and interest groups, all with different ideas about tourism development. The ITA would need to address the concerns of these various groups if development and publicity work were to be successful. Finally, as mentioned earlier, the Irish Tourist Association was largely dependent on voluntary contributions by local authorities for its existence. If the ITA failed to meet local needs, then the authorities might cease to allocate money to the group.

As a result, the Irish Tourist Association's first priority was to carry its message that tourism was a national interest to local communities in order to establish local branches and support. The ITA argued that local organization would ensure progress on the national development front; guarantee regional improvements in lighting, sewerage, roads, and entertainment facilities; and attract tourists and their currency. While tourism was a national campaign, it would be unsuccessful unless local committees took charge of efforts in their areas.[33]

After meeting with J. P. O'Brien and other ITA representatives, the Killarney Tourist Association was created on 26 January 1924, making it one of the first and most important of the ITA's local branches. Like the ITA as a whole, the Killarney branch included such community leaders and leading businessmen as Senator William O'Sullivan, later chairman of Cosgrave's party in the Seanad (senate); the major local landowner, Lord Kenmare; several representatives of the Killarney Urban District Council; Howard Harrington (who attained his post as president of the ITA in 1926 largely because of his association with the Killarney branch); and others associated with local tourism. Like the ITA, the Killarney Tourist Association cited the betterment of Ireland as the primary reason for developing tourism. At the group's formation, Major Ross Kinloch MacGillycuddy, another major local landowner, stressed that the "object of this admirable association" should "appeal to every patriotic Irishmen" because it would encourage "the tide of travel to flow once again to our beautiful and ancient land" and would bring with it valuable foreign currency.[34] It was a tune that tourism interests sang repeatedly over much of the next seventy years—tourism was in the country's national interest, and patriots should do whatever they could to attract and please visitors.

Killarney was at the forefront of tourist impressions of Ireland, so the ITA was entirely justified when it endeavored to establish a local branch in the lakeside village before making similar efforts elsewhere. Killarney was an area that poets and travel writers alike had enthused about for nearly two hundred years, a beauty spot that headed almost every potential tourist's list of places to see in Ireland. While the government was keen to avoid becoming too deeply involved in tourism, it did not hurt that there was a widespread consensus that Killarney was the country's most notable tourist attraction. With Killarney firmly integrated into the ITA, the new body was well placed to maintain important political clout and to secure its position as the only organization approved by the minister of industry and commerce to receive money under the 1925 Local Government Act.

In addition to this successful effort to establish a local branch at Killarney, and even before passage of the Local Government Act, J. P. O'Brien and members of the ITA executive visited many other local authorities and community groups to encourage the formation of similar branches. Besides promising local groups regional publicity materials—the ITA's main function—the body quickly began trying to address local concerns in order to underline the extraordinary power of tourism to cure the nation's ills. With the exception of a handful of places such as Killarney, Tramore, and Glengarriff, local communities were not concerned with tourism per se, but they definitely favored the infrastructure improvements that the ITA suggested tourism could inspire; better roads, sewerage, and the development of a safe water supply were all required if tourism was to prove a viable undertaking, and more immediately, these things made life better for residents.

Dingle, today one of Ireland's leading tourist destinations, was little more than a run-down fishing village and a rural backwater in the wake of the Civil War. The *Kerryman* newspaper, which represented an influential pro-tourism voice during the 1920s, noted that Dingle's "isolated situation" and the nature of its soil effectively removed it from any list of viable sites for industrial development. As a result, the paper urged the town to focus its efforts on developing tourism, fisheries, and forestry.[35] In December 1924, J. P. O'Brien wrote to local community leaders to suggest that they form a committee to address tourism issues. He argued that this need was pressing because the Great Southern and Western Railway had already expressed interest in taking over the Dingle railway—a narrow-gauge rail line famous for its rather terrifying path through the mountains toward Dingle town. The town followed O'Brien's advice and a committee, chaired by the parish priest of Dingle, Canon John McDonnell, was nominated.[36] After a handful of meetings, which stressed the lack of good roads, poor sewerage, and the shortage of hotels, the committee lapsed into nonexistence.[37] Yet the ITA, helped along by the *Kerryman,* did not give up and continued to urge Dingle residents to take tourism seriously. ITA representatives also carried the message to Dublin that Dingle needed improvements. The sewage system was "positively dangerous," a "menace to public health." Among other things, sewage from the local fever hospital flowed down one of the town's streets, resulting in "unusual recurrent cases of fever."[38] Partly because of the ITA's pressure, the government moved to repair the sewage system in 1925.

Early in 1926, McDonnell once again urged Dingle community leaders to develop a local ITA branch. He "pointed out the importance of the tourist business in the district. Dingle would get all the overflow visitors from Killarney."[39] McDonnell chided the townspeople, saying that he "was amazed at the apathy of the people." He stressed the area's great natural beauty and its historical attractions such as the Gallarus Oratory and the views at Slea Head, and then noted that the roads were in a bad state and must be improved if the area were to attract large numbers of tourists.[40]

The committee was soon reestablished with McDonnell as chairman, and this time it had more staying power, largely because it was the only representative body in Dingle and therefore provided the only way in which the town could effectively make its case to the Kerry County Council and, more important, the central government. At its second meeting in March 1926 the re-formed branch passed a "strong resolution" calling for the "the bad state of the streets of Dingle" to be brought to the attention of the relevant authorities.[41] Almost immediately, just days after the passage of the resolution by the local ITA branch, there was "a decided improvement" in Dingle's streets. The new ITA branch was heartily praised in the *Kerryman* and was urged to continue focusing "attention on other local grievances with a view to having them rectified. Public cleanliness is an all-important factor, not only from the point of view of sanitation, but also as an attraction to the tourist. Nothing is so repulsive or more calculated to create a bad impression in the minds of tourists than muddy streets."[42]

The local ITA branch did continue to address local grievances, exerting at least as much of its energy on improving the welfare of the community itself as on publicizing the area's tourist attractions. In July 1926, for example, the group concerned itself with flooding in a local river that was "the dumping ground for every tin can and old bucket within three miles' radius of the town." This constant trash disposal impeded the flow of the river and caused an overpowering stench during the summer months. During the winter the river overflowed as a result of blockages brought about by the heaps of rubbish and caused widespread flooding that damaged local businesses and private homes. The local tourism committee argued, "As the Tourist Association is the only local body functioning at present, it should receive all practical support from the public. Though it has no financial resources nor executive powers, that it has a considerable weight has already been clearly manifested."[43] The precise nature of the grievance mattered relatively little; it was only important to the townspeople that "tourism" represented an excellent argument in favor of fixing whatever problem happened to arise.

Local improvement efforts by the ITA and its affiliated branches were certainly not limited to the area immediately surrounding Killarney, nor were they restricted to the period immediately following the ITA's formation. The town of Kinsale in County Cork, site of a famous battle in 1601 and near to the famously scenic Old Head of Kinsale, represents a prime example of further ITA efforts to address local grievances over an extended period. In this case the local representative body was the Kinsale Development Association, which concerned itself with all forms of local development, including signposting, hygiene, road building, industrial development, and tourism. In this capacity the Kinsale Development Association addressed the ITA on numerous occasions beginning around 1930 and continuing into the 1940s, even after the Irish Tourist Board was established in 1939.

The first appeal by the Kinsale Development Association concerned improvements to the main road between Cork City and Kinsale. The road had suffered considerable wear and tear in the years since its original grading in 1913. By April 1930 the Kinsale group had already received a grant from the Road Board for half the cost of repairs and was beginning to lobby the Cork County Council for funds to cover the remaining costs. Kinsale Development Association leaders argued in the main that the "very bad state" of the road was "militating severely against the commercial and tourist traffic in our district."[44] In addition to a published flyer urging the council to support its scheme, the Kinsale Development Association sent an envoy, Ernest E. Wolfe, to the ITA annual meeting in Dublin to generate publicity for the road improvements.[45] Wolfe worked hard, keeping Kinsale's plight front and center on the meeting agenda and stressing the potential revenue that Kinsale might generate from the brisk tourist trade that a satisfactory road would allow.[46] The strategy worked. Combined publicity and public pressure inspired action by the County Council at its budget meeting in February 1931. The Cork-Kinsale road project was allocated as much as £30,000 versus considerably smaller grants for similar projects in other parts of the county, which, when combined, earned a meager £12,500 in assistance.[47] Two years later, the Kinsale Development Association adopted a similar strategy to encourage improvements to the Kinsale-Garrettstown Road and then again, beginning in 1938, to stimulate development of the Kinsale water scheme that was designed to modernize the town's woefully inadequate water system.[48]

For most citizens, then, in the years immediately following the Civil War (and even down to the 1970s), tourism was an avenue toward local improvement, an excuse for enhancements in rural areas that otherwise showed little promise of development. By arguing that road or sewerage improvements might bring tourist revenue, it was possible to justify expenditure and to raise local claims to a higher place on the already packed agendas of local and central government bodies. In fact, the success of these arguments set a precedent that was expanded throughout the years covered by this study, and that made "tourism" a common argument for everything from enhanced signage to an end to logging, to environmental protection in rural areas, to the way in which housing developments should be designed. Tourism represented a national solution to local problems and was increasingly defined as a "national interest" by local communities during the late 1920s and the 1930s because of this fact.

The ITA's immediate effort to connect itself to local authorities had two important ramifications. First, it ensured that the ITA was always responsive to local concerns. Because councils considered their budgets annually, the central tourist organization was under constant pressure to meet local demands—a pressure that frequently caused the ITA difficulty. For example, in late 1926 County Kerry branches of the ITA became dissatisfied with the amount of publicity they were receiving in ITA publications. The problem began when two Killarney representatives informed the Kerry County Council that the central office of the ITA "gave no value for the money they got last year. The manner in which Killarney was advertised in the guide issued by them was most unsatisfactory, and as far as advertising outside or in the liners, not a single pamphlet dealing with Killarney was seen."[49] Initially, after the landowner and ITA supporter Major MacGillycuddy advised the council that it would not be wise to desert the national body, the council decided to provide the Killarney branch of the ITA with enough funding to produce its own guide, independent of the national organization, while continuing to provide annual funds to the national body. The interim decision did not last, however, and on 1 January 1927 the County Council resolved to withhold funds "as a protest against the remissness of the Central Executive of the Irish Tourist Association."[50]

Far beyond the damage inflicted by the subtraction of the annual contribution made to the ITA by the Kerry County Council, the loss of support from this vital tourist center had wider implications. Other councils, not blessed with Killarney's international reputation as a tourist destination, were often reluctant to support the ITA in the first place. Kilkenny, for example, made no great rush to join when its support was first solicited early in 1925. In response to the Kilkenny County Council's obstinacy, the ITA wrote to inform them "Kilkenny is now practically the only centre of importance which remains completely unorganised from the tourist point of view." The association observed that although Kilkenny lacked the same attractions found at Killarney, the ITA was especially anxious to provide publicity for the "underdeveloped resorts of Ireland." Despite this plea, the Kilkenny County Council deferred any decision to a later meeting.[51] A favorable decision by Kilkenny officials to support the ITA was delayed until 1927.[52]

In these circumstances, when such historic places as Kilkenny were already on the fence, for Kerry, the very epicenter of tourism, to withhold funds could well prove disastrous for the ITA. If the ITA could not serve its biggest client, how would it assist those areas with fewer scenic attractions? To avoid wider unpleasantness, the ITA quickly began courting the Kerry County Council. To assuage the concerns of the important regional legislators, on 29 January 1927 the ITA altered its bylaws to allow local authorities that contributed more than £100 per annum to nominate a member to its board of directors. While this decision greatly increased the size of the board, it also left local authorities with the impression that they would have a much greater say in tourism policy.[53] The dispute with the Kerry County Council was resolved shortly thereafter.[54]

The second major implication of the close relationship between ITA leaders and local authorities was the organization's ability to speak for local interests—a capability that served it well even into the 1950s and early 1960s. Forced into constant contact with local power brokers, often bending over backward to meet demands such as the one described above, the ITA was made intimately aware of local concerns and could then relay them to the central government in Dublin.

Inside the Coven

While the Irish Tourist Association was increasingly effective at bringing its message of national renewal through tourism to local communities, it was certainly not universally successful. For those outside of tourism centers even the promise of infrastructural improvement rang hollow. During the 1920s and 1930s counties like Roscommon and Cavan simply did not attract tourists, so it was difficult to imagine that tourism might have any positive benefits there. It was hard to connect the dots between farmers and hoteliers—difficult to imagine that farmers received income from hotels and restaurants that catered to tourists, let alone that once foreign currency entered the pockets of Irish entrepreneurs, it eventually made its way into those of employees and then on to Irish shops and businesses. Even those with college degrees did not always make the connection. In fact, some of the staff hired by J. P. O'Brien to manage tourism from the ITA's Dublin office did not fully understand the role that successful tourism could play in a national or regional economy. For example, well-known civil servant C. S. (Todd) Andrews,[55] who worked at the ITA in the late 1920s after receiving an accounting degree from University College, Dublin (UCD), "conceived [of tourism] as . . . operating for the benefit of foreign visitors rather than for its native Irish employees. At that time tourism was very much in its infancy, and its commercial possibilities were still unexplored. I did not appreciate its value as an invisible export or its potential contribution to the national economy."[56] Perhaps as a result, Andrews did not approve of the idea "of an Ireland swarming with tourists."

As the Todd Andrews example suggests, being employed by the Irish Tourist Association did not necessarily imply a deep devotion to tourism. In fact, the ITA office staff were hired more for their political connections than for any passion for the development of tourism—a striking contrast to the ITA's membership and executive committee, whose passion for tourism knew no bounds. After being instructed to set up the ITA's first office in 1925, O'Brien immediately fell back on his republican connections and surrounded himself with "a coven of ex-IRA men who had opposed the government in arms."[57] O'Brien, like many republicans following the Civil War, was intensely loyal to his anti-treaty colleagues. Advertisements were placed, but the successful candidate was hired based on word of mouth among republicans. Andrews, for example, was determined not to emigrate after completing his degree at UCD. He ferreted around for work and eventually, in 1926, ran across an ITA advertisement for an organizer. After consulting with Seamus Moore, a friend and newly elected TD (Teachta Dála, member of the Irish parliament), Andrews was accorded a meeting with Jack O'Brien. It did not take long for the two men to discover that they knew one another from the Civil War. Andrews remembers that their first post–Civil War meeting largely involved "recalling our previous meetings, reminiscing on the Civil War, and discussing the new departure in the republican movement brought about by the formation of the Fianna Fáil party." While O'Brien did not find Andrews suitable for the advertised position, he immediately offered him a job as the ITA's accountant, even making a special request to the ITA executive in order to secure an extra £1 per week for Andrews.[58]

When Andrews started work, he found that he was by no means the only ex-IRA man on the premises. O'Brien's second-in-command was a man named David Barry who had served with the IRA in north Cork. Barry's primary role was to solicit funding from hotels, travel agencies, local authorities, and other businesses. The small staff also included Sean Fitzpatrick, a former adjutant of the Third Tipperary Brigade of the IRA, whose experience with printing qualified him to handle the ITA's publishing requirements. While no longer active members of the IRA, the entire staff were dedicated supporters of Éamon de Valera. In contrast to O'Brien's staff, the

ITA board, then headed by J. C. Foley, who was a close friend and backer of W. T. Cosgrave, was made up of "men of substance" who were "all strong supporters of the Free State regime and some were active politically."[59]

Although none of the above-mentioned staff was active in the republican movement while working for the ITA, the Free State's continued political turmoil did find its way into the ITA office when Andrews was asked to hire somebody to help increase the number of brochures and guidebooks. Andrews, perhaps unwisely, hired a young man whom he had met as part of University College Dublin's Republican Club, Frank Ryan. Ryan had little if any interest in tourism—indeed, he was actively fighting against the state that he now worked to promote to largely English visitors. This detail did not bother Andrews, who simply warned Ryan not to store IRA documents or other materials in the ITA offices. Ryan disregarded the warning, however, and it was not long before Criminal Investigations Division (CID) raided the Tourist Association offices, where they found a cache of IRA files. When asked, Andrews denied any knowledge of the documents, of Ryan's ownership of them, or even of the police raid, saying that "from time to time I lost my sight and hearing, and . . . I must have been blind and deaf during the raid and the subsequent interrogation."[60] Ryan was arrested and held overnight but then released. He quickly resigned his post at the ITA.

The Many Meanings of Tourism

Even in places like Killarney where tourism was broadly considered an important part of life, there were differences of opinion about how it should be developed. For most tourism supporters the development of tourism was directly connected to the desired development of Irish industry and to the construction of a vibrant economy in the wake of Ireland's period of armed conflict. But debate about tourism was also caught in the "confused baggage of ideas" inherited from nineteenth-century nationalists, which called for both the preservation of traditional society *and* industrialization.[61] On the one hand, some, such as many Gaelic-language enthusiasts, wanted to preserve Irish life as it had always been (at least in their imaginings). For these individuals tourists represented "a formidable influx of foreignism" and a "deadly threat" to traditional rural life.[62] Meanwhile, on the other hand, O'Brien and the ITA promised that tourism "developed on proper business lines can be made a source of untold revenue" for County Kerry and Ireland more generally,[63] and they stressed that revenue from tourism would be vital if Ireland was to be able to recover from its economic misfortunes.[64] It followed that local ITA branches, like the one at Cobh, stressed the need for "the co-operation of all residents of all classes of society."[65]

The expectation that "all classes" of society should contribute to tourism development had a dark side; the pro-tourism faithful showed little tolerance for statements or activities that might undermine their efforts. Tourism was a national duty and to question tourism development policy was considered unpatriotic behavior. Given the conflicting messages that nationalists transmitted about the desire for industrialization and the dream of maintaining a rural society, conflict was almost inevitable: the two ideas simply do not easily connect. Modernization cannot occur without altering the way of life experienced in rural areas; the need for faster production necessarily accelerates life, reduces the number of workers required to make a larger number of products, and alters attitudes toward time. Tourism, the ITA's great harbinger of modernity, was no different from other modernizing forces in its general effects.

Since at least the early 1900s the tourist experience in Killarney invariably involved a boat trip between the upper and lower lakes aboard a small boat rowed by at least two of the local "boatmen." Along the way tourists visited the "Meeting of the Waters" at Old Weir Bridge, negotiated some mild rapids, and listened to the boatmen spin their unique version of local lore. Tourists who did not have the time for the longer journey also tended to make use of the boatmen's services by traveling to the various islands of the lower lake.

With the foundation of the ITA, tourism developers imagined almost infinite growth of the industry and began looking for ways to service more and more visitors in an increasingly efficient manner. During the 1920s most Killarney tourists were English men and women who arrived aboard excursion trains run by the Great Southern and Western Railway Company. Trains left London for Holyhead, tourists traveled across the Irish Sea on a ferry, and then the railway whisked them across the Emerald Isle to Killarney. Each season thousands of visitors poured in, made the rounds of Ross Castle, the Gap of Dunloe, and Muckross Abbey, and paid a visit to the boatmen on the famous lakes. Given the tight train schedule, and the fact that the trips

1. Killarney boatmen row tourists to the famous "Meeting of the Waters." Courtesy of Bord Fáilte Éireann–Irish Tourist Board.

were marketed as efficient holidays for busy English visitors, the excursionists enjoyed only a very short stay at Killarney before their train raced them back to London. Recognizing the potential logjam that a growing flood of tourists might cause, and believing that tourists ultimately wanted an efficient and thoroughly "modern" experience, the Killarney branch of the ITA argued that it would be necessary to introduce motor launches to the Killarney lakes—a view that was violently rejected by the boatmen.

The ITA first seriously considered the motor-launch idea on 16 October 1925 after hearing comments made by representatives from the Great Western Railway, who promised to double the number of Killarney tourists in 1926 if the efficiency of the boat trip could be improved.[66] The Killarney tourist authorities were stunned by the idea of such tourist traffic and quickly agreed to add the motorboats. As far as the ITA was concerned, "Killarney must not and cannot be kept back."[67] If tourists wanted motor launches, then they should have them.

The boatmen were horrified. Even before the Great Western proposal was made, the boatmen expressed the belief that motorboats should not be allowed on any of the Killarney lakes because even if initially limited to the lower lake, they "would soon spread out their influence, putting the boatmen out of business"—a plea that had evidently brought immediate assurances from the ITA (in 1924) that no such outcome would ever be allowed.[68] Just one year later, however, the association completely reversed itself. Insult was added to injury when Howard Harrington accused the boatmen of being unpatriotic.[69] The boatmen did not appreciate having their patriotism and local pride questioned by an American interloper, and they quickly lashed out in a letter to the *Kerryman,* claiming that local hoteliers cared only for their own pocketbooks, not for the town's or country's good fortune, and that others in the association merely hoped to advance their own social and political fortunes through membership. Harrington, they complained, "is only a very short time here, but he acts already as if he found Killarney and owned it."[70] What right had a "blow-in" to question their patriotism and local pride or to undermine time-honored tradition? The boatmen represented 150 native residents of the community, and their way of life mattered enough that they were willing to fight the proposed change, hinting that physical violence was not out of the question. Although the association replied by offering the boatmen a monopoly on the motor-launch business, assuring them that the ITA had no desire to put anybody out of work, the boatmen were impervious to argument on the matter.

The conflict soon widened. The *Kerryman* attacked the boatmen and picked at each of the boatmen's arguments, demeaning them as "expressions of undiluted vulgarity . . . intended for savage sarcasm [but amounting] to nothing more than coarse buffoonery symptomatic of the low-caste mentality responsible for them."[71] As far as the *Kerryman* was concerned, "'Advance Killarney!' must be the slogan; and it cannot advance if we are satisfied to wage war on progressive methods."[72] Press attacks on the boatmen did not end at the Kerry border. The *Irish Independent,* one of Ireland's leading national newspapers, argued that Killarney's tourist development was threatened by "the short-sighted policy of the local boatmen in opposing the introduction of motorboats."[73] In turn, press coverage inspired letter writers who insisted, "Attacking men like Mr. Harrington of Dunloe will do no good. He is at any rate an Irishman who is proud of his Irish ancestry and not like some of the so-called Irish-Irelanders, who send their children to England to acquire an English accent."[74]

At its heart, then, the motor-launch issue had become a nexus for discussion of precisely what it meant to be Irish. For the Irish Tourist Association and the promodernization media, motor launches were a way to increase tourist income and to make Killarney prosperous and Ireland a modern, forward-looking nation. For the boatmen the issue went deeper. Motorboats represented a direct attack on everything they knew and understood. The motorboats were an emasculating result of modernity. Worse still, the boats were suggested by an *English* company and were being pushed down the people's throats by an *American* newcomer. It was a debate about tradition versus modernity, about time-honored ways of earning a living versus a mind-numbing new world, and about insiders versus outsiders defining how life should be lived. In this instance tradition won out and the motor-launch debate retreated into unspoken memory. The available sources do not explain why the ITA dropped the issue, but the outcome probably owed more to financial considerations than to anything else. Although the local landowner, the Earl of Kenmare, approved of the use of motor launches on the lower lake, he did not offer to purchase the boats.[75] Likewise, with the boatmen obviously unwilling to purchase new launches, the onus fell on the ITA, which lacked the required funds. Killarney's lakes would have to wait until the 1950s to absorb the exhaust of motorized pleasure craft.

Investing in Tourism

Even while juggling political differences between the ITA executive and its staff, the Frank Ryan distraction, conflict over how tourism development should proceed, and the shoestring budget of roughly £10,000 per annum, the association forged ahead with its efforts to promote tourism and to publicize Irish attractions. By 1929 the ITA was producing thirty-six separate publications each year, covering places such as Killarney, Cork City, and Dublin among others—totaling some 1.5 million pieces of literature—as well as a monthly travel magazine called *Irish Travel*.[76] While most of these were local guides, the ITA also published a comprehensive *Official Guide to Ireland* starting in 1925. The *Official Guide* offered visitors information about Irish antiquities, language, and culture, and then highlighted sites and sights in all regions of the country.

The considerable cost of publishing the guides was supplemented by advertising placed by various clients. Foremost among these were hotels, railway companies, and Irish resorts. There were also ads, however, for linen manufactures, the Abbey Theatre, whiskey, cigarettes, and even portrait companies.[77] Irish businesses had a variety of motivations for supporting the Irish Tourist Association. For those directly dependent on tourist traffic, like hoteliers, ITA publications were an obvious advertising outlet and the association's success an important investment. For others, linen manufacturers for example, tourists represented a potentially valuable market sector. But corporate motives were not always obvious. Guinness, for example, has made quite a name for itself through creative advertising since at least the 1930s, yet its support of the Irish Tourist Association had little to do with a perceived advertising benefit. Instead, Guinness, perhaps the Free State's single largest private corporation, supported the ITA because the company believed that doing so was its patriotic obligation.

The Tourist Association, represented by its then president Senator Moran and by David Barry, first approached Guinness for support on 7 July 1925. They explained the aims of the association and showed Guinness officials a copy of the *Official Guide,* some ITA advertisements, and the organization's list of Irish hotels.[78] After the meeting Guinness officials noted that both an historic precedent and the reputable nature of the ITA membership supported giving a favorable response to the plea. Historically, Guinness had supported Frederick W. Crossley's late nineteenth- and early twentieth-century attempt at a tourist-development organization, also called the Irish Tourist Association, with a modest contribution of £25 in 1915.[79] In addition, the men noted that Senator Moran was "an important person in Dublin" whose interest in tourism was understandable and obvious.[80] More important, Guinness officials remarked that "the betterment of Ireland" had "become most fashionable."[81] Based on these points, the General Purposes Sub-Committee resolved to provide a £100 contribution to the association—one of the largest grants received by the ITA during this early period.[82] For Guinness, the ITA represented "one of those appeals" that required a positive response "on account of our position in Ireland." It was unlikely that the ITA would generate any real money for the brewery.[83]

"See Ireland First"

As noted previously, ITA officials encouraged cooperation with their movement, but cooperation could involve any number of activities ranging from providing money to actively assisting tourists. For most of those involved, the best way to support the tourism crusade was to "see Ireland first." According to the ITA, "a healthy option has been created in Ireland this year that the wisest, and certainly the most patriotic, thing Irish people can do is to see their own country in their holiday-time."[84] Viewing Ireland would not only acquaint Irish people with the Irish landscape and its "unique attractions," but it would assure that Ireland was not exporting its own people as tourists.[85]

The phrase "See Ireland First" paraphrased an older American tourism campaign, "See America First," and the choice of slogan is telling. In the United States, "See America First" was first used as the title for a Western tourism conference held at Salt Lake City in 1906. The words were subsequently utilized as the title of a magazine and in limited advertising campaigns conducted by the See America First League. It was only after American railway companies adopted the phrase that it truly ignited a mass movement, however. "See America First" was about making money, but it was also an expression of patriotism and of the desire to unify the American people. For the railway companies, tourism not only promised to help turn a profit, it represented an important component of nation building. The campaign worked. Tourist traffic aboard America's railways increased dramatically. The new national parks grew ever more popular. In fact, the program was so successful that there was even an unsuccessful attempt to copyright the phrase "see America first" so that it might remain associated with Glacier National Park.[86] In the same spirit, for the ITA the phrase "See Ireland First" represented both potential economic advantage and, just as important, the same nation-building mission behind its American inspiration.

The ITA's "See Ireland First" program involved posters, brochures, statements in the press, and tourist maps, but it also found its way more directly into every Irish home through the post office. The story is instructive of different views within government departments concerning tourism during the early days of the Free State. In May 1925 the Irish Tourist Association wrote to the Department of Posts and Telegraphs, requesting that post office mechanical stamping machines be fitted with die hubs bearing the words "See Ireland First" between May and September each year. J. Booth, a civil servant in the Department of Posts and Telegraphs, noted that fitting out the machines would cost the association £221, not including a fee for advertising. The department was concerned, however, because the advertisement did not relate directly to any government or official administrative project. Ordinarily this request might have been straightforward enough because the government would simply have charged the advertiser for use of the space, but in this case "the attraction of tourists by the Irish Tourist Association is likely to benefit the country materially, and the Minister for Posts and Telegraphs considers that the privilege of the advertisement should be free of charge."[87] H. P. Boland, then serving in the Department of Finance, did not see the matter in the same terms, however. He threw cold water on the scheme: "We [the Department of Finance] incline to the view that this means of advertising should be regarded primarily as available for governmental purposes, such as the Post Office Savings Bank, savings certificates, etc.," and should only be available to other interests, regardless of the potential national benefit, when the government could not find any product to advertise. As a compromise, the Department of Posts and Telegraphs decided to charge the ITA a nominal advertising fee of £20.[88] The terms were subsequently agreed, and the association continued to utilize this outlet into the 1930s.

The Need for Government Action

While the ITA was successful in establishing local branches, in obtaining support from local authorities, and in encouraging a growing number of people to contribute to the tourism campaign, tourism was not a political issue during either of the general elections held in 1927. Major candidates, whether from the ruling Cumann na nGaedheal party, the Labour party, or de Valera's newly formed Fianna Fáil, focused on agriculture and industrial development—as well as on attacking the other parties—rather than on tourism. Even Eugene O'Sullivan, an independent from County Kerry who was chairman of the Killarney branch of the ITA and ran in the first election of 1927,[89] seldom mentioned tourism as a campaign issue, instead focusing on the more politically salient issues of agriculture and fisheries.[90] Most of the voting public did not understand the significance of tourism, and even in County Kerry most voters displayed little interest.

As in 1924–25, the lack of public political interest during the late 1920s and early 1930s did not mean that the government completely ignored tourism. Cumann na nGaedheal was warmly supported by most of the ITA executive, and the party could not completely dismiss tourism as a result. The government was well aware that the 1925 Local Government Act created two closely related problems for the successful development of the tourist industry. First, the act did not *require* local authorities to contribute to the ITA. Second, local authorities determined their annual budgets on a yearly basis and so were able to regularly reconsider their contributions to the ITA, making it impossible for the association to engage in long-term planning.[91] As much as the government believed that the current legislation provided an efficient and economical approach to tourism development, they had to admit that the association's annual income of just over £10,000 in 1930 was inadequate for the job at hand.[92]

In May 1931 the government proposed legislation designed to push local authorities to give money to "one recognised [tourist] association," unless special permission was acquired from the minister for industry and commerce to forego payment. Under the new proposal local authorities would provide this funding over a multiyear contract, not in one-year installments, allowing the approved tourist-development organization to plan ahead.

Although the proposal was far from revolutionary, during the course of the Seanad and Dáil debates surrounding the bill, a variety of objections were raised that illustrate the poor understanding, even among Irish leaders, of tourism's economic role, the problems facing Irish tourism development, and the ideological divide between the two main political parties. Ministerial misunderstanding of tourism's economic role is primarily visible in concern over the concept of levying rates to support tourist development. Senator Thomas Linehan voiced a concern that was echoed by several others: "It seems very strange that the cost of developing that traffic, which will benefit the entire country and every class in the country alike, should be placed altogether on the ratepayers." In particular, farmers faced a significant burden under the legislation, and Linehan remarked, "The benefits derived from a development of tourist traffic are of interest to the farmers in a very small way only." Given these facts, the senator believed that, in the interest of fairness the necessary money should be provided out of the Central Fund in the form of government aid, not further taxation.

There were also justifiable concerns about whether Ireland could handle substantial tourist traffic. Fianna Fáil Senator Seán E. MacEllin, for example, noted, "I know that in the western districts of Ireland it can hardly be said that the tourist areas are ready for foreigners. The roads are almost impassable, and the sanitary accommodation is on the poor side. There are very few, if any, water supply schemes."[93] Indeed, these problems were very real. Even in the 1950s few hotels were available in most tourist centers. In Dublin during the early 1950s there were just twelve rooms with a bath, and far fewer rooms without baths than were needed;[94] the situation was undoubtedly far worse in the 1930s. Evidently it was unclear to MacEllin, and to others who agreed with him, that tourist-development legislation might help eliminate the shortage.

Lastly, there were a series of complaints that stemmed from the ideological divide and bitterness between the two major parties. Cumann na nGaedheal believed in tourism development as long as it did not cost the government anything. Meanwhile, Fianna Fáil was primarily concerned with the development of self-sufficiency, the creation of native industries,[95] and the use of tariffs to support Irish businesses[96]—hardly policies that coexisted easily with the ITA's close ties to English rail companies or with the industry's dependence on English tourists. Seán Lemass, later one of the greatest government advocates for tourism, expressed his party's objections to the legislation in an extensive Dáil debate. First, Lemass argued that devoting significant resources to tourism development was foolish because "we have not in this country either the climate or the facilities" to compete with continental destinations. In view of this situation Lemass asked why the country should spend time, energy, and money on external visitors when Irish tourism interests could direct their efforts toward attracting Irish visitors who would not only be interested in Ireland, but who would ensure Ireland's self-sufficiency by avoiding the export of Irish tourists to foreign destinations. Apparently Lemass had not yet absorbed the realities of tourism development since 1924, or, for that matter, looked at his mail, which had been stamped with "See Ireland First" for several years.

One by one, Cumann na nGaedheal ministers pointed out that the ITA *was* attracting many foreign visitors—most of them from Britain—despite having to compete with more sunny destinations. These visitors came to see beautiful scenery and to enjoy outdoor sporting activities such as fishing and hunting—the same activities that had attracted English visitors since Victoria and Albert popularized such pursuits in the 1840s during their frequent visits to Balmoral Castle in Scotland, as well as during their visit to Ireland in August 1849. One deputy pointed out:

> These results [the economic advantages of tourism] are not fully appreciated because the advantages in money spent are very often hidden. We have tourists coming into this country who do not merely spend money in travel and in living here for [a] time, but by acquiring objects which are made in the country, and these things are not always taken into consideration. A great deal of the business which is done with the tourists is not shown at all in the results given by the Tourist Association.[97]

Patrick Hogan, a deputy from County Clare, suggested that Lemass was not well informed about the activities of the ITA, and that the association was actually working to attract "every likely type of tourist." Another deputy added that the ITA had already been conducting a campaign "urging our people to patronize the many beautiful watering places we have in the country during the holiday season."

This defense of the association did not impress Lemass given that his party enjoyed little support from the powerful ITA executive. Lemass wanted to ensure that the ITA's existence was not cast in legislative stone, and he replied by asking whether the minister for industry and commerce would be willing to support another tourist organization, or whether the legislation would enshrine the ITA into Irish law as *the* national tourist body. Patrick McGilligan, the minister for industry and commerce, replied by saying that in the unlikely event that another tourist association emerged, the ITA's certificate could be revoked. This reply was enough for Fianna Fáil. As long as it was legally possible to withdraw the ITA's sanction without further legislation, Fianna Fáil had the option to support a new tourism organization that lacked the ITA's unfavorable political leanings. The Tourist Traffic Act subsequently passed on 27 May 1931.

A New Expression of Nationalism

Fianna Fáil won over 45 percent of the vote in the 1932 general election, taking seventy-two seats to Cumann na nGaedheal's fifty-seven, thus moving Ireland into a new chapter of its political history.[98] If the Irish people had voted for change, they certainly got it. De Valera's new government quickly moved to stop paying annuities to the United Kingdom as mandated by the Anglo-Irish Treaty. This move precipitated a spiraling exchange of tariffs and countertariffs.[99] The so-called "Economic War" was under way—a conflict that had a much greater impact on agriculture than it ever did on tourism. Despite the crisis over tariffs and countertariffs, the tourist business grew steadily throughout the 1930s, and the number of British tourists increased from just over 245,000 in 1932 to nearly 318,000 by 1936.[100]

Beyond failing to honor distasteful aspects of the Anglo-Irish Treaty, the new government pursued Fianna Fáil's long-term goal of creating indigenous industry in the hope of creating a self-sufficient Ireland. In the present context the most important Fianna Fáil efforts involved the creation of semistate companies. These included the Industrial Credit Company, Bórd na Móna (the Turf Board), the Irish Life Assurance Board, Industrial Alcohol Factories Limited, Aer Lingus, and the Irish Tourist Board.[101] As far as tourism is concerned, the last two of these were exceptionally important as well as intimately connected. Aer Lingus developed largely as a result of Seán Lemass's long-term fascination with aviation that began when, as a young man, he spent his free time watching airplanes taking off at Leopardstown racecourse.[102] Lemass believed that a national airline could prove a significant asset by ensuring national control of its external communications and by providing a second line of defense in case of emergency.[103] In addition, the existence of a national airline would protect the country's vital interests in trade and tourism if foreign airlines should choose not to serve Ireland.[104] But the airline's supporters had larger goals than defense or control of communications in mind, and they hoped, among other things, to make Ireland the international junction for air traffic between North America and Europe and to connect the Free State directly to other "principal countries."[105] In was an ambitious program, given that at the time Aer Lingus was operating only two aircraft, on two routes, using a temporary military airfield as its base of operations.

According to Michael Kevin O'Doherty, who served as private secretary to Lemass from 1944 to 1946 before moving to the Irish Tourist Board (where he worked in various capacities until the late 1960s), Lemass's interest in tourism developed directly from his passion for aviation.[106] For Aer Lingus to be successful it would need to carry as many people in and out of Ireland as possible, making tourists essential. Even so, it is equally important to stress Lemass's relationship with J. P. O'Brien, which stretched back to the Civil War when the two men had fought together. Lemass was intensely loyal, and O'Brien was a staunch believer in the central role of tourism in Ireland's national revival. There is every reason to believe that O'Brien used his important government contact to continue the ITA's tourism crusade.

Although Lemass had made certain that the ITA could be eliminated under the 1931 Tourist Traffic Act, when he became minister for industry and commerce he soon realized that such an action was virtually impossible because the ITA had firmly established itself as *the* national tourism body. Those who were interested in tourism were already ITA members and could not be called upon to create a new voluntary body. Perhaps more important, the ITA's long-standing policy of getting as close as possible to the local authorities made the ITA all but untouchable. Any attempt to undermine the ITA could be perceived as an attack by Dublin on local autonomy.

Any hope of extricating the tourism crusade from the hands of the Irish Tourist Association lay in creating a semistate body to handle tourism development. Several newly created semistate bodies, which Lemass preferred to call "state-sponsored,"[107] were already relatively successful; they made it possible to "substitute state enterprise when private initiative was lacking,"[108] while still maintaining a certain amount of state control even as the government was able to distance itself from day-to-day management concerns.

John Leydon, a very competent civil servant whose close working relationship with Lemass proved invaluable to the successful realization of many of the minister's plans, circulated Lemass's solution to the tourism question as an open letter to government departments on 18 May. Leydon stressed the minister's newfound belief in the importance of tourism "as a factor in the national economy and, more particularly, from the point of view of its effect on the balance of international payments." For Lemass it was no longer acceptable to follow the state's previous "passive" tourism policy. Leydon and Lemass argued that the ITA's inadequate budget, combined with the costly need to improve the poor condition and small number of Irish hotels, made it impossible for the ITA to continue to serve as the primary national tourism-advocacy body. Above all,

> the holiday habit has grown enormously in recent years and has received a new impetus from recent legislation giving workers holidays with pay. There can be no doubt that in future there will be almost unlimited scope for the development of tourist traffic in view of the fact that so many workers are now enjoying holidays with pay who never before enjoyed the privilege of a holiday. These people will require information as to how and where to spend a holiday and what the approximate cost will be, and naturally more accommodation will be necessary to receive them, and more attractions to secure their patronage.

The solution was to create "more effective machinery" that could better carry out tourism development: a statutory tourist body was needed.[109]

None of this meant that the Irish Tourist Association should be abandoned. On the surface Lemass and Leydon argued that to focus the ITA's efforts on advertising was justified because the proposed tourism company would be empowered to own and operate hotels—a potential conflict of interest if it were also creating publicity materials. There were two unstated reasons, however. First, to dissolve the ITA would risk alienating local authorities and important regional ITA branches, not to mention important business interests who were directly involved with the association, while to preserve the association might make it possible to make use of these connections to the benefit of the new tourist authority. Furthermore, the Irish Tourist Association had created the crusade to persuade people of the importance of tourism, and by so doing, it was symbolically connected to national perceptions of tourism. The new tourist legislation was designed to create greater government control over tourism development, and the legitimacy of this activity required channeling the ITA's symbolic monopoly to government advantage.

While well conceived politically, economically, and symbolically from Lemass's perspective, the proposal elicited immediate objections from within the Department of Finance, the Department of External Affairs, and even the Land Commission. These objections were based on differing ideas about the role of government, not on any opposition to tourism development as carried out by the ITA. As far as the Land Commission was concerned, no semistate body should have rights to the compulsory acquisition of land for hotels, guest houses, game, and so forth, because this right would directly conflict with the commission's powers to acquire land for the purpose of assisting the so-called congested districts. Likewise, the commission feared that any such acquisition of land might easily inspire corruption by allowing the Tourist Board to blatantly cater to specific interests.[110] On another front a civil servant within the Department of External Affairs pointed out that companies should create revenue for their shareholders—something that no "state company" was designed to accomplish. State-sponsored companies were "dressed up with capital, powers, objects, and articles, but with nowhere to go."[111] Meanwhile, civil servants in the Department of Finance argued that private enterprise should be counted on to develop tourism; government handouts were not the answer. If such enterprise had been lacking, it was because potential developers recognized that Irish resort tourism was not different enough from English destinations to warrant more substantial investment. If anything, the government should devote itself to improving local water and sewerage services and then offer grants to assist private interests, not create a new organization devoted to carrying out development on its own at great expense.[112] Likewise, a civil servant in the Department of External Affairs suggested increasing the rates allotted to the ITA in order to provide loans to local authorities for tourism and hotel development, to support cooperation with the association on training hotel workers, and to provide the association with the power to prosecute hoteliers who failed to live up to agreed hotel standards.[113] Despite these objections, no department nor any civil servant opposed the need to develop tourism. As far as most officials were concerned, it made sense to increase the advertising budget currently allotted to the Irish Tourist Association, even if a semistate development body were not created.[114]

Birth of a Tourist Board

Despite the opposition within government departments, Seán Lemass used the annual ITA meeting in Dublin on 25 October 1938 to announce that he would soon introduce substantial tourism legislation. The existing system was inadequate and the existing policy framework had to be abandoned in favor of something dramatic. He promised a budget of at least half a million pounds for the new organization and stressed that there were simply not adequate facilities in Ireland to handle any large influx of tourists. While the new tourist board would not "normally interfere with private enterprise," it would be empowered to build and operate hotels and to provide or assist in providing "services, amenities, amusements, or other attractions" for tourists. Beyond these tasks, the new tourist board would carry out publicity programs and would train tourism, restaurant, and hotel employees. Further, the Irish Tourist Board (ITB) was also to work with prospective tourist guides, assuring that visitors encountered the very best narration of Irish life. Should new tourism agencies be required, the new tourism body was empowered to create them. Finally, the ITB would administer a voluntary system of registration whereby boarding houses, restaurants, hotels, and cafes would sign on with the tourist authority so that tourists could be assured of a quality experience. Meanwhile, the Irish Tourist Association would continue to function with financial support from the Irish Tourist Board added to its previous income sources, but it would confine itself "to non-commercial activities, as it is not a body equipped for commercial enterprise."[115]

After Lemass's presentation the Irish Tourist Association remained confident in its position and was generally positive about the proposal. The only major concern was that the legislation might ultimately infringe on private enterprise by creating a government-supported tourism monopoly, but this objection was quickly set aside. Had not Lemass specifically said that there would be no such conflict? The new legislation represented no threat to tourism interests or to the ITA, while it would provide greater resources to the industry as a whole.[116]

The Tourist Traffic Act of 1939 created the Irish Tourist Board. This body had the power to acquire lands and the ability to inspect hotels and to prosecute proprietors whose premises were defined as "hotel," "guest house," "holiday camp," or "youth hostel" and who failed to meet the ITB's standards for each respective type of accommodation. The board could establish special tourism areas, operate hotel training programs, provide funds to local authorities for development projects, and operate its own hotels, not to mention engage in publicity activities such as the publication of guidebooks. If there was a catch, it was that the board was expected to do all of this on a budget of £45,000 per year, with access to only £600,000 in repayable loans.[117]

The tourist industry generally welcomed the act because it "puts our country ahead of all others in the matter of comprehensive legislative measures calculated to ensure at once the scientific development of our wonderful tourist resources and the elimination of sources of complaint and annoyance to tourists."[118] For tourism leaders this was legislation to be proud of, a powerful statement that Ireland was moving in the right direction—the direction of modernity—and was far outstripping other countries by creating a tourism body concerned with more than just publicity. Ireland was acting like a mature state that could be proud of its ability to deal with the big issues.

When J. P. O'Brien assumed his post as the newly appointed chairman of the Irish Tourist Board and began taking steps toward beginning operations, it seemed that the Irish Tourist Association had been widely successful in convincing much of the country that tourism was an important national interest; the government had finally committed itself to investing in tourism development, and the road ahead seemed clear. Of course, there were still differing opinions about the symbolic meanings of tourism, but the ITA's view of tourism now appeared to dominate. The future seemed bright for Irish tourism until Germany invaded Poland, and then nothing was certain anymore.

2

Developing Irish Tourism, 1939–1958

The newly created Irish Tourist Board barely had time to set up its offices in Dublin before tourism was once again the topic of widespread debate. The reality of war imposed new priorities on the Irish state that did not include tourism. Above all, de Valera's government wanted to remain nonaligned.[1] Neutrality was widely seen as the best way of symbolically asserting Irish independence from Britain, and many viewed it as the "acid test" for Ireland's freedom.[2] In addition, the state was not immediately under threat, and there was little to justify suffering through the horrors of war.[3] Ireland was still recovering from the struggle for independence and subsequent civil war, it faced widespread unemployment, it lacked an adequate industrial base to develop a munitions industry,[4] and it could not afford the spending required to support a war-ready military.[5]

To preserve its neutrality while maintaining domestic stability, the government implemented a widespread censorship program in the hope of keeping "'the temperature down,' both internally and between Ireland and the belligerents." Politicians hoped that the program would maintain the unity of the population by suppressing potentially divisive comments or threats to public order.[6] In order to further ensure stability, the government paid particular attention to managing the country's scarce provisions. The demand for consumables simply was not met by the supply. Gas, coal, clothes, tea and sugar, bread, and coffee were all rationed.[7] The rationing program was such a high priority that it led to the first major cabinet changes since 1932.[8] Seán Lemass became minister of the newly created Department of Supplies, Seán MacEntee was the new minister for Industry and commerce, and Seán T. O'Kelly assumed control of the Department of Finance.[9] With few jobs, high emigration, and an endless string of difficult decisions to be made,[10] to say nothing of the fact that for much of the war tourists could not get to Ireland owing to grounded flights and dangerous seas, tourism was once again a low priority. This chapter traces the effort by tourist groups to convince the government and the public—both during the war and afterward, when a political crisis erupted over tourism policy—that ongoing development of tourism continued to be in the national interest. It was not until 1952 that tourism was once again widely considered an important national priority at government level, and the industry began to achieve increased public support only after an extended pro-tourism educational campaign. To reestablish tourist development as a national interest was an uphill battle, but it was one that ultimately set the basic policy framework for Irish tourism efforts through the late 1950s, and it shaped the appearance of Irish tourism throughout the rest of the twentieth century.

Tourism During Wartime

On 4 September 1939, one day after Britain declared war on Germany, J. P. O'Brien learned of the probable suspension of the Tourist Traffic Act "for as long as the Emergency Powers Act, 1939, continues in force."[11] The tourism chief wasted no time before writing to the minister for industry and commerce to argue that suspending the act would create unemployment and further disturb the country's economic situation. He claimed that sustaining the Irish Tourist Board would send a vital symbolic message to the Irish people by showing them that "carrying on" was important despite present difficulties. O'Brien did not deny that changes would need to be made. Given the likely drop in tourist receipts, the government had little reason to invest in large-scale publicity, but it *was* fair to expect a dramatic increase in tourism following the war, and the country would benefit greatly by using the lull in tourist traffic to prepare for a predictable postwar boom. The best course forward, argued O'Brien, was to continue supporting both the ITA and the Tourist Board so that these bodies might study existing amenities and possible future development, launch a hotel-grading scheme, dispense loans for resort and hotel improvements, and even initiate especially important development programs. O'Brien admitted that the continuation of his salary might create a "source of embarrassment to the government," but he offered to take on additional government-related work to fill administrative gaps when needed while still ensuring that vital tourism development continued. He concluded by pointing out that the remaining members of the ITB would be occupied in assisting the Irish Tourist Association with a survey of Irish holiday facilities.[12]

O'Brien's letter did not inspire an immediate recommendation from the Department of Industry and Commerce on the suspension issue. Instead, the minister simply circulated a memo exploring the pros and cons of each possible course of action. In favor of suspension the minister noted that the public, "who will be called upon to bear greatly increased burdens due to war conditions, will expect all possible economies to be effected, and particularly the elimination of expenditure on nonessential services like tourist traffic development, and that in any event the amount of useful work which could be done during the war conditions is very small."[13] Still, said the minister, O'Brien's argument in favor of extending the board had merit and should be afforded serious consideration. Given his close contacts with government officials, and especially with Seán Lemass, O'Brien undoubtedly knew that MacEntee's memorandum failed to present a strong case in favor of continuing tourist development during the war years, and in November he followed up his earlier letter with a detailed memorandum explaining why the Tourist Board should continue to operate and precisely what it would accomplish if allowed to function. According to O'Brien, tourism already comprised a considerable segment of the economy, bringing wealth "to all parts of the country and all classes of our people," while directly supporting some twenty thousand Irish citizens. In particular, seaside towns and many Gaeltacht (Irish-speaking) areas depended on tourism. If the ITA and ITB ceased operations, numerous Irish people would be unrepresented, unemployed, and deprived of income. O'Brien added that state support of tourism "is almost essential to counties like Kerry, Donegal, and Galway, as is the guaranteeing of minimum prices for wheat and beet in many inland counties." The tourism chief did not ignore the obvious fact that tourist economies depend on tourists, but tourists need not come from outside of Ireland, and it was in fact perhaps better if they did not. Government promotion of domestic tourism would contribute to the health and welfare of the Irish people by educating them "to save up during the year for holidays which would give them a change of environment amidst opportunities for healthy recreation," as well as teaching them about their own national territory through the continuation of the ITA's "See Ireland First" campaign. There could be no better time to promote Ireland for native tourists than a period when the Irish "people cannot go abroad." In other words, to continue the Tourist Traffic Act would avoid crippling the Irish tourist industry and avoid reducing it "to the unorganised and comparatively impoverished position of the industry in 1925," while simultaneously creating more responsible and educated Irish citizens. O'Brien insisted that the impressive benefits of tourist development could be attained using few resources and little government expenditure. Above all, the Tourist Board would execute an extensive planning program designed to make postwar development at Ireland's holiday resorts possible. More immediately, nearly all Irish resorts required substantial enhancement of health and sanitation facilities as well as road safety provisions—all improvements that could be supported under wartime unemployment relief schemes. The ITB's planning program would thus identify both long-term development projects and labor-intensive schemes that might provide Irishmen with work during the Emergency. O'Brien argued that it would be important to establish local committees to direct development projects. These would not only provide a local presence but would also encourage greater investment by local authorities: an essential component of any development project, whether in wartime or peacetime.

Beyond these recommendations, O'Brien suggested that the Tourist Board could implement the hotel-grading scheme specified in the Tourist Traffic Act, identifying facilities requiring improvements *before* the predicted postwar boom in tourism. By doing this during a period of relatively low tourist traffic, hotels would be able to raise their standards to match board requirements before the expected rush of postwar visitors. The wartime period would also give the board time to move ahead with a hotel-training scheme and the improvement of transport arrangements throughout Ireland. Publicity, Gaeltacht holidays, and inland-fishery development also required immediate attention. Indeed, the only major component of the 1939 tourist legislation that the board did not plan to address was the designation of "special areas" of the country well suited to tourism development and protection. Instead of making the designations, the board would study the potential impact of such action, carefully examining the implications for local economic and social development whenever the designations were made.

In short, the Irish Tourist Board would function as a tourism think tank, putting into effect limited development schemes only if and when they could contribute to the overall employment situation during the wartime crisis. The plan was designed to be successful despite tight finances and would cost the government a mere £9,000 per year in operating costs and £75,000 in repayable advances for development projects versus the £45,000 annually and £600,000 in loans assigned in the 1939 act.[14] From O'Brien's perspective tourism development still represented the national interest, and he went out of his way to offer a plan that would create employment in the near term while ensuring the country's ability to attract and cater to a flood of future tourists.

Despite O'Brien's aggressive efforts, the government had not made a decision at the end of January 1940, though Seán MacEntee was now firmly in favor of continuing the ITB's efforts. The minister offered three arguments in favor of leaving the board in place, all based on O'Brien's memorandum. First, the industry was increasingly important to the Irish economy and should be safeguarded. Second, the board enjoyed widespread popular support among "all sections of the community" because it filled "a long-felt want." And third, MacEntee did not believe it worthwhile to endanger the survival of the Irish Tourist Association by inadvertently encouraging local authorities to reduce or abolish their contributions to the group.[15] In short, tourism remained a national interest, and therefore continued development was the only logical course of action.

While the Department of Industry and Commerce now firmly supported the pro-tourism line, the Department of Finance and the Department of Local Government had more conservative and indeed backward-looking ideas about the national interest. The Department of Local Government and Public Health, which had statutory control over funding provided to the ITA through the 1925 Local Government Act and the 1931 Tourist Traffic Act, objected primarily to the argument that the ITA would somehow cease to function if the ITB were suspended until after the war. According to this department, any actions taken by the government vis-à-vis the Tourist Board would "not have an appreciable influence on local authorities." If financial problems arising from the Emergency caused the local authorities to cut their expenditures on tourist publicity, they would cease to fund the ITA, whether the ITB continued to operate or not.[16]

Meanwhile, as far as Finance was concerned, the Emergency was not the time to begin preparing for the postwar world. According to Finance officials, the Tourist Traffic Act was predicated on an assumption of peacetime conditions, and now that the world situation was anything but peaceful, the act was no longer viable. The minister for finance maintained that the Emergency

> has caused serious unemployment, entailed substantial additional expenditure without countervailing savings, and has reduced revenue, thereby rendering necessary a supplementary budget under which heavy additional taxation has been imposed. Further, it has been found necessary to float a loan of £7,000,000 to provide for the liquidation of short-term debt incurred, and to meet capital commitments, some of which, e.g., defense expenditure, are non-productive.

It was necessary to assume that the war would not end quickly, important to anticipate "further sacrifices on the part of the community, if services of an absolutely essential kind are to be maintained." To continue to finance the Tourist Traffic Act "would be not unlikely to create the impression in the country that economy was considered by the government to be neither necessary nor desirable." Besides, if the government adopted a policy of intelligent spending designed to help people weather the crisis, Irish citizens would continue to take holidays, and the Irish tourist industry would be more than supported by its virtual monopoly on home traffic during the Emergency. To postpone planning and development until after the war would not unduly handicap the Irish tourist industry because other states would be equally debilitated as a result of hostilities. Lastly, the resources required to undertake even small development projects were not available given the realities of rationing.[17]

That Finance immediately positioned itself against the ITB is not surprising because this key governmental body in 1939–40 was little different from the Department of Finance in 1922. As historian Ronan Fanning has pointed out, "the single outstanding characteristic of the first thirty-five years of the department's history is the absence of change, a remarkable continuity reflected both in the department's organisation and personnel."[18] Not only was J. J. McElligott the department's most important civil servant throughout these years, but there was also a general unwillingness to explore new ideas, and "early Finance men may have felt that they had little enough to learn from outsiders."[19] Established orthodoxy governed the department's response to new ideas, and its officials acted in accordance with conventions handed down from generation to generation. Finance's very recruiting system ensured such continuity by the fact that new blood was brought into the department at the tender age of eighteen, immediately after leaving secondary school and before any untoward influences, such as higher education, might creep in.[20] Beyond all else, McElligott and his longtime colleagues sought stability. McElligott's first understanding of how the national economy and government fiscal policy should function developed "after two years of chaos and disorder . . . [had] threatened to tear the infant state apart."[21] In his mind the best way to ensure stability was to continue along tried and true tracks, deviating little from known quantities. For Finance, just as for the Killarney boatmen, rapid tourism development represented a source of change and risk—a fact that led to a consistent anti-tourism stance throughout the 1930s, 1940s, and 1950s (before the *Economic Development Plan* of 1958). The Department of Finance frequently made efforts to limit state funding for tourism, yet, just as Finance lost the fight in 1938 to limit state funding for the proposed tourist board, it repeatedly proved unable to suspend the Tourist Traffic Act during the war years or to tamp down funding requests in the early 1950s. On 28 February 1940 the government agreed with the Department of Industry and Commerce concerning the desirability of renewing the board's remit for another year.[22] Then, on 15 July 1941, the government again extended the board's life until 31 March 1944 in spite of continued pleas by the Department of Finance.[23]

Why did Industry and Commerce consistently win the tourism battle throughout the war years? Part of the answer certainly lies in the decreasing power experienced by the Department of Finance following its "years of ascendancy" between 1924 and 1932.[24] After 1932 a series of new economic policies, "anathema to Finance orthodoxies," were put in place, resulting in a marked increase in the number of civil servants and giving "big spending departments, such as Industry and Commerce and Agriculture," increased power.[25] But there were other reasons as well, and the influence of the Irish Tourist Association was significant. The association had no qualms about lobbying the government in order to attain its goals, and it was very adept at speaking to government concerns. In the case of extending the Tourist Traffic Act, the ITA argued that tourism would help alleviate unemployment. Immediately preceding the 1941 debate that ultimately extended the board's life until 1944, the association argued that carrying out "certain resort improvements . . . would provide productive employment for a large number of workers"—such as the provision of footpaths, roads, promenades at seaside resorts, water and sewerage improvement schemes, the construction of swimming pools, the building of recreation halls, road improvements, enterprises aimed at limiting coastal erosion, and the clearance of unwanted vegetation near bathing beaches. While acknowledging the difficulties that led the government to scale back Tourist Board activities, ITA directors unanimously urged that "certain improvement works at resorts, particularly schemes which afford large-scale employment for unskilled workers, should be included in any emergency unemployment schemes to be approved by the government." The choice of these schemes should

> keep specially in mind those areas in the country which are situated on the seaboard, and which for natural reasons are the least prosperous. The population of such areas find it difficult, even in normal times, to earn a livelihood; they were largely dependent on holiday traffic in past years to supplement their frugal resources and are now suffering from the cutting off of this source of income. In addition, it is important to note that, in the main, these areas do not benefit from the special measures adopted in recent years for the assistance to agriculture. Not having suitable land, they could not engage in the production of such commodities as wheat and beet with the advantage of guaranteed sale prices. On the other hand, for the purchase of essentials such as bread, flour, and sugar, they have had to contribute substantially to the guaranteeing of the minimum prices above mentioned.

Gaeltacht areas faced similar concerns.[26]

In effect, the Irish Tourist Association, just as it had done in the 1920s when it lobbied for improvements to isolated towns like Dingle and Kinsale, functioned as a voice for outlying areas. This position carried with it a considerable amount of political muscle that could not safely be trifled with, especially when political stability was foremost on the government's priority list. Furthermore, the Tourist Board and ITA argument about employment schemes was difficult to ignore. When massive unemployment forced thousands to emigrate, it was not politically expedient to disregard potentially viable work-creation projects, especially ones that would aid economically challenged regions of the country. And finally, any policy decision that allowed the Irish Tourist Association to disappear would alienate important members of the community while also frustrating key areas of the country like Cork and Kerry. These were ties to the localities that, especially in a time of crisis, the national government could ill afford to break.

Consideration of the national interest and of the vital role that tourism could play in Irish affairs was foremost in the minds of tourist authorities, especially the leaders of the ITA, who continued to believe that tourism development was a powerful way to display nationalist pride. More than ever, they enthused, tourism "was of vital importance" to ensuring "the livelihood of thousands of their people, particularly in poor coastal districts" dependent on tourist traffic. After agriculture, tourism was the country's largest employer, and any failure to support it would prove disastrous.[27]

Holiday Savings Clubs

In spite of wartime conditions, local authorities provided funds to the Tourist Association throughout the early 1940s. While grants were noticeably diminished in 1940–41 (just under £14,000 versus the roughly £18,000 per year received before the war),[28] revenue from local authorities never dropped below £13,500 during the course of the Emergency.[29]

Armed with this slightly diminished budget, the Tourist Association focused its efforts on developing a holiday savings-club program that was designed to educate workers about how best to use their limited financial resources while also teaching them about their national territory. The scheme was based on similar nineteenth-century programs that helped mill workers from England's industrial centers enjoy an annual seaside holiday at resorts such as Blackpool.[30] While the association could only dream of the success enjoyed by these early English savings programs, they nevertheless believed the clubs to be an excellent way to promote native resorts, and the ITA began contacting labor unions, business executives, and workers in 1940.[31] By paying money into a large pool, workers were able to earn interest and to lower the rates at Irish resorts, ensuring themselves of affordable holidays in areas to which they might not otherwise be able to go. The scheme was designed to educate workers about the benefits of saving money for more substantial getaways rather than confining themselves to short evening trips to Howth or Bray. According to the lord mayor of Cork city, the scheme also functioned to "make people appreciate the beauties of our own country."[32] During the first year of its efforts the ITA gave presentations to the Irish Transport and General Workers' Union, employees of the Dublin Flour Mills, the Irish Brewers' Association, and the Civil Service Clerical Association, among others.[33] In 1941 alone 22 clubs were formed, and by 1945, 178 clubs, representing 45,000 workers, had been created.[34] In the immediate postwar years the program continued to grow, ultimately reaching 205 clubs by 1948 and including 47,000 workers.[35]

Exploration and Development

While the Irish Tourist Association tried to retrain Irish workers, J. P. O'Brien and the Irish Tourist Board attempted to move ahead with their planning and development efforts only to face almost immediate criticism. Hotel grading was the first planned program to be abandoned. While the grading scheme would have required the expensive training of inspectors, the primary problem was pressure on the government from the Irish Tourist Association and the Irish Hotels Federation, a collection of hoteliers who banded together during the 1920s to push their interests both within the ITA and at government level. These groups argued that any grading program that might require extensive alterations or adaptations of existing premises, especially on short notice, would be an undue hardship.[36]

At the same time that it encountered opposition to hotel grading, the ITB could not move ahead with its development and planning efforts fast enough to satisfy the ITA and local authorities. As early as November 1941 the Tourist Association expressed concern that ITB-directed development projects were not progressing as expected. The limited progress resulted in insignificant unemployment relief and did little to forward the tourist industry.[37]

The only visible development project began at Tramore in 1942. The scheme made use of local labor and a detachment of the Construction Corps for (among other things) an aggressive program of site leveling, drainage, and reclamation of land.[38] Invoking its powers of compulsory acquisition for the first time, the board also purchased several properties in the area.[39] By 1944 the scheme employed some two hundred members from the Construction Corps, and work was expected to last for at least two more years at a total cost of £40,000.[40] By 1945 the development was "practically completed," allowing the board to begin working on further plans "for commercial development of the property" at Tramore.[41]

At the same time that the Tramore scheme was being undertaken, the board suggested further development programs at other resort towns, including Portmarnock, Bundoran, and Lisdoonvarna—all of which promised to provide high employment and a long-term financial return through the construction of bathing, recreation, and amusement facilities. Like Tramore, each of these places was already a notable tourist attraction.[42] For Tramore, the program was undoubtedly considered a success, and there is no reason to believe that the ITA was displeased with the ITB scheme there, once undertaken. Other observers, especially in areas like Kilkenny where tourism had not yet caught on as a promising new industry, were far less pleased. Ultimately the development schemes helped to spark the single most damaging controversy in the history of Irish tourism. This battle derailed the board's development program, brought about a complete revamping of the ITB, and, sadly, began to destroy the effectiveness of the single most notable voice in tourism development to this point—J. P. O'Brien.

The Crisis

Despite the success of efforts to retain government support for wartime tourism development, the entire pro-tourism project nearly collapsed in the late 1940s. The crisis in Irish tourism had its roots in three areas: personal animosity toward J. P. O'Brien and the Tourist Board among members of the Irish media; the extension of the ITB's development policy to include the purchase and management of hotels immediately following the war; and the acquisition and subsequent grounding of a number of Constellation aircraft bought by Aer Rianta (then leased by Aer Lingus) to fly between Shannon and New York.

Since entering the tourist industry in 1924, J. P. O'Brien was one of Ireland's most important tourism figures, and with the establishment of the Tourist Board he became the industry's most visible leader. While tourism was a nexus for a variety of voices and interests from local groups to private interests to the central government, O'Brien was the face of tourism policy and the creative force behind much of the industry's early growth and later expansion.[43] Given his prominence, it is not surprising that O'Brien became a minor celebrity—a ubiquitous figure in nearly all newspaper articles relating to tourism. While this renown was undoubtedly flattering to the Corkman, his friend Todd Andrews later recalled that it led O'Brien to acquire "what William James called 'the moral flabbiness born of the exclusive worship of the bitch goddess success.'" O'Brien made powerful friends whom he tended to meet in the lounge bars of Dublin hotels, and he "developed a way of life which was alien to his upbringing and real sentiments." Unfortunately, these "friends" were often more interested in O'Brien because of his connections: powerful businessmen made use of an inadequately compensated public official to secure political access. At the same time he made enemies, several of whom were important media figures like R. M. Smyllie, editor of the *Irish Times,* and, most visibly, a man named E. T. Keane, who owned and edited a provincial paper called the *Kilkenny People.*[44]

Keane was born in Listowel on 16 July 1867 and began his journalism career with the *Munster News* at an early age. He developed a keen interest in politics that he exercised as a founding member of the Kilkenny branch of Sinn Féin. By 1917 Keane was friends with W. T. Cosgrave, and after supporting the nationalist politician in the election of December 1918 had his newspaper suppressed. After the Anglo-Irish Treaty was signed in December 1921, Keane took his stand with the pro-treaty forces.[45] The journalist was not above using his newspaper as a political organ, and his willingness to do so made him "'a living legend in his own lifetime' and 'arguably the outstanding provincial editor of this century.'" Keane distinguished himself as "an irreconcilable political opponent" of Fianna Fáil. During the Emergency the government found him impossible to deal with. He refused to follow directions and persistently published "censorable matter," but he was tolerated because of his now advanced age and long record as a distinguished newsman. Among other things, Keane published an anti-Axis editorial after German bombs fell on Dublin and Belfast—an action that was clearly in violation of the government's neutral position. When the censors demanded that he supply them with copies of all leading articles in advance of publication, Keane replied by not publishing any leading article at all, while including an editorial entitled "The Liberty of the Press" that was subsequently suppressed.[46]

Among his strong opinions Keane displayed an antipathy for tourism, and he was especially upset that the Tourist Board continued to function during the war while providing what Keane considered an excessive salary to J. P. O'Brien. Beginning in 1942, Keane launched his own personal anti-tourism crusade, using the pages of his paper to lambaste the tourism industry, the Irish Tourist Board, and O'Brien. The attack began in March with an editorial entitled "Where Jobs Accumulate and Men Decay." The piece attacked Fianna Fáil for allowing civil servants to draw excessive wages, using de Valera's comment that no civil servant should ever earn more than £1,000 per year as an example of party hypocrisy. Keane's primary example was O'Brien, whom he declared to be "overpaid and overemployed."[47] By 18 April, Keane's commentary on O'Brien became more personal, and he began referring to him as "Mr. J. P. O'Brien, B.A. (pass)." While Lemass had told the people that they would need to tighten their belts, the Tourist Board had been allowed to continue its spending. As far as Keane was concerned, the Irish Tourist Board was "one of the greatest fakes ever thrust upon this unfortunate country," led, "as everyone expected," by O'Brien with a shocking salary of £1,500 per year plus travel and expense allowances. Keane declared that the Tourist Board had "flopped," and he neglected to acknowledge that O'Brien had voluntarily reduced his own salary in keeping with the troubles of the day. Keane observed snidely that J. P. O'Brien's "is the only name in the telephone directory that has his letters 'B.A.' after it, but he forgot to add the word 'pass.' Man, in his time, plays many parts, but few men so many parts as this luminary." The newsman concluded that it was a "gross injustice" that people's tax dollars should be used to support the "up-keep of a useless and expensive contraption like this Tourist Board and for the payment of salaries to the holders of sinecures."[48]

Keane was in no way finished. Over the coming years—indeed, until his death in 1945—the editor attacked O'Brien and the board in at least twelve different articles. He called the leaders of the Irish Tourist Association the "Playboys of the Western World" because they enjoyed a well-catered annual meeting in Dublin in 1943,[49] and he declared the Irish Tourist Board to be little more than "a sanctuary for Fianna Fáil politicians."[50] O'Brien was compared to Hamlet,[51] he was ridiculed as the "high priest" of the board,[52] and the addition of the word "pass" with every reference to him assured that the head of the Tourist Board suffered attacks on his intelligence at every turn. Between the insults, Keane did manage to make a collection of thoughtful comments about board policy. He criticized the board's hotel evaluation program when it was finally announced in 1944;[53] he challenged the amount of alcohol consumed at ITA and Tourist Board functions;[54] he pointed out the government's lack of attention to the TB epidemic in favor of tourism development;[55] and he suggested that the board's development scheme at Tramore was marked more by the laying of concrete than by the improvement of the area's sublime and beautiful assets.[56] However valid these criticisms were, and while Keane may well have been an extraordinary figure in the provincial press of Ireland before this controversy, his conduct in this case was juvenile, cruel, and destructive.

On a personal level the attacks dramatically affected O'Brien. While initially they "only raised smiles," as the articles and years came and went, the cruel words eventually "succeeded in wrecking O'Brien's self-confidence by making him the subject of national ridicule."[57] Early in 1946 O'Brien sought legal advice from the eminent Dublin attorney Arthur Cox about how to stop the *Kilkenny People* articles. (Although Keane died in 1945, the paper remained unfriendly to tourism until the early 1950s.) O'Brien was told that in any libel action taken in Ireland the "plaintiff invariably became the defendant," and he was advised not to take any action against the paper.[58] With easy access to drink through his many meetings in hotel bars, to say nothing of the large quantity of alcohol that was ubiquitous at tourism-development functions, O'Brien gradually began to seek escape in drink and was increasingly absent from meetings. Tragically, J. P. O'Brien, the most prominent single voice in early Irish tourism development, was descending into the grip of alcoholism.[59]

The ITB's development program continued despite the unfavorable press. The purchase of property at Tramore was followed by still more acquisitions including land at Ardmore, Arklow, Ballynahinch and Recess, Bundoran, Courtown, Dollymount, Garryvoe, Glengarriff, Kilkee, Killarney, Lisdoonvarna, Newtown, Termonfeckin, Portmarnock, Rosses Point, Salthill, Skerries, and Youghal.[60] In the immediate postwar years, the Tourist Board believed that "the provision of additional accommodation is . . . considered the most urgent requirement. In normal circumstances the board could rely on private enterprise to meet increased demands, but in this case experience has shown that special measures involving the board's direct intervention are necessary." The proposed intervention involved the "conversion and enlargement" of properties that had been acquired at some of the previously mentioned sites. To the board's credit, it did not envision running these properties itself because to do so would represent a clear conflict of interest. Instead, it was proposed that an interim company be incorporated to run the newly created hotels. As quickly as possible, the board would move to sell the hotels to private interests, divesting itself of all properties and eventually rendering the interim company obsolete. From the ITB's perspective the scheme was designed to "encourage private enterprise in the provision of adequate and suitable accommodation."[61] In May 1946 the proposed company, Fáilte Téoranta, was incorporated in order "to convert and operate for hotel purposes five houses situated on properties that had been purchased by the board." The hotels were open for business throughout the 1946 tourist season, and the board looked forward to expanding them further.[62]

As noted in chapter 1, one of the most prevalent concerns about the formation of the Irish Tourist Board in 1938–39 was the board's potential threat to private enterprise; some feared that the new authority might eventually acquire a monopoly of the tourist facilities in Ireland by establishing a stranglehold on the hotel business.[63] The development of the "Fáilte hotels," on the heels of three years of constant criticism of board policy by several Irish newspapers, sparked a powerful backlash. The *Irish Times* attacked board statements about the need for "luxury hotels." Smyllie, the paper's editor, insisted that the notion of "luxury" hotels in Ireland was ridiculous, and accused O'Brien of "suffering from *folie de grandeur* or some such aberration."[64] Unsurprisingly, the *Kilkenny People* also attacked the hotel scheme. The paper responded to reports about the board's plan with a withering condemnation: "It should also be a matter of deep concern to the public generally because the proposal, if it is to take effect, will establish a most pernicious principle. Why should a state subsidized but useless body be permitted to enter into competition with people who, through taxation, are obliged to pay a not inconsiderable proportion of the annual expenditure of the Irish Tourist Board?"

The paper proceeded to rail against the recent start of board inspections of existing hotel premises, claiming that the "horde of inspectors" had been "let loose" to "harass many hotel proprietors and even wipe out of business others on the flimsiest of pretexts"—destroying family businesses that had existed for generations—all in the name of catering to the "imaginary influx of mythical foreign tourists."[65] It was not bad enough that a state-funded body was going to compete with private hotels; the ITB was putting the competition out of business by using unjust inspections. And even more damning still, the tax dollars that were paying for these hotels were not being used to help either Ireland's war-torn European neighbors or the Irish people themselves.[66] The paper pointed out that while Ireland needed 60,000 new homes to meet workers' needs,

> there has been a great falling off in the number of new houses built during the last few years, but in spite of this, it has been found possible to provide large sums for the erection or reconstruction of high-class luxury hotels to cater for wealthy tourists who pay flying visits to this country. If it can be found possible to provide building materials for the erection or reconstruction of hotels for wealthy foreigners, many of whom are as mythical as their wealth, it ought to be possible to provide some materials for the more urgent need of housing our own people.[67]

The *Irish Independent*, the daily newspaper with the largest circulation in Ireland, adopted a similar view of the hotel scheme, noting the lack of adequate facilities to house the Irish themselves. Instead of feeding and housing tourists, "the Irish people should have first claim on the food and board in this country."[68] Just where were the government's priorities? How could anybody argue that the national interest rested with foreigners and not desperately poor *Irish* workers?

As indicated in the *Irish Independent*, many were skeptical about the desirability of attracting tourists in the first place—a concern made considerably more threatening by the fact that between 1946 and 1949 Ireland enjoyed a massive influx of tourists. The *Irish Press* declared, "A fortuitous chain of circumstances in 1946, over which we had no control, established us a highly lucrative tourist trade." The English "were hungry, had plenty of loose cash, and were tired of standing in queues for anything from a pin to a tin of pineapple."[69] As a result, in 1946 "visitor receipts"—the total income from tourist traffic—reached £18 million, or 4.5 times larger than the highest prewar figure. In 1947 tourist income climbed to £28 million and then peaked in 1948 at £33 million,[70] before falling back to £28 million in 1949.[71] Regrettably, accurate visitor numbers were not recorded until the mid-1950s, making it impossible to say precisely how many tourists were involved in expending these amounts. But the perception was that Ireland was under invasion by Britons and Europeans desperate to find steaks, dairy products, and countryside and cityscapes not marred by total war. The *Irish Times* reported that as a result of a publicity campaign conducted by the Tourist Board and the ITA, "the adverse conditions in other tourist resorts, and of continued 'austerity' in Great Britain, this country now is faced by imminent threats of tourist invasions on such a scale as may seriously overtax its powers of digestion."

This "invasion" would increase inflation dramatically and thus raise the cost of living. The paper explained that when British tourists brought their currency into Ireland it was promptly converted into Irish pounds. Thus for every £100,000 brought into Ireland "another £100,000 is added to Éire's already inflated currency—£100,000 that would not have been required if those 10,000 tourists had spent their money at home or in some other country!"[72]

Although the paper did not discourage tourist development (in fact, the editors encouraged it by saying that short-term losses would mean long-term gains), the threat of rising costs in a country still feeling the effects of war-time deprivations was hardly a prediction welcomed by the Tourist Board; the specter of inflation was not the best way to sell an expensive hotel development scheme. Indeed, the *Kilkenny People* had no qualms about attacking the very notion of tourism development under the present circumstances, alleging that thousands of pounds were being squandered by the "so-called tourist industry" and calling for restraint: "We have no objections to the

SUGGESTED I.T.A. SIGNPOST FOR O'CONNELL STREET.

2. Suggested ITA Signpost, *Dublin Opinion* cartoon, Sept. 1943.

development of the tourist industry when circumstances are more favorable, but at the present time we, perhaps very selfishly, feel we have little enough for ourselves and cannot give visitors to this country the *Céad Míle Fáilte* which would be extended to them in normal days in Éire."[73]

Even in Killarney, where tourism was always a priority, the hotel scheme generated little goodwill. This time the concern was not the board's potential threat to private enterprise; it was the fact that little had been done in Killarney itself. It was true that the Tourist Board had purchased property at Killarney (Muckross House no less), and that it had offered "numerous proposals for tourist development," but "practically all the Killarney proposals had been turned down by the board because . . . they would have required either partial or total subsidy by the state."[74] As a result, Killarney tourist authorities resolved that something needed to be done to "shake up" the Tourist Board; the buying of land at Killarney was not enough—the board needed to follow through with actual development.[75] As a result, the Killarney Urban District Council filed a formal condemnation of the board and demanded that immediate proposals be submitted for development at

Killarney.[76] The ITB responded immediately to these concerns by sending a photographer to the tourist center—in itself not a strange activity as the board made sure that a photographer visited every year in order to demonstrate the ITB's interest in the area. These photographs varied little from year to year, meaning that from five to twenty new plates nearly identical to the previous Killarney shots were added to the photo library each year. The 1948 trip was different. The photographer took over three hundred photographs that were, once again, more or less identical to all previous shots dating back to (at least) 1939. Perhaps the Tourist Board could not act on its development hopes for its property at Muckross House, but at least its photographer could spend several days and shoot numerous rolls of film in Killarney and the immediate area, demonstrating a good show of concern in the process.[77]

Beyond public view the board was also harshly criticized. Badly infected by the development bug, and inspired by a trip to Germany to study the Nazi's Kraft durch Freude program several years earlier,[78] the board presented a memo urging the adoption of an Irish recreational policy that would undermine "the natural tendency, particularly with more hard-working elements of the community . . . , to use free time for mere idleness." "Preventative measures" would ensure the "physical well-being" and "mental development" of the Irish people. In pursuit of this aim the Tourist Board detailed the lack of recreation facilities in rural Ireland and looked to numerous foreign examples to show what other countries were doing to promote recreation, defined by the board as "the *beneficial* use of leisure-time."[79] Efforts to define the way in which people spent their time when not working had been around since the Victorian period, when the middle classes created museums, codified field sports, and advocated an educational approach to seaside visits (studying tide pools, for example).[80] Nor was there anything strange about the concept of state-sponsored leisure during the 1930s and 1940s. Other countries had similar programs (a detailed list was included with the Tourist Board proposal). The Nazis, for example, used their leisure organization, Kraft durch Freude, to teach the German people both how to be better Germans and what to believe politically.[81] Nevertheless, the board's proposal stands out as one of the more curious artifacts of the Emergency period in Ireland because it went so much further than anything else proposed by tourist authorities before or since. Not surprisingly, it was a document that won the board few friends.

When the minister for local government and public health was asked to offer his comments on the matter, his verdict was far from muted. The minister demanded to know "why the Irish Tourist Board considered itself free to turn from those statutory functions which should be its sole preoccupation in order to address itself to a subject with which at best it cannot be more than remotely concerned" especially because "its labours so far have been conspicuous only by lack of any practical achievement." Rather than "amusing itself in drafting absurd totalitarian schemes," the Tourist Board should strive to enhance Ireland's tourist potential. Renaming the Irish Tourist Board document "Towards an Irish Totalitarian State," the minister demanded to know if the board felt that the Creator should have spent the seventh day doing something other than resting—a clear display of "mere idleness." While the members of the board might have delusions of competency, they had no right to compel the Irish people to play during their time off.[82]

J. P. O'Brien and the Irish Tourist Board simply could not catch a break. They were criticized for not attracting enough tourists and for attracting too many of them. They were attacked for threatening private enterprise and for not developing hotels fast enough or in the right places. And they were viewed as stepping beyond their statutory responsibilities in an effort to turn Ireland into a totalitarian state. Under the circumstances it is little wonder that O'Brien began to crack, a victim of his own "success" and notoriety.

It was not only the Tourist Board that was under attack. Aer Rianta and Aer Lingus also faced controversy that spilled over into tourism—partly because of the obvious link between the airlines and tourism development and partly because J. P. O'Brien served as a director on the Aer Rianta board from 1946.[83] Following V-E Day, Aer Lingus rapidly acquired a collection of new aircraft, and in 1947 and 1948 it expanded its routes to include Dublin-Manchester-Amsterdam, Dublin-Brussels, Dublin-Belfast-Glasgow, London-Shannon, Shannon-Paris, Dublin-Belfast-Liverpool, and even Dublin-Rome.[84] These routes alone (especially Dublin-Rome, which lacked any substantial clientele during the winter months) represented an expansion that was too rapid and too costly. Yet Aer Rianta still planned to launch a new transatlantic service between Shannon and New York for which they purchased several Constellation aircraft. From their inception the two airlines had never made a profit, and the purchase of new aircraft and the costs of expanding the number of routes had a profoundly negative impact on the airlines' accounts. In 1946–47, Aer Lingus suffered a net loss of almost £75,000, or just over 20 percent of total revenue. The following year losses increased to a mind-boggling £891,000.[85]

From the perspective of the opposition parties, the purchase of the Constellation aircraft was unrealistic and irresponsible in the same way that Fianna Fáil's tourism-development policies had been during the Emergency. While more suited to the Rome route, the Constellations were ultimately leased by Aer Lingus and used to fly between Dublin and London. Given their size and relative inefficiency over short distances, they were a poor choice.[86] The airline's marketing campaign emphasized the luxurious comfort of the huge planes but did little to attract enough passengers to make them profitable.[87] Horrified by massive losses, the new interparty government quickly cancelled the proposed North American route on the eve of its maiden flight—the night before St. Patrick's Day in 1948.[88] The Constellation aircraft were sold shortly thereafter amid a considerable controversy that was linked all too easily in the minds of many with the "Fáilte hotel" controversy.[89]

Given all of this dissension, it is hardly surprising that when Fianna Fáil lost the general election in 1948 and was replaced by an interparty government, O'Brien was quickly fired and a new pro–Fine Gael Tourist Board director named W. F. Quinlan was appointed. The widespread distaste for tourism following the crisis surrounding the industry made tourism politically unpopular and dramatically undermined the effort to emphasize the national importance of the industry. During the next four years the Tourist Board was presented with the task of liquidating its properties. Just two years after its formation, Fáilte Téoranta reported that it had made a profit of £6,000 on its five Tourist Board hotels. Although the company itself hoped to continue, in October 1949 the government decided that it should be "wound up."[90] While the ITA and members of the ITB maintained that tourism was a vital national concern, neither group was in a position to successfully argue the point; an outside voice, unsullied by the tourism crisis, was needed to convince the Irish people and their government that tourism should remain a crucial concern for the nation.

America and the Irish National Interest

Even as the Tourist Board lay crippled by the postwar tourism crisis, a growing constituency recognized that tourism represented Ireland's "best hope of improving dollar earnings"[91] following British action to avoid a breakdown in trade between sterling and dollar countries.[92] In Ireland tourism represented the second most important dollar source behind emigrants' remittances and legacies. Whereas remittances totaled £3.5 million in 1947, tourism earned an impressive £1.8 million—considerably more than any other dollar income source. Better still, tourism revenues exploded following the war and had climbed to £2.7 million by 1948, whereas remittances declined to £3.1 million.

It was difficult to ignore the potential for tourism growth given that Ireland was "only receiving a mere trickle of the potentially enormous flow of Irish-American tourists and their dollars." But there remained two major problems: inadequate transportation to bring tourists to Ireland and a lack of entertainment facilities to occupy them upon their arrival.[93] Worse, the tourism crisis had left tourism development politically untenable for the Fine Gael–led government, and it is questionable whether any major changes would have taken place in the structure of tourism administration had not the American government strongly pressed Irish officials to improve the Irish tourist industry.

Ireland began receiving American aid through the European Recovery Program, or Marshall Plan, in July 1947.[94] Although Ireland did not receive substantial Marshall Plan money for tourism development, the Economic Cooperation Administration viewed tourism as an important component of the effort to rebuild countries such as France,[95] and Colonel T. J. Pozzi, the chief of the Travel Development Section of the Economic Cooperation Administration (ECA), believed that Ireland possessed similarly attractive tourist potential. With this idea in mind, he visited Ireland to survey the industry in 1949.[96] Following a tour arranged by the Irish Tourist Board,[97] Pozzi encouraged the ITB to launch a publicity campaign in America,[98] and he offered numerous suggestions for persuading tourists passing through

Shannon airport to stay in Ireland, including the installation of a movie theatre at Shannon, the dramatic expansion of shopping facilities at the airport, and the provision of far more duty-free items for purchase. In addition, he informed Irish officials that the most important task facing the industry was "to raise the quality of the hotel accommodation . . . to the level that will be acceptable to the ordinary United States tourist, and then to construct enough additional accommodation to take a further expansion in numbers."[99]

When his suggestions were not efficiently implemented, Pozzi lost patience with the Irish authorities and pointed angrily at the government's inaction and at the inefficiency of the Tourist Board itself. The ECA official doubted the ability of the board's members and expressed grave concern about the qualifications of Quinlan to handle the challenges ahead.[100] By 1950 there had still been little action and Pozzi's frustration continued to grow. Finally, in a meeting with the minister of external affairs, Pozzi "gave what he called a very private but at the same time a very definite warning that the amount of Marshall aid in 1950–51 would depend on the action which would be taken by the government." Although ECA administrators were generally friendly toward Ireland, "their patience had been exhausted," and Pozzi demanded that "effective government action in this field by way of reconstruction of the Tourist Board and otherwise was essential to avoid a complete deterioration" of relations with Washington: "If Ireland did not show some real interest in increasing her dollar earnings in the line which seemed most feasible, the ECA could hardly be expected to continue their aid at the forecast level."[101] In effect, Pozzi and the ECA were telling the Irish government that tourist growth was in Ireland's national interest, in terms of both improving dollar earnings and ensuring the continued receipt of Marshall Plan aid. Whether the task was politically popular or not, the government had to take immediate steps to restructure the ITB, hire more qualified staff, and mount an aggressive tourist-development campaign.

Tourism as Foreign Policy

At the same time that foreign pressure was brought to bear on the Irish government to develop tourism, a growing number within the Department of External Affairs believed that tourism might prove a useful foreign policy tool. The concept of mixing the activities of tourist authorities and those of the Department of External Affairs was first put forward during Dáil debates concerning the 1931 Tourist Traffic Act. At that time P. Hogan, a TD from County Clare, suggested that Irish representatives in England, America, Germany, and France could be called upon to hit "the people in those countries in the eye, so to speak, with the fact that we have a country worth seeing." From Hogan's perspective it was not that Irish consular officials should go out of their way to deliver leaflets, but rather that they should be in a position to distribute materials when relevant—to use existing resources to extend the reach of tourist advertising. Hogan's view was not universal, however, and others dismissed the idea. While Irish consulates abroad would certainly lend whatever aid was required to the Tourist Association, it was not the duty of Irish ambassadors to offer such assistance.[102]

At the end of World War II the Department of External Affairs suggested that tourism could be used to promote Irish political objectives through what it called "cultural propaganda." External Affairs noted that the new strategy "covers a wide range of activities—book, art, photographic, and film exhibitions; exchanges of students and lectureships; lecture tours; the preparation and distribution of books and publicity material to public and university libraries; and so on." These products would "make the country better known and understood" by informing outsiders about "every aspect of the country's national life and activity." The approach had a number of advantages: it was "not 'suspect' as obviously political propaganda tends to be"; there were no diplomatic limitations to be observed, and no complicated political questions to work through. Cultural propaganda would help make foreign intelligentsias "generally friendly and sympathetic." The department observed, "Our experience during the war showed how important it is to us to have—at least in the more important countries—a nucleus of public opinion which knows something about this country and has some understanding of, and sympathy with, our national aims and points of view. The influence of such a group can be of even [more] decisive importance in times of difficulty."[103]

This policy was all the more desirable because various governments, urging the development of closer cultural relations, had already contacted the department. External Affairs successfully advocated the establishment of a

Cultural Relations Committee, and although sources are spotty concerning the early activities of the committee, it is clear that relations were forged between External Affairs, the Irish Tourist Association, and, later, Bord Fáilte (the Irish Tourist Board). As it became more established during the 1950s, the Cultural Relations Committee included members of Aer Lingus, Bord Fáilte, the Department of External Affairs, Irish Rail (Córas Iompair Éireann or CIÉ), the Export Board (CTT), and later Radio Telefís Éireann (RTÉ), and it carried out joint operations intended to improve the image of Ireland abroad.[104]

Effective Action?

Thus, by the first months of 1950 it was very clear that something had to be done about tourism, whether the necessary actions would be politically unpopular or not. Government statistics made clear that tourism was now Ireland's second most important industry behind agriculture and was the country's leading export[105]—facts that could not be ignored because the economy was quickly plunging into a "huge" trade deficit.[106] Furthermore, Pozzi and the ECA continued to argue that the government was ignoring a primary national interest and a guaranteed source of valuable dollar income.

In February the minister for industry and commerce finally took tentative action by requesting a proposal from the Irish Tourist Board outlining its vision for the future. The subsequent report advocated a new five-tier structure for the board, including divisions concerned with hotels and catering, publicity, transportation, general promotion, and finance, along with substantial pay increases in order to secure the best talent available, and an expanded advertising campaign.[107] While the minister for industry and commerce, Dan Morrissey, agreed broadly with the proposed structure and the need for increased spending, he was largely ambivalent about the proposal.

Morrissey's colleagues at the Department of Finance were anything but ambivalent and charged that the scheme was little more than an excuse for increases in pay and personnel which "only incidentally . . . suggest[ed] how the board might approach the problem of maintaining and expanding the tourist industry." As far as Finance was concerned, nothing in the plan justified the requested £3 million. As an alternative, the minister suggested that substantial improvements could be attained simply by revamping the existing hotel-grading scheme, developing hotel-training programs, and pro-viding easy credit for private organizations interested in improving existing tourist facilities. Finally, he argued that an expanded publicity campaign in the United States might also be implemented by using repayable advances rather than a substantial budgetary increase. The minister justified these suggestions by arguing that "it would be unwise to spend large sums on advertising the attractions of this country abroad before positive improve-ments had been effected in standards of accommodation, etc. Such a policy would lead to speedy disillusionment of visitors and would undermine the prospects of developing an assured dollar income from tourism."[108]

Following the inability of either the Tourist Board or the government to offer a coherent direction, three other groups were formed to provide their opinions. The first was sponsored by the European Travel Commis-sion (which Ireland joined at its foundation in 1948) under the aegis of the Marshall Plan and involved a three-month trip to America by Irish tourism officials, including Kevin O'Doherty of the Tourist Board, to visit a num-ber of hotels. Although O'Doherty was impressed by the high standards of American accommodations, he soon concluded that it would be far more helpful if a group from the Irish Hotels Commission made a similar tour. Such a trip might open the hoteliers' eyes to the sort of improvements neces-sary if Ireland were going to compete for American dollars. A group from the Irish Hotels Commission was established in March to visit both Irish and American hotels under the auspices of the Organization for European Economic Cooperation and the ECA.[109]

The Hotels Commission's report was given to the Department of Indus-try and Commerce at the end of September 1950. Although the commis-sion's report offered a series of suggestions, including the production of more tourism films and the publication of more professional publicity mate-rials that featured both historical and scenic information, its major concern was directed at the atrocious state of Irish accommodations. "Almost all" lacked central heating, 80 percent were without a private bath/toilet, Cobh was more akin to a Third World port than a suitable place to greet wealthy American travelers, Irish hotels were manned by untrained staffs (which the commission blamed on emigration), and the Tourist Board was attempting to improve the situation by using a faulty inspection policy implemented by guileless inspectors. The Hotels Commission suggested four principal solutions. First, the statutory tourist authority should contain at least three members of the hotel and catering industry who would be equipped to develop an effective grading scheme. Second, the tourist authority should be able to levy taxes in order to guarantee an adequate budget. Third, the tourist authority should execute its own publicity activities, ensuring continuity across the industry by eliminating the need for communication between a public body (ITB) and a private one (ITA). And finally, the tourist authority should provide grants for the reconstruction, improvement, and development of hotels.[110]

The third and most important of the three fact-finding bodies consisted of a group of American hoteliers led by Robert K. Christenberry, president of the Astor Hotel in New York, and the group's report represents an extraordinary example of an outside voice effectively interjecting itself into the debate about Ireland's national interest. The "Christenberry report" was submitted to the Irish government in July and August 1950 and has been widely recognized as an important contribution to the tourism debate during the early 1950s.[111] Although few of the committee's suggestions had been adopted three years after the release of the report, the document nevertheless provided government officials with a well-argued and extensive, if often less than complimentary, commentary on the state of the tourism industry in Ireland from an outside perspective. Above all, Christenberry believed that Ireland had all of the raw materials necessary to create an excellent tourist destination, and that such an undertaking would have dramatic benefits for the country, but there was much work to be done. While still in the United States, prospective American visitors found it nearly impossible to find "authentic information concerning the country." What information was available came in the form of "a flood of confusing brochures describing every section of Ireland, but very little of it containing the essential information" that the tourist would need.[112] Once in Ireland, American visitors faced "the trip by tender to the pier at Cobh, the customs inspection in the bleak and windy shed, the lack of even the most primitive sanitary facilities, [and] the currency inspection under the leaky roof of a dismal crowded room." Upon leaving Cobh by rail, the tourist found advertisements for Norway, Austria, and Britain, but not Ireland, "Never before have we found competitive advertising so strategically

placed," the committee noted sardonically. Once beyond these early horrors, the tourist would experience more frustrations staying in substandard
hotels, riding on filthy trains, dining on dull food, and vainly seeking evening entertainment.

The Christenberry report offered a variety of very specific suggestions
for improving the structure of Irish tourist development and for enhancing
the country's ability to attract American dollars. Above all, the Christenberry
committee urged the complete restructuring of tourism administration by
November 1950. To begin with, there should be one tourism organization
in Ireland, and it was advisable to merge the ITB and ITA into a single
body. In a break with the past, appointments should be based on professional qualifications, and candidates drawn from business, advertising, and
the hotel and hospitality industry. Above all, appointees should be "completely divorced from politics." No longer could the industry afford to have
longtime republicans like O'Brien or anti-treaty stalwarts like Quinlan. At
the same time it was considered important that the new chairman be Irish.[113]
Christenberry's argument in favor of instituting an ethnic hiring criterion is
completely understandable given Ireland's rapidly declining economic situation at the beginning of the 1950s. To have placed a foreigner in such a
prominent position would have undermined the entire tourism project.[114]
Indeed, Christenberry fully acknowledged the political difficulties inherent
in any major tourism initiative, and for this reason the *new* tourist agency
should be renamed in order to avoid any association attached to the old Irish
Tourist Board.

In order to ensure success, Christenberry argued, the new board should
take full advantage of ECA technical assistance over a period of six months,
making use of the international expertise available in order to bring the
body up to high standards quickly. It was also important that the new tourism organization receive adequate funds. Penny-pinching was ill-advised
and would do little more than cripple the new body before it could take
its first steps. Clearly, the increased staff and higher salaries required "a far
larger budget and a more realistic method of raising funds. It means that the
government will have to get completely in the swim of tourism instead of
merely wetting its feet." While Britain and Bermuda devoted $350,000 and
$200,000 respectively to promoting their tourist products in the American

market alone, Ireland spent a meager £30,000 in all markets in an effort to attract visitors.

Furthermore, Christenberry pointed out that authorities had made no real effort to sell tourism to the Irish people since the war: "Despite the importance of this one industry in the nation's economy, the average Irishman knows practically nothing about its value," in stark contrast to Switzerland, where "every citizen is aware of tourist spending and what it means to him personally." In Christenberry's mind the success of tourism required that the "Irish people themselves" have sympathy for tourist development. The battle for tourism was now centered in the halls of power, but it really needed to be fought in the country as a whole. If Irish men and women themselves did not recognize tourism as a national interest, if they did not understand "the dollar economy involved," then they would not play their part in developing tourist facilities and welcoming visitors.[115]

In sum, the Christenberry report provided the government with a clear blueprint for a new tourist authority and offered concrete suggestions about the work that was required. Yet few of Christenberry's suggestions were adopted. Tourism remained "political" until the late 1950s, and the Irish Tourist Association continued its activities until 1964. Although the budget for tourism was increased dramatically, it fell far short of what was really required, and instead of centralizing tourist development with one board, Ireland ended up with *three* tourist boards. Even the suggested cooperation between the ECA and Irish tourism bodies failed to materialize—a victim of the board's "non-cooperation."[116] Even so, over the coming months the document was seldom absent from discussion. The committee of American hoteliers did push government officials to further acknowledge what Pozzi and the ECA had been already arguing fiercely, namely, that tourism development should be taken more seriously. In the wake of all of the scandal and a general perception that the board had made few gains, few Irish citizens really believed that spending money on a tourist board was worth the investment; Christenberry made a strong counterargument.

Behaving "Like Ostriches"

In the immediate aftermath of the Christenberry report the government created a cabinet committee to address the tourism issue, consisting of the

Taoiseach, the Tanaiste, the minister for external affairs, the minister for defense, and the parliamentary secretary to the minister for industry and commerce. The committee advocated immediate steps to publicize Ireland as a stopping place for Americans making the Holy Year pilgrimage to Rome, efforts to promote Ireland through Irish-American organizations, the provision of improved souvenirs, enhanced cooperation between the ITA and Tourist Board, and the appointment of a new ITB chairman. Nevertheless, few if any members of the committee seriously discussed substantial revision of tourist-development policies or organization.[117] Above all, the committee flatly rejected the idea that the ITA should be disbanded because

(a) both organisations [ITB and ITA] have separate sources of income;
(b) the association has an established tradition with a record of achievement;
(c) tourism is a sphere of activity well suited to co-operative effort and to organisation by persons whose purpose is not profit but community service; [and]
(d) there is public interest in the association of a proprietary or representative nature.[118]

The ITA's political significance is clearly visible from this list. With its important local connections and influential membership, the organization was almost untouchable, its preservation almost a national interest in itself. Far from disbanding the ITA, the Taoiseach believed that it should "be strengthened financially."[119]

The Department of Industry and Commerce enthusiastically greeted Christenberry's notion that the Tourist Board should launch a widespread campaign to educate the Irish people about the importance of tourism, because "it is necessary to explain the value of tourism and how tourist earnings benefit the country and the individual. In the schools, on farms, and in workshops and offices, propaganda for tourism must be set in motion."[120] Yet the department was reticent about restructuring the board, apparently believing that throwing money at the Tourist Board would solve the problem, with no restructuring required. Selling tourism to the public would eventually assuage the problem created by the tourism crisis, but in the meantime radical change was out of the question.

Meanwhile, outside of government circles frustration was increasing. Within the Tourist Board, Roger Greene, whom Colonel Pozzi had suggested as the ECA's choice for a board chairman in 1949,[121] resigned in disgust in June 1950. Greene told the *Irish Times* that his resignation was the result of "dissatisfaction with the government's attitude" and had nothing to do with the common feeling that the Quinlan-led board was notable for its "incompetency and neglect" of its duties. Greene claimed that he and the board had presented numerous reports to the government, only to have them ignored, and his resignation certainly illustrates growing frustration within the ITB.[122] The ITA was similarly irritated. Speaking at the association's annual general meeting, J. P. O'Brien, who was in the midst of an ill-fated attempt to start his own travel agency, Irish Express,[123] blamed the various government departments and stressed that the "government should do much more than the merely advisory part towards increasing hotel accommodation in the country."[124]

The media, and particularly the *Irish Press,* were also increasingly critical of government inaction. The *Press* blamed a decline in tourist traffic during 1950 on the "lack of leadership and organisation" from the "arch-villain," the Irish Tourist Board.[125] The paper reasoned that anyone with a "sense of responsibility" should recognize the need for prompt and efficient improvement in tourist-development policy because "no country, particularly a small and poor one like ours, can afford to throw away a huge source of revenue such as poured into Ireland in 1946, 1947, and 1948." It was no longer acceptable to "behave like ostriches" by ignoring competition for tourists from other countries like Great Britain, while failing to do everything possible to ensure a continuation of the impressive tourist receipts of the late 1940s.[126]

In addition, the ECA continued to be greatly dissatisfied with the rate of progress. Throughout January, February, and March 1951, Marshall Plan representatives attempted to work with the Tourist Board on various development projects, primarily the distribution of grants, but they found it "impossible to get the ITB representatives to take any effective part in the discussion."[127] By 1 February the Department of External Affairs realized that Ireland was in danger of forfeiting "the goodwill" of the ECA mission because of the failure to make headway on tourism development.[128] By 7

February the mission began to threaten to withdraw a £100,000 grant for tourism development, as well as various agricultural grants totaling almost £1 million altogether.[129] When External Affairs was finally able to push the board into a meeting in mid-March, the tourist authority, which was tied up in efforts to promote government acceptance of its restructuring ideas, was unprepared to offer adequate feedback to the ECA, and consequently, the Marshall Plan money for tourist development, as well as the mission's willingness to provide advice, were placed in further doubt.[130]

When the government finally introduced legislation early in 1951, the proposals of the Christenberry report were little more than a distant memory for Fine Gael and its government partners. The new legislation included a dramatic increase in spending, provision for a *larger* board—not the lean and mean board suggested by Christenberry—and small changes to the ITB's hotel-registration scheme.[131]

The Lemass Solution

Consideration of the Fine Gael tourism bill was terminated in June 1951 by the dissolution of the Dáil for elections that produced a Fianna Fáil victory, and Seán Lemass, again minister for industry and commerce, did not present his bill until early 1952. During the period between Fianna Fáil's return to power and the introduction of a dramatically revised Tourist Traffic Act, Lemass "undertook a very careful and thorough review of policy in relation to tourist development," even inviting Christenberry to return to Ireland to brief him on the now famous report.[132] Above all, Lemass wanted to reach a decision about the fate of the ITA, the structure of the ITB, and what new roles, if any, should be given to tourist authorities.

Lemass had another consideration in mind as well—how to help his ailing friend and former Civil War comrade J. P. O'Brien.[133] Since losing his job in 1948, O'Brien had made an unsuccessful effort to establish his own travel agency. When this effort failed, he was faced with the problem of supporting a wife and children in decent comfort, not to mention his worsening alcoholism. Lemass quickly decided to establish a tourism publicity board, in addition to the existing Tourist Board, for his friend O'Brien to manage.

Lemass justified the need for a separate publicity board by noting that local authorities were able, under the 1939 Tourist Traffic Act, to establish their own associations and to seek approval from the minister to divert publicity payments to the local group. While this had never been an issue before, in 1950 a local publicity association was established in Sligo and had been subsequently authorized by the former minister for industry and commerce, Dr. Thomas F. O'Higgins. Given this precedent, it seemed likely that other local authorities might do the same, resulting in a dramatic decrease in Tourist Association income that would cripple the ITA and Ireland's tourist publicity effort as well. Adding further support to this argument, O'Higgins had also decided to end Tourist Board contributions to the ITA, further robbing the voluntary organization of valuable income. The new publicity board would circumvent the threat of ITA dissolution while providing the Dáil with statutory control over publicity. The proactive approach begged the question: Why not wrap up the association immediately? Lemass explained the step not only by citing the risk "of controversy and agitation," but also by asserting that the ITA represented something "of real value" by virtue of its long history. It was better to arrange for the association's "continued participation in tourist publicity work in conjunction with the Tourist Board" by ensuring the ITA a place on the board of directors for the statutory development and publicity boards.[134]

Lemass's embrace of the multiboard structure did not inspire universal approval, to say the least. One official even declared it "evidence of political cowardice on the part of the minister."[135] T. K. Whitaker, a high-ranking member of the Department of Finance, agreed and argued that instead of two boards, the publicity functions could be carried out within the larger vehicle of a single tourist board made up of "separate committees," with O'Brien as deputy chairman. Likewise, McElligott, also of Finance, insisted that the publicity board should be a subsidiary of the tourist board and should not have a separate staff.[136] The minister of finance was "horrified" at the extent of expenditure planned in the new legislation,[137] and his department worked to limit grants-in-aid to the proposed boards—an effort that Lemass was "not prepared to accept."[138] Ultimately Lemass secured the budget of £250,000 and £3,000,000 in loan guarantees that he had requested.[139]

Far more damning in the longer term than Department of Finance rejection, however, was that the Tourist Board itself responded with anger over the proposed separation of publicity activities from the main ITB structure.

Lemass was unsympathetic and quickly replied that he had never given any consideration to granting the board power over the new publicity body, which in his view would need to be able to "run its own ship."[140] The board's opposition to the separate publicity body should have sparked some concern at Industry and Commerce, yet no anxiety was visible.

The new tourism development structure became a reality even before legislation was presented to the Dáil. By October 1951 the publicity body was already functioning, leaving only its name to be seriously debated.[141] After an extensive discussion about possible names that included considerable bickering about the nuanced meanings of various Irish words, it was decided to call the publicity board "Fógra Fáilte" and the tourist-development board "An Bord Fáilte."[142] These names were not especially popular, and a number of TDs expressed reservations about the need for a Gaelic name in the first place; former minister for industry and commerce Dr. O'Higgins sneered that "it cannot be suggested that the change to an Irish name assists the saving of the language . . . I take it that we are not going to endeavour to teach tourists the Irish language."[143] He followed up this jibe by predicting that the name might confuse tourists from England and elsewhere, fatally undermining the tourist-development effort. Although teaching tourists the Irish language was not Lemass's reason for using an Irish name, he appears to have felt that it was important for the government to stress the country's unique Gaelic past and present, pointing at every turn to Ireland's rich heritage, especially at a time when the nation's fortunes were in decline. To use Gaelic names sparked memories of a proud past, deflecting attention from the failed Irish Tourist Board and the failing Irish economy.

Back to Business

With the passage of the Tourist Traffic Act of 1952, the two statutory tourist bodies quickly got to work developing tourism products and trying to educate the Irish people about the industry's national importance. The national education program took two forms. Most dramatically, the tourist authorities inaugurated a new Irish homecoming festival called "An Tóstal," which was held annually between 1953 and 1958.[144] Although An Tóstal was most obviously intended to increase dollar earnings and to extend the tourist season by drawing a sizeable portion of the nation's twenty million "exiles" back to Ireland, the event was supposed to increase internal awareness of tourism while educating Irish people about the importance of the industry, the country's proud cultural heritage, and the way in which Irish landscapes should look. An Bord Fáilte boasted that the "pre-eminent" position of tourism would be "clearly recognised by all" as a result of Tóstal festivities.[145] In newspaper articles and advertisements the Irish were encouraged to plant flowers, paint their homes, clip hedgerows, and generally tidy their surroundings. As Taoiseach John A. Costello said when opening the 1955 Tóstal,

> its secondary but closely related object is to provide opportunities for national spring cleaning, whereby to promote individual, local, and national conceit in, and responsibility for, the neatness, attractiveness, and order of our cities, towns and villages, of our houses, gardens, and public buildings, and to stimulate our own interest in, and appreciation of, our culture, shrines, and holy places and the beauties of our own land.[146]

Ireland's national festival was intended as an important component of a national retraining scheme in which tourism was strongly positioned as a national interest and its development regarded as a patriotic duty. According to tourist authorities, "the success of An Tóstal depends on the individual citizen" and represented "a first-class business proposition for the nation." If successful, the festival would create "a better Ireland for generations to come."[147]

The second reeducation program (launched at the same time that An Tóstal was being planned) consisted primarily of a booklet entitled *What Does Tourism Mean to You?*, which featured the slogan "Tourism is everybody's business—the tourist is everybody's guest." The publication lectured the reader: "Tourism is a living, dynamic activity which touches many aspects of our national life," but which could "flourish only when there is a general public appreciation of its value." The booklet attempted to define tourists and to describe the role of the industry in the economy by graphically suggesting that it was the country's largest single export in 1949,[148] listing Ireland's main tourist attractions, stating the significance of domestic tourism, and drawing attention to the fundamental importance of the general public in the industry's success. According to the publishers, "Every one of us can help the visitor feel at home in Ireland by extending to him that extra courtesy and consideration to which every guest is entitled"—a task made easy because "it is a natural instinct with the Irish people."[149]

The campaign to teach Irish citizens about the importance of tourism did not end with the demise of An Tóstal. In fact, the message that "Tourism is Everybody's Business" remained a staple component of Bord Fáilte Éireann's (BFÉ) activities into the late 1970s, when BFÉ created a short film that again emphasized the financial significance of tourism to the Irish economy—by then responsible for one in every ten jobs and worth £230 million per annum—and suggesting annual spring-cleaning, the development of local festivals, and the friendly treatment of tourists. Ultimately, the board claimed, tourism "enriches our own lives" by sparking the creation of improved roads, parks, a healthier environment, and "pride in our way of life, history, and scenery."[150] Much as in the 1920s, so too in the 1950s, tourism still constituted a harbinger of local improvements and a conduit to a better life.

Bord Fáilte Éireann

In spite of the launch of numerous new programs, the two-board structure collapsed in 1954 as a result of J. P. O'Brien's declining health and an almost total lack of communication between O'Brien and the director of An Bord Fáilte, J. A. Nugent.[151] As previously noted, Nugent and his team already resented Fógra Fáilte before the passage of the 1952 Tourist Traffic Act, and it certainly did not help that Nugent and O'Brien refused to speak to one another from the outset. Nugent was a Fine Gael appointee who had started with the Irish Tourist Board in 1950, while O'Brien was a longtime member of Fianna Fáil—politics and the legacy of the Civil War remained a significant and damaging component of tourist administration.[152]

In August 1954, two months after Fine Gael returned to power at the head of another interparty government, the two statutory tourist organizations jointly agreed to request legislation to dissolve Fógra Fáilte in favor of a single statutory tourist body. When presenting the requested legislation in February 1955, the new minister of industry and commerce, William Norton, argued that "the existence of these two bodies results in unnecessary duplication of staffs and lack of central direction. This must give rise to overlapping and must weaken the effective control and direction of staff and of functions. Such a situation can only give rise to unhealthy rivalry between the two bodies and perhaps clashes of personality."[153]

The desire for a single statutory body did little to diminish the power of the Irish Tourist Association. As always, the ITA engaged in its usual heavy lobbying efforts to guarantee its continued position in Irish tourism development. This time the association asked for official recognition in the new legislation, a "position of dignity" that "granted more power and a definite status" to the ITA.[154] Toward this end ITA leaders successfully persuaded the County Council Chambers to pass a resolution demanding specific reference to the Irish Tourist Association in the new bill.[155] Norton provided this recognition by noting "the special position of the Irish Tourist Association in connection with tourism," and he proposed "to give the association suitable representation on the new board" as long as local authorities continued to provide the ITA with significant funds.[156] The association remained politically untouchable.

After passage of the 1955 Tourist Traffic Act, An Bord Fáilte and Fógra Fáilte were merged into a single statutory tourist body called Bord Fáilte Éireann; there would be no further significant legal changes in the shape of the statutory Irish tourist organization until the late 1990s. Unlike the previous statutory bodies, the new tourist board was less driven by a single top-level figure and instead drew much greater attention from its board of directors, who now began to take a more direct interest in various policy options, leaving the chairman to address questions of day-to-day administration.[157] Even more important, the days of political appointments also quickly came to an end. Whereas O'Brien, Quinlin, Nugent, and an interim director named J. F. Dempsey were all political appointees, Timothy J. (T. J.) O'Driscoll, who took office in 1956, was not. Instead, O'Driscoll was a tough-minded man from Cork who had little patience for politics of the ordinary kind. Before his long career as director-general of Bord Fáilte Éireann, O'Driscoll had been a star athlete; later, as a civil servant, he had been involved in the establishment of CIÉ under the tutelage of John Leydon. After getting involved in an insider-trading scandal, the Corkman was transferred from his post at Industry and Commerce to another department based in the Phoenix Park, a position that did not satisfy the ambitious O'Driscoll. Rather than await reassignment, the future Bord Fáilte leader cycled back to the offices of Industry and Commerce, discovered that his desk was still vacant, and simply transferred himself back to his old job. According to Kevin O'Doherty, who worked extensively with O'Driscoll, the Corkman was a "very dominant character," a "real go-getter," and "he could get things done." O'Driscoll was precisely the man that Bord Fáilte needed. Whereas the accepted approach to securing employment during this period was to know somebody, O'Driscoll refused to see anybody who presented references before establishing his or her qualifications. He simply wanted the best people he could find and did not care about their politics.[158]

With tourism now separated from its once clear links to the major political parties, tourist revenue increasing (by 1958 revenue had reached £34.6 million, the highest on record), and a host of development and promotional projects being aggressively pursued by the Tourist Board, the tourism industry seemed ready to take off. Adding further fuel to the fire, the *White Paper on Economic Expansion* of 1958 afforded the industry a prominent place in government economic priorities and pledged £1 million in grants to assist in tourism development through 1968.[159] In turn, the *Second Programme for Economic Expansion* called for a doubling of tourism revenue between 1960 and 1970.[160]

In many ways it was a new era for tourism development in Ireland—a period of setting goals and expecting to achieve them. The more objectives that were set, the more tourists were needed to meet them, and the more attentive policy makers had to be to industry demands. While the government had previously debated the status of tourism as a national interest, the industry was now assured of a place in government thinking; tourism was again considered an important national priority.

3

Change and Continuity, 1958–1994

Between 1958 and the early 1990s Ireland underwent massive social and economic change. Society became increasingly urbanized as traditional rural industry collapsed and workers left agriculture,[1] tuberculosis was eradicated, and infant mortality was reduced.[2] Even Irish Catholicism, once widely considered a defining characteristic of Irishness, changed dramatically as church influence declined and mass attendance dropped precipitously in the late 1980s and the 1990s.[3] During the second half of the century as a whole, the Irish economy dipped and climbed like a vicious rollercoaster. The 1950s were marked by a lackluster economy and dizzying emigration.[4] The 1960s featured a dramatic economic improvement and a virtual end to the mass exodus of the previous decade. The brief prosperity did not last. After the shock of the first world oil crisis of 1973, joblessness climbed once more and did not drop below 13 percent again until 1994.[5] Despite this painful problem, there was reason to hope for a brighter future, even if it did not seem likely at the time. In 1973 Ireland joined the European Economic Community (EEC), opening the door to vital economic assistance. The eventual implications would be significant (see chapter 7).

As Ireland slowly moved from widespread poverty and underdevelopment to become a somewhat awkward modern country on the cusp of a great transformation during the 1990s, tourism became an increasingly important component of the Irish economy and an ever more obvious national interest.[6] New tourism enterprises and growth targets after the first *Programme for Economic Expansion* in 1958 reflected this growing recognition. At the same time, the government voted larger and larger budgets to the Tourist Board and so showed its deepening belief in the value of tourism.[7] Naturally, expanding government interest and increasingly aggressive goals meant that tourism administration grew more complicated. From the 1960s tourism plans had to balance the elements of development, the environment, and carefully targeted ad spending. Marketing programs needed to cater to the tastes of a widening number of audiences; advertising had to be tailored to match a dizzying array of visitor gazes. At the same time Irish tourism had to compete with countries such as Spain, whose tourism growth outpaced all others in Western Europe during the 1950s.[8] These new pressures forced Bord Fáilte Éireann (BFÉ) to expand its market research efforts and to become increasingly savvy in its approach to promoting the country.

Even as tourism budgets and planning pressures increased, Irish tourism retained many of the concerns that had existed since 1923. The industry remained a nexus for discussion about the national interest and identity. Although there was now considerable consensus about the importance of the industry in economic terms, there were still diverse local and regional interests, still divisions over precisely how Ireland should be presented to the world, still shortages of accommodation, an infrastructure needing constant improvement, and the problem that Irish tourism remained a highly seasonal product. Just as in the two earlier periods of post–Civil War tourism development, the years after 1958 saw a diverse collection of individuals and groups using tourism as an excuse to push local grievances at central government level. At the same time the government's newfound dedication to tourism development meant that it was no longer willing to leave local tourism administration to a body outside its control. In 1964 the ITA was finally disbanded and replaced by Regional Tourism Organisations with direct administrative links to Dublin. Finally, just as Marshall Plan administrators had earlier tried to coerce the Irish government into further tourist development, so too the European Union pushed tourism in Ireland as a path toward economic development and self-sufficiency in the 1980s and 1990s. Outside pressures, just as much as inside voices, continued to define tourism as a national interest.

During the years between 1924 and roughly 1955 the national tourism debate had centered on whether tourism was desirable and for what reasons, unfolding in a more or less linear manner. By 1958 there were few who doubted the importance of tourism, yet there remained divisions about how to shape the industry and about precisely why tourism was important to the nation. At the same time, more and more people were concerned about how Ireland should be represented to the world at large. Tourism officials gradually became more adept at dealing with the challenges posed by the new dialogue. They improved their ability to collect information, made an effort to improve national control of local development efforts, launched more and more spectacular marketing initiatives, and actively used tourism as a means of defining and expanding the national community—all as the diverse voices present during the pre-1958 period continued to make themselves heard.

A "True Patriot"

By 1962 tourism revenue reached nearly £47 million and was climbing rapidly every year. Not surprisingly, local groups desperately wanted to secure as much of this meaty pie as possible and continued to exert considerable influence over tourism development. For some, tourism represented a potential source of great wealth, but for many others it presented a solution to the pressing problems of poverty, underdevelopment, and massive emigration—all shockingly obvious on the western seaboard.

Father John J. Scanlon arrived in the rural parish of Tuosist in 1961, and his interest in tourism can stand for that of many small rural communities along the western seaboard. Situated on the Kerry side of the Cork-Kerry border in the Caha Mountains, Tuosist is rugged, rural, and stunningly beautiful. It sits in a rocky and heather-strewn landscape, dotted with forested areas, more welcoming to midges than men. While most tourists know the Healy Pass and the Coast Road, they seldom stop for more than a few moments to snap photographs and take in the view of Hungry Hill, Glanmore Lake, the Cascade waterfall, and the other quickly accessible scenic attractions of the area.

Scanlon had no sooner arrived at his cottage, devoid of modern sanitation or electricity, than he realized that his parish faced a crisis; the community was "dying . . . , or more correctly, almost dead."[9] In 1841 the area had been home to 7,485 people. By 1926 the population had fallen to 1,800, and by 1963 it had dropped still further to just 860. Worse still, the emigration that was destroying the community showed no sign of stopping. There were 150 bachelors in the parish and just 25 marriageable young women

Upon reaching eighteen, young women immediately left for England, leaving behind aging parents who generally followed their children as soon as the young people had established themselves in a new life abroad. In 1963 as many as sixty houses lay vacant, collapsing quickly as moisture seeped into the support structure. Beyond the specter of constant emigration Scanlon perceived another major problem: mounting foreign ownership. While Irish industrialists and tourist authorities expressed little interest in the parish, he feared that German and English developers were actively purchasing large tracks of land, and predicted that Tuosist would soon be most notable for proliferating "Trespassers will be prosecuted" signs.[10]

At first Scanlon thought that the solution was to find a matchmaker who would arrange marriages that might help to prop up the dwindling population. Scanlon wanted to find a diplomat and an authority on Tuosist family history. The successful candidate was expected to smoke a pipe—to "lend authority to his statements"—as well as to "know the parishioners of Tuosist like the back of his hand." Impossible job qualifications, to be sure, and it did not take Scanlon long to recognize that a matchmaker was not going to solve the rural crisis anyway. Something more proactive was required.

In Scanlon's mind tourism became the most viable solution. Tuosist has little arable farmland, and without electricity or running water, to say nothing of better road access, industrial development was out of the question. Even so, the parish did have scenic beauty in spades. Writing to Bord Fáilte, to the Department of the Taoiseach, and to Erskine Childers, the minister for transport and power, Scanlon argued that the famous Healy Pass, Glanmore Lake, Glenbeg Lough (famous for trout fishing), the groves of Dineen, the mountains, the seas—all give variety for the tourist; no wonder then that tourists who pass through are amazed by its beautiful scenery and disgusted with the tourist bodies who even have left the very name of Tuosist off the maps.

Scanlon wondered why Bord Fáilte was "doing big things elsewhere in places such as Killarney and Ballybunion" while ignoring Tuosist, robbing the parish of vital revenue by encouraging tourists to pass from Glengarriff to Kenmare or Killarney without stopping to spend a few days in this scenic Shangri-La. He suggested that the government could improve the situation dramatically by bringing electricity and improved sanitation to area homes, thus allowing the rapid development of tourist accommodation and enhancing the attraction of the area to visitors.[11] It was a heartfelt plea, not at all unlike those from Kinsale and Dingle during the 1920s, 1930s, and 1940s.

The plight of Tuosist caught the attention of Listowel-based playwright John B. Keane,[12] who interviewed Scanlon and published an extended article on Tuosist in the *Sunday Press*. For Keane the plight of Tuosist was one of national importance, and the fight to save the parish was every bit as nationalist in its inspiration as Easter Week had been. Keane held that

> [a] patriot is not a man who boasts about the Irish heritage, Irish culture, the Irish language as such. Idealist, yes, but not patriot. A patriot is a man who contributes in a practical way to the development of his own country. A man who stays at home and marries at home in spite of the overwhelming difficulties is a true patriot.
>
> He is a patriot who fights with his heart and mind for the countryside which gave him birth. He is a patriot who helps communities less fortunate than his own. Men of consequence and substance who take an interest in places like Tuosist are the real practical patriots.

Keane was writing to the government, to wealthy investors, to men of influence, in the hope that he could make them see Scanlon's plight and feel a desire to help, if not for Tuosist, then for Ireland. "Money and incoming people will bring the natives back," he insisted. "If a man is drowning, won't you give him priority?" Tourism would surely "make all the difference" by supplementing farm income, sparking marriages, ensuring the development of "a well-appointed guesthouse," and allowing Scanlon to return to his spiritual tasks of conducting christenings and marriages and saying Sunday mass.[13]

The government took Scanlon's comments seriously, applauding his efforts to install signposts along key parish roadways and assuring the priest of "the great importance that the government attaches to the development of tourism, not only in the national interest, but as a means of promoting the economic welfare of rural areas." Scanlon was told that the position of Tuosist would be systematically considered.[14]

After its referral from the Department of the Taoiseach's office, Scanlon's plea found a willing audience in the members of the Kerry Development

Team. After considering his proposals (which also included a handful of agricultural suggestions), the team determined that tourism was the region's most promising prospect and that the erection of holiday chalets should be encouraged. The chalets would be ideal for financially pinched families from Great Britain, Europe, and America, while requiring little staff and increasing the "spending population" of Tuosist.[15]

If the British and American markets were seriously to be considered, the erection of saleable chalets first demanded electrification. After receiving direction from the minister of transport and power, the Electricity Supply Board (ESB) quickly began to consider electrifying at least that part of Tuosist parish near Lauragh and its immediate vicinity.[16] In the meantime Scanlon continued writing letters, explaining that "the poor mouth excuse of lack of money carries no weight, as the tourists in many ways will pour it back again into the national purse."[17] The rural priest was difficult to ignore, and by February 1964 the ESB confirmed that its staff would be able to extend power to thirty households in the parish.[18] It was a significant victory, but certainly did not guarantee Scanlon's ultimate success.

The next major challenge was to win approval from Bord Fáilte for the chalet scheme. Such support would have seemed likely because Tourist Board development policy was now based on the provision of loans and grants, and special monies were available for development in the western counties, where tourism was increasingly seen as the most promising harbinger of economic relief. On 19 June 1962 a general program was approved under which money was to be provided to develop farmhouses to serve as bed-and-breakfasts, while further schemes were planned to develop chalets in Gaeltacht areas.[19]

Unfortunately, Tuosist was a small and relatively isolated parish without a significant preexisting service industry, nor was it a Gaeltacht district. Thirty electrified homes near the Kenmare River hardly represented a sound investment. Tourist authorities wanted to support larger projects, such as communities of holiday homes, rather than isolated groups of two or three, along with promotional policies designed to attract substantial numbers of visitors. Yet the logic was more than just economic. By the early 1960s, Bord Fáilte was fully aware of the importance of scenic beauty and was beginning to view itself as an environmental watchdog organization. In particular, the success of the Tidy Towns program, inaugurated in 1958 (see chapter 6), demonstrated to the board that building and planning controls were beneficial to the tourism industry; the board believed that "a rash of isolated building could be injurious to the scenic amenities of the area."[20] Given the circumstances, Tuosist was not a viable site for substantial board investment.

Scanlon did not give up. While little money was forthcoming to develop holiday cottages, the priest was eventually able to secure Bord Fáilte assistance in creating a brochure advertising the attractions of Tuosist. The brochure featured photographs of area scenery and families seated around gas lamps recounting ancestral stories or perhaps remembering the beautiful sites/sights witnessed during the day's adventures. The text attempted to sell the area as "a holiday with a difference," desirable precisely because it was not modern in any way. Prospective visitors were informed, "You will find the people in Tuosist living the same kind of life as they have lived for decades past." The very fact that electricity was still not widely available in 1971 ensured that "the ancient art of story-telling has not been displaced by the impact of radio and television—the local people have it at their fingertips, and it is fascinating to hear the stories take shape from the lips of a seanechaidh." This was an area where poetry was as obvious as the staggeringly beautiful scenery, and boating and pony-trekking also beckoned the visitor.[21]

Scanlon's efforts were not a complete failure. He did, after all, bring electricity to a small area of his parish, prompt the development of two small hotels, and successfully publish a tourism brochure. Given that Scanlon was essentially a single voice calling out from the Kerry wilderness, these were no small achievements. The guidebook and limited tourist accommodation did not end the exodus from Tuosist, and Scanlon's dream of large-scale tourism development was never realized, but his voice had been taken seriously, echoing through the halls of government and prompting inquiries by Bord Fáilte, the Department of Transport and Power, the ESB, and the Kerry County Council. Even when local pleas were unsuccessful, they demanded the government's ear and inevitably drew the attention of tourist authorities.

Not all local interests were represented by single individuals. Local authorities, development companies like the Shannon Free Airport Development Company, bodies like the Kilmainham Restoration Society, and other tourism-related groups and organizations all exercised a significant influence on tourist authorities and/or the government. Negotiations with Belfast during the 1960s, for example, were partly influenced by local interests in the border counties who demanded assistance with canal-development programs, the foundation of the Enniskillen airfield, and increased ease of movement for anglers interested in fishing the numerous lakes in the "Lakelands" area.[22]

Local pressure often prompted swift action by tourist authorities, as in 1972 when hoteliers in Clare became upset with a Bord Fáilte booklet entitled *Where to Eat in Ireland: Traveler's Guide to 100 Selected Restaurants*. After the initial complaints it did not take long for the Irish Hotels' Federation to call on the Tourist Board to cease distributing the guide. Despite the protests, BFÉ insisted that *Where to Eat* was little more than an indicator of top restaurants. Even so, within days of the federation's demand, Bord Fáilte suspended distribution of twenty thousand copies of the booklet.[23] It was more beneficial for the statutory Tourist Board to placate the federation and the Clare hoteliers than it was to risk alienating either group further. Local demands were certainly not limited to the distribution (or not) of guidebooks; they ranged from County Clare's insistence that BFÉ work to develop angling tourism because it would be the "savior of Clare tourism,"[24] to complaints by others about the omission of their region from a Bord Fáilte slideshow.[25] Just as in earlier days, tourism authorities were constantly reminded that tourism development concerned more than a handful of Tourist Board officials.

"Eight Little Monsters"

Given the continued importance of local interests, the rapidly expanding size of the industry, and the growing government investment, it was only a matter of time before government interest in tourism clashed with the now old-fashioned and inefficient Irish Tourist Association. From the government's perspective it was now important to directly control local tourism efforts as well as those at the national level.

The conflict finally erupted when in early 1963 the local tourism promoters in west Cork, headed by Michael R. Boland, contacted Bord Fáilte about establishing a tourism-development association for that region under the terms of the 1931 Tourism Traffic Act. Because the request fit neatly into a growing government and Tourist Board desire to create local associations as a means of bypassing the ITA, a meeting was quickly arranged between Tourist Board chief T. J. O'Driscoll and Cork County Manager Michael Conlon to discuss the proposal.[26] The meeting was intensely productive and quickly resulted in a plan to establish the West Cork Tourist Development Company, a plan that was subsequently expanded to cover the county as a whole. On 1 March, Conlon invited interested parties to an emergency meeting of the Cork County Council to discuss an immediate realization of the plan. The ITA was not amused. By the time the emergency County Council meeting took place, the ITA, still comprising powerful figures from Irish political and social life, had intensely lobbied all members of the Cork County Council to reject the proposed organization, fiercely arguing against any county contributions to the new body. Boland was furious that the proposal had been torpedoed, and he complained bitterly to the Taoiseach himself.[27]

The association's response to the west Cork proposal was not surprising. Although the ITA had settled easily into running tourism bureaus in both North and South following the 1952 Tourist Traffic Act, its leaders guarded their diminished role with an iron fist. Unless it showed constant vigilance, the ITA feared that grants from local authorities would dry up, bringing about the demise of the organization. Any attempt to establish alternative local organizations was thus greeted with outright hostility.

The ITA's survival strategy could not have clashed more sharply with the policy of Bord Fáilte and the Department of Transport and Power in encouraging local associations through development grants—grants that guaranteed a local voice and also ensured that the new associations were dependent on the central tourism organization rather than on local authorities. This new government policy had been announced in October 1961; in addition to endorsing local tourism organizations, the policy document also advocated a merger of the two national tourism bodies, or at the very least, a complete retooling of the ITA "in light of current conditions." More than any minister before him, Erskine Childers wanted to see the abolition of the ITA, and in February 1963 he ordered his department to investigate the means available for dispensing with the association.[28] The minister believed that it was "essential to have a central organisation coordinating this growing local effort, eliminating overlap and breaking new ground."[29] While the ITA lobbied intensively to attain statutory responsibility for local coordination,[30] Childers did not think that its leaders were "suited to this task as regards staffing, constitution, or methods of administration." In addition, he was appalled by the Cork story and could not imagine entrusting "a task of leadership" to the association. In the minister's eyes the ITA was little more than an excuse for lavish annual gatherings in Dublin and had not contributed substantially to tourism development for many years.

The very reasons that had enabled the Irish Tourist Association to survive since 1924 made disbanding it difficult. O'Driscoll, for example, expressed a desire to avoid conflict with the ITA, while Childers recognized that "it is clearly a delicate business in view of the previous contribution of the ITA to tourist development and the prestige which still attaches to the director's position. A number of them are our people." The minister wondered whether the ITA could be reshaped into some kind of "advisory National Tourist Association, with appointed officers to exchange information and represent the combined forces of tourism," and he hypothesized that the time was right for a change given that longtime ITA director J. Fitzpatrick was nearly ready to retire.[31] Lemass agreed to the idea, assuming that it could be "applied harmoniously," and suggested that Childers should move ahead.[32]

On 11 April 1963 the minister met with a deputation from the ITA and outlined his thoughts concerning the future of local and regional tourism promotion, including his views on the future of the association. Childers called the current two-body structure "a misapplication of effort to have all this background and knowledge—and in particular, the invaluable local connections through the local authority representatives—devoted to what I feel are rather limited functions." A single statutory body would also avoid confusing the public and local associations, and it would improve communication, especially given the growing number of local tourist organizations. Childers proposed the creation of six or seven regional bodies representing homogenous geographical areas "that would constitute a viable unit in terms of promotion as a holiday area." The new regional tourism bodies "would have a good measure of discretion in regard to the servicing and generation of traffic within their own areas." They would operate information services, improve local tourism amenities, publish regional brochures, and run regional publicity campaigns. Most important, each regional body would be composed of men with "experience, energy, and representative quality." Although each of the regional tourism organizations would have "a degree of autonomy," Childers firmly intended that Bord Fáilte would oversee the various groups and provide a degree of centralized control.[33]

Of course, from the ITA's perspective the new plan offered little to love and was not greeted warmly. As far as the old tourist body was concerned, the ITA continued to symbolize the national importance of the tourist movement, and this symbolism was worth fighting for. One member immediately leaked the minister's new plan to the press despite the very clear "confidential" stamp on the cover letter that Childers supplied to the deputation. It is not clear whether the leak was motivated by a well-considered desire to humiliate the minister and rally support for the old standard bearer of Irish tourism, or whether it was simply an emotional outburst, but it did have the effect of embarrassing Childers, who quickly notified the Taoiseach of the ITA president's formal apology for the leak.[34]

Meanwhile, the press quickly jumped on the leak and began reporting the impending death of the Irish Tourist Association, not with merry glee but with a hint of nostalgia. Even the *Irish Press*, which was founded by Éamon de Valera in 1931 to ensure positive coverage of Fianna Fáil and its policies,[35] was not overwhelmingly positive about the death of the old voluntary organization once hated by the party. Instead, the paper noted the unpromising prognosis for the ITA and stressed that the association had "earned much good-will, not alone by the establishment of its bureaux, but also among county councils, many of which have annually contributed funds to the organisation."[36] There was no immediate welcome for the minister's proposal and no formal government statement, just the slightly premature publication of an obituary for the forty-year-old parent body of post–Civil War Irish tourism—a body that had not quite yet uttered its audible death rattle.

Undaunted by the unfortunate ITA leak, the Department of Transport and Power officially announced the new regional plan on 15 October.[37] Unlike the initial proposal made to the ITA deputation, the plan called for the creation of eight Regional Tourism Organisations (RTOs): Dublin Regional

Tourism (Dublin city); Eastern Regional Tourism (Dublin, Kildare, Louth, Meath, and Wicklow); South-Eastern Regional Tourism (Carlow, Kilkenny, Tipperary South, Waterford, and Wexford); Southern Regional Tourism (Cork and Kerry); Mid-Western Regional Tourism (Clare, Limerick, and Tipperary North); Western Regional Tourism (Galway and Mayo); North-Western Regional Tourism (Donegal, Leitrim, and Sligo); and Midland Regional Tourism (Cavan, Laois, Longford, Offaly, Monaghan, Roscommon, and Westmeath). Childers stressed that the plan would seek to tap the interest, goodwill, energy, and experience of "tourism-conscious people" in the service of their respective regions. Each RTO would be incorporated as a company under the 1931 Tourist Traffic Act and would be supported by the relevant county council. Local authorities, local development associations, and other tourism concerns would receive membership, as would business people and private citizens if they so desired, all under the guidance of Bord Fáilte. The bodies would deal with regional publicity and provide local contacts, foster interest in tourism by local authorities, and educate the people about the benefits of tourism; they would also organize local amenities and work to improve facilities, encourage coordination among all local groups, and run special campaigns to attract tourists and encourage constructive county planning.[38]

Not long after the announcement, Kevin O'Doherty, then Regional Development and Travel Facilities manager, was assigned the task of establishing the new Regional Tourism Organisations. O'Doherty, a tall, physically powerful, and intensely hard-working man who started his professional life with the tourist board after a stint as Seán Lemass's private secretary, had an encyclopedic knowledge of regional politics and the personalities involved in tourism. He found a situation in which meetings had already been held and disputes and deepening rivalries were beginning to emerge. Counties that historically disliked one another—Wexford versus Carlow and Cork versus Kerry, for example—found the prospect of working together difficult enough, but when the specter of disproportionate representation within the new RTOs was introduced into the equation, they became positively hostile.

O'Doherty decided to tackle the most challenging rivalry first: Cork and Kerry. To successfully bridge the gap, the longtime Bord Fáilte man needed a director acceptable to both counties. He wanted to find someone who was outside the usual collection of tourism-development suspects, who was thoughtful and energetic, and who recognized the difficulties. As luck would have it, O'Doherty found his man during an early meeting at the Imperial Hotel in Cork when Liam Devlin, a graduate of University College Cork, a member of the Harbour Board, and a successful small businessman, spoke from the back of the room. Devlin's questions were intelligent and well articulated, and he quickly caught O'Doherty's eye—especially because Devlin immediately recognized that the RTOs could easily become "eight little monsters" if not carefully constituted, eight little monsters all with their own individual interests and concerns, no more the subordinates of Bord Fáilte than the ITA had been. Devlin proved an inspired choice, and he "took to it like a bird," cleverly circumventing the problem of giving either Cork or Kerry top billing by naming the RTO "Ivernia." With the most difficult counties out of the way, O'Doherty easily moved on to establish the other seven companies, finishing with Dublin on 2 March 1964. Despite the many potential snares, all eight Regional Tourism Organisations were incorporated in less than eighteen months.[39]

As efficient as the establishment of the RTOs was, problems remained in relation to both the operation of the eight organizations and the fact that some members of the Irish Tourist Association remained hostile to the new structure. Even before all eight companies were established, there was "some misunderstanding as to the nature and scope of the regional organisations."[40] As far as Bord Fáilte was concerned, each regional body existed primarily to pursue development activities, leaving the bulk of the marketing to emerge from the Baggot Street Bridge offices of the national Tourist Board. In the rush to establish the RTOs, however, Galway-Mayo and Wexford-Waterford were not adequately briefed about the extent of their authority, and both immediately began working to attract as much attention to their own regions as possible, effectively usurping central control over publicity in these areas. Naturally other regions soon followed suit, quickly establishing a de facto promotional role for the local bodies. In effect, the RTOs were in fact emerging as the feared "eight little monsters," running their own operations to a degree not envisaged by Bord Fáilte or Erskine Childers.[41]

Adding to the headaches, the Irish Tourist Association refused to die quietly, even as several of the top jobs in the new RTOs went to longtime ITA members in order to facilitate a smooth transition. Many of the directors were "befogged by the suddenness of the demise of the ITA" and believed that the organization should continue, if only in an advisory capacity. The selection of RTO directors was especially troubling to some members of the ITA. As previously noted, Bord Fáilte made the initial selection of RTO directors. "If a region consisted of two counties, the aim was to have 7 or 8 people and to spread the representation over the counties concerned—to get people generally, commercial and tourist interests, people who were prepared to serve, people who attended the formation meetings of the regional organisations," and, of course, people who were popular enough with the Tourist Board to be invited to serve. This heavily top-down composition at the start, even if elections were planned to occur just two years later, struck some in the ITA as "a kind of qualified democracy" carried out by a board that had little understanding of voluntary organizations and by appointees who in many cases lacked any comprehension of such groups. It was suggested that many of those who had been appointed were involved in for-profit tourism businesses (travel agencies, for example), rather than people "who are putting something into it without hope of reward."[42] For ITA members tourism was a national interest, tourism promotion a nationalist act, and these new RTOs seemed to be motivated more by personal profit than by patriotic duty.

In spite of an agreement that the ITA would voluntarily wrap itself up, no such decision was taken at the extraordinary meeting called on 6 May 1964. Instead, nine of the fifteen directors present voted to continue the ITA until the annual meeting in the fall, when the final terminating vote would be rendered. The final months of the association were filled with acrimony and were notable only for remarks such as one made by Eamon Quinn, an ITA board member, who angrily declared that "Bord Fáilte are not a fit and proper body to administer the tourist industry."[43] The ITA had been in existence for over forty years, despite numerous challenges, and its members believed deeply in the patriotic purposes of the group. In the end, however, the ITA's success in shaping popular consensus about the national importance of tourism was paradoxically the cause of the association's demise. The group had become little more than a relic of the past, while tourism was the road to the future.

The Growth of Government Interest

When the Irish Tourist Association finally succumbed, the industry was growing more rapidly and had a larger impact on the economy than at any previous time in Irish history. Beyond the creation of the RTOs, the government showed a slowly growing faith in the tourist industry. In 1958 the industry received a significant stamp of approval with its inclusion in the *White Paper on Economic Expansion* and was allocated at least £1 million in grants "to help the development of major resorts"[44]—support that continued to grow stronger when tourism income reached £42.4 million in 1960 (up by £4.6 million over the previous year),[45] £46.9 million in 1961,[46] and £49.5 million in 1963.[47]

Encouraged by these increases, the government included tourism in the *Second Programme for Economic Expansion*. This time the plan called for a doubling of tourism revenue between 1960 and 1970. Faced with such a big challenge, tourism interests—including Bord Fáilte, various hoteliers, RTO representatives, trade union officials, and travel agencies—passed a resolution calling for complete cooperation, effective communication, and the full devotion of resources to attaining the government's objective.[48] Partly as a result of this newfound solidarity—combined with greatly expanded marketing efforts in Europe and North America,[49] a growing list of tourist sites (see chapters 4–6), expanding tourist accommodation, and more rapid transatlantic travel—during the period covered by the *Second Programme*, tourism revenue increased from £39 million to £97 million—growth of more than 5 percent per annum.[50] Just as exciting, growth came not only in the British market, always Ireland's most important single source of tourism revenue, but also from the United States. In 1962, some 85,000 Americans traveled to Ireland.[51] By 1967 this number grew to 140,000 and by 1970 it had reached 230,000—a clear indication that tourism development efforts were increasingly effective.[52]

From the perspective of the Department of Transport and Power this increase was dramatic and important, especially because it both assisted the balance of payments and provided a significant economic stimulus. Irish markets expanded, vital revenue flowed to the rural west, and development companies benefited through the constant construction of new hotel and resort facilities.[53] While the government had been aware of the far-reaching benefits of tourism for many years, the age of planning inaugurated in 1958 now painted these bonuses in much brighter colors, and the *Third Programme* showed even more government confidence in tourism development by setting £112 million as the revenue target for 1972.[54]

In spite of the apparent growth in government confidence, industry observers remained concerned that the government had yet to show a firm dedication to supporting tourism through even larger grants, and they feared that officials might just as easily withdraw funding, especially if there were a change in administration. In late 1965 and early 1966 reports from within the government suggested that there was to be no major increase in tourism spending in the new budget. This news left insiders surprised and upset. *Irish Travel Trade News,* the major industry journal, expressed shock. It declared that the government's projected tightfistedness was "nothing more than a piece of monumental cheeseparing," and noted that the Tourist Board would be forced to carefully reconsider all of its financial allocations, scaling back publicity spending and resort development—areas that Ireland could ill afford to shortchange.[55] Ultimately the 1966 Tourist Traffic Act did provide the industry with a financial boost. Nonrefundable grants for development schemes were increased to £3.25 million, and a £5 million ceiling on the board's overall budget was removed.[56]

Even with the spending increases the government was still not providing funds fully commensurate with the importance of tourism. In 1966 the Organisation for Economic Cooperation and Development (OECD) released a report urging member countries, including Ireland, to increase tourism spending. The report noted that tourism was "among the fastest growing economic activities" in many of the twenty-one member nations. Ireland received 18 percent of its export earnings from tourism, placing it in third place behind Spain (42 percent) and Austria (24 percent). The OECD argued that increased spending would not only boost the number of tourists but also have significant benefits "from the social, educational, and cultural point of view," while generally contributing "to a better understanding among nations." Flexible and well-funded tourism development was essential.[57]

Some members of the industry hailed the international body's comments and also argued loudly for increased spending. The Eastern Regional Tourism Organisation was one of the most prominent critical voices and attacked the Department of Finance in the press, declaring that the minister's "actions appear to be aimed at keeping tourists away from our shores." Picking up on a point that the OECD had made in its report, Eastern Regional chairman J. A. Corr argued that improved research and development were essential to future success in this industry. Corr fumed that "the state allocation for the industry is completely unrealistic in relation to its real value," and he demanded that the government "come to their senses and provide the necessary funds for the industry." More than simply failing to spend enough, Corr insisted that the government had managed to increase costs in Ireland, making Irish holidays more expensive, while also failing to provide adequate resources to allow the industry to prepare for the coming of jumbo jets to Dublin airport in 1970. The government, in short, was undermining the national interest. He concluded, "If government attitudes are not quickly revised on these matters, then Ireland will find itself in a high price bracket, competing in one of the world's most competitive industries—the consequences could prove irretrievable."[58]

While the government did offer a small £500,000 increase to the board's development grants in 1968,[59] this action did little to silence criticism about low tourism spending. In 1970 P. J. Breen, chairman of the South-Eastern Regional Tourism Organisation, declared that "tourism in Ireland is being starved to death by a lack of financial support," with spending defined by short-term considerations. Development was "artificially retarded," opportunities were "not being converted into business," and vital growth-promoting projects were "being axed or shelved for indefinite periods"—all results of the "grossly inadequate" resources allocated to Bord Fáilte. Even T. J. O'Driscoll, who ordinarily made his financial complaints behind closed doors, had publicly protested about the situation, said Breen. The South-Eastern regional manager concluded "the blunt situation is that unless there is a sizable increase in the amount of monies being made available to tourist development bodies, their future must be called seriously into question. . . . Crisis point has been reached."[60]

The government was not deaf to the complaints, and in 1972 the amount allocated for resort development was increased by £750,000, and an additional £2 million was provided for the expansion of accommodation.[61] Three years later, another £750,000 was injected into the fund for development grants, together with £3 million more for the creation of more lodgings.[62] Government spending increased even more dramatically in 1983, when £30 million (from £16 million) was allocated for accommodation, while development funds were raised to £14 million (from £4.75 million).[63] In 1987 another £10 million was added.[64]

But it was in 1988 that the government truly put its money on the table when its *Programme for National Recovery* "set about creating an environment which would encourage investment in tourism." The plan featured tax incentives, grants, and EU support, and it led to an increase in tourism investment from £25 million in 1987 to £200 million in 1992. Investment expanded even more rapidly thereafter. By 1993 some £770 million had been pumped into the industry over five years, £380 million of which came from the state purse; this was more than had been invested during the previous twenty years combined. Spending did not slow thereafter, and a further £707 million was spent between 1994 and 1999.[65] Indeed, during the course of the 1990s, the government showed an astounding willingness to spend money on tourism marketing. For example, the Irish government invested some £30 million in the Tourism Brand Ireland campaign,[66] and then created a £14.5 million fund devoted exclusively to marketing in 1999.[67] Now that tourism was a £2.5 billion industry, the government no longer appeared to have any qualms about investing aggressively.[68]

Government decisions to spend such huge amounts of money on tourism were not entirely precipitated by industry pressure, however. As during the late 1940s and 1950s, outside factors also contributed to government decision making. This time the primary outside factor was the European Union. When Ireland joined in 1973, European powers had yet to establish a unified continent-wide policy on tourism, and the EU paid little notice to the industry until a commissioner was finally given responsibility for it in 1980. It was only in 1990 that the EU began to pay serious attention to tourism, allotting 5 million ECUs to support its "European Tourism Year" program. Spending was subsequently increased to 5.64 million ECUs in 1992 and then to 7 million in 1993.

Much of the early tourism-development support that Ireland received from the EU was provided in the form of European Regional Development Funds—monies given to "contribute to the correction of the principal regional imbalances within the community by participating in the development of structural adjustment of regions whose development is lagging behind and in the conversion of declining industrial regions." Of these funds, slightly less than 2 percent was devoted to tourism, most of this going to the United Kingdom and Italy. Ireland received European Regional Development Funds beginning in 1983, though only 0.9 percent was allotted specifically to tourism. Most of this money was devoted to the improvement of Irish ports and the development of cultural and heritage sites.

Beginning in 1987 the EU revamped its structural-funds program, a reorganization that coincided with renewed Irish government interest in tourist development (other than publicity) resulting from growing unemployment throughout the 1980s. From 1989 to 1993 the government invested some £450 million in the improvement of Irish tourist facilities, much of which (£380 million, or 53 percent) came directly from the EU.[69] The result of this influx of cash was a veritable explosion in the number and quality of tourist sites available to visitors. Tourist routes were improved, existing facilities expanded, and new tourism centers constructed.

Although dramatic infrastructural advances had taken place before 1989, with the expansion of EU tourism-development monies at the outset of the 1990s, projects were undertaken that would have been unimaginable earlier. Starting in 1989, for example, groups that included local residents and the Dublin city branch of An Taisce (National Trust for Ireland) began to take an interest in developing the Temple Bar area of Dublin. A proposal was circulated advocating the redevelopment and renovation of Dublin's "Old City," the cornerstone of the plan being the proposed reinvention of the "Temple Bar" area that had been owned by Córas Iompair Éireann (Irish rail) from 1966 and was slated for development as a transportation hub. By the mid-1980s, however, it was home to a significant community of citizens, nearly all of whom wanted to see the area turned into a cultural center rather than a bus or train station.[70] As a result, a new proposal was hatched through which the area would become a kind of Parisian "Left Bank," including cobbled streets, cultural venues, and artsy shops and restaurants, as well as a mix of housing.[71] In 1991 the interested parties successfully convinced the government and Dublin city to allow development of the area and a company called Temple Bar Properties was established under a government act to administer an urban pilot project and organize a development programme for the area.[72] Bord Fáilte soon moved the Temple Bar project to the very top of its list of investments (much of this money was drawn from European Union development funds), and it spent some £2 million in 1993 alone on the enterprise. Temple Bar was by far the largest development undertaking funded by the Tourist Board during this period, well ahead of the second highest funded site, a heritage project in Cobh that received about £450,000.[73] By the late 1990s the Temple Bar area had become one of Europe's leading short-term tourist attractions, plagued only by its success as a center for "hen and stag parties."[74] Partly as a result of this success, as well as because of the renewal of Grafton Street (whose renovation began somewhat earlier when it was permanently pedestrianized in 1985),[75] Dublin has become the third most successful city in Europe (following London and Paris) in terms of the number of tourist "bednights."[76]

While increased spending is one indication of official views about the importance of tourism, another is the way in which the cabinet addressed tourism. The Department of Industry and Commerce handled tourism until October 1961; at that point responsibility was transferred to the Department of Transport and Power.[77] Because a dedicated minister did not have responsibility for tourism, industry officials believed that their enterprise was not truly important to the government. In 1973 the National Tourism Council, essentially a pro-tourism lobby, suggested that tourism should be serviced by its own parliamentary secretary. It argued that tourism "did not appear to be fully recognised as a major industry either in the extent of government assistance or in the tax concessions which would be appropriate. . . . The ratio of official assistance, when related to the generation of foreign earnings by tourism—this country's second largest overseas revenue earner—is negligible." Furthermore, the existing ministerial structure meant that issues like landing rights and airfares were not adequately addressed by the government. As far as the National Tourism Council was concerned, tourism legislation was outdated, the preservation of Irish culture was neglected, the environment was spoiled, and other tourism issues were generally ignored. In order to ensure that these issues were addressed in the interests of tourism and, for that matter, Ireland, the industry should receive its own minister, as in the case of agriculture.[78] A year later, the president of the Irish Hotels Federation expressed a similar concern, declaring that tourism was "at the bottom of the cabinet list of priorities."[79] In response to these demands and as a reflection of genuine official interest, the government finally acknowledged the industry fully by forming a new Department of Tourism and Transport in 1977, abandoning its original plans to give tourism responsibilities to the newly created Department of the Environment.[80] Since 1977 responsibility for tourism has been moved two more times. First, between 1997 and 2002 tourism was assigned to the Department of Tourism, Sport, and Recreation.[81] This department was disbanded in 2002, however, and responsibility for tourism was then given to the Department of Arts, Sport, and Tourism, where it remains at the time of this writing, a symbol of the government's strong continuing concern about tourism.[82]

Pursuing New Markets and Growing Professionalism

Whether tourism funding was adequate or not, higher spending demanded greater results. More than ever before, tourism administrators needed to develop strategies that would attract ever-increasing tourist numbers. This requirement had two effects. First, it assured that tourism developers had to become increasingly professional in their activities, always striving to expand existing markets and to develop new ones. Second, it fueled increased debate about the shape of the Irish tourism product—the topic of the next three chapters.

While it has been claimed that the Irish decided "to sell out Irish culture to a predominantly English audience,"[83] the truth is far more complicated. It is certainly true that the English market has long dominated Irish tourism planning. The Irish Sea did not impose any language barrier, London was less than one day distant by train, and the British railway companies were more than willing to invest their own resources in developing the lucrative route between London and Killarney. As early as 1925 the Irish Tourist Association spoke of "new and stronger ties of friendship" between Ireland

and England, thus already pushing the recent conflict out of mind.[84] Even as British servicemen were murdered in an ambush at Cobh,[85] British railway companies sent representatives to meet with the Irish Tourist Association.[86] Promises of 1,000–1,500 excursionists each weekend and of 1,500–2,000 longer-term visitors to Killarney were hugely attractive to the young Tourist Association, and the group bent over backwards to assist the railway companies as a result.[87]

Despite the eagerness to attract as many English tourists as possible, the political relationship between Ireland and its former colonizer was sometimes difficult. On occasion, the influx of English tourists sparked minor conflicts. In 1939 the IRA painted anti-English slogans near tourist facilities in Killarney, including these three examples: "England, damn your concessions, we want our country," "Down with England," and "We want no uninvited guests." The Irish government refused to act, not wanting to "fire the first shot in a new war with the IRA," and some British travel agencies responded by pulling Irish Tourist Association advertising from their shelves, a move that prompted tourism interests in Killarney to demand an end to these IRA activities.[88] Similarly, in 1963, when a comparable incident brought about the cancellation of a trip by some young English servicemen to Achill Island, it inspired horror both at the local and the national levels. An anxious Taoiseach, Seán Lemass, wrote to Erskine Childers that in future, "whenever arrangements contemplated by them [Bord Fáilte] appear likely to involve political consideration[s], they should consult with you [as the responsible government minister] in advance."[89]

From time to time, conflict arose over the incursion of British financial interests into the Irish marketplace. In 1925 Killarney hoteliers complained when a collection of English journalists visited Killarney, only to have their attention monopolized by the English railway companies, which not only operated the train routes but also owned the largest hotel in town, prompting local businessmen to cry foul because they "did not get a look in." Likewise, local hotel owners complained that they could not realistically compete with the railway's practice of offering combined rail and hotel rates, which had the effect of underbidding Killarney-based hoteliers and thus completely excluding local competitors.[90] While the *Kerryman* agreed with the local businessmen and urged the ITA to take the issue up with railway officials, the situation did little to deflect cooperative efforts or the ITA's strong desire to cash in on a growing stream of English tourists.

In another representative incident in 1951, the English publisher Edward J. Burrow and Company offered to publish a guidebook for Kilkenny at no expense to the local authority, a proposal that prompted criticism from the Irish Tourist Association and Irish Tourist Board. One concerned individual declared "it a terrible thing that an English firm could produce a guide book and that the Irish Tourist Board, to the upkeep of which the Kilkenny County Council contributed a share . . . , had done nothing."[91] The *Kilkenny People,* long critical of Irish tourist authorities, chided both the ITA and Irish Tourist Board for their lack of action and commended the County Council for demanding board action.[92] Ultimately the publication went forward, prompting R. Burke of the County Council to say in disgust, "After a quarter of a century's freedom it is a sad thing that such guides cannot be produced in Ireland."[93] One year later, when the first preparations for An Tóstal were being made, several "show cards" and a full-color poster were also printed in England as a result of the inadequate printing facilities in Ireland combined with an Irish printers' strike. This created a minor furor within the Department of Industry and Commerce as civil servants demanded to know why An Bord Fáilte and Fógra Fáilte were not working together to pursue all possible avenues for printing their publicity materials in Ireland.[94] Jan de Fouw, the graphic designer responsible for much of Fógra Fáilte's and subsequently Bord Fáilte's graphic output, recalls that the English print run was horrifying to many because it meant that "the national identity was reproduced on foreign paper."[95] In keeping with this concern, de Fouw, Guus Melai (who designed the logo for An Tóstal; see chapter 4), and their Dutch colleagues, who had come to Ireland in search of work and an opportunity to make their mark in graphic design, were asked to leave their names off the various design projects they undertook in Ireland because doing so "was only stirring up feelings and waves which we could do without."[96] When Fógra Fáilte began publishing *Ireland of the Welcomes,* officials insisted that the entire publication be produced in Ireland—a requirement that severely limited the use of color and the design complexity of the publication for a number of years—and without de Fouw's name in the credits.[97]

Despite the occasional conflict, early ITA support for developing the English market was far more characteristic of relations between the two states in this area than the handful of incidents like those mentioned above. It was generally agreed that tourists from Britain and Northern Ireland would always form Ireland's largest market segment, and that efforts should be made to ensure that Britannia continued to send its tourists across the Irish Sea and the border.[98] Britain and Ireland showed an exceptional willingness to work together, actively seeking greater cooperation between their respective tourist bodies throughout the 1950s and beyond.[99]

From the very beginning of tourism development after the Civil War, the tourist authorities also dreamed of attracting visitors from the lucrative American and continental European markets. Guidebooks were translated into German and French, and some companies even wrote guides specifically to cater to foreign tastes rather than producing translations. In 1932, for example, Guinness published a Francophone guidebook that focused on the types of Guinness, the adaptation of stout to fit French tastes, and the proper way to serve the tasty black liquid, as well as the correct color, taste, and pouring technique necessary to serve the ultimate pint of stout.[100] English-language guides, meanwhile, addressed the brewery's history and spent far less time on the aesthetics of the beverage produced there.[101] No stranger to marketing, Guinness hoped to exploit the French love for good food and drink by appealing to their supposed aesthetic and gastronomic sensibilities.

Even so, expanding promotional efforts to the continent or to the United States was a daunting and expensive challenge. While Europe was not far away, it was culturally and linguistically diverse. Meanwhile, America was thousands of miles distant—a serious problem when transatlantic transport was limited to slow-moving steamships—and the United States both geographically huge and culturally varied. As Michael Gorman realized soon after beginning work at Fógra Fáilte, the marketing of Ireland in the United States was like tackling all of Europe at once.[102] Given small budgets, the authorities had to monitor their efforts, gradually expanding their marketing campaigns as transportation improved, financial support increased, and experience was acquired.

The Irish Tourist Association began to pursue the American market as early as February 1924. At the monthly ITA meeting in Cork, George Harris, a passenger agent from the White Star Line in Cobh and one of the original members of the ITA executive, stressed that it was both "desirable and urgent" to launch a major marketing effort in America.[103] Over the next three years several ITA members, including Howard Harrington, the association's president and himself an American, journeyed to the United States to meet with travel agents and others of importance.[104] In 1927 the Tourist Association opened a bureau in New York City when the Great Western Railway Company offered space in its offices. The association hoped that its new offices would allow for a more efficient distribution of literature and other publicity in the States.[105] The thought was right, but with an annual budget of only about £15,000, and with the reality that American tourists would need to commit to at least two weeks of steamship travel in order to make the journey, very little was actually accomplished.

Following World War II, Marshall Plan officials and the Christenberry committee urged the Irish authorities to move into the American market.[106] An Tóstal was partly an effort to attract Irish-Americans back to Ireland as tourists. As tourist-development efforts grew throughout the 1950s, Bord Fáilte continued to explore ways to expand its promotional efforts in America. In 1956 the board's director-general traveled to the United States to explore the possibilities for expansion, and he urged the addition of a Chicago-area office.[107]

The Irish tourist authorities were similarly interested in continental markets, and as early as 1938–39, when the first major Tourism Traffic Act made its way through the Oireachtas, senators expressed their hope that the new Tourist Board would pursue the continental market. Citing Ireland's long isolation from continental culture, senators suggested that tourism might draw Ireland back into Europe.[108] After Bord Fáilte received larger financial grants from the government during the 1960s, its leaders were able to increase efforts to attract continental tourists. Whereas materials had once been distributed either through the Department of External Affairs (see below) or Aer Lingus in places other than Britain and the United States, Bord Fáilte now opened offices in Italy, Austria, and France. When the Bord Fáilte office was opened in Paris during the late 1960s, the board spared no expense. Careful attention was paid to geographic location, and the new office was sited adjacent to the Paris Opera in order to ensure substantial foot traffic. Next, the board hired a leading French advertising and marketing company to publicize the event. They placed full-page ads in *Paris Match* featuring the slogan "Ireland is not on the Mediterranean, thank God!": an indication that a trip to Ireland set the tourist apart from the growing hordes on Spanish beaches. The board leased a chateau, complete with lakes in both the front and the back, near Paris, and they threw a massive party—the invitation to which included a box of smoked Irish salmon. In front of the estate visitors were directed by a member of the Irish police, a tricolor flew on the flagpole, an Irish army piper played as visitors entered, descendants of the old Irish Brigade in period uniform greeted guests, Owen Dillion of the Shelbourne Hotel prepared traditional Irish cuisine, contemporary poets recited the works of Yeats and other Irish writers, fly fishermen demonstrated the art of fly-casting on one of the lakes, and a professional Irish golfer offered lessons in a nearby field. While contemporary marketing organizations might use many of these tactics today, in the 1960s the program was revolutionary. The Tourist Board was willing to do "anything to make it [the Irish tourism product] stick out," remembers Michael Gorman, Bord Fáilte's European publicity manager at the time.[109]

Beyond opening new travel bureaus, Bord Fáilte launched major marketing campaigns in the Benelux countries in 1968,[110] increased its foreign-language publications with a particular emphasis on German-language materials,[111] and held travel workshops in major European markets (like Germany) that were intended to educate travel agents about the attractions of an Irish holiday.[112] Bord Fáilte also improved the market research efforts that it had begun in the early 1950s; it clearly wished to enhance its understanding of the likes and dislikes of potential customers in foreign markets. The first survey was conducted in 1955 and included 3,000 travelers, allegedly representing the views of some 7,500 people. When asked what pleased them most about their Irish adventures, most replied, "The Irish people themselves."[113] This fact set Ireland apart from popular destinations such as Paris where few tourists encountered actual French people.[114] Officials learned that 10 percent of Americans came to Ireland to visit relatives, and that Belleek china, Waterford crystal, and Limerick lace were among the most popular

Irish souvenirs.[115] In subsequent years additional questions were added about visitor nationality, purpose of visit, length of stay, why Ireland was chosen over other potential holiday destinations, how visitors used their time in Ireland, and how they allocated their expenses.[116] The surveys revealed that word of mouth was by far the biggest motivation for coming to the Emerald Isle, that Americans made more use of travel agents than Britons, and that Dublin and County Kerry were by far the most popular destinations.[117] The board eventually established a research department and adopted increasingly scientific approaches to its survey work. In 1973, for example, Bord Fáilte conducted an extensive survey of *Attitudes of American and English Tourists Towards Shopping in Ireland and Irish Merchandise.* Unlike the first surveys, which were conducted by schoolgirls in airport-based interviews, this one was done through small random samples of British and American tourists divided into groups of six respondents. The board then used "non-directive" interviews to gauge participant opinions, striving for self-directed discussions in order to avoid influencing results. Interviewers typically began by asking basic questions about country of origin, occupation, length of stay, reason for travel, and the type of holiday desired. Shopping was almost inevitably listed as one of the activities included in an Irish holiday, and this answer allowed discussion to shift to perceptions of Irish shops, impressions about Irish products, window displays, mythology about specific crafts, brand recognition, women's attitudes to Irish clothes, and, finally, the motivation for purchase.

The results of the souvenir survey revealed numerous differences between British and American travelers that allowed the authorities to further differentiate their products by market. For example, it became clear very quickly that American travelers were drawn primarily from one social group, were defined by social class rather than ethnic background, and had a series of interests in common. They anticipated a romantic and relaxing holiday rather than one that was intellectually stimulating or purposeful, showed surprise at the amount of history to be found in Ireland, and looked forward to beautiful scenery, tranquility, and friendly people. In contrast, English tourists came from two distinct groups. The first of these was the upper-middle and upper class; members of this group came to Ireland with a substantial level of interest and knowledge about Irish culture. The second group, drawn from among the middle and lower-middle class, was inclined to be economical and chose Ireland primarily as a suitable destination to take their children. Even so, both groups of English visitors looked forward to beautiful scenery, tranquility, and escape—to say nothing of a "more 'natural' life rhythm." Although both Americans and Britons agreed in anticipating beautiful scenery, the British found little that was exotic or exciting about travel in Ireland. Decisions were made at the last minute and trips were shorter. The feeling that Ireland was not exotic spilled over into British attitudes toward shopping. While Americans actively sought out Aran sweaters, for example, English visitors thought them "bulky and unfashionable," and experienced little of the rustic charm cited by American visitors. British visitors spent little money on Irish products while in the country, and they were far more apt to criticize souvenir shops that they found "cheap, trashy, [and] filled with foreign (Japanese) goods."[118]

In the 1990s Bord Fáilte took another step forward in its study of foreign markets. By this time annual reports contained detailed information about visitor statistics for North America, Britain, Northern Ireland, and all of the major continental markets, including Spain, Italy, Germany, France, the Benelux countries, and Switzerland. These data were supplemented by a series of publications entitled *Know Your Market*; each book painstakingly explored the activities popular with each nationality. For example, Italians spent most of their time in Dublin, but by the mid-1990s they were increasingly interested in car rentals and were moving beyond the city in larger numbers. Italians were far more interested in hiking or walking than in other activities and enjoyed visiting historical sites.[119] In contrast, the French favored the southwest and showed less interest in historic sites, though they too enjoyed hiking and walking. French visitors were disproportionately interested in the Irish way of life.[120] Meanwhile, the main interest of Americans was in sightseeing and in finding distant ancestors. They expected a friendly welcome and an opportunity to view Ireland's historic places and scenic sites.[121] Armed with such visitor information, tourist officials could target specific social and national groups with a precision not previously imagined.

Conclusion

The Irish government was never completely disinterested in tourism, but the status of the industry as a primary national interest only developed over time.[122] From the 1920s onward officials recognized that tourism might bring valuable revenue into Ireland, but there were fundamental divisions about what role the government should take in promoting tourism. As tourism revenue increased, pressure was brought to bear by various sectors of Irish society, and as foreign bodies from the Marshall Plan administration to the OECD and the European Union stressed the importance of tourism, government officials increasingly recognized the vital place of the industry in Irish economic and social life. But one other point must also be made. Throughout the period between the Civil War and the start of the Celtic Tiger, Ireland was a very poor country. Regardless of the potential financial gain offered by tourism, officials had finite resources to invest in tourism expansion, especially before 1960. With numerous challenges facing the nation, tourism was not always the most apparent or easily understood concern of government officials, for whom the national interest seemed more obviously aligned with addressing agricultural productivity, manufacturing growth, emigration, the Northern question, and a number of other major issues. As a result, the entire period between 1924 and 1994 was often marked by debate about the relative importance of tourism as well as about the precise results to be sought through tourism development.

Although it was only quite recently that tourism rose to the top of government spending priorities, the gradual increase in expenditure that followed passage of the 1952 Tourist Traffic Act sparked a significant increase in the exchange of ideas about the precise "product" that tourist developers would present to outsiders, about the very nature of Irishness. This increased interchange focused attention on the definition of Irish culture, history, and landscape and it involved a wide cross-section of society that was, if anything, even more extensive than that which participated in the national interest debate. It is to this dialogue that we must now turn.

4

Culture, Language, and Tourism

Introduction

Language and culture are two of the most obvious components of national identity.[1] Nearly all nations feature their own festivals, traditions, costumes, dances, sporting events, and any number of other defining characteristics, while language both reflects these cultural artifacts and allows them to be perpetuated through ongoing education. The trend in nationalism studies, to say nothing of nationalist discourse itself, is to stress national consensus and homogeneity in cultural and linguistic concerns. Scholars have fiercely debated when common culture developed, seeing it variously as almost timeless[2] or modern and invented,[3] but they are less prone to examining the contested nature of culture *within* a specific national group. Language is generally presented as integral to either the perpetuation of timeless traditions or the invention of new ones,[4] and the tendency is to focus on transnational conflicts over language or to describe specific nationalist movements without addressing the diversity of opinion within a single nation.[5] In Ireland, for example, considerable attention has been paid to the importance of the Gaelic League[6] and the Gaelic Athletic Association,[7] but less attention has been given to the fact that these movements were not universally important across Irish society.[8] Despite the attention paid to the language revival in the story of the Irish nationalist movement, for example, the success of the revival effort was limited, and the story of the Gaelic League is very much that of a minority of the population. While in 1986 the number of Gaelic speakers in Ireland had climbed to 1,043,000 from 541,000 in 1926, the former figure still represented only about 31 percent of the population—up from 19 percent sixty years earlier.[9] In other words, since the 1920s, if we believe these census figures,[10] the percentage of Irish speakers in the Republic of Ireland has never risen above about one third of the population, leaving one to wonder why the vast majority of the Irish people exercised little interest in a language that conventional wisdom holds rests at the center of Irish identity. In one sense the numbers were a success story, of course. The number of Gaelic speakers *had* increased, and the language continued to play a significant role in a substantial number of lives. Yet if Gaelic was as central to Irish identity as the language revivalists believed, why is the entire Republic not a Gaeltacht?

While it is true that both language and culture have played tremendously important roles in various nationalist movements—the Catalan, Quebecois, Welsh, Cornish, and Flemish nationalist movements are five relevant examples—the Irish case demonstrates that ambivalence and debate has been as common as homogeneity and consensus. The first three chapters demonstrated that Irish perceptions of their common interests changed over time according to economic and political circumstances, and they also made clear that definitions of these interests varied among different groups and individuals; the same was true of ideas about both language and culture. While revivalists wanted to protect the Gaeltachts from the threat of modernization, the native speakers themselves were more interested in employment and economic improvement. Likewise, "traditional" Irish culture inspired more ambivalence than consensus. It was one thing to hold gatherings such as Puck Fair in Killorglin, Co. Kerry, for Irish people, another thing to present the filth, drinking, and brawling endemic at the event to outsiders.

As noted in the introduction, although there was certainly considerable debate about the specifics of how Ireland should be promoted, there was consensus that the country should always be presented in the best possible light, and anger was widespread when the presentation of Ireland fell short of the ideal. This chapter examines the role played by tourism in debates about Irish language and culture. At every turn those involved in promoting the country as a tourist product wanted to present the "best" that Ireland had to offer, but in doing so, they were forced to balance differing ideas about what the "best" of Ireland was, as well as to display widely diverging ideas about how to protect authentic Irishness from unwanted change. The dialogue detailed here unfolded in two phases corresponding to the debate about tourism as a national interest. During the first phase, which corresponded with the debate detailed in chapters 1 and 2, the question of selling Irishness centered on the tourist threat to the language revival. While tourism interests saw Gaelic as a tourist attraction, and the influx of tourists as potentially beneficial to the Gaeltachts, language enthusiasts feared that an influx of "foreignism" might undermine efforts to save the Irish language by introducing Anglophone tourists into Gaelic-speaking areas and encouraging the use of English rather than Irish. The second phase, which began in earnest during the 1950s, corresponded to the growing consensus that tourism development was a national interest and featured a push to present Ireland as in accord with widely internalized stereotypes of friendliness, warmth, a relaxed attitude toward life, and the innate ability to tell a great story—an objective that sometimes clashed uneasily with the realities of Irish life.

Phase I: The Tourism Threat

From the very first efforts of the Irish Tourist Association to develop the tourist industry in the Cork and Kerry region, tourism was presented as a potential savior of the Gaeltachts. During 1925–26, when the ITA strove to establish a Dingle branch of the association, the Dingle Peninsula was portrayed as a likely tourist hotspot. It was an area with majestic coastal scenery and unequalled "archaeological wealth," and it was "one of the few [areas] in which the true Gaelic atmosphere can be found in its original purity."[11] The region promised to be especially enticing to language enthusiasts interested in visiting historic sites while studying the Irish language in quiet surroundings. The ITA believed that visitors did not want to see Irish people imitating the "Anglo-Saxons"; they wanted to see authentically Irish people, and the association's view was supported by advice from American tourists that the Irish should "never forget . . . to keep alive the glorious Gaelic traditions of Ireland."[12]

Of course the ITA was also subject to local pressure, and it was clear from early on that many people in the Kerry Gaeltacht were anxious to see tourism developed quickly. From the initial establishment of the Dingle branch of the ITA, its members urged the creation of a special advertising campaign that would inform visitors of the Gaelic "purity" to be found on the peninsula. Not only were these Dingle residents excited about the idea of language tourism in their backyard, but they were also actively upset that the ITA had not done more to provide them with legions of Gaelic-seeking tourists.[13]

Reflecting the association's belief in the marketability of the Irish language and the pressure exerted on that body by those in Gaelic-speaking areas, the 1929 ITA guidebook stressed the deep roots of the Gaelic language and informed tourists that "the Irish people maintained their language, customs, and literature down to modern times," thus preserving a continuity with the past. The guide presented a positive appraisal of the Gaelic revival: "Today the Irish language is the official language of the country and is taught in all the schools. Already the revival movement has given [the country] a talented group of novelists, poets, and dramatists, whose works are an augury of its continued success."[14] Gaelic was something to be heard and enjoyed by tourists, a clear sign of unchanging Irishness as well as of the success enjoyed by nationalists in keeping this past alive.

Not only did the ITA mention the Gaeltacht in its guidebooks for Ireland as a whole, and Kerry in particular, but the association also published a special guide encouraging tourists to visit the Gaeltacht and endeavored to circulate it to government offices in the hope of attracting civil servants to visit Connemara, Kerry, and other Irish-speaking areas.[15] The guide stressed the attractions of the regions for sportsmen, drew attention to bathing opportunities, and focused on the astonishing scenery. While these attractions did exist, there was also a considerable amount of outright fiction in the booklet. The ITA's enthusiasm led its leaders to claim that Gaeltacht roads "are now beyond reproach by the motorist," and that "accommodation is available to satisfy the most fastidious and the plainest tastes—from modern, excellently appointed and managed hotels to farmhouses in which clean and comfortable accommodation can frequently be had."[16] These promises represented a vast exaggeration of the truth.

Archie Bell, a travel writer from Ohio, took a particular interest in Gaelic during his 1928 trip to Ireland, noting with pleasure when he met a waitress who "spoke Irish as fluently as she did English." Bell was excited because he had noticed that relatively few Irish adults were able to speak the native tongue. He explained how matters stood:

As with Mussolini at Rome, the hope of the Irish government lies with the future generations. The children are learning Irish in the schools. Teachers are attending special sessions all over the country to polish up. Political speeches are frequently delivered in the native tongue. Street signs are printed in both English and in Irish. Some of the newspapers have at least one editorial each day in Irish. Young people who speak and read it are supposed to get better jobs in official offices. But the fact remains that while interest in the language is increasing every day, the majority of the adults cannot speak it.[17]

For Bell the experience of meeting a Gaelic speaker was unique and authentic, but it was more than that. Throughout his narrative Bell wrote about the revitalization of Ireland without ever mentioning English rule or the fight for independence, let alone the Civil War. For Bell history ended in the late Middle Ages; Ireland was defined by pretty scenery and amusing myths and stories, not by poverty and disease, emigration, political conflict, and a legacy of violence. The Irish language connected the present with a distant mythical past. The language movement and the prospect that more and more Irish people would be directly connected to this ancient soft-focus Celtic arcadia was a very positive thing; it would recreate Ireland in the green-tinted pastels of ancient history.

A "Deadly Threat"

In contrast to the ITA's faith in the value of marketing Gaelic, or the desire for development commonly voiced in the Gaeltachts themselves, by the 1930s a growing number of revivalists found tourists threatening because the visitors did not speak Gaelic. As early as 1934, Seán MacEntee, then minister for finance, produced an extensive memorandum responding to a proposal for development of the Gaeltacht as a tourist centre. He believed that the industry "must be regarded as the largest source of potential wealth for these areas," but he also stressed that even in this light the government's primary responsibility was to ensure the preservation of the Irish language.[18] MacEntee did not speak Irish himself, but Gaelic preservation was very important to him. His family spent holidays at Dunquin, Co. Kerry, the children were raised to be Irish speakers, and his wife, Kate Browne, taught Gaelic at various schools including University College Dublin.[19] As minister for finance, the challenge was to balance economic reality with this dedication to the revival. In his memo, MacEntee explained that any successful policy should harmonize "the economic and language interests" of the nation. The problem was that previous experience suggested that it was necessary to isolate the Gaeltacht in order to guarantee linguistic security. The language survived in the Gaeltachts precisely because they were remote and isolated. In order to maintain this isolation it was necessary to develop schemes calculated to attract only *the right kind of tourists:* Irish-speaking tourists. MacEntee was skeptical about the idea of developing Gaelic communities as holiday centers where Anglophones might come to hear and learn Irish. If Anglophone families were to arrive en masse in the Gaeltachts, even given their heartfelt desire to learn the language, they would soon lapse into English. The visitors would tend to interact with one another, not with the local families. As a result, "the presence of such [English-speaking] families in the heart of the Gaeltacht would only endanger the hold the language has at present as a vernacular in the Gaeltacht." MacEntee suggested that a more radical approach was required in which extensive development of special holiday villages would be undertaken in Dingle, Connemara, and Donegal. The program would constitute "a drastic reorganisation of the whole area." Tourists would stay in these new developments among Irish speakers employed to converse in the native tongue with the visitors, and no English speaking would be tolerated. The idea was modeled on a "successful" program adopted by Father Lawrence Murray in Rannafast, Co. Donegal, who maintained a watchful eye over visitors to his village, ensuring that no English-speaking tourists were allowed into the homes of Irish speakers. MacEntee's plan would keep damaging Anglophones at bay by using the authority of government departments and local disciplinarians like Father Murray. Such a program would be expensive, but MacEntee felt strongly that "the holiday industry in the Gaeltacht should not be approached from the aspect of profit-making"; instead, what was needed was a state program that would guarantee the success of the language revival while also bringing money into poor areas.[20]

The 1939 Tourist Traffic Act threatened to create an unprecedented influx of Anglophone tourists, and the perceived risk sparked a positively xenophobic response among many observers. One letter-writer protested emphatically against the proposed scheme of tourist development and the expenditure of public moneys thereon, while no effective steps are being taken to protect the Gaeltacht from *such a formidable influx of foreignism. For it is a deadly threat to the Gaeltacht, if not to the whole Gaelic revival movement.* Of the huge increase in visitors expected, 99 per cent will be English-speakers from Great Britain, America, Australia, and New Zealand. Add their influence to the predominance of English already in our midst and the position of Gaelicism will be pitiful.[21]

Others agreed, prophesizing that "an enormous influx of British and American tourists is bound to be a great Anglicising agent in what is left of the Gaedhealtacht." This was a problem for the language, but it sparked another concern as well because it made certain that the money and energy needed to make tourism one of the state's main industries would be used not to build "a prosperous Irish nation" but to arrange "Ireland to suit the tastes of British and American tourists. Not tourists of the thoughtful, discriminating type—but tourists of the average, unthinking sort, whose wants are luxurious hotels, fishing, and jazz dancing, who leave every "beauty spot" defiled with rubbish, and whose idea of Ireland is a place where ridiculous peasants will amuse them."[22] The development of tourism, at least for those who spoke out about the Tourist Traffic Act, represented a betrayal of all that was fundamentally Irish. The danger to the language movement was just one of many negative outcomes, and some defense of those things most Irish was sorely needed. While it might not be necessary to "close the frontiers of the Gaeltacht, as Hitler might do," it was certainly the case that the government, "pledged and elected to restore the language, should hesitate before financing a scheme that, if launched before any measures are taken to strengthen the Gaeltacht, will almost certainly destroy the language in its native territory."[23]

Of course the Irish Tourist Association saw things much differently. As far as the association, and specifically the Killarney branch, were concerned, increased tourist traffic would mean "increased employment in the Gaeltacht, thereby helping to stop emigration of Irish speakers and [to] preserve the language," not to mention increasing the amount of farm produce consumed, much of it grown by Gaelic-speaking farmers. The xenophobic response was itself anathema to true Irishness. As Fred Crowley, a TD and director of the ITA, put it, "The Celtic race had a reputation for being capable of absorbing rather than being absorbed."[24] If Cu Uladh, the most prolific of the antitourism language enthusiasts, would come to Kerry, he would see "districts where the language, to a great extent, was a living force, and the people there were very anxious to have visitors and tourists, and the visitors and tourists were delighted to hear the Irish language spoken." The Gaels had played a part "in the national struggle in every shape and form for the past 500 years," and nobody should feel any "apprehension that [an] increased number of tourists will injure" the Irish people. Indeed, the further development of Irish customs would attract more tourists while making Ireland still more Irish.[25]

The conflict between the ITA and the "Gaelic Leaguers"[26] made its way into the Oireachtas during the late stage of the debate concerning the Tourist Traffic Act; the tone, however, was almost entirely favorable to tourist development. Senator Donnchadh Ó hEaluighthe, for example, stressed that his experience in Gaeltacht areas suggested that tourism brought valuable revenue and employment to Irish speakers and that the proposed legislation would help the congested districts, not harm them. Seán Lemass echoed this view, saying that the legislation would be "wholly beneficial" to the Gaeltacht areas.[27] Yet, as positive as most of the discussion within the government was, even here there were voices of concern. C. S. Almond, a civil servant in the Department of Finance, echoed the fears voiced by the Gaelic Leaguers. Almond warned that tourist development would have "serious repercussions" for the language movement, and argued that the language "is finding difficulty in combating the strong forces of cinema, the dance-hall, jazz, etc." Faced with an influx of tourists and a "programme of development which must have as its foundation the encouragement of all the forces which militate against the Irish language," the result could only be the extinction of Gaelic.[28]

Developing Language Tourism

Following passage of the act, the Irish Tourist Board and the ITA were faced with developing tourism in Gaeltacht areas while addressing the Gaelic Leaguers' concerns. As far as the Tourist Association was concerned, tourism remained "the only industry whose development could be made to supplement the income of large numbers of uneconomic holders in Gaeltacht areas."[29] As a result of this view, the association continued to push visitors toward the Gaeltacht regions, and its publications changed little from past efforts, continuing to draw attention to the many visitors who "annually flock to learn from them [Gaelic speakers in the Dingle area] the pure, musical Gaelic which they speak."[30]

The Tourist Board, on the other hand, was pushed toward considering potential schemes as part of its program of planning and development during the Emergency. The board began investigating Gaeltacht tourism after de Valera encouraged its leaders to explore the possibilities available. The request came following the taoiseach's receipt of a memorandum from An Fear Mór, a six-foot, six-inch-tall Gaelic enthusiast who had previously established the Ring Irish College and published several popular Irish-language textbooks.[31] An Fear Mór was particularly interested in Bunbeg, Co. Donegal, as a likely development site, and the Tourist Board was encouraged by the taoiseach to survey the area. The board was less than excited about the task, apparently doubting its qualifications to adopt the project, and the ITB urged the creation of a public company, similar to Aer Lingus or the Turf Board, to administer it—a view that was angrily denounced by the Department of Finance, which insistently recalled, "It was always contemplated that the improvement of holiday facilities in the Gaeltacht would be one of the main tasks of the board."[32]

In November 1944, J. P. O'Brien submitted the board's proposal to de Valera and expressed the opinion that "the district is in every way suitable for a first experiment in the provision of improved and enlarged accommodation for Irish summer courses." Using the Ring Irish College as a model, the board argued that it would be necessary to develop a set of buildings to provide classrooms, dining facilities, and accommodation for at least a hundred adults. In order to ensure that the plan would earn a profit and therefore be covered by the requirements attached to their wartime operating agreement, tourist authorities visualized using the buildings as a fosterage school during the academic year. There were also to be facilities for a vocational-education program to teach "domestic economy" to local housewives, who would be called upon to cater for visitors.[33] As it stood, the board's survey discloses shortcomings at all centres in the matter of accommodation, catering, public health services, and recreation amenities. Generally speaking, they have not kept pace with the times, and their survival depends on a substantial program of improvement in respect of the matters above mentioned. The system of control operating in practically every case is such that no improvement can be expected without some impetus and encouragement from some government source.[34]

Three years after receipt of the board's proposal, the minister of industry and commerce appointed a four-man committee comprising civil servants in the Departments of Finance, Lands, Industry and Commerce, and Education to assess the report. The group's assessment was overwhelmingly negative. While the Irish Tourist Board suggested that the entire Bunbeg development could be accomplished for £30,000, the committee expected the project to cost more than £100,000. Furthermore, the board's claim that the project could be profitable within a short period of its completion was sharply challenged, and the interdepartmental committee concluded that it would take at least *thirty years* before the necessary loans would be paid off. Indeed, the Bunbeg college would probably operate at a yearly deficit of at least £6,200. Given the cost, as well as serious doubts about the ability of the program to attract an adequate number of students, the interdepartmental committee recommended that the Tourist Board's plan be dismissed.

Development through Grants

In assessing the Tourist Board's proposal, the interdepartmental committee surveyed all of Ireland's Gaeltacht areas, paying particular attention to the amenities available. The committee found areas with flawless scenery and attractive recreational facilities, but also other districts that lacked running water, adequate sanitation, and lighting. Most visitors were accommodated in private homes, and overcrowding, unsuitable toilet facilities, and poor catering were endemic. Worse still, very few families were in any financial position to meet the economic challenge that would have to be overcome if they were to improve their homes in order to accommodate visitors—Irish or otherwise. The committee therefore advocated the provision of grants and loans to homeowners in Gaeltacht areas so that they could improve their homes. These loans would cover improved sanitation, enhanced water supplies, and the addition of guest rooms. The government should also step up efforts to provide a piped water supply and sewerage systems to Gaeltacht villages. It would be desirable to extend rural electrification schemes to as many Irish-speaking areas as possible. In addition, strong efforts should be made to provide "housewives who keep visitors"—women with "some training in domestic economy, with special regard to general cleanliness, the maintenance of the house and surroundings, the provision of a variety in food and its cooking, and [knowledge about] the importance of the economics of the guest-house, of the proper rearing of fowl, and the production of an adequate supply of eggs and milk." The committee also advocated the destruction of "dilapidated structures, neglected outhouses, sheds, unsightly waste materials, etc." Buildings should be painted, and trees and shrubs planted. Local committees needed to be encouraged to take control of their surroundings so that the natural beauty of Gaeltacht areas was not marred by the presence of eyesores—all concepts that were adopted several years later during An Tóstal and ultimately during the Tidy Towns and Villages Competition. Finally, the interdepartmental committee stressed that roadways in Gaeltacht areas were generally "unsatisfactory." The government should improve roads as well as improve access to beaches, boat launches, and swimming facilities.[35] In effect, the accommodations, people, and landscape of the Gaeltacht areas needed to be improved for the benefit of tourists: if Irish speakers, those "virtuous countrymen,"[36] were to be acceptably Irish, they needed to be properly trained and their lands suitably groomed.

Throughout the 1950s and beyond, it was the interdepartmental committee's suggestion for the provision of grants and loans that was adopted to develop the Gaeltacht. In October 1952 the minister for local government approved a program to improve "roads of tourist value in the Gaeltacht and the congested districts." The program was supposed to last for eight years, and expenditure in any given year was not to exceed £400,000.[37] Similarly, in 1959 the government passed a Housing (Gaeltacht) Amendment Bill "to give a new kind of financial assistance to families in the Gaeltacht areas" and to "provide accommodation for visitors to these areas, particularly students of the Irish language."[38] In 1965 Irish-speaking regions were once again under study to determine how to "foster the growth of farmhouse holiday accommodation." Far from frowning on the idea as too expensive or expansive, the Department of Finance responded to a somewhat truncated Bord Fáilte proposal by arguing that it should be extended to as many western districts as possible. The old concern about Anglophone tourists undermining the Irish language was completely surpassed by a feeling that the Gaeltacht might be particularly appealing to foreign visitors.[39] Nobody publicly challenged the proposal.

From the 1950s to the 1990s and beyond, the government promoted rural development, not language preservation. From the perspective of the state there were more pressing concerns than the language movement, and development monies were increasingly designed to assist the congested districts because they were economically challenged, not because of the desire to protect the language per se. This policy of firm support for economic development over language preservation was fully in keeping with the government's larger failure to make compulsory Irish seem important.[40] For those who genuinely cared about the language movement, it was a painful pill to swallow. The government was allowing the language to die "by stealth,"[41] and while occasional antitourism comments were made as late as the 1950s about allowing Anglophones into the Gaeltachts, such comments were notable more for their anachronistic presence in an ever-more-modern Ireland than for their widespread public acceptance.[42]

Phase II: Representing the Best of Irishness

As fear about the negative cultural implications of tourism waned, three simultaneous developments occurred that focused attention on Ireland's image: the number of tourists to Ireland rose, the government's interest in tourism increased, and the Tourist Board's development activities expanded. From the central government level, where cultural propaganda was an important component of Ireland's foreign policy, to average Irish men and women, there was a real desire to ensure that the world's impression of Ireland did not mimic the *Holiday* magazine article mentioned in the introduction. Not only would such an image undermine the tourist industry; it would also reflect badly on the Irish people themselves.

Many historians and literary critics frequently cite the widespread use of negative stereotypes to describe the Irish. At various points these scholars note that the Irish were often seen as rustic, simian, plebeian, and drunken.[43]

When not presented as potentially violent and threatening, the Irish were often seen as clowns, rogues, comic heroes, or "stage Irishmen."[44] Many perceived the Irish as inferior to the English, a fact made intuitively obvious by their "inferior" brogue.[45] Just as in the Raj, these stereotypes helped to justify colonial rule because the Irish were considered to be little more than "hapless dupes, hapless petitioners, and victims of discrimination" who required England's paternalistic assistance.[46] Yet this emphasis on the negative fails to acknowledge the variability of opinion. For example, Roy Foster demonstrates that Irish stereotypes were always rife with contradiction and negative characterizations were usually based more on class than upon race. "Marginal men" who were dissatisfied with their lives at home in England— men such as Thackeray, Shelley, Trollope, Lord Randolph Churchill, and even Frederick Engels—often saw Ireland as a realization of the dreams and fantasies that left them uncomfortable at home. Yet, just as these men were prone to viewing Ireland through romantic green-colored glasses, so they were equally disturbed when the Irish nationalist movement threatened the status quo. Trollope, for example, viewed the Irish as his kinsmen, yet he was violently opposed to Home Rule and defended the British government's actions during the Famine. He even tried to dismiss the "Irishness" of his character Phineas Finn when Irishness increasingly symbolized something to him that was more disturbing and divisive than he had previously imagined. "The qualities of perception which make Trollope the best 'Irish' novelist of the mid-century had by old age been thrown into reverse," states Foster.[47] Stereotypes, in other words, could be used as a matter of convenience, providing an "other," whether positive *or* negative, as circumstances warranted.

The ability to pick and choose stereotypes was not limited to "marginal men" (or to "Micks on the make" for that matter). Following the Irish Civil War, the Irish rejected unappealing characterizations of Ireland and Irishness and adopted more positive ones to serve new purposes. Most Irish people opted for a harmonious vision of Ireland that was rooted in older stereotypes, including Irish warmth and friendliness, a relaxed attitude toward life, and the innate ability to tell a great story—the same things that had often been appealing to Foster's "marginal men." Images were chosen because they matched tourist perceptions, offered visitors something different from what the tourists were used to, *and,* perhaps more important, because many Irish people believed in the images. During the 1920s the ITA used the welcoming and friendly image of Irishness to contrast with the horrors of recent war and expressed confidence that, despite Ireland's recent civil strife, tourists would "meet with a hearty 'Céad Míle Fáilte'" upon entering the country.[48] The threat of violence surrounding the general elections in 1927 was similarly dismissed because "the Irish people maintain their proud traditions for hospitality and kindness to their visitors."[49] Such reassuring words were not limited to tourist publications; they were frequently repeated in newspaper articles and speeches. Seán Lemass, for example, informed the Irish Tourist Association, "We are the heirs of a great tradition of courtesy and hospitality which has survived throughout all the centuries of our history, and the observing of that tradition today should be the keynote of those engaged in the tourist movement."[50] This same confidence was expressed by Taoiseach Jack Lynch in 1968, when he argued that for the Irish "hospitality to strangers is almost a way of life," a tradition "summed up in the Irish welcome 'Céad Míle Fáilte'—a hundred thousand welcomes. It means much more than the provision of food and drink and accommodation for the tourist. There is a genuine friendly interest to make the stranger feel at home."[51] None of these comments was made directly for the benefit of tourists, but rather they were offered by one Irishman to another.

Ultimately the Irish welcome, Irish hospitality, and the friendliness of the Irish people made Ireland a unique and desirable place, bolstering the Irish self-image. Many experienced a feeling of pride when the American humorist Will Rogers, for example, commented glowingly about the extraordinary welcome that Americans received in Ireland during 1926: "I have been in twenty countries, and the only one where American tourists are welcomed wholeheartedly by everybody is in Ireland . . . ; they don't owe us and they don't hate us." Finally, he quipped, "This endorsement is on the level and calls for no appointment from Tammany Hall whatever."[52] Comments like this one raised Ireland above other European destinations, displaced more unpleasant stereotypes, and fueled the patriotic zeal of tourism officials.

Post–Civil War travel writing also reflected these refurbished images. For example, Bell, the travel writer from Ohio, reminisced about the "lurid tales" presented by an engaging jarvey (hackney coach driver) "with the skill of a veteran novelist."[53] Years later, British comedian Tony Hawks told of his adventures hitchhiking around Ireland with a refrigerator to fulfill a drunken bet, claiming that such an undertaking would only be possible in the Emerald Isle. "In some parts of the world," he writes, "a stranger pulling a fridge on a trolley into a bar on a Friday night might be a recipe for a good kicking, but here I felt it more likely [that] if set upon, I would be held down and sung to."[54] In virtually all cases travel writers found the Irish eccentric, engaging, and endearing.

Kitsch and the Rural Image

From the vantage point of early twenty-first-century America, it might seem perfectly logical to assume that Irish tourism officials would adopt images of leprechauns, people dressed in green, rainbows, and pots of gold. The lexicon of American images of Ireland includes an inventory of green beer, Lucky Charms cereal, horror movies about demented leprechauns, and bath soap that promises to make the user smell as fresh as a soft morning in Ireland (never mind that a soft morning in rural Ireland is more likely to smell of livestock than soap). Indeed, Ireland's tourist shops are packed with kitsch, but tourism authorities have seldom made use of these products in any official capacity. Before the Irish Tourist Board was formed in 1939, Killarney was often described as a "fairyland"[55] and Irish scenery as "fairy-like," but the ITA made no effort to play up leprechaun-based "Paddywhackery." Likewise, the ITB, Fógra Fáilte, and Bord Fáilte have similarly avoided mindless kitsch. In fact, when Bord Fáilte did publish a folder that emphasized Irish folklore and the important role of the "little people" in Irish storytelling, it presented an essay by W. B. Yeats that described Ireland's fairy mythology in literary terms, and the booklet did not reflect the frivolity of the cereal-hawking little people in popular culture.[56] Low-class kitsch was avoided because tourism officials believed strongly that the "lazy leprechaun" idea of Ireland should be avoided. It was acceptable to exploit "native charm and character" as well as legends, antiquities, the native language, and traditional dress, but these should never be allowed to overshadow "a modern progressive outlook on life." Any projection of Ireland should show "the sophisticated side of Irish life" and break with "sentiment in a deliberate way."[57]

In 1950 the government formed a subcommittee to assess Ireland's tourist industry, and after looking into the matter, the committee immediately complained that the souvenirs offered at Irish shops were unsatisfactory. In particular, "the bog-oak pipe, the shillelagh, and the Birmingham broach should be driven from shops and shop windows." These items reflected an undesirable stereotype of Irishness, not an "appropriate and tasteful design in harmony with Irish culture and history." Likewise, the "caubeen and pipe type of advertisement" was to be avoided in favor of campaigns focusing attention on the many places of natural beauty in Ireland.[58] Rather than catering to the lowest common denominator, the authorities exhibited a sense of national pride in their perception of the mementos that should be made available. Moreover, some officials believed strongly that souvenirs should be manufactured in Ireland—providing employment to Irish people and establishing a reputation for the quality of Irish crafts. During the late 1950s, Bord Fáilte undertook a special initiative to increase the number of suitable souvenirs available; it oversaw an increase from 30 to 120 product lines by 1957, as well as substantial growth in the number of shops stocking these gifts.[59]

The fact that tourist authorities avoided leprechauns certainly does not mean that they rejected presentations of the Irish people as culturally distinct and different. In particular, Irish people have been portrayed as rural and agriculturally centered. The "Pre-1960s Types" collection in Bord Fáilte's photographic archive offers a striking illustration of the images of Irish people that were most often presented to tourists. The photographs include Irish men and women gathering and stacking turf, harvesting various crops, making hay, collecting and stacking kelp, driving horse-drawn carts, weaving, participating in livestock fairs, dressed as Mummers or Wren Boys, managing sheep, working on currachs (traditional boats), fishing, plowing, and so forth. The traditional "Kinsale cloak" worn by many women in west Cork through the 1940s was also a popular photograph and found its way into numerous guidebooks and travel narratives as well. Ultimately Irish people were presented in striking contrast not only to their industrial neighbors in Britain or on the continent but to the denizens of Dublin and Cork city as well. In many of these images work, and hard work at that, is clearly being done, but the tasks, clothing, and traditions reflect, or seek to project, a timeless Irishness.

It would be wrong to interpret these images purely as a desire to capture a past age or a reflection of foreign perceptions of Irishness—donkey carts,

3. A farm family harvesting turf near Downing, County Donegal. Courtesy of Bord Fáilte Éireann–Irish Tourist Board.

currachs, and turf cutting remain very much a part of the lexicon of Irish tourism, as is clear in the Tourism Brand Ireland campaign (see introduction). Instead the images represent a vision of what the tourism developers of the 1920s to the 1950s imagined Ireland to be. Of course, Ireland really *was* rural during this period. When Jan de Fouw, the Dutch graphic designer who was largely responsible for defining the look and content of *Ireland of the Welcomes* from 1952 into the 1990s, made home movies of his travels around Ireland, he captured people wearing shoes made of rawhide, donning handwoven trousers, and working their land in a manner that had been current since the years immediately following the Great Famine.[60] In some ways the tourist images used into the 1960s showed Ireland as it was and had been for decades. On the other hand and more important, this imagery illustrated Ireland as the nationalist imagination wanted it to be portrayed: Irish *poverty* was reformatted to symbolize Irish *purity*.

Shortly after the Civil War the Irish Coinage Committee recommended the issue of coins bearing images of Irish animals and wildlife, clearly showing the symbolic significance of rural settings.[61] Not everybody agreed with the choice. Reflecting the long-standing debate surrounding modernization, some urged the use of industrial symbols. Coinage Committee chairman W. B. Yeats dismissed this suggestion by musing, "we have so few industries & doubt the decorative value of a porter bottle." Others feared that the coins suggested "paganism," "Freemasonry," and Ireland as a "land of devil-worshippers." Still others, including Maud Gonne, denounced the designs because an English artist, Percy Metcalfe, created them. Despite the objections, the coins were generally approved of.[62] Allegations of devil-worship aside, the salience of rural Ireland was real and did not diminish with the change of government in 1932. In what is perhaps his most quoted policy statement, Éamon de Valera declared to radio listeners on Easter Sunday 1943,

> That Ireland which we dreamed of would be the home of a people who valued material wealth only as a basis of right living, of a people who were satisfied with frugal comfort and devoted their leisure to things of the spirit; a land whose countryside would be bright with cosy homesteads, whose fields and villages would be joyous with sounds of industry, the romping of sturdy children, the contests of athletic youths, the laughter of comely maidens; whose firesides would be the forums of the wisdom of serene old age.[63]

De Valera was dreaming about precisely the same things that were depicted in tourist guidebooks. To show a rural Ireland in which the people diligently worked the land and appeared forever content was not just a message for tourists and foreign governments; it was a message to the Irish people themselves—a way of bolstering the native self-image during a time of economic hardship.

There was one additional reason for depicting an overwhelmingly rural and traditional Ireland: tourism had the potential to bring untold riches into underdeveloped areas that could no longer hope to support themselves on agriculture or fishing. As I have stressed in earlier chapters, by pushing tourists into small western-seaboard communities, and especially the Gaeltachts, the authorities hoped to stem the tide of emigration. Today, far outstripping any desire to stress symbolic links to the land, the focus on rural images grows directly from the need to pump money into rustic communities. The development of "agri-tourism" is only the most recent movement to assist underdeveloped areas. During the 1980s the government was faced with extremely high out-migration from such places. Between 1981 and 1986 alone rural population growth was cut in half, and rural unemployment climbed steeply during this period. Seventy-five percent of the agricultural products that were produced were in excess supply in the European Union, driving farm prices down and continuing to exacerbate the emigration problem.[64] The future for rural Ireland seemed desperately bleak. Only 35 percent of the rural population could find agricultural employment; part-time farming did not provide an adequate way of life because there were no jobs to supplement the meager income produced. Service-sector work was also limited; even in areas where tourism was important, the work created was seasonal.[65]

In the 1980s ACOT (the socioeconomic section of the Agricultural Advisory Service) began to promote the concept of more diversified tourism in rural areas.[66] In particular, this body advanced the idea of developing agri-tourism that involved attracting tourists to working farms in order to experience rural life. The program was to be locally run, but it experienced early problems. Few efforts were made to develop acceptable medium-range planning objectives, and community members failed to combine their resources to mount adequate marketing campaigns.[67] Still, by 1988, Bord Fáilte became convinced that agri-tourism might be viable if adequately administered. The Tourist Board's 1994–99 sustainable-development plan expressed a desire to create "rural tourism areas" that "generally lie outside the tourism centres and cater for a market segment that is seeking a quiet holiday where tourists can get to know a local area intimately, immersed in the traditions of rural Ireland."[68] Rural tourism has the added advantage that it keeps tourists in a specific area for longer periods, ensuring that their funds flow directly into the local community for an extended time. Just as tourism developers in the 1940s hoped to use language tourism as a means of promoting economic development in Gaeltacht areas while also encouraging the language, so too contemporary tourism interests hope to advance economic growth in sparsely populated rural districts.

Festivals and Irish Tourism

Markets and fairs have been a part of Irish life for many hundreds of years and initially emerged as "a response to a local need to exchange surplus produce." More than simply places of business, fairs brought people from different social backgrounds and geographic locations together, helping to shape Irish society in new ways: "town met country; farmer met trader; and the influences of the wider world were introduced into the local culture."[69] Later, the larger fairs attracted not only people from around Ireland but also from Britain and even the continent.[70] By the late nineteenth century the number of markets and fairs held throughout Ireland began to decline.[71] This downturn sped up during the twentieth century as fairs covered larger market areas, trains ceased running to many old parochial centers (especially after 1960), respectability gained an ever stronger hold on society (demanding an end to the drunken revelries that held sway during earlier times), and traditional sites of economic activity were replaced by multipurpose stores.

Today those fairs and festivals that remain—"like the 'Auld Lammas Fair' of Ballycastle in County Antrim or Puck Fair in Killorglin in County Kerry—do so as much for social or touristic as for commercial purposes."[72] In fact, beginning in the early 1950s with the first mounting of An Tóstal, fairs and festivals emerged throughout Ireland in order to attract tourists rather than cattle or horse traders. Organizers developed new traditions that allegedly represented time-honored examples of Irish culture. Whereas traditional fairs were often bawdy gatherings, filled with drink, thinly veiled bestial sexuality, violence, and the presence of marginal groups like Irish Travellers, tourist festivals presented a happier side of Irish culture, celebrating food, theatre, music, and friendliness. The official desire to present Ireland as a land of welcoming people and joyous, time-honored customs combined with the economic need to draw an ever-increasing number of visitors and with the tourists' dream of experiencing a little piece of authenticity.

Puck Fair and the Problem with Traditional Entertainment

Puck Fair was originally a cattle fair held every August in Killorglin: a little town at the head of Dingle Bay in County Kerry. In some ways Puck Fair was a relic of an earlier age when many fairs adopted animals as symbols of the festival and the commercial spirit of the event.[73] On the first day of the fair, Gathering Day, a wild goat, captured in the mountains above Killarney, is crowned king and hoisted onto a tall tower to preside over the fair. The second day is primarily given over to cattle trading, and the third, Scattering

4. Fair authorities place King Puck on his platform at the start of the 1955 Puck Fair. Courtesy of Bord Fáilte Éireann–Irish Tourist Board.

Day, sees the dethroning of the king and his release back into the Kerry mountains. The actual act of crowning the goat is undertaken by a small girl, the "Green Queen," who reigns with Puck (though not on the tower). The sexual overtones of a young girl and a well-endowed goat are not explicitly pointed out in the ceremony, but they are carefully emphasized in Muriel Rukeyser's account of the event.[74] In practice, the three-day fair was marked by incessant drinking and dancing,[75] to say nothing of the distressing accumulation of muck that one might expect from a large number of livestock.[76] Traditionally Puck Fair was also the site of frequent fighting—often attributed to the presence of Irish Travellers sparring with rival Travelling families as well as with unfriendly locals. Despite the ethnic or cultural ill-will between the Travelling community and landed locals, the fair was reportedly made a "real Irish fair" only by the "Tinkers"—whose presence brought two culturally diverse components of Irish society into close contact.[77]

Many Irish people were ambivalent about mixing "traditional" fairs and tourism. In her account of a 1958 trip to Puck Fair,[78] Rukeyser recounts numerous comments by Irish people, most of them from Kerry itself, arguing that Americans should not visit Puck Fair because "it's so materialistic. It's all about drinking."[79] Another local observer went further, describing the three-day festival as "all hatred and dreariness" marked by "long, slow, slugging fighting, breaking everything it passes through."[80] One Killorglin resident even predicted that the author "won't be able to stand it. She's American, after all."[81] Even as Rukeyser prepared to leave following the final day of the fair, she was asked by one of her Kerry friends to "go easy on Puck."[82] Although Rukeyser would not necessarily have been aware of it, attitudes toward Irish Travellers were also undergoing a dramatic change in the years following World War II. No longer viewed as free spirits as they were before the early 1950s, the Travelling people were increasingly seen as dirty, dangerous, and repulsive—outsiders from mainstream Irish society, despised people to be hidden away, not celebrated.[83] Puck Fair's intimate association with Irish "Tinkers" certainly added to the widespread ambivalence about presenting the fair to tourists.[84] For many locals Puck Fair was simply too dirty, too violent, too bestial, too primordial for any outsider to understand.

Despite local concerns, the fair was included in tourist guidebooks and in much travel writing. During the 1920s and 1930s the Irish Tourist Association made a point of drawing attention to the fair, including it in their *Official Guide to the Kingdom of Kerry*.[85] During the immediate postwar period the Puck Fair Committee made a point of publishing a souvenir guide for the event, including photographs of King Puck and a debate about the origin of the fair.[86] Travel writers like Sean O'Faolain also maintained an interest in the curious tradition of crowning a goat. O'Faolain made a point of mentioning the fair in his *Irish Journey,* and the Irish-born travel writer Leslie Daiken demonstrated an interest in the fair through numerous articles and a BBC radio broadcast.[87]

As the number of tourists in Ireland began to increase, the authorities became somewhat less enthusiastic about promoting Puck. In Fógra Fáilte's

Ireland Guide, published in about 1953, Puck Fair received an extensive description.[88] In 1958, when Rukeyser visited the fair, Bord Fáilte's annual calendar of events not only listed Puck Fair, it provided readers with a description of the event and the various groups known to participate.[89] This complete listing continued into the 1960s,[90] but by 1973 it was scaled back to a mere name-and-date listing. It was not that the format of the calendar of events had changed to exclude descriptions—the Dublin Horse Show, for example, retained a detailed caption; rather, the authorities appear to have become increasingly tentative about recommending that tourists "do" Puck.[91] Indeed, the Tourist Board's *Ireland: 1980* guide, which offered visitors descriptions and photographs of the country's attractions, did not suggest Puck as a suitable August activity.[92] Although Puck continued to be included in Bord Fáilte's *Ireland Guide* as part of descriptions of Killorglin, it was no longer prominently placed in "what's on" schedules—despite the fact that by this time it bore little resemblance to its earlier incarnation after having been reinvented as a tourist fair, albeit with the same sexual overtones and mass drunkenness of thirty years before.[93] But the fair was treated as a curiosity taking place over "three days in August"—three *undefined* days. What had happened?

It seems likely that Puck Fair began to fall from favor because it did not offer an altogether acceptable picture of Ireland or Irishness. Tourist authorities could not have legions of American tourists realizing, as Rukeyser did in 1958, that they were going "to an orgy."[94] Leslie Daiken did not see Puck Fair as offensive. He recognized that Puck was a "bucolic fiesta which must be the last survival in these Islands of a pagan orgy of hard drinking—tempered with dancing, singing, and those occasional faction-fights which invest the balmy, midnight air with yells of priapine frenzy."[95] But Daiken saw something else that he believed to be more important, a relic of the romance of ancient Ireland. His gaze focused on the timeless tradition involved, and he worked, through his travel articles and a BBC radio presentation entitled "Where Puck Is King," to share the fair's "character and particular atmosphere." Puck Fair was, he insisted, uniquely Irish, "the only ritualistic congregation of men and women of goodwill in all north-west Europe where a wild goat is tamed for kingship."[96] He romanticized the event as something that "every poet in Ireland" comes to see "because every native of Kerry is at heart a poet." Although the fun was often "fast and free," in Daiken's mind it was "never a riot or bacchanal, but nimble as a Kerryman's tongue with spontaneous jollity; friendly as a big family party; honestly countrified like any true fair-day ought to be."[97]

Tourist authorities were less convinced. In fact, when Daiken contacted Michael Gorman, then editor of *Ireland of the Welcomes,* about publishing an article on Puck Fair, the editor responded with interest but with the caveat that Daiken should "keep the *Ireland of the Welcomes* readership in mind and only stress those aspects of Puck Fair which are universally acceptable as attractions."[98] This was *not* the Ireland to which Bord Fáilte wanted to direct tourists, *not* the Ireland that it wanted to feature in the glossy pages of its travel magazine, and *not* the Ireland that it wanted to emphasize in its calendar of events. Puck Fair could not be eliminated from official guides because it was still something of interest to many tourists. More important, it was Killorglin's only claim to fame—beyond the town's geographic location at the beginning of the "Ring of Kerry" scenic motoring tour—and the Tourist Board's mission was to promote tourism and related employment throughout Ireland. Puck was also, until the launch of An Tóstal and the ancillary festivals that sprang, Athena-like, from it, one of Ireland's few remaining fairs. Once more fairs and festivals became available, Puck was easily downplayed in favor of more respectable entertainment like the Cork Film Festival or Galway Oyster Festival. New "traditions" were required to replace their more dated and much less respectable antecedents.

Inspiration

An Tóstal: Ireland at Home was the single largest tourist development project undertaken during the 1950s and it stands as an excellent example of how Irish identity was influenced both from within and without Ireland. While actual events were planned in Ireland, the idea and inspiration for An Tóstal came from abroad. Juan Trippe, the president of Pan-American Airlines, first suggested the concept for a new tourist festival in 1951,[99] the same year that Britain held its Festival of Britain. Trippe's idea fell on receptive ears partly because just one year before the Cabinet Sub-Committee on Tourism had argued that Ireland should promote "an event of international significance which would appeal to our own people at home and abroad" and that would be "somewhat on the lines of the proposed Festival of Britain."[100] Holding an Irish version of the Festival of Britain allowed the Irish to demonstrate themselves to be on par with their neighbors across the Irish Sea. At the same time, the festival idea allowed the Irish to create events that reflected a more widely acceptable Irish culture while also addressing issues raised during the tourism crisis of 1948–51.

Although the Irish were certainly inspired by the Festival of Britain, the two events were fundamentally different. An Tóstal was far more focused on tourism earnings than the British festival, which was primarily a "pat on the back" to reward the British people for winning the war while also providing a "tonic for the nation" during a period of economic and political difficulty."[101] In contrast, the success of Tóstal hinged on "an emotional desire on the part of people of Irish descent to visit Erin" and events were designed accordingly.[102] The Irish tourist festival was intended to lengthen the tourist season (hence the fact that it was planned for the early spring) and to attract people of Irish ancestry back to the Emerald Isle from America, England, and the various Commonwealth countries. In a strict sense, then, any failure to immediately attract legions of tourists would mean that An Tóstal had failed (despite subsequent rationalizations of government and tourism officials).

History was a central theme of both the British and Irish festivals, yet here too important variations were prominent. Festival of Britain organizers planned an event that offered an "autobiography" of the nation. A carefully chosen history was offered and the people were presented as quiet, unassuming, and tough—rather like the hobbits in J. R. R. Tolkien's *Lord of the Rings* trilogy, first published three years later in 1954–55. History was defined in terms of timeless traditions that would carry the people forward toward a bright future; indeed, modernity and progress were stressed above all. There were conflicts, of course, and local festivals in Cornwall, Wales, and Scotland gave primacy to local distinctiveness rather than the narrative designed by central planners in London, but the more centralized administration of British events assured that a picture of timeless traditions and "unity through diversity" predominated. Even where divergent historical narratives were notable, few questioned the desirability of modernity.[103] History mattered, but only insofar as it contributed to the glories of the present and the promise of the future.

Meanwhile, An Tóstal, though first proposed in 1951, was presented as a vestige of Irish history—a surviving exemplar of a long and ancient tradition of Irish festivals. An Tóstal was a descendant of "great festivals of long ago— Tara, Tailteann, Carmain, Uisneach, and all the rest." The new tourist festival was designed to revive this long tradition.[104] Of course, in reality, Tailteann, a sort of medieval Olympic Games, had not been held since 1169 (with the exception of a short-lived revival in the 1920s), Tara was more associated with medieval governance than hedonistic enjoyment, and the other two events were pagan religious holidays and bore virtually no similarity to the very modern and mostly secular An Tóstal.[105] None of this mattered. Indeed, when explaining the choice of the name An Tóstal, organizers said that they hoped it would inspire memories of "Ireland's earliest national assemblages."[106] Of course the term, which translates as "a gathering," had probably never been used in antiquity. It was chosen after representatives of Bord Fáilte argued that a Gaelic title should be given to the festival and a five-pound note was offered to the government's translation office for suggestions.[107] Several days later "An Tóstal" emerged as the leading recommendation and was soon presented as a clear link with the ancient past. As a way of making Tóstal's lineage graphically obvious, organizers commissioned the design of an emblem that was to symbolize "ancient Irish festivals and gatherings." That Guss Melai, a Dutch designer, developed the logo was carefully kept under wraps.[108] The insignia included a "traditional Irish harp," the fore pillar and head of which included ornamentation drawn from the Book of Kells—ornamentation "inspired by the Celtic decoration engraved on the old Irish harps."[109] The An Tóstal logo not only graphically linked this very modern tourist gathering to the distant past, it also linked modern Ireland symbolically to the musical and artistic outpourings of a previous age. Whereas the Festival of Britain was intended to point British attentions toward a bright future,[110] An Tóstal pointed festival-goers backward toward an unobjectionable past. "Ireland at Home" was offered to visitors as being just as traditional as Puck Fair, if not more so; yet there were no aspects of Tóstal that needed to be downplayed in order to stress "only those aspects [of Irishness] which are universally acceptable." An Tóstal was inherently suitable for all audiences.

An Tóstal drew attention to the national community and celebrated the achievements of the *Volk* in a manner that was much different than in Britain

5. Publicity poster for the 1954 An Tóstal, featuring Guss Melai's famous Tóstal harp. Courtesy of Bord Fáilte Éireann–Irish Tourist Board.

Both festivals put the national "cultural attractions . . . on display,"[111] but in Ireland local communities created these attractions, not a centralized committee as in Britain.[112] From the moment that the Irish government accepted the Tóstal idea, the two statutory tourist bodies launched an aggressive campaign to hire an organizer, publish spectacular publicity materials, and plan a series of monumental parades and other events around Dublin, but it was local "Tóstal Councils" that actually developed the majority of the events. An Tóstal lacked the traveling exhibits and regional displays that were a core component of the Festival of Britain and the Tóstal's organizational structure assured that the festival reflected a truly grassroots sense of Irish identity.

New Traditions for a Modern Age

What cultural attractions did the committees include? Tóstal Councils developed a wide variety of events that included sporting events, parades, musical concerts, plays, pageants, exhibits, and so forth. The 1953 Tóstal opened during Easter Week with a special mass at the Pro-Cathedral in Dublin, presided over by Archbishop John Charles McQuaid.[113] This mass was followed by a massive military parade down Dublin's abnormally clean streets—"one of the biggest reviews in Ireland's history," including members from all three of the Irish armed services, and an inspection of the troops by Irish President Seán T. O'Kelly. This was followed by the raising of the Tóstal flag, a tribute by Taoiseach Éamon de Valera at the 1916 memorial, the release of carrier pigeons instructed to bring goodwill to the country, and the lighting of candles throughout Dublin. Similar displays occurred simultaneously in Cork city, and a torchlight procession took place at the Hill of Slane, where a massive bonfire was lit to symbolize Saint Patrick's introduction of Christianity to the Irish people.[114]

When selecting events, "the strongest possible emphasis" was placed "on Gaelic life, history, language, and culture." Both the Gaelic Athletic Association and the Gaelic League were called upon to provide "complete cooperation." Promoters, both regional and national, were invited to develop events under the headings "nationality," "culture," and "constitutional and civic life," with national traditions, language, music, art, drama, folklore, recreation, and leisure all given special attention.[115]

Pageants were an important component of Tóstal schedules, allowing organizers to send a dramatic message to visitors about Irish life and history. During the first year a special "Tóstal Show" was presented at the Theatre Royal in Dublin that dramatized important phases of Irish history defined by the theme "four green fields," symbolizing the four provinces of Ireland. County Waterford went one better, providing two historical pageants, including one that dealt with the Danish invasion and another featuring that of the Normans.[116] In the following year national organizers planned a more elaborate event and presented a monumental "Pageant of Saint Patrick" that spanned two days and four locations, including Drogheda, Navan, Slane, and Tara. At each site an aspect of the Saint Patrick story was presented, ranging from the saint's arrival in Ireland, to his arrest at Slane, to his eventual peaceful conversion of the Brehons and Druids at Tara.[117] Organizers used 500 costumes for the choir alone and employed the services of 1,300 volunteers to carry the event off. In addition, 1,000 pigeons, 24 wolfhounds, and 30 horses, as well as deer and other game, were integrated into the event.[118] As it happened, the occasion attracted fifty thousand largely Irish spectators to Tara alone, despite bitterly cold March weather.[119] The spectacle impressed government officials, who suggested that a similar pageant might be included in subsequent Tóstals, but only at five-year intervals, as it was too expensive a proposition for annual repetition.[120]

Despite the heavy costs, organizers opted to include the pageant in the 1955 schedule, though it was staged at Croke Park rather than across the broad canvas of the Boyne Valley. This time the pageant functioned as the Tóstal opener and told of Patrick's meeting with the high-king of the Druids in the Court of Tara and of "his over-throwing of the forces of paganism." Saint Patrick was played by leading Dublin actor Anew McMaster, and the pageant was written and produced by Micheál MacLiammóir, and directed by Hilton Edwards of Dublin's Gate Theatre, assuring that the luminaries of Dublin's theatre world were all involved.[121] The 1956 pageant was also presented at Croke Park, but organizers broke with previous practice in telling the story of Cuchulainn, the great Irish warrior so feared by his adversaries that even after his death, when his body was propped up facing the enemy, Cuchulainn's foes dared not approach until they saw crows pecking at the dead warrior's corpse. A thousand actors presented six performances of the epic play under the floodlights at Dublin's great Gaelic sports ground.[122]

Sporting matches were among the most commonly promoted Tóstal events. As the official souvenir guidebook stressed, "Every tourist knows that Ireland is a sporting country," and it drew particular attention to the fact that "Ireland is home to one of the world's greatest amateur sporting organisations." From the perspective of festival promoters Gaelic sport was important because "they are the games of the people"—as popular in Ireland as baseball in America or Australian Rules football in Australia. Of Ireland's four million inhabitants, some three million, it was said, "are either present or past members or else consistent supporters" of the Gaelic Athletic Association (GAA). To know the Irish people was to know Gaelic sports and especially hurling. In spite of the fact that the geographical centers of hurling strength are traditionally found only in a handful of mostly southern counties (especially Kilkenny, Tipperary, Cork, and Clare), the sport nevertheless was "in the blood and bone of the Irish breed," and, even at the elite level it was allegedly played purely "for the love of the game and for the honour of the county, parish, or little white-walled village, as the case may be." Just as important, the focusing of visitor attention on Gaelic games offered another instrument allowing tourist authorities to point toward Ireland's ancient cultural traditions. "Men were hurling [in Ireland] when the gods of Greece were young," boasted the guidebook. Hurling was "immortal," and even restrictive colonial policies could not suppress it.[123]

Of course, Fógra Fáilte made it abundantly clear in their souvenir handbook that Gaelic sports were not the only game in town. Equestrian sports, angling, motor sports, hunting, running, sailing, hiking, and a wealth of other activities were also present in abundance, making it impossible to "give a comprehensive view of sport in Ireland in the course of a few pages."[124] Fundamentally, the message was that Ireland offered something for everybody—whether in sporting interests or in serious cultural activity. Indeed, the Tóstal guidebook drew attention to a number of aspects of Irish life, including its people, landscape, work habits, and cultural achievements. Visitors were to be made to understand Ireland not only through the games its people played, but also by the success of Irish industry since independence and the long list of literary, visual, and musical accomplishments of its people. The guidebook did not attempt to present Irishness as a simple combination of friendliness and good humor, but instead claimed that the Irish "character tends to be a baffling one," marked by dramatic changes in mood from gaiety to somber melancholy. Only a long stay in Ireland would reveal the complex national personality of its people.[125]

Before this discussion returns to specific Tóstal events, it should be noted that while Irish sport was a prominent feature of festival events, organizers also placed a substantial emphasis on the Irish work ethic. The world of labor was not only considered important to understanding the Irish people, it was also viewed as essential to understanding the achievements of independent Ireland. Having outlined the prevalence of agriculture, the Tóstal guide noted that although "there was no systematic establishment of manufacturing industries until the independent Irish state was founded," since that time "substantial advances have been made towards effecting a satisfactory economic balance between agricultural and manufacturing enterprise."[126] For tourism organizers it was a matter of substantial pride that "considerable progress has . . . been made in a comparatively short time towards increasing the industrialisation of Ireland."[127] This satisfaction was not limited to the tourist guidebooks. For example, Kilkenny launched a substantial "industrial exhibition" as part of its 1953 Tóstal effort,[128] even including a special pageant devoted to the county's industrial success.[129] In both 1953 and 1954 the Cork Tóstal Council combined forces with the Cork Chamber of Commerce and the Cork Regional Group of the Federation of Irish Manufacturers to host a "Cork Makes It" exhibition featuring products manufactured in Cork city and its environs.[130] Limerick presented an annual parade celebrating Irish industry.[131] Far from the workplace being absent, as Barbara O'Connor mistakenly suggests in an article about Irish tourist representations,[132] "Ireland at Home" showed visitors a nation of men (and to a much lesser extent women) who worked hard but knew well how to enjoy a bit of *"craic"* when not building a vibrant and successful nation.

An Tóstal was primarily about showing the nation's guests a good time. Ireland was nowhere more successful than in its extraordinary output of music, literature, and theatre. Both Irish music and Irish literature and theatre personified the message of ancient cultural achievement advanced by Tóstal organizers. Gaelic-language writing was traced to an epic, pre-Homeric literary tradition.[133] Anglo-Irish writing, although more recent, grew from "certain racial or national qualities," and traits such as "Irish humor" were the result of "several perceptibly indigenous strains" that combined to create something uniquely Irish.[134]

Perhaps most important of all, Irish music was clearly a major element of ancient Irish life. The Muireadach high cross at Monasterboice, for example, included a thousand-year-old carving of harp and pipe players seated around Christ. When such representations were taken "in conjunction with the numerous references in early mediaeval manuscripts, they make it clear that music entered largely into the life of the ancient Irish."[135] The corpus of folk music that resulted from this almost timeless tradition formed "an integral part" of Irish heritage and, not surprisingly, played a substantial role in Tóstal events. When announcing Tóstal in *Ireland of the Welcomes,* Fógra Fáilte made a point of including photographs of pipers, a choir, and a symphony, as well as of featuring a harp and a young dancer done in spot color to draw attention to them.[136] De Valera's opening speech delivered in Cork city drew attention to Ireland's musical tradition and addressed the numerous musical events planned to occur there, including an opera, a *cailidh,* sacred music performances, recitals, and so on.[137] Indeed, Cork was one of the first areas to create a special competition in the form of a choral contest that ultimately continued to be held after the demise of An Tóstal in the late 1950s.[138] Eventually other localities added music and theatre festivals to their Tóstal schedules as well, including Dublin's Festival of Grand Opera, the Wexford Music Festival, Dublin's International Festival of Music and the Arts, the Cork Film Festival, and the Dublin Theatre Festival.[139]

In spite of the wide variety of events offered to potential Tóstal tourists, very few made the trip and the festival was far from the success of its British cousin. Between 1953 and 1958 both the government and the Tourist Board saw one visitor target after another hopelessly missed. Instead of massive crowds of excited tourists, more often than not the scene was of "flags and bunting bedraggled, bands playing bravely, no sign of tourists, and ministers of state standing under umbrellas saying their piece."[140] As early as 1954 there was debate about the early spring timing of the event, but it was pointed out that the "point was to extend the tourist season," and no changes were made.[141] In planning for the 1956 Tóstal, Bord Fáilte argued that it should be staged from 6 to 21 May, and the event was moved one month forward.[142] It proved no more successful, however, in attracting tourists. Despite the poor showings, the minister for industry and commerce announced in 1955 that the event would run through at least 1958, thus putting off any serious discussion of dissolving An Tóstal.[143]

In July 1958 a committee was convened to discuss the future of "Ireland at Home." After much deliberation the group concluded that Tóstal had not been successful in extending the tourist season and therefore did not justify the considerable expense. Rather than abandon the festival idea outright, however, the committee suggested that the Tóstal period be *extended* to run all the way from June through September. It was argued that this approach would attract visitors to the country while retaining the growth of civic pride and the successful local events that had developed under the rubric of An Tóstal. Furthermore, seaside resorts would be able to create special events in July and August rather than in the dreary spring months when few tourists ventured to the seaside, while urban centers could launch indoor events such as film festivals either earlier or later in the season as desired.[144] Now Bord Fáilte's message was that Ireland was a land of festivals.[145]

The story of Ireland's tourism festivals does not end with the emergence of the "Ireland of the Festivals" idea. Almost immediately, virtually all the local events began to lose money, requiring Bord Fáilte to step in to provide financial support. The Tourist Board's first grants were given in 1962, and it promised to continue funding the events for three years. Initially, the board offered £26,000, spread among eight festivals, including major celebrations in Dublin, Cork, Wexford, and Waterford, as well as several angling events and the Yeats Summer School in Sligo. In the following year £28,000 was given to the same festivals. By 1964 the number of events securing aid had increased to eleven, with total grants now estimated at £30,000 and with the larger festivals receiving in the range of £4,000 each. During the first two years of the program Bord Fáilte estimated that the festivals benefiting from its aid took in some £100,000 in tourism earnings. The larger events were more bullish still. The Dublin Theatre Festival estimated an annual income of £100,000 on its own, earned from 2,700 foreign tourists in attendance at its events. Likewise the Cork Film Festival cited £21,000 in earnings over eight days. The Cork Choral Festival was far less successful, however, running a deficit of some £900. Bord Fáilte hoped that its grant program would inspire corporate sponsorship, allowing the board to eventually end the scheme. Guinness, for example, already supported the Festival of Kerry, the Wexford Festival, the Dundalk G & G Festival, the West Cork Festival at Clonakilty, Bundoran's Lobster Festival, the Kilkenny Beer Festival, the Sligo Festival, and many others. If similar corporate interest could be generated, perhaps through tax incentives, the Tourist Board predicted a bright future.[146]

As it happened, the 1965 review of festival policy found it impossible for the Tourist Board to cease financial subventions, and it was decided to continue the program through 1970. Tourist Board chief T. J. O'Driscoll stressed that decisions about aid would be based increasingly on the level of local support—financial and otherwise. Only those communities strongly behind their tourism festivals could realistically expect substantial assistance from the Tourist Board. Meanwhile, even as its director-general noted that board finances were being stretched more thinly each year, he encouraged the expansion of Ireland's festivals by local groups in order to "offer scope for the generation of tourist traffic in volume" and for giving "special attention" to "festivals which are distinctively Irish in character." Each festival should establish a local company and a tighter administrative structure to ensure financial solvency.[147]

Bord Fáilte never escaped the need for the provision of festival grants, but the number and the professionalism of the events do seem to have increased. By 1970 the Dublin Tourism RTO decided to begin developing a weeklong St. Patrick's Day celebration, modeled largely on U.S. ideas about "Ireland's national holiday."[148] After a brief decline in the mid-1990s,[149] the event has steadily gained momentum since that time, and in 2002, Dublin visitors were treated to four days of fireworks, parades, dancing, and music.[150] Likewise, outstanding events like Wexford's Opera Festival and Kerry's "Rose of Tralee" contest have also persisted.[151] Today hundreds of festivals, large and small, enliven the Irish countryside every year, designed to attract tourists without any of the unsavory aspects of Ireland's ancient markets and fairs.

Conclusions

While there has long been kitsch available for purchase in Ireland's souvenir shops, the stuffed shamrocks, pots of gold, and wee ceramic leprechauns are only one small piece of the tourism puzzle. The conscious desire to present the "best" of Ireland was far more prevalent. Tourism developers, whether at the local or national level, all hoped to present a positive image of the Irish people and to stave off economic malaise, yet beyond this consensus, different opinions about how best to define "Ireland" for tourists were obvious. Was it a Gaelic-speaking country or an Anglophone one? Were the Irish a modern nation with family-friendly values or a traditional country in which man and beast were intimately linked?

The story of the cultural presentation of Irishness for tourists suggests two main conclusions. First, as with the debate surrounding tourism as a national interest, the presentation of Irish culture was a collective process. Language enthusiasts were every bit as vocal as tourism advocates, even if their view ultimately failed to win the day. Those who enjoyed traditional fairs added their voices to the debate just as did those who favored more modern and respectable tourist festivals. Outsiders such as tourists, Pan-American Airlines, Dutch graphic designers, and Festival of Britain planners all had an influence on events in Ireland just as did those who had lived in Ireland all their lives; tourism product development was a collective process. Second, cultural images were not unchanging artifacts of the colonial past. While older images were maintained when they met contemporary needs, it was just as possible to abandon older ideas when demands changed. Just as the conception of Ireland's "national interest" evolved with time, so too did ideas about the cultural appearance of the nation itself. In short, tourist images were hardly a "weight" around Irish necks. Instead these images were a canvas upon which the Irish (including tourist authorities and local communities) could paint their own vision of themselves: a vision of friendly, welcoming, industrious, and independent people.

5

Tourism and the Past

Like language and culture, history plays a significant role in imagining the nation. National groups find their "ultimate moorings in history."[1] A shared past provides the nation with legitimacy, allowing nationalists to catalog the numerous challenges successfully faced by their ancestors, to recount the countless glorious deeds carried out over time, and to lay claim to territory that has been (or should have been) in the possession of the nation since the beginning of time.[2] The past creates a structure for "the world as a product of the interplay of various communities, each possessing a unique character and history, and each the result of specific origins and developments."[3] Nationalists need only remind their compatriots of the past to inspire a desire to relive old glories, thus revitalizing the nation for a new age.[4]

Just as genuine Irish culture provided a challenge to the positive stereotypes of Irishness, so too the realities of Irish political history posed a formidable barrier to the portrayal of Irish welcoming friendliness to all visitors. On the one hand, Ireland's modern history was largely defined by nationalist struggle against English rule, while on the other, English tourists represented the single largest source of tourism earnings in Ireland: some £24.3 million per annum in 1962.[5] At the same time, memory of Ireland's Civil War was still rife during the 1950s and even the 1960s. Thus, while in theory nationalists need only point to a few specific historical events in order to energize their countrymen and countrywomen, the Irish case suggests that matters can be significantly more complicated. While it is one thing to agree that a nation has a common past, it is another thing altogether to agree on precisely what that past was. Which stories are most important? Who are the heroes and who the villains? In a country like Ireland where civil war has blighted the national memory, which faction should take precedence? Yet the challenge of presenting Irish history to tourists was not limited to problems with historic memory. Access to the Irish landscape, and to historic sites, was contested. Limited funds, or at least a failure by government officials to provide adequate funds, and the necessity of linking site-development efforts to international trends also played a role in shaping the Irish heritage product.

This chapter examines the presentation of Irish history to tourists from 1923 to the end of the century. The initial development of historic sites for tourist consumption mirrors closely the larger debate about the position of tourism as a national interest. The first portion of this chapter traces the efforts by preservationists and antiquarians to obtain legislation to protect Ireland's historic places. The chapter then recounts the early efforts of the statutory tourist authorities to develop and present historic sites to visitors, paying particular attention to both the choice of sites and the narratives chosen to accompany them. Careful notice is paid to the strong desire to avoid all controversy, while also exploring, as a focal example, the development of Kilmainham Jail as a museum—a project that at first seems to fly in the face of the usual conservative approach to developing historic sites. It is argued that the Kilmainham development was possible only because the story of the prison was manipulated to reduce controversy while presenting Irish history as a unified struggle for liberty and freedom. The final section examines how larger trends in the presentation of "heritage" have helped to define the character of Ireland's heritage tourism products.

The Past as Irish Tourist Attraction

Although the heritage industry is relatively recent,[6] the use of historic sites as a tourist attraction is not. In the ancient world, Egyptian and Greek ruins fascinated Roman tourists.[7] Much more recently, "modern" tourists from across Europe were fascinated by ancient ruins from at least the early nineteenth century and found these places both mysterious and romantic. In Ireland, Victorian visitors were attracted to places like Glendalough, Newgrange, Clonmacnois, and Monasterboice, drawn by aesthetics, not historical narrative. From the very beginning of the tourist movement after the Civil War, the Irish Tourist Association recognized the potential attractiveness of historic sites and made a conscious effort to present places like the Gallarus Oratory on the Dingle Peninsula and the various ruined castles and monasteries near the Killarney lakes to interested tourists. The first editions of *Ireland: Official Publication* made a point of addressing, in words and pictures, Ireland's impressive collection of historic sites. The guide informed visitors that "Ireland is of special interest to the antiquary, the number of ancient monuments of many kinds being extraordinarily great."[8] Throughout the 132-page guidebook the ITA included images of churches, high crosses, round towers, Neolithic sites, the Gallarus Oratory, the Rock of Cashel, and other notable ancient sites.

Early visitors displayed interest in the past, though for most tourists this interest appears to have been limited to the scenic attributes of ruined buildings—continuing the Victorian love affair with "romantic" ruins—and the legends and stories attached to many of the sites; more contemporary events were seldom mentioned.[9] Archie Bell, the travel writer from Ohio, thrilled at his driver's exciting tales of the origins of castles and of the various Killarney-area ruins, not to mention the ruins of Brian Boru's castle, various ancient burial places, and the stunning detail in the Book of Kells.[10] Likewise, "Kuklos," an English travel writer, expressed awe at the sight of the Gallarus Oratory and drew attention to the local legends about fairies guarding the beehive huts at Dunquin near Slea Head, Co. Kerry.[11] Little attention was paid, either by tourists or the Tourist Association, to the actual history of the sites/sights in question.

Government officials were conscious at a very early stage of the importance of preserving historic sites, although the fact that tourism had not yet achieved widespread recognition as a national interest meant that tourism was seldom, if ever, used as a justification for preserving ancient ruins. As early as 1925, academics began to call for the Irish Free State to "take its place among the other nations of Europe" by passing an act that would preserve ancient sites. Officials argued,

> It is hardly necessary for us to dwell here upon the importance of the preservation of ancient monuments; that is admitted by the common consent of the civilised world. In Ireland such preservation is doubly necessary: first, because education in the past has not been such as to develop in the people at large an understanding of the value of ancient monuments; and secondly, because of the great importance of Irish antiquities for an understanding of the early civilisation not merely of Ireland but also of Europe.

If anything, the Civil War made Irish antiquities even more valuable "as survivors from the wreck."[12]

The desire to put Irish preservation into a European context is telling and it demonstrates that the symbols of national identity are not created in isolation. The preservation movement was European in scope and was almost always tied in one way or another to a nationalist impulse. Although Pope Pius II passed the first preservationist edicts during the fifteenth century,[13] most European countries generated either nationalist preservation groups or state-sponsored monuments acts beginning in the middle of the nineteenth century. France, for example, passed its hugely influential Historic Monuments Act in 1887 following a growing nationalist preservation movement with roots in the French Revolution.[14] In Germany, Göethe expressed preservationist ideas as early as the 1770s, but the first widespread interest in saving ancient structures emerged only after German unification and during a period of pronounced German nationalist feeling. State-sponsored monuments acts followed later.[15] In virtually every case, preservationists insisted on the national importance of preserving the past. Victor Hugo, for example, declared that "long histories make great peoples," indicating that physical markers of the past serve to remind people of their glorious history.[16] Likewise, Bismarck reportedly insisted that it was "of greatest harm to a nation when it allows the living consciousness of its connection to its heritage and history to fade."[17] Built structures represented, insisted German preservationists, a corporeal link to the past. Thus University College Dublin archaeologist R. A. S. MacAlister,[18] one of the primary architects of early Irish preservation, echoed the larger discourse when he stressed that preservation and archaeological study represented "a truer patriotism."

The introduction of monuments legislation shortly after the Civil War was both a means of expressing the modern state's connection to the glorious Irish past *and* a way of putting the new state into the same orbit as the major European powers. Failure to establish monuments legislation would have represented not just the rejection of the anguished pleas of a few hypereducated intellectuals but also the rejection of the widely accepted discourse of modern European nationalisms. Ireland would have been alone in Europe—hardly a viable strategy at a time when the new Irish government hoped to introduce Ireland into the pantheon of nation-states.

While there had been isolated calls for the protection of Irish monuments before 1921, all responsibility for such efforts rested with the British government.[19] Whereas English legislation was careful not to diminish the rights of landholders by depending on goodwill rather than enforced restrictions, legislation addressing Ireland placed more control in the hands of the Office of Public Works than it did landowners.[20] The first Irish preservation act, the Irish Church Act, was passed in 1869. England had to wait thirteen years for a similar statute. This legislation placed many Irish churches under the protection of the government. The Ancient Monuments Protection Act of 1882 assured the preservation of further sites and a special Irish monuments act was passed in 1892 in order to add still more relics. By 1904, 189 Irish monuments were protected and £1,000 per year was provided for the upkeep of important ancient and monastic sites.[21]

Perhaps as a result of the long struggle over Irish property, from the very beginning of debate regarding a Free State monuments act concerns were raised that any protection of ancient monuments would interfere with property rights, a contention that preservation advocates took immediate exception to. As far as preservationists were concerned, "a man is regarded rather as a steward of his property than as absolute owner." These sites were of national importance, and it was not acceptable that any landowner should deprive future generations of the ability to enjoy these places.[22]

During the 1920s, perhaps even more than access, the biggest danger to Ireland's ancient sites was from individuals who freely removed inscribed stones or other monuments either for sale or for their own enjoyment. In an impassioned letter to the Irish president, MacAlister stressed that legislation was required immediately to guarantee the preservation of Ireland's ancient sites, in spite of the country's difficult financial and tenuous political situation. He made particular reference to inscribed stones, which he considered "especially valuable national heritage" because "every specimen is unique; and every specimen lost or destroyed is a definite national loss." MacAlister cited his recent visit to Loughcrew megalithic cemetery, where he discovered that one sculptured slab had been removed: "What has become of it is impossible to say; but everyone who could hire a donkey could easily have removed it and sold it."[23] Many other sites were threatened by farmers who raided the ruins for construction supplies or who plowed through ancient earthworks while trying to improve tillage land.

Protecting Irish Heritage

The major challenge in drafting legislation was to develop language that would provide the required protection while not being offensive to or undermining the rights of landowners. The solution to this problem rested largely with the development of an acceptable definition of the type of monuments to be protected. In the context of the time, it was a fairly easy decision. Although the English Georgian Society began advocating for the protection of eighteenth-century structures beginning in 1933, before the 1940s and 1950s most European preservationists focused on buildings constructed before 1700.[24] The Irish were no exception. Whether in Ireland or elsewhere, older buildings tended to inspire less political or aesthetic controversy while at the same time drawing attention to a long heroic past. Thus Irish legislators assumed a very specific and chronologically limited definition of "ancient monuments"; monuments were

> held to comprise all remains bearing upon the racial characteristics or the social, political, artistic, or religious history of the Irish people. It shall include religious history of the Irish people. It shall include religious and secular buildings of all kinds, whether still in use or not, and ruins thereof; fortifications and other structures of stone or earth; lake-dwellings; burial mounds or other sepulchral monuments of all kinds and their contents, including the bodies or bones of the dead; inscribed and sculptured stones; dolmens, stone circles, and all other megalithic monuments; written records in any language, on paper, parchment, or other writing materials; and all portable weapons, garments, implements, utensils, and ornaments whatsoever, in stone, pottery, metal, bone, wood, or other materials, as well as human bones, shells, and animal bones, the contents of ancient midden heaps and cave deposits. The year 1800 A.D. shall be deemed "ancient," except in the case of manuscripts in the Irish language, when the limit shall be 1850 A.D.[25]

While it was not widely discussed, this definition conveniently eliminated consideration of most sites tied to the long struggle for Irish independence, minimizing potential conflict with the British and ensuring that painful political differences and social divisions within Irish society would remain absent from discussion.

Although initially proposed in 1925, appropriate legislation languished behind other priorities until it was finally passed in 1930. The new act made it illegal to damage protected historic sites or to export valuable items of historic significance, and, most important, it outlined the government's ability to claim guardianship over major sites.[26] According to the act, the commissioners of public works could, with approval from the Department of Finance, acquire important sites, either by using legal force or by being entrusted with care of the site by deed. Local authorities could also be entrusted with the care of major sites, though supervisory responsibility was always vested in the Office of Public Works. Guardianship did not necessarily ensure that a given site would be made accessible to the public unless the government owned the monument, although the bill did provide the commissioners with access rights. Finally, in cases where the commissioners believed that a national monument faced imminent damage or destruction, they could file a preservation order, imposing an immediate halt to harmful activity and forcing the landowner to allow access to the Office of Public Works in order to repair any damage.[27]

Role of the Tourist Board

In spite of the importance assigned to historic sites in ITA guidebooks, tourism authorities spent precious little energy on the improvement or development of such sites before 1952. For this situation there were three reasons. First, the 1939 Tourist Traffic Act was primarily designed to promote the improvement and construction of hotels and tourist resorts, not historic sites. Second, the Office of Public Works had statutory authority over Ireland's national monuments, and Public Works was concerned with restoration and preservation, not the promotion of tourism; in fact, it was standard policy to erect signs warning people to stay away from historic sites; little or no effort was made to provide interpretative signage.[28] Finally, government officials gave scant attention to the fact that historic sites were of particular interest to tourists. The prevailing wisdom was simply that tourists wanted to enjoy natural scenery and take pleasure from the Irish coastal resorts, not visit ancient piles.

Despite official ambivalence, the Irish Tourist Association, with some assistance from the Irish Tourist Board, used the war years to develop a catalogue of potential postwar tourist attractions throughout Ireland. Thirty-three surveyors carried out the project. These men conducted "a thorough exploration of every parish [through] contact[s] with local authorities, development committees, sporting, archaeological, cultural, and other organisations, with clergy, teachers, Gardaí, and various other individuals";[29] their efforts marked an even more ambitious undertaking than the association had tackled in 1926 when the ITA attempted to complete a photographic survey of the country.[30] As far as the association was concerned, the facilities survey represented "one of the most important activities undertaken by the ITA since its inception." The project took four years and was finally completed in September 1945.[31]

Even after the ITA survey, government thinking remained static during the 1940s, and it was not until the release of the reports of the Christenberry and Hotels Commission that official attitudes about the relationship between historic and cultural sites and tourism began to shift. In his report Christenberry explained that most Irish-Americans came from poor agricultural areas and lacked any real knowledge of Ireland's historic and religious shrines. It followed that Irish castles would have a "positive appeal" for Americans, while the country's cathedrals, churches, and shrines would attract Irish-American Catholics.[32] At the same time the Irish Hotels Commission stressed that religious and historical sites were of particular interest to American tourists and urged that "a complete survey of our guide-book literature should be undertaken with the least possible delay, and that historical and archaeological societies should be invited to co-operate in the preparation of new issues."[33]

Whether as a result of these reports or not, when Seán Lemass began to consider comprehensive tourism legislation following Fianna Fáil's 1951 election victory, he made it clear that "the proposal for the exploitation of national monuments and shrines" was an especially important part of his tourism-development plans. As a result, Lemass provided powers of compulsory acquisition to An Bord Fáilte in the 1952 Tourist Traffic Act, and he also directed the Tourist Board to erect signage, enhance access to historic sites, and improve the quality of tourism literature. In spite of considerable debate and outright opposition from the Office of Public Works, which considered the provision of such powers to the Tourist Board to be "fundamentally unsound,"[34] the new powers were included with the rest of the new tourism legislation.

Even before passage of the 1952 tourism act, An Bord Fáilte had undertaken an assortment of development projects. Initially, board activities were limited to the erection of signposts to "some of our most important tourist attractions and many of our finest archaeological sites." It was hoped that the program would increase interest in historic places in almost every county in Ireland. At the same time men such as the Rev. Denis Ó Floinn, a professor of Irish at Maynooth College, urged An Bord Fáilte to put up signs intended to provide tourists with "a coherent idea" of the "glorious history" at the country's various historic sites. An Bord Fáilte soon followed this advice and approached the local authorities in Kerry, Donegal, and Wicklow to encourage them to assist in the campaign by erecting signs provided by the Tourist Board.[35]

In order to carry out the signage project, the Tourist Development Board hired Patrick Hartnett, an archeologist employed by the National Museum who was best known for his excavation of the Fourknocks passage tomb in County Meath, to compose straightforward informational signs, including data about when, by whom, and why a given structure was created.[36] Narratives that might have proven in any way contentious were stripped from the information presented to tourists. Even so, by contextualizing a site like Mellifont Abbey, with its famous Cistercian ruins, the board redefined the monuments there to say something about medieval Irish Christianity, showing continuity between Catholicism in that distant era and the faithfulness of contemporary Ireland.[37]

Early Efforts

Little was done to improve historic sites, beyond the erection of signs, until July 1953. An Bord Fáilte recognized that both the Office of Public Works and, to a lesser extent, the local authorities were opposed to having the Tourist Board undertake any activities related to the preservation of historic sites. Before commencing any major projects and in an effort to address conflicting opinions, An Bord Fáilte held a series of meetings with advisory committees in Cavan, Donegal, Galway, Louth, Offaly, Roscommon, Sligo, Tipperary, Waterford, Wicklow, Cork, Dublin, Kildare, Limerick, and Meath; the purpose of these meetings was "to explain in detail how An Bord Fáilte might be of assistance in problems concerning monuments in their district and to inspect with the members as many sites as possible."[38] During the course of these and subsequent meetings, the tourist authorities took note of sites that might warrant publicity as well as locations that would require development work in order to prepare them to accommodate increased tourist traffic. Tourism officials paid special attention to determining the identity of the relevant landowners at each site, because "unrestricted access to the sites" would come only as a result of "goodwill." Board officials were very much aware that "we must clear the ground by securing the goodwill of the local people, otherwise nothing can be done. With all the powers of the National Monuments Act . . . , we cannot appropriate private property."[39] Although this was not strictly true, given that compulsory acquisition of national monuments was permitted under both the 1930 Monuments Act and the 1952 Tourist Traffic Act,[40] the reality was (and is) that a clear line was drawn between public and private land—a line that the government has been loath to cross, regardless of the archeological, scenic, or historic importance of the sites involved. While the government was willing to forcefully acquire land for low-income housing and even industrial development, it was not willing to exercise the same authority in the name of historic or scenic sites (see chapter 6).[41]

Once the goodwill of local landowners was obtained, the Tourist Board undertook an assortment of limited projects from 1954 to the early 1960s and provided development grants after that. At different times the Tourist Board provided lighting for the Lusitania Memorial at Cobh,[42] improved parking facilities at various sites, developed the approach to the cloisters at Mellifont Abbey,[43] cleaned up graveyards and cleared vegetation,[44] built a small shelter and toilet facilities at Newgrange,[45] and carried out other related projects. The ITB seldom (if ever) overlapped in its operations with those of the Office of Public Works as Public Works had feared, and the board did not become directly involved in large-scale restoration work.

The conservative nature of Tourist Board (and Office of Public Works) activities from the 1950s through the 1970s was defined primarily by budgetary constraints. Not only did the board lack adequate funding for development projects, but Public Works was similarly strapped for cash. Kevin O'Doherty, responsible for the Tourist Board's development efforts during the 1950s, recalls that the National Monuments Division of the Office of Public Works had an annual budget of just £4,000 during the early 1950s—an amount easily spent on one minor project.

More aggressive development, like the reconstruction of Bunratty Castle or the restoration of Kilmainham Jail, had to be accomplished through private initiative. At Bunratty Castle, one of Ireland's most famous and popular tourist attractions since it opened in 1960, restoration and development was made possible by the energy of the site's owner, Lord Gort, by archeologist John Hunt, and the by Shannon Free Airport Development Company. Although the project had to be approved by the Office of Public Works (Public Works approval was reluctantly given) and received development grants from Bord Fáilte, it was certainly not a government project; this was also true of the other Shannon-area castle developments at Knappogue, Dunguaire, and Craggaunowen. The idea, first put forward in 1962, to create an historic park and to hold medieval banquets at Bunratty was also the product of private initiative by the group noted above.[46]

Choosing Sites and Narratives

It was relatively easy for the Office of Public Works and Department of Finance to focus their preservation efforts because they were primarily concerned with sites brought to their attention as needing immediate protective action. Likewise Bord Fáilte was limited by significant budget constraints and was thus forced to restrict its activities to access development, occasional minor restoration (as at Mellifont Abbey), and the installation of signage. Even so, other considerations often had to be taken into account. Were sites long-standing stops on the tourist trail, as were Glendalough or Clonmacnois? Were there larger political or memory questions to be considered? Just how expensive would any restoration be? A site's status as one that was particularly important in the story of the Irish nation did not necessarily equate to government recognition that restoration was in the "national interest." The authorities were more than willing to ignore restoration requests when the history involved might prove contentious.

While sites were chosen for development on a case-by-case basis, and while no documents survive that lay out a clear selection process, sites designated for development were overwhelmingly ancient or medieval in nature. Taken as a whole, these sites reflect larger European preservation trends while also suggesting a vision of Ireland that is at once timeless and pious, a land of saints and scholars, heroic chieftains, and ancient mysteries. It was equally important to the tourist authorities that sites be easily understandable to visitors. For example, early consideration was given to tourist development at the Hill of Tara, but it was determined that it would be too costly to make the collection of grass-covered mounds understandable to tourists; at the very least, a full-time guide would be needed at the site.[47] It also appears that the board consciously decided *against* developing some sites, such as the passage tombs at Loughcrew, in order to "save them for ourselves."[48]

Even if there was a reluctance to develop a few choice sites, others virtually demanded attention. The monastic "city" at Glendalough, Co. Wicklow, was one such place. During the height of Victorian tourism this site, with its beautiful round tower, its curious oratory named for the site's founder St. Kevin, and the stunning mountainous panorama surrounding the ruins, was always a favorite of visitors from England.[49] Post–Civil War tourist organizations showed a similar level of interest, and Bord Fáilte accumulated a disproportionate number of Glendalough photographs in its photographic archive—not because of political pressure, as at Killarney, but because the site simply lent itself to the gaze of tourist and camera alike.[50] In 1951 Córas Iompair Éireann led tours to the monastic city, and most visitors reportedly found it to be a high point of their trip.[51]

Even popularity did not guarantee prompt and thorough restoration. Although Glendalough was among the seven hundred sites under Office of Public Works protection in 1949,[52] it remained largely neglected and uncared for. In 1951 Peadar S. Doyle, TD, submitted a question to the Office of the Taoiseach and then to the minister of finance that noted that Glendalough was "losing its natural beauty due to the absence of a responsible authority for preserving the surroundings." Doyle wondered if An Taisce, the Irish National Trust, would take action, or whether the relevant government department would step in to ensure the proper level of maintenance and preservation.[53] Doyle was not the only critic. The Rev. Denis Ó Floinn referred to the government's "shameful disregard for our holy places" and argued that if located in continental Europe, Glendalough would be beautifully presented to visitors, who would find a "coherent idea" of the site's history.[54] Public Works contended that its officials had no "executive functions or funds," and argued that the local authorities should take responsibility for sites like Glendalough. For academics like Michael J. O'Kelly of University College Cork, it was not a question of finger-pointing but of preserving this "irrevocable" link "with the country's whole cultural inheritance, ecclesiastical and secular." It was not possible to excuse allowing sites like Glendalough to "crumble to dust or become overwhelmed in a jungle of overgrowths."[55]

After the passage of the 1952 Tourist Traffic Act, Bord Fáilte went some distance toward correcting the problem at Glendalough by constructing a new parking area and making other access improvements, while also developing ground plans to assist in the exhibition of the site. The plans showed "the original layout and existing remains," noting "the various periods to which these remains belong and [assisting] visitors in their examinations of the buildings by indicating clearly the various sections—cloister, nave, etc."[56] It was a substantial step forward but still failed to meet the complete satisfaction of Erskine Childers, the future president of the Republic, who was so filled with development ideas that he had a habit of jotting them down on a notepad that he kept for the purpose by his bedside.[57] Among his ideas Childers proposed a development at Muckross House (see below) and another at Glendalough. Monastic history fascinated Childers, and he wrote to the taoiseach in 1962 that a museum featuring Irish missionary work from the fourth to the eighth centuries should be built behind the Royal Hotel at Glendalough. The displays would stress Ireland's proud history as a home for saints and scholars as well as its heritage of bringing spiritual knowledge to the heathens beyond its shores. Such a museum would address the conversion of England and the foundation of English cathedrals by the Irish, the scientific studies carried out by Irish monks during the time of Charlemagne, and the efforts of Irish saints such as St. Dunstan, St. Fiacra, and St. Columbanus (Columcille) to convert heathens on the continent and in Britain. Childers enthusiastically noted that much of the material, including photographs, translations, dioramas, maps, and "modern devices for dramatising journeys and fields of activity," including "a film or two . . .

[and] tape recordings, etc," would have to be constructed.[58] It was certainly a creative proposal, perhaps even before its time, but it was not greeted with enthusiasm. Lemass did "look into" the scheme, perhaps out of friendship or loyalty, but he ultimately dismissed it because the topic was too controversial. According to the taoiseach, historians believed the scanty source material to be "unreliable":

> For example, historians may feel that statements about the conversion of England to Christianity by us may need some qualification if a true impression is to be given to the public; there are conflicting opinions, in fact, about the conversion of Ireland to Christianity (one is that the mission to Armagh was distinct from the mission to Tara—that it was significantly earlier and undertaken by a different missionary). In the present controversial state of this matter it may be felt premature for the Office of Public Works to formulate an official state version of this very important part of our history.[59]

While it is now difficult to imagine holding back the development of a museum because of inconclusive evidence (such a thing certainly seems unlikely in the present age of mushrooming heritage centers), at the time the state's unwillingness to take a firm stand on an official state history was fully in keeping with its lack of interest in providing state funding for the restoration of Kilmainham Jail or for other modern-history sites. The development of historical sites had to meet a series of criteria that included low cost, willing landowners, and a complete lack of controversy.

While the absence of development of more recent sites of historical significance is striking, it must be made clear that the revolutionary struggle was not forgotten. During the period from the foundation of a statutory tourist authority through the 1960s, the struggle with England was very much a part of public culture in the form of a campaign by the Dublin Brigade of the Old IRA to establish a Garden of Remembrance near the Rotunda Hospital,[60] calls for the restoration of Kilmainham Jail, and a massive commemoration of the Easter Rising in 1966. In each case the major focus was on the role that memory work would have for domestic consumption, though tourism did have an important place in the Kilmainham Jail Restoration Society's original proposal.

The tendency to avoid modern history in the development of tourist sites can be explained by three likely causes. First, in the wake of the Civil War there was a desire to relegate unpleasant divisions into the dark recesses of the unspoken past. As late as the 1950s Ireland's political leaders continued to be divided by memories of the Civil War. Living together peacefully required pushing this bleak chapter of the nation's history into the background. It was not that the past was forgotten, only that "silence was better than hypocrisy," and it was easier than feeling disgust at having done to fellow Irishmen what the British had done so recently to them.[61] Second, after 1959, when state finances began to improve, the commemoration of Ireland's revolutionary struggle had immediate policy implications for the country's relationship with Northern Ireland. With the ascension of Lemass to the taoiseach's office in 1959, Irish policy toward Northern Ireland changed to one of advocating cooperation. This change, combined with the primacy of tourism as a point of common effort, made it important for the Republic to carefully consider the implications of tourism activities in light of the government's desire to create a smooth working relationship with the North. Finally, and perhaps most obviously, the overwhelming majority of tourists in Ireland have always been from mainland Britain. Given this dependence on tourists from across the Irish Sea, it is hardly surprising that Irish tourist promoters have not gone out of their way to emphasize conflict with Britain.

Nevertheless, occasional development proposals were made and private initiatives were free to move ahead. In 1938, Arthur R. Vincent and his wealthy American in-laws, who had purchased Muckross House for Vincent and his wife as a wedding present, gave the house in Killarney to the state. The estate was expansive, covering ten thousand acres of scenic land around the Killarney lakes, and Vincent believed that it would provide a valuable park for the Irish people and thus serve as a fitting memorial to his late wife.[62] Faced with possession of the new lands, the state was immediately plunged into uncertainty about what to do with the property. At various points the space was considered for commercial development, a hostel (Vincent's preference), a religious retreat, a biological research station, a dairy instruction center, a country residence for the president of Ireland, a hotel, a convalescent home, a civil-service training facility, and a folk museum.[63] It is the folk museum proposal that will concern us here.

Like the missionary museum at Glendalough, the folk-museum concept was born during one of Erskine Childers's late-night epiphanies in 1962. Initially he suggested a "museum of the Irish heritage from the sixteenth century to the present day," including American presidents of Irish heritage; the inventor of the torpedo, turbine, and submarine; the first steel worker in the Ruhr valley; famous Irish actors and playwrights; and so on.[64] In the following year Childers expanded dramatically on his idea for both the house and its grounds. He suggested that the grounds be developed to include extensive footpaths so that tourists could enjoy beautiful views of the Killarney lakes, and that the gardens be expanded and embellished. Careful study was to be done to ensure a balance between motor access and the traditional jaunting-car route to and from the house. Picnic facilities were to be developed and located in such a way as to limit their impact on the surroundings. Muckross House itself would be turned into a museum featuring rotating exhibits from various state museums, including Irish silver, lace, furniture, tweeds, and couture, as well as traditional cottage implements, domestic ware, etc. Waterford glass and Waterford chandeliers would receive prominent placement, as would Irish ceramics, art, and historic portraits. Photographic exhibits would display Celtic crosses and Irish abbeys, while "first-class" Irish souvenirs would be available. More striking still, Childers suggested that a room be set aside to display material from the "1916 Rising or the general struggle for independence," and that another room be devoted to "national progress." Beyond merely displaying artifacts of Irish history and culture, Childers dreamed of developing Muckross as a first-class museum, and he therefore suggested that scholars be brought in to advise, local experts be consulted, lectures on Irish history be offered, conferences be run, garden tours be given, and Irish dancing, song, and orchestral music be performed.[65] The plan was nothing if not ambitious, and Childers immediately began working to develop support, enlisting the backing of Arthur Vincent, who expressed disgust at the other leading suggestion—that Muckross House be used as a training facility for civil servants.[66] An Taisce also favored the folk-museum proposal, dreaming that the Muckross estate might cater to American visitors captivated by the museum and to artists who would be inspired by the outdoor scenery and the beautiful objects within.[67] Similarly, at least one visiting Irish emigrant wrote to the *Irish Independent* to express his hope that the estate would be developed as a park rather than used for some other, less public purpose.[68] Local tourism interests also supported the museum plan.[69]

In spite of Childers's enthusiasm, the Vincent endorsement, and the other public support for the museum, the Department of Finance was outspoken in its opposition. As far as Finance was concerned, the museums in Dublin, Bunratty Castle, and the proposed folk museum at the Royal Hospital, Kilmainham,[70] were more than enough to satisfy the demands of visitors, while the proposed training facility might also serve as a hotel during the summer months, providing an enhanced return on the government's investment. At Killarney, Finance officials said, scenery should take precedence, not museum exhibits.[71]

In the end, however, Childers won the day. Widespread public support for a parklike facility at the Muckross estate trumped the Department of Finance. After opening to the public in June 1964, the "Bourne Vincent Memorial Park" attracted twenty thousand people to the house during the first year of public access.[72] In spite of a brief conflict in 1968 with local jarveys,[73] the museum and grounds have continued to be a popular addition to the tourist trail. Bord Fáilte cited the facility as a "successful experiment in interpretation and historical representation" in its 1981–85 tourism plan, hinting that others interested in developing heritage sites would do well to follow the Muckross model.[74] In 1989 the verdict was similarly positive, with *Irish Travel Trade News,* the industry journal, noting that the house, by then the headquarters for the Kerry Folklife Association and displayed in the "great house tradition," with some rooms devoted to interpretive displays, could be expanded to become even more attractive. Farm outbuildings could be turned into craft workshops, museums of folk life, displays of farm machinery, theatres for traditional entertainment, and even barn space for preserving "distinctive Kerry cattle."[75] Although the 1916 Rising and independence-struggle display was apparently never introduced, probably because it would have been too controversial, the Childers proposal proved attractive to tourists and a beneficial addition to the Killarney-area product mix, thus demonstrating that public pressure, well-organized political effort, and an unthreatening rural message could overcome opposition and achieve success.

Representations

When the past was to be presented to outsiders—in guidebooks, for example—every effort was made to assure that the representation that was offered was the *right one:* one that would not offend outsiders while also assuring equanimity within Ireland itself. The group best positioned to oversee such concerns was the Cultural Relations Committee that was established following World War II to undertake Ireland's "cultural propaganda" program (see chapter 2). Ireland faced a significant problem: it was largely unknown abroad. Even American St. Patrick's Day celebrations featured French and Scottish beverages over Irish ones. There were then no major Irish rock-and-roll bands, no offshore Irish pubs, and no Irish dancers thumping out their Celtic rhythms on the world's stages as would be the case during the tourism boom of the 1990s (see chapter 7). "We wanted to get Irish things known. Create an image of Ireland. It was something that was in everybody's interest, including [that of] the Department of External Affairs," recalls Michael Gorman, who was a member of the Cultural Relations Committee in 1958. From the beginning each member of the committee was on an equal footing—the government did not attempt to dominate the agenda—though tourism was a focal point for discussion because it was important to the Tourist Board, Aer Lingus, and CIÉ, while simultaneously creating a wider audience for Irish exports.[76] Though the Department of External Affairs originally proposed the creation of the Cultural Relations Committee, the semistate bodies, not External Affairs, soon dictated the group's agenda and scope. In 1960, for example, the department received five proposals about ways to expand publicity activities abroad. In considering the various suggestions, government officials were surprised to find that "our own proposals are by comparison [to those of the Tourist Board, etc.] extremely modest, palliatives rather than cures."[77] Tourism interests were literally shaping the government's approach to cultural propaganda and molding its effort to present Ireland in a favorable light internationally.

In keeping with the tourism industry's leading role in framing cultural policy, the Department of External Affairs did not usually intervene in the content of tourist publications. Instead, the department focused its efforts on ensuring that Irish consulates around the world were well stocked with tourist materials. In 1953, for example, the committee made certain that Fógra Fáilte's *Ireland of the Welcomes* magazine was distributed to cities in the United States, Canada, Brazil, Australia, Italy, Spain, the Netherlands, Sweden, England, France, and Belgium—a list that was maintained and expanded throughout the 1950s and 1960s.[78] Likewise, the Cultural Relations Committee made certain that guidebooks, tourist maps, and brochures were also widely available abroad.[79] Foreign consulates frequently requested additional materials, and a number of ambassadors took a special interest in distributing pamphlets and flyers to receptive parties.

The Department of External Affairs showed a strong interest in how Ireland was portrayed in guidebooks, magazine articles, and other publications, however: part of the reason that the department was so responsive to public pressure concerning the *Holiday* magazine feature (see introduction). Interest in the content of tourist publications was not limited exclusively to public scandals. On a day-to-day basis External Affairs commented on a variety of publications and in so doing they showed a desire to balance the need to avoid controversy with the need to maintain goodwill among the still politically divided population of the Republic. For example, Conor Cruise O'Brien, who served in the cultural wing of the Department of External Affairs during the early 1950s, was asked to comment about a guidebook called *Ireland for Everyman,* published by J. M. Dent and Sons of London. O'Brien replied that the "guide sections are good" but that the "brief outline of Irish history would be better omitted if it could not be improved." He argued that the period from the Act of Union forward was "seriously lacking" in balance, "and sections of it use language which would be quite in place in, say, a history of the French Resistance Movement by a German journalist." O'Brien complained that Emmet's rising was referred to as "'a mere street riot'—a reference which will certainly be regarded here as gratuitously offensive to Irish feeling." Likewise, the Great Famine was treated as little more than an economic catastrophe, with no indication of the Irish view that it was both economic and political and that the British deserved much of the blame. O'Brien took issue with a description of the 1867 Fenian Rising as "an outrage," saying that "if the Fenian risings were outrages, then all rebellions and revolutions against legally constituted authorities are outrages, and all governments now existing, based as they are on some series of outrages in the past, are really illegal conspiracies."[80] Four days after O'Brien submitted his comments, the J. M. Dent and Sons managing editor apologized and promised that the history section would be either dramatically revised or omitted from all future editions of the guide.[81]

Saving the "Bastille of Ireland"

Although the Irish government showed little interest in developing controversial sites of any kind, from the mid-1930s there *were* calls for the construction of sites commemorating recent revolutionary history. The most prominent of these requests was made by the Dublin Brigade of the Old IRA, which also called for the creation of a Garden of Remembrance at the Rotunda Gardens near Parnell Square in Dublin.[82] While it took thirty-one years for the idea to be realized, the government ultimately did create the garden with relatively little public controversy.[83]

Kilmainham Jail was potentially much more problematic. It was first opened in 1796 and functioned as an active prison until 1924. The jail was a product of the late-eighteenth-century prison-reform movement that placed an emphasis on punishing the mind (rather than taking revenge on the body), while also improving hygiene and thus humanitarian acceptability. The vast majority of convicts who passed through the prison were confined there for assault, burglary, shoplifting, rape, highway robbery, murder, bigamy, cattle stealing, and other such "common" crimes. During the Great Famine, for example, many afflicted people actively courted arrest in order to obtain relief, and the prison soon became vastly overcrowded. While life in the prison was unpleasant, at least there was food to eat. Even so, it is the political prisoners incarcerated there from the first day of prison operation who are placed front and center in the museum's narrative. The list of famous inmates includes Henry Joy McCracken, the Sheares brothers, Lord Edward Fitzgerald, Robert Emmet and Anne Devlin, Charles Stewart Parnell, members of the Young Irelanders, Fenians, and Invincibles, T. M. Healy, Michael Davitt, the 1916 leaders, Éamon de Valera, members of the IRA during the War of Independence, and numerous "Irregulars" during the Civil War.[84] Indeed, the first four Free State executions (November 1922) of anti-Treaty prisoners took place in the prison yard on the opposite side of a wall from the site used by British troops to kill the 1916 leaders.[85]

Given the prison's long history as an unwelcome home for Ireland's various nationalist heroes, the site was doubly challenging as regards tourist development. First, it raised troubling memories of the long conflict with England, and more damning still, the execution of Irregulars in the prison yard strongly associated Kilmainham with the still festering psychological wounds of bloody civil conflict. Given the desire to avoid these memories, it is hardly surprising that, when the prison was decommissioned in 1924, nobody called for its preservation. For most people Kilmainham Jail was a site of suffering more synonymous with oppression than heroism, better ignored or, at the very least, used for purposes other than official memory. At various points Kilmainham was utilized as a storage facility for materials being used in the Shannon Electricity Scheme,[86] was suggested for conversion to office space,[87] and avoided outright demolition only because the government was unwilling to foot the bill.[88] Nobody considered it important to preserve the prison.

By the late 1930s various groups showed increasing interest in Kilmainham. The most important development was a formal proposal by the National Graves Association, a republican organization devoted to the preservation of nationalist gravesites throughout Ireland, to develop the site as a memorial and museum to house artifacts related to the 1916 Rising.[89] The plan proposed the installation of a plaque at the site where members of the Irish National Invincibles were hanged in 1883 for the Phoenix Park murders.[90] At the site of the 1916 executions, a few hundred feet away, there was to be an eighteen-inch wall surmounted by grave-railings along with a fountain. A plaque was to proclaim, "On this hallowed spot the executed leaders of the Rising fell [followed by their names]."[91] The proposal made no mention of the Civil War executions that occurred roughly forty feet to the south, nor did it draw attention to the site where James Connolly had been shot, located on the opposite end of the stone-breakers' yard from the rest of the 1916 killings. The latter omission may have been the result of poor research by the Graves Association or of Connolly's Marxism, which was periodically raised as an issue during this period of intense anticommunism. Perhaps a different plan was simply judged undesirable from an architectural or political standpoint: better that the leaders be commemorated *together* in order to spatially demonstrate Irish unity in the fight for freedom. As will be noted below, just such a concern later provided the motivation behind the Kilmainham Jail Restoration Society's unwillingness to allow a separate Connolly memorial.

The commissioners of public works had no immediate objection to the Graves Association proposal, even suggesting to the Department of Education that a museum be developed at the site. Public Works officials estimated that the scheme would cost £600 to implement. In order to stock the museum with artifacts it was suggested that the "National Risings Collection" be relocated from the National Museum in Kildare Street to a new jail museum. The Department of Education rejected the proposal, however, on the grounds that the collection was a popular attraction at its present location, where it could be adequately cared for, whereas if moved to Kilmainham, the collection would likely deteriorate in the increasingly run-down prison buildings. Instead, Education officials suggested that the site could be maintained in its current condition, and paintings of revolutionary leaders mounted in their corresponding cells in order "to recall the history of the liberation movement," while the great hall of the jail could be fitted up to display the automobile collection then housed at Kildare Street. This was intended as a constructive suggestion, but it was quickly tabled at the onset of the Emergency in 1939.

Consideration of Kilmainham's restoration did not reemerge until the immediate aftermath of the war when the Office of Public Works commissioned an architectural inspection of the buildings. The results were distressing. Though the inspectors found that the walls were in no immediate danger of collapse, they alarmingly observed that "there is constant danger from falling slates, glass, and plaster, and . . . timber floors and roofs are far from safe." Under the circumstances the commissioners suggested that it would be extremely costly to repair and maintain the buildings: "Any considerable expenditure merely for the purpose of removing their present dangerous condition would not be worthwhile." Because the Department of Education was still unwilling to consider establishing a museum at the site, and given that the Office of Public Works believed that the building would not make acceptable office space, the commissioners recommended a limited preservation program. Their plan would have preserved those cellblocks having historical significance, as well as the yard where the 1916 executions had occurred, while the rest would have been disposed of for building purposes.[92]

This suggestion did not demand dramatic expense, but it functioned to pay lip-service to remembering Ireland's revolutionary history—a concern of at least a minority of the population during the immediate postwar years. Again, however, little happened.

By 1953, while the prison was rapidly descending into ruin, commemoration plans resurfaced. This time the Department of the Taoiseach initiated discussion of a prison-restoration and museum-development project—not because de Valera wanted to relive his days as a prisoner at Kilmainham, but as an employment scheme.[93] Unemployment in Ireland was reaching crisis levels and emigration was now a national disease. The restoration of Kilmainham Jail could provide jobs while meeting the republican desire to remember Ireland's proud fighting past. The planning committee adopted the old National Graves Association proposal, but once again little happened and the condition of the site continued to deteriorate with alarming rapidity. By 1955 the commissioners of public works warned that the public should no longer be allowed any access to the site. Slates were blowing off the roof, glass and plaster were falling, and ceilings were caving in. The situation had now reached a crisis. Kilmainham Jail was collapsing and would not last for many more years if the government persisted in its disinclination to act. If there was to be a solution, somebody or some organization outside the government would have to provide it.

The Restoration Society

The Kilmainham Jail Restoration Society began to gestate in the mind of a young North Dubliner named Lorcan C. G. Leonard in 1952. Leonard had become interested in the prison while waiting for a bus ten years earlier; he perceived a "friendliness" at the site that was almost certainly absent for most visitors, both past and present. Ten years later, Leonard and his friend Tommy O'Brien jointly agreed that the Invincibles had been unfairly exiled from Irish history and that something should be done about it. "Even radical republican thought . . . maintained an ignorance of them. Evidently, the efforts of the Invincibles were too 'earthy' for even their refined palates." The men's answer to this historical quandary was to plan a documentary film about the Invincibles and to use the proceeds to install a memorial at the jail. Among other potential collaborators Leonard contacted "Cre" O'Farrell,

Sean Dowling, and Paddy Stephenson. These men told Leonard that he was "dealing with a dangerous subject which is best left alone." Dowling eventually agreed to take part as long as his name was never formally associated with the project. The next step was to film key locations inside the prison itself—a task made impossible by the unwillingness of the Office of Public Works to provide access. The film project immediately foundered, but Leonard's interest in the prison did not.

Not long after the death of the movie idea, Leonard received word that the Office of Public Works was accepting bids from demolition companies to tear down the prison. Leonard was horrified: "This was indeed the last act of the philistines, who had already provided a rash of 'Mother Éire's' and Celtic crosses from one end of the country to the other to prove, I suppose, the respectable and Catholic character of the 'four glorious' years." Leonard quickly approached a friend and fellow member of the Old Dublin Society, Paddy Stephenson, who agreed to participate in any "mass action" to preserve the penitentiary.[94] Discussing the matter further, they hatched a plan to restore the site by using volunteer labor and donated materials in order to establish a museum, and communicated this intention to Sean Dowling, later chairman of the restoration campaign. They asked for help "in an effort to save Kilmainham Jail from the ravishes [*sic*] of time and the indifference of politicians," for "what was once [a] monument to heroic endeavour is now the silent mocking cavern to the indifference of our times." Good Irish men and women simply could not allow "the most holy spot in Ireland" to vanish into thin air.[95]

In September 1958, Leonard brought a small group together at Jury's Hotel in Dublin to discuss restoration plans. There was skepticism about the viability of a volunteer effort, but the participants kept talking. It did not take long for the group to agree that "in order to preserve unity of purpose, nothing relating to events after 1921 would be introduced into any activity, publicity, or statements in connection with Kilmainham." With a common understanding of the road ahead taking shape, Leonard began recruiting workers—primarily from among known republicans. Leonard and his colleagues believed that members of the Old IRA would furnish the bulk of volunteers because these men "needed no instruction on Kilmainham or its unique position" as a building of major significance in the republican history of Ireland.

Support began to mount. The Congress of Irish Trade Unions informed the fledgling society that the TUC would not frown on voluntary efforts to restore the jail, though it was unwilling to offer an official endorsement. Likewise, the Building Trades Council agreed to back a voluntary restoration effort. The Old IRA was also willing to aid the plan, but only on condition that "nothing of or relating to the period after 1921 would be identified with the Kilmainham project."[96] Dublin Corporation had already shown an interest in preserving the building and probably also supported the proposed idea, although Leonard does not specify whether he or his colleagues had contacted city councilors.[97] With all of the essential groups lined up in support of the plan, or at least not in opposition, the time had arrived to submit a proposal to the government.

While Leonard was pushing forward with his voluntary restoration scheme, the National Graves Association was also petitioning the government on behalf of the jail. As in 1938, it advocated plaques, a fountain, and grave-railings, but it now added the new elements of a pathway to the site of the graves of the Invincibles and a museum in the nineteenth-century great hall that would house "national relics, mementos, documents, guns, and other articles associated with our fight for freedom." Seán Fitzpatrick, the secretary of the association, told the press, "There is no place more intimately and dramatically associated with our fight for independence than Kilmainham, and no matter what else may be done in the way of memorials to our past, we all want Kilmainham restored and preserved. It is really the focal point of our centuries-long struggle."[98]

Likewise, the Old IRA Literary and Debating Society also lobbied the government to act on the restoration. Writing to de Valera, leaders of the Old IRA argued that the matter should be "treated as urgent," for the decaying jail should not be allowed to disappear:

> There is a craving for knowledge of local and national history waiting to be satisfied, and where better in a properly organised museum than in Kilmainham; make it the capitol's showplace for our people and a tourist attraction. Make that stone-breaking yard where our leaders died a Garden of Remembrance. We look forward to the day when that gaunt pile will be converted into a place of national pilgrimage, where the story of Ireland's long fight for freedom could be told better than [in] any history books.[99]

When Leonard's proposal appeared late in 1958, it must have been a welcome sight for Department of Finance officials. With pressure from the Graves Association and the Old IRA on the one hand and a lack of any real interest in spending money on an ever-more-expensive restoration program on the other, the new voluntary proposal appeared to be the best of all possible worlds.[100] The plan offered "a major step forward in civilian initiative" and promised returns "of immeasurable value to future generations, not to mention the immediate asset of a tourist attraction." The plan was also financially bold. Its authors estimated that the restoration could be accomplished in five years at a cost of £60,000 to £70,000 using entirely volunteer labor.[101] The plan left little room for government objection, and it was formally approved by the Department of Finance in February 1960.[102]

Above all, the Restoration Society viewed the jail as a national shrine, but they also believed that it would become a successful tourist site as well and they placed tourism at the forefront of their proposal. By 1958 many displayed a growing awareness of the important role that tourism could play in stimulating the lagging economy, especially following the publication of the *Programme for Economic Expansion*. Stressing tourism made it possible for the Society to both delineate a potential revenue stream and to hold the restoration up as an important element of national renewal. Thus restoring Kilmainham was to be a nationalist activity on multiple levels: it meant reclaiming and commemorating the nationalist past while at the same time striking a symbolic blow at the economic malaise of the 1950s. Thanks to the Society's proposal, tourism and Kilmainham were now closely joined, thus ensuring that the prison would become more than a site for domestic cultural consumption.

A Unifying Symbol

There was very little public conflict concerning the reconstruction—with one exception. Although the Civil War issue had been erased early in the process, the treatment to be accorded to the Marxist leader of the Citizen Army, James Connolly, remained a stumbling block. In September 1966 the Labour party proposed the erection of a special Connolly memorial in the yard where he had been executed—on the wall opposite from where the other executed 1916 leaders had fallen. Such a memorial was absent from the

Graves Association proposal, and it was similarly excluded from the Restoration Society's plans. According to Sean Dowling, chairman of the Restoration Society, the unwillingness to provide a separate memorial *on that spot* was not politically motivated in any way. Dowling argued, "James Connolly belonged to the whole Irish people and not to any political party, not even to the one he founded." As a result, the society "decided . . . that no separate plaque to any leader would be permitted in the execution yard, but that the Labour party might erect a plaque to the memory of Connolly anywhere else in the jail." For the Labour party this solution was unacceptable. Its leaders charged in their reply that the Restoration Society was clearly "subservient" to Fianna Fáil and alleged that "the republican party" was using the prison for its own ends—accusations that were strenuously denied by Dowling.[103] Perhaps as a measure of the popularity of the restoration project, the public in general sided with the society. One Labour supporter argued, "A separation [of the 1916 leaders] would diminish both Connolly and the other signatories [of the proclamation of the republic]."[104] Another letter writer, who did not specify his political affiliation, "fully agree[d] with the committee's decision to keep the execution yard a sacred place, free from all references to present-day political parties."[105] By now Kilmainham Jail was not just the project of a few republicans anxious to remember 1916 rebels, the Invincibles, or activists in the War of Independence; it was instead a commemoration of Irish national identity, a symbol not only of the nation's past but also of its present.

What made the site so powerful in cultural terms was that its restoration was almost entirely a grassroots effort—just as had been proposed. During the reconstruction of the prison the Kilmainham Jail Restoration Society received only small contributions from the Irish government. In 1966, Seán Lemass wrote to Dowling to inform him that monies collected from the pool at the newly opened Garden of Remembrance near Parnell Square would be donated to the society—a grand sum of some £50.[106] In addition, the government did provide £1,000 per year through the Office of Public Works to cover insurance for the workers,[107] and furnished roughly a hundred glass display cases for the museum.[108] Government officials, however, were far less forthcoming when the society requested roof slates valued at £1,500.[109] Overwhelmingly the costs of restoration were met through voluntary contributions from individuals, businesses, and other organizations willing to support the project—a significant indication of how popular the restoration eventually became. Not only did the voluntary nature of the project allow the society to work around unpleasant memories, but it also reshaped the central memory of the prison into that of a site representing the *whole* of Ireland. The project would not have been possible without government approval, but the lack of government funding or other major official involvement kept tourist authorities well clear of the enterprise. This made it possible to evade the fact that the conflict commemorated had been with the British—Ireland's single largest tourism market, valued at some £24.3 million annually in 1962.[110] In addition, the Civil War was removed from the table as a subject of contention, and only positive memories of Irish nationalist activity were specifically invoked. Most important of all, it was the voluntary effort of disparate nationalist groups that made the reconstruction possible—men from both sides of the Civil War conflict and from all age and social groups.

From the beginning the Restoration Society drew careful attention to the workers. In their first newsletter the leaders of the group boasted that the number of workers now included "over two hundred tradesmen and skilled workers giving of their spare time, working hard night after night and on Saturday afternoons. Praise is silenced. Let what must be said of this magnificent effort be said afterwards—now is the time for work and effort." Of course, these sentiments did not stop them from pointing out that the workers were of "all ages and walks of life," that "lads of 15 and 17 years" were present along with 80-year-old veterans, Dublin dock workers, and even an ex-British army sergeant.[111] When Lemass visited the site in 1964 to survey progress, he was lavish in his tribute: "The work of restoration to the buildings was of national importance. The work already carried out by voluntary labour was . . . truly remarkable."[112] He was echoing a sentiment that the media had stressed as early as 1962. The *Dublin Evening Mail,* for example, featured a story that consisted of short biographical sketches of the workers, and not, as might have been expected, of the numerous illustrious prisoners who had served time in the jail. Among the commonplace figures mentioned was Jim Bruce, who had worked on the prison since September 1960, focusing his attention on the roof; Damien and Raymond Cassidey, who had "devoted their evenings to rebuilding the jail since reconstruction began"; and Joe Magill, a bricklayer "who has found more bricks than enough to lay in his hours after work."[113] For a time at least, heroism was about giving something back to Ireland through the rebuilding of an historic site. Another paper went so far as to boast, "Who said idealism is dead in Ireland? Go to Kilmainham Jail any evening, even with snow on the ground, and you will find a living proof that the idealism of 40 years ago is still very much alive."[114] Even in 2003, the Dúchas guide to the prison recalled the restoration as "an epic feat of voluntary effort and enthusiasm achieved without the support of government grants."[115]

Through comments such as these, the voluntary labor to reconstruct the jail was itself integrated into the mythology of the prison, in effect adding to the register of heroes associated with the site. These workers may not have fired on an enemy, but they had taken aim at the economic and spiritual malaise that gripped Ireland in the 1950s, and they stood as flesh-and-blood reminders of the improving fortunes of the early 1960s. During the 1950s industrial output fell, the country's GNP dropped, unemployment climbed at an alarming pace, and between 1951 and 1956 the population fell 2.1 percent.[116] When "remarkable" growth replaced distressing decline in the early 1960s, the workers were already in place to symbolize the reversal.[117] Their labors were born of a need to draw people into a national rebuilding program, and their progress physically illustrated the success of those efforts at a time when the *Programme for Economic Expansion* was beginning to turn around the economy. The restoration project held up the spectacle of everyday Irish people physically demonstrating their national pride through distinctly corporal memory work. In striking contrast to the tens of thousands who emigrated during the 1950s, these ordinary Irish people were not only staying put but also constructing Kilmainham as a totem of the national struggle while they themselves became symbols of that struggle. The enemy was different, but the nationalist zeal was still very much alive.

Paul Connerton has argued that collective memory is engendered through physical participation in the memory process.[118] This is nowhere more true than in connection with Kilmainham Jail, where the whole process of voluntary restoration created memories of a collective past devoted to nation-building in both violent and peaceful forms. By participating in this protracted process, volunteers created a new history of the jail, with their own actions of swinging hammers and clearing rubble not only permitting the prison to persist as a site of memory, but also making the restorative action itself part of the memory continuum. Kilmainham was originally built by the British to imprison Irishmen. By reconstructing it, the Irish built a site that could enshrine their past as one of unified struggle against imperial oppression and of the improvement of Irish lives.

The preservationists intended to create Kilmainham as a memorial to Irish revolutionaries and as a tourist attraction, but for this goal to be achieved, the enterprise had to be undertaken by Irish citizens themselves because only a grassroots voluntary effort could circumvent the challenges facing the construction of any tourist site devoted to modern Irish nationalist memory—not the least of which was government unwillingness to pay for any large restoration project. By removing the Civil War as a source of contention immediately, by linking revolutionaries of diverse political views together in one group, and by not allowing any single nationalist figure to be appropriated for contemporary political ends, the restorers of the prison developed a uniquely "national" site, dedicated to Ireland as a whole. Finally, the fact that Kilmainham was reconstructed through voluntary effort ensured that Irish tourist authorities remained distanced from memories of earlier historical struggles, unencumbered by the past as they tried to entice the old enemy into taking relaxing Irish holidays. Indeed, Bord Fáilte maintained this distance by not mentioning Kilmainham or any related revolutionary sites or events in the pages of its tourist magazine until the 1980s.[119]

Since its restoration Kilmainham Jail has evolved to meet modern tourist tastes by incorporating more elements of Irish history, including attitudes to crime and prison reform, the Great Famine, and even the Irish Civil War. Yet even with these new additions, the jail remains Ireland's primary tourist site devoted to revolutionary history. Kilmainham not only projects its history as a prison for Irish nationalists since the late eighteenth century but also stands as a symbol of continuing Irish nationalism even after the end of armed struggle—a shrine to Irish nationalist feeling both before and after the revolution.

Packing in the Flash

Particularly in the last ten or fifteen years, it has ceased to be enough to develop historic sites because an idea came easily in the night or because a committee of volunteers felt a desire to commemorate the past. Today sites must be designed to match the tastes of tourists raised on Disney-like heritage centers featuring flashy multimedia presentations, holograms, and interactive displays. While a small visitor center, access improvements, and electric lighting were enough to make Newgrange acceptable for tourists in the 1950s,[120] today sheer visitor numbers and tourist tastes have led Dúchas to develop an impressive visitor center, complete with a full-sized replica of the passage tomb, multimedia presentations, diorama displays, and a building designed to resemble the great megalithic tombs. It is as much like going to Disneyland as it is visiting an historic site. Similarly, the Céide Fields and Corlea Trackway feature buildings designed to communicate meaning, with the Trackway housed in a massive Celtic cross and Céide Fields combining "physical grandeur, antiquity, and death" in a "single, simple, and very ancient architectural image" that springs like the pyramids at Giza from the Irish countryside.[121] Further demonstrating contemporary tastes, the 1798 Center at Enniscorthy features a less than dignified debate between the holographic heads of Edmund Burke and Thomas Paine, disembodied voices, and marching drummers complete with interactive TV screens in their instruments.

The need to develop these more "contemporary" attractions was brought home to Bord Fáilte following a scathing report by the Ventures Consultancy during the late 1980s. The report found that Ireland's

> existing product is tired and unprofessional. . . . Many of your new proposals are 'copy-cats' of existing attractions. . . . Ireland's history is complex, and many facets are being overlooked. . . . Your interpretation and interpretive planning is unimaginative and lacks originality and variety. . . . Projections of visitor numbers are unrealistic, marketing planning is poor, and market research is almost non-existent.[122]

As a result, the Tourist Board adopted a framework of "themes and subsidiary storylines" that could be developed. These included *Living Landscapes, Religion and Ritual, War and Conquest, Earning a Living,* and *The Spirit of Ireland*. Existing attractions and proposed new ones were worked into this framework, consultants were hired to assist in development, and a heritage-marketing consortium company was established. The result was a dramatic increase in the number of tourist attractions charging an admission fee (from 85 in 1983 to 219 in 1993), a doubling in the number of admissions to such sites (from 3.4 million to 6.9 million), and a dramatic increase in visitor spending.[123] Among other emphases, the board drew renewed attention to the Gaelic language (including the marking of additional Gaeltacht holidays), monuments, music, and literature and song, and to traditional activities like fishing, the development of agriculture, and leisure activities. Just as important, the tourist authorities began considering new ways in which to present heritage, including the use of interactive media systems to "enhance interest and understanding."[124] In order to meet government targets for the doubling of tourism revenue, Bord Fáilte focused its attention on modernizing, diversifying, and expanding its heritage product.

A large part of the task of producing heritage extends beyond determining the products and narratives to be presented to the interpretation of those stories. The Glendalough proposal was problematic, not because stories were unavailable but because the government was unwilling to decide on a fixed narrative that would interpret the evidence available. Likewise, the restoration of Kilmainham Jail was made possible because all parties agreed at the outset that the site would present an unambiguous story of Irish *unity* in the fight against oppression. Heritage requires "more than preservation: its significance should be conveyed to the visitor, leading to an enriched understanding of the context of the present."[125] In order to be successful, interpreters must translate the past into a modern language, linking the present to the past with common symbols. This goal is accomplished by using "a range of methods, media, materials, and management" that work together as "'culture brokers' or mediators between tradition and modernity.[126] As popular culture changes, the brokers used for accomplishing translation evolve to meet new tastes—an evolution that has been tremendously obvious in the development of the tourism product offered by the Guinness Brewing Company.

Lovely Day for a Guinness

For Guinness, tourism represents a successful form of advertising. Since opening in December 2000, the Guinness Storehouse became (perhaps)

Ireland's leading tourist site, building on the sound reputation of the company's previous tourist facility, the Hopstore.[127] The Storehouse is nothing if not modern, making use of so many "culture brokers" as to leave the visitor exhausted by the time he reaches the rooftop tasting room, high atop a giant pint-glass-shaped atrium. The facility is a virtual assault on the senses, with running water, loud noises, multimedia presentations, interactive displays, music, artifacts, and no less than three bars. This facility did not develop in a vacuum and actually represents the most recent in a series of Guinness tourism attractions.

The company initially recognized the potential value of advertising after the launch of its first campaign in Scotland in April 1928. Under the guidance of S. H. Benson, the campaign materials featured the now-famous slogan "Guinness is good for you" and displayed "a picture of a large glass of stout with a typical Guinness head." A poster was circularized to all doctors in the advertising area along with "free samples for 'medical use.'"[128] This campaign was followed up with parodies of *Alice in Wonderland*, with rugby sponsorships, and later with Gilroy's famous "Guinness for Strength" and "Lovely Day for a Guinness" posters, with their toucans, lions, and other animals thirsting for stout.[129] The result was a 7.3 percent increase in Scottish sales, even as sales in Britain as a whole dropped by 6.8 percent. Although the Great Depression caused sales to drop precipitously in the 1930s, the success in Scotland ensured that Guinness continued extensive use of advertising.[130]

At least from the incorporation of the company in 1886, Guinness recognized that visitors enjoyed seeing the inner workings of the massive St. James's Gate Brewery. In 1887, 4,000 people toured Guinness.[131] By the early highpoint in 1919 this number had climbed to 19,600 visitors and the company had distributed almost 20,000 guidebooks.[132] Numbers declined thereafter as political tension increased with the onset of the War of Independence. Interested parties had only to "present a suitable letter or introduction" to receive a tour through St. James's Gate. Evidently a fair number of such letters existed because tours departed every fifteen minutes, Mondays to Fridays, from eleven A.M. to three P.M.[133]

Following the tourism boom after World War II and the news that Fianna Fáil was going to push through new tourism legislation, Guinness began planning to improve its tourism product. A memo was circulated that suggested that more guides be trained, enabling "more inexperienced men to see how a star performer puts across the patter to his audience." It was also noted that the company should conduct occasional visitor surveys in order to make certain that tourists were impressed by their visit.[134] In the following year a script was crafted in order to standardize the information provided to visitors, most of which covered the history of the brewery and the brewing process, but which also addressed the various benefits given to employees, including full medical support and inexpensive food. It was stressed that "although an old firm, we [Guinness] are not afraid to keep our plant modernised"—a claim that echoed the wider emphasis on Ireland's modernity in contemporary tourist guidebooks and the An Tóstal program.[135] Guides were even told how to answer many of the frequent questions asked by tourists, including the origin of the water used and the flavor of Guinness in the United Kingdom vis-à-vis Ireland. When asked about the water, guides were instructed to "kill the belief that Guinness is made from Liffey water"; instead, they were to inform visitors that the water is actually drawn from a special well in County Kildare. Those who asked about taste were to be told that "the results of tasting by our expert tasters do not show that Guinness brewed in one brewery is superior to Guinness brewed in another."[136] While the company's presentation for tourists was carefully considered, the organization did not expend any effort in mounting fancy displays. It was not an unsuccessful formula, and the brewery was attracting fifty thousand visitors per year by 1958 and sixty thousand in 1959. The brewery prided itself on its tour leaders, bragging that "our guides are prepared to meet all sorts of people, grave and gay, and to be ready for such jobs as lifting the Seven Dwarfs of 'Snow White' to enable them to see into a vessel, or finding another way round for the German wrestling giant, Gargantua, whose height of eight feet would not allow him to use the passenger tunnel to the lower level." The formula was so successful that "rarely is anybody disappointed."[137]

Besides staging the tours, Guinness continued to use its marketing budget to promote sporting events and festivals during the 1950s, often citing a perceived public obligation rather than advertising objectives. Likewise, in 1958 the company restored its windmill because of its "sense of public duty to preserve an historic landmark."[138] Support of the first Galway Oyster Festival in 1954 was justified in the same way, by the claim that the company was assisting a "wholly local, voluntary, and otherwise admirable organising committee."[139] While this may have been the case, there was undoubtedly a significant advertising and tourism benefit as well, giving Guinness every reason to support An Tóstal as well as the eventual catalog of festivals from Wexford to Cork that the company pulled under its wing.[140]

By 1960 the brewery tour had become so successful that tourists were carried along on a narrow-gauge railway called the "Planet," and in 1963 the company expanded its tourism efforts still further by opening a souvenir shop at the Victoria Quay stocked with glass tankards, penknives, glass cloths, and other collectables.[141] In 1966 the brewery inaugurated its first museum, though access was limited only to special parties. The museum represented a striking contrast with those of today. Rows of glass cases displayed various artifacts, including the "most interesting exhibit in the museum," a display of coopers' tools with illustrations of how they were used. Photographs, old bottles, a steam engine, and a Geoghegan narrow-gauge steam locomotive, old ledgers, and foreign labels filled out the exhibits.[142] It was a step toward providing still more attractions to tourists and was probably very much like other museum displays in Ireland at the time, showing objects and displaying a limited amount of written material but lacking the coherent narratives found in future efforts.

At the same time that the museum was opened on Waltling Street, a committee began to study the visitors' route through the brewery, looking for potential sanitation and safety problems, while also comparing the Guinness experience with those of the Carlsberg brewery in Copenhagen, the Heineken brewery in Amsterdam, and the Pripps brewery in Stockholm. It was hoped that the group would learn more about what Guinness was doing well while making it possible to adopt potentially attractive features used at these other breweries. Ultimately the committee reported "tours of brewery premises can be deadly dull," making the inclusion of entertainment at Pripps easily understandable. It was a message that was not lost on Guinness and that eventually came to dominate the thinking behind the company's tourism ventures. The committee was pleased to report that Guinness visitors were allowed access to a larger portion of the brewery than the other

6. Guinness operated a narrow-gauge train called "The Planet" as part of its brewery tour during the early 1960s. Courtesy of Guinness Ireland Archives, St. James's Gate, Dublin 8.

corporations allowed, but it noted that the bottling plant should be included and a larger effort made to interpret the facility through the use of models, as was being done at Carlsberg. Finally, it was felt that the museum should be opened to a larger number of visitors, although the committee was divided about the relative merits of doing so, given the cost of the improvements that would be required. Regardless of whatever changes might be made, "it is essential that a visitor leaving St. James's Gate should realise he has been to a brewery."[143]

By the 1980s the number of tourists had climbed still higher, and the leading of large numbers of tourists through the brewery was becoming ever more challenging. Furthermore, fashions had changed. Museums and heritage centers now demonstrated historical events or industrial processes using

7. The Guinness Hopstore used the latest display technology to tell the story of Guinness stout during the 1980s and 1990s. Courtesy of Guinness Ireland Archives, St. James's Gate, Dublin 8.

manikins. Beginning in 1984, Guinness began constructing a new facility for tourists that fit new demands, investing £1.5 million in restoring and modifying the old hop-storage facility at St. James's Gate. When it finally opened on 27 July 1988, John Davies, the Guinness managing director, told gathered dignitaries that the exhibition "cleverly harnesses modern display technology to tell its story in a graphic and entertaining way"—the story being the evolution of Guinness as a company from its humble origins in the late 1750s among Dublin's many breweries of that day and the process used when making Guinness. Beginning on the first two floors, visitors were ushered through a display illustrating the making of beer, on through the original gates of the brewery, and into a collection of text panels, models, reconstructions, and bits of brewery equipment. Next, visitors learned about the history of the company, its place in the contemporary world, Guinness advertising, and the elaborate transport systems used to carry Guinness from the quay at Dublin to pubs around the world. The visit was completed with a pint of Guinness in the basement bar.[144] It was a site placed firmly at the forefront of museum design—it even smelled like a brewery, thanks to the aroma left after two hundred years of hop storage.

Storehouse

By the late 1990s, however, the Hopstore was obsolete. Inanimate reproductions and immobile text panels were out of date, and the three-floor facility was simply too small to handle the still growing number of tourists. Guinness made the decision in 1998 to abandon the Hopstore and to develop a massive six-story visitor facility in an old storehouse building—a large steel-beam structure originally built by A. H. Hignett in 1903.[145] The eighty-year-old Dublin-based architectural firm Robinson Keefe Devane completed the refurbishment at a cost of £24 million.[146] The steel-beam construction, still modern-looking one hundred years after its initial assembly, was augmented with a glass roof, endless escalators, and a glass elevator giving the upper floors an exceptionally bright and spacious feeling. The company used the steel-frame structure of the building, as well as assorted industrial equipment, to give the building a functional industrial feeling.[147] The new tourist facility also featured a 360-degree bar on the top level, two additional bars lower down, a visitor center, a cultural venue, the Guinness Ireland Archives, and a training facility for Guinness employees.[148] The "conceptualisation, identity, advertising, Web design, literature, and events programs" were all assigned to Imagination Group USA, a U.S.-based design and marketing company, at an additional cost of £6 million. When it was finally opened three years after work had begun, the Storehouse sought to "interpret one of the world's best known brands in a totally new and unexpected way," giving visitors a chance to learn "about the brewing process and the huge impact the business has made in Dublin and overseas."[149] This learning process was accomplished through "new set-piece exhibits and presentations in film, digital media, sound, and projections" in order to "fully immerse the visitor in the ongoing story of the famous brand."[150]

If nothing else, the Storehouse certainly was a change from past Guinness tourism efforts. Upon entering, visitors are greeted with a loud industrial-like noise and a massive waterfall designed to show the importance

8. Visitors to the Guinness Storehouse are greeted by a display featuring the ingredients used to make stout. Photograph by the author.

of water, as displays nearby describe hops, barley, and malt. Video screens depict Guinness as a central component of Irish culture, firmly linked to great moments in Gaelic football and hurling history as well as to memorable moments in Irish advertising. Further along, visitors sit on office furniture as images from the brewery's history are flashed on the walls around them and a voice recounts the story of Arthur Guinness's first purchasing an old brewery in order to establish his own, with the business gradually moving from the brewing of ales to that of stouts. As visitors ascend still higher, they reach an interactive advertising display that allows more patient tourists to view Guinness commercials dating from the 1950s to the present, reliving proud moments like an impressive drag-racing slug and talented bicycle-riding fish—both of which enjoy Guinness, despite the fact that Guinness is definitely *not* good for slugs! Finally, after climbing six floors, the tourist arrives at the Gravity Bar, where she can enjoy a pint while gazing on a 360-degree view of Dublin.

While the facility enjoyed a hugely successful launch and a significant boost when President Bill Clinton of the United States visited a few days later,[151] feelings about the site were mixed. *Irish Times* columnist Joe Humphreys was horrified by the company's attempt at "colonising our national heritage" and turned up his pen at the entire enterprise, declaring Guinness to be a "corporation that believes its own hype." It all seemed terribly impersonal to him because the visitor traverses the six-floor experience alone. "The idea seems to be to create a distance between the punter and the product in an effort to further heighten the mystique," he observed sourly, and then complained that many of the displays appealed little to adults while captivating the "under-sixes," inevitably creating battalions of Guinness drinkers and legions of alcoholics.[152] Guinness was disgusted at the reporter's comments, declaring that the company, at over 240 years of age and the drink of choice for millions, was every bit the major part of Irish culture suggested by the facility's narrative. Furthermore, the allegation that the Storehouse was little more than a giant sales pitch was wholly off the mark. This was a site that offered value for money because "visitors can easily spend several hours exploring the building" and enjoying their pint—or a glass of soda for those uninterested in Guinness. Moreover, it was incorrect to claim that the Storehouse might encourage underage drinking. After all, the company spokesperson asked rhetorically, "Does the Chamber of Horrors at Madame Tussaud's in London encourage young people to go on a rampage of torture and murder? We have to accept that parents with young families will quite reasonably try to satisfy their insatiable desire for knowledge by visiting attractive locations with a long history and tradition." Theirs was an authentic heritage site, an educational facility, and it was suitable for visitors of all ages.[153]

Humphries was not the only critic of the Storehouse. Shortly after the previously cited editorial appeared, Dr. Michael Loftus wrote to the *Irish Times* to express his agreement: "The most disturbing aspect is allowing youth of all ages to view the massive promotion of a potent, addictive drug. How sad. Where is the responsibility?"[154] Others disapproved of the near canonization of Guinness creator Arthur Guinness and the site's other "mawkish tributes" to the Irish brew.[155] The painful admission fee was also singled out for scorn; the *Irish Times*, for example, declared the facility to be the worst value in Ireland, saying, "Charges you 13.50 to watch some Guinness ads and have a pint. Yet gets more visitors than any other tourist attraction in Ireland. One word: suckers!"[156]

Ultimately, the Guinness story demonstrates the changing face of heritage, the increasingly international voices and fashions involved in translating it, and the almost inevitable conflict that develops as a result. Heritage is, after all, the most recent shape of historical debate both inside and outside of the nation. Although Humphreys did not explicitly say it, by questioning the brewer's right to "colonise" Irish heritage and the desirability of displaying the Guinness product to young people, he was challenging long-held stereotypes about the Irish and alcohol.[157] Is it desirable that Irishness be associated with a beer? Should the face of a nation be so closely linked to an opaque beverage? Is the success of Guinness advertising ultimately a horribly negative thing for the Irish image? The very success of the Guinness Storehouse, whether the facts it presents are accurate or not, makes these questions that much more prevalent, while continuing debate surrounding Irish heritage and history into a new millennium.

Conclusion

Since the foundation of the Irish Free State tourism has continually raised questions about the preservation, presentation, and exploitation of Irish history. What topics should be discussed and *how* should they be discussed? Is it permissible to present history that is contested, or to appropriate symbols to create links between certain products (especially when that product is an alcoholic beverage) and national identity? Should historical narratives be used to unify a people or as a way to reflect divisions that have made the nation what it is today?

This chapter reveals a long-standing uncertainty about the answers to the above questions. Irish people hoped to use the past to reflect well on modern Ireland by stressing earlier accomplishments while avoiding unpleasant recent memories. When the recent past was addressed, it was done in a manner that glossed over the more unpleasant realities, again presenting Ireland, both to foreign tourists and to the Irish themselves, in a positive light.

Perhaps it is unsurprising that the authorities and interested citizens tried to use the past to offer a pleasant image of Ireland, but the government's tendency to distance itself from the production of heritage, even "positive" heritage, is more striking. While money was certainly in short supply, the development of sites that celebrated Irish unity and achievement might have functioned to create strong feelings of national pride—much as the impressive structures built in nineteenth-century Germany were used to "nationalize the masses."[158] Instead, the government fostered a deeply ambivalent relationship with history, even as the tourist authorities recognized the value of the past for attracting tourists. Perhaps it is this ambivalence, as much as a lack of funds or the importance of landownership in nationalist thought, that has left authorities unwilling to make use of their powers to compulsorily acquire land or, at the very least, to "encourage" landowners to provide suitable access to important historic structures resting on their property.

6

Creating the Tourist Landscape

Territory and landscape make nations tangible. National landscapes are imagined to have unique characteristics that symbolically represent the native spirit of the *Volk*. While nationalists must develop national histories and culture, landscape requires the provision of a spatial knowledge of national geography that in turn enhances an exact understanding of what it is to be English, German, French, or Irish.[1] But nationalists often do more still, striving to preserve their landscape, to present it in a specific way, and to enhance access to the land so that it becomes possible to provide generation after generation, as well as foreigners and locals alike, with a personal understanding of the national territory.

Irish landscape is generally associated with the rugged western seaboard—an association that developed because it allowed Ireland to be defined against England, as well as against the eastern seaboard that was corrupted by Anglicization, urbanization, and industrialization.[2] Yet, given the important political role assigned to Irish scenery, Irish history does not abound with examples of the hiking clubs and healthy-living societies that developed as a way to teach those in places like Germany and England about their homelands.[3] Instead, tourist-related activity has partly substituted for the nationalist-minded hiking clubs.[4] The Irish Tourist Association, Bord Fáilte, and local authorities interested in tourism development actively worked to shape Ireland for both native and tourist consumption, an effort that was helped and hindered by groups and individuals outside of the tourist industry. The long history of conflict over land and the constitutional right to landownership ensured that tourist officials constantly had to deal with landowners. While officials could and did provide a nearly endless series of suggestions, advice, and even legislation, ultimately the creation of Irish landscape was the product of a horizontal dialogue that occurred across Irish society.

This chapter explores the interaction of the government, tourist authorities, and the Irish people themselves by addressing the importance of landscape in tourist discourse, questions about land access rights and ownership, efforts to develop and shape Irish landscapes and townscapes, Tourist Board attempts to redefine ecosystems to match perceived tourist demands, special undertakings to conserve environments, and the way in which landscapes have been manipulated through their photographic presentation. In the end readers should recognize the myriad factors involved in creating the way in which Ireland is visualized as well as the role that the negotiating of landscape has played in continually reimagining Irish national identity.

The Importance of Irish Landscape

Almost from the first moment that travelers visited Ireland, they were attracted to the scenery. Since the 1750s virtually every travel writer has voiced strong enthusiasm for the landscape, singing the praises of the Killarney lakes and gazing in awe at the rugged rocks and cliffs of the western seaboard. Archie Bell was so awestruck in 1928 that he urged visitors to travel slowly so that they might feel and absorb the beauty around them; the basic message has changed little since.[5] Of course there were also critical voices. In the early 1950s Heinrich Böll equated the greenness with forsakenness,[6] and in the late 1980s Eric Newby, who bravely rode around Ireland on a bicycle in January, complained often about the driving rain that obscured his view.[7] Most recently, Pete McCarthy protested bitterly about "slapdash construction of suburban housing in places where there are no suburbs."[8] Yet even this moaning reveals the powerful attraction of Irish scenery and the disappointment when it failed to meet expectations, a point further emphasized by the fact that virtually every major tourist market in Ireland cites landscape and scenery at or near the top of the list of the country's attractions.[9]

Members of the Irish Tourist Association recognized the strong pull of the landscape for tourists from the beginning. ITA guidebooks always stressed the many beauty spots of Ireland—the sheer quantity of which created a mecca for tourists.[10] During the initial push to establish local branches, areas like Dingle, Waterville, Kenmare, and Killarney were especially valuable focal points for ITA efforts precisely because of their scenic attractiveness. Representatives were fond of saying that Ireland's scenery was among the finest in the world, that there was little reason to visit America, France, or Switzerland when Ireland offered more diversity spread over a much smaller area, thus making it possible to really experience the whole instead of tidbits here and there.[11]

For the Irish Tourist Association it was not enough merely to feature attractive photographs or glowing textual accounts of Ireland's beauty; they also believed that it was necessary to protect the landscape from the visual signs of modernization while at the same time developing the land for consumers. As early as the 1920s, ITA leaders advocated the belief that it was important for Ireland to preserve and improve the landscape in order to attract visitors. Even as tourism advocates dreamed of a tourism-inspired modernity, they also sought to guarantee that development projects fit a specific set of aesthetic assumptions about what belonged in Irish landscapes and townscapes. Furthermore, the association worked to create a network of signposts around the country that would allow tourists to find their way through the labyrinth of narrow country lanes.

Beginning as early as 1925, the ITA lobbied for the improvement of urban areas, including the destruction of derelict sites. According to the association, "one such eyesore spoils the effects of an otherwise unkept secret. If councils have not powers to deal arbitrarily with such matters, they should take steps to secure them."[12] Simply removing abandoned buildings was not enough, and the Tourist Association touted the efforts of those areas that were pushing for urban cleanliness, applauding Clonmel, for example, for its effort to create cleaner streets and provide "a general brightening-up of the aspect of the town."[13]

The association also took an interest in urban development projects in other countries. For example, P. C. O'Mahony, a member of the Killarney branch of the ITA, enthusiastically pointed to the Yorkshire seaside resort at Scarborough as an example of what Irish towns should emulate. O'Mahony noted that the local corporation "controls practically everything" in order to ensure that the town remains clean, attractive, and inviting. Disused buildings were quickly disposed of or refurbished, beachside bungalows were kept in smart repair, and streets were looked after by a team of full-time staff.[14] Picture-postcard perfection was the rule, not the exception.

The ITA paid careful attention to the type of structures that were erected, hoping to make sure that Ireland did not develop buildings out of keeping with its image. Talk of constructing high-rise hotels to cater to American visitors, for example, was strongly questioned. "It would certainly look a bit odd to see a huge building in, say, O'Connell Street, Dublin, towering over the other houses like a giant looking down on a lot of dwarfs." It was not that skyscrapers were inherently bad or unaesthetic; after all, as the author pointed out, the Nelson Pillar was equally out of place on O'Connell Street. Rather, the point was that tourists seek unfamiliar sights. Only tourists completely unfamiliar with tall buildings would find such a structure interesting, and neither British nor American visitors fit such criteria.[15]

The association also pushed for major alterations to the modern Irish landscape. Beginning in 1926 the ITA lobbied for the implementation of a nationwide reforestation scheme. The group argued, "The necessity for a considerable amount of tree planting is an obvious one from the scenic point of view—trees are an essential part of inland scenery." Such a scheme would dramatically improve the national health, and the Irish climate would be "favourably affected by an increase in our areas under timber." Moreover, it was the government's duty to "repair the ravages of recent years by initiating a scheme of compulsory planting."[16] Once planted, trees should be cared for in a manner that ensured their aesthetic appeal. The association reported that tourists had already commented to ITA representatives about the "disfigurement of the countryside caused by careless lopping of trees." Trees should be planted, but at the same time the local authorities should be given the power to make certain that any and all pruning was "done more skillfully."[17] This scheme, if implemented, would have completely redefined the appearance of the areas into which it was introduced, altering Irish scenery to mirror more closely that of America or even continental Europe.

Given its tiny budget and its lack of statutory authority, the Irish Tourist Association was in no position to act as anything other than a lobby for environmental preservation and responsible development. The later statutory tourist boards, on the other hand, had more power to undertake landscape-altering schemes and devoted considerable energy to redefining Irish scenery. While more will be said about the board's various activities in a moment, suffice it to say here that at various points the Tourist Board undertook environmental studies, worked to redefine Irish townscapes, acted as a quasi-environmental watchdog organization, attempted to retrain the Irish people to accept a specific aesthetic of Irish spaces, forwarded an extensive signposting campaign, and even altered whole ecosystems in order to meet tourist desires.

The concern about Irish scenery extended beyond the efforts of tourist organizations. Newspaper letter-writers frequently used tourism as a reason for action or inaction on landscape-related concerns. In 1946, for example, one man wrote to the *Irish Times* to complain about widespread logging between Bray and Enniskerry, just south of Dublin. "We have become so obsessed by the profit motive that it is useless to suggest that Ireland's natural beauty is a thing worth preserving for its own sake," the author grumbled. Continuation of the current "orgy of destruction" would virtually assure the loss of tourism revenue.[18]

Lord Sligo of Westport, Co. Mayo, also cited tourism as a reason for careful consideration of how to treat the Irish landscape. In 1960, Lord Sligo opened Westport House to tourists for the first time, attracting some two thousand visitors in the first weeks of operation. The building was the first private "great house" in southern Ireland to open as a tourist attraction, and Lord Sligo had big plans, including a large-scale publicity campaign and a concerted effort to improve the amenities available to house visitors. Yet, just as he was set to develop his property as a major tourist attraction, efforts were well advanced to build a fifteen-acre factory adjacent to the house. Sligo insisted that he was not worried about the factory per se; indeed, he favored any project that would bring employment to his town. But he was concerned that it would severely alter the view from his estate, thus badly damaging its potential as a tourist attraction.[19] The danger was profound because it could not "be too strongly emphasised that the average tourist comes here [to the west of Ireland] partly because he does *not* have to look at factories—quite likely, he works in one employing several thousands." During 1961, Lord Sligo expected 10,000 visitors to Westport House, and "the possibility of explaining away a factory on our front-door step to 10,000 people, who might have paid to visit this house, causes us some concern."[20]

Among the people of Westport, Lord Sligo's plight received little sympathy. The Westport Urban Development Council unanimously passed a resolution calling for the factory's construction and declared the resolution their "best night's work yet." The community had long wanted a factory, and as far as the council was concerned, Sligo had no say in the matter. At certain points the language became heated and threatening. Members went so far as to say that Lord Sligo should not be permitted to walk on a public footpath near the harbor.[21] Within months the tone had gotten so unpleasant that the *Irish Times* referred to the debate as "the war at Westport." As far as the townspeople were concerned, tourism revenue would be beneficial, but they had seen precious little of it during the first year that the house was open to visitors, and they did not imagine that further wealth would be forthcoming. Meanwhile they believed that the factory would employ some five hundred local men, bringing "new life and business to Westport." The factory would "transform the town."[22]

The Westport situation is but one of many similar stories of conflict between proposed growth projects and the need to maintain an essentially premodern landscape for tourists—a dialogue that stretched even into the very heart of Irish tourism at Killarney. As far back as William Thackeray's visit in the 1840s, Killarney was notable for "a hideous row of houses" that informed the visitor that he had reached Killarney.[23] Today Killarney has expanded into a massive expanse of bed-and-breakfasts, hotels, and small homes. The travel writer Pete McCarthy describes the scene accurately and with much humor:

"Killarney—Looking Good," says the sign, but whichever direction you approach from . . . you are greeted by rows and rows of B&Bs. Many are suburban semis [semi-detached] . . . that, Tardis-like, have miraculously created the space to accommodate big-boned American families reared on hormone-enriched all-you-can-eat buffets. Others are grander, executive-style homes that look like they were assembled last week from a doll's house kit. All are festooned with signs proclaiming their attractions. "All Rooms En-Suite! TV! Car Space! Tea and Coffee Making Facilities!" they shout. But why stop there? People shouldn't sell themselves short. Tourism's a cut-throat business. You need to get all your selling points up there on the board. "Sheets On All Beds!" "Legs Keep Bed Off Floor!" "Drawer To Put Underpants In!" "Walls!"[24]

The development that prompted the expansion of the town from Thackeray's row of ugly cottages into a holiday metropolis created strong feelings even among those interested in promoting Irish tourism. Just as with the Killarney boatmen's objections to motor-launches, the growth of holiday homes was often greeted with hostility. Dublin-born, London-based travel writer Leslie Daiken is a case in point. His articles urge an approach to Irish travel based on impulse and "Edwardian rhythms."[25] He was among the first writers to advocate a horse-drawn caravan tour of Cork—promoting Con Murphy's horse-drawn caravan business as an ideal source of the perfect Irish holiday and anticipating Bord Fáilte's recognition of the attractiveness of this type of vacation.[26] While Daiken was all for getting to one's holiday destination quickly, once there he asked, "Is there anything quite so good for the body, mind, and senses than to climb into an open barouche, nod to the coachman, and 'do the tour,' passing under those branches drooping with heady perfume, indifferent to the sun-intoxicated flies that follow the old nag's ears as, clop-clopping to the rhythm of the *Fiacre* ballad, he leads us in and out of streets and laneways that no limousine or motorcycle looks quite right in." There was no better way to see Ireland than in a jaunting car, exploring Dublin through its "Bloom's Cabs" or seeing Killarney or the Mountains of Mourne at a horse's pace.[27] He viewed jaunting cars as "a symbol of unchanging Ireland" and dreamed that they might "long continue so, as they have done all these years at Killarney," even as he tirelessly promoted tourism in Ireland and urged more and more visitors to make the trip.[28] In Daiken's mind Kerry represented the last place "in these islands where you can call for a wagonette and have a uniformed coachman drive you into breath-taking scenery."[29] As a result, he focused much of his energy on promoting the region.

Given Daiken's apparent dedication to tourism development,[30] the horror with which he reacted to the success of tourism is striking. In 1961, after doing research on the current tourism market in Killarney, proposing articles to a handful of publications about the area, and learning about the sale of a large portion of the lakes to an American (see below), Daiken became greatly disenchanted by the changes that he saw taking place in this tourism center. All at once, in an unpublished article, Daiken urged tourists to "see Killarney before they murder it." He grieved,

If you have tears, prepare to shed them now—for the "developers" are in. And you can imagine what that means. Most Irish people who love their country's natural beauty (and who used to nourish an honest hatred for the Saxon invader) now reserve their righteous anger and fury for this new menace—the soulless speculators and magnates who, by remote control, are turning the world-famed beauty spots of Éireann into "developed areas," replacing the dignified emblem of an Irish Wolfhound for that of a Hot Dog.

Daiken gave "Killarney ten years before it becomes a second Blackpool," and noted that he had once believed Killarney would escape the ravishes of the profit hounds, leaving the "ineffable, unspoilt, heavenly vistas of Killarney's lakes and fells" to "go on forever," but he now realized this was a mere pipedream. It was not only that an American had purchased Killarney (Daiken made no secret of his disgust about this fact); it was also the "Germanisation of Killarney," the disappearance of the area's former solitude, the omnipresent concern about "how many more beds can we squeeze into this region at 'x' hundred £ per bed per annum." Killarney was becoming little more than another European tourist center, and this "Europeanisation of Killarney" was "a death-blow to the very impulse that attracts the English-speaking-world."[31]

Whose Landscape?

Even as Daiken was being horrified by rapid and excessive growth in Killarney, a few miles away in Tuosist, Father John Scanlon desperately hoped to attract development and to replace the increasingly depopulated landscape of his parish with family homes and productive farms. In chapter 3, Scanlon's quest to attract tourism revenue during the early 1960s was explored as an example of a local voice actively trying to use tourism as a harbinger of modernity, wealth, and a barrier against the endless cycle of emigration. In 1971, Scanlon again contacted the government when he learned that one of the larger local farms was on the market. While tourists might see "unspoilt virgin scenery," the painful reality was that "old folk" and "lonely bachelors" were selling their "small rocky holdings to foreigners for a few thousand and then . . . [migrating] to the nearest town . . . or cross the seas." Scanlon was horrified. He could not fathom selling to foreigners, and he believed that tourism development would solve the problem.[32] It was not enough that beautiful landscapes existed in Ireland; they should be owned, farmed, and enjoyed by the Irish themselves.

While Taoiseach Jack Lynch appreciated Scanlon's plea, he replied to the concerned priest that there was little chance of Bord Fáilte's or the government's purchasing the land. According to Lynch, "the right to private property enshrined in our constitution is interpreted as the right to dispose of it freely as well. It is only on very rare occasions . . . that this right can be invaded."[33] Scanlon was mortified and promptly replied that "we lovers of our country would have something to leave to posterity as a proof of our genuine patriotism" if the land were purchased by the state.[34] In Scanlon's mind the constitution was irrelevant. Only continued Irish ownership of Irish land really mattered.

Brian Lenihan, minister for transport and power, followed up the taoiseach's letter by noting that although Bord Fáilte had statutory authority to purchase property, it did so only through grants to local authorities in order to facilitate large-scale development. Tuosist was simply not "in a major resort" and therefore was not eligible for resort-development funds. While tourist authorities were in contact with the Kerry County Council and were willing to encourage preservation of the area, they simply could not provide any financial assistance.[35]

The foreign threat perceived by Scanlon was not limited to rural farms. In 1962 an American businessman contacted the Office of the Taoiseach on behalf of a wealthy American investor asking to purchase Blarney Castle, a site long popular with tourists. The man argued that his employer "would use every means possible to bring to Ireland an enormous increase in visitors by creating a desire on the part of Americans to see Ireland and to kiss the Blarney Stone." Beyond making just a simple purchase, the investor hoped to restore the old castle and "build a great hotel" to cater to legions of American tourists.[36] Mercifully, the taoiseach dismissed the offer out of hand. The castle was considered a national monument, and the taoiseach was unwilling to apply the same legal criteria that he had urged for Tuosist.

The story was much more complicated at Killarney, however, where an American real-estate investor actually purchased the Kenmare estate, containing some 8,300 acres of Ireland's most beautiful scenery, including two of Killarney's three lakes, Ross Castle, and the old abbey of St. Finian Lobhar—for a mere £100,000. The investor, J. Stuart Robertson, was born in Glasgow, married a Killarney girl, and subsequently moved to the United States, where he attained considerable success in real estate. Robertson purchased the property in August 1956 amid concern from local interests that he might permanently alter time-honored agreements such as jarvey access to the Gap of Dunloe or the ban on motor-launches on the lake.[37] Robertson assured the locals that this would not be the case and added that he was interested in using the site to breed Irish horses for export.[38]

The sale sparked an immediate outcry from almost all sectors of Irish society. The Killarney Tourist Association started a fund to purchase the site, and Sinn Féin suggested that the descendants of evicted tenants should receive the land as compensation for the losses incurred by their relatives in the late nineteenth century.[39] Bord Fáilte suggested that the land should be purchased "on a national basis," and pointed out "this was an opportunity, which might not recur, of establishing the future of Killarney which is our best known tourist attraction." The land could easily be added to the previously existing Bourn Vincent Park that abutted it in many places.[40] Yet in spite of the various appeals by Sinn Féin, the Tourist Board, the ITA, the Royal Irish Academy, the Royal Dublin Society, the Irish Hotels Federation, and the Hotel and Restaurant Association, to say nothing of numerous individuals,[41] the government refused to consider purchasing the land because to do so would create "a most embarrassing precedent for them." Yet the political potency of the sale was not lost on government officials, and they promised to ensure that the "national interest" would not be undermined by the sale, and that no tawdry development would be allowed.[42] Legislation to protect beauty spots and tourist amenities, for example, might prove a viable way to guarantee the protection of "special areas" while not forcing the government to directly challenge the Irish constitution.[43]

As it happened, Robertson sold the estate early in 1961 to an Irish-American millionaire named John McShain, who no doubt pleased the citizens of Killarney by calling Robertson "a complete promoter" interested in little more than financial gain. McShain promised that he would not develop the site for commercial purposes, but would instead use the existing Kenmare family home as a private holiday residence. The only change would be the installation of a modern heating system and a complete refurnishing with Irish antiques purchased at sales in the area.[44]

No Unauthorized Entry

Private landownership often forces tourists in Ireland to confront "No Trespassing" signs, as Pete McCarthy discovered while searching for an ancient burial site in County Cork. After finding the site, McCarthy discovered a sign that read: "Notice is hereby given that the occupier of this property excludes the duty of care to all visitors. No unauthorised entry is allowed."[45] The travel writer considered climbing the gate, but he imagined "some beefy farmer lurking behind the net curtains, with ginger hair growing out of his ears and nostrils, just itching to exclude the duty of care to some trespassing English bastard," and he therefore decided to move on in search of a stone circle.[46] Once again he located the site with some difficulty, only to discover that it was located in a paddock marked with a warning about a bull. At every turn McCarthy was confronted with a view of land that emphasized private ownership and restricted access over public consumption and accessibility—a conflict that reflects two distinctly different readings of the "national interest," one giving primacy to attracting tourist dollars, the other projecting the politically charged nineteenth-century notions of the "three Fs" and peasant proprietorship.[47] These dueling views have placed tourism interests, the government, and local families in direct conflict since the 1920s.

The Irish government first tried to address the ownership dilemma in relationship to historic sites in the 1930 National Monuments Act, then again in the 1952 Tourist Traffic Act. Both of these laws authorized first the Office of Public Works, then An Bord Fáilte, to acquire land. From a preservation standpoint the 1930 Monuments Act worked fairly well, requiring only three amendments as of 2002, but the two acts did very little to solve ownership and access concerns because the government was rarely willing to fully use the powers of compulsory acquisition included in both pieces of legislation.[48] Little conflict resulted when this legislation functioned properly. For example, in 1938 it was reported that a cairn in Oldcastle Townland, Co. Cork, was in jeopardy because the landowner planned to remove the structure in order to facilitate more efficient plowing. The Office of Public Works responded by filing a preservation order that was subsequently approved. As was generally the case, the farmer accepted the order and no damage was done to the site.[49] In situations where the landowner was more intransigent, however, problems quickly arose because the government was unwilling to risk an expensive lawsuit. The battle of wills inherent in such a scenario inevitably raised questions about rights to Irish lands as well as to the historic sites found on the property. If the government was unwilling to demand control over the most beautiful areas of the country, or the most historic ones, did that ultimately mean that the country's scenic and historic gems were the private possessions of a privileged few rather than all Irish men and women?

The Battle for Poulnabrone

The questions of ownership and access were raised most prominently during a protracted struggle over ownership of the Poulnabrone dolmen in the Burren of County Clare during the 1980s and 1990s. The dolmen, a type of megalithic tomb in which several standing stones support one massive capstone, stands in a field of limestone pavement near the Corofin-Ballyvaughan road in the heart of the Burren. Poulnabrone is "one of Ireland's most photographed dolmens."[50]

The Poulnabrone story began in 1981 when Dr. Peter Harbison, then archeologist for Bord Fáilte, called the Office of Public Works in order to urge the speedy acquisition of the dolmen and its immediate surroundings so that a suitable car park could be constructed and the site preserved as an important national historic site.[51] Public Works quickly affirmed its willingness and began to determine how much land should be acquired.[52] The initial signs were positive and the needed steps were taken completely according to plan; the landowner, Thomas Byrnes, even agreed to hand the dolmen over to the state.[53] By May 1982, however, the situation began to spin out of control. First, the Clare Archaeological and Historical Society reported structural problems at the site. Smaller stones around the base of the monument had been moved, risking the structural integrity of the whole dolmen. Given Poulnabrone's "situation and its graceful appearance," the society urged immediate action.[54] Perhaps sensing that the level of alarm about the dolmen's condition might raise its market value if the process were slowed, Byrnes and his lawyer began to ignore Office of Public Works correspondence. Matters got worse still when a group of "visitors" locked ten of the farmer's cattle into a nearby shed, where they remained undiscovered for three days without access to food or water. The farmer was enraged, and correspondence between Bord Fáilte, the Office of Public Works, and the farmer became heated.[55] By 1985 the Office of Public Works was exceedingly frustrated by the lack of progress.[56]

Despite the setbacks, Public Works continued to push for state acquisition of Poulnabrone, a task made even more difficult because the government and the farmer had fundamentally different ideas about what ownership of the dolmen should mean. For Public Works the owning of a national monument entailed serious responsibility because the landowner was effectively a guardian of the nation's past. From the government's perspective the purchase offer of £2,000 was more than generous under the circumstances,[57] and would even provide the farmer with a certain existential equanimity by making him "happy in the knowledge that he was co-operating in the preservation of an important part of our heritage."[58] The offer held little promise for the disgruntled landowner, however. According to the farmer's lawyer, Jennifer Foley, Byrnes "was like any other person who owned property . . . ; he would not part with any of it except for a price, and the fact that it was a national monument meant absolutely nothing to him."[59] If Poulnabrone was to pass into government hands, the farmer was going to receive a fair market value for the land, payment of legal costs and applicable taxes, and assurances that the site would be fenced off so that tourists would not trespass on his land.[60]

At wits end and fearing reports that the dolmen's structural integrity was deteriorating still further, the government was forced to act.[61] The Office of Public Works applied for a "guardianship order" on 21 November 1985. Although the order did not change ownership of the site, it did allow Public Works to carry out all necessary restoration activity.[62]

Following the completion of a major restoration project at Poulnabrone, attempts to purchase the site continued and the price inched ever skyward, hitting £60,000 in 1989.[63] Byrnes and the government each hired firms to evaluate the value of the property and predictably reached vastly different conclusions: The Public Works set the value at £10,000, while the firm hired by Foley valued the land at £50,000 because it "could be very valuable" for "commercial development."[64]

From the tourism perspective things proceeded to get worse. Early in 1993, Thomas Byrnes's insurance company advised the farmer that the constant traffic of visitors to the dolmen presented a substantial insurance risk and instructed him to take "every possible precaution to prevent people from gaining access to his lands." It did not take long for the farmer to construct a barbed-wire fence to stop the invasion of his property "by trespassers for the purpose of viewing the dolmen." Although he promised not to interfere with the structure in any way, he would now use "every possible means" to prevent tourists from viewing it.[65] The Office of Public Works quickly contacted the Department of Agriculture in the hope of attaining a suitable insurance package that might protect Byrnes and others like him, while keeping the dolmen open to its adoring public.[66]

By 1994 the dolmen was again accessible to tourist traffic, but now a new challenge was present—Byrnes had decided to use the site as a means of generating profit by standing near the fence and demanding a contribution from all visitors. This action brought a series of complaints—especially when "a scruffily dressed man" began approaching women in their cars to demand money—but there was little that could be done.[67] The dolmen was privately owned and therefore out of government control; Byrnes was free to collect whatever fees he wished. The cost of public liability insurance was extremely high, and while the Office of Public Works hoped that "the few farmers who are charging admission fees will cease the practice," it was nevertheless understandable.[68]

Finally, after twenty years of dead-end negotiations and seemingly endless confrontations with the landowner, the sordid mess drew to a close in 2001 after Byrnes and his lawyers set the asking price at £300,000.[69] Exhausted by the long battle for Poulnabrone, the Office of Public Works, now called Dúchas, asked the Department of Finance for permission to purchase the property for the amount asked. Finance approved the purchase just four days after receiving the Dúchas request.[70] At last Poulnabrone was in state hands, leaving Dúchas to begin drafting a plan for proper development of the site.

Perhaps the most striking issue raised by the Poulnabrone dolmen story is the attitude taken by public and private interests toward the desirability of acquiring historic sites by compulsory purchase. Under the 1930 National Monuments Act and the 1952 Tourist Traffic Act, compulsory acquisition of important sites was legal, and both Bord Fáilte and the Office of Public Works expressed a desire to purchase Poulnabrone, but neither of the two bodies was willing to exercise the statutory muscle at their disposal to force the issue. Private landownership trumped national aspirations.

Developing Irish Landscapes

In spite of challenges involving ownership and access, from the 1950s onward there was rarely a moment when the statutory tourist authorities were not directly seeking to train the Irish people to accept a specific view of land, to reshape the landscape, and to protect particularly scenic areas while at the same time developing sites to make them more friendly to outsiders.

During the Emergency in the early 1940s the vast bulk of Irish Tourist Board activity was directed toward resort and hotel development, and relatively little attention was paid to worries about landscape preservation and improvement, unsightly buildings, or related concerns. This priority was primarily because the listing of "special areas," as covered in part IV of the 1939 Tourist Traffic Act, was suspended during the first part of the Emergency and only reconsidered for implementation in 1944.[71]

It was not until the early 1950s that statutory tourist authorities became overtly concerned with improving urban and rural landscapes. Beginning in 1951 the Tourism Development Board implemented a national signposting campaign, launched its program called "Tourism Is Everybody's Business, the Tourist Is Everybody's Guest," became increasingly involved in planning decisions, and even began an angling-development scheme that altered whole ecosystems to fit tourist demands—all of which were designed to improve the landscape for visitors.

Signposting

In one story in their famous collection about an English resident magistrate negotiating Irish country life, Edith Somerville and Martin Ross observed, "In that part of Ireland in which my lot is cast signposts do not exist. The residents, very reasonably, consider them to be superfluous, even ridiculous, in view of the fact that everyone knows the way, and as for strangers, "haven't they tongues in their heads as well as another?" It all tends to conversation and an increased knowledge of human nature."[72] This attitude was not limited to the stomping grounds of "the Irish R.M.," and the same state of Irish signage was found in much of the Irish countryside. From the 1920s onwards, the Irish Tourist Association encouraged the erection of signposts as "a necessary advancement for the development of motor touring."[73] The resulting program was funded by the central government but carried out by local authorities;[74] unfortunately, it did not prove far-reaching enough, and the majority of Irish roadways were left unsigned and therefore incomprehensible to tourists and nonlocals alike. By the 1950s, when the amount of motor traffic began to increase steadily, the perplexing Irish road network had become a growing tourism liability, prompting the Tourism Development Board to undertake a nationwide signage campaign designed to order the Irish countryside for tourist consumption.

Bord Fáilte was required by statute to undertake signposting activities in the Republic of Ireland, incurring expenditure for the creation of signs and any further activities "in connection with the signposting of roads and the designation of recognised tourist routes, as the board may consider desirable in the interests of the development of tourist traffic."[75] In addition, the Tourist Board was also expected to erect interpretive signs in the vicinity of national monuments, both pointing the way toward important sights/sites and explaining them upon the visitors' arrival.[76]

The Tourist Board began its signposting program in 1951 in conjunction with the Automobile Association, which had started its own signposting scheme in late 1950. By July 1951 the route between Dublin and Belfast, the Dublin-Killarney road, and the route to Waterford from Dublin were all clearly marked, and plans were made to complete a series of advance-direction signs between Waterford, Cork, and Killarney as well as along the Dublin-Sligo road.[77]

The Tourist Board's efforts were directed by Kevin O'Doherty, who was responsible for studying the best approaches to signage, the acquisition of signs, and the distribution of these signs to relevant local authorities for erection. O'Doherty's first activity was to travel to Windsor, near London, to learn everything that he could about road signage from the acknowledged experts. He quickly discovered that the best road signage available was far beyond the means of his organization to acquire. An Bord Fáilte amounted to a group of "very small boys with very small budgets," and the massive illuminated overhead signs then becoming popular in Britain were simply not viable in Ireland.[78] Regardless of the utility of the impressive British signs, Ireland was forced to adopt a more conservative approach. The Tourist Board acquired three types of signs, including "advance direction signs," "fingerpost indicators," and "signs to national monuments." The first of these warned travelers on Irish trunk roads about approaching turns and about the direction in which they would need to go so as to reach their destination. Fingerposts complemented these signs at the turns themselves. And finally, national-monument signs were "intended to be partly descriptive, the aim being . . . to enable visitors touring the country to select monuments which may be of interest to them." In each case signs were presented in both English and Gaelic, with Gaelic presented on top.[79]

From the outset the relationship between Bord Fáilte and local authorities on the signage issue was tense. From O'Doherty's perspective, although signage was essential for tourist development, it was the responsibility of local authorities, not the Tourist Board. For tourist authorities, however, the inclusion of signage in the Traffic Act represented a cynical ploy by the Department of Local Government to indulge local unwillingness to develop a signage network. It was not that local authorities were opposed to tourism, but rather that they lacked initiative. O'Doherty recalls needing to fight with local authorities to accept signs; then, because the signs originated from An Bord Fáilte and not their employer, the engineers responsible for installing the signs argued that the signage represented a tourist-development activity and should earn them additional wages. This demand directly clashed with the Tourist Board's belief that the installation of road signs was already a local responsibility. As a result, once local authorities began to install the signs, resentment about low pay and management issues guaranteed that the signs were not always installed correctly or in the right locations; the placement of mileage signs and directional signage often bore little in common with actual mileages or directions to given locations.[80]

Despite the challenges, the signposting efforts of Bord Fáilte gradually gathered steam. By March 1954, 3,360 fingerpost signs had been ordered, with almost 2,900 already having been distributed; 290 of them were for national monuments.[81] On 14 March 1956 the 10,000th signpost was erected to guide visitors to Our Lady's Church at Glendalough. Also by that time the variety of signs had been expanded to include mileage markers and town or village names.[82] The program ultimately continued through the 1960s, with some 36,000 signs having been posted by 1965.[83]

Everybody's Business

When tourist authorities first informed the Irish people "Tourism Is Everybody's Business" in 1952, they hoped to teach ordinary people about how they could help foster the tourism industry. The advice was to provide courteous and friendly service and to work tirelessly to make yards, hedges, and built structures presentable by planting flowers, trimming bushes, and painting buildings.[84] While this counsel had roots in the activities of the Irish Tourist Association, it was probably motivated by foreign influences as well. For example, when the Irish Tourist Board sent a committee to Germany to study the Kraft durch Freude (KdF) program in 1937, the committee observed the KdF's large-scale program to improve the attractiveness of German homes and villages by planting flowers and removing unsightly structures.[85] Likewise, tourism officials were also aware that the more recent Festival of Britain encouraged the improvement of people's surroundings by promoting the removal of damaged buildings and the redesign of bombed-out landscapes.[86] Given such inspiration, there was little doubt among tourism developers that aesthetic reform was desirable and that Ireland should seek to remove unfortunate reminders of past or present poverty.

In keeping with this opinion, the Tourist Board applauded the efforts of tourism interests in Arklow, who took the ITB's advice and launched a program "to beautify our town and make it a pleasant healthy place for ourselves and an attractive happy resort for visitors." Among their activities, the Arklow Tourist Association created lantern slides depicting the townscape in the way that it *should* look. Members of the group also contacted their local authority in order to demand improved street lighting, additional public seating, and improved signposting, along with regular Sunday street cleaning.[87] Arklow's response inspired Bord Fáilte to expand its effort, working to encourage individuals, societies, and clubs to plant trees along streets, create memorial groves, and develop communal woodlots and "decorative shelterbelts"—all in the hope of improving Irish scenery through the addition of more trees.[88]

In the following year the government agreed to support the An Tóstal festival. The public was told that An Tóstal would bring people to Ireland, creating new friends for the country, but that to be successful, the effort demanded that "we must be proud of what we have to show and therefore we must plan and prepare. Everyone can help, by decorating homes, by removing eyesores, by writing to friends abroad, by showing courtesy to our visitors, [and] by aiding in the setting up and activities of local Tóstal committees."[89] Civic pride was essential and local committees were the "most effective weapon" for creating it.[90] Newspaper readers were urged to "trim your lawns and plant flowers," and were informed that An Tóstal would "result in the brightening up of towns and villages and the clearing away of eyesores."[91]

A number of towns energetically adopted Tourist Board suggestions. Cork city went to great lengths to provide visitors with an attractive display. Shields of important Munster families were mounted on lampposts in the city's main thoroughfare. Plots of flowers, shrubs, and other plants were laid throughout the city; flags and banners were flown, and there were even plans to attain a variety of special lighting fixtures to ensure that the city would be attractive after the sun had set.[92] Even smaller towns were excited; for example, Portumna in County Galway enlisted the help of local schoolchildren to "brighten" and "decorate" the town.[93]

The public-education component of An Tóstal was judged to be a resounding success, and Bord Fáilte strove to expand the ability of the festival to promote civic pride and the implementation of local improvements.[94] Under the direction of Jim O'Brien, a former ITA member, the Tourist Board launched a new "Tidy Towns and Villages Competition" as part of the 1958 An Tóstal. There were no large prizes and little publicity, yet the idea was popular enough to attract fifty-three entries in the first year alone.[95] O'Brien's enthusiasm was infectious and spread like a pandemic of aestheticism as he crisscrossed the countryside from village to village and town to town, making comments about each place into a cassette recorder and finally reporting on the winners.

The Tidy Towns concept extended local Tóstal activities, like painted window-box competitions in County Cork, to the whole of Ireland and promoted the idea that houses should be brightly painted, flowers planted, litter collected, and derelict buildings removed, all the while hastening the development of civic responsibility.[96] The Tidy Towns and Villages idea immediately resonated at both the local and national levels. The minister for local government was especially smitten by the idea and promptly encouraged "earnest consideration" of the project by each local authority and "the desirability of taking part in the competition." Participation was "clearly in the national interest . . . so that there may be widespread awakening of civic consciousness in the direction of making and keeping towns clean, tidy, and generally attractive." In keeping with the Tidy Towns idea, the Department of Local Government urged measures to clear derelict sites, improve sanitary conditions, remove litter, and otherwise embellish townscapes by providing litter receptacles, planting trees and shrubs, maintaining public sanitary conveniences, and painting public buildings, to say nothing of working closely with shopkeepers to make further improvements.[97]

Backed by strong support, the Tidy Towns Competition quickly took hold. There were 82 entries in 1959 and 213 in 1960, and officials fully expected more towns to enter in subsequent years.[98] By 1964 Bord Fáilte reported that "Irish villages and towns looked markedly neater and more colorful than at any time in the past," and it attributed the improvement to the Tidy Towns Competition.[99] When the annual event was first launched, most Irish towns were dirty and lacked color, having the personality of "wet cement," but the new competition sparked an aesthetic revolution in Ireland's urban spaces that left behind pastel-painted buildings, flower boxes, and carefully cropped vegetation.[100]

Recognizing the potential for still further improvement, the Tourist Board expanded the competition, adding categories for resorts and coarse-fishing centers as well as awarding a prize for rural roadside properties. The latter category is particularly interesting because "contestants" did not register to compete, as was true in the other categories; rather, Bord Fáilte officials simply noted particularly attractive properties "which set an example to others in the district" while driving around the country. It was a less than subtle way of encouraging rural dwellers, using peer pressure and competition, to maintain their land and houses in a manner acceptable to tourists and the tourist authorities. While the Tourist Board was not really able, despite holding the required statutory authority, to forcibly acquire land, its officials were capable of pushing landowners to comply with the "national interest" in aesthetic terms by offering prize money and the opportunity to upstage the neighbors—all at the bargain price of just £7,500 in 1963.[101] In the following year Bord Fáilte further expanded the number of "surprise prizes," recognizing the potential that the awards had to influence the appearance of rural homesteads.[102]

Many local authorities and community organizations caught the Tidy Town bug. Meetings were held in community centers around the country to discuss ways to improve the chances of winning the competition. Enthusiastic citizens in Clonakilty, Co. Cork, for example, met regularly in the late 1960s and early 1970s to discuss Tidy Town results and their tactics for improvement. In October 1970 members of the Clonakilty Town Council decided to use the Bord Fáilte report on their town to pressure "the owners of property mention[ed] in the report as being unsightly and to ask them for their co-operation for the coming year." In the same year the council also employed the report to press the post-office authorities to improve the aesthetic appeal of the post office and the space immediately surrounding it. The report was further used to identify specific hedges and other shrubs requiring attention.[103]

Towns elsewhere took a similar interest. The urban council in Ennis, for example, launched its 1986 Tidy Towns campaign by promoting a special environmental seminar in a local hotel that included speakers from the Shannonside RTO and the secretary of the Keep Kilkenny Beautiful Committee—the local group that spearheaded the "Marble City's" successful 1985 campaign.[104] By February 1986 the Ennis Urban Council further increased its efforts to win the coveted Tidy Town title by investing £250,000 in such improvements as twice-weekly trash collection, maintenance of open spaces, and a program of environmental works.[105]

Kilkenny's approach to the competition was not limited to a well-organized and hard-working committee or costly campaigns by the local council, but also included local competitions, including one that pitted storeowners against one another to determine the most attractive storefront in the city. The competition pushed banks to completely abandon unsightly plastic signage in favor of cut stone. Each year the committee met to develop a "plan of campaign" that included monthly targets and plans to carry them out. While the committee itself was comprised of volunteers, the Kilkenny County Council did what it could to assist these efforts. Indeed, the group went so far as to carefully plan council-housing schemes so as to include the provision of liberal amounts of open space, parks, and trees—an action that earned a special award from Bord Fáilte.[106]

The composition of Tidy Towns committees varied across Ireland. Sometimes they were entirely driven by local authorities and at other times they were voluntary. Local church leaders frequently conducted the campaigns. Even more often, Tidy Towns efforts were the domain of women anxious to demonstrate their organizational abilities on a public stage. They sought to show Ireland that its women were far more than just good housekeepers; they were stewards of Irish places and spaces, with control over the aesthetic appeal of their country. It was a way for women to express both local and national pride and to be rewarded accordingly.[107]

The Tidy Towns concept was so successful from Bord Fáilte's perspective that the organization continued adding additional categories to the competition. By the end of the 1970s prizes had been added for best estate village, market town, fishing village, historic town, seaside town, city village (areas like Clonskeagh or Rathmines in Dublin), and commuter town—not to mention the overall prize and the surprise prizes included previously.[108] In 1980 the authorities even introduced awards for primary and post–primary school grounds, hoping to make certain that even schoolyards personified the right view of Irishness.[109] The number of towns participating also increased dramatically. In 1979, 754 towns and villages took part.[110] By 1984 the number of entries had climbed to 804, while a similar National Gardens Competition attracted 1,300 entries.[111]

Although tourist authorities did not view all Irish towns and villages as identical, they did have ideas about the essence of these places. Irish towns were "disarming in their simplicity," sometimes hinted at when "a distant church spire or castle gives warning," but otherwise nestled cleanly into the landscape. Irish towns featured "gaily-painted" gateways, "rows of white-washed stones," and farmhouses "with pink-washed walls and slated roofs." Even petrol stations were painted in "gay colours."[112] On approach, visitors should experience a smooth transition between "the open countryside" and "the closed, contained spaces of the narrow streets or village square." Townscapes should provide a contrast with distant views of hills, mountains, lakes, and seas. In essence, a "village might be called the 'snug' of the countryside [a snug is a quiet corner of a pub where conversation and contacts flourish in sociable surroundings]." Expanding the concept of the warm and welcoming pub, villages should possess individuality, emphasized by the use of creative color schemes possessing "all the charm and confidence of folk art."[113]

When judging towns, Bord Fáilte adjudicators never wished to forget the unique attributes of any town while applying a range of common criteria. For example, while judges were particularly interested in the harbor in seaside towns, the river in riverside villages, and the juxtaposition of mountain and town in hilly regions, they were especially vigilant in the search for those attributes not acceptable in *any* Irish town. Checklist in hands, judges drove slowly into these towns, paying careful attention to the approach. Were there unkempt hedges or rock walls? Was litter strewn along the roadside? Once inside the village, the judges then explored the town, looking for public spaces, attractive paint, flowers, and the integration of appealing built spaces with natural features. Plastic signage or even overhead telephone and electricity wires might badly damage a competitor's chance of dominating the competition, and Bord Fáilte made a point of informing towns that the "mess of overhead wires" quickly destroyed the appearance of Irish streetscapes and should be dealt with quickly by urban-development boards and local councils: such outward displays of modernity were unacceptable. Signage should be "traditional" and avoid unsightly plastic. It was even better if Gaelic were integrated into signage texts. Modern conveniences, while required *inside* Irish hotels, bed-and-breakfasts, and guest houses, were to be kept invisible from those walking down an Irish street. After all, tourists visited Irish towns to find out what it means to be Irish, noted one Bord Fáilte Tidy Towns judge, and the presentation of these towns was therefore an essential means of transmitting the right image.[114]

The competition was not entirely about presenting an image to visitors, but also stressed the presentation of that same image to locals as well by creating "a better place in which to live." The challenge was to retrain Irish people to work with one another toward a common objective. For any Tidy Towns committee to function, the traditional Irish tendency toward "jealousy and bickering" must be avoided, allowing "everyone, from the smallest child to the most senior citizen," to take part in the national improvement effort. Sound leadership, cooperation, and solid community relations, combined with local pride and a desire for color, cleanliness, good repair, politeness, and friendliness to all, along with school and youth involvement and a desire to succeed—all could be combined to create both a tidy town and better Irish men and women.[115] By pushing people to join together to improve their towns for visitors, the Tourist Board hoped to reshape the Irish people themselves. Aesthetic sense had to be changed, mutual appreciation and toleration fostered, and a sense of local and national pride instilled. The work of creating a tidy town extended far beyond the pursuit of an ever-increasing cash prize to that of fostering a better national community—from the built environment on up. This important enterprise was not a project that ever ended, and at the outset of the 1970s Bord Fáilte commented approvingly on the record number of Tidy Towns entries before stressing the need for persistent effort by all bodies involved in managing Irish landscapes and cityscapes in order to guarantee the continued Irishization of Irish spaces.[116]

Altering Ecosystems for Tourism

Beyond promoting improvements to built environments, tourist authorities exerted considerable energy toward molding ecosystems to match the demands of tourism. Even in the 1920s the Irish Tourist Association recognized the potential of angling tourism.[117] In 1926 the association launched a program to improve trout fishing in Killarney's lakes, beginning with a letter to the Department of Fisheries asking about the best approach to enhancing trout fishing in the area. The minister suggested that the ITA ask local anglers about the stock in the lakes, the average size of fish available, and the ease of catching fish before actually undertaking fish-planting operations.[118] These activities were subsequently carried out, and eventually a hatchery program was implemented with assistance from the Department of Fisheries, including the initial hatching of twenty thousand trout ova.[119] Later the program was expanded and an additional forty thousand ova were purchased, composed primarily of white trout, as recommended by the minister.[120]

While these early ITA efforts differed very little from long-time fish-farming practices, Bord Fáilte had a different idea and undertook an expansive and dramatic campaign to improve angling facilities, especially along the border with Northern Ireland. It was widely felt that the counties of Cavan, Monaghan, Longford, and Roscommon offered little to tourists. There were no dramatic sea cliffs, no wave-battered beaches, and while there were great expanses of bogland, these places were viewed as fruitful areas for turf harvesting but not for tourist development. On the other hand, numerous lakes and rivers had never been developed for angling tourism. In addition, Erskine Childers, a member of the cabinet and a TD for Athlone-Longford, took a particular interest in the area, and in his energetic fashion he urged Lemass to allow the Tourist Board to pursue an angling-development program there.[121] The first such program was approved in January 1953 and was operated in partnership with the Inland Fisheries Trust.[122] It was noted that the number of coarse fish was causing a dramatic deterioration in the quality of trout angling as well as a reduction in the length of the angling season in larger lakes. Local angling associations made some effort to address the problem, but they were largely unsuccessful. The plan devised by An Bord Fáilte and Inland Fisheries was to take place over five years and involved "a partial scheme of coarse fish elimination and trout salvage on inflowing rivers and streams in Lough Corrib and Mask and a somewhat complete operation on Lough Arrow." The Inland Fisheries Trust initiated the program in January 1953 with financial support from the Tourism Development Board.[123] During 1956 alone, 10,000 pike (one of which weighed 46 pounds) and 276,000 perch were removed from the seven lakes covered by the scheme, killed, and buried next to the lake. Several million perch ova were also removed. As predators were reduced, trout stocks climbed.[124]

Ironically, at the very moment when the program was proving most successful, doubts began to surface about its wisdom. Not all fishermen enjoyed catching trout or salmon as did the Irish. For example, the French enjoyed pike fishing, while English anglers had a soft spot for perch and other coarse fish—in striking contrast to Irish and American anglers, who sought brown and rainbow trout respectively. These other markets might prove more lucrative if the predatory fish were *not* removed from Irish waters.[125] It was estimated that Britain alone was home to at least two million coarse fishermen. This realization brought a sudden change in policy. The new "long-term fishery development program," implemented in April 1957, designated some areas for coarse fishing while continuing to exterminate predatory fish in others. Initial activities included the expansion of available accommodation and increased access to fishing areas, as well as the restocking of lakes with coarse fish. Efforts were also made to improve game fishing on the Shannon.[126] In the first months of the program thirty-five coarse-fishing centers were established. Classes were offered to local women at vocational schools in Leitrim, Donegal, and Westmeath on the proper way to prepare coarse fish—courses made necessary because the Irish themselves had no experience actually cooking such fish.[127]

Two years after the new plan went into effect, fifty-five coarse-fishing centers had been established and a series of twelve sea-angling festivals had been organized.[128] A special guidebook devoted to marketing the new coarse-fishing holidays highlighted what had been accomplished. Officials did not

> guarantee that as soon as you come to Ireland, you will start catching numbers of big fish; we cannot even guarantee that you will catch a fish at all, for fish are queer, unpredictable creatures, as every angler knows, and we want to be perfectly straight with you. We do, however, declare without fear of contradiction that your chances will be better here than elsewhere, that you will have a vast number of well-stocked, almost virgin waters at your disposal, and that the Irish people will do their best to see you enjoy yourself. The size of the catch is up to you—and up to the fish.[129]

Anglers took the bait. In 1959 fish-mad tourists spent as much as £675,000, compared with the £431,500 they had spent just a year earlier—an impressive return on the £54,000 invested in the plan.[130]

Ultimately, what is vitally important about the angling-development programs, beyond the obvious economic yield, is the fact that the tourist authorities were not content merely to shape Ireland's towns and villages or to take part in the planning of such projects. In addition, they extended their interest to altering aspects of Ireland's natural environment. In this instance foreign tastes were wholeheartedly catered to, and Irish lakes were molded to match the tourist gaze. The Irish public does not appear to have expressed significant interest in the angling programs. Whereas there was great popular awareness of the Tidy Towns Competition and widespread interest in landownership issues, Ireland's fish were left to dangle, unloved except by those—a growing fraternity of foreign visitors—who would pursue and eat them.

Conservation, Planning, and Development

It would be incorrect to assume that tourist authorities have spent the past eighty years looking only for ways to alter Irish landscapes and townscapes to meet tourist demands without also exerting effort to conserve environmentally sensitive areas, limit pollution, and promote responsible development. During the 1970s and 1980s Bord Fáilte was particularly active in encouraging responsible planning decisions, lobbying for environmental conservation, and even working to define how developments should look.

Up to 1963, Irish planning initiatives were not terribly successful. Following the Civil War, planning was overshadowed by the need for survival. Unemployment was a much larger concern than responsible building and design; housing problems necessitated quick action, not an extended muddle over design issues.[131] Significant planning legislation was passed in 1934, but there was "an absence of an adequate will to implement it."[132] During the 1940s there were increasing calls, primarily from architectural groups, to consider organized planning programs when constructing new buildings in Irish cities, especially Dublin. In 1942 these demands spawned a National Planning Conference that included representatives from twenty-five different organizations, including the Irish Tourist Board. The conference demonstrated Irish capacity to produce a broad planning movement, but unfortunately it generated little lasting success owing to political and ministerial apathy and "the inability of the government to come to terms with such a radical movement with interdepartmental implications." By 1944 any drive to update planning legislation had all but dissolved.[133] The first widely implemented legislation was passed in 1963. It was designed to achieve certain major objectives; these included the development of a more flexible planning system operated by local authorities and the devising

of the means that would better enable local authorities to promote industrial and commercial development, to preserve amenities in both town and
country, and to fairly determine the compensation payable to landowners
for the specific restrictions imposed on them.[134] In the present context it is
especially noteworthy that the 1963 Planning and Development Act was
intended to help preserve amenities as well as to develop them—a substantial change from past practice because nature reserves, the protection of
animal and plant species, and the protection of natural environments simply
were not major issues before the 1960s.[135]

The foundation of An Taisce, the National Trust for Ireland, in 1948
also represented a substantial shift in Irish thinking about conservation. An
Taisce sought to "preserve, for the benefit of the nation, lands of natural
beauty, buildings of national historic or artistic interest, and, as regards land,
to preserve (as far as practicable) its natural aspect and features and animal and plant life."[136] Initially the group consisted of some 250 members
and concerned itself with "nature conservation and matters such as the flora
in the Burren, County Clare, the state of the area surrounding Killarney,
Kanturk Castle in County Cork, [and] the possibility of using Powerscourt
House as a Georgian museum."[137] As time passed, An Taisce acquired some
lands, began to manage a handful of Ireland's "big houses," and functioned
as a lobby for environmental concerns, pushing the government to consider
the impact of development on both plant and animal life as well as the aesthetic appeal of the countryside. Still, the body had no statutory role and was
thus limited in its ability to carry out major projects.

Although the Irish Tourist Board was included in the 1942 Planning
Conference (it was represented there by J. P. O'Brien), the body does not
appear to have shown significant concern for planning or conservation issues
in its day-to-day practices until at least the 1960s.[138] The Tourist Board's
planning role, however, was dramatically altered by the 1963 Local Government (Planning and Development) Act, which recognized a number
of specified bodies—including An Taisce and Bord Fáilte—to oversee the
conservation aspects of the legislation because its framers "recognised the
close connections between the quality of the environment and the tourist
industry"—an outgrowth of the new consensus about the national importance of tourism.[139] The Tourist Board and other designated bodies were

given responsibility to review development plans that might have a detrimental environmental or aesthetic impact within certain limitations (there were special exemptions for agricultural development such as piggeries).[140] Should any objection be made to a specific development plan, it could be appealed to the assigned bodies for review.[141] The Tourist Board's inclusion not only ensured that planning questions were constantly on Bord Fáilte's plate; it also provided the board with some power to back up its growing interest in conservation and environmentalism.

By the early 1970s the Tourist Board was thoroughly absorbed in its planning role, and besides reviewing planning petitions under the 1963 Planning Act, it became involved in projects designed specifically to define the physical shape of Irish development. In 1972, Bord Fáilte joined with the International Council of Societies of Industrial Design, the Kilkenny Design Workshop, and Córas Trachtala (the Irish Export Board) to promote a seminar attended by designers from around the world; their job was to study Irish tourist areas and to make suggestions about ways to improve existing structures and the aesthetics of future tourist development. The seminar was based on the idea that tourism "should be seen as a continuing social and educational process" in which tourists are conditioned to read a landscape in a given way, and children and young adults are made to understand the land in a particular manner defined from above. Tourism itself was considered as a way to demonstrate to visitors how local people live, but at the same time tourism must "appear to remain" secondary to other activities. At no point should the Irish people feel themselves to be "inhabitants of a tourist museum."[142]

After the consortium completed a survey of the Irish countryside, it released a detailed report covering everything from the style and physical placement of accommodation to the most attractive and functional designs for road signs. Every aspect of correct design for tourism needed to be integrated into the Irish landscape without announcing itself. Colors and materials should be chosen to match the local scenery, and furnishings should be made locally to assure continuity—an activity that would require ongoing effort to train locals to "be aware of and protective of their natural resources."[143] The group advocated a variety of changes to Irish roadways in order to exploit their scenic potential, including the planting of vegetation to enhance particular views or to camouflage undesirable ones.[144] Footpaths were suggested as an ideal way to promote "greater appreciation of the countryside."[145] Road signs, so much a part of Tourist Board efforts to carefully translate the network of roadways into a form easily consumable by tourists, were to be made more easily readable. In particular, "directional, informational, and utility signs could include Irish characters for the sake of atmosphere and national morale, but they should be properly designed from the point of view of legibility and recognition."[146] Perhaps even more interesting, the committee advocated changing the green color of Irish postboxes to something more visible lest tourists be unable to find them[147]—a somewhat startling suggestion because the boxes, many still displaying the royal crest from the days before independence, had been hastily painted green after the Anglo-Irish Treaty of 1921 in order to proclaim Ireland's newfound freedom.[148] Ultimately the report furnished a comprehensive series of design suggestions that were intended to balance the need to present a uniquely national landscape, increased automotive traffic, and the constant growth of tourist demand.

The International Council of Societies of Industrial Design report, however, had relatively little, if any, real impact. In 1989, Bord Fáilte, in conjunction with An Taisce, published yet another document that covered much of the same ground, carefully detailing how buildings should be constructed and where they should be sited. This time special emphasis was placed on using whitewashed siding and thatched roofs—materials that would "help ensure that Ireland's landscapes continue to be a source of delight not only for those who live and work there but also for the visitors for whom they are a major attraction."[149] Traditional cottages should be refurbished to meet new demands while maintaining the timeless qualities of the Irish countryside.[150] New structures should be positioned in such a way as to carefully blend in—placed in the same careful manner that Irish builders had reputedly used for hundreds of years.[151]

In spite of the initiatives of tourism authorities, Irish efforts toward responsible development have been less than successful. Travel writer Pete McCarthy recently reiterated common criticisms:

> I am not the first to observe that the landscape of rural Ireland has been badly defaced these last thirty years by the slapdash construction of suburban housing in places where there are no suburbs. . . . But before sneering at Irish bad taste, smug outsiders who live in twee English villages, like me,

should bear in mind that the bungalow blight is simply the logical outcome of Ireland's history of poverty; a poverty for which English landlords living across the sea in their carefully preserved villages must shoulder their fair share of the blame.[152]

While McCarthy's view of history probably contains some truth, a lack of older homes has little to do with the blight of new developments—the very developments upon which he is commenting in this passage. These are the result of often inadequately exercised planning restrictions, not of English oppression. Since at least 1968 planning efforts have been burdened by allegations of corruption. Erskine Childers, for example, was forced in 1968 to refute allegations by one Dáil deputy who alleged that property values were being raised by corrupt use of the planning process.[153] More recently, during the months in which this book was being researched, Ireland was rocked by a series of allegations stemming from the Flood tribunal that clearly revealed corruption in the building industry, to say nothing of the government and civil service.[154]

Besides the presence of corruption (at least in recent years), there was often conflict between local authorities and central planning bodies like An Foras Forbartha (the National Planning Board), to say nothing of a certain amount of public apathy.[155] Even in the area of environmental controls the Irish public showed less inclination for concern than those in other European countries.[156] Even so, Bord Fáilte took an ever-increasing interest in the protection of the environment in the early 1970s. In 1972 the Tourist Board, in conjunction with An Foras Forbartha, released a massive study of Ireland's coastal areas. This study not only surveyed the natural characteristics and beauty of coastal areas but also assessed the potential of these areas to support tourism development, paying particular attention to Ireland's Gaelic-speaking districts. The report suggested ways in which such areas could best be used, noting especially those areas whose beauty warranted protection, but also identifying those best suited to industrial development or urban expansion. Foreign investment in coastal districts was also considered, but its scale and significance were downplayed—Ireland was not being purchased by Europeans as Father Scanlon had once feared.[157]

In the years following this report, and with the tourist authorities' expanding interest in planning, environmental concerns were seldom absent from Bord Fáilte's annual reports. In 1974 Bord Fáilte argued that industrial development should be kept well clear of scenic areas so that foreigners and Irish people alike need not see drab industrial structures while consuming the beauties of the Irish countryside; the landscape should be divided into development zones, with some areas carefully protected and others sacrificed to progress.[158] Annual reports also provided opportunities to raise awareness of environmental threats. For example, in 1979 Bord Fáilte insisted that

> an attractive environment is the cornerstone of the Irish tourist industry. While the main tourist areas are recognised as designated areas in the Tourist Development Plan and are a primary concern, there continue to be many threats to the rural and urban environment. There is often a widespread indifference to the whole issue of conservation. Changes in the use of land and water resources as a result of industrialisation, new agricultural techniques, urbanisation, etc., and the frequent low standards in the treatment of sewage and industrial waste, poor road standards, and inadequate management of public facilities such as toilets, public spaces, and refuse dumps, pose an ongoing threat to the environment and overall quality of life.
>
> The efforts of community and voluntary groups at national, regional, and local level in tackling such problems must be commended. Hopefully, it is a sign of the awakening of a general understanding of the benefits of a clear and healthy environment, but much remains to be achieved.[159]

The message had not changed in 1981, when the board reported some progress and increasing public awareness of environmental threats, or in 1985, when Bord Fáilte drew attention to the problem that pollution was more widespread than previously feared.[160] Between the late 1960s and early 1990s Bord Fáilte repeatedly stressed the need for careful management of the countryside and the protection of Ireland's natural amenities. As long as the environment remained "the cornerstone of Irish tourism," it was essential for tourism authorities, the government, and the Irish people to take green-space issues seriously.[161] Indeed, the 1994–99 *Tourism Development Plan* envisioned environmental protection as a centerpiece of the drive to create "sustainable tourism." While the report claimed that there now existed "an unprecedented level of environmental awareness in Ireland," it also conceded that there was "no room for complacency" because "our superior environment is mainly due to a historically low level of development rather than to any preconceived plan."[162]

Representations of Irish Landscape

Photographic and literary representations of Irish landscape offered for tourist consumption have changed remarkably little with time, yet this fact makes the particular framing or choice of subject in tourist photographs no less important. Whether captured in 1926, 1972, or the mid-1990s, images of the Gap of Dunloe near Killarney, for example, almost always feature the roadway meandering through the rugged, rocky mountains, taken from slightly up the hillside, and featuring a jaunting car.[163] Even so, images were often produced to match new marketing demands. For example, during the 1960s motor touring became a major emphasis of Tourist Board marketing efforts, and as a result, photos of automobiles were increasingly introduced into tourist guidebooks and advertising—generally showing a motor car in the foreground and a happy couple enjoying the scenery either from the car itself or from a slight distance. These images clearly demonstrated to potential visitors that Ireland's richest beauty spots could be easily reached in the comfort of an automobile, and the photos were further enhanced by texts stressing the relative dearth of motor traffic on Irish roadways.[164] Once motorcars became a standard part of the lexicon of tourism photography, they did not disappear; the fundamental ingredients remained largely the same. If there was any major shift in official Tourist Board photography, it had more to do with the skill of the photographers, the use of models rather than actual tourists (beginning in 1960 and probably influenced by the appearance of John Hinde Studios in the marketplace), and, of course, a much wider usage of color images as printing techniques improved during the 1960s and 1970s.

Ireland was perhaps best known through postcards produced by John Hinde Studios. Hinde possessed an unparalleled understanding of tourist tastes. In particular, he recognized the need for vivid color, clearly expressing the notion *"I wish I was there."*[165] Hinde's images presented an idealized Ireland, one that tourists inevitably wanted to remember, regardless of how often it had rained during their trip. From the publication of his first postcards in 1957, Hinde broke with photographic and artistic traditions:

9. and 10. Photographs of the Gap of Dunloe near Killarney were almost always shot from the same handful of vantage points, as these images from 1972 and 1996 illustrate. Courtesy of Bord Fáilte Éireann–Irish Tourist Board.

"By introducing bright foreground colours in his cards . . . He stuck primary colours prominently in the foreground to accentuate to viewers that, yes, they were looking at a COLOUR photograph . . . He was shrewd enough to realise that an audience used to seeing black and white pictures didn't just want to see a bit of colour tinting, it wanted to see A COLOUR PHOTOGRAPH."[166]

In order to make certain that his images matched his aesthetic objective, Hinde's photographers bent over backwards to *construct* images of Irish landscape, rather than simply presenting narrow views as was true in most travel photography. It was not a case of waiting days for the correct lighting, as photographers have done since the first camera appeared in the 1820s; rather, objects were introduced to each image based on what the photographer felt *should* be present. Hinde's photographers always carried foxglove in their cars so that it might be planted in the foreground of photographs, even when the flower would not grow naturally in the spot in question.[167] More striking still, models were carefully dressed to provide the necessary authenticity to an image. In the early 1990s, during an exhibition of Hinde postcards at the Museum of Modern Art in Dublin, David Noble, a well-known Hinde Studios photographer, recalled a ten-day photo shoot in the Aran Islands during which he hoped to capture a shot of fisherman carrying their currach into the sea while another mended his nets in the foreground. Despite telling the men what he hoped to capture, the local models arrived directly from church and dressed in their Sunday best: hardly the picture of rugged fishermen in wellies and Aran sweaters that Noble imagined. Making matters worse, when an effort was made to outfit one of the locals in a suitable sweater, the only such garment available in all of the Aran Islands was moth-eaten and too small.[168]

As in Hinde's photographs, where the touristic desire for color and authenticity was carefully catered to, stories in *Ireland of the Welcomes* were chosen to meet the demands of an external gaze. From the beginning, the magazine's designer, a Dutchman named Jan de Fouw, exerted considerable influence on content because "as an outsider, I had more of an open eye to what was interesting in Ireland than the Irish themselves."[169] There was a conscious effort to escape the "Killarney syndrome" and to cover other aspects of Irish scenery and culture, usually with a bent toward personal-interest stories.

The coverage of Ireland's extensive boglands provides a case in point. Before the 1960s and 1970s these areas were not presented to tourists as desirable places to visit. Many of the Irish themselves were deeply ambivalent. Those who grew up on the bog were viewed as little more than "bog-trotters" and represented "the symbol of poverty and backwardness," "ignorance and illiteracy." The bog was "itself in the Irish mind . . . a symbol of aridity and barrenness."[170] Beginning in the 1930s the great expanses of turf began to inspire a different set of ideas among a handful of officials, who increasingly viewed these areas as a potential source of fuel, even while others maintained a healthy dose of "amused skepticism."[171] In 1934 the government established the Turf Development Board, renamed Bord na Móna in 1946.[172] In subsequent years the Turf Board discovered how to efficiently mine Ireland's peat resources, constructed massive turf-burning power stations, and proudly presented the program as an Irish industrial-development success story, taking what was useless and making it into something exceedingly valuable.[173] The bogs were not romantic spaces and certainly were not worthy of the tourist gaze, unless it was to see Irish cleverness at work.

By the early 1970s, however, the bogs were increasingly romanticized, and they were seen more and more as uniquely Irish. In 1970, *Ireland of the Welcomes* published an issue featuring "a day on the bog" that dealt with the time-worn tools used by farmers to harvest turf for their fires, enthused about the wonderful conversations that might be had with farmers as they cut turf, and declared the bog to be "a grand place when the weather's right."[174] Another article in the same issue described the bogs as a "national liability for at least a thousand years" that was made useful only after the acceptance of nationalist demands that the bogs be used to promote Irish freedom. Today, the author enthused, "the patriot's dream has come true. Research and mechanisation have turned turf production into a large-scale national industry. Bord na Móna (the Turf Board) has had a more dynamic effect on Ireland than practically anything that has happened in its history."[175] The Tourist Board was beginning to understand that tourists, especially those from America, found bogs unique, romantic, and interesting, but at the same time there was a need to continue using them as a symbol of Ireland's modernity—in striking contrast to the bog-trotter stereotype.

Six years later, the romanticization of the bog continued apace. Irish poet Seamus Heaney was called on to write about his experiences on the bog. Though he acknowledged the great financial benefits of Bord na Móna, his prose reflected a far more romantic view of these places than was current previously. While Heaney admired the enterprise embodied by the exploitation of the bog, he maintained an "irrational attachment to the unspoiled wastes." The bog was not just beautiful; it was a catalogue of Ireland's long past, "Jungian ground" which functioned as a kind of "geological memory-bank," a "treasure trove" of objects "retrieved bit by bit by the turf-cutter." The bog was a "dark casket" containing "clues to our past and to our cultural identity."[176] For Heaney it was a conflict between his head and his heart, the old struggle between an Irish identity that was forward-looking and modern, and a sense of Irishness rooted in a timeless past of the imagination. No longer were bogs a liability; instead, they constituted a storehouse of the Irish past, a direct link to timeless ancestors, and a beautiful unspoiled retreat from the present. It would be wrong to portray Heaney's view as one defined by tourists—his extensive catalog of bog-related poetry clearly shows his personal connection with these spaces—but the fact that Bord Fáilte chose to publish the poet's comments illustrates the growing tourist interest in these places. Finally, in 1987, the editors of *Ireland of the Welcomes* devoted an entire issue to the bog. This time readers learned about the types of bog, read poetry celebrating these uniquely Irish places, perused accounts of unique bog flora and fauna, discovered the archeological inheritance provided to the Irish people, and were made aware of the back-breaking but romantic experience of hand-cutting turf. Bord na Móna did not inspire outright criticism, but the uneasy relationship between conservation and exploitation was acknowledged in more blunt fashion than in previous issues. This time an author wrote that the case for environmentalism was long a difficult one to "impress upon Irish people—especially those who live beside the peatlands." For them, the bog represented a resource to be exploited; their attitudes were "utilitarian." Abstract concepts such as "ecosystems and biotopes" held little sway. Yet, on the other hand, the author added that more bogs should be preserved intact, thus casting aside the notion that the only use for Ireland's peatlands was the generation of a few more megawatts.[177]

The bog has become an openly contested space, a symbol of Ireland's successful ability to straddle both ancient and modern living, to debate and discuss its places, spaces, and past. Bogland is no longer synonymous with backwardness; instead, it is thoroughly romanticized and celebrated for the ecosystem, history, and unique scenery available there. It was a transformation that had little to do with Bord na Móna propaganda and far more to do with the tourist gaze and with official desires not only to satisfy that gaze but also to bring tourist money into areas like Roscommon, which previously had little to offer tourists in the way of scenic grandeur or famous historic sites/sights.

Conclusion

From the first publications of the Irish Tourist Association to the most recent books and films by Bord Fáilte and Tourism Brand Ireland, Irish landscapes and townscapes have been one of the most important aspects of the tourism product. Tourists have flocked to places like Killarney in order to consume beautiful spaces, and tourist authorities have responded by working to physically shape Irish landscapes, whether through development and improvement projects or through conservation. Likewise, local voices like those of Father Scanlon and Lord Sligo, to say nothing of the numerous Tidy Towns committees, have also sought to ensure that Irish aesthetics and economics fell into line, presenting Irish landscapes and townscapes in a uniquely "Irish" way. Tourist guidebooks and postcards reflect a gradual trend toward niche-marketing (motor touring, for example), the growing importance of new technology (such as color photography), and even changing ideas about which landscapes are desirable and appealing (the bog).

From the 1920s the Irish looked upon their physical spaces as a way to portray Irishness to the world, and tourism developers encouraged their fellow citizens to actively consider the foreign gaze when building new structures or maintaining old ones. Most expressed a palpable desire not only to attract tourism income but also to show Ireland in the most positive light possible. The alteration or preservation of physical spaces was viewed in nationalist terms every bit as much as in economic ones. At the same time attitudes about the importance of earning a living *in* Ireland, as in the case of the Gaelic language revival, were never far from the surface for many groups. Landownership represented a potential source of revenue, a fact that could produce behavior that was either selflessly patriotic or an outright insult to the greater good, as in the case of Poulnabrone, depending on circumstances.

In the final analysis this chapter suggests that the Irish landscape has been an important area of debate about Irishness. The active effort by many Irish people to shape their physical space had the effect of melding environmental and aesthetic trends with economic concerns and long-standing attitudes toward landownership; the result was a long-running dialogue about uniquely Irish places and spaces.

7

Tourism and the Tiger, 1994–2007

Beginning in 1987, Ireland experienced arguably the most dramatic transformation in the country's entire economic history; the "Celtic Tiger" of the mid- and late 1990s sparked hitherto unimaginable economic development, construction, and job growth. Unemployment, once the bane of Irish life, virtually disappeared. Beginning in 1994, some one thousand jobs were added each week, more than fifty thousand per year. By 2000, Ireland was *importing* workers while attracting many of its native sons and daughters home from "exile." The change was so dramatic that when this book was being researched, potential immigrants faced long lines at the immigration office, many opting to camp out, joining the queue in the earliest hours of the morning in order to assure service. Job growth reflected stunning economic expansion. Irish growth rates exceeded all others in Europe and often surpassed the four "Asian Tigers." In 1995, the country enjoyed a 10 percent increase in gross domestic product (GDP), while in 1996 the gross national product (GNP) was three times higher than at any point in the previous decade, averaging 5.4 percent in the four years to 1997. Growth rates were the highest in the world, some 7.5 percent per year, and inflation was low. The national debt was reduced to 69 percent of the GNP in 1997. Irish living standards soon rose to match the European average for the first time.[1] Although tourist postcards continued to feature the slogan "Rush Hour in Ireland" atop a sheep-strewn roadway, life actually moved at a pace closer to the speed of now nearly ubiquitous BMWs.

The tourist industry both contributed to and was altered by the Celtic Tiger. By 1994, the debates about how to present Ireland to visitors and the desirability of doing so had established an efficient and modern tourist industry. Tourism products were in place. Marketing was sophisticated. The Irish image was welcoming and friendly. The Irish people built it; now the tourists came in unimaginable numbers. From 1994 onward Irish tourism expanded by as much as 18 percent each year—staggering when compared with the international average of only 4.5 percent during the same period.[2] Although England was always Ireland's largest single source of tourism revenue, profound growth in the English market continued during the boom period. Between 1993 and 1997, for example, the number of British tourists increased by 17 percent, from 1,783,000 to 2,590,000.[3] These numbers reached 3,494,000 in 2000. At the same time, revenue increased from £401.6 million in 1993 to £873.4 million in 2000.[4] Growth in the North American market was equally impressive with revenue growing 18 percent between 1993 and 1997, while the number of American visitors increased by 16 percent. While just 422,000 North Americans visited Ireland in 1993,[5] by 2000 this number grew to 1,058,000. The increase in North American earnings was notable, moving from £316.6 million in 1996 to £541.8 million in 2000.[6] The numbers were similarly positive from Europe, which had only become a substantial segment of the Irish tourist market in the 1980s.[7] In 1987, 382,000 Europeans, mostly from France and Germany, visited Ireland.[8] By 1997 this number reached 1,168,000,[9] and by 2000 it hit 1,451,000. Earnings increased from £457.7 million to £578.1 million during the same period.[10]

The Irish made Ireland Irish and then successfully sold their new identity to the world, but there was nothing fixed about the new product. The two great tourism-related debates remained. What does it mean to be Irish and how should Irishness be balanced with the nation's interests? This concluding chapter examines both the continued transformation of the Irish tourism industry since 1994 and the struggle to reconcile Irishness with economic demands. After examining why tourist numbers increased so dramatically during the 1990s, the chapter outlines continued government efforts to reformulate the tourist industry to more closely meet the national interest. The final section illustrates that the challenge of balancing culture, economic need, and disparate ideas about the meaning of Irishness remain an important part of Irish national discourse.

Coming of the Golden Horde

It is virtually impossible to identify any single cause for the explosive increase in tourist traffic to Ireland during the 1990s. Instead, several specific conditions of possibility combined to create an environment ripe for dramatic growth. These include: the long-term effort of tourism advocates and others to create a successful tourist industry (see chapters 1–6); the advent of government spending commensurate with the industry's significance (see chapter 3); increased political stability in Northern Ireland; the sudden "pop culture" notoriety that resulted from a proliferation of popular Irish rock bands and Irish-themed films; and the significant increase in the number of Irish pubs and products around the world. When these factors combined with a favorable economic situation in the United States and Britain, as well as with a continued expansion of Irish tourist products and accommodation, the pump was primed for previously unimagined expansion. The country had something to sell and the infrastructure necessary to sell it. It is worth examining several of these factors in turn.

The End of Violence

Despite a general trend after World War II toward tourism growth, Irish tourism suffered a series of severe difficulties in the 1970s related to two oil crises (1973 and 1979) and, more important, violence in Northern Ireland.[11] In the years after partition, tourism tended to draw Northern Ireland and the Republic closer together. The Irish Tourist Association and its Northern counterpart, the Ulster Tourist Development Association (UTDA) had close ties during the 1920s and 1930s.[12] During the 1940s, cross-border tourism cooperation was in contrast to the official "cold war" that raged between North and South and represented a rare *public* display of collaboration during a period when the two states were officially divided by a deep chasm of mutual antagonism.[13] Cooperation continued, albeit behind closed doors during the 1950s,[14] and tourism topped the agenda during the famous meetings between Irish Taoiseach Seán Lemass and Northern Ireland Prime Minister Terence O'Neill in January 1965. The two men agreed on the value of developing cross-border tourism links, and it was decided to explore several areas for cooperation; these included the possibility of joint promotion abroad, the encouragement of "inter-flow between the two parts of Ireland," the abolition of the *triptyque* system for private cars at the border, and consideration of permitting the free passage of hired cars through border checkpoints.[15] It was critical to eliminate any hassles that travelers might encounter.[16] There was also discussion of launching a joint venture to develop Enniskillen Airfield, a regional airport that would facilitate more efficient travel to Sligo, Donegal, and Leitrim, as well as attracting more tourists to Fermanagh and Tyrone.[17] Finally, the two leaders affirmed that their respective ministers with authority for tourism development, Erskine Childers in the South and Brian Faulkner in the North, should hold joint talks in the near future.[18] This promising state of affairs lasted until the onset of the Troubles in 1968.

Throughout the 1970s and 1980s, there were regular meetings between officials from both North and South; tourism was almost entirely at the mercy of the political situation, however. After the IRA cease-fire took effect in August 1994, the road was cleared for an increased tourism push in Northern Ireland as well as for an expansion of North-South tourism cooperation. In November of that year authorities from both countries announced that a £6million cross-border marketing campaign would be launched in 1995 in the hope of attracting an additional 92,000 tourists. While details were not immediately announced, it was agreed that the two tourist boards would collaborate on an "Ireland Vacations" television campaign in Britain, America, France, Germany, and Holland. As always, the campaign would include houses, gardens, literary tours, museums, castles, and heritage and cultural attractions. The cease-fire represented what Charlie McCreevy, Dublin's minister for tourism and trade, called an opportunity to "maximise the island's greatest asset—the natural beauty and heritage." McCreevy's Northern counterpart agreed, predicting, "tourism has the capability and imagination necessary to seize the opportunities which now present themselves." And opportunities there were: by October 1994 the Northern Ireland Tourist Board (NITB) had already experienced an increase of over 90 percent in visitor inquiries as compared with the previous year.[19]

In the following year a more significant program was announced that called for an integrated island-wide "Tourism Brand for Ireland" to be launched in 1997. It was anticipated that the plan would cost £5 million to kick off and some £20 million to £30 million annually thereafter. Bord Fáilte and the NITB would collaborate on the project[20]—ultimately reaching a level of cooperation that was celebrated by a special award granted by England's *Observer* newspaper in 1996; the award recognized the two boards as "a model of cross-border cooperation, as they have combined their respective strengths to promote an industry that remains central to Ireland's long-term economic development."[21]

Bord Fáilte was very excited about the new program, envisioning it as "a critical change in focus for the marketing of the island of Ireland over the next five years." Tourism Brand Ireland represented the first time that "all of Irish tourism will be able to unify behind a single market initiative, a tourism brand which will contain the same central message, with variations and modifications which meet the needs and expectations of individual markets and cultures." The program, it was argued, would provide a powerful tool, strengthening the island's market position and allowing Ireland to attain its ultimate tourist potential.[22]

On 11 November 1996, Tourism Brand Ireland was launched, eighteen months after the initial market research had commenced. I have already described the emotionally evocative video that represented the first installment of the new marketing program (see introduction); it was only one part of a "complete portfolio" of materials compiled to communicate the central message of the campaign—that Ireland was not so much a place as "an emotional experience." In all cases the term "Ireland" was used, always in English, without denoting North or South.[23] It was as though past conflicts between the two Irelands never existed, as though sectarianism was not even a memory.

The development of the new program brought the long period of Troubles-related pessimism to an abrupt halt. In Northern Ireland, for example, tourism numbers began climbing very soon after the first announcement of the cease-fire, and a new spirit of cooperation between North and South on tourism matters arose shortly thereafter. Despite occasional outbreaks of violence, the new environment even caused tourism officials in Belfast to be buoyant with optimism after tourism shot up 67 percent in just one year,[24] and these officials subsequently launched a campaign to promote the proliferation of bed-and-breakfasts on the Falls Road, the working-class neighborhood most closely associated with the IRA.[25] As far as many tourists were concerned, there were no longer any reasons *not* to travel to Ireland. Crossing the border no longer required special paperwork as it had before 1965, Northern Ireland was safe for visitors, and there was little reason to fear traveling freely across the whole island—a fact that tourism authorities could publicize widely.

Even so, there were further challenges. While decommissioning and the creation of a new policing body attracted most of the news coverage, establishing cross-border groups to handle tourism, fishing, and the rest also proved controversial. In April 1998, John Bruton, leader of the Fine Gael party, explained that the purpose of these efforts was to build a "structure of co-dependence which makes conflict impossible" by replacing the "traditional aspirations which made conflict inevitable up to now." The problem was that the various parties involved could read efforts toward this end differently. When unionists proposed developing joint cooperative ventures with Scotland, nationalists viewed the suggestion as a clear attempt to strengthen the union, while nationalist efforts to develop cross-border ventures were seen as an extension of Lemass's original policy to use cooperation to move toward a united Ireland. The "game of suspicion would gradually corrode the new institutions."[26]

At the end of November 1998, Tony Blair, the British prime minister and one of the driving forces behind the process that led to the Good Friday Agreement, flew to Ireland to launch a joint British-Irish council that would address issues spanning the Irish Sea as laid out in the agreement. Blair used the meeting to begin pushing for the establishment of cross-border cooperative bodies. Although there was considerable enthusiasm for the possibility of expanded all-Ireland marketing,[27] tourism and transport were already proving problematic because the Ulster Unionist Party (UUP) was unwilling to accept all-Ireland distribution of European development funds—money that would invariably benefit the Republic disproportionately.[28] Unionists insisted that tourism be removed from the list of cross-border bodies in favor of the development of separate organizations that would work together in the same manner that had been in place since the mid-1960s.[29] During their discussions Blair and Trimble left tourism on the table, but when they agreed to the establishment of six cross-border bodies on 24 November 1998, tourism was omitted from the list.[30]

By 1 December all consensus had eroded and there was talk that the devolution of powers called for by the Good Friday Agreement might not take place. Challenges existed on both sides of the border. While nationalists in Northern Ireland viewed North-South bodies as a "counter-weight" to the unionist majority, unionists were reluctant to agree to extensive cooperation for the same reason. Meanwhile, the government in Dublin resisted the establishment of cross-border bodies out of a reluctance to restrict departmental authority.[31] Two days later, Tony Blair returned to Belfast to find a solution to the impasse.[32] By the following morning, 4 December, a tentative agreement was reached on four North-South implementation bodies: trade and business development, transport, EU programs, and tourism. The plan was certainly not complete, and the deadlock was not yet forgotten, but progress did seem to be at hand.[33] The parties reached a final agreement on 18 December, following yet another eighteen-hour series of negotiations ending in what one delegate called "a victory for common sense." This time six cross-border bodies were agreed, with one more now included as "an unofficial seventh cross-border body to regulate tourism." This seventh body would be created through the merger and privatization of the Northern Ireland Tourist Board and Bord Fáilte.[34]

Relatively little changed in 1999 in terms of cross-border tourism cooperation. To be sure, Northern Ireland enjoyed a dramatic tourism expansion, showing growth of almost 20 percent between 1999 and 2000. Further growth was predicted following the establishment of the new cross-border company.[35] Tourism Ireland Ltd. was incorporated in December 2000 after the circulation of a memorandum outlining the functions of the North/South tourism company,[36] and it was given responsibility for all international marketing beginning in 2002. The new publicity body comprised one hundred former Bord Fáilte employees and thirty from the Northern Ireland Tourist Board, with another twenty to be hired by the Northern authorities. The new company acquired "ownership and management of Tourism Brand Ireland, strategic all-island destination marketing in all markets outside the island of Ireland, and responsibility for the entire overseas office network." Although Tourism Ireland Ltd. was assigned the task of delivering international marketing materials, Bord Fáilte and the Northern Ireland Tourist Board remained in charge of developing the underlying products. The two national boards also retained control over marketing domestic tourism, research and planning, niche marketing, regional marketing, the implementation of sports-tourism initiatives, festivals and cultural events, the grading of hotel premises, and the development of sustainable tourism.[37]

With North and South working together, there was no longer any reason for tourists to stay away. The new structure would pose challenges and the success of the new venture would depend on a "positive attitude and a willingness to co-operate," but in the short term Irish tourism was freed of a significant stumbling block.[38]

Popular Culture and Irish Products

Ireland's growing status as a center of popular culture, in contrast to its earlier obscurity, aided the new publicity effort. Following the foundation of Bord Fáilte in the 1950s, it became painfully obvious to tourism promoters that Ireland was largely unknown beyond the shores of Éire: "Ireland didn't exist outside Ireland." Americans, of course, celebrated St. Patrick's Day, but tourist authorities believed that there was little Irish about the American version of the holiday; even the whiskey consumed was Scottish. From a tourism standpoint continental Europeans often confused Ireland with Iceland, a cold, dreary, and frozen rock somewhere in the Atlantic Ocean.[39] In an attempt to correct this misunderstanding, the Export Board, Fógra Fáilte, Aer Lingus, and the Department of External Affairs formed a cultural relations section during the 1950s in order to "get Irish things better known." The group worked to market Irish products like Jameson's whiskey and Guinness stout; they strove to create a widespread belief in the "genuine Irish welcome" and to make it clear that Ireland was not a desolate rock in the North Atlantic, but rather a green, vibrant, and quickly developing yet timelessly rustic country.

As it happened, the group's efforts proved remarkably successful. Guinness and Jameson's whiskey are now ubiquitous. Surveys conducted by Bord Fáilte consistently show that tourists overwhelmingly cite the "Irish people" as one of the highlights of their travels and primary reasons for traveling.[40] And, of course, prefabricated Irish pubs now dispense their libations in virtually every city around the world, made to order by a Dun Laoghaire–based company specializing in selling all the right kitsch.[41]

Ireland also received a dramatic boost as a prospective tourist destination when filmmakers started to represent the country in popular films. John

Ford's *Quiet Man* (1952) inspired untold numbers of American tourists to visit Cong, County Mayo, after initial release of the movie. Subsequent showings on television and eventually VHS and DVD further enhanced the picture's impact. Some years later, David Lean's *Ryan's Daughter* (1970) sparked a similar increase in tourism around the Dingle Peninsula. Yet these early Irish-centered films represented only the tip of a much larger iceberg.

In 1973, the Arts Council of Ireland was empowered to assist the creation of an Irish film industry. In 1977, the Arts Council took advantage of this power by providing film script awards to indigenous writers. The film *Poitín* (1978), directed by Bob Quinn, was the first beneficiary of the new monies and helped inspire the creation of the Irish Film Board in 1981. Between 1981 and 1987 the Film Board helped fund work by major directors such as Neil Jordan and John Boorman, establishing them as significant figures in cinema and going some way toward making Ireland an attractive location for and subject of major films. Between 1988 and 1992, the government further increased efforts to attract filmmakers by offering special incentives to those willing to make their movies in Ireland, with significant results; movies included: *The Courier* (1988), *Reefer and the Model* (1988), *The Field* (1990), *The Commitments* (1991), *Into the West* (1992), and *Far and Away* (1992). Although the box office for these films was not always huge, they helped further establish Ireland as a film center.[42] More movies followed, including blockbusters such as Mel Gibson's Oscar-winning epic *Braveheart* (1994) that was set in Scotland but largely filmed in the Wicklow Mountains outside of Dublin. More often than not, movie audiences found a rustic, simple, friendly Ireland that was little removed from the tourist board image that was by now well established. The impact on Irish tourism was dramatic. Naoise Barry, film commissioner for the Irish Film Board, summed up the situation by saying, "Irish cinema has a huge impact on Ireland's tourism industry. [Major films] will be seen by millions around the world for years to come. Ireland's rural landscape has enormous appeal to film-maker and tourist alike."[43] In 2007, Fáilte Ireland (see below) estimated that film and television representations of Ireland were responsible for as much as €250 million in tourism revenue annually.

At the same time, especially among a younger audience, the popularity of rock bands like U2 and The Corrs should not go unnoticed. Quite simply, during the 1990s, U2 became the most popular rock band in the world. Their records and CDs sold many millions of copies, their songs received staggering airplay, and their concerts packed massive stadiums and outdoor venues around the world—each show resembling a gargantuan revival meeting, a tribal gathering, more than merely a rock concert. In the present context the group's success is important because

> it is difficult to read or hear anything relating to U2 without confronting sooner or later that they are an "Irish" band. If individual members do not raise the issue, commentators, journalists, or fans feel compelled to. Although it is impossible to define the category of "Irishness," a large part of the band's significance and impact depends specifically upon its national status in an increasingly multinational world, and particularly on the great variety of connotations which trail that identity into the twenty-first century.[44]

Unlike most Irish bands, U2 remains based in Dublin—Bono (Paul Hewson) and The Edge (Dave Evans) living just south of the city in the wealthy suburb of Killiney.[45]

For music fans across Europe and America the country of U2, the Pogues, The Corrs, Van Morrison, Enya, Sinéad O'Connor, the Chieftains, and Riverdance represented a significant cultural draw throughout the 1990s—something on which Dublin Tourism has tried to capitalize in recent years with a Dublin music-scene walking tour that traverses the city from one important musical site to the next. Rock music and the continuing popularity of traditional Irish music have made Ireland "hip," and when combined with the Celtic Tiger image of Ireland as a country on the make, it is unsurprising that young people flooded in. The Emerald Isle is no longer a destination purely for families and the more mature, but now exerts a strong attraction for younger visitors—a fact that makes itself abundantly clear when wandering Dublin's streets or traveling around the country.

Fáilte Ireland

In contrast to the 1990s, the first years of the new millennium were difficult ones for the Irish tourist industry. The initial "crisis descended from the skies" and had "the potential to torpedo much of the economy and much of what has been achieved in growth."[46] Foot-and-mouth disease, a viral infection that causes high fever as well as blisters on the tongue and feet of cloven-hoofed animals, struck Great Britain with a vengeance beginning on 20 February 2001. Because the disease spreads quickly and is virtually untreatable, the only recourse is to destroy whole herds of livestock. The first outbreak was in Essex, England, and within weeks 2,024 more farms were afflicted.[47] The Countryside Agency put the cost at between £800 million and £2.4 billion in livestock losses, while British tourism suffered a still worse fate, losing between £2 billion and £3 billion.[48] Ireland was spared the horrors of widespread destruction—only one farm, in Proleek, County Louth, was actually hit by the disease—but tourism still suffered. To avoid a widespread epidemic, the Irish government shut down the countryside and many attractions. Livestock could not be moved, hill walking was banned, national parks were closed, angling was stopped, equestrian sports were forbidden. In effect, the country was closed to tourism. Forty-one days after the outbreak, the government finally announced that the country was open again.[49] By August authorities were breathing a sigh of relief. Tourism numbers were down by 2.4 percent, largely because of a significant drop in English tourists, but overall "it could have been worse."[50]

Yet natural disaster was not the only threat to the tourist industry. The September 11 terrorist attacks in New York City, in the skies over western Pennsylvania, and in Washington, D.C., sent shock waves around the world. It was not simply that nearly three thousand people were dead for reasons that most people did not understand, but that passenger planes were used as weapons. The image of planes flying into buildings was like something drawn from a Hollywood action film and it was more than many travelers could stomach—even when world governments, especially the United States, dramatically enhanced airline security. The impact was severe; in the United States alone, the airline sector lost 20 percent of its value overnight. Flights were cut, jobs were eliminated, and travelers stayed home—at least initially. Expanded airline security only made travel seem that much less desirable.[51]

For tourism officials in Ireland, the horror was twofold. Just as was true for millions of people around the world, the attack prompted shock and grief. Closer to home, the second horror was the reality that the devastation at Ground Zero in New York "will resonate in the Irish industry well into next year." Bord Fáilte predicted "big losses" for the Irish tourism sector,[52] and Dr. James McDaid, the minister responsible for tourism development, predicted as much as a 17 percent drop in tourist traffic extending well into 2002.[53] A drop in tourism revenue, in turn, meant lost jobs and lost livelihoods.

While foot-and-mouth disease and terror attacks were visible threats, the Irish tourist industry faced another challenge as well: the Irish were slowly losing their reputation for friendliness, especially in Britain. Always the largest market for Ireland's tourist product, the number of British holidaymakers dropped slightly in 1999 from 970,000 tourists to 940,000. Faced with what authorities hoped was not a long-term downward trend, Bord Fáilte hired an Edinburgh consultancy firm to examine the problem. The firm's report was worrying.[54] As far as tourism authorities were concerned, "nothing in the entire array of the Irish tourist product is more important than the quality of the Irish welcome," yet the report made clear that many prospective tourists no longer felt the same welcome they had come to expect.[55]

The problem was probably not a fundamental shift in Irish character, but rather the collective impact of daunting change. As noted above, Ireland went from being poor and backward to relative affluence almost overnight. At the same time, tourist numbers far exceeded the actual population of the country itself. With the world turned upside down, it hardly seems surprising that the people of Ireland needed time to adjust. They needed to undergo the kind of dialogue detailed in these pages. They needed to collectively assess what it meant to be Irish in a land of BMWs, widespread tourism, and the sudden availability of a hitherto unimaginable standard of living.

Finally, there was at least one other factor that required the attention of authorities: the reality that tourism marketing in both Northern Ireland and the Republic was, for the first time, to be conducted by the same organization: Tourism Ireland Ltd. As noted, the creation of a single body to handle all foreign marketing of Ireland was a symbol of peace and cooperation, and the developments that prompted the creation of Tourism Ireland played an important role in the tourism boom of the 1990s. Yet Tourism Ireland had another effect as well, this one more worrisome for those still working for Bord Fáilte. Specifically, Tourism Ireland Ltd. assumed one of the tourist board's most important tasks—overseas marketing, raising the not insignificant question of whether the old structure for Irish tourism development was still relevant in the twenty-first century.

As foot-and-mouth disease, the disappearing welcome, the impending launch of Tourism Ireland Ltd., and eventually 9/11 struck home, government and tourism officials considered how best to address the challenge of developing tourism in a new millennium. Minister for Tourism Dr. James McDaid asked himself an unsurprising question: was it time to shake up the bureaucratic structure of Irish tourism? Bord Fáilte was a more professional and sophisticated organization than it had been in 1953, but was it suited to new realities? The desire to centralize control by creating Dublin-led Regional Tourism Organisations had gone wrong almost immediately during the mid-1960s; was it now time to assume *real* centralized control? Could a new organization reverse the perception problem while developing new marketing strategies that would continue to expand Ireland's tourism marketplace? Might a new tourism organization, freed from its history and armed with a new structure, ultimately create new attractions and new plans? Now that Tourism Ireland handled overseas marketing, was Bord Fáilte structured in the most productive fashion for handling domestic tourism development? For McDaid, the answer seemed overwhelming: it was time to create a new tourism organization and time to retire Bord Fáilte.

For their part, Bord Fáilte officials and staff were content to proceed as they had always done, setting goals, striving to achieve them, and, when faced with a problem such as the disappearing welcome, looking for ways to quietly encourage changed behavior. As a case in point, to solve the problem of the disappearing welcome, Bord Fáilte used the same strategy that so successfully redefined the Irish landscape: they launched a new competition, the "Irish Welcome Awards," which rewarded those who truly embodied the old "Céad Míle Fáilte" as opposed to the new "Frosty Fáilte."[56] As far as many in Bord Fáilte were concerned, the old structure was far from broken and the evidence to support this view was clear to see; in 2001 British travel agents voted to award Bord Fáilte the prestigious Travel Trade Gazette Award for top tourist/destination board in the world.[57]

Neither awards nor the status quo was acceptable to McDaid and his colleagues in the Department of Arts, Sport, and Tourism. In late August or early September 2001, the government contacted the directors of Bord Fáilte and CERT, the Council for Education, Recruitment and Training, suggesting that the two organizations amalgamate.[58] Like Bord Fáilte, CERT was a product of the staggering tourism development efforts of the 1950s and 1960s. The government formed the council thirteen years after the Christenberry report (see chapter 2) had recommended a formalized structure for training hotel workers, thus taking responsibility for training away from Bord Fáilte and so freeing the tourist board to single-mindedly pursue development and promotion work.[59] As time passed, CERT established training centers around Ireland at Killybegs, Sligo, Galway, Limerick, Tralee, Cork, Waterford, Tallaght, Dublin, and Athlone. Students could pursue courses in cooking, waitressing, housekeeping, tourism, bartending, reception, and management, among other careers.[60] Given the striking lack of government records or Dáil debate about the organization, as well as a surprising lack of contentious news coverage, CERT apparently sparked relatively little controversy and was successful in reaching a large client base. In 1992 alone CERT provided training to some 10,000 students.[61] In 1995, during the first years of the Celtic Tiger, no fewer than 98 percent of CERT graduates found employment, despite the fact that the number of students rose to 11,500.[62] The organization was the very model of accomplishment.

Successful or not, McDaid was convinced that "one agency, capable of delivering more integrated, streamlined programs and services, might provide the best delivery model for supporting the future development of the industry in line with Government objectives." On 5 September 2001 officials from both the tourist board and from CERT notified McDaid that they accepted the new initiative.[63] At the same time the two bodies released a statement noting that they would spend the coming weeks carefully studying how best to effect the merger.[64] On the surface, everything appeared entirely copasetic.

Behind the scenes and off the record, fear was widespread among tourist board staffers. As the majority of research for this book was completed, tourist board officials worried about what jobs would be allotted the planned "National Tourism Development Authority" (more commonly called "Fáilte Ireland") and whether they and their friends would have a place in the new body. Many were unclear about the division of labor between Tourism Ireland and the development authority. At the same time, Tourism Ireland acquired roughly one-half Bord Fáilte's staff and these men and women worried about whether the move from a semistate body to a private one would negatively impact their incomes and pensions.[65] For many who had given their lives to tourism development, nothing seemed certain anymore.

The staffs were left to worry for roughly a year before the minister presented any significant new information. Finally, in September 2002, a new minister for arts, sport and tourism, John O'Donoghue, announced that legislation creating the new tourism body would receive fast-track treatment so that the new board would be in place in time for the 2003 tourist season.[66] The minister presented his bill on 21 November 2002. While Fáilte Ireland would not handle international marketing, it nevertheless maintained many of Bord Fáilte's old responsibilities. The new board would "encourage, promote and support the development and marketing of tourist facilities within the state" by overseeing education (CERT's former role), developing tourism products, grading and registering hotels, engaging in research and planning, pursuing advertising and publicity activities within the Republic, and providing advice and consultancy services. Of particular interest, Fáilte Ireland would also have the ability to establish tourism-related companies—a risky role that had caused considerable problems during the Fáilte Hotels controversy that nearly destroyed Irish tourism during the late 1940s.[67]

The legislation passed easily through the Seanad, although questions were raised about ministerial authority and the process for selecting Fáilte Ireland officials.[68] The bill was subsequently presented to the Dáil on 12 February 2003 where it received a warm welcome. One by one Dáil ministers expressed their approval of the new legislation, while also noting the successes of Bord Fáilte and CERT. As Jack Wall, a Labour TD, put it, "Bord Fáilte and CERT deserve to be congratulated for their work over many years. Bord Fáilte did an amazing amount of work to promote tourism in Ireland. CERT has had a major influence with regard to the training of personnel in the tourism industry."[69] Unlike past argument over the creation of new tourism bodies, Fáilte Ireland simply did not inspire very much debate. At the dawn of the new millennium, almost all considered tourism to be a national interest and few doubted that changed circumstances might warrant a new development board.

Now four years old, Fáilte Ireland appears to be a success. Armed with more funding than any previous Irish tourist board, the new body is tremendously active in sponsoring events, pursuing environmental initiatives, lobbying for the construction of facilities such as conference centers and sports complexes, and developing new tourism products. On the training front, CERT's remit to oversee training programs also continues, complete with regular workshops to help train those already active in the industry. Even competitions such as the Irish Welcome Awards continue, attempting to assure that Ireland's tourism product is safe.[70] Far from the revolution that many in Bord Fáilte feared as they awaited legislation in 2002, in many respects Fáilte Ireland represents striking continuity with the past.

"The Dingle Wrangle"

Despite the creation of a new tourist board and widespread consensus about the importance of tourism, the long-running debates about national identity and the national interest continued unabated during the first years of the twenty-first century. Not only does tourism remain a nexus for debate and discussion, national discourse continues to involve many of the issues described in these pages.

There is no better example of this still ongoing dialogue than the heated conflict over the name ascribed to the town of Dingle, the little fishing village that, as early as 1924, ITA advocates believed had the potential to become a major tourist draw. As described in chapter 1, most Dingle residents were ambivalent about tourism at first. In fact, the only way that Irish Tourist Association officials were able to establish a local branch was to promise that tourism was synonymous with the improvement of infrastructure. During the 1920s better roads, drainage, and sewerage trumped all other concerns. The national interest, at least as far as Dingle residents were concerned, was closely tied to an improvement in the standard of living. Although the notion that tourists might actually flood into Dingle was impossibly abstract to most residents, the townspeople were anxious to get whatever they could from the ITA and the central government.

During the 1960s tourism and government officials earmarked monies to develop hotels, resort facilities, and beach access for tourists[71]—a timely investment because the release of David Lean's film *Ryan's Daughter* in 1970, filled with beautiful area scenery, quickly attracted the attention of an ever-increasing tide of visitors and prompted the construction of still more facilities. The appearance, in 1983–84, of a friendly dolphin, which area entrepreneurs soon named Fungie, prompted Dingle's final rush toward tourism greatness. In 1987, just one sailor carried tourists out to see Fungie, twelve passengers at a time. By 1991 the number of boats, which varied widely in size, reached fifteen. Tourism was now the town's largest source of income. "Dingle" was a tourist brand, synonymous with beautiful scenery, a fun-loving porpoise, and a higher density of ancient sites than virtually anywhere else in the world.[72] If the people of Dingle doubted the significance of tourism in 1924, by 2004 public skepticism was virtually nonexistent.

Consensus did not mean an absence of debate about either the national interest or national identity. During the spring of 2005 Dingle catapulted into the national and international spotlight as the result of a heated, sometimes nasty, debate about precisely what to call the town. The incident started in 2003 when the Oireachtas passed the Official Languages Act. Just as politicians during the early days of Irish independence sought to save the Irish language by promoting its use in government offices and in schools, and by considering the creation of Gaelic language preserves free of tourists (see chapter 4), the new legislation was intended to "promote the use of the Irish language for official purposes in the state."[73] One section of the act stipulated that English language place names would no longer be acceptable in Gaeltacht areas, so the minister for community, rural, and Gaeltacht affairs, Éamon Ó Cuív—Éamon de Valera's grandson—insisted that the town of Dingle change its name to "An Daingean," an Irish word meaning "fort." The name "Dingle" would no longer appear on "maps, road signs, statutory instruments and official correspondence." As far as the minister was concerned, the legislation was clear and there was little room for discussion. When asked about the change, Ó Cuív huffed, "It is An Daingean, full stop. The days of walking both sides of the street are over. It's a nonsense not having linguistic criterion attached to the Gaeltacht."[74]

Despite the minister's definitive sense of closure, by changing the name from "Dingle" to "An Daingean," Ó Cuív reignited debates about core versus periphery, urban versus rural, Ireland's relationship to its colonial history, and the importance of tourism relative to a uniquely Gaelic Irishness.

While the monetary stakes were much higher than at any previous point in the history of Irish tourism, the fundamental debate about Irishness was little changed.

For those living in Dingle town, about 1,800 residents, the name change represented a direct attack by Dublin authorities on both the villagers' sense of identity and their primary source of income. One pub owner told the *New York Times* that the change "was thrown upon us with the stroke of a pen." For many, such top-down management inspired memory of English rule from Dublin. For the editorial board of the *Irish Examiner,* the change was "not only an intolerable subversion of our democracy but a show of contemptible arrogance by Government and local authorities, that has not been witnessed since the days when we were ruled from Dublin Castle."[75]

The historical value of the Dingle name also captured the imagination of some townspeople. One group of activists formed an informational campaign to fight the change: the Dingle Name Campaign. While combating centralized control and a perceived attack on democracy was at the heart of their argument, history was also a factor. The group took pains to trace the history of "Dingle" from the twelfth century forward, pleading, "The Minister and his department have said that Dingle is a corrupted place name, and that it doesn't mean anything. Dingle has been known as Dingle for the past 750 years. How long must a town have its name before it has meaning?"[76] Every native resident grew up in a place called "Dingle"; for these people the word meant "home."

Above all, campaigners argued that the name change would cripple Dingle's tourist industry. From the beginning, local tourism officials feared that Gaelic language signs would confuse tourists and lead to disaster. Tourists were "getting dizzy in the head" trying to make sense of new road signs. A local west Kerry councilor, Michael O'Shea, added, "We might write to Minister Ó Cuív and tell him that foreigners do not understand the Irish language. Perhaps a new sign should now be put up on the N86: 'If you don't understand Irish, don't go beyond this point.'"[77] Justifying their fear, the Dingle Name Campaign conducted a survey over the St. Patrick's Day bank holiday in 2007 and found that eight of every ten visitors had trouble finding Dingle town.[78] Activists argued that businesses were dying and Americans were unable to find the town—even the time-honored act of asking directions did not work as many Kerrymen had yet to internalize the name change.[79] Dingle faced a significant problem. Lost tourists meant lost livelihood. Tourism had helped stop emigration from Dingle; now the old specter loomed again. For what? The government "spent millions promoting the Dingle Peninsula brand" and they were now willing "to throw it away."[80]

For those in favor of the name change, inconvenience and short-term confusion were a small price to pay for saving the Irish language and Irish heritage. Sean Ó Cathasaigh, a native Gaelic speaker from Dingle living in Maynooth, County Kildare, wrote to the *Irish Times* to express his support for the change. While many might "denigrate our native language," the Irish should take pride in acknowledging "our native treasure."[81] Finian McGrath, an Independent TD from Dublin, expressed a similar sentiment, noting that he would not expect the French or Spanish to provide Anglicized versions of their place names, so why should the Irish bow to tourist pressure? For McGrath, the tourist industry faced little threat because "clever and sensible marketing will brand 'An Daingean' internationally in a matter of weeks."[82] Raé Kearns, of Trim, County Meath, lamented the loss of authentic Gaelic names in favor of "bland, soulless inventions that have usually no historical or environmental relevance to the area." Anglicized names represented the loss of "a very important part of our linguistic and environmental heritage."[83] Kearns did not agree that changing the name "Dingle" was desirable, but he nevertheless advocated a careful consideration of naming—deliberation that was not given to the small Kerry town. Finally, the minister behind the change, Éamon Ó Cuív, weighed in to insist on the correctness of the conversion. The name change would simplify matters for tourists because only a Gaelic name would appear on signs and maps. Answering the anti-change activists' question about how long it takes for a name to develop meaning, the minister admitted that the name "Dingle" has a long history, but insisted that "An Daingean" represents the "authentic" name for the community. Evidently 750 years is not enough time to establish authenticity for a "foreign" word. Ó Cuív went on to insist that tourism would not suffer from the change; indeed, the display of national pride and the marketing of authentic Gaelic Irishness might actually increase tourist interest.

In short, most of the old notions of Irish identity were represented in the debate. For some, authentic Ireland should be understood as pre-Norman;

for others, it is the product of history. The idea that Ireland is defined by common economic interests, especially tourism, was prevalent in the anti-name-change arguments, while the idea that Ireland is more culturally defined dominated the pro-change view. Ultimately the two views represented polar opposites and, for the debate participants, it was a zero sum game.

The Dingle Wrangle seemed largely insoluble. Name change opponents fought using every tool at their disposal. First, they sought to control the media. The Dingle Name Campaign published a website in order to make their position as widely known as possible. The tone of this site was calm and serious. It featured a history of Dingle, presented a reasoned anti-change argument, republished newspaper articles and letters to the editor, and reassured language campaigners by providing Irish-language material to interested readers. Anti-change advocates readily gave interviews. Editorial pages disproportionately reflected an anti-change position. Perhaps most damning, foreign papers took a negative view of the change. For example, Melbourne, Australia's *Sunday Herald Sun* began an article on the debate with the line "Tourists, beware"—precisely the opposite of the welcoming and friendly view of Ireland that tourism advocates spent the better part of a century developing.[84]

But the anti-change campaign's most significant action was to demand a plebiscite about the name change. In October 2005 the Kerry County Council agreed to hold an election and they subsequently did so one year later.[85] Roughly 1,222 residents were allowed to vote, mostly inhabitants of the town itself, and 1,095 of these opted to do so. Of those who voted, 1,005 voted in favor of a bilingual name: Dingle Daingean Uí Chúis. The vote cost €10,000, but for anti-change campaigners it seemed well worth the expense.

Despite the overwhelming vote, Ó Cuív continued to insist that no bilingual name would be legally acceptable under the Official Placenames Act.[86] The villagers were not amused. Angry letters appeared on the letters pages of Irish newspapers, ministers got an earful from constituents, and editorial writers decried the government's "subversion of democracy."[87]

After considerable ministerial wrangling, it was finally reported that a deal was struck on 20 June 2007 between Jackie Healy-Rae, TD, and An Taoiseach Bertie Ahern to reinstate the town's bilingual name. Healy-Rae, fresh off a narrow election victory in May, was anxious to deliver on a campaign promise. Ahearn was almost certainly well aware that "people are sick of the whole situation."[88] After three years of fighting, the democratic process won out, but the debate itself was not, nor could it be, solved. For more than eighty years tourism inspired debate about the nature of Irishness and Irish interests; the Dingle Wrangle was yet another chapter in this debate and the existence of a new tourism authority did nothing to stop dialogue.

Conclusion

All too often we forget that history is not simply about a few great men or about the results of high-level political squabbling. Authors write within the context of their times. Artists and musicians respond to or react against contemporary trends. To a large degree, politicians must act within the confines of public opinion. Yet despite these realities, there is a tendency to discuss national identity as though Wizard of Oz–like characters control society while sitting in offstage control booths. Critics often present tourism as an unstoppable force that robs social groups of agency and leaves permanently altered societies in its wake. Scholars often present national identity as the creation of a few educated elites. The narrative of Irish history is dominated by a handful of nationalists, groups, and writers while everyday men and women, who have also played an important role in shaping Irish history, are forgotten.

The story told here offers a different narrative. Through tourism-inspired discourse, government officials, rural priests, community groups, foreign governments, tourists, and others came together to develop and create the image of Ireland that is presented to visitors today. Each group played an important role and none of the developments described in these pages would have been possible without the combined effort of all. In many ways, the development of the tourist industry was a significant triumph for the Irish people, who created their own identity and offered it to the world largely on their own terms. This is not the story of a people locked in a postcolonial prison as some suggest; it is the story of a nation actively involved in creating its own past, present, and future.

From the Irish Civil War to the present, tourism facilitated debate about Irish national identity along two separate but closely related axes. First, there was debate about the shape of Ireland's "national interest." While social scientists and historians have tended to dismiss the notion of a national interest as little more than an indication of the importance of the *rhetoric of nationalism* in an age of nation-states, the concept is actually more fundamental than that. Having a single "national" interest perpetuates an idea of unity by fostering dialogue. In Ireland there was often little agreement about precisely what the Irish nation wanted or needed, in spite of an underlying assumption of unanimity. From government officials all the way to parish priests, there were myriad opinions about what was best for the Irish people. At the local level, concerns like the need for sanitation or road improvements and the expansion of employment opportunities often seemed to overwhelm other concerns. If roads were made better, Irish towns more livable, and Irish people employed, then the community as a whole would benefit. In the halls of power, the national interest tended to revolve around growing the economy, filling the dollar gap, saving the Irish language, and placating Marshall Plan officials.

The question of modernization loomed large on both sides of the national interest debate. While improved transportation and the influx of tourists might have dramatic benefits, so too it could potentially destroy traditional culture such as the language or timeless fairs and festivals. Motor-launches on the Killarney lakes might bring benefits to the community, but they might also destroy a way of life. The development of tourist hotels might improve the economy but the new structures might also blight the landscape. Pro-modernization forces eventually won the battle for tourism, but even then the challenge of balancing the realities of modernity with the need for timelessness forced debate about the country's national interest.

Even as tourism prompted the debates noted above, it also led to discussion about the very things most often cited as core components of national identity. Whether the issue was landscape, culture, or history, virtually all Irish men and women wanted Ireland to be presented in the best possible way, and this required deciding precisely what "way" that was. Traditionally, Irish townscapes existed in black and white, derelict sites littered the landscape, and there was little attention paid to clearing away trash—all attributes that would negatively impact any tourism program, to say nothing of foreign attitudes toward the Irish people. Tourist authorities, local groups, architects, and others combined their efforts to alter the appearance of Irish landscapes, redefining townscapes as brightly colored and clean, promoting the removal of derelict sites, and urging anti-litter campaigns. Likewise, traditional Irish fairs and festivals were coarse and sometimes violent affairs—qualities that would lend weight to negative stereotypes of Irishness rather than promote the more jovial and pleasant depictions of the national character preferred by many in the Tourist Board and beyond. Once again tourist authorities and local committees addressed the problem by creating new traditions while casting their gaze into antiquity for inspiration. Irish history provided a very similar problem. Much of the recent Irish past was defined by struggle and conflict, including agonizing civil war. The narrative that was developed for historical sites—both for tourist and local consumption—glossed over these divisions, even when the site was intimately associated with partisanship and conflict as at Kilmainham Jail. Ireland's past was most often viewed in terms of saints and scholars while ancient historic sites assumed greater value than more recent monuments. Tourism created a dialogue about the Gaelic language revival as well, an issue that went to the very heart of the notion of a Gaelic Ireland. Was Irishness better served by protecting the language from foreign influences and by keeping tourists at bay, or by attracting visitors to the Gaeltachts? Would the rural Irish benefit more by developing a revenue stream or maintaining a distinctive language-culture in an essentially premodern form? Then, in the past few years, should economic considerations or a desire to save the language triumph in places like Dingle?

In all of these cases, the various participants prioritized aspects of identity, ultimately determining the "official" form that Irishness would take, a shape that was to be presented to the Irish and their visitors alike. While the discussion might have been about a tourist product, it was never possible to limit the material results of these discussions to a narrow imaginary space, a sort of tourist museum. When landscapes were changed, regardless of the reason, the alteration could not help but modify the relationship of those living in close contact with these spaces. When new festivals were created, people quickly became invested in them, whether as participants or observers. When a narrative of Irish history was decided upon, its historic sites became the destination for school field trips as well as the tourist gaze, educating Irish children and their parents, domestic tourists, and foreign visitors alike about Ireland's past. When tourism development was prioritized over self-conscious language protection, the impact was profound in Gaeltacht communities like Dingle that were transformed from communities in decline to internationally known tourism centers, only to continue being the focus of heated discussion over the merits of money versus culture.

None of this is to say "tourism changed the Irish people." The reality was never so simple, nor so vulgar. At every turn Irish groups and individuals made decisions, hashed out their thoughts on a public stage, made determinations about how they viewed themselves and how others should view them. As noted above, the interpretations of Irishness discussed here were not entirely imposed from above, nor were they merely colonial fragments hung like cowbells around the necks of Ireland's men and women. The Irish people were active participants in the creation of their own identity, not the victims of a relentless tourist gaze or the unyielding drive of policy-makers.

While not every voice has been included in these pages, the stories that have been are representative and reveal an impressive level of participation across social groups and geographic space. To be sure, after the advent of the Irish Tourist Board, most (though not all) tourism initiatives came from the "top," but proposals were not necessarily accepted and always required willing participation by local groups. Central tourism authorities could not "go it alone" and constantly had to concern themselves with developing effective ways to work with local realities. Dublin could create plans, but it was groups and individuals in Cork, Kerry, Galway, Mayo, Waterford, Sligo, Wexford, Tipperary, and all of Ireland's other counties who had to carry them out. The Tidy Towns Competition would have failed had it not been for local interest. Language preservation would more than likely have trumped Gaeltacht development schemes were it not for calls from rural and Gaeltacht areas for financial help. Kilmainham Jail would have been destroyed in the early 1960s if a group of nationalist-minded volunteers had not stepped in to refurbish it, rewriting the site's historical narrative in the process. Ultimately the negotiation of Irishness and Irish interests that occurred as a result of tourism was a horizontal and perpetually recurring process.

Of course, dialogue was not entirely internal. Even as identity was debated across Irish society it was also partly defined through dialogue with outsiders. At the heart of tourism, after all, are tourists. Visitor expectations had to factor into discussion. If American tourists wanted to find long lost relatives, expected to experience historic sites, and dreamed of purchasing Irish products, and if English tourists were more interested in the scenery and a quick getaway, both tastes had to be taken into consideration. Likewise, as tourism spending increased, so too did the need to consider what French, German, Italian, Spanish, and other groups of European tourists wanted to find. Foreign voices were not only those of tourists—foreign governments also had comments to make, pressures to apply. From the Marshall Plan to European Development Grants, international interests have concerned themselves with the Irish identity and the Irish national interest, helping to push the notion that Ireland needs tourism and to pay attention to what is required to attract tourists. The Irish could pick and chose which voices to hear, which initiatives to implement, which products to produce, but they did so while in constant contact with the outside world—a contact that tourism did a great deal to promote.

The story told in *Making Ireland Irish* is a complicated one and it does not lend itself to a clear summation of continuities and changes. Over the time-span covered by this study there was a general trend toward consensus about the importance of tourism, the need for increased government spending, and the idea that everybody should play a role, however small, in making the national tourism project work. As time passed, there was also a diversification of Ireland's tourism products that have, among other things, expanded to include a greater recognition of the country's long struggle for independence, suggesting a growing acceptance of the past.

There is more to see in Ireland than ever before, but old issues persist. No Trespassing signs still mar the landscape. Puck Fair continues to take place every August, even if in an altered form. Litter proliferates like proverbial rabbits. Regional concerns still plague central tourism authorities. Heritage sites remain primarily ancient and religious in nature, though more "nationalist" sites have appeared in the last fifteen years. The language question still makes international headlines. But, through it all, the Irish scenery continues to dominate tourism marketing just as Céad Míle Fáilte has remained a perpetual component of advertising materials.

Rather than reading the narrative presented here as a relentless march toward the present, or even in terms of specific continuities and changes, we should read this story as one of continual discussion and we should place the utmost importance on the dialogue itself. As early as the 1930s there were those who wanted to see more sites devoted to Irish martyrs: they did not mysteriously emerge in the late 1950s to urge restoration of Kilmainham. Rather they gradually earned a more dominant voice as conditions changed. Likewise, as early as the 1920s there were calls to remove derelict sites and to clean up litter, though what success was attained had to wait until ecological concern attracted widespread attention and financial resources increased. And, of course, there are still those who fear that tourism will destroy the Gaeltachts. This is a story about opinions whose fortunes wax and wane. Different understandings of Irish national identity rise in prominence at various points only to diminish in importance later on. It follows that self-identification changes as well as people redecide exactly what it means to be Irish.

Notes

Bibliography

Index

Notes

Introduction

1. Neil Steedman, "£3m Tourism Brand Ireland Is Launched," *Irish Travel Trade News,* Nov. 1996, 13.

2. Irene Furlong, "Frederick W. Crossley: Irish Turn-of-the-Century Tourism Pioneer," in *Irish History: A Research Yearbook,* no. 2 (Dublin: Four Courts Press, 2003), 162.

3. Hartmut Berghoff and Barbara Korte, "Britain and the Making of Modern Tourism: An Interdisciplinary Approach," in *The Making of Modern Tourism: The Cultural History of the British Experience, 1600–2000,* ed. Barbara Korte, Hartmut Berghoff, Ralf Schneider, and Christopher Harvie (Basingstock, UK: Palgrave, 2002), 1–20.

4. Jeremy Black, *The British Abroad: The Grand Tour in the Eighteenth Century* (New York: St. Martin's Press, 1992).

5. Gerhard Stilz, "Heroic Travellers—Romantic Landscapes: The Colonial Sublime in Indian, Australian and American Art and Literature," in Korte et al., *Making of Modern Tourism,* 85–107, especially page 85.

6. Alain Corbin, *The Lure of the Sea* (Berkeley: Univ. of California Press, 1994).

7. Peter Womack, *Improvement and Romance: Constructing the Myth of the Highlands* (London: Macmillan Press, 1989). Also see Charles Withers, "The Historical Creation of the Scottish Highlands," in *The Manufacture of Scottish History,* ed. Christopher Whatley and Ian Donnachie (Edinburgh: Polygon, 1992), 143–56.

8. Ian Ousby, *The Englishman's England: Taste, Travel and the Rise of Tourism* (Cambridge, UK: Cambridge Univ. Press, 1990), see chap. 3.

9. Penelope Durell and Cornelius Kelly, eds., *The Grand Tour of Kerry* (Allihies, Beara, Co. Cork: Cailleach Books, 2001), 21.

10. Durell and Kelly, *Grand Tour of Kerry,* 23.

11. Ibid., 29.

12. Melissa Fegan, "The Traveller's Experience in Famine Ireland," *Irish Studies Review* 9, no. 3 (2001): 161–372, see page 361.

13. Orvar Löfgren, *On Holiday: A History of Vacationing* (Berkeley: Univ. of California Press, 1999), 16–17.

14. Shelley Baranowski and Ellen Furlough, eds., *Being Elsewhere: Tourism, Consumer Culture, and Identity in Modern Europe and North America* (Ann Arbor: Univ. of Michigan Press, 2001), 6.

15. Löfgren, *On Holiday*, 19.

16. Piers Brendon, *Thomas Cook: 150 Years of Popular Travel* (London: Secker and Warburg, 1991). For a short summary, see W. H. Bradley, "Around the World with Thomas Cook," *British Heritage*, 1988, 56–61.

17. Furlong, "Frederick W. Crossley," 163; Donal Horgan, *The Victorian Visitor in Ireland: Irish Tourism, 1840–1910* (Cork: Imagimedia, 2002), 23.

18. English numbers are drawn from P. J. G. Ransom, *The Victorian Railway and How It Evolved* (London: Heinemann, 1990), 79 and 110. Irish numbers are drawn from Donal Horgan, *Victorian Visitor*, 24–27.

19. Brendon, *Thomas Cook*, 64–65 and 167–68.

20. Furlong, "Frederick W. Crossley," 173–74.

21. Ibid., 174–75.

22. This account of Crossley's activities is based on Furlong's superb article, one of the very few scholarly treatments of nineteenth-century Irish tourism. It should be of interest to anybody anxious to learn more about early Irish tourist development.

23. Quoted in Joe J. Lee, *Ireland, 1912–1985: Politics and Society* (Cambridge: Cambridge Univ. Press, 1989), 56.

24. For Finnish numbers, see ibid., 69; Spanish Civil War statistics are available in Stanley G. Payne, *The Spanish Civil War, the Soviet Union, and Communism* (New Haven: Yale Univ. Press, 2004), 336n. 14.

25. Baranowski and Furlough, *Being Elsewhere*, 1.

26. Louis Turner and John Ash, *The Golden Hordes: International Tourism and the Pleasure Periphery* (London: Constable and Co., 1975).

27. James Buzard, *The Beaten Track: European Tourism, Literature, and the Ways to Culture, 1800–1918* (Oxford: Clarendon Press, 1993).

28. Paul Fussell, as quoted in Baranowski and Furlough, *Being Elsewhere*, 3.

29. Dean MacCannell, *The Tourist: A New Theory of the Leisure Class* (Berkeley: Univ. of California Press, 1999), 45.

30. Walter Benjamin, *Illuminations: Essays and Reflections* (New York: Schocken Books, 1968), 217–52.

31. Rudy Koshar, "'What Ought to Be Seen': Tourists' Guidebooks and National Identities in Modern Germany and Europe," *Journal of Contemporary History* 33, no. 3 (1998): 323–40.

32. Michel Peillon, "Tourism—the Quest for Otherness," *Crane Bag* 8 no. 2 (1984): 165–68.

33. Tom Selwyn, ed., *The Tourist Image: Myths and Myth Making in Tourism* (Chichester, UK: John Wiley and Sons, 1996), 23.

34. Robert E. Wood, "Tourist Ethnicity: A Brief Itinerary," *Ethnic and Racial Studies* 21, no. 2 (1998): 218–41.

35. Catherine A. Palmer, "Tourism and Colonialism: The Experience of the Bahamas," *Annals of Tourism Research* 21, no. 4 (1994): 792–811. Spurgeon Thompson makes a similar argument about Irish tourism. See his "The Postcolonial Tourist: Irish Tourism and Decolonization since 1850" (Ph.D. diss., Univ. of Notre Dame, 2000).

36. Simon Abram, "Performing for Tourists in Rural France," in *Tourists and Tourism: Identifying with People and Places,* ed. Simon Abram, Jacqueline Waldren, and Donald V. L. Macleod (Oxford: Berg, 1997), 31.

37. Moya Kneafsey, "Tourism and Place Identity: A Case-Study in Rural Ireland," *Irish Geography* 31, no. 2 (1998): 111–23, see page 121.

38. Moya Kneafsey, "Rural Tourism and Identity: Stories of Change and Resistance from the West of Ireland and Brittany," in *New Directions in Celtic Studies,* ed. Amy Hale and Philip Payton (Exeter: Univ. of Exeter Press, 2000), 167–96, see page 172.

39. Thompson, "The Postcolonial Tourist," 3–4.

40. Frank O'Connor was a pseudonym for Michael O'Donovan. He was born in Cork and raised in poverty by a loving mother. His father served in the British army and was largely absent from O'Donovan's life. As a young man, he fought as a Republican in the Civil War and was eventually interned in Gormanstown in 1923. O'Donovan's first collection of short stories, *Guests of the Nation,* recounted his wartime experiences, contrasting the ideals he fought for with the painful realities of war. O'Donovan was harshly censored during the 1940s and became increasingly bitter as a result. This bitterness extended to the Clare County Council, which refused to build a monument to Marriman, one of O'Donovan's favorite poets. He emigrated to the United States in 1951, after his marriage collapsed and life in Ireland became unbearable. While in the United States, he lectured widely at American universities and produced three critical works on Irish literature. He returned to Ireland in 1960 and died six years later. See Brian Ó Dalaigh, ed., *The Stranger's Gaze: Travels in County Clare, 1534–1950* (Dublin: Clasp Press, 1998).

41. "IRA Protest on O'Connor's Article," *Irish Press,* 21 Jan. 1950.

42. Letter from John J. Byrne, [?] Dec. 1949, Department of the Taoiseach [hereafter cited as DT], S14716A, National Archives of Ireland, Dublin.

43. "US Magazine Asked to Apologise," *Irish Independent,* 7 Jan. 1950.

44. Letter from Killarney Urban District Council Resolution and letter to the Taoiseach, 23 Jan. 1950, DT, S14716A, National Archives of Ireland, Dublin.

45. "Libeling a People," *Catholic News,* 26 Nov. 1949.

46. While O'Connor's accuracy does not matter in our context, much of what he wrote was relatively correct. The Catholic Church did hold considerable power (as became very clear during the Mother and Child controversy just four years later). Poverty was appalling. Dublin was in such poor shape that Georgian buildings literally collapsed upon themselves. Infant mortality was horrendous. There was little in the way of industry. A vast number of men and

women fled Ireland in search of better prospects during the 1950s. Of course, O'Connor made a number of not insignificant errors as well. His discussion of Irish history, for example, was riddled with inaccuracy. The Civil War was not caused by partition and the Allies did not maintain essential military bases in southern Ireland during the Second World War (although they certainly wanted to).

47. Francis McCoy, "Backstage with Mr. Frank O'Connor," Dec. 1949, DT, S14716A, National Archives of Ireland, Dublin.

48. "How O'Connor Article Was Concocted," *Irish Press,* 21 Jan. 1949.

49. Department of External Affairs, memorandum, 18 Jan. 1950, Department of Foreign Affairs [hereafter cited as DFA], 366/117, National Archives of Ireland, Dublin.

50. Department of External Affairs, article draft and letter, 25 Sept. 1950, DFA, 366/117/1, National Archives of Ireland, Dublin.

51. Ernest Gellner, *Nations and Nationalism* (Ithaca, N.Y.: Cornell Univ. Press, 1983); and E. J. Hobsbawm, *Nations and Nationalism since 1780* (Cambridge: Cambridge Univ. Press, 1990).

52. Partha Chatterjee, *The Nation and Its Fragments* (Princeton, N.J.: Princeton Univ. Press, 1993).

53. Benedict Anderson, *Imagined Communities: Reflections on the Origin and Spread of Nationalism* (London: Verso, 1991). See also Alan Williams, ed. *Film and Nationalism* (Piscataway, N.J.: Rutgers Univ. Press, 2002).

54. Michael Billig, *Banal Nationalism* (London: Sage Publications, 1995).

55. Tim Edensor, "National Identity and the Politics of Memory: Remembering Bruce and Wallace in Symbolic Space," *Environment and Planning* 29 (1997): 175–94.

56. Oliver Zimmer, *A Contested Nation: History, Memory and Nationalism in Switzerland, 1761–1891* (Cambridge: Cambridge Univ. Press, 2003).

57. Stuart B. Schwartz, ed., *Implicit Understandings: Observing, Reporting, and Reflecting on the Encounters Between Europeans and Other Peoples in the Early Modern Era* (Cambridge: Cambridge Univ. Press, 1994), 3.

1. Introducing a National Interest, 1922–1939

1. Tom Garvin, *1922: The Birth of Irish Democracy* (New York: St. Martin's Press, 1996), 83; and Michael Farry, *The Aftermath of Revolution: Sligo 1921–23* (Dublin: Univ. College Dublin Press, 2000), 205.

2. Michael Hopkinson, *Green Against Green: The Irish Civil War* (Dublin: Gill and Macmillan, 1988), 273.

3. Terence Brown, *Ireland: A Social and Cultural History, 1922 to the Present* (Ithaca, N.Y.: Cornell Univ. Press, 1985), 15.

4. D. George Boyce, *Nationalism in Ireland* (London: Routledge, 1995), 340.

5. Quoted in Boyce, *Nationalism in Ireland,* 339.

6. "The Cobh Outrage: Hopes of Capture; Hunting for Missing Men; Free State Forces in the South," *Kerryman*, 5 Apr. 1924.

7. Farry, *Aftermath of Revolution*, 202.

8. C. S. Andrews, *Man of No Property: An Autobiography*, vol. 2 (Dublin: Mercier Press, 1982), 26.

9. Jeffrey Prager, *Building Democracy in Ireland: Political Order and Cultural Integration in a Newly Independent Nation* (Cambridge: Cambridge Univ. Press, 1986), 99.

10. Garvin, *1922*, 88.

11. Sasha David Pack, "Spain in the Age of Mass Tourism, Modernization, and Dictatorship, 1945–1975" (Ph.D. diss., Univ. of Wisconsin-Madison, 2004), 24–25, 53–58, especially page 56.

12. Brown, *Ireland*, 16.

13. "Tribute to a Senator," *Irish Independent*, 7 Jan. 1924.

14. "Tourist Traffic, An All-Ireland Movement: What Other Places Have Done," *Kerryman*, 26 Apr. 1924.

15. Irish Tourism Memorandum and Association Articles of Association, 1924, Dissolved Companies, D7282, National Archives of Ireland, Dublin.

16. "Obituary. Death of Former President of ITA, the Late Mr. J. C. Foley, LL.D.," *Irish Travel*, June–July 1933, 123.

17. "Activities of the ITA," *Irish Travel*, Sept. 1925, 9–10.

18. "Mr. Howard S. Harrington: Appreciation by His Old Staff," *Kerryman*, 11 Sept. 1926.

19. Irish Tourism Memorandum and Association Articles.

20. Michael Kevin O'Doherty, interview by author, Dublin, 29 Apr. 2002. Also see C. S. Andrews, *Man of No Property*, 67.

21. C. S. Andrews, *Man of No Property*, 66 and 71.

22. Harvey Levenstein, *We'll Always Have Paris: American Tourists in France since 1930* (Chicago: Univ. of Chicago Press, 2004), x. See also Pack, "Spain in the Age of Mass Tourism," 58.

23. Dáil Debate, 5 (12 Dec. 1923), 1802. All Dáil and Seanad debates are available online at <http:\\www.oireachtas.ie>.

24. Dáil Debate, 6 (19 Mar. 1924), 2175.

25. Dáil Debate, 9 (20 Nov. 1924), 1322.

26. According to Mary E. Daly, the role of government was seriously debated in the first twenty-five years after the Anglo-Irish Treaty. Some believed that the state should not interfere with industrial development, while others felt that such intervention was necessary and desirable. Daly argues that a new industrial elite emerged in the 1920s and 1930s that was intensely dependent on government assistance. Mary E. Daly, *Industrial Development and Irish Society: 1922–1939* (Syracuse, N.Y.: Syracuse Univ. Press, 1992), 177–80.

27. "Tourist Plans: Conference Called by the Minister of Industry," *Kerryman*, 20 Dec. 1924.

28. Dáil Debate, 10 (10 Mar. 1925), 847.

29. *Irish Independent,* 7 Jan. 1924.

30. Dáil Debate, 10 (10 Mar. 1925), 847.

31. *Local Government Act, 1925* (Dublin: Government Publications, 1925).

32. "Tourist Development: National Association," *Kerryman*, 24 Jan. 1925.

33. "Notes and News," *Irish Travel,* Sept. 1925, 2–4.

34. "Irish Tourist Association: Killarney Branch Formed," *Kerryman*, 26 Jan. 1924.

35. "Dingle Doings: The Tourist Trade," *Kerryman*, 27 Dec. 1924.

36. "Dingle Rural Council: Tourist Development," *Kerryman*, 13 Dec. 1924.

37. "Irish Tourist Association: Dingle Branch," *Kerryman*, 23 May 1925.

38. "Dingle Doings: Sewerage," *Kerryman*, 17 Oct. 1925.

39. "Irish Tourist Association: Dingle Branch," *Kerryman*, 20 Feb. 1926.

40. "Dingle Branch, Irish Tourist Association: Committee Appointed," *Kerryman*, 27 Feb. 1926.

41. "Tourist Development Association, Dingle Branch: Condition of Streets; Question of Urbanizing," *Kerryman*, 13 Mar. 1926.

42. "Dingle Doings," *Kerryman*, 27 Mar. 1926.

43. "Dingle Doings," *Kerryman*, 24 July 1926.

44. Cork-Kinsale Road, 23 Apr. 1930, Kinsale Development Association [hereafter cited as KDA], U274/6, Cork Archives Institute, Cork, Ireland.

45. L. O'Connell to ITA, 3 Apr. 1930, KDA, U274/6, Cork Archives Institute, Cork.

46. J. P. O'Brien to L. O'Connell, 14 Apr. 1930, KDA, U274/6, Cork Archives Institute, Cork.

47. Clipping from unknown newspaper, "Main Road Grants," 20 Feb. 1931, KDA, U274/6, Cork Archives Institute, Cork.

48. L. O'Connell to Secretary of Roads Board, Department of Local Government, 31 May 1933, KDA, U274/6, Cork Archives Institute, Cork; and "Kinsale Notes: Kinsale Tourist Development and Water Scheme," [?]1938, KDA, U274/2, Cork Archives Institute, Cork.

49. "Advertising Tourist Resorts," *Kerryman*, 24 Dec. 1926.

50. "Killarney Tourist Association," *Kerryman*, 1 Jan. 1927.

51. "Tourist Development," *Kilkenny People,* 7 Nov. 1925.

52. "Kilkenny County Rates," *Kilkenny People,* 5 Mar. 1927.

53. "Tourist Association: Directors from Local Bodies," *Kilkenny People,* 29 Jan. 1927; and "Tourist Traffic: Irish Association's Important Decision," *Kerryman*, 29 Jan. 1927.

54. "Tourist Trade: Preparing for the Coming Season," *Kerryman*, 19 Feb. 1927.

55. During his varied career, Todd Andrews established Bord na Móna (the Turf Board), acted as chairman of Córas Iompair Éireann (Irish rail), and was a director of Radio Telefis Éireann (RTÉ).

56. C. S. Andrews, *Man of No Property,* 67–68.

57. Ibid., 71–72.

58. Ibid., 67–68.

59. Ibid., 70–71.

60. Ibid., 73–74.

61. Daly, *Industrial Development,* 10–11.

62. Cu Uladh, "Gaeltacht and Tourists," *Irish Press,* 31 Sept. 1938.

63. "Irish Tourist Association," *Kerryman,* 1 Nov. 1924.

64. *Irish Travel,* Sept. 1925, 2–5.

65. T. C. O'Reilly, letter, Jan. 1926, Seamus Fitzgerald Papers [hereafter cited as SFP], PR6/673 (1) and (2), Cork Archives Institute, Cork.

66. "Killarney Tourist Association: Proposed Motor Boat Service," *Kerryman,* 24 Oct. 1925.

67. "Kerryisms," *Kerryman,* 17 Oct. 1925.

68. "Killarney Lakes: Boatmen Against Motor Boats," *Kerryman,* 17 May 1924.

69. "Killarney Tourist Association," *Kerryman,* 24 Oct. 1925.

70. "Launches on the Lakes: The Reply of the Boat-Men's Association," *Kerryman,* 31 Oct. 1925.

71. "Kerryisms," *Kerryman,* 7 Nov. 1925.

72. "Kerryisms," *Kerryman,* 17 Oct. 1925.

73. Republished as "Success of the Tourist Season: Killarney Pleased, All Expectations Beaten," *Kerryman,* 31 Oct. 1925.

74. "Killarney and Motor Launches: Letter from Mr. Wm. Ahern, UDC," *Kerryman,* 14 Nov. 1925.

75. "Motor Launches on Killarney Lakes: Letter from Lord Kenmare," *Kerryman,* 21 Nov. 1925.

76. "Activities of the ITA," *Irish Travel,* Feb. 1929, 128–29.

77. *Ireland: Official Publication* (Dublin: Irish Tourist Association, 1929). One-third of the ITA's annual income came from contributions made by local authorities. The rest was made up of subscriptions by hotel and rail companies, dues paid by two hundred members, and grants from a handful of other companies. C. S. Andrews, *Man of No Property,* 70.

78. Board Memo No. 4345, 9 July 1925, GDB/C009/0405, Guinness Ireland Archives, Dublin.

79. While no comprehensive history of the first Irish Tourist Association has been written, interested readers should consult the organization's major publication: the *Irish Tourist.* Donel Horgan's *Victorian Visitor in Ireland* also contains limited information as does Irene Furlong's "Frederick W. Crossley."

80. Moran owned both Moran's Hotel and the Dolphin Hotel. He also served on the Ports and Docks Board.

81. Board Memo No. 4345.

82. General Purposes Sub-Committee Minutes, 17 Aug. 1926, GOB/C006/0121, Guinness Ireland Archives, Dublin.

83. Board Memo No. 4345.

84. "Notes and News," *Irish Travel,* Aug. 1926, 291.

85. "Ireland as a Tourist Resort," *Kerryman,* 21 Aug. 1926.

86. Marguerite S. Shaffer, *See America First: Tourism and National Identity, 1880–1940* (Washington D.C.: Smithsonian Institution Press, 2001).

87. J. Booth, letter, 8 May 1925, Department of Finance [hereafter cited as DF], S041/0012/25, National Archives of Ireland, Dublin.

88. H. P. Boland to J. Booth, 27 May 1925, DF, S041/0012/25, National Archives of Ireland, Dublin.

89. After the assassination of Kevin O'Higgins, the government called a second general election following passage of an aggressive Public Safety and Electoral Act. The new legislation required all members of the Oireachtas (Irish legislature) to take an oath of allegiance—a clever way to press de Valera to either accept constitutional politics or return to the political wilderness. The new legislation also allowed Cosgrave to take an aggressive and democratic stand against continued Republican violence. Fianna Fáil agreed to the new requirement and entered the Oireachtas in August 1927. For a very readable account, see Stephen Collins, *The Cosgrave Legacy* (Dublin: Blackwater Press, 1996); see also John Horgan, *Seán Lemass: The Enigmatic Patriot* (Dublin: Gill and Macmillan 1997), 46.

90. For a fairly typical example of O'Sullivan's campaign rhetoric, see "Mr. Eugene O'Sullivan's Candidature: Meeting at Kenmare," *Kerryman,* 28 May 1927. O'Sullivan briefly mentioned tourism on 21 May, arguing, "Our neglected fisheries and our tourist trade are amongst the nation's prime assets, and must be attended to in a competent and business-like way." "Mr. Eugene O'Sullivan. Chairman Killarney Urban District Council to Stand for Kerry as an Independent Candidate," *Kerryman,* 21 May 1927.

91. Seanad Debate, 14 (6 May 1931), 896–97.

92. Income during the period 1926–30 was as follows:

    1926—£2,227

    1927—£5,169

    1928—£8,827

    1929—£10,245

    1930—£10,222.

Letter to James McNeill, 1931, DT, S5482, National Archives of Ireland, Dunlin.

93. Seanad Debate, 14 (6 May 1931), 896–97.

94. O'Doherty interview, 29 Apr. 2002.

95. Roy Foster, *Modern Ireland: 1600–1972* (London: Penguin, 1988), 540.

96. John Horgan, *Enigmatic Patriot,* 52.

97. Dáil Debate, 38 (22 Apr. 1931), 19–20.

98. Collins, *Cosgrave Legacy,* 53. See also Lee, *Ireland, 1912–1985,* 175–78, for more details about the campaign.

99. Lee, *Ireland, 1912–1985,* 178.

100. Tourist traffic numbers are far from precise until at least the 1950s; however, it is fair to assume that the trends represented in early figures are accurate. In 1926, estimates were that 184,320 Britons visited Ireland. By 1932, this number had increased to 245,468, and by 1936 the estimate had risen to 317,979. The number of American visitors also rose, moving from just over 8,000 in 1926 to 10,840 in 1936. "The 1936 Tourist Season Has Set New Records," *Irish Travel,* Nov. 1936, 26.

101. Brian Farrell, *Seán Lemass* (London: Gill and Macmillan, 1983), 41.

102. See John Horgan, *Enigmatic Patriot,* 88.

103. Quoted in ibid., 88–89.

104. Bernard Share, *The Flight of the Iolar: The Aer Lingus Experience, 1936–1986* (Dublin: Gill and Macmillan, 1986), 7.

105. Quoted in John Horgan, *Enigmatic Patriot,* 88–89.

106. O'Doherty interview, 29 Apr. 2002.

107. John Horgan, *Enigmatic Patriot,* 87.

108. Farrell, *Seán Lemass,* 41.

109. John Leydon, letter, 18 May 1938, DFA, S084/0020/38 (Main File), National Archives of Ireland, Dublin.

110. Memo by Sean Ua Morain, 1938, DFA, S084/0020/38 (Part 2), National Archives of Ireland, Dublin.

111. Minute from Mr. Lynd, 22 May 1938, DFA, S084/0020/38 (Part 1), National Archives of Ireland, Dublin.

112. Minute by C. S. Almond, 6 May 1938, DFA, S084/0020/38 (Main File), National Archives of Ireland, Dublin.

113. Minute from Mr. Lynd, 22 May 1938.

114. Minute by C. S. Almond, 6 May 1938.

115. "Tourist Traffic Board for Ireland," *Cork Evening Echo,* 25 Oct. 1938.

116. "Killarney Discusses Tourists: New Government Bill Examined by UDC," *Cork Evening Echo,* 5 Nov. 1938.

117. *Tourist Traffic Act, 1939* (Dublin: Government Publications, 1939).

118. "The Irish Tourist Board: New Appointment by Government Recognizes Importance of Irish Tourist Industry," *Irish Travel,* Sept. 1939, 313.

2. Developing Irish Tourism, 1939–1958

1. Brian Garvin and Geoffrey Roberts, eds., *Ireland and the Second World War: Politics, Society and Remembrance* (Dublin: Four Courts Press, 2000), 11.

2. Garvin and Roberts, *Ireland and the Second World War,* 13.

3. Donal Ó Drisceoil, *Censorship in Ireland 1939–1945: Neutrality, Politics, and Society* (Cork: Cork Univ. Press, 1996), 3.

4. Lee, *Ireland, 1912–1985,* 259–60.

5. Ibid., 265.

6. Ó Drisceoil, *Censorship in Ireland,* 6.

7. Tony Gray, *The Lost Years: The Emergency in Ireland, 1939–45* (London: Little, Brown and Co., 1997), 7.

8. Ronan Fanning, *The Irish Department of Finance, 1922–58* (Dublin: Institute of Public Administration, 1978), 312.

9. John Horgan, *Enigmatic Patriot,* 100–101.

10. Garvin and Roberts, *Ireland and the Second World War,* 32 and 34.

11. Tourist Traffic Act, 1939—Question of Suspension, 7 Sept. 1939, DT, S10946, National Archives of Ireland, Dublin.

12. J. P. O'Brien to J. Leydon, 5 Sept. 1939, DT, S10946, National Archives of Ireland, Dublin.

13. Tourist Traffic Act, 1939—Question of Suspension.

14. Memorandum for the Government from J. P. O'Brien, 20 Nov. 1939, DT, S10946, National Archives of Ireland, Dublin.

15. Department of Industry and Commerce Memorandum, 29 Jan. 1940, DT, S10946, National Archives of Ireland, Dublin.

16. Ibid.

17. Department of Finance Memorandum, circa Jan. 1940, DT, S10946, National Archives of Ireland, Dublin.

18. Fanning, *Irish Department of Finance,* 626.

19. Lee, *Ireland, 1912–1985,* 572.

20. Ibid., 573.

21. Fanning, *Irish Department of Finance,* 627.

22. Irish Tourist Board Annual Report and Accounts, Year Ended 31st March 1941, 25 June 1941, Tourism, Transport, and Communications [hereafter cited as TTA], 5/1/2, National Archives of Ireland, Dublin.

23. Cabinet Minutes. G.C. 3/49, 29 Feb. 1944, DT, S10946, National Archives of Ireland, Dublin. See also Department of Industry and Commerce Memorandum, 18 Feb. 1944, DT, S10946, National Archives of Ireland, Dublin.

24. Fanning, *Irish Department of Finance,* 629.

25. Ibid., 631.

26. Irish Tourist Association memorandum to Minister for Industry and Commerce, 16 Apr. 1941, DT, S10946, National Archives of Ireland, Dublin.

27. "Holidays in 1941," *Irish Travel,* Feb. 1941, 86.

28. Department of Local Government, *Department of Local Government Report, 1940–41* (Dublin: Government Publications, 1941), 20.

29. Department of Local Government, *Department of Local Government Report, 1943–44* (Dublin: Government Publications, 1944), 20.

30. For the most thorough discussion of English savings clubs, see Susan Barton, *Working-Class Organisations and Popular Tourism, 1840–1970* (Manchester: Manchester Univ. Press, 2005). Interested readers should also see John K. Walton, *Blackpool* (Edinburgh: St. Martin's Press, 1998), 53–54.

31. Account of Success of Holiday Savings Clubs Established by Irish Tourist Association in Industrial and Commercial Concerns, [?] 1948, Ms 33, 718/H (231), National Library of Ireland, Dublin. Cited with the permission of the Board of the National Library of Ireland.

32. "With the ITA Holiday Savings Clubs: Close of the Cork Campaign," *Irish Travel,* Mar. 1942, 92.

33. "Irish Tourist Holiday Savings Club Scheme," *Irish Travel,* Jan. 1941, 66.

34. Account of Success. Cited with the permission of the Board of the National Library of Ireland. See also Irish Tourist Association's Twentieth Anniversary Issue: 1925–45, 1945, Todd Andrews Papers [hereafter cited as TAP], P91/B/10, University College Dublin Archives, Dublin.

35. List of ITA Accomplishments, 1963, DT, S13087G/63, National Archives of Ireland, Dublin. By the early 1950s, the savings club program was no longer viable. Even as the Organization for European Economic Cooperation advocated forming European-wide savings clubs, An Bord Fáilte declared that such savings clubs "would not meet with success in this country as Irish people generally like to make individual holiday arrangements." See Debate summary, 3 Feb. 1953, TTA 3/1/7, National Archives of Ireland, Dublin.

36. "Irish Hotels Federation Report of the Third Annual General Meeting," *Irish Travel,* Dec. 1940, 63.

37. "Irish Tourist Association Annual General Meeting, Thursday, Oct. 23rd, 1941," *Irish Travel,* Nov. 1941, 19.

38. Memo: The Tourist Industry, 10 Feb. 1945, DT, S13087A, National Archives of Ireland, Dublin.

39. Irish Tourist Board Annual Report and Accounts, Year Ended 31st March, 1943, 23 June 1943, TTA 5/1/2, National Archives of Ireland, Dublin.

40. Industry and Commerce Memorandum, 18 Feb. 1944.

41. Irish Tourist Board Annual Report and Accounts, Year Ended 31st March, 1945, 28 June 1945, TTA 5/1/2, National Archives of Ireland, Dublin.

42. Industry and Commerce Memorandum, 18 Feb. 1944. For additional information about the Portmarnock, Bundoran, and Lisdoonvarna plans, see J. P. O'Brien memorandum, 10 Feb. 1945, DT, S13087A, National Archives of Ireland.

43. O'Doherty interview, 29 Apr. 2002.

44. C. S. Andrews, *Man of No Property,* 76.

45. "Death of Mr. Edward T. Keane," *Kilkenny People,* 19 May 1945.

46. Ó Drisceoil, *Censorship in Ireland,* 181.

47. "Where Jobs Accumulate and Men Decay," *Kilkenny People,* 21 Mar. 1942.

48. "Here We Are Again!" *Kilkenny People,* 18 Apr. 1942.

49. "The Playboys of the Western World," *Kilkenny People,* 23 Jan. 1943.

50. "The Irish Tourist Board," *Kilkenny People,* 31 Mar. 1945.

51. "Let Us Praise Famous Men: Tourist Bigwigs on Parade; Sausages and Highbrows," *Kilkenny People,* 4 Nov. 1944.

52. "Really, Mr. Condon!" *Kilkenny People,* 2 Sept. 1944.

53. "The Tourist Ramp Costs," *Kilkenny People,* 25 Mar. 1944.

54. "Staggered Holidays," *Kilkenny People,* 26 Feb. 1944.

55. "A Square Deal for the Taxpayers," *Kilkenny People,* 24 July 1943. Also see "The Tourist Ramp," *Kilkenny People,* 4 May 1946.

56. *Kilkenny People,* 2 Sept. 1944.

57. C. S. Andrews, *Man of No Property,* 76.

58. Michael Kevin O'Doherty, interview by author, Dublin, 30 July 2002.

59. Michael Gorman, interviews by author, Dublin, 6 Aug. 2002 and 11 Oct. 2002.

60. The cost of these properties averaged roughly £12,000 each. For a detailed accounting, see National Archives of Ireland, DF, F200/7-14/45.

61. Tourist Development Program, 29 June 1946, TTA 5/1/2, National Archives of Ireland, Dublin.

62. Irish Tourist Board Annual Report and Accounts, Year Ended 31st March 1947, 27 June 1947, TTA 5/1/2, National Archives of Ireland, Dublin.

63. "Killarney Discusses Tourists. New Government Bill Examined by UDC," *Cork Evening Echo,* 5 Nov. 1938.

64. C. S. Andrews, *Man of No Property,* 76.

65. "The Tourist Ramp," *Kilkenny People,* 27 Jan. 1945.

66. *Kilkenny People,* 4 May 1946.

67. "More Vital Than Luxury Hotels," *Kilkenny People,* 15 June 1946.

68. "Tourist Board and Tourists," *Irish Independent,* 1 May 1946.

69. "The Future of Irish Tourism," *Irish Press,* 12 Oct. 1950.

70. Preliminary Report of the Irish Hotels Commission, 30 Sept. 1950, DT, S13087C, National Archives of Ireland.

71. "Tourism a Major Asset of Nation," *Irish Independent,* 27 Oct. 1950.

72. "Heavy Tourist Spending Will Increase Living Costs," *Irish Times,* 18 Apr. 1946.

73. "The Tourist Ramp," *Kilkenny People,* 19 Apr. 1947.

74. Memorandum: Killarney, 16 Jan. 1948, DT, S13087A, National Archives of Ireland, Dublin.

75. KTA chairman's address to Killarney Tourist Association annual general meeting, 12 Dec. 1947, DT, S13087A, National Archives of Ireland, Dublin.

76. Memorandum: Killarney, 16 Jan. 1948.

77. Photographs K.1/48–K.107/48 include the Killarney area. Another two hundred photographs, running to K.301/48, cover remaining Killarney-area tourist sites in the Dingle and Ring of Kerry areas. (The archive's indexing system uses the first number to define the photograph's position on a roll and the second number to denote the year in which the image was taken.)

78. Shelley Baranowski, *Strength Through Joy* (Cambridge: Cambridge Univ. Press, 2004), 62. Nazi Germany's Kraft durch Freude (Strength Through Joy) program was designed to raise "the productivity and political loyalty" of workers by improving factory conditions, encouraging development of the Volkswagon (People's Car), and promoting a holiday program that, at its height, accounted for nearly ten million overnight stays in German hotels during 1936—11 percent of total bednights for the year. The program went a long way toward help-ing to structure leisure time by providing inexpensive outings to workers. See Rudy Koshar, *German Travel Cultures* (Oxford: Berg, 2000), 121, 123–25.

79. ITB memorandum, "Towards an Irish Recreational Policy," Feb. 1944, DT, S13087A, National Archives of Ireland, Dublin, emphasis mine.

80. See Peter Bailey, *Leisure and Class in Victorian England: Rational Recreation and the Contest for Control* (Buffalo, N.Y.: Univ. of Toronto Press, 1978); Robert W. Malcolmson, *Popular Recreations in English Society, 1700–1850* (Cambridge: Cambridge Univ. Press, 1973); also see Walton, *Blackpool*.

81. See Baranowski, *Strength Through Joy.*

82. Minister of Local Government and Public Health memorandum, 29 Apr. 1944, DT, S13087A, National Archives of Ireland, Dublin.

83. Share, *Flight of the Iolar,* 106.

84. Mícheál Ó Rain, *Are Lingus: 1936–1986: A Business Monographic* (Dublin: Magill Print/Aer Lingus, 1986), 13–14.

85. Ó Rain, *Are Lingus,* 14.

86. Ibid., 14–15.

87. Share, *Flight of the Kolar,* 104–5.

88. Ó Rain, *Are Lingus,* 15.

89. O'Doherty interview, 29 Apr. 2002.

90. Memorandum: Fáilte Téoranta, 21 Nov. 1949, DT, S13904B, National Archives of Ireland, Dublin.

91. Minute, 30 Nov. 1949, DFA, 366/115 Pt. 1, National Archives of Ireland, Dublin.

92. Fanning, *Irish Department of Finance,* 397.

93. First Interim Report on Tourism of the Inter-Departmental Working Party on Dollar Earnings, 1950, DT, S13087C, National Archives of Ireland, Dublin.

94. Bernadette Whelan, *Ireland and the Marshall Plan, 1947–57* (Dublin: Four Courts Press, 2000), 17.

95. Levenstein, *We'll Always Have Paris,* 114–19.

96. "Colonel Pozzi in Ireland," *Irish Travel,* July 1949, 198.

97. O'Doherty interview, 29 Apr. 2002.

98. "Colonel Pozzi in Ireland."

99. Interim Report, 1950, DT, S13087C, National Archives of Ireland, Dublin.

100. Memo to Mr. McCarthy, 30 Dec. 1949, TTA 5/2/14, National Archives of Ireland, Dublin.

101. DFA Memorandum, 27 July 1950, DT, S13087C, National Archives of Ireland, Dublin.

102. Dáil Debate, 22 Apr. 1931.

103. Department of External Affairs, Memorandum for the Government: Cultural Publicity Abroad, 2 June 1947, DT, S13773A, National Archives of Ireland, Dublin.

104. Summary of Meeting with Michael Gorman, 18 June 1959, DFA, 366/263, National Archives of Ireland, Dublin.

105. "Christenberry Report," July–Aug. 1950, DT, S13087D, National Archives of Ireland, Dublin.

106. Denis O'Hearn, *Inside the Celtic Tiger: The Irish Economy and the Asian Model* (London: Pluto Press, 1998), 37.

107. Department of Industry and Commerce memorandum, 15 Feb. 1950, TTA 5/2/14, National Archives of Ireland, Dublin.

108. Department of Finance memorandum, 16 Feb. 1950, TTA 5/2/14, National Archives of Ireland, Dublin.

109. Briefs for Minister of Industry and Commerce, Feb. 1951, TTA 2/4, National Archives of Ireland, Dublin; and O'Doherty interview, 29 Apr. 2002.

110. Preliminary Report of the Irish Hotels Commission for American Tourism, 30 Sept. 1950, DT, S13087C, National Archives of Ireland, Dublin.

111. James Deegan and Donal Dineen devote three pages to the Christenberry report in their twenty-five-page summary of Irish tourism development between 1922 and 1960. They acknowledge that the report's influence on government policy is difficult to determine. See James Deegan and Donal Dineen, *Tourism Policy and Performance: The Irish Experience* (London: International Thompson Business Press, 1997), 17–19. Linda King is far less guarded and argues that the report had a profound impact, especially in the area of advertising content. Linda King, "'Guaranteed Irish'—Aer Lingus and the Representation of Ireland" (paper presented at *Ireland's Heritages: Critical Perspectives on Consumption, Method and Memory,* Galway-Mayo Institute of Technology, Castlebar, 19 Oct. 2002).

112. Christenberry report. Tourist guides took this scattered approach as a result of the ITA's close connection to local authorities and the need to universally please all counties, not the belief that everything and every place in Ireland was equally important to tourists. Areas like Killarney were able to exert more pressure than the Roscommons or Cavans of the country, but minor regions *also* contributed to the Association's small budget and could not be ignored.

113. Quinlan was appointed primarily for his pro–Fine Gael politics and he seems to have lacked any substantial tourism background.

114. Much of the graphic design work done in Ireland during the 1950s and 1960s was by Dutch designers like Jan de Fouw who produced, among other things, *Ireland of the Welcomes* from 1952 into the 1990s. De Fouw and his fellow countrymen were encouraged to keep a low profile and to avoid putting their name on their publications because doing so sparked negative commentary in the pages of Irish newspapers. *Home Movie Nights: Jan de Fouw,* directed by Alan Gilsenan, Dublin: RTÉ, 2001; and also Jan de Fouw, interview by author, Dublin, 14 Oct. 2002. For a more complete outline of the story of Dutch influence on Irish design, including an account of de Fouw's influence, see Conor Clarke, *Oranje and Green: Holland-Ireland, Design Connections 1951–2002* (Amsterdam: BIS Publishers, 2002).

115. Christenberry report.

116. DFA Minutes, 31 Jan. 1951, DFA, 366/115 Pt. 1, National Archives of Ireland, Dublin.

117. Report of Cabinet Subcommittee on Tourism, 10 July 1950, DT, S13087C, National Archives of Ireland, Dublin.

118. Memorandum: The Irish Tourist Board and Tourist Publicity, 1950, DT, S13087C, National Archives of Ireland, Dublin.

119. Ibid.

120. Memorandum from Irish Tourist Board to Minister for Industry and Commerce, 13 Dec. 1950, DT, S13087C, National Archives of Ireland, Dublin.

121. Memo to Mr. McCarthy, 30 Dec. 1949, TTA 5/2/14.

122. "Tourist Board Scheme Delayed by Minister," *Irish Times,* 9 Oct. 1950.

123. O'Doherty interview, 29 Apr. 2002.

124. "Irish Tourist Association Annual General Meeting and Luncheon," *Irish Travel,* Nov. 1950, 27–33.

125. *Irish Press,* 12 Oct. 1950. This is a reference to a leadership shake-up at the Tourist Board that took effect on 1 October during which J. A. Nugent was made the new chairman. As noted above, there were not, however, any massive changes to board structure or responsibilities. See Annual Reports and Accounts, Year Ended 31st Mar. 1951, 1951, DT, S13904C, National Archives of Ireland, Dublin.

126. "The Future of Irish Tourism Part II," *Irish Press,* 14 Oct. 1950.

127. DFA Minutes, 31 Jan. 1951.

128. DFA Minutes, 1 Feb. 1951, DF, 366/115 Pt. 1, National Archives of Ireland, Dublin.

129. DFA Minutes, 7 Feb. 1951, DFA, 366/115 Pt. 1, National Archives of Ireland, Dublin.

130. DFA Minutes, 14 Mar. 1951, DFA, 366/115 Pt. 1, National Archives of Ireland, Dublin.

131. Draft of Tourist Traffic (Amendment) Bill, 1951, TTA 2/4, National Archives of Ireland, Dublin.

132. Dáil Debate, 129 (27 Feb. 1952), 1120–22.

133. Liam Cosgrave was the only minister to make veiled reference to the personal reasons behind the formation of the publicity board. Cosgrave commented that "[i]t is essential in a matter of this kind to avoid any merely personal considerations or any question of personalities and to recognize that the interests of the tourist industry transcend both personalities and the importance of any of these organizations, however long established or however well-intentioned the members of them may be. The industry is far too important to allow it to be handled in a way which will result in either confusion or overlapping of functions." Part of Cosgrave's statement referred to the perpetuation of the Irish Tourist Association; however the "personal considerations" mentioned were undoubtedly a reference to the friendship between Lemass and O'Brien. Ibid.

134. Dáil Debate, 129 (27 Feb. 1952), 1136–39.

135. Dáil Debate, 219 (6 Mar. 1952), 1608. Actually, Lemass was responding to a powerful ITA effort to preserve "the identity of the ITA." See ITA Directors Are Perturbed, 26 Oct. 1951, TTA 14/2, National Archives of Ireland, Dublin; and Industry and Commerce Memorandum, Nov. 1951, TTA 5/2/3, National Archives of Ireland, Dublin.

136. Department of Industry and Commerce Minutes, 6 Dec. 1951, TTA 2/7 vol. 1, National Archives of Ireland, Dublin.

137. Report of Inter-Departmental Meeting, 1 Dec. 1951, TTA 5/2/3, National Archives of Ireland, Dublin.

138. Note to McElligott from D. P. Shanagher, 19 Dec. 1951, TTA 2/7 vol. 1, National Archives of Ireland, Dublin.

139. This finding contradicts Joe J. Lee's suggestion that Finance was able to dramatically handicap Industry and Commerce efforts to forward tourist development [Lee, *Ireland, 1912–1985,* 308].

140. D. P. Shanagher to J. A. Nugent, 18 Dec. 1951, TTA 2/7 vol. 1, National Archives of Ireland, Dublin.

141. The idea that a new name was required for the Irish Tourist Board was one of the few suggestions made in the Christenberry report that was wholeheartedly adopted by the government. This acceptance was owing to the need to distance the new body from the failed board of the 1940s. Given the speed with which the publicity board was launched, it is hardly surprising that out of a desire to begin work O'Brien began using stationary headed "Tourist Publicity Board of Ireland" without receiving official sanction first. O'Brien's action sparked immediate anger in the Department of Industry and Commerce, and the publicity chief was quickly ordered to cease using the English-language letterhead because Lemass wanted to use an Irish name for the new board. See Note from Agnew to Slattery, 8 Oct. 1951, TTA 2/7 vol. 1, National Archives of Ireland, Dublin. The minister felt that it was "desirable that we should get away from the unimaginative kind of name that we established in 1939," no doubt because

such "unimaginative" names were all too closely associated with the failed 1939 board. See Dáil Debate, 129 (27 Feb. 1952), 1124.

142. At the end of October, O'Brien suggested that the name "Fógra Fáilte" might be ideal. J. Agnew, a civil servant at Industry and Commerce, replied that "fógra" was unsuitable because it translated as "notice" or "warning"; the numerous other names that were suggested, however, including Fáilte Éireann and Forás Fáilte, failed to generate substantial support. The names offered for the Tourist Board itself, including Turas Éireann, Cuaird Éireann, Forás Taisteal, and Taisteal Éireann, likewise proved unpopular. See Memo from Agnew to Slattery, 20 Oct. 1951, TTA 2/7 vol. 1, National Archives of Ireland, Dublin; and Points in Regard to the Attached Draft Heads, 1951, TTA 2/7 vol. 1, National Archives of Ireland, Dublin.

143. Dáil Debate, 129 (6 Mar. 1952), 1607.

144. For a detailed discussion of the background and content of An Tóstal, see chapter 4. The festival's profound impact on Irish landscapes is addressed in detail in chapter 6.

145. "An Tóstal," *Irish Tourist Bulletin,* Nov. 1952, DT, S14995A, National Archives of Ireland, Dublin.

146. Taoiseach's Speech at Opening of Tóstal at Cork, 8 May 1955, DT, S15297B, National Archives of Ireland, Dublin.

147. "An Tóstal: A Word of Advice," *Dublin Opinion,* Dec. 1953. This "advice" was contained in an advertisement placed by the tourist board in the satirical magazine *Dublin Opinion.* There was nothing satirical about the advertisement, however, and it succinctly states what the board was saying in its own publications and press statements.

148. According to the booklet, tourism was responsible for £28 million in total exports. As a whole agriculture brought in £40.5 million but the board's figures divided this into specific categories, the largest of which were cattle exports valued at £20 million. Exports were further divided into "other live animals" (£7 million), "eggs" (£5 million), "drink" (£5 million), and "poultry" (£3.5 million). *What Does Tourism Mean to You?* 1952, DT, S14995A, National Archives of Ireland, Dublin.

149. *What Does Tourism Mean to You?*

150. *Tourism Is Everybody's Business,* produced by Joe Byrne, Aiden O'Hanlon, and Brian Keogh for Bord Fáilte Éireann, 1978, Irish Film Center Archives, Dublin.

151. Gorman interviews, 6 Aug. 2002 and 11 Oct. 2002. O'Brien passed away in 1956. See Acknowledgement of a Subscription to the J. P. O'Brien Memorial Fund, May 1956, SFP, PR6/1027, Cork Archives Institute, Cork.

152. O'Doherty interview, 29 Apr. 2002; Gorman interview, 11 Oct. 2002.

153. Dáil Debate, 148 (9 Feb. 1955), 48.

154. Memorandum, 21 July 1955, TTA 14/4, National Archives of Ireland, Dublin. Following the 1952 Tourist Traffic Act, the ITA was primarily responsible for running tourist bureaus in Ireland and no longer published its own guidebooks, magazines, or other materials.

155. Resolution from County Council Chambers, 12 Feb. 1955, DT, S15766, National Archives of Ireland, Dublin.

156. Dáil Debate, 148 (9 Feb. 1955), 48.

157. O'Doherty interview, 30 July 2002.

158. Gorman interview, 11 Oct. 2002.

159. Memorandum, 11 Feb. 1959, DT, S16596A, National Archives of Ireland, Dublin.

160. BFÉ Press Release, 17 Sept. 1964, DT, S13087H/95, National Archives of Ireland, Dublin.

3. Change and Continuity, 1958–1994

1. Tony Varley, Thomas A. Boylan, and Michael P. Cuddy, eds., *Rural Crisis: Perspectives on Irish Rural Development* (Galway: Center for Development Studies, Univ. College Galway, 1991).

2. J. W. O'Hagan, *The Economy of Ireland: The Performance of a Small European Country* (London: Macmillan, 1995), 27.

3. Tom Inglis, *Moral Monopoly: The Rise and Fall of the Catholic Church in Modern Ireland* (Cork: Cork Univ. Press, 1998).

4. Brian Fallon, *An Age of Innocence: Irish Culture, 1930–1960* (Dublin: Gill and Macmillan, 1998), especially page 257.

5. See O'Hearn, *Inside the Celtic Tiger*; and O'Hagan, *Economy of Ireland*. The unemployment statistic cited here is found in O'Hagan, *Economy of Ireland*, 40.

6. It has often been suggested that the 1960s represented a "quantum leap into modernity"; however, Brian Fallon argues that developments in the 1950s and even the 1940s were far more profound. Fallon's view is definitely borne out in tourism development. While there was dramatic growth in the 1960s, the foundation was laid earlier and changes that took place during the 1960s and 1970s seldom had the profound impact of the institutional developments covered in chapter 2. See Fallon, *An Age of Innocence*, especially 257–71.

7. No legislation after 1955 attempted to accomplish anything as dramatic as the 1939, 1952, or 1955 acts had done and instead covered budgetary increases and minor issues such as the grading of caravan parks. See Deegan and Dineen, *Tourism Policy and Performance*, 38 and 41.

8. Pack, "Spain in the Age of Mass Tourism," 106.

9. Father John Scanlon to Erskine Childers, 29 July 1963, DT, S17316/63, National Archives of Ireland, Dublin.

10. John B. Keane, "A Matchmaker Wanted for the Deserted Village," *Sunday Press,* 10 Nov. 1963.

11. Father John Scanlon to Erskine Childers.

12. Keene's sympathy with the plight of bachelor farmers was recorded in *The Chastitute,* a humorous story of John Bosco's unsuccessful attempts to hire a matchmaker able to help end his fifty-three-year battle with religiously inspired sexual guilt, social ineptitude, bad luck,

and virginity. See John B. Keane, *The Chastitute: A Play In Two Acts* (Dublin: Mercier Press, 1981).

13. *Sunday Press,* 10 Nov. 1963.

14. Runai Aire to Father John Scanlon, 1 Sept. 1963, DT, S17316/63, National Archives of Ireland, Dublin.

15. Ó Cearbhaill from Father John Scanlon, 18 Sept. 1963, DT, S17316/63, National Archives of Ireland, Dublin.

16. Seán Lemass to Father John Scanlon, 26 Sept. 1963, DT, S17316/63, National Archives of Ireland, Dublin; and 18 Sept. 1963, DT, S17316/63.

17. Father John Scanlon to Electricity Supply Board, 7 Jan. 1964, DT, S17316/95, National Archives of Ireland, Dublin.

18. Note from Electricity Supply Board, 18 Feb. 1964, DT, S17316/95, National Archives of Ireland, Dublin.

19. Memorandum: Problems of Small Western Farms, 29 July 1963, DT, 98/6/149, National Archives of Ireland, Dublin.

20. Memorandum: Father Scanlon's letter, 24 Sept. 1963, DT, S17316/63.

21. Tourism brochure: "Take a Holiday 'Away from It All' in Tuosist," circa 1970, DT, 2002/8/299, National Archives of Ireland, Dublin.

22. For a detailed discussion of cross-border tourism dialogue, see Eric G. E. Zuelow, "'Ingredients for Cooperation': Irish Tourism in North-South Relations, 1924–1998," *New Hibernia Review* 10, no. 1 (2006): 17–39.

23. "Hoteliers and Catering People Upset by Bord Fáilte Booklet," *Clare Champion,* 10 Nov. 1972.

24. "Angling—The Saviour of Clare Tourism," *Clare Champion,* 25 Mar. 1983.

25. "Bord Fáilte Accused of Neglecting East Clare," *Clare Champion,* 24 May 1985.

26. Department of Transport and Power Information Sheet: Irish Tourist Association, Feb. 1963, DT, S13087G/63, National Archives of Ireland, Dublin.

27. Michael R. Boland to Erskine Childers, 11 Mar. 1963, DT, S13087H/63, National Archives of Ireland, Dublin.

28. Department of Transport and Power Information Sheet.

29. Erskine Childers to Seán Lemass, 21 Mar. 1963, DT, S13087G/63, National Archives of Ireland, Dublin.

30. J. Fitzpatrick to Erskine Childers, 4 Jan. 1963; Note from Irish Tourist Association to Department of Transport and Power, 1963, DT, S13087H/63, National Archives of Ireland, Dublin.

31. Erskine Childers to Seán Lemass, 21 Mar. 1963.

32. Seán Lemass to Erskine Childers, 28 Mar. 1963, DT, S13087G/63, National Archives of Ireland, Dublin.

33. Statement by Erskine Childers to Deputation from Irish Tourist Association, 11 Apr. 1963, DT, S13087G/63, National Archives of Ireland, Dublin.

34. Erskine Childers to Seán Lemass, 19 Apr. 1963, DT, S13087G/63, National Archives of Ireland, Dublin.

35. The paper was designed to be both a party newspaper—De Valera remained on the paper's board of directors throughout his career in politics—and a commercial enterprise. Following Seán Lemass's tenure as the paper's managing director, it began to reflect an ideological split within Fianna Fáil. The paper sided against the party's protectionist wing and supported the new Whitaker/Lemass belief in free trade and the promotion of outside investment. Given the paper's new forward-looking direction, it is interesting that it did not immediately welcome the demise of the ITA in favor a more efficient and modern tourism development structure. See John Horgan, *Irish Media: A Critical History since 1922* (London: Routledge, 2001), 28 and 68.

36. "Talks to Be Held on Fate of ITA," *Irish Press*, 19 Apr. 1963.

37. "Bord Fáilte to Take over ITA," *Irish Press*, 16 Oct. 1963.

38. "New Tourist Plan Is Vital to Economy," *Irish Press*, 18 Oct. 1963.

39. O'Doherty interview, 30 July 2002. Also see Minutes, ITA Council of Director's Meeting, 20 Feb. 1964, SFP, PR6/1031(2), Cork Archives Institute, Cork.

40. Minutes, ITA Council of Director's Meeting, 20 Feb. 1964.

41. O'Doherty interview, 30 July 2002.

42. Minutes, ITA Council of Director's Meeting, 20 Feb. 1964.

43. "ITA Says No Closing Down Yet," *Irish Press*, 7 May 1964.

44. Bord Fáilte, *Bord Fáilte Annual Report and Accounts, Year Ending 31st March 1959* (Dublin: Bord Fáilte, 1959).

45. Bord Fáilte, *Bord Fáilte Annual Report and Accounts, Year Ended 31st March 1961* (Dublin: Bord Fáilte, 1961).

46. Bord Fáilte, *Bord Fáilte Report for the Year Ended 31 March 1962* (Dublin: Bord Fáilte, 1962).

47. Bord Fáilte, *The Irish Tourist Board Report for the Year Ended March 31 1964* (Dublin: Bord Fáilte, 1964).

48. Bord Fáilte Press Release, 17 Sept. 1964, DT, S13087H/95, National Archives of Ireland, Dublin.

49. Bord Fáilte, *The Irish Tourist Board Report for the Year Ended March 31, 1965* (Dublin: Bord Fáilte, 1965).

50. Department of Transport and Power Memorandum, 12 June 1970, DT, 2001/6/316, National Archives of Ireland, Dublin.

51. Bord Fáilte, *The Irish Tourist Board Report for the Year Ended 31 March 1962*.

52. Bord Fáilte, *The Irish Tourist Board Report for the Year Ended March 31, 1966* (Dublin: Bord Fáilte, 1966); Bord Fáilte, *The Irish Tourist Board Report for the Year Ended March 31, 1970* (Dublin: Bord Fáilte, 1970).

53. Department of Transport and Power Memorandum.

54. "Targets Are Set High: Third Programme Issued," *Irish Travel Trade News*, Feb. 1969, 1 and 8.

55. "Bord Fáilte Hit by Big Financial Set Back in '66," *Irish Travel Trade News*, Feb. 1966, 1.

56. *Tourist Traffic Act, 1966* (Dublin: Government Publications, 1966).

57. "Is Rate of Investment in Irish Tourism Sufficient?" *Irish Travel Trade News*, Oct. 1966, 2.

58. "Rate of State Investment in Tourism Too Low," *Irish Travel Trade News*, Dec. 1968, 10.

59. *Tourist Traffic Act, 1968* (Dublin: Government Publications, 1968).

60. "Tourism Being Starved to Death by Lack of Financial Support," *Irish Travel Trade News*, May 1970, 18.

61. *Tourist Traffic Act, 1972* (Dublin: Government Publications, 1972).

62. *Tourism Traffic Act, 1975* (Dublin: Government Publications, 1975).

63. *Tourism Traffic Act, 1983* (Dublin: Government Publications, 1983).

64. *Tourism Traffic Act, 1987* (Dublin: Government Publications, 1987).

65. Bord Fáilte, *The Fáilte Business 2000: The Role of Tourism in Economic Growth* (Dublin: Bord Fáilte, 2000), 32.

66. Frank McNally, "All Ireland Tourism Campaign Launched," *Irish Times*, 12 Nov. 1996.

67. "Allocation for Tourism up 21 Percent," *Irish Times*, 12 Nov. 1999.

68. Bord Fáilte, *Fáilte Business*, 2.

69. Deegan and Dineen, *Tourism Policy and Performance*, 156–65.

70. Gerry Smyth, *Space and the Irish Cultural Imagination* (New York: Palgrave, 2001), 82.

71. "'Old Dublin' Must Be Developed as Tourism Centre," *Irish Travel Trade News*, May 1989, 44–45.

72. Smyth, *Space*, 82.

73. Bord Fáilte, *Bord Fáilte Report for the Year Ended March 1993* (Dublin: Bord Fáilte, 1993).

74. "Matt McNulty Is New Temple Bar Chairman," *Irish Travel Trade News*, Aug./Sept. 1999, 29.

75. An Taisce, *Grafton Street Sustaining the Magic. What Future for Dublin's Favorite Shopping Street?* (Dublin: An Taisce, 1995).

76. Ruth McManus, "Dublin's Changing Tourism Geography," *Irish Geography* 34, no. 2 (2001): 103–23, see page 107.

77. Transport, Fuel, and Power, Transfer of Administration and Ministerial Functions Order, No. 2, 28 Oct. 1961, DT, S13987G/61, National Archives of Ireland, Dublin.

78. "Should Tourism Have a Government Spokesman Queries NTC Chairman," *Irish Travel Trade News*, July/Aug. 1973, 6.

79. "Minister Blamed at Tourism Meeting," *Irish Travel Trade News*, Nov. 1974, 1 and 4.

80. "Tourism Industry Gets Ministerial Recognition," *Irish Travel Trade News*, Oct. 1977, 1.

81. "Ahern Makes Substantial Changes in Departmental Responsibilities," *Irish Times,* 27 June 1997.

82. Mark Hennessy, "Lobbying Saves Walsh, Smith: Five New Faces to Figure at Cabinet Table as Ahern Sacks Four Ministers," *Irish Times,* 7 June 2002.

83. Thompson, "The Postcolonial Tourist," 4–5.

84. "British Pressmen Visit Killarney. Address of Welcome," *Kerryman,* 23 May 1925.

85. *Kerryman,* 5 Apr. 1924.

86. P. J. Courtney, "Railways and Tourists," *Kerryman,* 19 Jan. 1924.

87. "Killarney Tourist Development. Great Western of England Representatives at Killarney," *Kerryman,* 26 Sept. 1925.

88. Department of Justice to Maurice Moynihan, 19 July 1939, DT, S11345, National Archives of Ireland, Dublin.

89. Seán Lemass to Erskine Childers, 6 Aug. 1964, DT, S13087H/95, National Archives of Ireland, Dublin.

90. "Kerryisms," Kerryman, 23 May 1925.

91. "English Firm Leaves Tourist Board in Shade," *Kilkenny People,* 22 Sept. 1951.

92. "The Tourist Board," *Kilkenny People,* 22 Sept. 1951.

93. "ITA and English Company," *Kilkenny People,* 24 Nov. 1951.

94. See [?] McCarthy, Minute, 16 Feb. 1953, TTA 12/3, National Archives of Ireland, Dublin; and [?] O'Riordain, Minute, 19 Nov. 1952, TTA 12/3, National Archives of Ireland, Dublin.

95. De Fouw interview, 14 Oct. 2002.

96. Gilsenan, *Home Movie Nights.*

97. De Fouw interview, 14 Oct. 2002.

98. Points for the Minister on the Memorandum dated 16th February submitted to the Government by the Minister for Finance in regard to Tourist Industry, [?]1950, TTA 5/2/14, National Archives of Ireland, Dublin; and A New Approach? 28 Sept. 1950, DT, S13087C, National Archives of Ireland, Dublin.

99. Department of External Affairs, British Travel and Holidays Association, [?]1955, DFA, 366/215, National Archives of Ireland, Dublin.

100. *Le Guinness: Son Brassage, Ses Properties, Ses Qualities* (Dublin: Guinness, 1932), 14 and 17, Guinness Ireland Archives, Dublin. See also *Guinness, Brasserie de Renommée Mondiale: L'histoire du Célèbre Stout aux Cinq Millions Hectolitres de Ventes Annuelles* (Dublin, circa 1950), 5 and 17, Guinness Ireland Archives, Dublin.

101. *Guinness Dublin* (Dublin, 1939, 1948, 1955), Guinness Ireland Archives, Dublin.

102. Gorman interview, 11 Oct. 2002.

103. "Irish Tourist Association: Meeting in Cork, Work in America, Branch Formed in Dingle," *Kerryman,* 13 Dec. 1924.

104. See "Ireland for Tourists: The Whole Country Organised; Elaborate Publicity Work," *Kerryman,* 2 May 1925; and "Killarney Tourist Association: Election of Officers,

Future Town Clerk to Be Secy, Killarney in the Films, Delightful Pictures of Killarney," *Kerryman*, 23 Jan. 1926.

105. "Irish Tourist Association: Bureau in New York," *Kerryman*, 24 Dec. 1927.

106. "Christenberry Report."

107. Bord Fáilte, *Bord Fáilte Éireann Newsletter* (Mar.–Apr. 1956), 1.

108. Seanad Debate, *Tourist Traffic Bill, 1938—Fifth Stage*, 20 July 1939.

109. Gorman interview, 11 Oct. 2002.

110. "Big Success for BFÉ Benelux Promotion," *Irish Travel Trade News*, Mar. 1968, 1.

111. For an example, see Bord Fáilte, *Urlaub Made in Ireland* (Frankfurt: Bord Fáilte, 1969).

112. "Importance of German Market Emphasized by Frankfurt Workshop," *Irish Travel Trade News*, June 1971, 2.

113. Bord Fáilte, *Bord Fáilte Éireann Newsletter* (Nov.–Dec. 1955), 1.

114. Levenstein, *We'll Always Have Paris*, 145 and 207.

115. Bord Fáilte, *Newsletter* (Nov.–Dec. 1955), 1.

116. Bord Fáilte, *Bord Fáilte Éireann Newsletter* (July–Aug. 1956), 1.

117. Bord Fáilte, Survey of Visitors, Summer 1956, DF, F120/1/57, National Archives of Ireland, Dublin.

118. Bord Fáilte, *Attitudes of American and English Tourists Towards Shopping in Ireland and Irish Merchandise: A Qualitative Investigation* (Dublin: Bord Fáilte, 1973).

119. Bord Fáilte, *Know Your Market: Italy* (Dublin: Bord Fáilte, 1997).

120. Bord Fáilte, *Know Your Market: France* (Dublin: Bord Fáilte, 1998).

121. Bord Fáilte, *Know Your Market: North America* (Dublin: Bord Fáilte, 1998).

122. There has been a tendency in some of the scholarly literature to claim that government interest in tourism did not develop until the late 1980s because the industry was not a spending priority. (Desmond Gillmor, "Recent Trends and Patterns in Irish Tourism," in *Irish Tourism Development*, ed. Proinnsias Breathnach [Maynooth: Geographical Society of Ireland, 1994], 3.) Although it is true that grants for tourism development were often smaller than the industry wanted and that really substantial government investment had to wait until the late 1980s, I hope that it has been clear that gauging government interest should not be based entirely on the amount of money allocated for development. It is more precise to consider financial allocations in conjunction with a willingness to include tourism in government development programs, the government role in tourism policy development, and the position afforded tourism in the cabinet. The resulting picture shows a growing recognition of tourism's important role as a national interest spanning some forty years, not as a sudden epiphany in 1988.

4. Culture, Language, and Tourism

1. Miroslav Hroch, "From National Movement to the Fully-formed Nation: The Nation-building Process in Europe," in *Mapping the Nation*, ed. Gopal Balakrishnan (New York: Verso, 1996), 78–97, especially page 79.

2. Anthony D. Smith, *The Ethnic Origins of Nations* (Oxford: Blackwell, 1986).

3. Gellner, *Nations and Nationalism*; and Eric Hobsbawm and Terence Ranger, eds., *The Invention of Tradition* (Cambridge: Cambridge Univ. Press, 1986).

4. Gellner, *Nations and Nationalism*; and Anderson, *Imagined Communities.*

5. Catalan nationalists base their claim for independence on the issue of linguistic rights, believing that the very definition of "Catalan" would lose any clarity if the language were to disappear. See Daniele Conversi, "Language or Race?: The Choice of Core Values in the Development of Catalan and Basque Nationalisms," *Ethnic and Racial Studies* 13, no. 1 (1990): 50–70, see pages 53 and 57. Flemish nationalists stress their language rather than shared values, dress, or other markers of national difference. See Jan Blommaert, "Language and Nationalism: Comparing Flanders and Tanzania," *Nations and Nationalism* 2, no. 2 (1996): 235–56, see pages 237–38. Finally, Quebecois nationalism emphasizes language as a primary marker of identity—a stance that won concessions from the Canadian government and assured that Quebec remains effectively a unilingual state within a state. See Milton Taras, "Nations and Language-Building: Old Theories, Contemporary Cases," *Nationalism and Ethnic Politics* 4, no. 3 (1998): 79–101, especially 87–89.

6. Colman Ó Huallachain, *The Irish and Irish: A Sociolinguistic Analysis of the Relationship between a People and Their Language* (Dublin: Irish Franciscan Provincial Office, 1994); Reg Hinley, *The Death of the Irish Language* (London: Routledge, 1990).

7. Mike Cronin, *Sport and Nationalism in Ireland: Gaelic Games, Soccer and Irish Identity since 1884* (Dublin: Four Courts Press, 1999).

8. Timothy Gerard McMahon, "The Social Bases of the Gaelic Revival, 1893–1910," (Ph.D. diss., Univ. of Wisconsin-Madison, 2001).

9. Central Statistics Office, *Statistical Abstract, 1990* (Dublin: Government Publications, 1990), 55.

10. It is very likely that a large percentage of those who claim to be Irish speakers actually know only a few words or phrases. In other words, the census data probably *overestimates* the strength of the language revival, and these numbers are worthy of caution.

11. "Dingle as Tourist Centre. Inch—Ireland's Finest Strand," *Kerryman,* 3 Oct. 1925.

12. "Kerry Roads and Hotels," *Kerryman,* 28 Aug. 1926.

13. "Tourist Development," *Kerryman,* 29 Jan. 1927.

14. Irish Tourist Association, *Ireland: Official Publication* (Dublin: Irish Tourist Association, 1929).

15. Gavon Campbill to Department of Finance, 14 July 1930, DF, E109/31/30, National Archives of Ireland, Dublin; and J. P. O'Brien to government, 12 June 1930, DF, E109/31/30, National Archives of Ireland, Dublin.

16. Irish Tourist Association, "Holidays in the Gaeltacht: See Ireland First," circa 1930, DF, E109/31/30, National Archives of Ireland, Dublin.

17. Archie Bell, *The Spell of Ireland* (Boston: L. C. Page and Co., 1928), 75.

18. Sean MacEntee, Memorandum: Development of the Tourist Industry in the Gaeltacht, 20 Nov. 1934, DT, S7839A & B, National Archives of Ireland, Dublin. The memorandum to which MacEntee was responding is missing from the National Archives and the relevant Taoiseach file.

19. Máire Cruise O'Brien, *The Same Age as the State* (Madison: Univ. of Wisconsin Press, 2004), 50, 78–79, 80, and 115.

20. MacEntee, Memorandum: Development of the Tourist Industry in the Gaeltacht, 20 Nov. 1934.

21. *Irish Press,* 31 Sept. 1938, emphasis mine.

22. R. Jacob, "Gaeltacht and Tourists," *Irish Press,* 5 Oct. 1938.

23. Cu Uladh, "Gaeltacht and Tourists," *Irish Press,* 3 Oct. 1938.

24. "Tourist Bill Will Benefit Gaeltacht," *Irish Press,* 1 Oct. 1938.

25. "Kilarney Discusses Tourists. New Government Bill Examined by UDC," *Cork Evening Echo,* 5 Nov. 1938.

26. This term was used by Donnchadh Ó hEaluighthe during debate about the bill in the Seanad. See Seanad Debate, *Tourist Traffic Bill, 1938—Fifth Stage,* 20 July 1939. It is not clear whether the anti-tourism authors were members of the Gaelic League or whether the Gaelic League took any official stance on the legislation.

27. Ibid.

28. C. S. Almond, Minute, 25 May 1938, DFA, S084/0020/38, National Archives of Ireland, Dublin.

29. ITA Memorandum to Minister for Industry and Commerce, 16 Apr. 1941, DT, S10946, National Archives of Ireland, Dublin.

30. Irish Tourist Association, *Official Guide to the "Kingdom of Kerry"* (Dublin: Irish Tourist Association, [?]1940).

31. O'Doherty interview, 30 July 2002.

32. Department of Finance Note, 1 Feb. 1944, DF, F200/17/44, National Archives of Ireland, Dublin.

33. Inter-Departmental Committee on Development of Gaeltacht Resorts, Report on Development of Gaeltacht Resorts, Feb. 1948, DF, F200/17/44, National Archives of Ireland, Dublin.

34. Irish Tourist Board, Gaeltacht Summer Colleges, 6 Jan. 1944, DF, F200/17/44, National Archives of Ireland, Dublin.

35. Ibid.

36. Nuala C. Johnson, "Making Space: Gaeltacht Policy and the Politics of Identity," in *In Search of Ireland: A Cultural Geography,* ed. Brian Graham (London: Routledge, 1997), 181.

37. Cabinet Minutes, 28 Oct. 1952, DT, S13087E1, National Archives of Ireland, Dublin.

38. Minute from Donnelly to Hayes, 8 Mar. 1959, TTA 2/27, National Archives of Ireland, Dublin.

39. Department of Finance, Memorandum for the Government: Observations of the Minister for Finance on the Memorandum of the Minister for Transport and Power Regarding Proposals for Assisting the Economies of Small Farm Areas in the West of Ireland through Tourism, 7 Apr. 1965, DT, 98/6/149, National Archives of Ireland, Dublin.

40. Lee, *Ireland, 1912–1985,* 671.

41. Ibid., 673.

42. "Tourism Is Not Good for the Irish Language—DJ at Dingle Court," *Kerryman,* 29 Nov. 1958.

43. L. Perry Curtis, Jr., *Apes and Angles: The Irishman in Victorian Caricature* (Washington, D.C.: Smithsonian Institution, 1997), x–xxxi and 157; Richard Stivers, *Hair of the Dog: Irish Drinking and Its American Stereotype* (New York: Continuum, 2000), see pages 1–10 for a brief summary of the drunken Irish stereotype.

44. Maureen Waters, *The Comic Irishman* (Albany: State Univ. of New York Press, 1984), 1–6.

45. Seamus Deane, *Strange Country: Modernity and Nationhood in Irish Writing since 1790* (Oxford: Clarendon Press, 1997), 54–56.

46. Michael de Nie, "'A Medley Mob of Irish-American Plotters and Irish Dupes': The British Press and Transatlantic Fenianism," *Journal of British Studies* 40, no. 2 (2001): 213–40, especially page 239. For more on British colonial ideas about the people of India, see Thomas R. Metcalf, *Ideologies of the Raj* (Cambridge: Cambridge Univ. Press, 1995).

47. Roy Foster, *Paddy and Mr. Punch: Connections in Irish and English History* (London: Oxford Univ. Press, 1995), 281–305.

48. *Kerryman,* 21 Aug. 1926.

49. Irish Tourist Association, "The Irish Elections, 1927," *Irish Travel,* June 1927, 197.

50. "Genuine Irish Welcome," *Irish Travel,* May 1932, 191.

51. Jack Lynch, Address by the Taoiseach, 13 Aug. 1968, DT, 99/1/131, National Archives of Ireland, Dublin.

52. Will Rogers, "American Tribute. Ireland's Welcome for the Tourist," *Kerryman,* 21 Aug. 1926.

53. Bell, *The Spell of Ireland,* 29.

54. Tony Hawks, *Round Ireland with a Fridge* (New York: St. Martin's Griffin, 1988), 93.

55. "Kerryisms," *Kerryman,* 15 Oct. 1927.

56. Bord Fáilte, *Ireland: Fairies* (Dublin: Bord Fáilte, 1976).

57. Draft letter from Michael Kevin O'Doherty to [?], Apr. 1950, Michael Gorman private collection.

58. Report of Cabinet Sub-Committee on Tourism.

59. Bord Fáilte, *Bord Fáilte Éireann Newsletter,* Nov. 1957, 3.

60. Gilsenan, *Home Movie Nights.*

61. Brown, *Ireland,* 75.

62. Roy Foster, *W. B. Yeats, A Life, Part Two: The Arch-Poet* (Oxford: Oxford Univ. Press, 2003), 332–35.

63. Brown, *Ireland,* 113.

64. Cuddy, 33–34.

65. Ibid., 42.

66. Quinn and Keane, 190.

67. Ibid., 192.

68. Bord Fáilte, *Developing Sustainable Tourism: Tourism Development Plan 1994–1999* (Dublin: Bord Fáilte, 1995), 3.

69. Denis A. Cronin, Jim Gilligan, and Karina Holton, eds., *Irish Fairs and Markets, Studies in Local History* (Dublin: Four Courts Press, 2001), 14.

70. D. Cronin, Gilligan, and Holton, *Irish Fairs and Markets,* 135.

71. Ibid., 16.

72. Ibid., 124. See also Patrick Logan, *Fair Day: The Story of Irish Fairs and Markets* (Belfast: Appletree Press, 1986), 65.

73. Logan, *Fair Day,* 20.

74. Rukeyser describes how a ten-year-old girl, the Green Queen, crowns Puck (69–70), then proceeds to stress the extraordinary sexuality of the girl's royal partner: "The huge white balls were before my eyes, great in their power and whiteness . . . Energy bulged here, a double bulge robed in the smoothness of white fur, hidden and trumpeting, open and recondite, worlds creating worlds, something secret and understood . . . He swung there, strong, white, the crowned world rising up through worlds, crowned by a girl's arm, still and held in his kingship, with the great bells slung between his horns, the great testicles slung between his legs." Muriel Rukeyser, *The Orgy* (New York: Coward-McCann, 1965), 71–72.

75. During a conversation I had while researching this book, one local publican proudly told me about his approach to the event. He boasted that all stools and tables were removed from his bar before the fair; it was simple geometry: more people could be plugged into the pub than would be possible if furniture were present. He went on to say that he would stock up on huge quantities of extra alcohol, hire a substantial short-term staff, and forego sleep for the entire event. It is a very lucrative, if exhausting, weekend for local public houses.

76. Logan, *Fair Day,* 56–57.

77. D. Cronin, Gilligan, and Holton, *Irish Fairs and Markets,* 136.

78. In the front space of the original 1965 edition of *The Orgy,* Rukeyser's publisher inserted the following disclaimer: "The goat is real, Puck Fair is real; the orgy is real. All the characters and the acts of this book, however, are—of course—a free fantasy on the event." The author steadfastly denied the publisher's statement, however, claiming that the work was "a documentary account of three days of living under an extraordinary power." According to Rukeyser, she drew all of her reporting directly from the notes taken during her August 1958 trip. Indeed,

"The only thing in it I did not write and I cannot vouch for is the publishers' disclaimer." See Murial Rukeyser, "Not a Novel," *New York Review of Books* 4, no. 9 (3 June 1965).

79. Rukeyser, *Orgy*, 25.

80. Ibid., 28.

81. Ibid., 104.

82. Ibid., 184.

83. I would like to thank Dr. Aoife Bhreatnach for sharing her research on changing perceptions of Irish Travellers with me during numerous conversations in the winter/spring of 2002. Interested readers should see Aoife Bhreatnach, *Becoming Conspicuous: Irish Travelers, Society and the State, 1920–70* (Dublin: Univ. College Dublin Press, 2007).

84. Logan, *Fair Day*, 113.

85. Irish Tourist Association, *Official Guide to "Kingdom of Kerry"* (Dublin: Irish Tourist Association, 1934), 95.

86. "Souvenir of Your Visit to Puck Fair, Killorglin," circa 1946, MS 33,488, List 34, National Library of Ireland, Dublin. Cited with the permission of the Board of the National Library of Ireland.

87. Sean O'Faolain, *An Irish Journey* (London: Reader's Union, 1941), 128. Leslie Daiken, "Fair at Killorglin," newspaper clipping, MS 33,488, List 34, National Library of Ireland, Dublin. Cited with the permission of the Board of the National Library of Ireland.

88. Fógra Fáilte, *Ireland Guide* (Dublin: Fógra Fáilte, [?]1953.

89. Bord Fáilte, *Ireland: Calendar of Events, 1958* (Dublin: Bord Fáilte, 1958).

90. Bord Fáilte, *Ireland: Calendar of Events, 1961* (Dublin: Bord Fáilte, 1961).

91. Bord Fáilte, *Ireland: Calendar of Events, 1973* (Dublin: Bord Fáilte, 1973).

92. Bord Fáilte, *Ireland: 1980* (London: Bord Fáilte, 1980).

93. Logan, *Fair Day*, 113.

94. Rukeyser, *Orgy*, 15.

95. Daiken, "Fair at Killorglin."

96. Leslie Daiken, *Where Puck Is King,* script for BBC radio broadcast, London, 1960, MS 33,483 (48), National Library of Ireland, Dublin. Cited with the permission of the Board of the National Library of Ireland.

97. Leslie Daiken, "Kerry in August: Where Puck Is King," *Ocean Times,* 8 July 1962. See also Leslie Daiken, "Puck Fair (Synopsis)," 1 Feb. 1960, MS 33,483 (48), National Library of Ireland, Dublin. Cited with the permission of the Board of the National Library of Ireland.

98. Michael Gorman to Leslie Daiken, 4 Sept. 1959, MS 33, 472 box 3, folder 11, National Library of Ireland, Dublin. Cited with the permission of the Board of the National Library of Ireland.

99. O'Doherty interview, 29 Apr. 2002. The administration of An Tóstal is covered by Irene Furlong, "Tourism and the Irish State in the 1950s," in *The Lost Decade: Ireland in the 1950s,* ed. Dermot Keogh, Finbarr O'Shea, and Carmel Quinlan (Douglas Village, Cork: Mercier, 2004).

100. Subcommittee on Tourism memorandum, 1950, DT, S13087C, National Archives of Ireland, Dublin.

101. The Festival of Britain served many roles beyond those listed here. For example, it was also designed to reflect the Labour Party's agenda for the country and was held as a centennial commemoration of the Great Exhibition of 1851. Becky E. Conekin, *'The Autobiography of a Nation': The 1951 Festival of Britain* (Manchester: Manchester Univ. Press, 2003), 2, 4, 8, and 28.

102. An Tóstal Proposal, [?]1951, DT, S15297A, National Archives of Ireland, Dublin.

103. Conekin, *Autobiography*.

104. "An Tóstal" (Ireland at Home): April 5th–26th, 1953, TTA 12/1, National Archives of Ireland, Dublin.

105. P. W. Joyce, *A Social History of Ancient Ireland*, vol. 2 (New York: B. Blom, 1968 [1913]).

106. Fógra Fáilte, *An Tóstal: Official Souvenir Guide* (Dublin: Fógra Fáilte, 1953), 96, in Michael Gorman private collection.

107. O'Doherty interview, 29 Apr. 2002.

108. De Fouw interview, 14 Oct. 2002.

109. Fógra Fáilte, "An Tóstal: Ireland at Home Brochure," 1953, DT, S15297A, National Archives of Ireland, Dublin.

110. Conekin, *Autobiography*.

111. An Bord Fáilte, An Tóstal Proposal, [?]1951.

112. Conekin, *Autobiography*.

113. An Bord Fáilte, *Irish Tourist Bulletin*, Dec. 1952, 6, DT, S14995A, National Archives of Ireland, Dublin.

114. Colm O'Laoghaire, *Ireland Invites You*, 16 mm, 20 min., 1953, distributed by Universal Irish News, Irish Film Center Archives.

115. An Bord Fáilte, *Irish Tourist Bulletin*, June 1952, 3, DT, S14995A, National Archives of Ireland, Dublin.

116. An Bord Fáilte, *Irish Tourist Bulletin*, Dec. 1952, DT, S14995A.

117. Aodh O'Neill, "Pageant of St. Patrick," 7 Dec. 1953, DT, S15297B, National Archives of Ireland, Dublin.

118. An Bord Fáilte, *Irish Tourist Bulletin*, Feb. 1954, 3–4, DT, S14995B, National Archives of Ireland, Dublin.

119. O'Doherty interview, 29 Apr. 2002.

120. Report of Meeting, 2 Sept. 1954, TTA 12/5, National Archives of Ireland, Dublin.

121. Bord Fáilte, *Some Highlights of An Tóstal, 1955* (Dublin: Bord Fáilte, 1955). While the Tóstal guide did not mention it, all three of these individuals were born in England. McMaster was born in Birkenhead, Cheshire, in 1891. He began acting in 1911 and founded a touring Shakespeare company in 1925. This group ventured widely, especially in areas often neglected by theatre groups such as the Near East and Irish provinces. During World War

II, McMaster's company toured Ireland, then traveled to Australia following the war. He returned to Dublin in 1951 where he again led a traveling theater group around Ireland. He has been described as the "last of the great Irish actor-managers." McMaster died in 1962. MacLiammóire (1899–1978) was born in London. While at school in London, he became interested in Gaelic and joined the London Gaelic League. He eventually moved to Ireland in 1927. Edwards (1903–1982) was also born in London. He first toured Ireland in 1920 with Anew McMaster's Shakespeare company and then returned to London where he joined the Old Vic. In 1927 Edwards returned to Dublin to perform once more with McMaster and then decided to open his own theatre, the Peacock in Abbey Street. He joined the Gate Theatre in 1930 and went on to direct more than four hundred productions. Henry Boylan, *A Dictionary of Irish Biography,* 3rd ed. (Niwot, Colo.: Robert Rinehart, 1998).

122. Bord Fáilte, *Bord Fáilte Éireann Newsletter,* Jan.–Feb. 1956, 3.

123. *An Tóstal: Official Souvenir Guide,* 98–100.

124. *An Tóstal,* 102.

125. Ibid., 34–38.

126. Ibid., 53.

127. Ibid., 56.

128. "Kilkenny's Industrial Exhibition," *Kilkenny People,* 4 Apr. 1953.

129. "An Tóstal Closes in Kilkenny," *Kilkenny People,* 2 May 1953.

130. Diarmuid O Braoin, "Comhairle Tostail Corchaighe," 1954, Organising Secretary's Report, 30 June 1954, SFP, PR6/1325 (14), Cork Archives Institute, Cork.

131. "Industrial Parade Will Be Bigger Than Ever," *Limerick Leader,* 16 Mar. 1955. I would like to thank Dr. Aoife Bhreatnach for bringing this reference to my attention.

132. O'Connor argues that Irish people are represented as prone to talking, drinking, laughing, and playing music, but certainly not to working. When work is represented, she claims, "it is transformed into something very different from the alienated experience which it very often is through a process of romanticisation." Labor is made organic, boiled down to milking cows or cutting turf. She claims that this imagery is a result of colonization and that the prevalence of country people in tourist imagery is a trait Ireland shares with many other "'primitive' societies" in which the peasant is turned into a tourist attraction. Barbara O'Connor, "Myths and Mirrors: Tourist Images and National Identity," in *Tourism in Ireland: A Critical Analysis,* ed. Barbara O'Connor and Michael Cronin (Cork: Cork Univ. Press, 1993), 72–73.

133. *An Tóstal: Official Souvenir Guide,* 70.

134. *An Tóstal,* 74.

135. Ibid., 64.

136. Malachy Hynes, "A Foretaste of Tóstal," *Ireland of the Welcomes,* Nov.–Dec. 1952, 3–8.

137. Éamon de Valera, Speech Draft, 5 Apr. 1953, DT, S15197A, National Archives of Ireland, Dublin.

138. Braoin, "Comhairle Tostail Corchaighe."

139. Bord Fáilte, *Ireland of the Festivals* (Dublin: Bord Fáilte, 1959).

140. "An Tóstal—Latest News," *Leinster Express,* 2 Aug. 1958.

141. (1) Future of An Tóstal (2) Commencement Date in 1954 and Subsequent Years, [?]1954, TTA 12/5, National Archives of Ireland, Dublin.

142. Bord Fáilte Éireann Favored 6th–21st May for the 1956 Tóstal, [?]1955, TTA 12/5, National Archives of Ireland, Dublin.

143. Industry and Commerce Minute, 3 Sept. 1955, TTA 12/5, National Archives of Ireland, Dublin.

144. Confidential Memorandum on An Tóstal Review, 24 July 1958, TTA 12/5, National Archives of Ireland, Dublin.

145. Bord Fáilte, *Ireland of the Festivals.*

146. "Probe: The Festivals—What Now?" *Irish Travel Trade News,* May 1965, 2.

147. "Bord Fáilte to Spend £30,000 on 11 Festivals," *Irish Travel Trade News,* Sept. 1965, 7.

148. "Week-Long Festival Celebration Plans," *Irish Travel Trade News,* Mar. 1970, 18. For a more detailed overview of Dublin Tourism's handling of the Dublin Saint Patrick's Parade, see Mike Cronin and Daryl Adair, *The Wearing of the Green: A History of St. Patrick's Day* (London: Routledge, 2002), 184–85.

149. Cronin and Adair, I>Wearing of the Green," 241.

150. Eithne Donnellan, "Manager Mick Becomes Green Marshal for St. Patrick's Day," *Irish Times,* 31 Jan. 2002.

151. *The Rose of Tralee: The Truth in Her Eyes,* produced by Celtic Production/Telegael for Bord Fáilte, 1991, Bord Fáilte Photographic Archives.

5. Tourism and the Past

1. Prasenjit Duara, *Rescuing History from the Nation: Questioning Narratives of Modern China* (Chicago: Univ. of Chicago Press, 1995), 3.

2. Duara, *Rescuing History,* 4. As early as 1320, Scottish nobles and clerics drew on history to explain why Scotland was distinct from England. The "Declaration of Arbroath" traced the Scots from "Greater Scythia" through Spain and finally to Scotland, all the while unified as a people and governed by good qualities that were constantly under attack by outsiders. Even today, Scots look back on the "Declaration" as a clear statement of their proud past. Of course, not every "nation" can look back on fourteenth-century expressions of nationalism; some have had to work much harder. See James G. Kellas, *The Politics of Nationalism and Ethnicity* (New York: St. Martin's Press, 1991), 23–28, especially page 28. After the Second World War, for example, Austrians felt compelled to differentiate their sense of identity from that of the Germans in order to distance themselves from a legacy of mass murder and imperialism. For Austrian nationalists, it was not enough "to promote a distinctly Austrian national present"; it was required that they

draw on evidence from the past to reinforce difference. Nationalist historians focused on ancient demarcations from Germany, working to show that they had never really been part of the German nation. See Peter Thaler, "National History—National Imagery: The Role of History in Postwar Austrian Nation-Building," *Central European History* 32, no. 3 (1999): 277–310.

3. Anthony D. Smith, "Nationalism and the Historians," in *Mapping the Nation,* ed. Gopal Balakrishnan (London: Verso, 1996), 175.

4. Anthony D. Smith, "Gastronomy or Geology? The Role of Nationalism in the Reconstruction of Nations," *Nations and Nationalism* 1, no. 1 (1994): 18.

5. Bord Fáilte, *Report for the Year Ended 31 March 1962,* 13.

6. G. J. Ashworth, "Is Heritage a Globalisation of the Local or a Localisation of the Global?" (paper presented at *Ireland's Heritages: Critical Perspectives on Consumption, Method and Memory,* Castlebar, Co. Mayo, Ireland, 19 Oct. 2002); and Michael Hunter, ed., *Preserving the Past: The Rise of Heritage in Modern Britain* (Stroud, Gloucestershire: Alan Sutton Publishing, 1996), 1.

7. Maxine Feifer, *Tourism in History: From Imperial Rome to the Present* (New York: Stein and Day, 1985), 7–26.

8. Irish Tourist Association, *Ireland,* 1929, 12.

9. For a discussion of the beginnings of the Victorian fascination with ruins, see Ousby, *Englishman's England.*

10. Bell, *The Spell of Ireland,* 29–30 and 52.

11. "'Kuklos,' Awheel in Kerry: 'The Most Beautiful County in the British Isles'; English Writer's Cycle Trip through the 'Kingdom'; Interesting Impressions and High Appreciation," *Kerryman,* 29 Oct. 1927 (originally published in the *London Daily News*).

12. Department of Education Memorandum, [?]1925, DT, S5004A, National Archives of Ireland, Dublin.

13. Gerald Baldwin-Brown, *The Care of Ancient Monuments* (Cambridge: Cambridge Univ. Press, 1905), 128.

14. Baldwin-Brown, *Care of Ancient Monuments,* 73–74.

15. Rudy Koshar, *Germany's Transient Pasts: Preservation and National Memory in the Twentieth Century* (Chapel Hill: Univ. of North Carolina Press, 1998).

16. Baldwin-Brown, *Care of Ancient Monuments,* 74–75.

17. Koshar, *Germany's Transient Pasts,* 31.

18. Professor R. A. S. MacAlister was perhaps the most vocal Irish advocate of preservation in Ireland. Born in Dublin in 1870, he attended school in both Rathmines and Germany before attending Cambridge University. MacAlister edited the journal of the Royal Society of Antiquaries between 1910 and 1918, then served as the society's president between 1924 and 1928. His archeological experience extended beyond the British Isles; he served as director of excavations for the Palestine Explorations fund between 1900 and 1909. Following his time in the Middle East, MacAlister returned to Ireland, where he became the first professor

of Celtic archaeology at University College Dublin—a post he held until 1943. He was also the first chairman of the National Monuments Advisory Council in the Free State following passage of the Monuments Act in 1930. MacAlister was in Germany at the very moment that calls for preservation were growing louder, and he was at Cambridge when the first preservation legislation was passed in England. When this familiarity with the larger preservation discourse is combined with his own interest in Celtic archaeology and languages, it is hardly surprising that MacAlister began warning against the destruction of Irish monuments as early as the 1890s. For more, see Boylan, *Dictionary of Irish Biography,* 230. Irene Furlong briefly describes MacAlister's late-nineteenth-century preservationist concerns in her article "Frederick W. Crossley: Turn-of-the-century Tourism Pioneer."

19. R. A. S. MacAlister, *Ancient Ireland: A Study in the Lessons of Archaeology and History* (London: Methuen and Co., 1935), x.

20. Andrew Saint, "How Listing Happened," in Hunter, *Preserving the Past,* 115–33.

21. Baldwin-Brown, *Care of Ancient Monuments,* 156–57.

22. Memorandum, [?]1925, DT, S5004A).

23. R. A. S. Macalister to the Department of the Taoiseach, 19 May 1926, DT, S5004A, National Archives of Ireland, Dublin.

24. Gavin Stamp, "The Art of Keeping One Jump Ahead: Conservation Societies in the Twentieth Century," in Hunter, *Preserving the Past,* 82–85.

25. Ancient Monuments Protection Act Draft, [?]1925, DT, S5004A, National Archives of Ireland, Dublin.

26. After cabinet consideration, the definition of *ancient monuments* changed relatively little in chronological terms, but dropped much of the initial specificity. *National Monuments Act, 1930* (Dublin: Government Publications, 1930).

27. *National Monuments Act, 1930.*

28. O'Doherty interview, 30 July 2002.

29. *ITA Twentieth Anniversary Issue,* TAP, P91/B/10, University College Dublin. Also see Kinsale Development Association Special Meeting Transcript, 10 Aug. 1942, KDA, U274/5, Cork Archives Institute, Cork.

30. *Anniversary Issue,* TAP, P91/B/10. Very little of the original ITA photographic collection remains, though a handful of undated glass plates are stored in the Bord Fáilte archive that are probably the remnants of the ITA collection. Bord Fáilte acquired the ITA's photo library during the early 1950s.

31. *Anniversary Issue,* TAP.

32. "Christenberry Report."

33. "Preliminary Report of the Irish Hotels Commission," 30 Sept. 1950, DT, S13087C.

34. Report of Meeting, 1 Dec. 1951, TTA 2/7 vol. 1, National Archives of Ireland, Dublin.

35. An Bord Fáilte, *Irish Tourist Bulletin*, July 1951, 3–4, DT, S14995A, National Archives of Ireland, Dublin.

36. O'Doherty interviews, 29 Apr. and 30 July 2002.

37. In his book *The Past Is a Foreign Country* (Cambridge: Cambridge Univ. Press, 1997), David Lowenthal makes a similar point, noting that the placement of signs around castle ruins leads visitors to read the site/sight as a particular historical narrative, defining the castle in a specific way that has little to do with the actual past of the monument. See pages 265–70.

38. An Bord Fáilte, *Irish Tourist Bulletin*, Dec. 1953, 8–9, DT, S14995B, National Archives of Ireland, Dublin.

39. E. M. Fahy to Paddy [?], 27 Sept. 1960, Cork Public Museum [hereafter cited as CPM], U180, Cork Archives Institute, Cork.

40. See note 48 in chapter 6.

41. "The War at Westport," *Irish Times*, 18 Jan. 1961.

42. Arts Council to the Taoiseach, [?], DT, 97/6/380, National Archives of Ireland, Dublin.

43. *Bord Fáilte Éireann Newsletter*, Nov. 1957, 4.

44. *Irish Tourist Bulletin*, Feb. 1954, 6, DT, S14995B.

45. O'Doherty interview, 30 July 2002.

46. Brian Callanan, *Leaders, Visions, and Networks, Ireland's Shannon Story: A Case Study of Local and Regional Development* (Dublin: Irish Academic Press, 2000), 58–64. A far more detailed, if less scholarly, account of the development of Bunratty Castle can be found in Bernard Share, *Bunratty: Rebirth of a Castle* (Dingle, Ireland: Brandon, 1995).

47. An Bord Fáilte, *Irish Tourist Bulletin*, Nov. 1953, 12–13; *Bord Fáilte Éireann Newsletter*, Mar. 1958, 2; Bord Fáilte, *The Irish Tourist Board Annual Report for the Year Ended 31 March 1962* (Dublin: Bord Fáilte, 1962); and O'Doherty interview, 29 Apr. 2002. Dúchas finally developed the Hill of Tara in the 1990s. The new installation includes an impressive multimedia presentation in a converted church. Amusingly, in the late 1960s, an Irish-American named William E. P. O'Donnell proposed that the Irish government should develop Tara, not as a tourist site but as a new site for the Oireachtas and an Irish college. O'Donnell argued that a long boulevard should be constructed between Tara and Slane to host massive St. Patrick's Day parades. "'Save Tara' Plea by American," *Irish Press*, 22 Jan. 1969.

48. Gorman interview, 11 Oct. 2002.

49. Donal Horgan, *Victorian Visitor*, 66.

50. See Irish Tourist Association, *Introducing Ireland* (Dublin: Irish Tourist Association, 1950); Fógra Fáilte, *Ireland: An Illustrated Guide to the Counties of Ireland* (Dublin: Fógra Fáilte, [?]1953); and Bord Fáilte, *Ireland: The Heritage of the Past* (Dublin: Bord Fáilte, 1968). The Bord Fáilte Photographic Archive maintains an extensive collection of early images of Glendalough in all seasons.

51. An Bord Fáilte, *Irish Tourist Bulletin*, Dec. 1951, 6–7, DT, S14995A, National Archives of Ireland, Dublin.

52. Thomas Bodkin, Extract from Report to the Government of Ireland on various Institutions and Activities concerned with the Arts in Ireland, 30 Sept. 1949, DT, S8488B, National Archives of Ireland, Dublin.

53. Peadar S. Doyle, Question for the Taoiseach, 31 Oct. 1951, DT, S8488B, National Archives of Ireland, Dublin.

54. *Irish Tourist Bulletin,* July 1951, 3–4, DT, S14995A.

55. "Ireland's Ancient Monuments, Lack of Interest by Schools Is Deplored," *Irish Independent,* 3 Oct. 1952.

56. *Irish Tourist Bulletin,* Nov. 1953, 12–13, DT, S14995B; and An Bord Fáilte, Annual Report and Accounts, Year Ended 31st March 1954, DT, S15647B, National Archives of Ireland, Dublin. See also An Bord Fáilte, *Irish Tourist Bulletin,* Aug. 1953, 5–6, DT, S14995B, National Archives of Ireland, Dublin.

57. O'Doherty interview, 29 Apr. 2002.

58. Erskine Childers to Seán Lemass, 16 May 1962, DT, S17301/62, National Archives of Ireland, Dublin.

59. Seán Lemass to Erskine Childers, 15 June 1962, DT, S17301/62, National Archives of Ireland, Dublin.

60. In many ways, the development of the Garden of Remembrance chronologically mirrors the restoration of Kilmainham Jail. The Old IRA first proposed a monument at the Rotunda Gardens during the mid-1930s but government action was put on hold by the Emergency. After the war, the site was converted into a tuberculosis hospital and it was not until Noël Browne, minister for health during the interparty government between 1948 and 1951, was able to locate an alternate site at which to base anti-TB efforts that the Remembrance proposal was actualized. Unlike Kilmainham, the Garden of Remembrance was an entirely government-led project. Like Kilmainham, it was formally opened during the fiftieth anniversary commemorations in 1966, but was not completed until the early 1970s. See the following Taoiseach files: S8114A-C/61, 96/6/193, 96/6/159, and 2000/6/83.

61. Anne Dolan, *Commemorating the Irish Civil War: History and Memory, 1923–2000* (Cambridge: Cambridge Univ. Press, 2003), 200.

62. "Muckross House," newspaper clipping, 13 Dec. 1963, DT, S6355C/63, National Archives of Ireland, Dublin.

63. E. Myers to Seán Lemass, 23 Sept. 1963, DT, S6355C/63, National Archives of Ireland, Dublin.

64. Erskine Childers to Seán Lemass, 16 May 1962.

65. Erskine Childers to Seán Lemass, 20 Nov. 1963, DT, S6355C/63, National Archives of Ireland, Dublin.

66. Ibid.

67. L. P. Leech, "The Bourne-Vincent Memorial Park," *Irish Press,* 3 Dec. 1963.

68. R. C. MacMillan, "Why Not the Lakes of Killarney for All?" newspaper clipping, 29 Nov. 1963, DT, S6355C/63, National Archives of Ireland, Dublin.

69. E. Myers to Seán Lemass, 23 Sept. 1963.

70. The Royal Hospital was eventually turned into the National Gallery of Modern Art and many of the artifacts originally planned for display in the Georgian building were moved to the Collins Barracks just down the Liffey.

71. Department of Finance, Memorandum for the Government, 20 Apr. 1963, DT, S6355C/63, National Archives of Ireland, Dublin.

72. "20,000 See Muckross House," *Irish Press,* 31 Oct. 1964.

73. Newspaper clipping, 3 Dec. 1968, DT, 96/6/150, National Archives of Ireland, Dublin; "Muckross Gate to Remain Closed," *Cork Examiner,* 9 Aug. 1968.

74. Bord Fáilte, *Tourism Plan 1981–85: Marketing and Development Guide Lines for the Irish Tourist Industry* (Dublin: Bord Fáilte, 1980).

75. "How to Sell Killarney," *Irish Travel Trade News,* May 1989, 46–47.

76. Gorman interview, 11 Oct. 2002.

77. Department of External Affairs, Memorandum, 20 July 1960, DFA, 366/263, National Archives of Ireland, Dublin.

78. See folder DFA, 366/166/1, National Archives of Ireland, Dublin.

79. See detailed records in file sequence: DFA, 366/166/1–15, National Archives of Ireland, Dublin.

80. Conor Cruise O'Brien to E. F. Bozman, 22 May 1952, DFA, 366/175, National Archives of Ireland, Dublin.

81. E. F. Bozman to Conor Cruise O'Brien, 26 May 1952, DFA, 366/175, National Archives of Ireland, Dublin.

82. Memorandum, 24 Feb. 1939, DT, S8114A, National Archives of Ireland, Dublin.

83. While the construction of the Garden of Remembrance sparked little controversy, there was considerable debate about the inscription that was to be included. This conflict extended the completion of the memorial long past its formal inauguration in 1966. After a text was finally agreed—no easy task (see letter from [?] to Jack Lynch, 10 Apr. 1969; Government Meeting Report, 5 Sept. 1969; Garden of Remembrance: Inscriptions on Carved Wall, 21 Sept. 1969, DT, 2000/6/83, National Archives of Ireland, Dublin)—there was a great deal of concern about what languages to use. Although the initial plan was to present a poem in Gaelic, chosen by a government-run contest, there was objection at both public and government level. See letter from [?] to Seán Lemass, 10 Apr. 1969, DT, 2000/6/83, National Archives of Ireland, Dublin. Although the Garden of Remembrance had never been considered as a potential tourist attraction, the idea of a Gaelic-only inscription troubled at least one reporter, who advocated translations of the poem in English, French, and "whatever other languages are considered necessary," because most would be unable to understand the Gaelic—a fact that was nowhere more true than for tourists. See Desmond Rushe, "How Many Could Really Translate It?" *Irish Independent,* 2 Nov. 1971. After all, the Garden would be "one of the very few attractions of its type we have for visitors" and "if only as a gesture of courtesy,

whatever inscription is there should be available in understandable languages." See Desmond Rushe, "The Winning," *Irish Independent,* 12 Nov. 1971.

84. *Ghosts of Kilmainham* (Dublin: Kilmainham Jail Restoration Society, 1963).

85. Pat Cooke, *A History of Kilmainham Gaol* (Dublin: Dúchas, 2001).

86. Letter from [?] to A. D. Codling, 27 Apr. 1928, DF, S002/0003/28, National Archives of Ireland, Dublin.

87. Department of Justice to [?], 2 Feb. 1929, DF, 13/9/29, National Archives of Ireland, Dublin.

88. Memorandum for the Government. Disposal of Kilmainham Jail, 17 June 1946, DF, S102/017/53, National Archives of Ireland, Dublin.

89. Reflecting the growing republican interest in the prison, the Irish Tourist Association drew attention to Kilmainham in 1938 by publishing an article in its monthly magazine, *Irish Travel,* entitled "A Visit to Kilmainham Jail, Dublin: The Bastille of Ireland." The article detailed the role played by the prison in Irish nationalist history, though it limited mention of the Civil War to a short note about female prisoners in 1923 without using the words "Civil War." See C. F. Ridgway, "A Visit to Kilmainham Jail, Dublin: The Bastille of Ireland," *Irish Travel,* Nov. 1938, 34; "Kilmainham Memorial Plans," *Sunday Press,* 4 May 1958.

90. The Invincibles were an offshoot of the Irish Republican Brotherhood who advocated political assassination. They are most significant for carrying out the Phoenix Park murders in 1882.

91. *Sunday Press,* 4 May 1958.

92. Memorandum for the Government. Disposal of Kilmainham Jail, 17 June 1946.

93. M. O. Muimhneachain to [?], 26 Aug. 1953, DFA, S102/017/53, National Archives of Ireland, Dublin.

94. Manuscript by Lorcan C. G. Leonard, "The Kilmainham Project as I Dreamt It and Lived It," 1960, Kilmainham Jail Archives, Dublin.

95. Lorcan C. G. Leonard to John Dowling, 9 June 1958, 1/G/1/2/14, Kilmainham Jail Archives, Dublin.

96. Leonard, "Kilmainham Project."

97. In 1956, Dublin Corporation received a planning application for a cinema to be constructed immediately adjoining the jail. The corporation declared that "it is of the utmost importance that its amenity ground be strictly preserved," and advocated using the jail as a museum. It was urged that "every precaution should be taken to safeguard the amenities of the hospital-jail complex in light of possible future fruition of these schemes." See Letter Regarding Kilmainham Jail, 15 Oct. 1956, DFA, S102/017/53, National Archives of Ireland, Dublin.

98. *Sunday Press,* 4 May 1958.

99. Old IRA Literary and Debating Society to Éamon de Valera, 27 Oct. 1958, DT, S6512D/63, National Archives of Ireland, Dublin

100. When the Restoration Society's plan was received, the government was again considering the Graves Association proposal in a slightly modified form. The estimated cost had risen to £20,000. See Proposal Submitted Concerning Jail by Cabinet Committee, 29 Oct. 1958, DT, S6512D/63, National Archives of Ireland, Dublin.

101. Outline Proposals for Restoration of Kilmainham Jail, 1958, DT, S6512D/63, National Archives of Ireland, Dublin.

102. Minute to Dr. O'Sullivan from [?Slavery], 1963, DT, S6512D/63, National Archives of Ireland, Dublin.

103. Seán Dowling to *Irish Times,* 27 Oct. 1966, Kilmainham Jail Archives, Dublin.

104. George Gilmore, "Connolly Plaque," *Irish Times,* 26 Oct. 1966.

105. J. P. Anderson, "Kilmainham Jail," *Irish Times,* 26 Oct. 1966.

106. Seán Lemass to Seán Dowling, 18 May 1966, DT, 96/6/193, National Archives of Ireland, Dublin.

107. Dáil Éireann, "Dáil Question Regarding Cost of Kilmainham Jail," DT, 96/6/159, National Archives of Ireland, Dublin.

108. Seán Lemass to Donogh O'Malley, 20 Feb. 1969, DT, 96/6/159, National Archives of Ireland, Dublin.

109. Seán Dowling to Seán Lemass, 15 Mar. 1969, DT, 96/6/159, National Archives of Ireland, Dublin.

110. Bord Fáilte, *Annual Report for the Year Ended 31 March 1962.*

111. *Kilmainham News,* 1960, Kilmainham Jail Archives, Dublin.

112. "Taoiseach's Sentimental Jail Visit—Pay Tribute to the Work of Renovators," *Sunday Press,* 3 May 1964.

113. "The 'Rising' Returns to Kilmainham," *Dublin Evening Mail,* 2 Jan. 1962.

114. Newspaper clipping, "Idealism Lives Again Among Workers at Kilmainham," n.d., Kilmainham Jail Archives, Dublin.

115. Cooke, *History of Kilmainham Gaol,* 41.

116. O'Hearn, *Inside the Celtic Tiger,* 38.

117. Ibid., 49.

118. Paul Connerton, *How Societies Remember* (Cambridge: Cambridge Univ. Press, 1989).

119. *Ireland of the Welcomes,* July–Aug. 1986, 39–40.

120. O'Doherty interview, 29 Apr. 2002.

121. David Brett, *The Construction of Heritage* (Cork: Cork Univ. Press, 1996), 131.

122. Quoted in Sean Browne, "Heritage in Ireland's Tourism Recovery," in *Cultural Tourism,* ed. J. M. Fladmark (London: Donheal Publishing, 1994), 14.

123. Browne, "Heritage," 14–15.

124. Ibid., 16 and 18.

125. Wiendu Nuryanti, "Heritage and Postmodern Tourism," *Annals of Tourism Research* 23, no. 2 (1996): 249–60, see page 253.

126. Nuryanti, "Heritage and Postmodern Tourism," 253–54.

127. When asked, Guinness declined to supply current visitor statistics. According to Bord Fáilte figures, the Guinness Hopstore—replaced by the Storehouse in December 2000—drew nearly 500,000 tourists in 2000. By 16 September 2001, the company reported that its new facility had welcomed one million visitors and expected another 180,000 by year's end. See "1m Visit Guinness Storehouse," *Irish Times,* 16 Sept. 2002.

128. S. R. Dennison and Oliver MacDonagh, *Guinness 1886–1939: From Incorporation to the Second World War* (Cork: Cork Univ. Press, 1998), 180.

129. Dennison and MacDonagh, *Guinness 1886–1939,* 185.

130. Ibid., 176.

131. "Viewing the Brewery," *The Guinness Harp,* May–June 1959, 17, in Guinness Ireland Archives, Dublin.

132. Registry Department, Board Yearly Reports, 1919–1924, Guinness Ireland Archives, Dublin.

133. *Guinness Dublin* (1939).

134. G. P. Adams, Memorandum: Guides' Talks to Visitors, 29 June 1951, GDB/PE03.01/0365, Guinness Ireland Archives, Dublin.

135. J. A. Mackeown, Guides' Talk (text), 7 Feb. 1952, GDB/PE03.01/0365, Guinness Ireland Archives, Dublin.

136. J. A. Mackeown, Memorandum: Guides' Talks—Supplementary Points, 1 July 1952, GDB/PE03.01/0365, Guinness Ireland Archives, Dublin.

137. "Guests of St. James's Gate," *Guinness Harp,* Mar.–Apr. 1958, 4, Guinness Ireland Archives, Dublin; R. T. Mooney, "Our Visitors: Sixty Thousand People Have Seen the Brewery During This Year," *Guinness Harp,* Oct.–Dec. 1959, 26, Guinness Ireland Archives, Dublin.

138. "Our Windmill Will Remain," *Guinness Harp,* Mar.–Apr. 1958, 3, Guinness Ireland Archives, Dublin.

139. L. A. Luke, "Galway Oyster Festival," *Guinness Harp,* Nov.–Dec. 1958, 15, Guinness Ireland Archives, Dublin.

140. "Laughter by the Liffey: Ireland's Annual Festival, An Tóstal, Meant Laughter and Music by Liffey-Side," *Guinness Harp,* July–Sept. 1959, 49, Guinness Ireland Archives, Dublin.

141. "Souvenir Shop," *Harp,* Autumn 1965, 49, Guinness Ireland Archives, Dublin.

142. H. S. Corran, "The Brewery Museum," *Harp,* Autumn 1966, 16–17, Guinness Ireland Archives, Dublin.

143. F. Edmundson, Report of the Committee on the Visitors' Route, Mar. 1971, Guinness Ireland Archives, Dublin.

144. *The World and His Wife* (Dublin: [?]1961), Guinness Ireland Archives, Dublin. See also *Your Guide to the World of Guinness at the Guinness Hopstore* (Dublin, circa 1990); and *Discover What's Brewing at the Guinness Hopstore* (Dublin: circa 1990).

145. "Ireland's New Golden Age," *Building Design,* 11 July 1997, 12.

146. "Refurbishment of Guinness Storehouse," *Building Design,* 1 Dec. 2000, 4.

147. Imagination Group USA, *Guinness Storehouse,* 2003, <http://www.imagination.com/usa/work/guinness.html> (accessed 9 Apr. 2003).

148. *Building Design,* 11 July 1997.

149. "Imagination Pulls Guinness Pint," *Design Week,* 22 Sept. 2000, 3.

150. Imagination Group USA, *Guinness Storehouse.*

151. "Storehouse Gets Celebrity Start," *Irish Marketing and Advertising Journal,* 1 Jan. 2001.

152. Joe Humphreys, "An Irishman's Diary," *Irish Times,* 10 Mar. 2001.

153. Pat Barry, "The Guinness Storehouse," *Irish Times,* 16 Mar. 2001.

154. Michael Loftus, "Letter to the Editor," *Irish Times,* 16 Mar. 2001.

155. David Abel, "Guinness Tour a Tough Swallow, Till the End," *Boston Globe,* 28 May 2003.

156. " . . . and the Worst Value," *Irish Times,* 12 Aug. 2003.

157. For an excellent discussion of these stereotypes, both in America and in Ireland, see Stivers, *Hair of the Dog.*

158. George L. Mosse, *The Nationalization of the Masses: Political Symbolism and Mass Movements in Germany from the Napoleonic Wars through the Third Reich* (Ithaca, N.Y.: Cornell Univ. Press, 1991).

6. Creating the Tourist Landscape

1. Pieter M. Judson, "Frontiers, Islands, Forests, Stones: Mapping the Geography of a German Identity in the Hapsburg Monarchy, 1848–1900," in *The Geography of Identity,* ed. Patricia Yaeger (Ann Arbor: Univ. of Michigan Press, 1996), 382.

2. Catherine Nash, "'Embodying the Nation': The West of Ireland Landscape and Irish Identity," in O'Connor and Cronin, *Tourism in Ireland,* 86–87.

3. David Matless, *Landscape and Englishness* (London: Reaktion, 1998); Scott Moranda, "Maps, Markers, and Bodies: Hikers Constructing the Nation in German Forests," The Nationalism Project, 2000, <http://nationalismproject.org/articles.html> (accessed 7 Aug. 2003); and Judson, "Frontiers."

4. Patrick J. Duffy, "Writing Ireland: Literature and Art in the Representation of Irish Place," in *In Search of Ireland: A Cultural Geography,* ed. Brian Graham (London: Routledge, 1997), 81. For those interested in related discussion of the visual representation of Ireland, see Adele M. Dalsimer, ed., *Visualizing Ireland: National Identity and the Pictorial Tradition* (Boston: Faber and Faber, 1993); and Fintan Cullen, *Visual Politics: The Representation of Ireland, 1750–1930* (Cork: Cork Univ. Press, 1997).

5. Bell, *The Spell of Ireland,* vii.

6. Heinrich Böll, *Irish Journal,* trans. Leila Vennewitz (New York: McGraw-Hill, 1967), 24.

7. Eric Newby, *Round Ireland in Low Gear* (London: Viking, 1987).

8. Pete McCarthy, *McCarthy's Bar* (Edinburgh: Hodder and Stoughton, 2000), 116.

9. Bord Fáilte, *Know Your Market: Britain* (Dublin: Bord Fáilte, 1998), 32–33; *Know Your Market: Switzerland/Austria* (Dublin: Bord Fáilte, 1994); *Know Your Market: Australia/New Zealand* (Dublin: Bord Fáilte, 1998); *Know Your Market: Austria/Switzerland/Eastern Europe* (Dublin: Bord Fáilte, 1998); *Know Your Market: Benelux 1997–1998* (Dublin: Bord Fáilte, 1997); *Know Your Market: Britain* (Dublin: Bord Fáilte, 1993, 1998); *Know Your Market: France* (Dublin: Bord Fáilte, 1998).

10. "Irish Tourist Development: Meeting at Waterville," *Kerryman*, 5 Dec. 1925.

11. For an example of this sort of comment, see "Tourist Development: Visit of English Railway Directors; Southern Beauty Spots; Reception at Parknasilla, Glengariff and Killarney," *Kerryman*, 9 July 1927.

12. "Notes and News," *Irish Travel*, Nov. 1925, 50.

13. "Notes and News," *Irish Travel*, Oct. 1925, 26–28.

14. "An Example for Ireland," *Irish Travel*, Oct. 1925, 42–43.

15. "Castles or Skyscrapers?" *Irish Travel*, Sept. 1925, 15. The author's negative comment about the Nelson Pillar is another indication of strong Republican feeling at the staff level in the Irish Tourist Association.

16. "Notes and News," *Irish Travel*, Jan. 1926, 94. Also "Notes and News," *Irish Travel*, May 1926, 187.

17. "Notes and News," *Irish Travel*, Apr. 1926, 162.

18. "Tourist Traffic," *Irish Times*, 25 Apr. 1946.

19. Marquis of Sligo to Seán Lemass, 30 Sept. 1960, DT, S13087F, National Archives of Ireland, Dublin.

20. Marquis of Sligo to national daily newspapers, 8 Dec. 1960, DT, S13087F, National Archives of Ireland, Dublin.

21. "'Green Light' for £2m. Factory on Council Site," *Mayo News*, 24 Sept. 1960.

22. *Irish Times*, 18 Jan. 1961.

23. McCarthy, *McCarthy's Bar*, 151.

24. Ibid., 151–52.

25. Leslie Daiken, "Strictly Personal. . . . " (manuscript), [?] June 1956, MS33,481(46), National Library of Ireland, Dublin. Cited with permission of the Board of the National Library of Ireland.

26. C. M. Murphy to Leslie Daiken, 28 May 1956, MS33,481(46), National Library of Ireland, Dublin. Cited with permission of the Board of the National Library of Ireland.

27. Leslie Daiken, "Vintage Vehicles," *GO Holiday Magazine*, Jan.–Feb. 1957, 23–25, MS33,488, National Library of Ireland, Dublin. Cited with permission of the Board of the National Library of Ireland.

28. Leslie Daiken, "Leslie Daiken Tells of His Boyhood Days in Ireland—and Re-Captures His Memories of Them—Round Trap Roundabout" (manuscript), 16 Jan. 1957,

MS33,487 box 5, National Library of Ireland, Dublin. Cited with permission of the Board of the National Library of Ireland.

29. Daiken, "Boyhood Days."

30. Daiken actively campaigned for an appointment as Bord Fáilte's principal representative in London so that he might improve the Board's effectiveness in the English marketplace. See Leslie Daiken to Niall Sheridan, 3 June 1956, MS33,485(50), National Library of Ireland, Dublin; Leslie Daiken to Niall Sheridan, 21 Mar. 1956, MS33,485(50), National Library of Ireland, Dublin; and Leslie Daiken to Niall Sheridan, 21 July 1956, MS33,485(50), National Library of Ireland, Dublin. All cited with permission of the Board of the National Library of Ireland.

31. Leslie Daiken, "By Killarney's Lakes and Fells: 'Heaven's Reflex'—or Hell's Perspex?" (manuscript), [?]1961, MS33,514, box Add. folder 51, National Library of Ireland, Dublin. Cited with permission of the Board of the National Library of Ireland.

32. John Scanlon to Jack Lynch, 2 Jan. 1971, DT, 2002/8/299, National Archives of Ireland, Dublin.

33. Jack Lynch to John Scanlon, 5 Jan. 1971, DT, 2002/8/299, National Archives of Ireland, Dublin.

34. John Scanlon to Jack Lynch, 21 Jan. 1971, DT, 2002/8/299, National Archives of Ireland, Dublin.

35. Brian Lenihan to Jack Lynch, 26 Feb. 1971, DT, 2002/8/299, National Archives of Ireland, Dublin.

36. Alvin Mansfield Owsley to Seán Lemass, 30 Mar. 1962, DT, S5004 E/62, National Archives of Ireland, Dublin.

37. This was not the first time that the sale of land at Killarney raised substantial concern. In 1899 the Muckross estate was placed on the market, sparking profound concern both in Ireland and in the Irish-American community. Irish-Americans, inspired by the recent creation of the first national parks in America, urged the Irish government to acquire the Muckross property and to declare it a national park rather than allow it to pass into foreign hands. As it happened, Guinness acquired the land, only to sell it to an American investor in 1910. See Marion R. Casey, "Ireland, New York and the Irish Image in American Popular Culture, 1890–1960" (Ph.D. diss., New York Univ., 1998), 233. The property subsequently passed through various American owners until it was finally bequeathed to the Irish government.

38. "American Has Bought Killarney Estate, Privileges to Be Continued," *Irish Independent,* 11 Aug. 1956.

39. Untitled newspaper clipping, *Kerryman,* 11 Aug. 1956, DT, S16047A, National Archives of Ireland, Dublin.

40. Bord Fáilte, Memorandum: Proposed Sale of the Kenmare Estate (Secret), 7 Aug. 1956, DT, S16047A, National Archives of Ireland, Dublin.

41. "National Appeal Advocated," *Irish Times,* 7 Aug. 1956.

42. Department of the Taoiseach and Killarney Tourist Association, 1956, DT, S16047A, National Archives of Ireland, Dublin.

43. M. O. Muimhneaohain, memorandum, 2 Aug. 1956, DT, S16047A, National Archives of Ireland, Dublin.

44. "Killarney Estate Not to Be 'Commercialized,'" *Irish Times*, 3 Feb. 1961.

45. McCarthy, *McCarthy's Bar*, 30. *Duty of Care* is a legal term that refers to the obligation imposed on an individual to adhere to a reasonable standard of care while performing acts that could be harmful. In this case, the term refers to harm that may result from unsupervised wandering on farmland and the owner's unwillingness to hazard the risk of allowing such access.

46. Ibid., 34.

47. In the nineteenth century, nationalists struggled to gain the "Three F's"—fair rent, fixity of tenure, and free sale—while nationalist leaders like Charles Stewart Parnell told Irishmen to "keep a firm grip on your homesteads and lands," creating a close link between political nationalism and the interests of Irish peasants. See Laurence M. Geary, "Parnell and the Land Question," in *Parnell: The Politics of Power*, ed. Donal McCartney (Dublin: Wolfhound Press, 1991), 90–101, especially page 95. For a concise overview of Parnell's relationship to the land question, as well as his larger political career, see: F. S. L. Lyons, *Parnell* (Dundalk, Ireland: Dundalgan Press, 1963).

48. Specifically, the Monuments Act provides: "The Commissioners may, with the consent of the Minister, acquire compulsorily or by agreement any national monument which they consider it expedient to acquire, and the Commissioners may so acquire a national monument whether they or a local authority are or are not the guardians thereof and whether a preservation order is or is not in force in regard thereto." *National Monuments Act, 1930* (Dublin: Government Publications, 1930).

Section 19 of the 1939 Tourist Traffic Act allowed the Irish Tourist Board to: "If and whenever the Board thinks proper to acquire compulsorily any land for the purpose of the exercise of any of the powers or the performance of any of the duties or functions conferred or imposed on it by this Act, the Board may, with the consent of the Minister, by order declare its intention so to acquire such land and every such order shall operate to confer on the Board full power to acquire compulsorily the land mentioned therein under and in accordance with this section." *Tourist Traffic Act, 1939* (Dublin: Government Publications, 1939).

The 1952 Tourist Traffic Act, sect 7, part 1, allowed: "Where the Board proposes to erect a notice or fence at, or to provide or improve means of access to, any historic building, site or shrine, or other place which, in the opinion of the Board is likely to be of particular interest to the public, and the owner refuses to permit the Board to carry out the proposed work, the Board shall have power to acquire, under section 19 of the Act of 1939, such land as the Board thinks proper to enable the work to be carried out." *Tourist Traffic Act, 1952* (Dublin: Government Publications 1952).

49. Cairn in Oldcastle Townland, Co. Cork—Issue of Preservation Orders, 1938, DF, S200/2/38, National Archives of Ireland, Dublin.

50. Peter Harbison, *Guide to National and Historic Monuments of Ireland* (Dublin: Gill and Macmillan, 1992), 68.

51. Phone record, 30 Nov. 1981, 94/3500/1, Office of Public Works, Dublin.

52. R. Nic Raighine to Peter Harbison, 10 Dec. 1981, 94/3500/1, Office of Public Works, Dublin.

53. Martin Bradley (Shannonside Tourism) to Office of Public Works, 20 Oct. 1981, 94/3500/1, Office of Public Works, Dublin.

54. John Costello to Secretary of the Office of Public Works, 11 May 1982, 94/3500/1, Office of Public Works, Dublin.

55. Martin Bradley to John Berkery, 31 May 1983, 94/3500/1, Office of Public Works, Dublin.

56. Martin Bradley to John Mahony, 22 Apr. 1985, 94/3500/1, Office of Public Works, Dublin.

57. Draft letter from M. Molloy to Jennifer Foley, 15 July 1985, 94/3500/1, Office of Public Works, Dublin.

58. Joan Phillips to Jennifer Foley, 13 Aug. 1985, 94/3500/1, Office of Public Works, Dublin.

59. Joan Phillips, memorandum, 23 Oct. 1985, 94/3500/1, Office of Public Works, Dublin.

60. Jennifer Foley to Office of Public Works, 29 Nov. 1985, 94/3500/1, Office of Public Works, Dublin.

61. J. Kevin Vaughn (Clare Co. Development Team) to Office of Public Works, 19 Feb. 1985, 94/3500/1, Office of Public Works, Dublin; "Guardianship Order for Poulnabrone Dolmen," *Clare Champion,* 10 Jan. 1986.

62. National Monuments: Acquisition Criteria and Information Check, 25 Oct. 1985, 94/3500/1, Office of Public Works, Dublin.

63. Jennifer Foley to Office of Public Works, 29 Jan. 1987 (OPW, 94/3500/3); [?] McMahon, memorandum, 8 Nov. 1989, 94/3500/3, Office of Public Works, Dublin.

64. Cyril de Courcy, "Report and Valuation of Lands at Poulnabrone Dolmen, Co. Clare," 1993, 94/3500/3, Office of Public Works, Dublin. Given the dolmen's location far from any other development, adequate transportation routes (the roadway that passes by is narrow and inefficient), or water sources, one wonders how this conclusion was reached. Indeed, the presence of a "national monument" would have made any such development illegal.

65. Jennifer Foley to Office of Public Works, 13 Mar. 1993, 94/3500/3, Office of Public Works, Dublin.

66. Report of Meeting Held at Ballyvaughn, Co. Clare on Friday 12th March 1993, Mar. 1993, 94/3500/3, Office of Public Works, Dublin. The monument's closure did not prevent Bord Fáilte from continuing to include photographs of the site in its various guidebooks—a

fact that certainly did little to reduce the tourist traffic climbing the farmer's barbed wire fence in order to make the "dangerous" trek across the limestone pavement. See Bord Fáilte, *Ireland Guide* (Dublin: Bord Fáilte, 1993), 256; and Bord Fáilte, *Ireland* (Dublin: Bord Fáilte, 1994), 12–13. There has been little effort by tourist officials to assure that sites presented in guidebooks and visitor centers are actually accessible to the general public. For example, the Burren visitor's center at Kilfenora uses images of a Penal-era painted red hand that likely served as a direction marker to a hedge school or hidden chapel in its multimedia presentation and display. When I went looking for the site, however, I soon discovered that the red hand appears to be located in the backyard of a local homeowner, surrounded by an eight-foot wooden fence with numerous "No Trespassing" signs posted along the full length of the wall.

67. Leslie J. Dlugokinski to Office of Public Works, 7 May 1999, 94/3500/3, Office of Public Works, Dublin.

68. Gerry Murray to Ms. McCann, 4 Nov. 1994, 94/3500/3, Office of Public Works, Dublin.

69. Note from Martin Luby, 30 July 2001, 94/3500/3, Office of Public Works, Dublin.

70. Martin Luby, 26 Jan. 2001, 94/3500/3, Office of Public Works, Dublin.

71. Department of Industry and Commerce Memorandum, 18 Feb. 1944, DT, S10946.

72. E. Æ Somerville and Martin Ross, *The Irish R.M.* (London: Abacus, 2000 [1928]), 458.

73. "Notes and News," *Irish Travel,* Feb. 1926, 114.

74. "Activities of the ITA," *Irish Travel,* July 1927, 240.

75. Draft Heads of Tourist Traffic (Amendment) (No. 2. Bill 1951, [?] July 1951, TTA 2/6, National Archives of Ireland, Dublin.

76. Report of Interdepartmental Meeting Held on 1st December 1951, to Discuss the Heads of the Proposed Tourist Traffic Bill. Amendments Requested by the Commissioners of Public Works, 1 Dec. 1951, TTA 2/7 vol. 1, National Archives of Ireland, Dublin.

77. *Irish Tourist Bulletin,* July 1951, 3–4, DT, S14995A.

78. O'Doherty interview, 29 Apr. 2002.

79. An Bord Fáilte, *Irish Tourist Bulletin,* Sept. 1953, 4–5, DT, S14995B, National Archives of Ireland, Dublin.

80. O'Doherty interview, 29 Apr. 2002.

81. An Bord Fáilte, *Annual Report and Accounts, Year Ended 31st March 1954,* Apr. 1954, DT, S15647B, National Archives of Ireland, Dublin.

82. Bord Fáilte, *Bord Fáilte Éireann Newsletter,* May–June 1956, 2.

83. Bord Fáilte *Irish Tourist Board Report for the Year Ended March 31 1965* (Dublin: Bord Fáilte, 1965).

84. An Bord Fáilte, *Irish Tourist Bulletin,* June 1951, 4–5, DT, S14995A, National Archives of Ireland, Dublin.

85. Baranowski, *Strength Through Joy,* 62. The third chapter of *Strength Through Joy,* "The Beauty of Labor," details the KdF's factory and community development programs.

86. Conekin, *Autobiography,* 153.

87. An Bord Fáilte, *Irish Tourist Bulletin,* Aug. 1951, 13–14, DT, S14995A, National Archives of Ireland, Dublin.

88. An Bord Fáilte, *Irish Tourist Bulletin,* Apr. 1951, 9, DT, S14995A, National Archives of Ireland, Dublin.

89. An Bord Fáilte, *Irish Tourist Bulletin,* Sept. 1952, 1, DT, S14995A, National Archives of Ireland, Dublin.

90. An Bord Fáilte, *Irish Tourist Bulletin,* Aug. 1952, 2, DT, S14995A, National Archives of Ireland, Dublin.

91. "An Tóstal," *Kilkenny People,* 14 Mar. 1953; "An Tóstal," *Kilkenny People,* 21 Mar. 1953.

92. "Decoration Plans for An Tóstal: City Streets Will Be Gay and Colourful," *Evening Echo* (Cork), 26 Mar. 1954.

93. An Bord Fáilte, *Irish Tourist Bulletin,* Dec. 1952, 6, DT, S14995A, National Archives of Ireland, Dublin.

94. Confidential memorandum on An Tóstal Review, 19 Feb. 1958, TTA 12/5, National Archives of Ireland, Dublin. Also Gorman interview, 11 Oct. 2002.

95. Bord Fáilte, *Annual Report and Accounts, Year Ending 31st March 1958* (Dublin: Bord Fáilte, 1958). Also O'Doherty interview, 30 July 2002.

96. O'Doherty interview, 30 July 2002.

97. Department of Local Government, *Department of Local Government Report, 1958–1959* (Dublin: Government Publications, 1959), 114–15. I would like to thank Dr. Aoife Bhreatnach for bringing this reference to my attention.

98. Bord Fáilte, *Annual Report and Accounts, Year Ending 31st March 1959*; and Bord Fáilte, *Annual Report and Accounts, Year Ended 31st March 1961.*

99. Bord Fáilte, *Report for the Year Ended March 31 1964.*

100. O'Doherty interview, 30 July 2002.

101. Bord Fáilte, *Board Report for the Year Ended March 31 1964.*

102. Bord Fáilte, *Report for the Year Ended March 31 1965.*

103. Records of Clonakilty Town Council, 1968–72, 6 Oct. 1968, Clonakilty Town Council Records, UDC1/10, Cork Archives Institute, Cork.

104. "New Approach to the Tidy Towns," *Clare Champion,* 14 Feb. 1986.

105. "On Target for a Tidier Ennis," *Clare Champion,* 28 Feb. 1986.

106. Kieran Hickey, ed., *Working to Win,* videocassette, circa 1988, distributed by Bord Fáilte, Bord Fáilte Photographic Archives, Dublin. The use of the phrase "plan of campaign" is particularly interesting as it draws a parallel line between the national work of creating tidy towns and the fight for land ownership during the late-nineteenth-century Land War.

107. O'Doherty interview, 30 July 2002.

108. Kieran Hickey, ed., *Our Tidy Towns—21 Years of Community Effort,* 16mm, 39 min., 1979, distributed by Bord Fáilte, Irish Film Center Archives, Dublin.

109. "Tidy Town," *Clare Champion,* 9 May 1980.

110. Bord Fáilte, *Bord Fáilte Report and Accounts for the Year Ended December 1979* (Dublin: Bord Fáilte, 1979).

111. Bord Fáilte, *Bord Fáilte Report and Accounts for the Year Ended December 1984* (Dublin: Bord Fáilte, 1984).

112. Dermot O'Toole, "Improving Our Towns," *Ireland of the Welcomes,* Nov.–Dec. 1961, 13–16.

113. George Bagnall, "Town and Village: Happy 21st Birthday, Tidy Town Scheme," *Ireland of the Welcomes,* Sept.–Oct. 1978, 10–15.

114. Eamon De Buitlear, ed., *There's Work to Be Done,* videocassette, unknown length, 1992, distributed by Bord Fáilte, Bord Fáilte Photographic Archive, Dublin.

115. Hugh Weir, "Making a Tidy Town," *Clare Champion,* 30 Oct. 1981.

116. Bord Fáilte, *Bord Fáilte Report for the Year Ended March 1973* (Dublin: Bord Fáilte, 1973).

117. *Kerryman,* 5 Dec. 1925.

118. "Killarney Tourist Association: Improving Killarney Lakes Fishing; Letter from Minister," *Kerryman,* 11 Dec. 1926.

119. "Killarney Tourist Association," *Kerryman,* 12 Mar. 1927; "Killarney Tourist Association," *Kerryman,* 9 Apr. 1927; and "Killarney Tourist Association," *Kerryman,* 21 May 1927.

120. "Killarney Tourist Association," *Kerryman,* 12 Nov. 1927.

121. O'Doherty interview, 30 July 2002.

122. Ibid. The Inland Fisheries Trust was a private organization and not officially recognized by the state. Nevertheless, it was supported by James Dillon, then minister for agriculture, and received some state funding as a tourism interest.

123. An Bord Fáilte, *Annual Report and Accounts, Year Ending 31st March 1953* (Dublin: Bord Fáilte, 1953).

124. Bord Fáilte, *Annual Report and Accounts, Year Ending 31st March 1957* (Dublin: Bord Fáilte, 1957).

125. O'Doherty interview, 30 July 2002.

126. Bord Fáilte, Angling Development and Exploitation Summary Details of Five-Year Plan, 1957, DF, F120/2/57, National Archives of Ireland, Dublin.

127. Industry and Commerce Memorandum for the Government. *Annual Report and Accounts, Year Ended 31st March 1958* (Dublin: Bord Fáilte, 1958); and Bord Fáilte, *Annual Report, 1957.* It is worth noting that a similar, though less expansive, program was also implemented in 1957 to destroy "vermin" responsible for the reduction of game animals and birds.

128. Industry and Commerce Memorandum for the Government. Bord Fáilte and Fógra Fáilte Reports and Accounts for the Year Ended 31st March, 1959, 11 Nov. 1959, DT, S15647B, National Archives of Ireland, Dublin.

129. Bord Fáilte, *Ireland for Coarse Fishing Holidays* (Dublin: Bord Fáilte, 1959), 5 and 15.

130. Department of Industry and Commerce Memorandum for the Government: Bord Fáilte and Fógra Fáilte: Reports and Accounts for the Year Ended 31st March 1960, 24 Oct. 1960, DT, S15647B, National Archives of Ireland, Dublin.

131. Michael J. Bannon, Kevin I. Nowlan, John Hendry, and Ken Mawhinney, eds., *Planning: The Irish Experience 1920–1988* (Dublin: Wolfhound Press, 1989), 13.

132. Bannon et al., *Planning*, 47 and 71–85.

133. Ibid., 64–65.

134. Department of Local Government, Explanatory Memorandum: Local Government (Planning and Development) Bill, 1962, DT, S16968C/63, National Archives of Ireland, Dublin.

135. Bannon et al., *Planning*, 91.

136. An Taisce, *The National Trust for Ireland* (Dublin: An Taisce, [?]1961), 2.

137. Bannon et al., *Planning*, 94.

138. National Planning Conference folder, 1943, DT, S 13469, National Archives of Ireland, Dublin.

139. Bannon et al., *Planning*, 99.

140. Bord Fáilte, *Bord Fáilte Report for the Year Ended December 1975* (Dublin: Bord Fáilte, 1975).

141. Bannon et al., *Planning*, 99.

142. Michael Gorman, Frank Height, Mary V. Mullin, and W. H. Walsh, eds., *Design for Tourism: An ICSID Inter Design Report* (Oxford: Pergamon Press, 1977), 10–11. I would like to thank Michael Gorman for providing me with a copy of this publication.

143. Gorman et al., *Design for Tourism*, 16–17.

144. Ibid., 33.

145. Ibid., 35.

146. Ibid., 40.

147. Ibid., 41.

148. *Seven Ages: Story of the Irish State (Program 1)*, RTÉ Online, 2000, <http://www.rte.ie/tv/sevenages/prog1.html> (accessed 13 Aug. 2003).

149. Philip Geoghegan, *Building Sensitively in Ireland's Landscapes* (Dublin: Bord Fáilte and An Taisce, 1989), 5–6.

150. Geoghegan, *Building Sensitively*, 9.

151. Ibid., 16–43.

152. McCarthy, *McCarthy's Bar*, 116.

153. Erskine Childers to Jack Lynch, 22 Mar. 1968, DT, 99/1/521, National Archives of Ireland, Dublin.

154. Although it had little to do with tourism, the Flood Report—released in September 2002, five years after it was launched in October 1997 following former Fianna Fáil TD Ray Burke's resignation over bribery allegations—revealed extensive corruption including

payments made by JMSE, an Irish construction company, to Burke. While the report certainly does not prove the long-running allegations of planning corruption, it does hint that there may have been at least a grain of truth in these rumors.

155. Bannon et al., *Planning,* 136.

156. Ibid., 139.

157. Niall Hyde, *National Coastline Study,* vol. 1 (Dublin: Bord Fáilte and Foras Forbartha, 1972).

158. Bord Fáilte, *Report for the Year Ended December 1974* (Dublin: Bord Fáilte, 1974).

159. Bord Fáilte, *Report and Accounts for the Year Ended December 1979* (Dublin: Bord Fáilte, 1979).

160. Bord Fáilte, *Report and Accounts for the Year Ended December 1981* (Dublin: Bord Fáilte, 1981); Bord Fáilte, *Report and Accounts for the Year Ended December 1985* (Dublin: Bord Fáilte, 1985).

161. Bord Fáilte, *Bord Fáilte Report for the Year Ended March 1992* (Dublin: Bord Fáilte, 1992).

162. Bord Fáilte, *Developing Sustainable Tourism,* 29.

163. Although the images included here are from a later period, the following photo series at the Bord Fáilte Photographic Archives further illustrate the point: K3/37, K.3A/37, K39–40/48, K42–47/48, K48–55/48, K8/57, K11/62–K34/62. There were some variations from later photographs, images taken from road level or from a jaunting cart itself, for example; the continuity is striking nevertheless.

164. Irish Tourist Board, *Ireland: Carefree Motoring* (Dublin: Bord Fáilte, 1969).

165. Luke Gibbons, *Transformations in Irish Culture* (Cork: Cork Univ. Press, 1996), 40.

166. *Hindesight* (Dublin: Irish Museum of Modern Art, 1993), 18–19.

167. *Hindesight,* 36.

168. Ibid., 38.

169. De Fouw interview, 14 Oct. 2002.

170. C. S. Andrews, *Man of No Property,* 114.

171. Ibid., 128.

172. Ibid., 130 and 133.

173. Turf harvesting was frequently included in tourism publications in this light. For an example, see the photographs in Irish Tourist Association, *Introducing Ireland* (Dublin: Irish Tourist Association, 1950). Similarly, Bord Fáilte declared that Irish bogs are a "valuable asset" that "yield turf for fuel and electric power." See Fógra Fáilte, "Ireland Invites You" (draft), 1953, DT, S15498, National Archives of Ireland, Dublin.

174. John Reader, "A Day on the Bog," *Ireland of the Welcomes,* Mar.–Apr. 1970, 8–11.

175. Stephen Rynne, "The Bog Transformed," *Ireland of the Welcomes,* Mar.–Apr. 1970, 12–15.

176. Seamus Heaney, "The Bog," *Ireland of the Welcomes,* May–June, 1976, 20–25.

177. "Bogland Special Edition," *Ireland of the Welcomes,* May–June 1987, 43.

7. Tourism and the Tiger, 1994–2007

1. Paul Sweeney, *The Celtic Tiger: Ireland's Economic Miracle* (Dublin: Oak Tree Press, 1998), 1–5.

2. Bord Fáilte, *Bord Fáilte Report and Financial Statements 2000* (Dublin: Bord Fáilte, 2000), 3.

3. Bord Fáilte, *Bord Fáilte Report for the Year Ended March 1993* (Dublin: Bord Fáilte, 1993), 12; and Bord Fáilte, *Markets: Perspectives on Irish Tourism 1993–97* (Dublin: Bord Fáilte, 1999), 7.

4. Bord Fáilte, *Report and Financial Statements 2000,* 17.

5. Bord Fáilte, *Markets,* 94.

6. Bord Fáilte, *Report and Financial Statements 2000,* 17.

7. Bord Fáilte, *Markets,* 17.

8. Bord Fáilte, *Bord Fáilte Report for the Year Ended March 1987* (Dublin: Bord Fáilte, 1987), 8.

9. Bord Fáilte, *Markets,* 17.

10. Bord Fáilte, *Report and Financial Statements 2000,* 17.

11. J. W. O'Hagan and M. J. Harrison, "UK and US Visitor Expenditure in Ireland," *The Economic and Social Review* 15, no. 3 (1984): 195–207.

12. "Notes and News," *Irish Travel,* [?]1926, 236–37.

13. For a detailed discussion of the North/South tourism relationship, see Zuelow, "'Ingredients for Cooperation.'" See also Michael Kennedy, *Division and Consensus: The Politics of Cross-Border Relations in Ireland, 1925–1969* (Dublin: Institute of Public Administration, 2000), 3.

14. Gorman interview, 11 Oct. 2002.

15. Report of Taoiseach's Visit to Belfast, 14 Jan. 1965, DT, 98/6/429. A "triptyque" was a complicated document that provided authorities with proof that the visitor's reason for travel was legitimate. It was often extremely frustrating to tourists, especially Americans, and was abolished throughout the rest of Europe during the early 1950s.

16. Report of Press Conference by Taoiseach, 16 Jan. 1965, DT, 98/6/149.

17. Jim Flanagan, "Cross Border Air Link," *Sunday Press,* 31 Jan. 1965.

18. Report of Taoiseach's Visit to Belfast.

19. "£6m Boost for North-South Tourism Drive," *Irish Travel Trade News,* Dec. 1994, 14.

20. "Ireland to Launch Tourism Brand in 1997," *Irish Travel Trade News,* Oct. 1995, 12.

21. "Joint Award for Bord Fáilte/NITB," *Irish Travel Trade News,* Nov. 1996, 19.

22. Bord Fáilte, *Bord Fáilte Report for the Year Ended March 1996* (Dublin: Bord Fáilte, 1996).

23. Steedman, 13.

24. Jane O'Sullivan, "Belfast Agreement Could Pave Way to Peace Payoff," *Irish Times,* 15 May 1998.

25. Dani Garavelli, "A Suitable Place for a Tourist?" *Scotland on Sunday,* 28 Mar. 1999.

26. John Bruton, "Agreement Must Be Focus of a New Loyalty," *Irish Times,* 20 Apr. 1998.

27. Frank Fitzgibbon, "Ireland Tourism Industry Confederation," *Sunday Times (London),* 8 Nov. 1998.

28. John Murray Brown, "Blair Flies to Ulster in Bid to Rescue Deadlocked Talks: Move to Secure Agreement on Setting up Cross-Border Bodies," *Financial Times (London),* 3 Dec. 1998.

29. Liam Clarke, "Blair Unveils UK-Irish Body in Dublin," *Sunday Times (London),* 22 Nov. 1998. The removal of tourism from the list of cross-border bodies came after early indications that tourism would be uncontroversial. See Jane O'Sullivan, "All-Island Body May Replace Bord Fáilte," *Irish Times,* 6 June 1998.

30. Martin Fletcher, "Trimble and Ahern Agree on Cross-Border Bodies," *Times (London),* 25 Nov. 1998.

31. John Murray Brown, "Mallon Urges Agreement on Cross-Border Bodies," *Financial Times (London),* 1 Dec. 1998, 11.

32. *Financial Times (London),* 3 Dec. 1998.

33. Clare Murphy, "Mallon Claims Deal Was Brokered by Blair," *Irish Times,* 4 Dec. 1998; and John Mullin, "Ulster Parties' Haggling Renewed as Blair Leaves," *Guardian (London),* 4 Dec. 1998.

34. Alison Hardie, "Ulster Parties Agree Power-Sharing Structure," *Scotsman,* 19 Dec. 1998. Some pundits declared the solution to be a slap in the face for Sinn Féin because the party had hoped for eight official bodies including tourism development. For nationalists, cross-border bodies represented a counterbalance to the dominance of unionist parties in the Northern executive.

35. John Murray Brown, "Peace Accord Benefits Tourism in Ireland," *Financial Times (London),* 28 Sept. 2000.

36. Implementation Group, *Establishment of New Tourist Development Authority* (Dublin: Department of Tourism, Sport, and Recreation, 2002), 30.

37. Implementation Group, *New Tourist Development Authority,* 6–7.

38. Ibid., 30.

39. Gorman interview, 11 Oct. 2002.

40. Bord Fáilte, *Tourism Plan 1981–85: Marketing and Development Guidelines for the Irish Tourist Industry* (Dublin: Bord Fáilte, 1980).

41. Cited in McCarthy, *McCarthy's Bar,* 365–66. Other companies, such as Bellatopia. com, offer items to "decorate your Irish pub or to entertain guests in your Ireland-themed rec room." *Ireland/Irish Pub Themed Items,* Bellatopia.com, 2003, <http://www.bellatopia.com/themes_irish_pub.shtml> (accessed 4 Aug. 2003).

42. Lance Pettitt, *Screening Ireland: Film and Television Representation* (Manchester: Manchester Univ. Press, 2000), 37–45.

43. Kate Homquist, "Shaking Up Our Quiet Movie Image," *Irish Times*, 3 Aug. 2006.

44. Smyth, *Space*, 164.

45. Ibid., 169.

46. Ella Shanahan, "Sending Out the Right Signals to Keep the Visitors Coming," *Irish Times*, 31 Mar. 2001.

47. "Origin of the UK Foot and Mouth Disease Epidemic in 2001," Department for Environment, Food and Rural Affairs (United Kingdom), <http://www.defra.gov.uk/foot-andmouth/pdf/fmdorigins1.pdf> (accessed 27 July 2007).

48. Alex Kirby, "F&M: The Rural Nemesis," BBC News World Edition, <http://news.bbc.co.uk/2/hi/in_depth/world/2001/review_of_2001/1697976.stm> (accessed 27 July 2007).

49. Sean MacConnell and Declan Fahy, "Foot-and-mouth Restrictions to Be Eased on Tourist Attractions," *Irish Times*, 2 May 2001.

50. Joe Humphreys, "A Bad Year but It Could Have Been Worse," *Irish Times*, 20 Aug. 2001.

51. Robert Looney, "Economic Costs to the United States Stemming from the 9/11 Attacks," *Strategic Insights* 1, no. 6 (Aug. 2002), <http://www.ccc.nps.navy.mil/si/aug02/homeland.asp> (accessed 27 July 2007).

52. Una McCaffrey, "Bord Fáilte Forecasts Big Losses in Already Ailing Tourism Industry," *Irish Times*, 13 Sept. 2001.

53. Dáil Debate, "Other Questions: Tourism Industry," 14 Nov. 2001.

54. Jim Dunne, "British Holidaymakers Think Irish Less Friendly," *Irish Times*, 20 Feb. 2001.

55. "Céad Míle Fáilte," *Irish Times*, 22 Feb. 2001.

56. Regina Daly, "Fáilte Ireland Search for Embodiment of Warm Irish Welcome," *Irish Times*, 3 Aug. 2004.

57. "Bord Fáilte Gets Top UK Award," *Irish Times*, 2 Nov. 2001.

58. Dáil Debate, "Written Answers," 14 Nov. 2001.

59. Deegan and Dineen, *Tourism Policy and Performance*, 19.

60. *Tourism and Travel in Ireland* (Dublin: Gill and Macmillan, 1993), 164–68.

61. "10,000 Trained in Tourism," *Irish Times*, 4 Jan. 1993.

62. "Work Found by 98 Percent of CERT Students," *Irish Times*, 17 Feb. 1995.

63. Dáil Debate, 14 Nov. 2001.

64. Jim Dunne, "Bord Fáilte and CERT Urged to Amalgamate," *Irish Times*, 6 Sept. 2001.

65. Jim Dunne, "Bord Fáilte Staff Seek Jobs and Pensions Assurances," *Irish Times*, 10 Dec. 2001.

66. Miriam Donohoe, "New Tourism Authority Bill to get Dáil Priority," *Irish Times,* 4 Sept. 2002.

67. *National Tourism Development Authority Bill, 2002, Explanatory Memorandum* (Dublin: Government Publications, 2002).

68. Seanad Debate, *National Tourism Development Authority Bill, 2002* 3 Dec. 2002.

69. Dáil Debate, *National Tourism Development Authority Bill, 2002,* 12 Feb. 2003.

70. Fáilte Ireland, *Annual Report 2005* (Dublin: Fáilte Ireland, 2005).

71. Department of the Taoiseach Memorandum, [?]1967, DT, 98/6/890, National Archives of Ireland, Dublin; and Bord Fáilte to the Department of the Taoiseach, 4 Mar. 1960, DT, S13087F, National Archives of Ireland, Dublin.

72. Steve MacDonogh, *The Dingle Peninsula* (Dingle, Ireland: Brandon, 2000), 77 and 80.

73. *Official Languages Act 2003* (Dublin, 2003).

74. Anne Lucey, "Minister Insists on Irish Version of Dingle," *Irish Times,* 20 May 2005.

75. "Alterations Subvert Democracy," *Irish Examiner,* 11 Jan. 2007.

76. *Dingle Name Campaign,* Dingle Name Campaign, 2007, <http://www.dinglename.com> (accessed 21 July 2007).

77. Lucey, "Minister Insists."

78. Eoin English, "Eight-in-ten Tourists Struggle to Find Dingle over St. Patrick's Weekend," *Irish Examiner,* 2 Apr. 2007.

79. "West Kerry 'Suffering Dramatic Fall in Business,'" *Kerryman,* 2 Feb. 2007.

80. Owen Bowcott, "Dingle Fights to Keep Its Name: Port Holds Referendum on Switch to Irish Version Change Could Confuse Tourists, Locals Claim," *Guardian,* 19 Oct. 2006.

81. Sean O Cathasaigh to the *Irish Times, Irish Times,* 18 June 2005.

82. Finian McGrath, TD, to the *Irish Times, Irish Times,* 22 July 2005.

83. Raé Kearns to the *Irish Times, Irish Times,* 4 Mar. 2006.

84. Shawn Pogatchnik, "Signs of the Irish Times," *Sunday Herald,* 4 Sept. 2005.

85. Anne Lucey, "Plebiscite to Be Held on Daingean or Dingle," *Irish Times,* 18 Oct. 2005; and Anne Lucey, "Ballot Includes 160 Not Living in An Daingean," *Irish Times,* 22 Aug. 2006.

86. Anne Lucey, "An Daingean Votes for Bilingual Name," *Irish Times,* 21 Oct. 2006.

87. *Irish Examiner,* 11 Jan. 2007.

88. Marian O'Flaherty, "Dingle Deal Struck—Healy-Rae Strikes Deal with Taoiseach to Restore Dingle Name," *Kerry's Eye,* 20 June 2007.

Bibliography

Archives

Bord Fáilte Photographic Archive

Ancient Sites and Monuments List, 1953– (black-and-white negatives)
Bord Fáilte Photographic Library color prints, 1990s, CD-ROM, vol. 3, 2002
Bord Fáilte Photographic Library Video Collection
Co. Kerry List, 1934–1985 (black-and-white negatives)
Types List, Pre-1960 (black-and-white negatives)

Cork Archives Institute

Clonakility Town Council
Cork Corporation Civic Reception Committee
Cork Public Museum
Kinsale Development Association
Seamus Fitzgerald Papers

Guinness Brewery Archives

Accounting Office Records
Annual Reports
Magazine/Guidebook Collection
Photographic Collection

Kilmainham Jail Archives

Kilmainham Jail Restoration

National Archives of Ireland

Department of Finance
Department of Foreign Affairs (Department of External Affairs)

Department of the Taoiseach
Department of Tourism and Transport/Industry and Commerce/Transport and
Power

National Film Centre of Ireland

Bord Fáilte travel and training films

National Library of Ireland Manuscript Collection

Dr. Sean Cooney Papers
Leslie Daiken Papers
Dillion Family Postcards, 1900–1940
Jacob Rosamond Papers

National Photographic Archives of Ireland

Lawrence Comparative Study
Wiltshire Collection

Public Records Office Northern Ireland, Belfast

Cabinet Minutes
Northern Ireland Tourist Board Annual Reports

University College Dublin Archives

Todd Andrews Papers

Department of Public Works/Dúchas—The Heritage Service

Poulnabrone Dolmen, Co. Clare. Tenure—Preservation Order, Guardianship

Private Collections

Michael Gorman, Dublin, Ireland

Libraries

Boole Library, University College Cork, Cork, Ireland
Cork City Library, Cork, Ireland
Madison Public Library, Madison, Wisconsin
National Library of Ireland, Dublin, Ireland
Trinity College Library, Dublin, Ireland
University of Washington Libraries, Seattle, Washington

University of Wisconsin-Madison Libraries, Madison, Wisconsin

Interviews

Clive Brooks, Bord Fáilte Photographic Library. Dublin, 17, 18, 22, 23 July 2002.
Jan de Fouw, graphic designer, *Ireland of the Welcomes*. Dublin, 15 Oct. 2002.
Michael Gorman, Bord Fáilte, retired. Dublin, 6 Aug. 2002 and 11 Oct. 2002.
Michael Kevin O'Doherty, Bord Fáilte, retired. Dublin, 29 Apr. and 30 July 2002.

Newspapers

Australian Financial Review (Australia)
Belfast and Irish News (Northern Ireland)
Belfast News Letter (Northern Ireland)
Belfast Telegraph (Northern Ireland)
Calgary Herald (Canada)
Catholic News (Ireland)
Clare Champion (Ireland)
Cork Examiner (Ireland)
Cork Evening Echo (Ireland)
Daily Telegraph (England)
Evening Herald (Ireland)
Financial Times (England)
Grand Rapids Press (United States)
Guardian (England)
Herald (Scotland)
Independent (England)
Irish Times (Ireland)
Irish Independent (Ireland)
Irish Press (Ireland)
Irish Weekly (Ireland)
Leinster Express (Ireland)
Limerick Leader (Ireland)
Kerryman (Ireland)
Kerry's Eye (Ireland)
Kilkenny People (Ireland)
Mayo News (Ireland)
Munster Express (Ireland)
New York Times (United States)

New York Review of Books (United States)
Ocean Times (Cunard Line)
Picture Post (England)
Toronto Star (Canada)
Seattle Times (United States)
Scotsman (Edinburgh)
Scotland on Sunday (Scotland)
Sunday Herald Sun (Australia)
Sunday Press (Ireland)
Sunday Times (England)
USA Today (United States)
Washington Post (United States)
Western People (Ireland)

Magazines

Building Design (England)
Design Week (England)
Dublin Opinion (Ireland)
Go (Britain)
Guinness Harp (Ireland)
Holiday Magazine (United States)
Irish Digest (Ireland)
Irish Marketing and Advertising Journal (Ireland)
Ireland of the Welcomes (Ireland)
Irish Travel (Ireland)
Irish Travel Trade News (Ireland)
Sunset Magazine (United States)
Traveltrade (Australia)

Videocassettes/Movies/Radio Transcripts

Byrne, Joe, Aiden O'Hanlon, and Brian Keogh. *Tourism Is Everybody's Business*. 16
    mm, 14 min., 1978. Distributed by Bord Fáilte.
Daiken, Leslie. *Where Puck Is King*. Script, 1960. Broadcast on BBC Radio.
De Buitlear, Eamon, ed. *There's Work to Be Done*. Videocassette, unknown length,
    1992. Distributed by Bord Fáilte.
Engel, Larry, and Steven Engel. "Ireland." *Going Places*. Videocassette, 58 min.,
    1998. Distributed by Thirteen/WNET Production.

Flaherty, Robert J., dir. *Man of Aran*. Videocassette, 75 min., 1934. Distributed by Academy Video.

Gilsenan, Alan, ed. *Home Movie Nights: Jan De Fouw*. Television broadcast, 2001. Distributed by RTÉ.

Hatton, Buddy. *Song of Ireland*. Videocassette, 60 min., 1990. Distributed by Quantum Communications.

Hickey, Kieran, ed. *Ireland—The Heritage of the Past*. 16 mm, unknown length, 1974. Distributed by Bord Fáilte.

———, ed. *Our Tidy Towns—21 Years of Community Effort*. 16 mm, 39 min., 1979. Distributed by Bord Fáilte.

———, ed. *Working to Win*. Videocassette, unknown length, circa 1988. Distributed by Bord Fáilte.

Hirshelwood, Simon. *The Beauty of Ireland: Donegal and Cork*. Videocassette, 52 min., 1997. Distributed by American Home Treasures.

———. *The Beauty of Ireland: Dublin and Kerry*. Videocassette, 52 min., 1997. Distributed by American Home Treasures.

Le Tour de France en Irlande. Videocassette, unknown length, 1998. Distributed by Bord Fáilte.

Marcus, Louis, prod. *Discovering Ireland*. Videocassette, unknown length, 1984. Distributed by Bord Fáilte.

———, prod. *Ireland Ours*. 16 mm, unknown length, 1973. Distributed by Bord Fáilte.

McAleese, Mary. *President's Message for St. Patrick's Day*. Videocassette, unknown length, 1998. Distributed by Bord Fáilte.

Mulkenrs, James, prod. *Ireland Invites You*. 16 mm, 13 min., [?]1966. Distributed by Bord Fáilte.

Nairn, Richard. *Ireland Naturally*. Videocassette, unknown length, 1991. Distributed by Bord Fáilte.

Nolan, Liam. *Return to the Island*. Videocassette, unknown length, 1964. Distributed by Bord Fáilte.

Ó Mordha, Seán, dir. *Seven Ages*. Videocassette, seven episodes, 2000.

O'Laoghaire, Colm. *Ireland Invites You*. 16 mm, 20 min., 1953. Distributed by Universal Irish News.

Steves, Rick. *Western Ireland, Dublin, and Belfast*. Videocassette, 51 min., 1997. Distributed by Small World Production.

St. Patrick's Festival, 1998. Videocassette, unknown length, 1998. Distributed by Bord Fáilte.

Williams, John, ed. *Ireland: Bird's Eye View*. Videocassette, unknown length, 1983. Distributed by Bord Fáilte.

Published Primary Sources

Andrews, C. S. *Man of No Property: An Autobiography*. Vol. 2. Dublin: Mercier Press, 1982.

An Taisce. *An Taisce—Annual Report, 1976*. Dublin: An Taisce, 1976.

———. *An Taisce—Annual Report, 1977*. Dublin: An Taisce, 1977.

———. *An Taisce—Annual Report, 1978*. Dublin: An Taisce, 1978.

———. *An Taisce—Annual Reports, 1979–1980*. Dublin: An Taisce, 1979–80.

———. *Grafton Street Sustaining the Magic. What Future for Dublin's Favorite Shopping Street?* Dublin: An Taisce, 1995.

———. *Heritage at Risk*. Dublin: An Taisce, 1977.

Authority and to Town Commissioners—Model Byelaws for Streets. Dublin: Department of Local Government, 1959.

Bell, Archie. *The Spell of Ireland*. Boston: L. C. Page and Co., 1928.

Böll, Heinrich. *Irish Journal*. Translated by Leila Vennewitz. New York: McGraw-Hill, 1967.

Bord Fáilte. *Access Dining in Ireland Guide 1995*. Dublin: Bord Fáilte Éireann, 1995.

———. *Accommodation Guide*. Dublin: Bord Fáilte Éireann, 1991, 1994.

———. *Advertising Supplement to Ireland 1980*. London: Bord Fáilte Éireann, 1980.

———. *The Angler's Guide to Ireland*. 5th ed. Dublin: Bord Fáilte Éireann, 1957.

———. *Annual Report and Accounts, Year Ending 31st March 1953*. Dublin: Bord Fáilte Éireann, 1953.

———. *Annual Report and Accounts, Year Ending 31st March 1956*. Dublin: Bord Fáilte Éireann, 1956.

———. *Annual Report and Accounts, Year Ending 31st March 1957*. Dublin: Bord Fáilte Éireann, 1957.

———. *Annual Report and Accounts, Year Ending 31st March 1958*. Dublin: Bord Fáilte Éireann, 1958.

———. *Annual Report and Accounts, Year Ending 31st March 1959*. Dublin: Bord Fáilte Éireann, 1959.

———. *Annual Report and Accounts, Year Ended 31st March 1961*. Dublin: Bord Fáilte Éireann, 1961.

———. *Attitudes of American and English Tourists Towards Shopping in Ireland and Irish Merchandise: A Qualitative Investigation*. Dublin: Bord Fáilte Éireann, 1973.

———. *Be Our Guest Hotels and Guesthouses: Illustrated Guide.* Dublin: Bord Fáilte Éireann, 1989, 1991, 1992, 1993.

———. *Bord Fáilte Corporate Profile.* Dublin: Bord Fáilte Éireann, [?]2000.

———. *Bord Fáilte Diary and Tourism Directory.* Dublin: Bord Fáilte Éireann, 1994, 1995, 1996.

———. *Bord Fáilte Report and Accounts for the Year Ended December 1978.* Dublin: Bord Fáilte Éireann, 1978.

———. *Bord Fáilte Report and Accounts for the Year Ended December 1979.* Dublin: Bord Fáilte Éireann, 1979.

———. *Bord Fáilte Report and Accounts for the Year Ended December 1980.* Dublin: Bord Fáilte Éireann, 1980.

———. *Bord Fáilte Report and Accounts for the Year Ended December 1981.* Dublin: Bord Fáilte Éireann, 1981.

———. *Bord Fáilte Report and Accounts for the Year Ended December 1982.* Dublin: Bord Fáilte Éireann, 1982.

———. *Bord Fáilte Report and Accounts for the Year Ended December 1983.* Dublin: Bord Fáilte Éireann, 1983.

———. *Bord Fáilte Report and Accounts for the Year Ended December 1984.* Dublin: Bord Fáilte Éireann, 1984.

———. *Bord Fáilte Report and Accounts for the Year Ended December 1985.* Dublin: Bord Fáilte Éireann, 1985.

———. *Bord Fáilte Report for the Year Ended December 1974.* Dublin: Bord Fáilte Éireann, 1974.

———. *Bord Fáilte Report for the Year Ended December 1975.* Dublin: Bord Fáilte Éireann, 1975.

———. *Bord Fáilte Report for the Year Ended December 1976.* Dublin: Bord Fáilte Éireann, 1976.

———. *Bord Fáilte Report for the Year Ended December 1977.* Dublin: Bord Fáilte Éireann, 1977.

———. *Bord Fáilte Report for the Year Ended March 1972.* Dublin: Bord Fáilte Éireann, 1972.

———. *Bord Fáilte Report for the Year Ended March 1973.* Dublin: Bord Fáilte Éireann, 1973.

———. *Bord Fáilte Report for the Year Ended March 1974.* Dublin: Bord Fáilte Éireann, 1974.

———. *Bord Fáilte Report for the Year Ended March 1986.* Dublin: Bord Fáilte Éireann, 1986.

———. *Bord Fáilte Report for the Year Ended March 1987.* Dublin: Bord Fáilte Éireann, 1987.

———. *Bord Fáilte Report for the Year Ended March 1988.* Dublin: Bord Fáilte Éireann, 1988.

———. *Bord Fáilte Report for the Year Ended March 1989.* Dublin: Bord Fáilte Éireann, 1989.

———. *Bord Fáilte Report for the Year Ended March 1990.* Dublin: Bord Fáilte Éireann, 1990.

———. *Bord Fáilte Report for the Year Ended March 1991.* Dublin: Bord Fáilte Éireann, 1991.

———. *Bord Fáilte Report for the Year Ended March 1992.* Dublin: Bord Fáilte Éireann, 1992.

———. *Bord Fáilte Report for the Year Ended March 1993.* Dublin: Bord Fáilte Éireann, 1993.

———. *Bord Fáilte Report for the Year Ended March 1994.* Dublin: Bord Fáilte Éireann, 1994.

———. *Bord Fáilte Report for the Year Ended March 1995.* Dublin: Bord Fáilte Éireann, 1995.

———. *Bord Fáilte Report for the Year Ended March 1996.* Dublin: Bord Fáilte Éireann, 1996.

———. *Bord Fáilte Report for the Year Ended March 1998.* Dublin: Bord Fáilte Éireann, 1998.

———. *Brochures on Irish Holidays, Holy Places, Ancient Monuments, and Battle of the Boyne.* Dublin: Bord Fáilte Éireann, 1962.

———. *Calendars of Events Including An Tóstal 1954–58.* Dublin: Bord Fáilte Éireann, 1954–58.

———. *Caravan and Camping in Ireland.* Dublin: Bord Fáilte Éireann, 1973, 1974, 1976, 1979, 1980, 1981, 1982, 1987.

———. *Caravan Sites, 1961.* Dublin: Bord Fáilte Éireann, 1961.

———. *Christmas Programmes in Ireland, 1970.* Dublin: Bord Fáilte Éireann, 1970.

———. *Coarse Fishing in Ireland. Fisherman! Clare-Lakelands for the Fishing Experience of a Lifetime.* Dublin: Bord Fáilte Éireann, [?]1979.

———. *Coarse Fishing in Ireland. Limerick. It's Child's Play!* Dublin: Bord Fáilte Éireann, [?]1979.

———. *Connemara Makes It Good to Have Holidays.* Dublin: Bord Fáilte Éireann, [?]1979.

———. *Cork, City, and County: Official Guide.* Dublin: Bord Fáilte Éireann, 1957.

———. *Developing Sustainable Tourism: Tourism Development Plan 1994–1999.* Dublin: Bord Fáilte Éireann, 1995.

———. *Direct Marketing and the Internet Marketing for Success: A Practical Guide for Tourism Businesses.* Dublin: Bord Fáilte Éireann, 1997.

———. *Discover Ireland: Holiday Breaks.* Dublin: Bord Fáilte Éireann, 1995 and 1997.

———. *Discover Ireland: Spring Guide '73: Inclusive Weekends, Breakaway Holidays.* Dublin: Bord Fáilte Éireann, 1972.

———. *Dublin 1991 Events.* Dublin: Bord Fáilte Éireann, 1991.

———. *EMU—A Simple Guide for Tourism Businesses.* Dublin: Bord Fáilte Éireann, 1998.

———. *Erriff and Delphi Fisheries.* Dublin: Bord Fáilte Éireann, [?]1979.

———. *The Fáilte Business 2000: The Role of Tourism in Economic Growth.* Dublin: Bord Fáilte Éireann, 2000.

———. *A Glimpse of Ireland.* Dublin: Bord Fáilte Éireann, 1992.

———. *Golf.* Dublin: Bord Fáilte Éireann, 1993.

———. *Grand Canal Festa.* Dublin: Bord Fáilte Éireann, 1971.

———. *Gulliver Ireland's Tourism Information and Reservations System.* Dublin: Bord Fáilte Éireann, 1992.

———. *Ireland.* Dublin: Bord Fáilte Éireann, 1994.

———. *Ireland: 1980.* London: Bord Fáilte Éireann, 1980.

———. *Ireland: 1981.* London: Bord Fáilte Éireann, 1981.

———. *Ireland. Accommodation for Anglers. Coarse Fishing and Sea Angling Centres.* Dublin: Bord Fáilte Éireann, 1962.

———. *Ireland: Angling Accommodation, Coarse and Sea Angling Centres.* Dublin: Bord Fáilte Éireann, 1964.

———. *Ireland: Books of Irish Interest.* Information Sheet No. 18. Dublin: Bord Fáilte Éireann, 1977.

———. *Ireland: Calendar of Events, 1958.* Dublin: Bord Fáilte Éireann, 1958.

———. *Ireland: Calendar of Events, 1959.* Dublin: Bord Fáilte Éireann, 1959.

———. *Ireland: Calendar of Events, 1960.* Dublin: Bord Fáilte Éireann, 1960.

———. *Ireland: Calendar of Events, 1961.* Dublin: Bord Fáilte Éireann, 1961.

———. *Ireland: Calendar of Events, 1962.* Dublin: Bord Fáilte Éireann, 1962.

———. *Ireland: Calendar of Events, 1963.* Dublin: Bord Fáilte Éireann, 1963.

———. *Ireland: Calendar of Events, 1964.* Dublin: Bord Fáilte Éireann, 1964.

———. *Ireland: Calendar of Events, 1965.* Dublin: Bord Fáilte Éireann, 1965.

———. *Ireland: Calendar of Events, 1970.* Dublin: Bord Fáilte Éireann, 1970.

——. *Ireland: Calendar of Events, 1973*. Dublin: Bord Fáilte Éireann, 1973.

——. *Ireland: Calendar of Events, 1974*. Dublin: Bord Fáilte Éireann, 1974.

——. *Ireland: Calendar of Events, 1976*. Dublin: Bord Fáilte Éireann, 1976.

——. *Ireland: Calendar of Events, 1979*. Dublin: Bord Fáilte Éireann, 1979.

——. *Ireland: Calendar of Events, 1980*. Dublin: Bord Fáilte Éireann, 1980.

——. *Ireland: Calendar of Events, 1981*. Dublin: Bord Fáilte Éireann, 1981.

——. *Ireland: Carefree Motoring*. Dublin: Bord Fáilte Éireann, 1969.

——. *Ireland: Carefree Motoring*. Dublin: Bord Fáilte Éireann, 1972.

——. *Ireland: Climate*. Information Sheet No. 2. Dublin: Bord Fáilte Éireann, 1977.

——. *Ireland for Coarse Fishing Holidays*. Dublin: Bord Fáilte Éireann, 1959.

——. *Ireland: Eighteenth Century Ireland Dublin*. Dublin: Bord Fáilte Éireann, 1976.

——. *Ireland: Fairies*. Dublin: Bord Fáilte Éireann, 1976.

——. *Ireland of the Festivals*. Dublin: Bord Fáilte Éireann, 1959.

——. *Ireland Guide*. Dublin: Bord Fáilte Éireann, 1993.

——. *Ireland: The Heritage of the Past*. Dublin: Bord Fáilte Éireann, 1968.

——. *Ireland. List of Caravan Sites, 1963*. Dublin: Bord Fáilte Éireann, 1963.

——. *Ireland. List of Caravan Sites, 1964*. Dublin: Bord Fáilte Éireann, 1964.

——. *Ireland: A Golfer's Paradise*. Dublin: Bord Fáilte Éireann, 1968.

——. *Ireland: Hill Walking and Rock Climbing*. Dublin: Bord Fáilte Éireann, 1976.

——. *Ireland: Holy Places*. Dublin: Bord Fáilte Éireann, 1976.

——. *Ireland: Horse Drawn Caravans*. Information Sheet No. 14. Dublin: Bord Fáilte Éireann, 1977.

——. *Ireland: Horse Riding Holidays*. Dublin: Bord Fáilte Éireann, 1976.

——. *Ireland: Hotels and Guest Houses 1964*. Dublin: Bord Fáilte Éireann, 1964.

——. *Ireland: Irish Crafts*. Dublin: Bord Fáilte Éireann, 1976.

——. *Ireland: Irish Recipes*. Information Sheet No. 29. Dublin: Bord Fáilte Éireann, 1977.

——. *Ireland: Land Arrangements for Travel Agents, 1972*. Dublin: Bord Fáilte Éireann, 1971.

——. *Ireland: Libraries, Art Galleries, Museums*. Dublin: Bord Fáilte Éireann, 1976.

——. *Ireland: Newspapers*. Dublin: Bord Fáilte Éireann, 1976.

——. *Ireland: Official List 1955: Hotels, Guest Houses, Holiday Camps, Holiday Hostels, Youth Hostels*. Dublin: Bord Fáilte Éireann, 1955.

————. *Ireland: Official List 1956: Hotels, Guest Houses, Holiday Camps, Holiday Hostels, Youth Hostels.* Dublin: Bord Fáilte Éireann, 1956.

————. *Ireland: Official List 1957: Hotels, Guest Houses, Holiday Camps, Holiday Hostels, Youth Hostels.* Dublin: Bord Fáilte Éireann, 1957.

————. *Ireland: Sailing in Ireland.* Information Sheet No. 9. Dublin: Bord Fáilte Éireann, 1977.

————. *Ireland. Seaside Resorts.* Dublin: Bord Fáilte Éireann, 1959.

————. *Ireland: Theatre and Historic Pageantry.* Information Sheet No. 19. Dublin: Bord Fáilte Éireann, 1977.

————. *Ireland: Tracing Your Ancestors.* Information Sheet No. 8. Dublin: Bord Fáilte Éireann, 1977.

————. *Ireland: Traditional Music.* Dublin: Bord Fáilte Éireann, 1976.

————. *Ireland West: Galway and Mayo.* Dublin: Bord Fáilte Éireann, [?]1979.

————. *Ireland, Your Holiday Guaranteed.* Dublin: Bord Fáilte Éireann, 1974.

————. *Ireland's Ancient Monuments.* Dublin: Bord Fáilte Éireann, [?]1964.

————. *Ireland's Ancient Monuments.* Dublin: Bord Fáilte Éireann, [?]1966.

————. *The Irish Tourist Board Report for the Year Ending 31st March 1960.* Dublin: Bord Fáilte Éireann, 1960.

————. *The Irish Tourist Board Report for the Year Ended 31 March 1962.* Dublin: Bord Fáilte Éireann, 1962.

————. *The Irish Tourist Board Report for the Year Ended 31st March 1963.* Dublin: Bord Fáilte Éireann, 1963.

————. *The Irish Tourist Board Report for the Year Ended March 31 1964.* Dublin: Bord Fáilte Éireann, 1964.

————. *Irish Tourist Board Report for the Year Ended March 1970.* Dublin: Bord Fáilte Éireann, 1970.

————. *Irish Tourist Board Report for the Year Ended March 31 1965.* Dublin: Bord Fáilte Éireann, 1965.

————. *Know Your Market: Australia/New Zealand.* Dublin: Bord Fáilte Éireann, 1998.

————. *Know Your Market: Austria/Switzerland/Eastern Europe.* Dublin: Bord Fáilte Éireann, 1998.

————. *Know Your Market: Benelux 1997–1998.* Dublin: Bord Fáilte Éireann, 1997.

————. *Know Your Market: Britain.* Dublin: Bord Fáilte Éireann, 1993.

———— *Know Your Market: Britain.* Dublin: Bord Fáilte Éireann, 1998.

————. *Know Your Market: France.* Dublin: Bord Fáilte Éireann, 1998.

———. *Know Your Market: Germany*. Dublin: Bord Fáilte Éireann, 1993.

———. *Know Your Market: Italy*. Dublin: Bord Fáilte Éireann, 1997.

———. *Know Your Market: North America*. Dublin: Bord Fáilte Éireann, 1998.

———. *Know Your Market: Spain*. Dublin: Bord Fáilte Éireann, 1993.

———. *Know Your Market: Spain*. Dublin: Bord Fáilte Éireann, 1997.

———. *Know Your Market: Switzerland/Austria*. Dublin: Bord Fáilte Éireann, 1994.

———. *Markets*. Dublin: Bord Fáilte Éireann, 1999.

———. *Miscellaneous Tourist Information Literature, Including the 'Discover Ireland' and 'Ireland: Information Sheet Seers,' 1967–73*. Dublin: Bord Fáilte Éireann, 1967–73.

———. *National Monuments of Ireland in Charge of the Commissioners of Public Works in Ireland*. Dublin: Bord Fáilte Éireann, 1964.

———. *Perspectives on Irish Tourism, Irish Travel Market 1994: A Report on Trip Taking in Ireland and Abroad by Irish Residents*. Dublin: Bord Fáilte Éireann, 1997.

———. *Perspectives on Irish Tourism Visits to Tourist Attractions 1996*. Dublin: Bord Fáilte Éireann, 1997.

———. *Pricing and Yield Management Marketing for Success—a Practical Guide for Tourism Businesses*. Dublin: Bord Fáilte Éireann, 1997.

———. *Reaching the Customer, Marketing for Success—A Practical Guide for Tourism Businesses*. Dublin: Bord Fáilte Éireann, 1997.

———. *Regions*. Dublin: Bord Fáilte Éireann, [?]1999.

———. *Relationship Marketing, Marketing for Success—A Practical Guide for Tourism Businesses*. Dublin: Bord Fáilte Éireann, 1998.

———. *Report and Financial Statements 2000*. Dublin: Bord Fáilte Éireann, 2000.

———. *Sea Fishing: Ireland*. Dublin: Bord Fáilte Éireann, n.d.

———. *Some Highlights of An Tóstal, 1955*. Dublin: Bord Fáilte Éireann, 1955.

———. *Spring Weekends 1975*. Dublin: Bord Fáilte Éireann, [?]1974.

———. *Tourism in the Irish Economy*. Dublin: Bord Fáilte Éireann, 1989.

———. *Tourism Plan 1974–77: A Four-Year Working Document for the Irish Tourist Industry. This Plan Is Supplementary to the Tourism Plan 1973–76*. Dublin: Bord Fáilte Éireann, 1974.

———. *Tourism Plan 1981–85: Marketing and Development Guidelines for the Irish Tourist Industry*. Dublin: Bord Fáilte Éireann, 1980.

———. *Tourism Towards 2000: Marketing Plan for Irish Tourism 1999*. Dublin: Bord Fáilte Éireann, 1999.

————. *Tourist Development Plan, 1976–80: Dublin Regional Tourism.* Dublin: Bord Fáilte Éireann, 1976.

————. *Tourist Development Plan, 1976–80: Eastern Region.* Dublin: Bord Fáilte Éireann, 1976.

————. *Tourist Development Plan, 1976–80: Midland Region.* Dublin: Bord Fáilte Éireann, 1976.

————. *Tourist Development Plan, 1976–80: Mid-Western Region.* Dublin: Bord Fáilte Éireann, 1976.

————. *Tourist Development Plan, 1976–80: National Plan.* Dublin: Bord Fáilte Éireann, 1976.

————. *Tourist Development Plan, 1976–80: North-Western Region.* Dublin: Bord Fáilte Éireann, 1976.

————. *Tourist Development Plan, 1976–80: South Eastern Region.* Dublin: Bord Fáilte Éireann, 1976.

————. *Tourist Development Plan, 1976–80: Southern Region (Cork/Kerry) Tourism.* Dublin: Bord Fáilte Éireann, 1976.

————. *Tourist Development Plan, 1976–80: Western Region.* Dublin: Bord Fáilte Éireann, 1976.

————. *Tramore Resort Plan.* Dublin: Bord Fáilte Éireann, 1971.

————. *Urlaub Made in Ireland.* Frankfurt: Bord Fáilte Éireann, 1969.

————. *Welcome to Ireland.* Dublin: Bord Fáilte Éireann, 1976 and 1979.

————. *Where to Eat in Ireland: A Traveller's Guide to 100 Selected Restaurants.* Dublin: Bord Fáilte Éireann, 1973.

BP Touring Service of Ireland. *Touring Guide to Ireland: Cork.* Dublin: BP, n.d.

British Tourist Authority. *Britain and Ireland, Car Ferry Routes.* London: British Tourist Authority, 1979.

CaraIreland Tours. London: Cara, 1973.

Central Statistics Office. *Statistical Abstract.* Dublin: Government Publications, 1990.

CIÉ Tours International, Inc.: Europe, Ireland, Great Britain. Dublin: CIÉ, 1971.

Clark, Gordon. *Tourist Trail: A Signposted Walking Tour of Dublin.* Dublin: Dublin Tourism, [?]1985.

Comeback for Erin? Dublin: National Tourism Council of Ireland, 1977.

Come Cruising on Ireland's River Shannon, the Most Wonderful Waterway in Europe. Dublin: Penguin, 1969.

Convery, Frank, and Sheila Flanagan. *Investing for Tourism in Ireland. Proceedings of the Tourism Investment Conference Held at University College Dublin, March*

29–31, 1994. Dublin: Dublin Environmental Institute, University College Dublin, 1994.

Cooke, Pat. *A History of Kilmainham Gaol.* Dublin: Dúchas, 2001.

Co-ordinating Committee for Killarney Tourist Industry. *See Killarney First.* Dublin: Bord Fáilte, 1972.

Cork/Kerry Tourism Organisation. *Cork/Kerry Tourism Marketing Plan as of 26/2/98.* Cork: Cork/Kerry Tourism, 1998.

Corrigan Kearns, Kevin. *Georgian Dublin—Ireland's Imperiled Architecture.* Newton Abbot, UK: David and Charles, 1983.

Coughlan, Stephen. *Tóstal Corcai. Festival of Cork, Souvenir Programme.* Cork: n.p., 1956.

Dalaigh, Brian O., ed. *The Stranger's Gaze: Travels in County Clare, 1534–1950.* Dublin: Clasp Press, 1998.

Department of Local Government. *Department of Local Government Report, 1939-40.* Dublin: Government Publications, 1940.

———. *Department of Local Government Report, 1940-41.* Dublin: Government Publications, 1941.

———. *Department of Local Government Report, 1941-2.* Dublin: Government Publications, 1942.

———. *Department of Local Government Report, 1942–3.* Dublin: Government Publications, 1943.

———. *Department of Local Government Report, 1943–4.* Dublin: Government Publications, 1944.

———. *Department of Local Government Report, 1944–5.* Dublin: Government Publications, 1945.

———. *Department of Local Government Report, 1945–47.* Dublin: Government Publications, 1947.

———. *Department of Local Government Report, 1947–48.* Dublin: Government Publications, 1948.

———. *Department of Local Government Report, 1948–49.* Dublin: Government Publications, 1949.

———. *Department of Local Government Report, 1949–50.* Dublin: Government Publications, 1950.

———. *Department of Local Government Report, 1950–51.* Dublin: Government Publications, 1951.

———. *Department of Local Government Report, 1951–1952.* Dublin: Government Publications, 1952.

———. *Department of Local Government Report, 1952–1953*. Dublin: Government Publications, 1953.

———. *Department of Local Government Report, 1953–1954*. Dublin: Government Publications, 1954.

———. *Department of Local Government Report, 1955–1956*. Dublin: Government Publications, 1956.

———. *Department of Local Government Report, 1956–1957*. Dublin: Government Publications, 1957.

———. *Department of Local Government Report, 1958–1959—Roads*. Dublin: Government Publications, 1959.

———. *Department of Local Government Report, 1958–1959. Appendix xxiii, Circular Letter No. L2/1959 of 2nd Feb. 1959 to Each Sanitary*. Dublin: Government Publications, 1959.

"Dingle Name Campaign." *Dingle Name Campaign, 2007*, <http://www.dingle-name.com,> accessed 21 July 2007.

Discover What's Brewing at the Guinness Hopstore. Dublin: Guinness Brewing Company, circa 1990.

Drumshanbo An Tóstal Committee. *Twenty-Second An Tóstal Druimseanbhoth*. Dublin: Bord Fáilte, 1974.

Dublin Corporation. *Dublin City Development Plan 1991*. Dublin: Dublin Corporation, 1991.

———. *Dublin City Development Plan 1999*. Dublin: Dublin Corporation, 1999.

Duff, Chris. *On Celtic Tides: One Man's Journey around Ireland by Sea Kayak*. New York: St. Martin's Griffin, 1999.

Durell, Penelope, and Cornelius Kelly, eds. *The Grand Tour of Beara*. Allihies, County Cork, Ireland: Cailleach Books, 2000.

———, eds. *The Grand Tour of Kerry*. Allihies, County Cork, Ireland: Cailleach Books, 2001.

Feehan, John, ed. *Tourism on the Farm. Proceedings of Two Conferences on Farm Tourism in Ireland: University College, Dublin, March 1992; Enniskillen Fermanagh, May 1992*. Dublin: Dublin Environmental Institute, University College Dublin, 1992.

Fine Gael. *Time for Action for the Repedestrianisation of Grafton Street*. Dublin: Fine Gael, 1976.

Fógra Fáilte. *An Tóstal: Ireland at Home, 1953. National Programme*. Dublin: Fógra Fáilte, 1953.

———. *An Tóstal: Official Souvenir Guide*. Dublin: Fógra Fáilte, 1953.

————. *Ireland Guide*. Dublin: Fógra Fáilte, [?]1953.

————. *Ireland: An Illustrated Guide to the Counties of Ireland*. Dublin: Fógra Fáilte, [?]1953.

————. *Ireland: Official List 1953: Hotels, Guest Houses, Holiday Camps, Holiday Hostels, Youth Hostels*. Dublin: Fógra Fáilte, 1953.

————. *Ireland: Official List 1954: Hotels, Guest Houses, Holiday Camps, Holiday Hostels, Youth Hostels*. Dublin: Fógra Fáilte, 1954.

Geoghegan, Philip. *Building Sensitively in Ireland's Landscapes*. Dublin: Bord Fáilte and An Taisce, 1989.

Ghosts of Kilmainham. Dublin: Kilmainham Jail Restoration Society, 1963.

Gorman, Michael, Frank Height, Mary V. Mullin, and W. H. Walsh, eds. *Design for Tourism: An ICSID Inter Design Report*. Oxford: Pergamon Press, 1977.

Guinness Dublin. Dublin: Guinness Brewing Co., 1939, 1948, 1955.

Guinness. Brasserie De Renommée Mondiale. L'Histoire du Célèbre Stout aux Cinq Millions d'Hectolitres de Ventes Annuelles. Dublin: Guinness Brewing Company, circa 1950.

The Guinness Brewery. Dublin: Guinness Brewing Company, circa 1955.

Harbison, Peter. *Guide to National and Historic Monuments of Ireland*. Dublin: Gill and Macmillan, 1992.

Harrington, John P., ed. *The English Traveller in Ireland: Accounts of Ireland and the Irish through Five Centuries*. Dublin: Wolfhound Press, 1991.

Hawks, Tony. *Round Ireland with a Fridge*. New York: St. Martin's Griffin, 1988.

Hooper, Glenn. *The Tourist's Gaze: Travellers to Ireland, 1800–2000*. Cork: Cork Univ. Press, 2002.

Imagination Group USA. "Guinness Storehouse," <http://www.imagination.com/usa/work/guinness.html,> accessed 9 Apr. 2003.

Implementation Group. "Memorandum of Understanding on the North/South Tourism Company." In appendix 6 of *Establishment of New Tourist Development Authority*. Dublin: Department of Tourism, Sport, and Recreation, 2002.

————. *Establishment of New Tourist Development Authority*. Dublin: Department of Tourism, Sport, and Recreation, 2002.

Inland Fisheries Trust. *Salmon and Sea Trout Fishing in Ireland*. Compiled by the Inland Fisheries Trust for Bord Fáilte Éireann. Dublin: Inland Fisheries Trust, 1966.

Ireland Flyaway Holidays 70. Dublin: Aer Lingus and BEA, 1970.

"Ireland/Irish Pub Themed Items," Bellatopia.com, <http://www.bellatopia.com/themes_irish_pub.shtml,> accessed 4 Aug. 2003.

Irish Tourist Association. *Angling and Golf*. Dublin: Irish Tourist Association, 1946.

———. *Cork Official Guide*. Dublin: Irish Tourist Association, 1932.

———. *Cork: A Short Survey of the Attractions and Holiday Facilities of Cork City and County*. Dublin: Irish Tourist Association, [?]1928.

———. *Dublin: Official Guide*. Dublin: Irish Tourist Association, 1933.

———. *Hike It or Bike It*. Dublin: Irish Tourist Association, [?]1944.

———. *Hotels and Boarding Houses in Cork City and County*. Dublin: Irish Tourist Association, 1927.

———. *Hotels, Restaurants and Garages in the Irish Free State: A Detailed List with Particulars of Accommodation and Charges*. Dublin: Irish Tourist Association, n.d.

———. *Introducing Ireland*. Dublin: Irish Tourist Association, 1950.

———. *Ireland: Official Guide*. Dublin: Irish Tourist Association, 1938 and 1947.

———. *Ireland: Official Publication*. Dublin: Irish Tourist Association, 1929.

———. *Ireland: Official Publication of the Irish Tourist Association*. Dublin: Irish Tourist Association, 1930 and 1932.

———. *Irish Curiosities. A Collection of Strange, Fascinating, Puzzling or Picturesque Oddities of Ireland Pictured and Described in This New I.T.A. Book*. Dublin: Irish Tourist Association, 1944.

———. *Irish Tourist Directory Comprising Hotels, Boarding Houses, Restaurants, Garages, and Other Business in the Irish Free State*. Dublin: Irish Tourist Association, 1934.

———. *Killarney: Beauty's Home: Official Guide*. Dublin: Irish Tourist Association, [?]1934.

———. *Killarney: Cill Airne/I.T.A. Official Guide*. Trallee, Ireland: Irish Tourist Association, [?]1949.

———. *Killarney: The Official Publication of the Irish Tourist Association*. Dublin: Irish Tourist Association, 1946.

———. *The Kingdom of Kerry: The Official Publication of the Irish Tourist Association*. Dublin: Irish Tourist Association, [?]1946.

———. *A Morning in Dublin*. Dublin: Irish Tourist Association, n.d.

———. *Official Guide to "Kingdom of Kerry."* Dublin: Irish Tourist Association, 1934, [?]1940.

———. *Welcome to Cork: A Short Survey of the Attractions and Holiday Facilities of Cork City and County*. Cork: Irish Tourist Association, [?]1927.

Irish Tourist Board. *Official List of Registered Premises for 1944. Hotels, Guest Houses, Holiday Hostels, Youth Hostels, Holiday Camps*. Dublin: Irish Tourist Association, 1944.

Kellogg's Fruit 'N Fibre Farmhouse B&B Guide. Huntingdon, UK: Kellogg, 1993.

Kerryweb Ireland. *"Cloghane and Brandon,"* <http://www.kerryweb.ie/destination-kerry/cloghane/cloghane.html,> accessed 12 Sept. 2000.

Kilmainham: The Bastille of Ireland. Dublin: Kilmainham Jail Restoration Society, 1970.

Le Guinness. Son Brassage, Ses Properties, Ses Qualities. Dublin: Guinness Brewing Company, 1932.

Living City Group. *Dublin—A Living City?* Dublin: The Living City Group, 1972.

Loughlin, Paul. *Product 1992. Getting the Product Right! A Presentation on the Progress Being Made in the Development of New Tourism Infrastructure. Bord Fáilte Tourism Industry Meeting, Burlington Hotel, Dublin.* Dublin: Bord Fáilte, 1991.

MacDonogh, Steve. *The Dingle Peninsula.* Dingle: Brandon, 2000.

McCarthy, Pete. *McCarthy's Bar.* Edinburgh: Hodder and Stoughton, 2000.

McKenna, Fionnuala. "Sunningdale Agreement, 8 January 1973," <http://cain.ulst.ac.uk/events/sunningdale/agreement.htm,> accessed 19 Mar. 2003.

National Coastline Study. Vol. 1. Dublin: S.N., 1972.

National Rehabilitation Board. *Guide to Accessible Accommodation in Ireland.* Dublin, 1998.

Neeson, Geraldine. *Our Heritage—Cork.* Dublin: Bruce Spicer, 1970.

Nelson, Justin, ed. *Faces and Places.* Dublin, circa 1987.

Newby, Eric. *Round Ireland in Low Gear.* London: Viking, 1987.

Northern Ireland Assembly. "Good Friday Agreement," <http://www.studiperlapace.org,> accessed 20 Mar. 2003.

O'Cahill, Donal, ed. *Killarney: Land and Lake.* 13th ed. Tralee: Donal O'Cahill, [?]1963.

O'Faolain, Sean. *An Irish Journey.* London: Reader's Union, 1941.

O'Sullivan, John F. *Glimpses of Paradise: A Guide History of Killarney.* Illfracombe: Stockwell, 1969.

Pictures and Answers: Things People Ask About Guinness. Dublin: Guinness Brewing Company, 1950.

Robertson, Manning. *Cautionary Guide to Dublin with 64 Illustrations.* Dublin: Royal Institute of the Architects of Ireland, 1933, 1934.

'Round Ballycotton Bay. Skibbereen: Star Printing, [?]1933.

Rukeyser, Muriel. *The Orgy.* New York: Coward-McCann, 1965.

Somerville-Large, Peter. *The Grand Irish Tour.* London: Hamish Hamilton, 1982.

Southern Regional Tourism Organisation. *Ivernia Interim Report—1971: Embodying End of Season Review 1971.* Cork: Southern Regional Tourism Organisation, 1972.

———. *Ivernia: Cork—Kerry.* Cork: Southern Regional Tourism Organisation, 1972.

"Storehouse Gets Celebrity Start." *Irish Marketing and Advertising Journal* 1 (Jan. 2001).

Taibln, Colm, and Bernard Loughlin, eds. *The Guinness Book of Ireland.* Enfield, Middlesex: Guinness and Bord Fáilte, 1995.

"Tourism—A Record." *The* Irish Times *Annual Review* 3 (Jan. 1966): 74–76.

Visitor's Guide to Dublin. Dublin: General Publications, [?]1969.

Walsh, Brendan. *Cycle Touring Ireland.* Dublin: Gill and Macmillan, 1997.

The World and His Wife. Dublin: Guinness Brewing Company, circa 1961.

Your Guide to the World of Guinness at the Guinness Hopstore. Dublin: Guinness Brewing Company, circa 1990.

Your Very Own Visitor Guide. The World of Guinness, Guinness Hopstore. Dublin: Guinness Brewing Company, circa 1990.

Secondary Sources

Unpublished Dissertations/Theses

Beyn, F. Emma. "Tourists, Travelers and Transients: Hostel Culture in Southwestern Ireland." Division III examination, Hampshire College, 1996.

Casey, Marion R. "Ireland, New York and the Irish Image in American Popular Culture, 1890–1960." Ph.D. diss., New York Univ., 1998.

De Nie, Michael William. "The Eternal Paddy: Irish Identity and the British Press, 1798–1882." Ph.D. diss., Univ. of Wisconsin-Madison, 2001.

Dolan, Anne. "Commemorating the Irish Civil War, 1924–2000." Ph.D. diss., Cambridge Univ., Cambridge, 2001.

Dunne, Paul. "Is Ireland the Ideal International Golfing Holiday Destination?" Master of Business Studies, Dublin Business School, 1995.

McMahon, Timothy Gerard. "The Social Bases of the Gaelic Revival, 1893–1910." Ph.D. diss., Univ. of Wisconsin-Madison, 2001.

Thompson, Spurgeon. "The Postcolonial Tourist: Irish Tourism and Decolonization since 1850." Ph.D. diss., Univ. of Notre Dame, 1999.

Zuelow, Eric G. E. "'Invasion of the Celts': The King's Visit and the Formation of Scottish National Identity." Master of Arts, Univ. of Wisconsin-Madison, 1999.

Other Unpublished Secondary Sources

Ashworth, G. J. "Is Heritage, a Globalisation of the Local or a Localisation of the Global?" Paper presented at *Ireland's Heritages: Critical Perspectives on*

Consumption, Method and Memory, Galway-Mayo Institute of Technology, Castlebar, Co. Mayo, Ireland, 19 Oct. 2002.

King, Linda. "'Guaranteed Irish'—Aer Lingus and the Representation of Ireland." Paper presented at *Ireland's Heritages: Critical Perspectives on Consumption, Method and Memory.* Galway-Mayo Institute of Technology, Castlebar, Co. Mayo, Ireland, 19 Oct. 2002.

Marcuse, Harold. "Shaping the Visitor Experience in Dachau, 1938–1968." In "Tourism, War and the Commemoration of Atrocity," ed. Rudi Hartmann, unpublished, 1999.

Published Secondary Sources

Abram, Simon. "Performing for Tourists in Rural France." In *Tourists and Tourism: Identifying with People and Places,* ed. Jacqueline Waldren, Simon Abram, and Donald V. L. Macleod, 29–50. Oxford: Berg, 1997.

Agnew, John. "European Landscape and Identity." In *Modern Europe: Place, Culture and Identity,* ed. Brian Graham, 213–35. London: Arnold, 1998.

Anderson, Benedict. *Imagined Communities: Reflections on the Origin and Spread of Nationalism.* London: Verso, 1991.

Arel, Dominique. "Language Politics in Independent Ukraine: Towards One or Two State Languages?" *Nationalities Papers* 23, no. 3 (1995): 597–624.

Ashworth, G. J., and P. J. Larkham, eds. *Building a New Heritage: Tourism, Culture and Identity in the New Europe.* London: Routledge, 1994.

Azaryahu, Maoz, and Aharon Kellerman. "Symbolic Places of National History in Zionist Mythical Geography." *Transactions of the Institute for Geography* 24 (1999): 109–23.

Bailey, Peter. *Leisure and Class in Victorian England: Rational Recreation and the Contest for Control.* Buffalo, N.Y.: Univ. of Toronto Press, 1978.

Balakrishnan, Gopal, ed. *Mapping the Nation.* London: Verso, 1996.

Baldwin-Brown, Gerald. *The Care of Ancient Monuments.* Cambridge: Cambridge Univ. Press, 1905.

Bannon, Michael J., Kevin I. Nowlan, John Hendry, and Ken Mawhinney, eds. *Planning: The Irish Experience 1920–1988.* Dublin: Wolfhound Press, 1989.

Baranowski, Shelley, and Ellen Furlough, eds. *Being Elsewhere: Tourism, Consumer Culture, and Identity in Modern Europe and North America.* Ann Arbor: Univ. of Michigan Press, 2001.

Barrington, Ruth, and Jim Dooge, eds. *A Vital National Interest: Ireland in Europe, 1973–1998.* Dublin: Institute of Public Administration, 1999.

Basch, Linda G., Nina Gleck Schiller, and Cristina Szanton Blanc. *Nations Unbound: Transnational Projects, Postcolonial Predicaments and Deterritorialized Nation-States*. Laughone, Pa.: Gordon and Breach, 1994.

Benjamin, Walter. *Illuminations: Essays and Reflections*. New York: Schocken Books, 1968.

Billig, Michael. *Banal Nationalism*. London: Sage, 1995.

Black, Jeremy. *The British Abroad: The Grand Tour in the Eighteenth Century*. New York: St. Martin's Press, 1992.

Blommaert, Jan. "Language and Nationalism: Comparing Flanders and Tanzania." *Nations and Nationalism* 2, no. 2 (1996): 235–56.

Boyce, D. George. *Nationalism in Ireland*. London: Routledge, 1995.

Boylan, Henry. *A Dictionary of Irish Biography*. 3rd ed. Niwot, Colo.: Robert Rinehart, 1998.

Bradley, W. H. "Around the World with Thomas Cook." *British Heritage*, 1988, 56–61.

Breathnach, Proinnsias, ed. *Irish Tourism Development*. Maynooth: Geographical Society of Ireland, 1994.

Brendon, Piers. *Thomas Cook: 150 Years of Popular Travel*. London: Secker and Warburg, 1991.

Brett, David. *The Construction of Heritage*. Cork: Cork Univ. Press, 1996.

Brown, Terence. *Ireland: A Social and Cultural History, 1922 to the Present*. Ithaca, N.Y.: Cornell Univ. Press, 1990.

Browne, Lance, and Kenneth A. Wright. *A Future for Dublin*. Bedford: Architectural Press, 1975.

Browne, Sean. "Heritage in Ireland's Tourism Recovery." In *Cultural Tourism*, ed. J. M. Fladmark, 13–25. London: Donheael Publishing, 1994.

Bruce, Steve. *The Edge of Union: The Ulster Loyalist Political Vision*. Oxford: Oxford Univ. Press, 1994.

Brunn, Stanley D., Ute Wardenga, and Anne Buttimer, eds. *Text and Image: Social Construction of Regional Knowledges*. Leipzig: Institut für Länderkunde, 1999.

Butler, R. W. "Evolution of Tourism in the Scottish Highlands." *Annals of Tourism Research* 12 (1985): 371–91.

Buzard, James. *The Beaten Track: European Tourism, Literature, and the Ways to Culture, 1800–1918*. Oxford: Clarendon Press, 1993.

Callanan, Brian. *Leaders, Visions, and Networks, Ireland's Shannon Story: A Case Study of Local and Regional Development*. Dublin: Irish Academic Press, 2000.

Cater, Erlet, and Stuart McMinn. "Tourist Typology: Observations from Belize." *Annals of Tourism Research* 25, no. 3 (1998): 675–99.

Chatterjee, Partha. *The Nation and Its Fragments: Colonial and Postcolonial Histories.* Princeton, N.J.: Princeton Univ. Press, 1993.

Chris Curtin, and Tony Varley. "Brown Trout, 'Gentry' and Dutchmen: Tourism and Development in South Mayo." In *Ireland from Below: Social Change and Local Communities,* ed. Thomas M. Wilson and Chris Curtin, 207–23. Galway: Galway Univ. Press, 1987.

Chubb, Basil. *The Politics of the Irish Constitution.* Dublin: Institute of Public Administration, 1991.

Clark, W., and B. O'Cinneide. *Tourism in the Republic of Ireland and Northern Ireland.* Belfast: Co-operation North, 1981.

Clarke, Conor. *Oranje and Green: Holland-Ireland, Design Connections 1951–2002.* Amsterdam: BIS Publishers, 2002.

Clifford, James. *Routes: Travel and Translation in the Late Twentieth Century.* Cambridge, Mass.: Harvard Univ. Press, 1997.

Cohrane, Feargal. *Unionist Politics and the Politics of Unionism since the Anglo-Irish Agreement.* Cork: Cork Univ. Press, 1997.

Colley, Linda. *Britons: Forging the Nation, 1707–1837.* New Haven, Conn.: Yale Univ. Press, 1992.

Collins, Stephen. *The Cosgrave Legacy.* Dublin: Blackwater Press, 1996.

Conekin, Becky E. *"The Autobiography of a Nation": The 1951 Festival of Britain.* Manchester: Manchester Univ. Press, 2003.

Confino, Alon. *The Nation as a Local Metaphor.* Chapel Hill: Univ. of North Carolina Press, 1997.

Connerton, Paul. *How Societies Remember.* Cambridge: Cambridge Univ. Press, 1989.

Connolly, S. J. "Popular Culture: Patterns of Change and Adaptation." In *Conflict, Identity, and Economic Development: Ireland and Scotland, 1600–1939,* ed. R. A. Houston, S. J. Connolly, and R. J. Morris, 103–13. Cambridge: Carnegie Publishing, 1995.

Conversi, Daniele, ed. *Ethnonationalism in the Contemporary World: Walker Connor and the Study of Nationalism.* London: Routledge, 2002.

Conversi, Daniele. "Language or Race?: The Choice of Core Values in the Development of Catalan and Basque Nationalisms." *Ethnic and Racial Studies* 13, no. 1 (1990): 50–70.

Corbin, Alain. *The Lure of the Sea.* Berkeley: Univ. of California Press, 1994.

Cormack, Mike. "Minority Languages, Nationalism and Broadcasting: The British and Irish Examples." *Nations and Nationalism* 6, no. 3 (2000): 383–98.

Cosgrove, Denis E. *Social Formation and Symbolic Landscape.* Madison: Univ. of Wisconsin Press, 1998.

Cronin, Denis A., Jim Gilligan, and Karina Holton, eds. *Irish Fairs and Markets.* Dublin: Four Courts Press, 2001.

Cronin, Michael. *Across the Lines: Travel, Language, Translation.* Cork: Cork Univ. Press, 2000.

Cronin, Mike. *Sport and Nationalism in Ireland: Gaelic Games, Soccer and Irish Identity since 1884.* Dublin: Four Courts Press, 1999.

Cronin, Mike, and Daryl Adair. *The Wearing of the Green: A History of St. Patrick's Day.* London: Routledge, 2002.

Cronin, Sean. *Frank Ryan: The Search for the Republic.* Dublin: Repsol Publishers, 1980.

Cullen, Fintan. *Visual Politics: The Representation of Ireland 1750–1930.* Cork: Cork University Press, 1997.

Curtis, L. Perry Jr. *Apes and Angles: The Irishman in Victorian Caricature.* Washington: Smithsonian Institution Press, 1997.

Dalby, Andrew. *Language in Danger.* New York: Penguin Press, 2002.

Dalsimer, Adele M., ed. *Visualizing Ireland: National Identity and the Pictorial Tradition.* Boston: Faber and Faber, 1993.

Daly, Mary E. *Industrial Development and Irish Society: 1922–1939.* Syracuse, N.Y.: Syracuse Univ. Press, 1992.

Darby, John. *Scorpions in a Bottle: Conflicting Cultures in Northern Ireland.* London: Minority Rights Group Publications, 1997.

De Nie, Michael. "'A Medley Mob of Irish-American Plotters and Irish Dupes': The British Press and Transatlantic Fenianism." *Journal of British Studies* 40, no. 2 (2001): 213–40.

Deane, Seamus. *Strange Country: Modernity and Nationhood in Irish Writing since 1790.* Oxford: Clarendon Press, 1997.

Deegan, James, and Donal A. Dineen. *Tourism Policy and Performance: The Irish Experience.* London: International Thomson Business Press, 1997.

Delany, Patrick, ed. *Dublin—A City in Crisis.* Dublin: Royal Institute of the Architects of Ireland, 1975.

Dennison, S. R., and Oliver MacDonagh. *Guinness 1886–1939: From Incorporation to the Second World War.* Cork: Cork Univ. Press, 1998.

Dillon, Michele. *Divorce: Moral Conflict in Ireland*. Lexington: Univ. of Kentucky Press, 1993.

Drisceoil, Donal Ó. *Censorship in Ireland 1939–1945: Neutrality, Politics, and Society*. Cork: Cork Univ. Press, 1996.

Duncan, A. A. M. *The Nation of the Scots and the Declaration of Arbroath*. Glasgow: Historical Association, 1970.

Durara, Prasenjit. *Rescuing History from the Nation: Questioning Narratives of Modern China*. Chicago: Univ. of Chicago Press, 1995.

Durie, Alastair J. "Tourism and Commercial Photography in Victorian Scotland: The Rise and Fall of G. W. Wilson and Co., 1853–1908." *Northern Scotland* 12 (1992): 89–104.

Edensor, Tim. "National Identity and the Politics of Memory: Remembering Bruce and Wallace in Symbolic Space." *Environment and Planning* 29 (1997): 175–94.

———. "Reading Braveheart: Representing and Contesting Scottish Identity." *Scottish Affairs* 21 (1997): 135–58.

Fallon, Brian. *An Age of Innocence: Irish Culture, 1930–1960*. Dublin: Gill and MacMillan, 1998.

Fanning, Ronan. *The Irish Department of Finance, 1922–58*. Dublin: Institute of Public Administration, 1978.

Farrell, Brian. *Seán Lemass*. London: Gill and Macmillan, 1983.

Farry, Michael. *The Aftermath of Revolution: Sligo 1921–23*. Dublin: Univ. College Dublin Press, 2000.

Fegan, Melissa. "The Traveller's Experience in Famine Ireland." *Irish Studies Review* 9, no. 3 (2001): 361–72.

Feifer, Maxine. *Going Places: The Ways of the Tourist from Imperial Rome to the Present Day*. London: Macmillan, 1985.

———. *Tourism in History: From Imperial Rome to the Present*. New York: Stein and Day, 1986.

Fishman, Joshua A. *Language and Nationalism: Two Integrative Essays*. Rowley, Mass.: Newberry House Publishers, 1973.

Fitzpatrick, David. *The Two Irelands: 1912–1939*. Oxford: Opus, 1998.

Forshee, Jill, Christina Fink, and Sandra Cate, eds. *Converging Interests: Traders, Travelers, and Tourists in Southeast Asia*. Berkeley: Univ. of California Press, 1999.

Foster, Roy. *Modern Ireland: 1600–1972*. London: Penguin, 1988.

———. *Paddy and Mr. Punch: Connections in Irish and English History*. London: Oxford Univ. Press, 1995.

————. "Remembering 1798." In *History and Memory in Modern Ireland,* ed. Ian McBride, 67–94. Cambridge: Cambridge Univ. Press, 2001.

————. *W. B. Yeats, A Life, Part II: The Arch-Poet.* Oxford: Oxford Univ. Press, 2003.

Fraser, T. G. *Ireland in Conflict: 1922–1998.* London: Routledge, 2000.

Fussell, Paul. *Abroad: British Literary Traveling between the Wars.* Oxford: Oxford Univ. Press, 1980.

Furlong, Irene. "Frederick W. Crossley: Irish Turn-of-the-Century Tourism Pioneer." *Irish History: A Research Yearbook.* No. 2, 162–76. Dublin: Four Courts Press, 2003.

Garrad, Larch S. "The Industrial Archaeology of Tourism." *Industrial Archaeology* 17, no. 1 (1982): 19–26.

Garvin, Tom. *1922: The Birth of Irish Democracy.* New York: St. Martin's Press, 1996.

Geary, Laurence M. "Parnell and the Land Question." In *Parnell: The Politics of Power,* ed. Donal McCartney, 90–101. Dublin: Wolfhound Press, 1991.

Geertz, Clifford. *The Interpretation of Cultures.* New York: Basic Books, 1973.

Gellner, Ernest. *Nations and Nationalism.* Ithaca, N.Y.: Cornell Univ. Press, 1983.

Gellner, Ernest, and Anthony D. Smith. "The Nation: Real or Imagined?: The Warwick Debates on Nationalism." *Nations and Nationalism* 2, no. 3 (1996): 357–70.

Gibbons, Luke. *Transformations in Irish Culture.* Cork: Cork Univ. Press, 1996.

Gillis, John R., ed. *Commemorations: The Politics of National Identity.* Princeton, N.J.: Princeton Univ. Press, 1994.

Gillmor, Desmond, ed., *The Irish Countryside: Landscape, Wildlife, History, People.* Dublin: Wolfhound Press, 1989.

————. "Republic of Ireland: An Expanding Tourism Sector." In *Tourism and Economic Development: European Experiences,* ed. G. Shaw and A. M. Williams, 221–41. Chichester, N.Y.: John Wiley and Sons, 1998.

————. *A Systematic Geography of Ireland.* Dublin: Gill and Macmillan, 1971.

Gold, John R., and Margaret M. Gold. *Imagining Scotland: Tradition, Representation and Promotion of Scottish Tourism since 1750.* Hampshire: Scholar Press, 1995.

Graham, Brian. "Historical Conservation and Revisionist Nationalism in Ireland." In *Building a New Heritage: Tourism, Culture and Identity in the New Europe,* ed. G. J. Ashworth and P. J. Larkham, 135–58. London: Routledge, 1994.

————, ed. *In Search of Ireland: A Cultural Geography.* London: Routledge, 1997.

Gray, Tony. *The Lost Years: The Emergency in Ireland, 1939–45*. London: Little, Brown and Company, 1997.

Gruffudd, Pyrs. "Back to the Land: Historiography, Rurality and the Nation in Interwar Wales." *Transactions of the Institute for Geography* 19 (1994): 61–77.

———. "Remaking Wales: Nation-Building and the Geographical Imagination, 1925–50." *Political Geography* 14, no. 3 (1995): 219–39.

Hall, C. M., and S. J. Page. *The Geography of Tourism and Recreation*. London: Routledge, 2000.

Hechter, Michael. *Internal Colonialism: The Celtic Fringe in British National Development, 1536–1966*. Berkeley: Univ. of California Press, 1975.

Heneghan, Philip. *Resource Allocation in Tourism Marketing*. London: Tourism International Press, 1976.

Hennessey, Thomas. *Dividing Ireland: World War I and Partition*. London: Routledge, 1998.

———. *A History of Northern Ireland*. New York: St. Martin's Press, 1997.

Hepburn, A. C. *The Conflict of Nationality in Modern Ireland*. New York: St. Martin's Press, 1980.

Herbert, David T., ed. *Heritage, Tourism and Society*. London: Mansell Publishing, 1995.

Hewison, Robert. *The Heritage Industry: Britain in a Climate of Decline*. London: Methuen London, 1987.

Hindesight. Dublin: Irish Museum of Modern Art, 1993.

Hindley, Reg. *The Death of the Irish Language*. London: Routledge, 1990.

Hopkinson, Michael. *Green Against Green: The Irish Civil War*. Dublin: Gill and Macmillan, 1988.

Horgan, Donal. *The Victorian Visitor in Ireland: Irish Tourism 1840–1910*. Cork: Imagimedia, 2002.

Horgan, John. *Irish Media: A Critical History since 1922*. London: Routledge, 2001.

———. *Seán Lemass: The Enigmatic Patriot*. Dublin: Gill and Macmillan, 1997.

Howe, Stephen. *Ireland and Empire*. Oxford: Oxford Univ. Press, 2002.

Huallachain, Colman Ó. *The Irish and Irish: A Sociolinguistic Analysis of the Relationship between a People and Their Language*. Dublin: Irish Franciscan Provincial Office, 1994.

Hunter, Michael, ed. *Preserving the Past: The Rise of Heritage in Modern Britain*. Stroud Gloucestershire: Alan Sutton Publishing, 1996.

Inglis, Tom. *Moral Monopoly: The Rise and Fall of the Catholic Church in Modern Ireland*. Cork: Cork Univ. Press, 1998.

Joyce, P. W. *A Social History of Ancient Ireland*. Vol. 2. New York: B. Blom, 1968 [1913].

Keane, John B. *The Chastitute: A Play in Two Acts*. Dublin: Mercier Press, 1981.

Kellas, James G. *The Politics of Nationalism and Ethnicity*. New York: St. Martin's Press, 1991.

Kelly, Deirdre. *Hands Off Dublin*. Dublin: O'Brien Press, 1976.

Kelly, Freida. *A History of Kilmainham Gaol: The Dismal House of Little Ease*. Cork: Dublin Mercier, 1988.

Kennedy, Michael. *Division and Consensus: The Politics of Cross-Border Relations in Ireland, 1925–1969*. Dublin: Institute of Public Administration, 2000.

Kirby, Alex. "F&M: The Rural Nemesis." *BBC News World Edition,* <http://news.bbc.co.uk/2/hi/in_depth/world/2001/review_of_2001/1697976.stm,> accessed 27 July 2007.

Kneafsey, Moya. "Rural Tourism and Identity: Stories of Change and Resistance from the West of Ireland and Brittany." In *New Directions in Celtic Studies,* ed. Philip Payton and Amy Hale, 167–96. Exeter: Univ. of Exeter Press, 2000.

———. "Tourism and Place Identity: A Case-Study in Rural Ireland." *Irish Geography* 31, no. 2 (1998): 111–23.

Kockel, Ullrich, ed. *Culture, Tourism, and Development: The Case of Ireland*. Liverpool: Liverpool Univ. Press, 1994.

Kofos, Evangelos. "National Heritage and National Identity in Nineteenth- and Twentieth-Century Macedonia." *European History Quarterly* 19, no. 2 (1989): 229–68.

Korte, Barbara, Hartmut Berghoff, Ralf Schneider, and Christopher Harvie, eds. *The Making of Modern Tourism: The Cultural History of the British Experience, 1600–2000*. London: Palgrave, 2002.

Koshar, Rudy. *German Travel Cultures*. Oxford: Berg, 2000.

———. *Germany's Transient Pasts: Preservation and National Memory in the Twentieth Century*. Chapel Hill: Univ. of North Carolina Press, 1998.

———. "'What Ought to Be Seen': Tourists' Guidebooks and National Identities in Modern Germany and Europe." *Journal of Contemporary History* 33, no. 3 (1998): 323–40.

Krapauskas, Virgil. *Nationalism and Historiography: The Case of Nineteenth Century Lithuanian Historicism*. New York: Columbia Univ. Press, 2000.

Krippendorf, Jost. *The Holiday Makers: Understanding the Impact of Leisure and Travel.* Oxford: Butterworth-Heinemann, 1987.

Krotz, Larry. *Tourists: How Our Fastest Growing Industry Is Changing the World.* Boston: Faber and Faber, 1996.

Kugelmass, Jack. "Bloody Memories: Encountering the Past in Contemporary Poland." *Cultural Anthropology* 10, no. 3 (1995): 279–301.

———. "The Rites of the Tribe: American Jewish Tourism in Poland." In *Museums and Communities,* ed. Ivan Karp, Christine Mullen Kreamer, and Steven D. Lavine, 382–427. Washington: Smithsonian Institution Press, 1992.

Kugelmass, Jack, and Annamaria Orla-Bukowska. "'If You Build It They Will Come': Recreating an Historic Jewish District in Post-Communist Kraków." *City and Society,* 1998, 315–53.

Kymlicka, Will. *Politics in the Vernacular: Nationalism, Multiculturalism, and Citizenship.* Oxford: Oxford Univ. Press, 2001.

Laitin, David. *Language Repertoires and State Construction in Africa.* Cambridge: Cambridge Univ. Press, 1992.

Lee, J. J. *Ireland 1912–1985, Politics and Society.* Cambridge: Cambridge Univ. Press, 1989.

Leed, Eric J. *The Mind of the Traveler.* New York: Basic Books, 1992.

Lloyd, David. *Ireland after History.* Cork: Cork Univ. Press, 1999.

Löfgren, Orvar. *On Holiday: A History of Vacationing.* Berkeley: Univ. of California Press, 1999.

Logan, Patrick. *Fair Day: The Story of Irish Fairs and Markets.* Belfast: Appletree Press, 1986.

Looney, Robert. "Economic Costs to the United States Stemming from the 9/11 Attacks." *Strategic Insights* 1, no. 6 (Aug. 2002), <http://www.ccc.nps.navy.mil/si/aug02/homeland.asp,> accessed 30 July 2007.

Loughlin, James. *The Ulster Question since 1945.* New York: St. Martin's Press, 1998.

Lowenthal, David. *The Past Is a Foreign Country.* Cambridge: Cambridge Univ. Press, 1985.

Lyons, F. S. L. *Parnell.* Dundalk, Ireland: Dundalgan Press, 1963.

MacAlister, R. A. S. *Ancient Ireland: A Study in the Lessons of Archaeology and History.* London: Methuen and Co., 1935.

MacCannell, Dean. *Empty Meeting Grounds: The Tourist Papers.* London: Routledge, 1992.

———. *The Tourist: A New Theory of the Leisure Class.* Berkeley: Univ. of California Press, 1999.

MacDonogh, Steve. *The Dingle Peninsula*. Dingle, Ireland: Brandon, 2000.

Malcolmson, Robert W. *Popular Recreations in English Society, 1700–1850*. Cambridge: Cambridge Univ. Press, 1973.

Massey, Doreen B. *Space, Place, and Gender*. Minneapolis: Univ. of Minnesota Press, 1994.

Matless, David. *Landscape and Englishness*. London: Reaktion, 1998.

Mazanec, Josef A., ed. *International City Tourism: Analysis and Strategy*. London: Pinter, 1997.

Mazon, Patricia, "Germania Triumphant: The Niederwald National Monument and the Liberal Moment in Imperial Germany." *German History* 18, no. 2 (2000): 162–92.

McCartney, Clem, and Lucy Bryson. *Clashing Symbols: A Report on the Use of Flags, Anthems and Other National Symbols in Northern Ireland*. Belfast: Institute for Irish Studies for the Community Relations Council, 1994.

McCrone, David, Angela Morris, and Richard Kiely. *Scotland—The Brand: The Making of Scottish Heritage*. Edinburgh: Edinburgh Univ. Press, 1995.

McDonald, Frank. *The Destruction of Dublin*. Dublin: Gill and Macmillan, 1985.

McIntosh, Gillian. *The Force of Culture: Unionist Identities in Twentieth-Century Ireland*. Cork: Cork Univ. Press, 1999.

McManus, Ruth. "Dublin's Changing Tourism Geography." *Irish Geography* 34, no. 2 (2001): 103–23.

———. "Heritage Tourism in Ireland—An Unholy Alliance?" *Irish Geography* 30, no. 2 (1997): 90–98.

McVeagh, John. *Irish Travel: A Bibliography*. Dublin: Wolfhound Press, 1996.

Melaugh, Martin. "The Sunningdale Agreement: Chronology of Events." *CAIN Web Service* (2002), <http://cain.ulst.ac.uk/events/sunningdale/chron.htm,> accessed 19 Mar. 2003.

Metcalf, Thomas R. *Ideologies of the Raj*. Cambridge: Cambridge Univ. Press, 1995.

Moranda, Scott. "Maps, Markers, and Bodies: Hikers Constructing the Nation in German Forests." *The Nationalism Project* (2001), <http://nationalismproject. org/articles.html,> accessed 7 Aug. 2003.

Mosse, George L. *Nationalism and Sexuality: Middle-Class Morality and Sexual Norms in Modern Europe*. Madison: Univ. of Wisconsin Press, 1985.

———. *The Nationalization of the Masses: Political Symbolism and Mass Movements in Germany from the Napoleonic Wars through the Third Reich*. Ithaca, N.Y.: Cornell Univ. Press, 1991.

National and Regional Tourism Planning: Methodologies and Case Studies. London: Routledge, 1994.

Nora, Pierre. "Between Memory and History: *Les Lieux de Mémoire.*" *Representations* 26 (1989): 7–25.

Nuryanti, Wiendu. "Heritage and Postmodern Tourism." *Annals of Tourism Research* 23, no. 2 (1996): 249–60.

O'Barr, William M., and Jean F. O'Barr, eds. *Language and Politics.* The Hague: Mouton and Co., 1976.

O'Beirne, J. W. *Romantic Story of Ireland's Greatest Park—The Phoenix.* Dublin: Bray Printing Co., 1934.

O'Brien, Harvey. "The Chastitute by John B. Keene." *Culture Vulture* (2002), <http://www.culturevulture.net/Theater/Chastitute.htm,> accessed 15 Apr. 2008.

———. "Culture, Commodity, and *Céad Míle Fáilte:* U.S. and Irish Tourist Films as a Vision of Ireland." *Éire-Ireland* 37, no. 1/2 (2002): 58–73.

O'Connor, Barbara, and Michael Cronin, eds. *Tourism in Ireland: A Critical Analysis.* Cork: Cork Univ. Press, 1993.

O'Hagan, J. W., ed. *The Economy of Ireland: Policy and Performance of a Small European Country.* London: Macmillan, 1995.

O'Hagan, J. W., and M. J. Harrison. "UK and US Visitor Expenditure in Ireland." *The Economic and Social Review* 15, no. 3 (1984): 195–207.

O'Hearn, Denis. *Inside the Celtic Tiger: The Irish Economy and the Asian Model.* London: Pluto Press, 1998.

O'Neill, Padraig. *Geographical Aspects of Tourism in the Republic of Ireland.* Galway: Social Sciences Research Center, Univ. College, Galway, 1979.

"Origin of the UK Foot and Mouth Disease Epidemic in 2001." Department for Environment, Food and Rural Affairs (United Kingdom), <http://www.defra.gov.uk/footandmouth/pdf/fmdorigins1.pdf,> accessed 27 July 2007.

Ousby, Ian. *The Englishman's England: Taste, Travel and the Rise of Tourism.* Cambridge: Cambridge Univ. Press, 1990.

Owen, Charles. *Britons Abroad: A Report on the Package Tour.* London: Routledge and Kegan Paul, 1968.

Paasi, Anssi. *Territories, Boundaries, and Consciousness: The Changing Geographies of the Finnish-Russian Border.* Chichester, UK: John Wiley and Sons, 1996.

Palmer, Catherine A. "Tourism and Colonialism: The Experience of the Bahamas." *Annals of Tourism Research* 21, no. 4 (1994): 792–811.

Patterson, Henry. *The Politics of Illusion: Republicanism and Socialism in Modern Ireland.* London: Hutchinson Radius, 1989.

Peillon, Michel. "Tourism—The Quest for Otherness." *Crane Bag* 8, no. 2 (1984): 165–68.

Pettitt, Lance. *Screening Ireland: Film and Television Representation.* Manchester: Manchester Univ. Press, 2000.

Pollard, John. "Patterns in Irish Tourism." In *Ireland: A Contemporary Geographical Perspective,* ed. A. J. Parker and R. W. G. Carter, 301–30. London: Routledge, 1989.

Prager, Jeffrey. *Building Democracy in Ireland: Political Order and Cultural Integration in a Newly Independent Nation.* Cambridge: Cambridge Univ. Press, 1986.

Ranger, Terence, and Eric Hobsbawm. *The Invention of Tradition.* Cambridge: Cambridge Univ. Press, 1986.

Riain, Mícheál Ó. *Aer Lingus: 1936–1986: A Business Monograph.* Dublin: Magill Print/Aer Lingus, 1986.

Roberts, Geoffrey, and Brian Garvin, eds. *Ireland and the Second World War: Politics, Society and Remembrance.* Dublin: Four Courts Press, 2000.

Rojek, Chris, and John Urry, eds. *Touring Cultures: Transformations of Travel and Theory.* London: Routledge, 1997.

Ross, Martin, and E. Æ Somerville. *The Irish R.M.* London: Abacus, 1928, 2000.

Rothery, Sean. *Everyday Buildings of Ireland.* Dublin: Department of Architecture, College of Technology, 1975.

Schwartz, Stuart B. Introduction to *Implicit Understandings: Observing, Reporting, and Reflecting on the Encounters between Europeans and Other Peoples in the Early Modern Era,* ed. Stuart B. Schwartz, 1–22. Cambridge: Cambridge Univ. Press, 1994.

Selwyn, Tom. Introduction to *The Tourist Image: Myths and Myth Making in Tourism,* ed. Tom Selwyn, 1–32. Chichester, UK: John Wiley and Sons, 1996.

"Seven Ages: Story of the Irish State" (Program 1). *RTÉ Online* (2000), <http://www.rte.ie/tv/sevenages/prog1.html,> accessed 13 Aug. 2003.

Shaffer, Margaret S. *See America First: Tourism and National Identity, 1880–1940.* Washington: Smithsonian Institution Press, 2001.

Share, Bernard. *Bunratty: Rebirth of a Castle.* Dingle, Ireland: Brandon, 1995.

———. *The Flight of the Iolar: The Aer Lingus Experience, 1936–1986.* Dublin: Gill and Macmillan, 1986.

Shaw, Gareth, and Allan M. Williams, eds. *The Rise and Fall of British Coastal Resorts: Cultural and Economic Perspectives.* London: Mansell, 1997.

———. "Tourism and Tourist Cultures in Europe." *American Behavioral Scientist* 36, no. 2 (1992): 155–71.

Shields, Rob. *Places on the Margin: Alternative Geographies of Modernity.* London: Routledge, 1991.

Simmons, Jack. "Railways, Hotels, and Tourism in Great Britain 1839–1914." *Journal of Contemporary History* 19, no. 2 (1984): 201–22.

———. *The Victorian Railway.* London: Thames and Hudson, 1991.

Simpson, Grant G. "The Declaration of Arbroath Revitalized." *Scottish Historical Review* 1, no. 4 (1977): 11–33.

Skelly, Joseph Morrison, and Michael Kennedy, eds. *Irish Foreign Policy, 1919–66: From Independence to Internationalism.* Dublin: Four Courts Press, 2000.

Skelly, Joseph Morrison. *Irish Diplomacy at the United Nations, 1945–1965.* Dublin: Irish Academic Press, 1997.

Smith, Anthony D. *The Ethnic Origins of Nations.* Oxford: Blackwell Publishers, 1998.

———. "Gastronomy or Geology? The Role of Nationalism in the Reconstruction of Nations." *Nations and Nationalism* 1, no. 1 (1994): 3–23.

Smith, Valene L., ed. *Hosts and Guests: The Anthropology of Tourism.* Philadelphia: Univ. of Pennsylvania Press, 1989.

Smout, Christopher. "Tours in the Scottish Highlands from the Eighteenth to the Twentieth Centuries." *Northern Scotland* 5, no. 2 (1983): 99–121.

Smyth, Gerry. *Space and the Irish Cultural Imagination.* New York: Palgrave, 2001.

Stabler, Mike, and M. Thea Sinclair. *The Economics of Tourism.* London: Routledge, 1997.

Stivers, Richard. *Hair of the Dog: Irish Drinking and Its American Stereotype.* New York: Continuum, 2000.

Sweeney, Paul. *The Celtic Tiger: Ireland's Economic Miracle.* Dublin: Oak Tree Press, 1998.

Tannam, Etain. *Cross-Border Cooperation in the Republic of Ireland and Northern Ireland.* New York: St. Martin's Press, 1999.

Taras, Milton. "Nations and Language-Building: Old Theories, Contemporary Cases." *Nationalism and Ethnic Politics* 4, no. 3 (1998): 79–101.

Thaler, Peter. "National History—National Imagery: The Role of History in Post-war Austrian Nation-Building." *Central European History* 32, no. 3 (1999): 277–310.

Thomas, Alys. "Language Policy and Nationalism in Wales: A Comparative Analysis." *Nations and Nationalism* 3, no. 3 (1997): 323–44.

Tourism and Travel in Ireland. Dublin: Gill and Macmillan, 1993.

Townshend, Charles. *Ireland: The Twentieth Century.* London: Arnold, 1999.

Tuan, Yi Fu. *Space and Place: The Perspective of Experience.* London: Edward Arnold, 1979.

Turner, Louis, and John Ash. *The Golden Hordes: International Tourism and the Pleasure Periphery.* London: Constable and Company, 1975.

Urry, John. "Holiday Making in Britain since 1945." *Contemporary Record* 5, no. 1 (1991): 32–44.

———. *The Tourist Gaze: Leisure and Travel in Contemporary Societies.* London: Sage Publications, 1990.

———. "*The Tourist Gaze* 'Revisited.'" *American Behavioral Scientist* 36, no. 2 (1992): 172–86.

———. "The Tourist Gaze and the 'Environment.'" *Theory, Culture and Society* 9 (1992): 1–26.

van der Borg, Jan, Paolo Costa, and Giuseppe Gotti. "Tourism in European Heritage Cities." *Annals of Tourism Research* 23, no. 2 (1996): 306–21.

Varley, Tony, Thomas A. Boylan, and Michael P. Cuddy, eds. *Rural Crisis: Perspectives on Irish Rural Development.* Galway: Center for Development Studies, Univ. College Galway, 1991.

Vellas, François, and Lionel Bécherel. *International Tourism: An Economic Perspective.* New York: St. Martin's Press, 1995.

Vigarello, Georges. "The Tour de France." In *Realms of Memory: Rethinking the French Past,* ed. Pierre Nora, 469–500. New York: Columbia Univ. Press, 1997.

Vogel, Harold L. *Travel Industry Economics: A Guide for Financial Analysis.* Cambridge: Cambridge Univ. Press, 2001.

Wall, Geoffrey, and Timothy J. Dallen. *Tourism and Political Boundaries.* New York: Routledge, 2001.

Walton, John K. *The English Seaside Resort: A Social History, 1750–1914.* New York: St. Martin's Press, 1983.

Waters, Maureen. *The Comic Irishman.* Albany: State Univ. of New York Press, 1984.

Weber, Eugen. *Peasants into Frenchmen: The Modernization of Rural France, 1870–1914.* Palo Alto, Calif.: Stanford Univ. Press, 1976.

Weinstein, Brian. *The Civic Tongue.* New York: Longman, 1983.

Whelan, Bernadette. *Ireland and the Marshall Plan, 1947–57.* Dublin: Four Courts Press, 2000.

White, Padraic A., and Ray Mac Sharry. *The Making of the Celtic Tiger: The Inside Story of Ireland's Economic Boom.* Cork: Mercier Press, 2000.

Wilford, Rick, ed. *Aspects of the Belfast Agreement.* Oxford: Oxford Univ. Press, 2001.

Williams, Alan, ed. *Film and Nationalism.* Piscataway, N.J.: Rutgers Univ. Press, 2002.

Withers, Charles. "The Historical Creation of the Scottish Highlands." In *The Manufacture of Scottish History,* ed. Christopher Whatley and Ian Donnachie, 143–56. Edinburgh: Polygon, 1992.

Womack, Peter. *Improvement and Romance: Constructing the Myth of the Highlands.* London: Macmillan Press, 1989.

Wood, Robert E. "Tourist Ethnicity: A Brief Itinerary." *Ethnic and Racial Studies* 21, no. 2 (1998): 218–41.

Wood, Robert E., and Michael Picard, eds. *Tourism, Ethnicity, and the State in Asian and Pacific Societies.* Honolulu: Univ. of Hawai'i Press, 1997.

Wood, Roy C., and Erwin Losekoot. "Prospects for Tourism Employment in Scotland." *Scottish Affairs* 34 (2001): 91–106.

Yaeger, Patricia, ed. *The Geography of Identity.* Ann Arbor: Univ. of Michigan Press, 1996.

Zuelow, Eric G. E. "Enshrining Ireland's Nationalist History Inside Prison Walls: The Restoration of Kilmainham Jail." *Éire-Ireland* 39 (Fall/Winter 2004): 180–201.

———. "'Ingredients for Cooperation': The Role of Irish Tourism in North-South Relations, 1924–1998." *New Hibernia Review* 10, no. 1 (2006): 17–39.

———. "National Identity and Tourism in 20th Century Ireland: The Role of Collective Re-Imagining." In *Nationalism in a Global Era: The Persistence of Nations,* ed. Mitchell Young, Eric G. E. Zuelow, and Andreas Sturm, 156–75. London: Routledge, 2007.

———. "The Tourism Nexus: The Meanings of Tourism and Identity since the Irish Civil War." In *Ireland's Heritages: Critical Perspectives on Memory and Identity,* ed. Mark McCarthy, 189–213. Hampshire: Ashgate, 2005.

Index